Advances in Computer Science and IT

Edited by
D. M. Akbar Hussain

Advances in Computer Science and IT

Edited by D. M. Akbar Hussain

This is a reprint of the book published in 2009 by Intech

Republished by InTech

Janeza Trdine 9, 51000 Rijeka, Croatia

Technical Editor Zeljko Debeljuh

Additional hard copies can be obtained from orders@intechopen.com

Advances in Computer Science and IT,
Edited by D. M. Akbar Hussain
p. cm.
ISBN 978-953-7619-51-0

For EU product safety concerns:
IN TECH d.o.o., Prolaz Marije Krucifikse Kozulić 3, 51000 Rijeka, Croatia,
info@intechopen.com or visit our website at intechopen.com.

Preface

This book has a unique title" Advances in Computer Science and IT", although it is not entirely new there is a trend of similar titles in many international conferences. However, for a book this title certainly has innovation and many articles presented in the text shows there uniqueness likewise the title.

The book presents some very interesting and excellent articles for this divergent title, the 22 chapters presented here cover core topics of computer science like Visualization of large databases, Security, Ontology, User Interface, Graphs, Object Oriented Software Developments and on the Engineering side Filtering, Motion Dynamics, Adaptive Fuzzy Logic, Hyper Static Mechanical Systems. It has also topics which are combination of Computer Science and Engineering like Meta Computing, Future Mobiles, Color Image Analysis, Relative representation and Recognition, Neural Networks. The book will serve a unique purpose through these multi-disciplined topics to share different but interesting views on each of these topics.

I would like to thank all the authors for their excellent contributions in the different areas of their expertise and it is their knowledge and enthusiastic collaboration which made possible to create this book, I hope it will be very valuable to the readers of all disciplines.

Editor

D. M. Akbar Hussain
Department of Electronic Systems
Aalborg University, Denmark
akbar786@ieee.org

Contents

Preface V

1. A New Object Selecting Technique for Visualization of Large Datasets 001
Navid Fallah and Ali Eydgahi

2. Beyond object-oriented software development 021
Adam Przybylek

3. Security Trade-off – Ontological Approach 039
Bialas Andrzej

4. A Model of Placing Liaisons in the Two Levels of an Organization Structure of a Complete Binary Tree Minimizing Total Path Length 065
Kiyoshi Sawada

5. Object Tracking under High Correlation for Kalman & $\alpha - \beta$ Filter 073
D. M. Akbar Hussain and Zaki Ahmed

6. Numerical Simulation of Converter Fed Squirrel Cage Induction Motors 093
C. Grabner

7. RGB Color Analysis for Face Detection 109
Qieshi Zhang and Jun Zhang

8. Mind Operator: Zone-Associated Relative Representation 127
Ching-An Hsiao

9. Adaptive implementation of nonlinear fuzzy image enhancement algorithms in the compressed JPEG images 145
Camelia Florea, Aurel Vlaicu, Mihaela Gordan and Bogdan Orza

10. Estimation of Per Unit Length Parameters of Multiconductor Lines by the Method of Rectangular Subareas 171
Saswati Ghosh and Ajay Chakrabarty

11. Alternative analytical method used in calculus of hyper static mechanical systems, in plotting the distribution of shear force, bending moment, displacements and rotations of section beam 183
Cornel MARIN, Viviana FILIP and Alexandru MARIN

12. Learning distributed selective attention strategies with the Sigma-if neural network 209
Maciej Huk

13. Numerical Integration Tools in Material Point Relative Motion Dynamics 233
Viviana Filip, Cornel Marin and Alexandru Marin

14. Slicing techniques to derive the User Interface Abstract Model 249
Daniela da Cruz and Pedro Rangel Henriques

15. IMAGE QUALITY ENHANCEMENT BY APPLYING GENETIC ALGORITHM IN MEDIAN FILTERING 277
Sandra Sovilj-Nikic

16. Direction of Arrival Estimation using the PRIME Algorithm 295
H.K. Hwang and Zekeriya Aliyazicioglu

17. Some sufficient conditions for graphs to be (g, f, n)-critical graphs 325
Sizhong Zhou, Hongxia Liu and Ziming Duan

18. Metacomputing with Federated Method Invocation 337
Michael Sobolewski

19. NEW STOCHASTIC DEPENDENCES PARADIGM AND ITS APPLICATION IN PROBABILISTIC MODELING 365
Jerzy K. Filus and Lidia Z. Filus

20. Introduction to AdaIndex—An Adaptive Similarity Search Algorithm in General Metric Spaces 381
Tao Ban and Youki Kadobayashi

21. Scenario Analysis of the Mobile Voice Services Market 397
HANNU VERKASALO, KIM LINDQVIST and HEIKKI HÄMMÄINEN

22. Next Generation of Electronic Patient Record: Moving from Information to Knowledge-based 415
Lau, Adela

1

A New Object Selecting Technique for Visualization of Large Datasets

Navid Fallah and Ali Eydgahi
University of Maryland Eastern Shore
Department of Engineering and Aviation Sciences
Princess Anne, MD 21853
aeydgahi@umes.edu

Abstract

This paper presents a new method for accelerating volume rendering of large datasets similar to urban areas. The proposed method improves the current algorithms by introducing a new technique which uses statistics about different objects to cover more general and comprehensive datasets. In this method, proximity, level of details, and statistics from previous moves are used to predict next position and to select objects for future use. This technique keeps track of previous moves and uses the application and viewer's specifications to produce probability areas. These areas help the method to predict next moves and the objects that have to be selected for future use. This technique simplifies the implementation and requires smaller memory footprint. A multi-resolution approach is introduced which is based on a special shape. By gathering statistics about different objects a unique shape is obtained that is used to select different objects and put them in the groups to be rendered with different resolutions. This way acceleration to produce high resolution visualization at interactive rate is achieved. The proposed technique solves the issues of redundant object downloading and redundant rendering on the server by downloading objects and images based on software and hardware specifications. This way it saves server and network resources to reduce the delay and to achieve interactive frame rate on client side. A visualization program based on the proposed method is presented.

KEY WORDS

Visualization, volume rendering, object selecting, simulation, multi-resolution, and large datasets.

1. Introduction

An increasing number of urban and geographic applications are now generating high resolution three-dimensional (3D) datasets. The sizes of these datasets are often too large to fit into memory or even on hard drive. This makes it almost impossible to keep the data on hard drive and load them into memory to perform interactive data visualization. One example is the Richtmyer-Meshkov Turbulent simulation [1], which is designed to study instabilities at the interface between two gases of different densities and produces datasets containing hundreds of time steps each being 7.5 gigabytes in size.

In the past few years, research has suggested that a considerable portion of a large dataset is often invisible due to the view angle and various aspects of data coherence could be exploited to reduce the amount of data that pass through the visualization pipeline [2]. An effective technique for reducing unnecessary rendering computation by eliminating invisible portions of data before visualization is presented as occlusion culling [3]. Guthe and Strasser [4] applied visibility test to multi-resolution volume rendering, Livnat and Hansen [5] introduced a view-dependent algorithm for iso-surface extraction, and several predictive approaches for structured datasets have been presented in [6]-[8]. Increasing gap between the available I/O, memory and computing bandwidth, and the rapidly increasing amount of data to be visualized requires new methods to select precisely the right objects to be loaded into memory.

Most of the desktop machines or laptops are not able to hold the large dataset due to their limited size of storage and memory. Therefore, techniques based on client-server architecture are used to solve this problem. One of the methods is unstructured grids introduced in [9]. The visibility sorting algorithm [10] is another technique, which sorts in object-space and image-space. This algorithm is fast, efficient, and flexible enough to handle geometry that are dynamically changing [11]. The hardware assisted progressive volume rendering introduced in [12] creates a progressive image transmission over the internet. In this method, a server renders objects and the produced images are sent to the client to be shown on screen. In this case, only a few images are stored on the client computers [12]. Having just the images on the client but not the objects slows down the exploration of interactive dataset. For example, when the view direction changes just a few degrees, the same objects with different angel have to be shown on screen and new images have to be rendered on server side and be sent to client. This uses both the server resources and network bandwidth and introduces new delays.

Direct volume rendering has become a standard technique for visualizing 3D datasets. This technique maps the data in the volume and projects it to 2D images. The direct volume rendering techniques using 3D texture mapping and hardware can visualize volumes of moderate sizes at interactive frame rates. The challenge is to allow interactive data exploration for even larger datasets. While the available texture memory in the high–end graphics hardware is limited to only several hundred megabytes, nowadays simulation applications can produce terabytes of data [13]. A practical solution for this issue is to reduce the amount of data being rendered. A possible technique [14] is to give the user a quick overview of the data. It is useful to first render the data at a lower resolution. As the user navigates through the data and requests further details in local regions of interest, if the rendering resources are available, different portions of the data are then retrieved and rendered at their higher resolution.

As visualization is an interactive process, sometimes rendering a lower resolution of data is sufficient for the user to get enough information about the area based on its distance. The capability to visualize data at different resolutions allows user to focus on specific area of interest and to spend more time and hardware resources for higher quality data for that area. Techniques have been introduced to provide hierarchical data representations for 3D volumetric data in [15]-[17] and for multi-resolution encoding and rendering of large scale in [18].

Level of detail (LOD) based visualization techniques as proposed in [19] allow rendering of the same objects using several different triangle meshes of variable complexity. Thus, the mesh complexity can be adjusted according to the object's relative position from the viewer, its visual importance in the rendered scene, and with respect to the available rendering power to guarantee stable interactive frame rates [20]. Although numerous ideas have been implemented on mesh simplification for geometric approximation [21]-[22], fewer approaches have been taken to address the problem of view-dependent simplification [20] for real-time rendering and performance optimization.

The proposed method in this paper, improves these methods by introducing new technique to predict and cover more general and comprehensive datasets. The method keeps track of previous moves and uses the application and viewers' specifications to produce probably areas. These areas help the method to predict next move and the objects that have to be selected for future use. The proposed method introduces a LOD technique which has been optimized for urban area visualization and requires minimum amount of necessary memory. This method is based on three layers of details. The first layer can be of different shape depending on the rendering objects. The second layer selects the objects for future use based on an algorithm specialized for this method and cache them into memory. The last layer downloads the objects over the network based on the same algorithm. The advantage of these layers of details is in their specific shape which is illustrated in the next sections.

2. The Proposed Method and its Data Structure

In the proposed method, different concepts have been employed to accelerate algorithms for visualizing large datasets. These include a customized data structure, a probability area based on different aspects of movement, different algorithm phases for organizing the dataset and selecting objects to visualize, and extending the algorithm to 3D and using it in network. A particular data structure to organize datasets and minimize the access time to objects is introduced. This data structure is optimized to have minimal overhead and best performance at different phases such as adding new objects to an existing dataset.

The data structure consists of three different types of objects. A prefixed is added to each type to distinguish between these objects. The first objects are Geo-Objects which have to be shown on screen. Geo-Objects simulate the real word objects and keep different information about each object such as shape, color, and location. The two other types of objects are Container-Objects and Linker-Objects. These two types construct the platform for data structure by pointing to each other and to relevant Geo-Objects. These objects are responsible to keep the integrity of the Geo-Objects.

Each Container-Object refers to specific geographic area and points to a group of Geo-Objects belonging to the same geographic location. These objects have to attach to each other in order to construct the dataset using Container-Objects. Each Container-Object by using Linker-Objects connects to all other Container-Objects around it. Container-Objects have pointer to point to all necessary Linker-Objects that are around it. Linker-Objects are pointing to Container-Objects that are next to them and other Linker-Objects. Connecting Container-Objects using this technique helps the algorithm to find nearby Geo-Objects in least amount of time.

Container-Objects have size-limit based on hardware and software specifications and requirements. By adding each Geo-Object to a specific location, the relevant Container-Object for that area points to that Geo-Object. When the size of the Geo-Objects that are being pointed with Container-Object exceeds the size-limit for that Container-Object, the Container-Object has to be broken down to smaller pieces and cover the same area with more Container-Objects to keep the balance. This feature is necessary to improve the memory performance and keep the access time as short as possible.

As a Container-Object breaks down, new Linker-Objects joins the new Container-Objects and other Container-Objects that are nearby. Separating these two responsibilities, maintain Geo-Objects with Container-Objects and establishes the links between these objects, which improves the memory and CPU performance while updating and maintaining the objects.

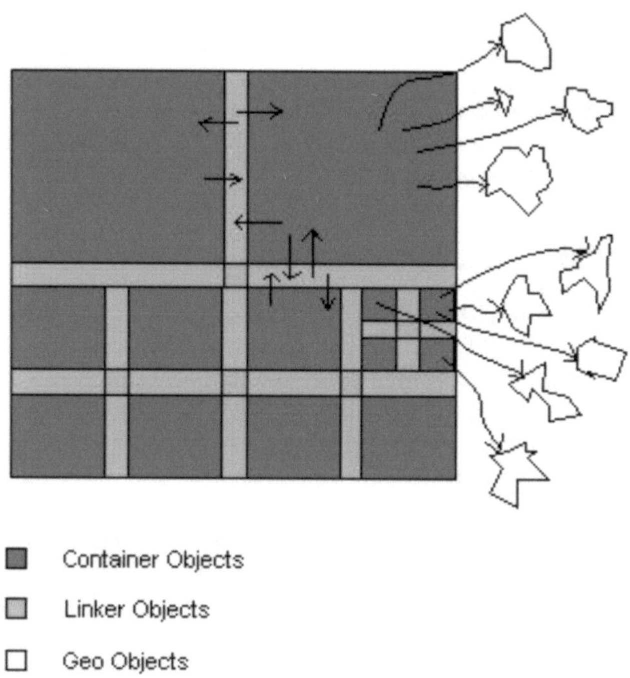

Fig. 1. Different types of objects used in the proposed data structure.

Figure 1 show the three different objects used in this data structure. The white objects represent Geo-Objects which will be rendered and will be shown on screen at the same time. Dark gray represent Container-Objects which points to Geo-Objects in their area. When a special area needs to be shown on screen, that container and the related Geo-Objects are loaded into memory to render. The bright gray represents Linker-Objects which links different containers. These objects are being used to find neighbors of a container when they need to be selected.

Handling the data structure consists of two phases. The startup phase and update phase which includes add or delete of Geo-Objects to/from an existing dataset.

The startup phase starts with an empty Container-Object which covers all the demanded area. Geo-Objects are being added to the container till the container reaches the size-limit. The size-limit of the container depends on the software and hardware specifications such as the rendering device, graphic card, and main memory. When the container reaches the size-limit, it is broken down to four new containers which each covers one-fourth of the old container area. This process continues until all the Geo-Objects have been added to the containers. Since each break produces 4 new containers, frequently breaking is not necessary and it improves the performance. Figure 2 demonstrates process of breaking a container into four new containers when size-limit is reached.

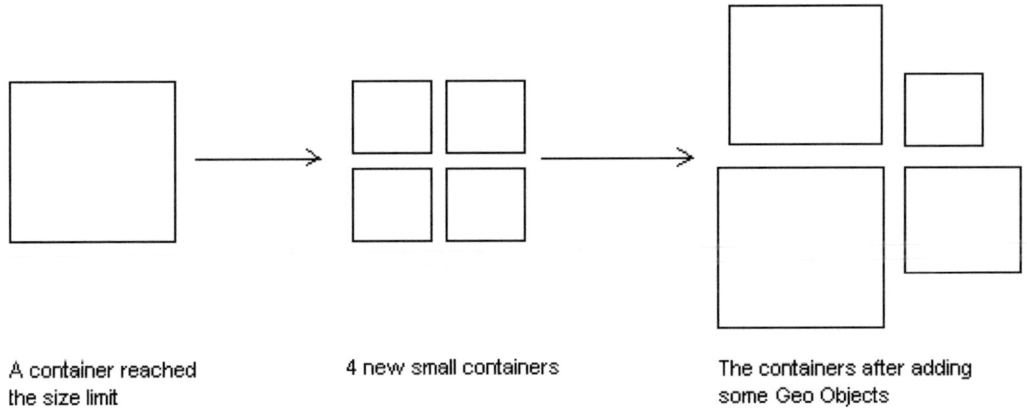

Fig. 2. The process of breaking a container which has reached the size-limit.

At the first phase while importing the dataset, the frequency of breaking the containers is high. This is only in the startup phase. Later changes on dataset need less effort and time. Thus, this method helps to speed up the access time and to retrieve data in less amount of time.

For the update phase, there are some Geo-Objects that need to be added or deleted. Process of adding Geo-Objects in this phase is the same process as adding Geo-Objects at the startup phase. Again, container-Objects are being broken to four new ones when they exceed the size-limit. By deleting Geo-Objects, the size of containers reduces. The containers that have less than one-eighth of size-limit have to be combined with their neighbors to make a new container in order to avoid wasting storage and memory spaces. If all four containers have one-eighth of size-limit, by combining them the new container will have half of the size-limit.

One of the advantages of this data structure is not being dependent on the shape and distribution of objects. The data structure does not waste storage by assigning extra space based on specific geographic distribution over the area. For example, a diamond-shaped distribution of objects seems to have wasted half of the containers as shown in figure 3. By using the proposed data structure, the memory is allocated just for the parts that contain Geo-Objects. Figure 4 demonstrates the same dataset representation using the proposed method. When a container is empty there is no need to allocate any storage and memory for the relevant Container-Object. Linker-Objects have to keep track of links and in this case they point to other linkers and as there is no container the pointers will be null.

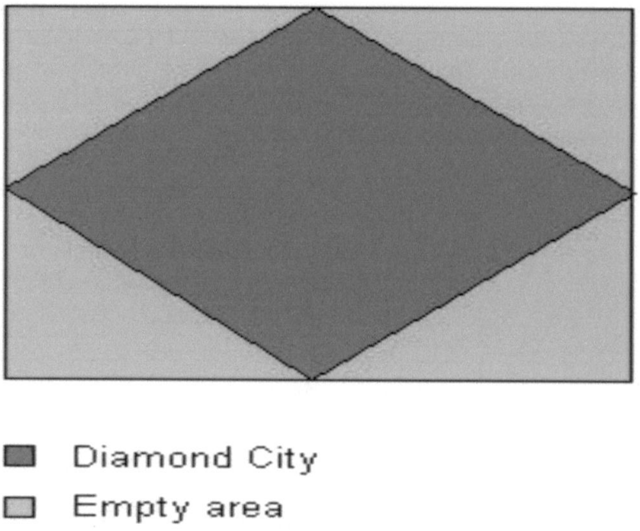

Fig. 3. Representation of a sample diamond dataset.

To speed up access time to objects, containers have to be numbered in specific order. This method of numbering helps to find any Container-Object in the area and its related containers such as its neighbors or children's of the same container in case the containers have to be merged. The merge is necessary when the four containers from the same parents have less than one-eighth of size-limit. An example of numbering process after a container is broken to new containers is shown in figure 5.

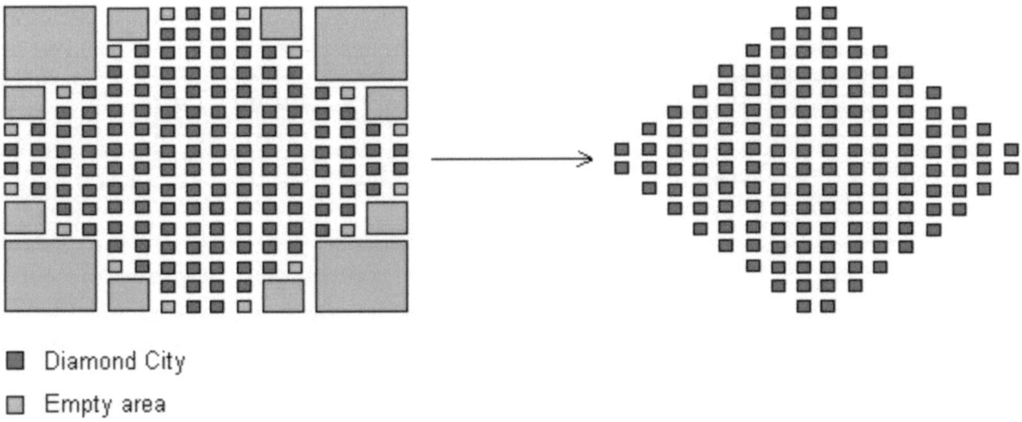

Fig. 4. Representation of a sample diamond dataset using proposed data structure.

For the first break, numbering process is as shown in figure 5. In this process, containers are numbered using two digits where the first digit is the number of main container. For example, by breaking container number 2 to four new containers, they are numbered as 20, 21, 22, and 23. This number specifies the relevant container in reverse method. For example, having container numbered 321, 3 means in the first break this container was a part of a container in South-East of the data set, 2 means that in second break this object was part of the container in South-West of the old 3 container, and finally, 1 means in the last break this container is in North-East of the old 32 container. By using this numbering method, any container or Geo-Object can be identified very fast and finding the neighbors of a container is achieved just by changing a digit in this string of digits.

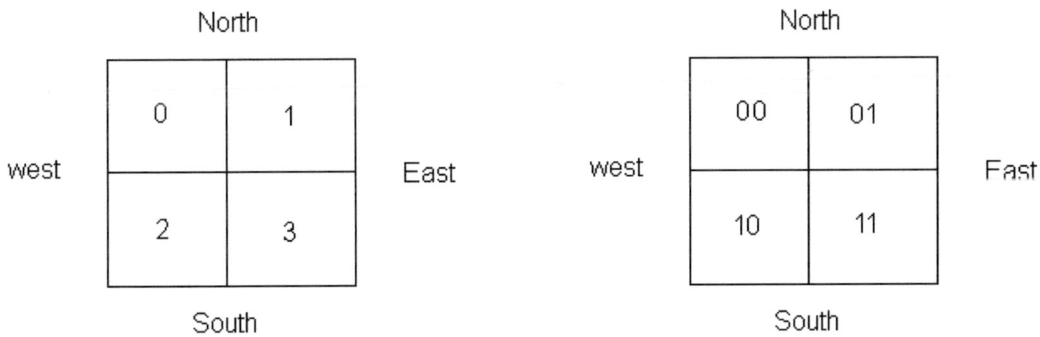

Fig. 5. Numbering a container after it is broken to four new containers.

The other advantage of this numbering is that each digit can be represented only by 2 bits as L_nD_n. For example, container numbered 32012203 can be stored in 16 bits. Bitwise instructions can be used to manipulate these numbers and to extract container information such as location and neighbors which reduce the calculation time. Figure 6 demonstrates a sample container that has been broken many times and its corresponding container numbering.

The algorithm for finding neighbors of a container is recursive and uses bitwise operations to locate them. As is shown in figure 5, the first bit for the left containers is always 0 and for right containers is 1. For the containers on top half of the second bit is 0 and for the down half it is 1. The first step in the process of finding the neighbors in left or right is to change the first bit. For example, to find 102 or 010010's neighbors, by changing the first bit the container 010011 or 103 is selected. To find the neighbor below or above, the second bit has to be changed which in this case it is 010000 or 100.

For the next step in the process of finding the neighbors, container numbers are represented as $(L_n D_n ... L_1 D_1 L_0 D_0)$ where L_i and D_i are the two bits of a digit. To find neighbor of a container that is located above or below, we consider:

$$L_0 = \overline{L_0},$$

$$L_1 = \overline{L_1},$$

$$L_i = \overline{(L_{i-1} \oplus L_{i-2})} \oplus L_i \quad \text{for i > 1}$$

Where bar symbol indicates logical not operation. This way, we find a neighbor in either above or below the container and then by changing the first bit, D_0, from 0 to 1 or from 1 to 0 the other neighbor is obtained.

To find the containers on left or right of an object, we consider:

$$D_0 = \overline{D_0},$$

$$D_1 = \overline{D_1},$$

$$D_i = \overline{(D_{i-1} \oplus D_{i-2})} \oplus D_i \quad \text{for i > 1}$$

This way, we find a neighbor in either left or right of the container and then by changing the second bit, L_0, from 0 to 1 or from 1 to 0 the other neighbor is obtained.

As an example, we consider 102 or 010010 container. Thus, L_0 is 1, L_1 is 0, L_2 is 0, D_0 is 0, D_1 is 0, and D_2 is 1. For the containers above and below, the L_0 will be 0, the L_1 will be 1, and the L_2 will be 0. Two new neighbors are 011000 or 120 and 011001 or 121. Left and right neighbors can be found with the same method.

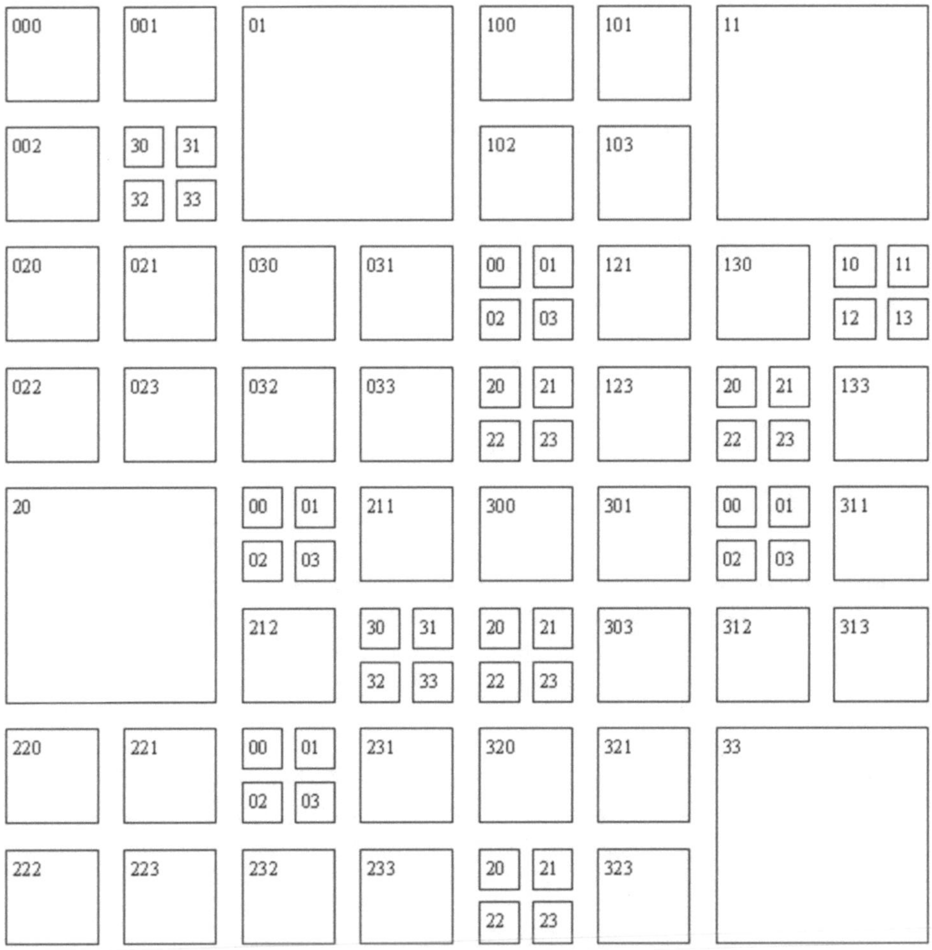

Fig. 6. Sample dataset demonstrating container numbering.

3. The Layers

In this paper, a specific shape called layer is introduced. The layer is obtained from probability of viewers changing their directions. The layer is used to identify and select proper objects that need to be processed. Different statistics and characteristics of movement such as speed and probability of turning to different directions are employed to generate layers. The layer is used to predict the viewer's next position and consequently enables the algorithm to deal with the objects that are affected by the move. This improves the performance, reduces the delay time, and makes it feasible for the real-time visualization of objects.

It is known that the probability of viewer moving forward is the highest, turning back is the lowest, and turning left or right is in between. Figure 7 shows a sample of layer.

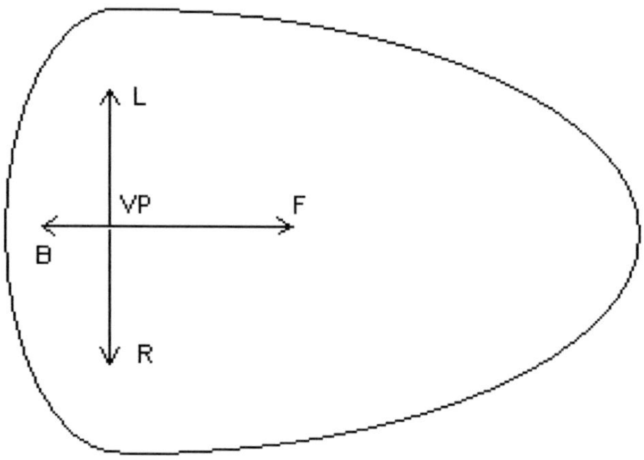

Fig. 7. A sample layer.

In figure 7, VP is the view point and F, B, R, and L represent the probability of going straight, turning back, turning right, and turning left. This is the best shape for layers and can be used for any kind of viewer. Viewer can be a car, airplane, human, or any type of object which simulate the viewer movement. The only difference between layers of different viewers is in their probability for turning. The shape is the same for all viewers and the algorithm is the same. The layer has to be customized and defined for each type of viewer.

There are two methods to generate the layers. The first one is to provide the probabilities while defining a new object as viewer. The second approach is to use the same probability for all directions as default. In this case, the program keeps track of movements and collects necessary statistics to generate probabilities and make corrections on the layers shape.

Since human moves slower than the other two viewers, it takes more time to get to farthest points and it is more likely for it to turn left or right than other two viewers. Therefore, it is necessary to have more details about nearer Geo-Objects and to select more Geo-Objects in left or right than other viewers. The airplane moves faster than the other two viewers and gets to farther points in less time. Therefore, selecting far Geo-Objects are inevitable and since it needs less detail in its left or right fewer Geo-Objects is selected in these directions.

The distance between the viewer and Geo-Objects around it creates layers with different sizes. Combining layers with different sizes produce a base layer which is used by the algorithm to determine proper resolution for each Geo-Object using multi-resolution and LOD concepts. Figure 8 shows a base layer created by four layers of different sizes.

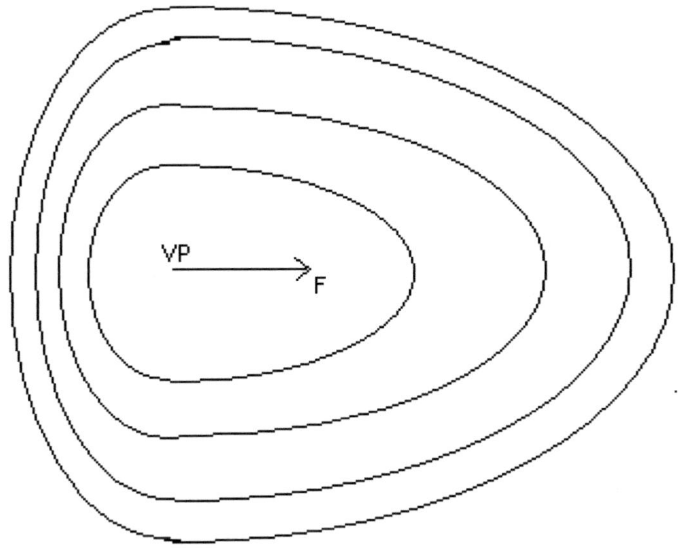

Fig. 8. A sample base layer.

The interior layer selects the Geo-Objects that have to be shown on screen and have to be rendered by an algorithm. Other layers select the Geo-Objects that do not need to be rendered but have to be cached to memory for later use. This technique speeds up the rendering process for next move when interior layer covers the Geo-Objects. The interior layer can contain several sub-layers depending on specification of an environment. The algorithm can render Geo-Objects in each sub-layer with different resolution and spend more time for Geo-Objects that are closer to viewer. Using this special shape helps to render or cache Geo-Objects into the memory more accurately by reducing the effort for caching the Geo-Objects that are less likely to be visited by viewer.

4. The Algorithm

The algorithm uses the probability area to select proper objects and applies the related future. Each layer is responsible to select the relevant objects for specific process. The size and number of layers depend on hardware and software specifications. Depending on the layer, the corresponding objects are selected either to render with proper resolution, to be cached into memory, or to be downloaded from the server.

This saves time by eliminating the delay time for downloading objects at rendering phase. Accurate prediction of required objects for future use is essential for reducing delay and achieving better interactive rate for visualization. The proposed layer is designed to achieve the better interactive rate.

The three rendering, caching, and downloading phases are parallel processes. These three processes use graphic hardware, memory, and network resources that are three different resources that do not interfere with each other and can work as a pipeline.

The algorithm selects the objects by moving the layer over the dataset. The objects in each layer are identified by moving the area based on the viewer speed and direction. This method employs queues for each layer to keep track of objects that have to be selected.

Selection process starts with the container which includes the viewer and pushes the container to the first layer's queue. In each step, first item in queue will be popped up and its neighbors will be selected and pushed to the proper queue. If they are in the same resolution area, they will be added to current queue. Otherwise, depending on their layer, they will be pushed to other queues either for lower resolution areas to be cached into memory or to be downloaded from the server. This will continue till all neighbor objects are selected and are placed in a proper area. The next step is to process the objects which includes rendering with proper resolution, caching into memory, or downloading.

The images from previous renders that are stored on hard drive or downloaded from the server are used to reduce the delay time. These images can be shown on screen while the algorithm works on the queuing or rendering process. The new images can be replaced on screen when the rendering is finished. These images can be downloaded from the server, or from previous rendering process that have been stored, or can be rendered while hardware resources are not in use. This can be done for containers that do not have images or the ones that have changed from the last time that they have been rendered.

5. An Example

A sample area is applied on sample dataset as is presented in figure 6 to demonstrate the object selection process. Figure 9 shows the sample probability area with two layers.

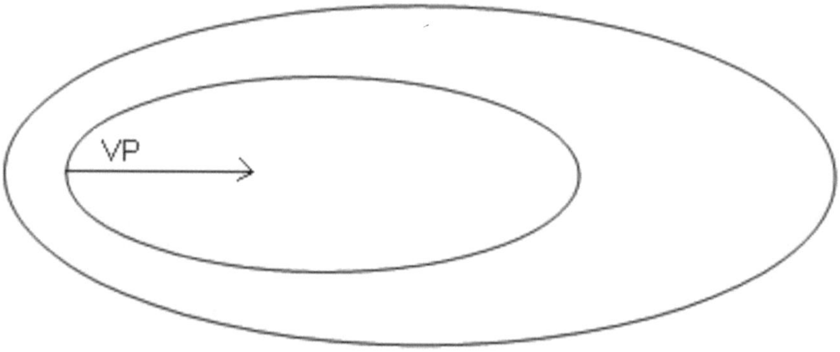

Fig. 9. Sample probability areas with two layers.

Figure 10 shows the result of applying the probability area in figure 9 to sample dataset in figure 6. The viewer is in north east of 023 container.

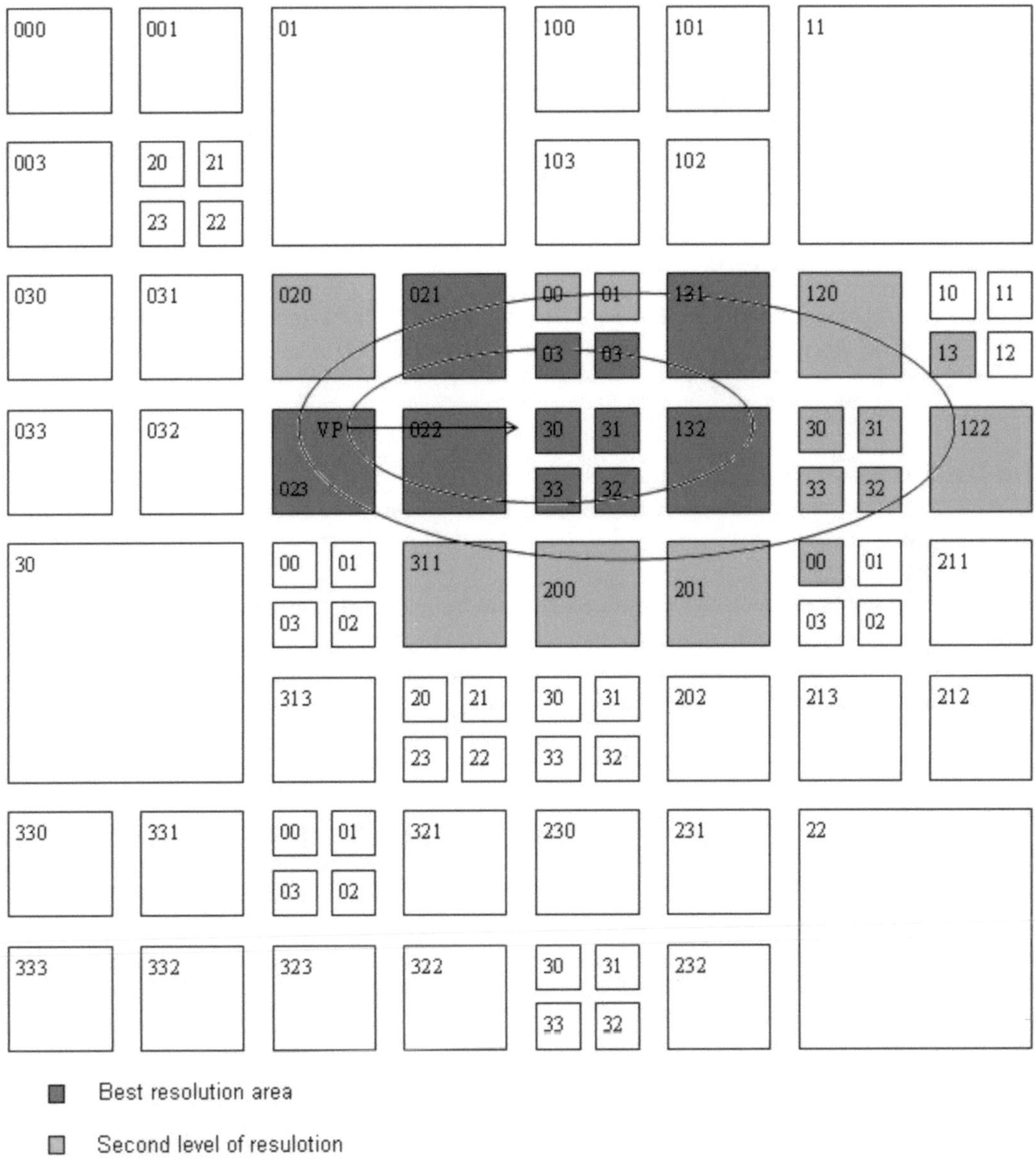

Fig. 10. Selected containers with the applied sample layers.

The algorithm starts with the container that includes the viewer. The algorithm pushes the container into the first queue, which is the rendering layer. The objects in this layer have to be rendered. The algorithm finds the neighbors of 023 container by modifying the digits in container's number. For the 023 container, neighbors are 020, 021, 022, 311, 3100, 3101, 30, 032, and 031. As 021 and 022 containers are in the same layer, they are pushed into the first queue. 020 and 311 containers are in next layer, and they are placed in the second queue. The rest of containers are not in probability areas and they are not placed in any layer and queue. For the next step as the 021 container is on the top of first queue, 1303 is pushed into the first queue and 1300 is pushed into the second one. For 022 neighbors, 1330 and 1333 are pushed into the first queue and 200 will be pushed into the second queue. For the next step, 1303, 1331, 1332, 131, and 132 are placed into the first queue and 1301, 201, 120, 1230, 1233, 2100, 1231, 1232, 1213, and 122 are placed into the second queue. The rest of containers are not in any layer. Selecting phase is complete as the area of each object is determined.

6. Implemented software

A program in java has been implemented to demonstrate the effectiveness of the proposed algorithm. The program consists of RLMain, RLFrame, DataSetCreator, DataSetViewer, RLImageApplet, and RLColorApplet classes. In this software the rendered images are shown on screen and rendering phase can be added as an extension.

The DataSetCreator class creates the dataset based on the proposed method and uses images as its input. This class puts the images in proper container and keeps images with three different resolutions.

The DataSetViewer class shows the dataset made by DataSetCreator class. This class shows images in the dataset with random resolution for sample and quick demonstration of the dataset produced by DataSetCreator. It also uses other classes to implement other functionality of the proposed method.

The RLImageApplet class uses the dataset produced by DataSetCreator class to implement the selecting phase of the proposed method. This class is a Java applet and selects containers, puts them in different resolution areas, and displays them on screen based on their proper resolution. There are three different resolution areas in the algorithm. A rectangle simulates the screen position on dataset and the area surrounded with the rectangle to clearly demonstrate the method. The probability area has two layers. The first layer is internal layer which selects the objects that are close to viewer. The objects in this area have to be rendered with the best resolution. The second layer selects the objects to be rendered with lower resolution as they are far from the viewer. These layers also select extra objects which are not in screen area and user is not able to see them. These extra objects are cached for future use to reduce the delay for later moves. Depending on the size of probability areas, some objects that have to be shown on screen may not be selected by any layer. In this case, the objects have to be selected as a new area and to be rendered with lower resolution.

The RLColorApplet class uses three different colors to simulate the proposed method. The screen simulation and probability areas are the same as RLImageApplet class. In this class to simplify the demonstration, each color represents a specific resolution area. The three colors and their corresponding layers are:

■ For the layer with the highest resolution.
■ For the layer with intermediate resolution.
■ For the layer with the lowest resolution.

Figure 11 shows the selected areas with RLImageApplet and RLColorApplet. The objects enclosed within the internal layer are rendered with the highest resolution. The objects in second area are displayed with lower resolution. Lowest resolution applies to the objects that are in screen rectangle but not selected by any probability area. The images in figure 11 represent the selected areas chosen by the algorithm before viewer moves.

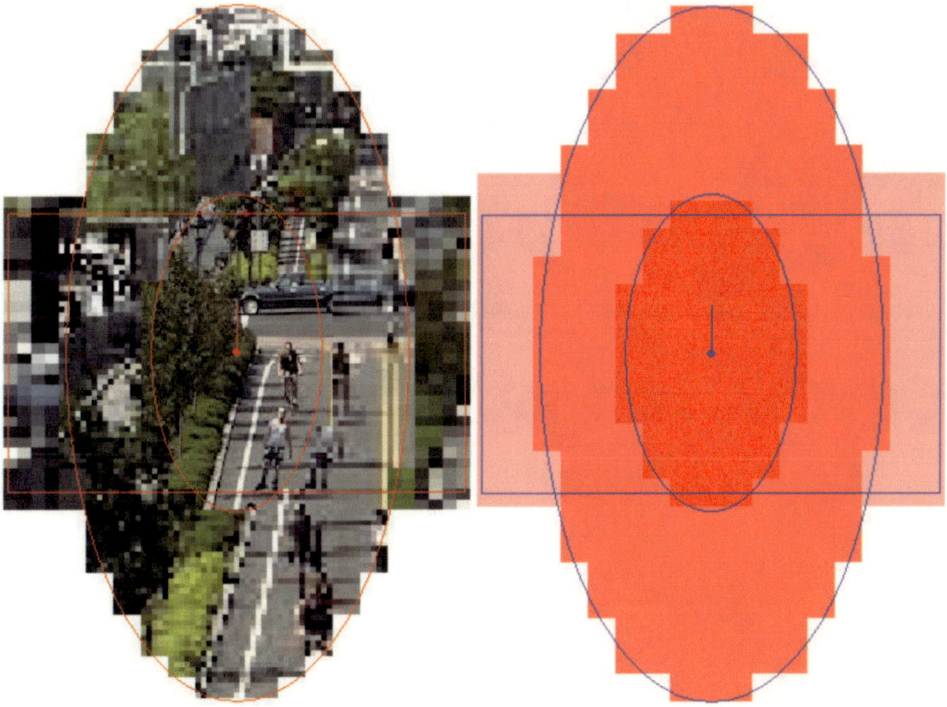

Fig. 11. Selected areas before viewer moves.

Figure 12 shows the selected areas after forward move. Since most of the necessary objects had been selected and rendered for previous move, the images in this figure show there are only few objects that need to be rendered and to be shown on screen for new position of the viewer.

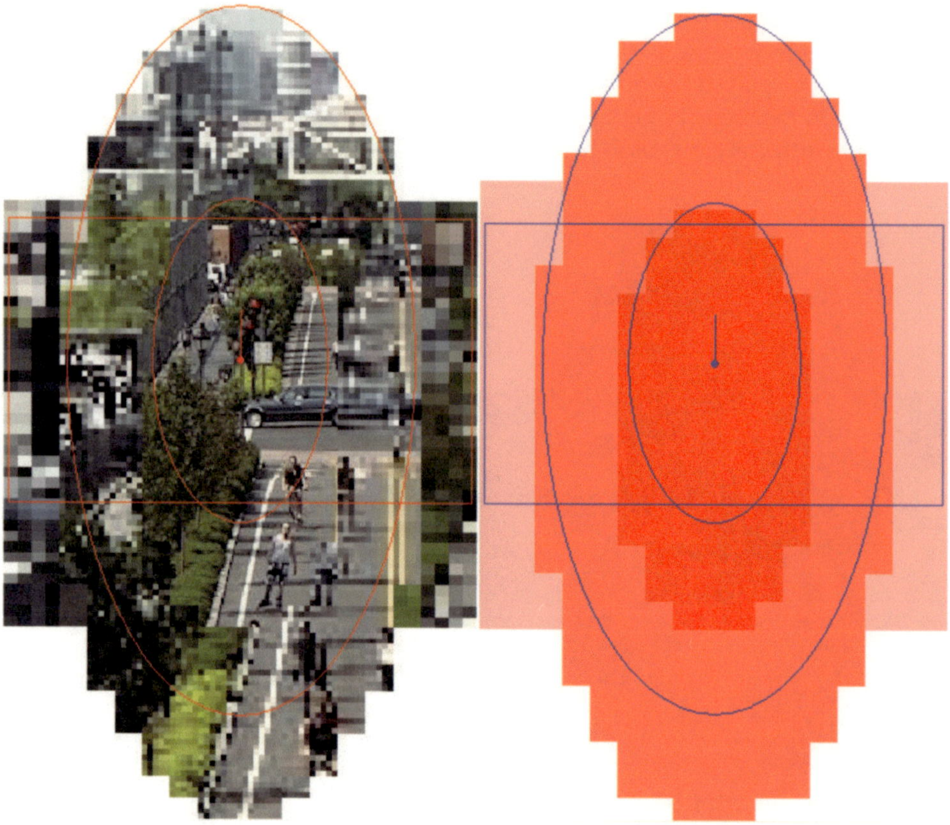

Fig. 12. Selected areas after forward move.

Figure 13 shows the selected areas after turning to the right. As probability areas represent, there are less objects ready on the sides other than front side of the viewer. In case of turning to the sides, more objects have to be selected and to be rendered with the proper resolution because it is a slower process than moving forward. Therefore, since the probability of turning to the sides is less than probability of moving forward, it provides minimum delay.

Fig. 13. Selected areas after right turn.

7. Conclusion

In this paper, a new method has been introduced to improve visualization of large datasets performance. A program based on the new method which utilizes proximity, level of details, and statistics from previous moves to predict next position and to select necessary objects for future use has been presented. This program is not dependent on the shape and distribution of objects and does not waste storage by assigning extra space based on specific geographic distribution over an area.

One of the advantages of the proposed algorithm is when datasets are too large to fit into local hard drive or when the geo-objects are frequently updated. If the available hard drive is large, more geo-objects can be kept on client side. But, if available storage size is small, geo-objects have to be downloaded more frequently. If geo-objects change repeatedly, as it is the case most of the times, the updated geo-objects have to be downloaded. Thus, it is not efficient to keep many geo-objects on hard drive. If the geo-objects are not changed frequently, objects can be stored on hard drive depending on storage capacity. This reduces the need for downloading geo-objects frequently and improves the performance.

The best shape for the probability area has been discussed to ensure the algorithm's interactive navigation. A set of effective view-dependent strategies has been suggested for selecting objects with small memory footprint and efficient use of network and server resource. Level of details, multi-resolution, and pipeline are the methods incorporated into the proposed technique to improve its performance.

8. Acknowledgment

This work was supported by NASA Langley Research Center Grant # NOC1-03033 under the Chesapeake Information Based Aeronautic Consortium (CIBAC).

9. Reference

A. A. Mirin, R. H. Cohen, B. C. Curtis, W. P. Dannevik, A. M. Dimits, M. A. Duchaineau, D. E. Eliason, D. R. Schikore, S. E. Anderson, D. H. Porter, P. R. Woodward, L. J. Shieh, and S. W. White, "Very High Resolution Simulation of Compressible Turbulence on the IBM-SP System," Proc. of the 1999 ACM/IEEE Conference on Supercomputing, Portland, Oregon, pp.70, 1999.

J. Gao, H. Shen, J. Huang, and James Kohl, "Visibility Culling for Time-Varying Volume Rendering Using Temporal Occlusion Coherence," Proc. of IEEE Visualization Conference, Austin, TX, pp. 147-154, 2004.

N. Govindaraju, A. Sud, S. Yoon, and D. Manocha, "Parallel Occlusion Culling for Interactive Walkthroughs using Multiple GPUs," University of North Carolina, Charlotte, Computer Science Technical Report TR02-027, 2002.

S. Guthe and W. Strasser, "Advanced Techniques for High-Quality Multi-Resolution Volume Rendering," Computer & Graphics, vol. 28, no. 1, pp. 51-58, 2004.

Z Liu, A Finkelstein, K Li, "Improving Progressive View-Dependent Isosurface Propagation," Computers & Graphics, vol. 26, no. 2, pp. 209-218, 2002.

L. Ibarria, P. Lindstrom, and J. Rossignac, "Spectral Predictors," IEEE Data Compression Conference, Snowbird, UT, 2007. To appear.

B. H. Feria, "Linear Predictive Transform of Monochrome Images," Image and Vision Computing, vol. 5, no. 4, pp. 267-278, 1987.

L. Ibarria, P. Lindstrom, J. Rossignac, and A. Szymczak, "Out-of-Core Compression and Decompression of Large n-Dimensional Scalar Fields," Proc. of Eurographics, Granada, Spain, pp. , 2003.

C. T. Silva, J. L. D. Comba, S. P. Callahan, and F.F. Bernardon, "A survey of GPU-Based Volume Rendering of Unstructured Grids," Brazilian Journal of Theoretic and Applied Computing (RITA), vol. 12, no. 2, pp. 9-29, 2005.

S. P. Callahan, M. Ikits, J. L. Comba, and C. T. Silva, "Hardware-Assisted Visibility Sorting for Unstructured Volume Rendering," IEEE Transactions on Visualization and Computer Graphics, vol. 11, no. 3, pp. 285-295, 2005.

F. F. Bernardon, S. P. Callahan, J. L. D. Comba, and C. T. Silva, "Interactive Volume Rendering of Unstructured Grids with Time-Varying Scalar Fields," Proc. of Eurographics Symposium on Parallel Graphics and Visualization, Lisbon, Portugal, pp. 51-58, 2006.

S. P. Callahan, L. Bavoil, V. Pascucci, and C. T. Silva, "Progressive Volume Rendering of Large Unstructured Grids," IEEE Transactions on Visualization and Computer Graphics, vol. 12, no. 5, pp. 1307-1314, 2006.

J. Gao, C. Wang, L. Li, and H. Shen, "A Parallel Multiresolution Volume Rendering Algorithm for Large Data Visualization," Parallel Computing, vol. 31, no. 2, pp. 185-204, 2005.

I. Boada, I. Navazo, and R. Scopigno, "Multi Resolution Volume Visualization with a Texture-Based Octree," The Visual Computer, vol. 17, no. 3, pp. 185-197, 2001.

D. Ellsworth, L. J. Chhiang, and H. W. Shen, "Accelerating Time-Varying Hardware Volume Rendering Using TSP Trees and Color-Based Error Metrics," Proc. of the 2000 IEEE symposium on Volume visualization, Salt Lake City, UT, pp. 119-128, 2000.

S. Guthe, M. Wand, J. Gonser, W. Strasser, "Interactive Rendering of Large Volume Data Sets," Proc. of IEEE visualization, Boston, MA, pp. 53-60, 2002.

T. Funkhouser and C. Sequin, "Adaptive Display Algorithm for Interactive Frame Rates During Visualization of Complex Virtual Environment," Proc. of the 20th Annual Conference on Computer Graphics and Interactive Techniques, Anaheim, CA, pp. 247-254, 1993.

R. Pajarola and C. DeCoro, "Efficient Implementation of Real-Time View-Dependent Multiresolution Meshing," IEEE Transactions on Visualization and Computer Graphics, vol. 10, no. 3, pp. 353–368, 2004.

P. Cignoni, C. Montani, and R. Scopigno, "A Comparison of Mesh Simplification Algorithms," Computer & Graphics, vol. 22, no. 1, pp. 37-54, 1998.

P. Lindstrom and G. Turk, "Evaluation of Memory-less Simplification," IEEE Trans. Visualization and Computer Graphics, vol. 5, no. 2, pp. 98-115, 1999.

C. Wang and H. Shen, "Hierarchical Navigation Interface: Leveraging Multiple Coordinated Views for Level-of-Detail Multiresolution Volume Rendering of Large Scientific Datasets," Proc. of Ninth International Conference on Information Visualization, Greenwich, UK, pp. 259- 267, 2005.

B. Shneiderman, "The Eyes Have it, A Task by Data Type and Taxonomy for Information Visualizations," Proc. of IEEE Visual Languages, Boulder, CO, pp. 336-343, 1996.

2

Beyond object-oriented software development

Adam Przybylek
University of Gdansk
Poland

1. Introduction

Dealing with complexity has been one of the fundamental goals of software engineering since its inception. The primary technique for managing the complexity of a software systems is **Separation of Concerns** (SoC) (Chu-Carroll, 2000), (Beltagui, 2003). SoC refers to the ability to decompose and organize the system into manageable concerns, which can be developed and maintained in relative isolation (Przybylek, 2007). A **concern** is a specific requirement or an interest which pertains to the system's development. Concerns can be classified into two categories: **core concerns** and **crosscutting concerns**. The former are usually responsible for the main functionality of a system. They are disjoined by nature and therefore their implementations can be precisely separated from each other. However, a typical system also consists of concerns like authentication, logging, error handling, data persistence, etc., which play a supporting role for core concerns. They capture non-functional requirements or technical-level issues that affect the system as a whole (Przybylek, 2007). Although they can be identified as distinct concerns, their implementations cut across the implementation of some core concerns and cannot be localized using traditional decomposition units such as procedures or classes (Przybylek, 2008). They are called crosscutting concerns and they are damaging to the software architecture.

A number of approaches have been proposed to achieve a better separation of crosscutting concerns. This chapter focuses on two the most prominent among them - aspect-oriented programming (AOP) and composition filters (CFs).

2. Background

2.1 Modularization

When solving a simple problem, the entire problem can be tackled at once. For solving a complex problem, the basic principle should be divided into easier to comprehend pieces, so that each piece can be conquered separately (Jalote, 2005). Implementation and maintenance costs generally will be decreased when each piece of the system corresponds to exactly one small, well-defined piece of the problem, and each relationship between a system's pieces corresponds only to a relationship between pieces of the problem (Yourdon & Constantine, 1979).

In software engineering, the unit to decompose a system is called a **module**. A module is a lexically contiguous sequence of program statements having a name by which other parts of the system can refere to it (Yourdon & Constantine, 1979), (Stevens et al., 1974). A module consists of two parts: an interface and a module body (implementation). An **interface** presents the services provided by the module. It separate the information needed by a client from the implementation details. A module body is the code that actually realizes the module responsibility. It hides the design decisions and is only accessible from within the module. The parts interface and implementation are also called public and private, respectively. Users of a module need to know only its public part (Riel, 1996). An interface serves as a contract between the module and its clients. This contract allows the programmer to change the implementation without interfering with the rest of the program, so long as the public interface remains the same (Riel, 1996). Designing a module so that the implementation details are hidden from other modules is called **information hiding** (Schach, 2007).

There are several reasons for structuring a program into modules:

- Modularization accelerates implementation by encouraging parallel development of different parts of a system.
- Modularization reduces the propagation of side effects when changes occur. Each change is localized to one specific module.
- Modularization makes the program easier to understand. Instead of trying to keep the entire program in mind at once, it suffices to check that each module meets its specifications under the assumption that all other modules also meet their specifications.
- Well-designed modules can be reused in other programs with no change.

The best known module properties to assess its quality are coupling and cohesion. **Coupling** is a measure of how strongly one module is connected to, has knowledge of, or relies on other modules. If two modules are loosely coupled, they are relatively independent, so changes in one module usually don't affect other modules. **Cohesion** is a measure of how tightly bound the internal elements of a module are to one another (Jalote, 2005). A module has high cohesion if all of its elements are related strongly and are necessary for achieving the functionality required. The goal of software engineer is to design the modules with high cohesion and low coupling. Such modules are easy to analyse, modify, test, and reuse.

2.2 From structured to object oriented programming

Various paradigms, that provide different modules to decompose a system, have been studied over years. The oldest decomposition unit are procedures and functions which are the focus of the **structured paradigm**. The structured paradigm merges the ideas proposed by:

- Dijkstra: SoC, layered architecture, structured control constructs, formal verification;
- Wirth: stepwise refinement, modular programming;
- Parnas: information hiding, modular programming;
- Hoare: designing data structures, verification of program correctness;
- Knuth: local variables, literate programming.

In the past, the structured paradigm proved to be very successful. However, as software grew in size, inadequacies of the structured techniques started to become apparent, and the

object-oriented (OO) **paradigm** was proposed by Dahl and Nygaard as a better alternative. The OO paradigm, which is currently the most popular, was created from a desire to close correspondence between objects in the real world and their counterparts in software. The object-oriented purism comes from the dogma that everything should be modeled by objects, because human perception of the world is based on objects.

An **object** is a software entity that combines both state and behavior. An object's behavior describes what the object can do and is specified by a set of operations. The implementation of an operation is called a **method**. The way that the methods are carried out is entirely the responsibility of the object itself (Schach, 2007) and is hidden from other parts of the program (Larkin & Wilson 1993). An object performs an operation when it receives a message from a client. A message is a request that specifies which operation is desired. The set of messages to which an object responds is called its message interface (Hopkins & Horan, 1995).

An object's state is described by the values of its attributes (i.e. data) and cannot be directly accessed from the outside. The attributes in each object can be accessed only by its methods. Because of this restriction, an object's state is said to be encapsulated. The advantage of encapsulation is that as long as the external behavior of an object appears to remain the same, the internals of the object can be completely changed (Hunt, 1997). This means that if any modifications are necessary in the implementation, the client of the object need not be affected.

In OO software development, a system is seen as a set of objects that communicate with each other by sending messages to fulfil the system requirements. The object receiving the message may be able to perform the task entirely on its own (i.e. access the data directly or use its other method as an intermediary). Alternatively, it may ask other objects for information, or pass information to other objects (Hopkins & Horan, 1995).

The most popular model of OOP is a classed based model. In this model, an object's implementation is defined by its **class**. The object is said to be an instance of the class from which it was created. A class is a blueprint that specifies the structure and the behaviour of all its instances. Each instance contains the same attributes and methods that are defined in the class, although each instance has its own copy of those attributes.

OO languages offer two primary reuse techniques: inheritance and composition. Software reuse refers to the development of software systems that use previously written modules. **Inheritance** allows for reusing an existing class in the definition of a new class. The new class is called the derived class (also called subclass). The original class from which the new class is being derived is called the base class (also called superclass). All the attributes and methods that belong to the base class automatically become part of the derived class (Cline et al., 1998). The subclass definition specifies only how it differs from the superclass (Larkin & Wilson 1993); it may add new attributes, methods, or redefine (override) methods defined by the superclass.

An object of a derived class can be used in every place that requires a reference to a base class (Cline et al., 1998). It allows for dispatching a message depending not only on the message name but also on the type of the object that receives the message. Thus, the methods that matches the incoming message is not determined when the code is created (compile time), but is selected when the message is actually sent (run time) (Hopkins & Horan, 1995). An object starts searching the methods that matches the incoming message in its class. If the method is found there, then it is bound to the message and executed, and the appropiate response returned. If the appropiate method is not found, then the search is made in the instance's class's immediate superclass. This process repeats up the class hierarchy until either the methods is located or there are no further superclasses (Hopkins & Horan, 1995). The possibility that the same message, sent to the same reference, may invoke different methods is called **polymorphism**.

A new class can be composed from existing classes by **composition**. Composition is the process of putting an object inside another object (the composite) (Cline et al., 1998). A composite can delegate (re-direct) the requests it receives to its enclosing object. Composition models the has-a relationship. It is claimed that composition is more powerful than inheritance, because (1) composition can simulate inheritance, and (2) composition supports the dynamic evolution of systems, whereas inheritance relations are statically defined relations between classes (Bergmans, 1994).

Inheritance is also called "white box" reuse, because internals of a base class are visible to its extensions. In contrast, composition is called "black box" reuse, because the internals of the enclosed object are not visible to the enclosing object (and vice-versa) (Oprisan, 2008). With composition, an enclosing object can only manipulate its enclosed object through the enclosed object's interface. Because composition introduces looser coupling between classes it is preferable to inheritance.

In the early days of OOP there has been a general agreement that single classes should be the primary unit of organization and reuse. However, over the years it has been recognized that a slice of behavior affecting a set of collaborating classes is a better unit of organization than a single class. In the face of these insights, mainstream programming languages have been equipped with constructs to group sets of related classes, for example name spaces in C++ or packages in Java (Ostermann, 2003).

2.3 Weaknesses of object orientation

The OO paradigm has been one of the most important contributions in the history of software development (Clarke & Baniassad, 2005). It was created from a desire to have language constructs for reflecting a natural view of the world. Although OOP improves software reuse and system maintenance, practical experience shows that OOP has not been as successful as expected. The main problem for OOP is that it does not have an efficient way of expressing crosscutting concerns.

As it turned out classes and packages are a powerful way only to modularize core concerns. Symptoms of implementing crosscutting concerns in OO languages are "code scattering" and "code tangling". **Scattering** occurs when multiple fragments of code that all do the same thing (or that do closely related things) are distributed across multiple modules. Code scattering causes that apparently small changes in requirements usually forces programmers to modify many modules. The term **code tangling** is often used to describe the situation where a class contains logic pertaining to more than one concern. Tangled code makes it difficult to see which code belongs to which concern. Code tangling and scattering negatively affect the software quality. In the result software is difficult to maintain and reuse (Kiczales et al., 1997).

3. The tyranny of the dominant decomposition

Every programming paradigm involves some kind of decomposition: starting with a high level depiction of the system's key elements and creating lower level looks at how the system's features and functions will fit together (Atlee, 2005). The manner in which a system is physically divided into modules can affect significantly the structural complexity and quality of the resulting system (Yourdon & Constantine, 1979), (Parnas, 1972). The most effectively decomposition is usually the one which minimizes dependencies among modules.

In software engineering, there are two common types of decomposition:

- procedural decomposition (in structured programming) - centers on identifying the major system functions and then elaborating and refining them in a top-down manner;
- object oriented decomposition - breaks a large system down into progressively smaller classes that are responsible for some part of the problem domain.

The exact nature of the decomposition differs between the structured and OO paradigm, but it feels comfortable to talk about what is encapsulated as a functional unit of the overall system (Kiczales et al., 1997). Therefore, both decomposition techniques can be generally treated as **functional decomposition**.

There are certain modularity problems that will never be solved satisfactorily with functional decomposition only, how sophisticated they may ever be. The main failure of functional decomposition is that it assumes that real-world concepts have intuitive, mind-independent, preexisting concept hierarchies. However, our perception of the world depends heavily on the context from which it is viewed: There is no conceptual lingua franca (Ostermann, 2003).

To illustrate the problem, consider the example (Fig. 1) presented by Ostermann. Each figure represents a particular concern of a software system. There are three options for organizing this space: by size, by shape, or by color. Each of these decompositions is equally reasonable, but they are not hierarchically related (Ostermann, 2003).

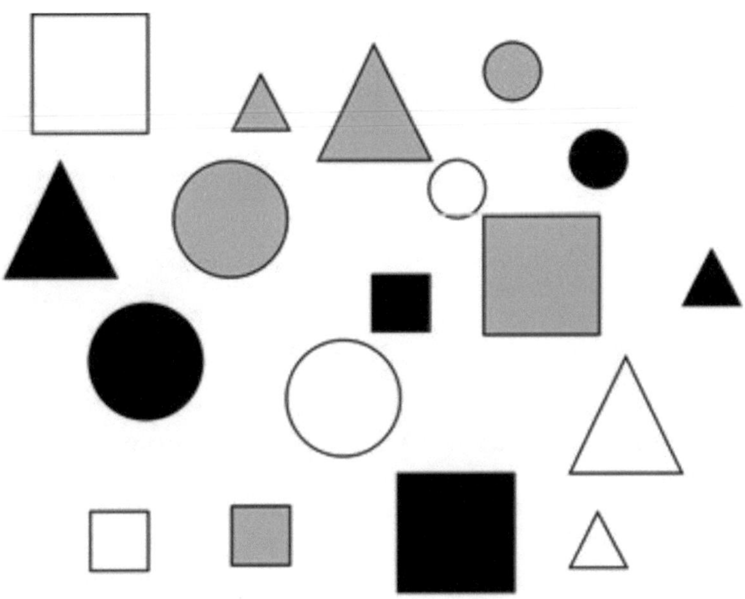

Fig. 1. Abstract concern space

With a mind-independent hierarchical decomposition, one fixed classification sequence has to be choosen. In Fig. 2, the classification sequence is color, shape, size. The problem with such a fixed classification sequence is that only the first element of the list is localized whereas all other concerns are tangled in the resulting hierarchical structure (Mezini & Ostermann, 2004). Fig. 2 illustrates this with the concern "circle", whose definition is scattered around the color-driven decomposition (Ostermann, 2003). Only the color concern is cleanly separated into white, grey, and black, but even this decomposition is not satisfactory because the color concern is still tangled with other concerns (Mezini & Ostermann, 2004).

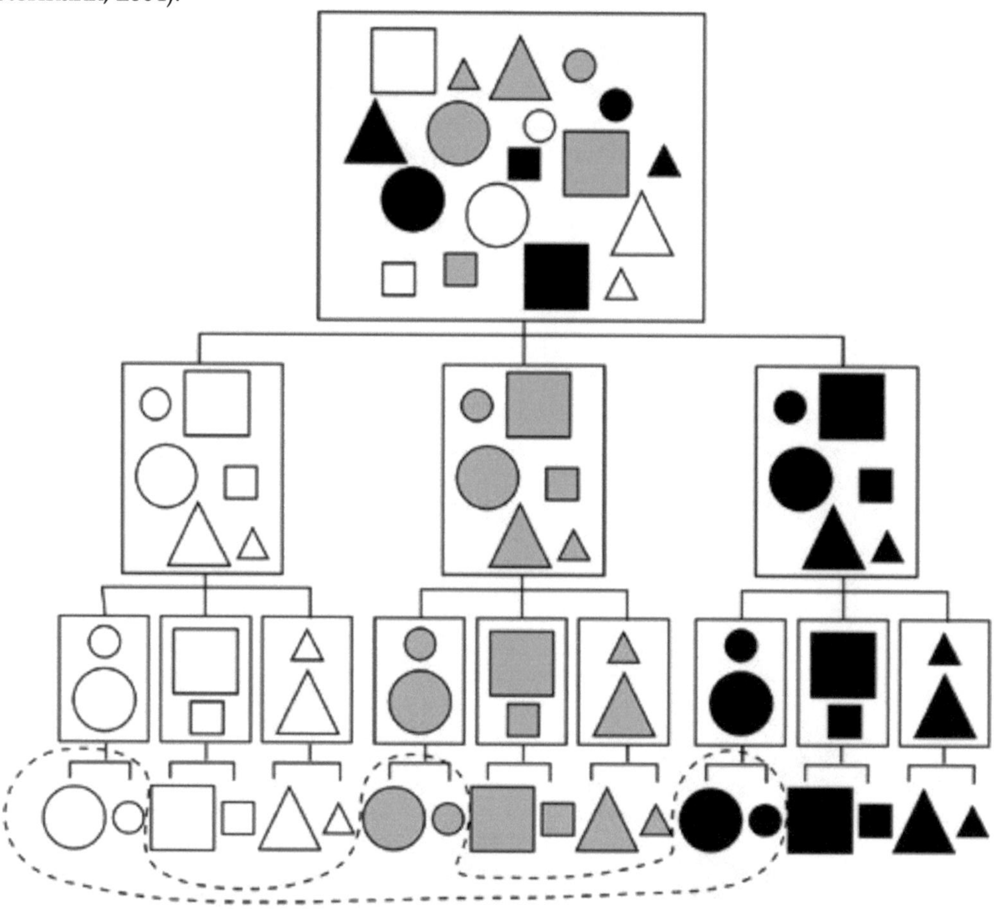

Fig. 2. Arbitrariness of the decomposition hierarchy

The presented problem is known as the "**tyranny of the dominant decomposition**" and it means that existing languages and formalisms generally provide only one, dominant dimension along which to separate e.g., by object or by function (Tarr et al., 1999). In the result, no matter how well a system is decomposed, implementation of crosscutting concerns will be scattered through the whole system and tangled into implementation of core concerns.

Several techniques have been invated to overcome this problem. The most prominent among them are aspect-oriented programming (AOP) and composition filters (CF's). Both paradigms builds on all the advantages of object orientation, so the term post-OO paradigm has been introduced to refer to them.

4. The aspect-oriented paradigm

4.1 Basic concepts

AOP grew out of the research work undertaken by Gregor Kiczales (Kiczales et al., 1997) at Xerox PARC (Palo Alto Research Center). It appeared as a reaction to the phenomena of code tangling and scattering. The aim of AOP is to improve SoC by introducing a new unit of decomposition, called aspect. Aspects allow programmers to implement crosscutting concerns in a well-localized way.

The first AOP language was AspectJ, developed by Kiczales and his team. To encourage the growth of the AspectJ technology and community, PARC transferred AspectJ to an openly-developed Eclipse project in December 2002. Since that time, AspectJ has matured into a stable and complete AOP platform. A program in AspectJ can be thought of being composed of two parts:

- the part implementing the core concerns;
- the part implementing the crosscutting concerns.

This model is called the asymmetric approach, which means that crosscutting concerns are encapsulated in a special kind of module, different from the base units.

AspectJ is an extension to Java. It brings new concepts such as an aspect, a joinpoint, a pointcut, an advice, an introduction, and a parent declaration.

An **aspect** is a module that encapsulates the behaviour and structure of a crosscutting concern. It can, like a class, realize interfaces, extend classes and declare attributes and operations. In addition, it can extend other aspects and declare advices, pointcuts, introductions and parent declarations.

A **joinpoint** is an identifiable location in the program flow where the implementation of a crosscutting concern can be plugged in. Typical examples of joinpoints include a throw of an exception, a call to a method and an object instantiation.

A **pointcut** is a language construct designed to specify a set of join-points and obtain the context (e.g. the target object and the operation arguments) surrounding the join-points as well. The purpose of declaring a pointcut is to share its pointcut expression in many advices or other pointcuts. A pointcut cannot be overloaded. The pointcut signature is follows:

```
[visibility-modifier] pointcut name([parameters]): PointcutExpression;
```

The visibility-modifier defines the visibility of the pointcut. The options for visibility are the same as for other Java artifacts. The PointcutExpression acts as a filter, matching join points that meet its specification. The name, which looks like a method, will be used shortly to handle actions performed when a join point is encountered by the Java runtime.

An **advice** is a method-like construct used to define an additional behaviour that has to be inserted at all joinpoint picked out by the associated pointcut. The body of an advice is the implementation of a crosscutting functionality. The advice is able to access values in the execution context of the pointcut. Depending on the type of advice, whether "before", "after" or "around," the body of an advice is executed before, after or in place of the selected joinpoints. An around advice may cacnel the captured call, may wrap it or may execute it with the changed context.

The simplicity format of advice is:

```
advice_type ([parameters]) [returning] : pointcut_name([parameters]) {
  //code to execute
}
```

An **introduction** is used to crosscut the static-type structure of a given class. It allows a programmer to add attributes and methods to the class without having to modify it explicitly. The power of introduction comes from the introduction being able to add methods to the interface.

A **parent declaration** may change the class's super-class or add implemented interfaces by defining an extends/implements relationship.

4.2 Examples

Scenerio 1 - Remote client monitoring

In some server application the need for a new requirement has occurred. IP addresses of remote clients must be logged. Logging is one of the most common crosscutting concern.

Two fundamental classes responsible for network communication are Socket and ServerSocket. ServerSocket runs on the server side and listens for incoming connections using its accept() method. When a client does connect, the ServerSocket::accept() method returns a Socket object, which connects the client and the server. The IP address of the remote client can be gained via the Socket::getInetAddress() method.

The logging concern can be implemented in an OO way by defining a new class that extends ServerSocket and redefines the original accept() method (Listing 1). After the original accept() method returns a new socket, the IP address is retrived from this socket and then logged. Moreover, every place where ServerSocket is instantiated has to be replaced by IPlogServerSocket.

```
class IPlogServerSocket extends ServerSocket {
  public Socket accept() throws IOException {
    Socket s = super.accept();
    String ip = s.getInetAddress().getHostAddress();
    System.out.println( new Date() +" [" + ip + "]" );
    return s;
  }
}
```

Listing 1. The IPlogServerSocket class

The above imlementation tangles the logging concern along with listening for incoming connection. The ancillary logging code doesn't belong to the class at the conceptual level, so it decreases the class cohesion. A better solution can be found when using the AO paradigm. With AspectJ-based logging, there is no need to extend the base class. All programmers need to do is define an aspect (Listing 2).

```
aspect IPMonitoring {
  pointcut clientConnect(): call(public Socket ServerSocket.accept()); //1
  after() returning (Socket s): clientConnect() { //2
    String ip = s.getInetAddress().getHostAddress(); //3
    System.out.println( new Date() +" [" + ip + "]" ); //4
  }
}
```

Listing 2. The IPMonitoring aspect

The most fundamental difference between the conventional and AO solution is a separation of concerns. Code related to logging is encapsulated in the IPMonitoring aspect. The joinpoints at which merging should be made are identified as the places where the ServerSocket.accept() method is called (line 1). The after-returning advice (line 2) runs after a successful return from accept(). Line 4 contains the actual logging code.

Scenerio 2 – Tracing a method's execution time
Tracing is a special form of logging where the entry and/or exit of selected methods are logged (Laddad, 2003). Suppose, the Matrix class is designed as shown at Fig. 3.

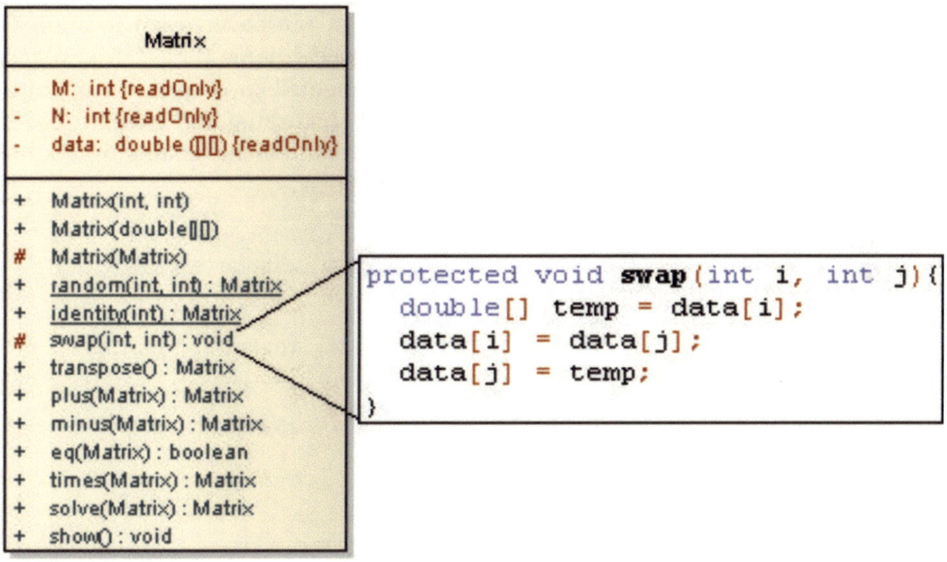

Fig. 3. The Matrix class

There is need to trace how long it takes to execute a method. OO solution requires embedding the tracing code in each method. For example, Listing 4 shows how the swap method is instrumented to mesure its execution time. Such instrumentation is very invasive.

```
public class Matrix {
//...
  protected void swap(int i, int j) {
    long start = System.currentTimeMillis();
    double[] temp = data[i];
    data[i] = data[j];
    data[j] = temp;
    long end = System.currentTimeMillis();
    double time = end - start;
    System.out.println("void Matrix.swap(int,int) - " + time);
  }
}
```

Listing 4. The swap method with tracing

The code needed for tracing is scattered, because almost the same code occures in each method. Alternatively, a new subclass could be created (Listing 5).

```
public class LogMatrix extends Matrix {
//...
  protected void swap(int i, int j) {
    long start = System.currentTimeMillis();
    super.swap(i,j);
    long end = System.currentTimeMillis();
    double time = end - start;
    System.out.println("void Matrix.swap(int,int) - " + time);
  }
}
```

Listing 5. Tracing in the subclass

However, code scattering and tangling are still present. Moreover, each location where Matrix is instantiated would have to be replaced by the new name (LogMatrix). But, what would happen if the tracing concern has to be implemented in several classes of a real system. Imagine how long it would take. Instead of disturbing the existing code it is sufficient to define an aspect that implements the new requirement (Listing 6). The tracing code is injected before and after the execution of each method.

```
public aspect TimeLogging {
  pointcut eachMethod(): (execution(* *.*(..)) && !within(TimeLogging);
  Object around(): eachMethod() {
    long start = System.currentTimeMillis();
    Object tmp = proceed(); //execute the original method
    long end = System.currentTimeMillis();
    double time = end - start;
    Signature sig = thisJoinPointStaticPart.getSignature();
    System.out.println(sig +" - "+ time);
    return tmp;
  }
}
```

Listing 6. The TimeTracing aspect

Scenerio 3 - Producer-Consumer

This scenerio uses the classical Producer-Consumer problem, where two processes (or threads), one known as the "producer" and the other called the "consumer", run concurrently and share a fixed-size buffer. The producer generates items and places them in the buffer. The consumer removes items from the buffer and consumes them. However, the producer must not place an item into the buffer if the buffer is full, and the consumer cannot retrieve an item from the buffer if the buffer is empty. Nor may the two processes access the buffer at the same time to avoid race conditions. If the consumer needs to consume an item that the producer has not yet produced, then the consumer must wait until it is notified that the item has been produced. If the buffer is full, the producer will need to wait until the consumer consumes any item.

Assume the existence of the cyclic queue as shown at Fig. 4. The method put(..) stores one object in the queue and get() removes the oldest one. Attribute nextToRemove indicate the location of the oldest object. The location of the new object can be computed using nextToRemove, number of items (numItems) and queue capacity (buf.length).

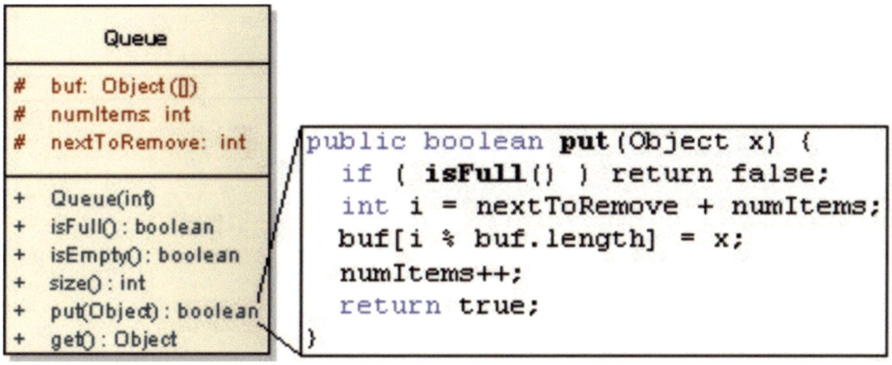

Fig. 4. The queue class

Stage 1 - Buffer

In order to use the queue as a buffer an adaption to a multi-thread environment is needed. Both put(..) and get() methods have to be executed in mutual exclusion. In addition, the buffer has to block a thread when the thread tries to add an element to a full queue or to remove an element from an empty queue. In Java these methods have to be wraped in synchronization code (Listing 8).

```
public class Buffer extends Queue {
  public Buffer(int capacity) {
    super(capacity);
  }
  public synchronized boolean put(Object x) {
    while ( isFull() ) try {
      wait();
    } catch (InterruptedException e) {}
    super.put(x);
    notifyAll();
    return true;
  }
  public synchronized Object get() {
    while ( isEmpty() ) try {
      wait();
    } catch (InterruptedException e) {}
    Object tmp = super.get();
    notifyAll();
    return tmp;
  }
}
```
Listing 8. The buffer class

The above implementation tangles the synchronization concern with the core logic. Moreover, the synchronisation code is scattered through the methods responsible for accessing the buffer. In the result the put(..) and get() methods contain similar fragments of code for cooperating synchronisation. A separation of synchronization concern can be achieved by using the aspect (Listing 9).

```
public aspect SynchronizedQueue pertarget(target(Queue)) {
  protected pointcut call_get(): call( Object Queue.get() );
  protected pointcut call_put(Object x):
    call( boolean Queue.put(Object) ) && args(x);

  Object around(Queue q): call_get() && target(q) {
    synchronized(this) {
      while( q.isEmpty() ) try {
        wait();
      } catch (InterruptedException e) {}
      Object tmp = proceed(q);
      notifyAll();
      return tmp;
    }
  }
  boolean around(Queue q, Object x): call_put(x) && target(q) {
    synchronized(this) {
      while ( q.isFull() ) try {
        wait();
      } catch (InterruptedException e) {}
      proceed(q,x);
      notifyAll();
      return true;
    }
  }
}
```

Listing 9. The SynchronizedQueue aspect

Stage 2 – Time buffer

After implementing the buffer a new requirement has occured: the buffer should save current date and time associated with each stored item. A Java programmer may use inheritance and composition as reuse techniques (Listing 10).

```
public class TimeBuffer extends Buffer {
  protected Queue delegateDates;
  public TimeBuffer(int capacity) {
    super(capacity);
    delegateDates = new Queue(capacity);
  }
  public synchronized boolean put(Object x) {
    super.put(x);
    delegateDates.put( new Long(System.currentTimeMillis()) );
    return true;
  }
  public synchronized Object get() {
    Object tmp = super.get();
    Long date = (Long) delegateDates.get();
    long time  = System.currentTimeMillis() - date.longValue();
    System.out.println(time);
    return tmp;
  }
}
```

Listing 10. The TimeBuffer class

The problem is that three different concerns are interwinded within put/get and so these concerns cannot be composed separately. It means that e.g. if a programmer wants a queue with timing he cannot reuse the timing concern from TimeBuffer; he has to reimplement the timing concern in a new class that extends Queue. A slightly better solution seems to be using AOP and implementing the timing as an aspect (Listing 11).

```
public privileged aspect Timing pertarget( instantiation() ) {
  protected Queue delegateDates;

  protected pointcut instantiation():
    target(Queue) && !cflow(within(Timing));
  protected pointcut init(Queue q): execution( Queue.new(..) ) && target(q);
  protected pointcut execution_get(): execution( Object Queue.get() );
  protected pointcut execution_put(): execution(boolean Queue.put(Object));

  after(Queue q): init(q) {
    delegateDates = new Queue(q.buf.length);
  }
  after(): execution_get() {
    Long date = (Long) delegateDates.get();
    long time  = System.currentTimeMillis() - date.longValue();
    System.out.println("<"+time+">");
  }
  after(): execution_put() {
    delegateDates.put( new Long(System.currentTimeMillis()) );
  }
}
```

Listing 11. The Timing aspect

This solution require only one change in the existing code - the instantation pointcut in SynchronizedQueue. It must be the same as in Timing.

5. Composition Filters

Composition Filters (CF's) was defined by Aksit and Tripathi in the late 1980s (Aksit & Tripathi, 1988), and originally implemented in the Sina language. The Composition Filters model can be thought of as the conventional OO model in which an object can be surrounded by input and output filters. **Filters** extend the message passing mechanism by manipulating incoming and outgoing messages. Incoming messages have to pass through all the input filters until they are dispatched and the outgoing through the output filters until they are sent outside the object (Bergmans & Aksit, 2001), (Czarnecki & Eisenecker, 2000). Dispatching here means either to start searching of a local method, or to delegate the message to another object. The filters together compose the enhanced behaviour of the object, possibly in terms of other objects. The resulting model and its elements are shown in Fig. 5.

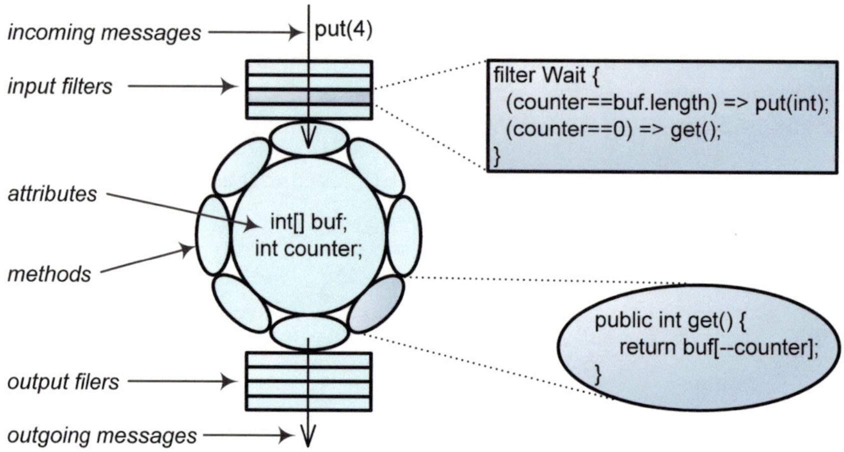

Fig. 5. The Composition Filters model

A filter definition consists of a **filter type** and **filter guards**. It has the following form:

```
filter filterType {
  condition => selector1, selector2, ..., selectorN;       //filter guard 1
  ...                                                      //filter guard 2
}
```

A selector is mainly used for matching messages. In addition it may modify certain parts of messages or indicate the targget object to which the message should be redirected. When the selector on the left hand matches, no further selectors should be considered.

A guard matches the message if (1) the condition evaluates to true, and (2) the message matches one of the selectors. As soon as the first guard is matched, the message is said to be accepted by the filter. A filter rejects a message if none of the filter guards matches the message. The filter type determines the semantics associated with acceptance and rejection of messages (Bergmans, 1994), (Bergmans & Aksit, 2001). In other words, it determines how to handle the messages after the matching process. Examples of predefined filter types are presented in Table 1.

filterType	**semantic**
Error	If the message is accepted, an exception is raised, otherwise the message continues to the subsequent filter.
Wait	If the message is rejected, it proceeds immediately to the next filter in the set. Otherwise the message is put in a queue, and delayed until the correspondent condition is satisfied. Re-evaluation of a Wait filter occurs at least at every change of the object state. In order to provide mutual exclusion, the pre-processor puts a synchronised block around every method for which a Wait filter is specified. However, while a message is blocked, the other messages can be processed.
Dispatch	The last filter in a filter set is always a Dispatch filter. When a Dispatch filter rejects a message, an exception is raised. In case of acceptance, the message is dispatched to the object that corresponds to the target of the matching selector (Bergmans, 1994).

Table 1. The predefined filter types

The running example of CF's is shown using scenerio 3 (Producer-Consumer) from Section 4.2. The presented source code is written in a simplified version of CF's.

Stage 1 - Buffer

The class definition in Listing 12 uses wait filter to provide the synchronization concern.

```
public class BufferCF {
  private Queue delegate;
  public BufferCF(int capacity) {
    delegate = new Queue(capacity);
  }
  filter Wait {
    delegate.isFull() => put(Object),
    delegate.isEmpty() => get()
  };
  filter Dispatch { true => delegate.* };
}
```

Listing 12. The Buffer definition in CF's

An arriving message is evaluated according to the Wait filter specification. The first guard matches the put(Object) if the buffer is full (i.e. the current number of elements in the buffer is equal to the capacity of the buffer). The second guard matches the get() message if the buffer is empty. When the message is rejected, it proceeds immediately to Dispatch filter. Otherwise the message is put in a queue, and delayed until the correspondent condition is satisfied. Re-evaluation of Wait filter occurs at least at every change of the object state. In order to provide mutual exclusion, the pre-processor puts a synchronised block around every method for which Wait filter is specified. However, while a message is blocked, the other messages can be processed.

The wildcard "*" matches all messages which are in the signature of the target. The filter guard "true => delegate.*" declares that all public methods in the delegate object are unconditionally allowed to execute.

Stage 2 – Time buffer

With CF's adding the timing concern requires to reimplement the synchronization concern. Moreover, the timing concern cannot be separate from the operation's core logic (Listing 13).

```
public class TimeBufferCF {
  private Queue delegate;
  private Queue delegateDates;
  public BufferCF(int capacity) {
    delegate = new Queue(capacity);
    delegateDates = new Queue(capacity);
  }
  public void put(Object x) {
    delegate.put(x);
    delegateDates.put( new Long(System.currentTimeMillis()) );
  }
  public Object get() {
    Long date = (Long) delegateDates.get();
    long time  = System.currentTimeMillis() - date.longValue();
    System.out.println(time);
    return delegate.get();
  }
```

```
  filter Wait {
    delegate.isFull() => put(Object),
    delegate.isEmpty() => get()
  };
  filter Dispatch { true => this.*, true => delegate.* };
}
```
Listing 13. The TimeBuffer definition in CF's

6. Discussion

The presented examples illustrate that OOP cannot deal effectively with implementation of crosscuting concerns. In each case the OO solution requires a significant rebuilding of the existing code. Invasive changes break the open-closed principle, which states that modules should be open for extension, but closed for modification. AOP and CF's bring a partial solution. They speed up evolving OO systems to new requirements. AOP usually allows developers to introduce new functionality without making any change to the existing modules. Moreover, it eliminates code tangling and scattering. However, no programming paradigm is without its own set of problems and pitfalls. Applying AO constructs makes the source code hard to understand, because classes are unaware of the presence of aspects. Aspects modify flow control and break encapsulation. Hence, the advantage of AOP over its ancestor is doubtful from the maintenance point of view. Although aspects makes it possible to separate crosscutting concerns, and in the result increase class cohesion, they increase the overall coupling. Aspects are tightly connected with the affected classes, so their reuse is limited.

Implementation of crosscutting concerns in each paradigm provides the following conclusions. AOP is the most beneficial in implementing development concerns such as tracing, debugging, profiling and testing. Development concerns are of interest only to the development team and have to be removed from a system prior to its release into production. AOP is also appropiate for prototyping. Aspects can easily enable and disable the additional functionality when new requirements are explored. AO solutions should also be considered when changes are made only for a moment (e.g. condition checking during the debugging process) and its implementation in an OO way would be invasive.

On the other hand, CF's is less powerful then AOP, but it extends the OO paradigm in a natural way. CF's improves delegation-based reuse and allow the developer to avoid composition anomalies.

7. Summary

Some difficulties in software development can't be overcome using the OO paradigm. Although OOP works well at modularizing core concerns, it falls short when it comes to modularize crosscutting concerns. The growing complexity of today's software makes it necessary for developers to deal with more and more crosscuting concerns. The goal of this chapter was to present how post-OO paradigms improves SoC. The principles of AOP and CF's were explained and illustrated by 3 scenerio of adapting software to new requirements. Both AspectJ and CF's solutions have the following advantages over its ancestor:

- the crosscutting concern is explicitly implemented: instead of being embedded in the code of core concerns;

- the evolution of the OO systems is simplified: new language constructs are offered;
- core concerns can be easily reused: crosscutting concern are not interwinded with core concerns.

Although the presented post-OO paradigms introduce new problems to software development, they indicate the direction in which the programming techniques should evolve.

8. References

Aksit, M. & Tripathi, A. (1988). Data Abstraction Mechanisms in Sina. *ACM Sigplan Notices,* vol. 23(11), 267-275

Atlee J.M. (2005). *Software engineering: theory and practice,* Prentice Hall

Beltagui F. (2003). Features and Aspects: Exploring feature-oriented and aspect-oriented programming interactions. *Technical Report No: COMP-003-2003,* Computing Department, Lancaster University, Lancaster

Bergmans, L. (1994). Composing Concurrent Objects - Applying Composition Filters for the Development and Reuse of Concurrent Object-Oriented Programs. *Ph.D. thesis,* University of Twente

Bergmans, L. & Aksit, M. (2001). Composing crosscutting concerns using composition filters. *Commun. ACM,* vol. 44(10), 51-57

Bergmans, L.; Aksit, M. & Tekinerdogan, B. (1999). Mapping Aspects to Components. University of Twente

Brito, I. & Moreira, A. (2004). Integrating the NFR framework in a RE model, *Proceedings of the 3rd Workshop on Early Aspects, 3rd International Conference on Aspect-Oriented Software Development,* Lancaster

Chu-Carroll M. (2000). Separation of concerns: an organizational approach, *Proceedings of the OOPSLA 2000 Workshop on Advanced Separation of Concerns*

Clarke, S. & Baniassad, E. (2005). *Aspect-Oriented Analysis and Design: The Theme Approach,* Addison Wesley, Boston

Cline, M.; Lomow, G. & Girou, M. (1998). *C++ FAQs,* Addison Wesley

Colyer, A.; Clement, A.; Harley, G. & Webster, M. (2004). *Eclipse AspectJ: Aspect-Oriented Programming with AspectJ and the Eclipse AspectJ Development Tools,* Addison Wesley, Boston

Czarnecki, K. & Eisenecker, U. (2000). *Generative Programming: Methods, Techniques, and Applications,* Addison-Wesley, Boston

Gradecki, J.D. & Lesiecki, N. (2003). *Mastering AspectJ: Aspect-Oriented Programming in Java,* Wiley, Canada

Hopkins, T. & Horan, B. (1995). *Smalltalk: An Introduction to Application Development Using VisualWorks,* Prentice Hall

Hunt, J. (1997). *Smalltalk and Object Orientation,* Springer

Jalote, P. (2005). *An Integrated Approach to Software Engineering,* Springer, New York

Kiczales, G. et al. (1997). Aspect-Oriented Programming, *Proceedings of the European Conference on Object-Oriented Programming (ECOOP).* LNCS, vol. 1241, 220-242, Springer

Laddad, R. (2003). *AspectJ in Action,* Manning

Larkin, D. & Wilson, G. (1993). *Object-Oriented Programming and the Objective-C Language,* Addison Wesley

Mezini, M. & Ostermann, K. (2004). Untangling Crosscutting Models with Caesar, In: *Aspect-Oriented Software Development,* Filman, E.E.; Elrad, T.; Clarke, S.; Aksit, M. (Ed.), Addison Wesley, Canada

Nora B.; Fadila A. & Said G. (2006). A Comparative Classification of Aspect Mining Approaches. *Journal of Computer Science,* vol. 2(4), 322-325

Oprisan, A. (2008). Aspect Oriented Implementation of Design Patterns using Metadata. *MSc Thesis,* University of Joensuu

Ostermann, K. (2003). Modules for Hierarchical and Crosscutting Models. *PhD thesis,* Technische Universität Darmstadt

Parnas, D.L. (1972). On the criteria to be used in decomposing systems into modules. *Communications of the ACM,* vol. 15(12), 1053-1058

Przybylek, A. (2007). Post Object-Oriented Paradigms in Software Development: a Comparative Analysis, *Proceedings of the 1st Workshop on Advances in Programming Languages at IMCSIT'07,* Wisla

Riel, A.J. (1996). *Object-oriented Design Heuristics,* Addison-Wesley, Boston

Schach, S.R. (2007). *Object-Oriented and Classical Software Engineering,* McGraw-Hill, Singapore

Stevens, W.; Myers, G. & Constantine, L. (1974). Structured Design, IBM Systems Journal, 13(2), 115-139

Tarr, P.; Ossher, H.; Harrison, W. & Sutton, S.M. (1999). N degrees of separation: multi-dimensional separation of concerns, *Proceedings of the 21st International Conference on Software Engineering*

Tarr P.; Harrison W.; Ossher H.; Finkelstein A.; Nuseibeh B. & Perry D. (2001). Workshop on Multi-Dimensional Separation of Concerns in Software Engineering. *SIGSOFT Softw. Eng. Notes,* vol. 26(1), 78-81

Yourdon, E. & Constantine, L.L. (1979). *Structured Design: Fundamentals of a Discipline of Computer Program and System Design,* Prentice-Hall, New York

3

Security Trade-off – Ontological Approach

Bialas Andrzej
Institute of Innovative Technologies EMAG
Poland

1. Introduction

The chapter presents the ontology creation process on the security trade-off methodologies example. The trade-off in the security investments is focused on finding an optimal solution with respect to the defined criteria. It is performed by the balancing of effects of security measures, which usually are opposing or conflicting. In such situation, finding an optimal solution is difficult and depends on the features of the applied methods and the application domain needs and constraints that vary from one domain to another.

The general motivation of the works is to support the researches on the security trade-off processes and methods using the advantages and new possibilities offered by the ontological approach. The security trade-off methods, developed separately in different application domains to meet their specific requirements, are diverse and there are many crosscutting issues in them. It is difficult to assess whether the given method can be used in the neighbour application domain because there is no common understanding of the method features and possibilities. Choosing the adequate method for the given application domain remains a challenge. Sampling and analyzing the knowledge dealing with these methods and their features is needed. In such situation, the ontological approach can be helpful, though two aspects of this issue exist. The ontological approach will be used to gain knowledge about the existing trade-off methods and tools, and some of them may be ontology-based as well. Generally, the ontology represents explicit formal specifications of the terms in the given domain and relations between them. The creation of ontologies allows to analyze, share and reuse knowledge in an explicit and mutually agreed manner.

The chapter deals with the preliminary works whose aim is to elaborate the Security Trade-offs Methods Ontology (STMO) and the related knowledge base. The STMO ontology concerns the basic trade-offs methods, especially risk-centred, best fitted for the selected application domains and used to support trade-off decisions in the security investments in these domains. The far-reaching aim of this work is helping to find the right method for the given application. This is the key issue requiring broad knowledge about the methods features and possibilities. The elaborated ontology has been designed for security experts from different application domains to choose the proper methods and tools, and indirectly to support their decision processes. More efficient trade-offs bring different benefits to stakeholders, e.g.: saving funds, improving security, better acceptance of measures, better management, improving the competitiveness and market position, etc.

The chapter discusses the first iteration of the STMO ontology incremental development process, aiming at the prototype creation. This prototype enables other, more extensive and long-term works, requiring deeper collaborative researches in the security trade-off methodologies, whose results can be concurrently incorporated into the developed target ontology and the related knowledge base. The presented there ontology prototype can be viewed as a general framework encompassing selected concepts and relationships and be able to sample knowledge concerning:

- needs and requirements of the application domains with respect to the trade-off processes support,
- identified trade-off methods, including risk-based ones, and their features.

Acquiring the knowledge will allow to define the basic criteria concerning the best fitted method for the given application.

Summing up, the first, main objective of this work is to provide a prototype of the ontology-based framework and tool:

- for researchers, to facilitate researches on the security trade-off methods and tools, aiming at their improvements and laying out their development directions, and to facilitate sampling, analyzing the related knowledge and making it available to the interested parties,
- for users and other interested parties, enabling them access to the knowledge about security trade-off methods in a concise way.

The second objective of this chapter is to present a complete example of the ontology creation process using the basic knowledge engineering principles and the proven, open for general use tool.

The Section 2 of this chapter presents an overview of the existing works concerning the ontological approach applied in the discussed security domain. To better understand the Security Trade-offs Methods Ontology elaboration process, the Section 3 gives an introduction explaining how ontologies are created. The STMO building process is discussed in the main section of the chapter, i.e. in the Section 4. The Section 5 sums up the achieved results and specifies the planned future researches.

2. An ontological approach within the security domain

Ontologies were elaborated recently in many disciplines where "a common understanding", "a common taxonomy" or "reasoning" are important, such as: web-based applications, medicine, public administration, biology and information security. The chapter concerns the latter issue. To get a common picture and background of the presented and planned research and development focused on the specialized security trade-off ontology creation, a short overview of existing works should be done.

Security ontologies are varied and express different issues in this domain. The first group of works concerns generally risk management issues. The paper (Ekelhart et al., 2007b) deals with the ISO/IEC 27001 standard implementation while the work (Ekelhart et al., 2007c) – quantitative risk analysis. Both deal with the knowledge base application supporting the information security management systems implementation. The similar issue, i.e. general aspects of security management is presented by (Martimiano & Moreira, 2005a). The work (Tsoumas et al., 2005) concerns the selection of controls while the work (Martimiano & Moreira, 2005b) discusses incident management issues. The paper (Atkinson et al., 2006) presents ontology-centred technology risk management architecture for the banking sector. This architecture is used for knowledge modelling and integrating different software components. This is another example of the ontological approach to the risk management applications.

The paper (Elahi & Yu, 2008) focuses on a goal-oriented approach for modeling and analyzing security trade-offs and incorporating them into the requirements analysis and architecture design. Goal orientation is also used to structure knowledge to assist designers in making security trade-offs. The authors aim to develop the conceptual modelling framework in the form of an ontology, which provides a required foundation for automated and formal reasoning.

The work (Vorobiev & Bekmamedova, 2007) discusses security and trust ontologies, expressing the risk analysis issues, security algorithm taxonomy, security functions, attacks and defence, and trust. In the work (Kim et al., 2005) the authors specify the extensive NRL (Naval Research Laboratory) security ontology, encompassing subontologies concerning the security of services, security agents, information objects, security algorithms, assurance and credentials. Additionally, they discuss ontology integration issues.

The work (Yavagal et al., 2005) presents an ontological approach to the modelling of the Common Criteria (ISO/IEC 15408) security functional requirements and their mapping to the specified security objectives. The work (Ekelhart et al., 2007a), related to the ontology available at the (Secure Business, 2008), is focused on the ontological representation of the Common Criteria (ISO/IEC 15408) security assurance requirements. The presented tool supports evaluators during the certification process in such activities like: planning an evaluation process, reviewing relevant documents or creating reports. The Author's papers concern also the Common Criteria methodology, presenting the Security Targets Ontology (Bialas, 2008) and the selected issues dealing with the security problem definition and solution using the introduced Specification Means Ontology (Bialas, 2009).

The examples of common security issues ontologies (CSL, 2008; DAML, 2008; Herzog, 2006; REI, 2008) can be analyzed using the Protégé Ontology Editor and Knowledge Acquisition System (Protégé, 2008). Please note the latter one (REI, 2008) presenting the REI ontology (precisely: the set of subontologies) which is used for the security policy development.

The review shows that the basic information security areas are represented by different ontologies. Their number is growing. Some of the mentioned ontologies concern risk management, even the security trade-off, but they are used as tools, e.g. supporting directly the risk management processes. None of these works is devoted to build the risk management methods taxonomy, trade-off methods taxonomy or the knowledge bases, classifying them, ordering their properties and helping to choose the right method for the given application.

Please note that there are some communities of professionals, e.g. (ENISA, 2009), (SARMA, 2009), which sample and manage the knowledge dealing with the risk management methods, but they do not use the ontological approach.

3. Ontology elaboration methodology and the used tool – introduction

In the computer science and information science, ontology is a formal representation of a set of concepts within a domain and the relationships between these concepts. It is used to

reason about the properties of that domain, and may be used to define the domain. (Wiki/ontology, 2009).
The ontology development, based on the basic knowledge engineering principles (Noy, 2001), begins with its domain and scope definition. It requires to investigate the matters that the ontology concerns (here: different aspects of the trade-off support). It allows to define the ontology competency questions (i.e. the questions that the ontology-related knowledge base is able to answer) and to identify the ontology terms within the domain. On this basis the definition of the hierarchy of classes and its properties can begin. The class hierarchy creates the taxonomy of terms in the discussed domain. Some classes have only an abstract meaning, some have instances, called also individuals. The ontology development needs permanent tests and finally the validation by ontology users. This way a prototype of the Security Trade-off Methods Ontology and the related knowledge base has been elaborated. As the development tool, the Protégé Ontology Editor and Knowledge Acquisition System from Stanford University is used (Protégé, 2008). The STMO will be expressed using the OWL (Web Ontology Language) language, precisely the OWL-DL (DL - Description Logics), which allows automatic reasoning, e.g. to compute the classification hierarchy.

4. Development of the Security Trade-off Methods Ontology (STMO)

The section presents the Security Trade-off Methods Ontology (STMO) elaboration process. Particular subsections discuss one step of this process, starting from the ontology domain and scope identification, through the concepts, properties and instances defining, to the ontology testing, validation and use. The STMO elaboration has two objectives:

- providing the common taxonomy of the security trade-off methods used in different application domains; allowing to better understand terms and relationships and to sample basic knowledge about the domain (the near objective, dealing with the STMO prototype presented in the chapter),
- creating on this basis the extensive knowledge database which can help to recommend the right method to solve the given problem in the considered application domain (the further objective, whose fulfilment is enabled by the STMO prototype).

4.1 Domain and scope of the ontology – determining the competency questions

The domain of the STMO ontology are the security trade-off methods, their features and applications, including related tools and their theoretical foundations. Please note that the trade-offs in security investments go beyond traditional cost-benefits and risk management approaches, though the risk issues still play the key role.
The analysis of the Security Trade-off Methods Ontology domain is focused on the following main issues:

- considered domains of applications,
- security trade-off methods,
- security measures implied by these methods,
- expected stakeholders' benefits of the use of the particular methods,

which are briefly discussed. The results of this discussion allow to identify important terms and to define the STMO concepts.

The targeted STMO ontology should consider a broad range of application domains where the security trade-off methods are used, e.g.:

- information security domain,
- financial sector (banking, insurance),
- critical infrastructures (transportation, telecommunications, fuel and energy),
- security-sensitive industry,
- public areas (citizens, governments, society),
- first responder organizations, anti-terrorism and anti-crime activities,
- health care sector,
- regulators (national; international),
- small business and others.

The concepts and relationships of the STMO ontology should express stakeholders' needs and requirements dealing with the security investments that can be encountered in these domains. The created ontology prototype will be open for any application domain but will be focused on the information security domain. Information technologies are the basis of business processes in other application domains, and their inherent risk has been a well known problem for years and for this domain many methods and tools have been developed. Other domains will also be considered though on a more general level of details. The concepts and relationships of the developed ontology should express different groups of methods supporting the trade-off processes, like:

- methods for risk management,
- methods for cost-benefit analysis,
- methods and frameworks for trade-off evaluation and decision support,
- other approaches, like scenario-based techniques, expert systems, process analysis, simulations & gaming, human factors models, etc.

The right method should provide the right (i.e. optimal with respect to the defined criteria) measures to solve the given problem within the considered application domain. Trade-offs has multidimensional character. For this reason, apart from the risk management issues including risk transfer and avoidance, the developed ontology should consider other factors, like: mitigation of uncertainties, impacts and cascading effects, trust, acceptance of measures by stakeholders, cross-cutting issues, integration into the regular systems or operations, supporting business processes, legal aspects, and different constraints. Security investment encompasses different kinds of the security measures used by the trade-off process. Sometimes they provide synergy but usually their impact is mutually opposing or even conflicting. Sometimes the measures implications have a financial or equivalent-to-financial dimension, sometimes they are difficult to express. The examples of the measures are:

- implementation of the selected technological solution enforcing security,
- fault-tolerant mechanisms, including redundancies,
- working out long-term security strategies based on the advanced risk management,
- regulations and legal acts,
- organizational and procedural measures,
- education, training and raising awareness.

The measures proposed by the methods used in the given application domain should bring different kinds of benefits for stakeholders, like:

- saving investment funds,
- gaining more financial return on security investment,

- improving their own security, competitiveness, market position, and supporting a long-term security strategy,
- selecting the best measures from alternatives and facilitating acceptance of the measures,
- prioritizing and scheduling decisions or selected measures,
- giving support to regulatory decisions and processes,
- improving confidence of societies in security measures, etc.

The scope of the STMO ontology is related to the ontology competency questions. They will be constructed around the main question: "How to find the right method to solve the given problem in the considered application domain?". The ontology-related knowledge base should be able to give an answer to this question (after defining the appropriate criteria) and to give an answer to the related, more precise questions, like: "Which is the method dealing with the anti-terrorism that considers escalation effects?", "Are there any goal-oriented methods considering spill-over effects?", "Which methods used for public areas of applications help to facilitate measures acceptance and provide detailed ROSI (Return on security investment) analysis results?", etc. Details of these answers depend on the maturity of the ontology and the gained knowledge. To solve this competency questions problem, a top-down method will be applied, beginning from the general issues, through step by step refining, to more precise issues.

4.2 Possible reuse of existing ontologies

During the ontology development the use of other, third-party ontologies should always be considered. The key issues are the range of compatibility, integration ability, quality, satisfied needs of the ontology users (who successfully validate or use it) and, first of all – the availability of the given ontology. The ontology reusability issue needs further investigation to better meet the needs and expectations of stakeholders.

On the discussed prototype stage of the STMO ontology development, no other ontologies will be reused. The open issue is to integrate, in the future, the STMO ontology with the external third-party ontologies, if they appear.

4.3 Identifying important terms in the ontology

The basic set of important terms encompassed by the STMO ontology is identified during the ontology domain analysis. The terms are grouped by domains of applications, used methods, proposed measures and their effects, as it was mentioned earlier in the subsection 4.1. They are supplemented by more detailed issues identified during the preliminary analysis of some representative methods. These terms are used to define the ontology concepts (classes) and their properties.

4.4 Ontology classes (concepts) and the class hierarchy

Generally, a top-down ontology development approach is applied, though the entire process was iterative and some bottom-up activities were undertaken. In order to assure the proper knowledge representation, it is necessary to perform the analyses of terms and relations between terms, e.g.: class-individual, class-subclass, class-superclass, abstract classes and classes having instances. The important decision to make is about what should be expressed by a class and what by a property. It is also necessary to take into consideration the possibility of the future evolution of class hierarchy, transitivity of class relations, avoiding common errors, naming convention, etc. Most class names (and properties names - subsection 4.5) are self explanatory, though their lengths should be limited.

For the STMO ontology prototype all concepts are grouped in the following main classes:

- the AppDomain class, representing different application domains,
- the SecMeasure class, representing security measures implied by methods,
- the Benefit class, expressing stakeholders' security benefits (positive effects) of the implemented measures,
- the MeasSideEffect class, expressing stakeholders' side effects (negative effects) of the implemented measures,
- the STOMethod class, expressing investigated security trade-off methods,
- the AuxiliaryConcept class, representing a set of auxiliary and diversified terms, whose individuals are used for main classes defining and the knowledge organizing and retrieving.

The first of the main classes, the AppDomain class, represents basic application domains of the security trade-off methods (and their subdomains, when needed). This class has subclasses that all together define the taxonomy of the considered application domains (Table 1).

Class	Subclass	Meaning
ATerrCrimeAD		Anti-terrorism and anti-crime activities
CritInfraAD		Critical infrastructures and their protection
	FuelEnerg	Fuel and energy sectors
	TeleComm	Telecommunications
	Transport	Transportation
FinancialAD		Financial sector
	Banking	Banking
	Insurance	Insurance
FirstRespAD		First responder organizations
HealthAD		Health care sector
InfoSecAD		ICT and information security
PubAreasAD		Public areas, including the citizens, governments, society
RegulatorAD		The regulators – organizations functioning on the national or international levels
SensIndustryAD		Security-sensitive industry
SmallBusinAD		Small business
OtherAD		Other, unclassified application domains

Table 1. Application domains (the AppDomain STMO ontology main class subclasses) - note that a subclass is also a class

This application domain taxonomy has a preliminary and open character. It will be refined and extended on the basis of the validation results and gained experience during the STMO ontology use. Probably, more subdomains for the public areas, financial sector, first responders, critical infrastructures ought to be distinguished.

The second main ontology class, i.e. the SecMeasure class, represents different kinds of the security measures implied by the considered methods, shown in the Table 2.

Class	Meaning
AdvancedTech	The implementation of the advanced technologies or infrastructure solutions
CoopFramew	The organized cooperation frameworks, such as: national or transnational cooperation, public-private partnership, emergency teams, exchanging the information about vulnerabilities, threats, risks, new technology solutions, sampling statistics, etc.
DevelopStrategy	Activities based on the elaborated security strategies, especially the long-term strategies
EduAware	Education, trainings and raising awareness activities
OrgProced	Different forms of the organizational and procedural measures
Redundancy	Different types of redundancies built-in to the systems
RegLegisStd	The regulation, legislation and standardization activities
RiskMngmt	The risks management implementation

Table 2. Security measures representation (the SecMeasure subclasses)

The third main ontology class, i.e. the Benefit class, expressing stakeholders' benefits, as the results of measures implied by methods, includes the issues shown in the Table 3.

Class	Meaning
AvoidEscalation	Disabling different forms of the threat escalation effects
FacilMeasAccept	Facilitating the selected measures acceptance
ImprovBussPosit	The general improvement of the business position, e.g. the competitiveness or market position
ImprovOwnSec	The improvement of the security of the stakeholder's organization, e.g. decreasing the number of incidents and related damages
ImprovPrivacy	The improved confidence of societies in security measures
LongTermSupp	Supporting the long-term business strategy
MonetaryReturn	More financial return on security investment
PosSocietImpact	The positive societal impacts of the security trade-off decision
PrioritizSchedul	The possibility to schedule and prioritize the implied security activities
RegDecisInfluence	The possible influence on the regulatory decisions and supporting the regulatory processes
RiskMngmtEffect	The risks management effects, e.g.: risk mitigation, risk transfer to a partner or insurer
SaveInvesFund	The saved investment funds
SelectOptions	The measures selection from the set of possible options
SpillOver	Additional, positive and indirect effects of the investment expenditures

Table 3. Possible benefits considered by methods – an ontological representation (the Benefit subclasses)

Apart from the benefits implied by the security measures, also their negative impacts (side effects) should be considered. They are expressed by the MeasSideEffect subclasses, shown in the Table 4.

Class	Meaning
DecrOperAbility	The decreased operational ability (the business efficiency lowers)
DecrPrivacy	The decreased privacy
DecrSecurity	The decreased security (e.g. in other areas)
ExceedInvesFund	The exceeded investment funds
LessReturn	The lower than expected financial return on security investment
NegBusinImpact	The negative impact on the business processes, increased business costs, decreased products quality, new barriers, obstacles as the consequences of the applied measures
NegSocietImpact	The negative societal impacts of the security trade-off decision

Table 4. Possible side effects considered by methods - an ontological representation (the MeasSideEffect subclasses)

The most important, fifth main class, i.e. the STOMethod, represents the investigated security trade-off methods. This is the central point of the entire STMO ontology. Currently, there are no STOMethod subclasses defined. Particular kinds of methods are distinguished by the STOMethod property, represented by the MethCategory class that will be explained later. The results of first investigation of the methods demonstrate that it is difficult to classify the given method into one category. Most of them have a complex, mixed-mode character. In the future, after investigating the representative number of methods and defining the criteria allowing to recommend given methods for particular application domains, some subclasses of the STOMethod, like: Best4ATerrCrimeAD, Best4CritInfraAD, etc. can be defined as the inherited classes using the Protégé built-in reasoning facilities.

The sixth main class, the AuxiliaryConcept class, includes varied issues. The individuals of the DecMakingLev class express different decision making levels (tactical, operational, strategic, national level, etc.). The MeasureScale, having subclasses: MonetaryScale, QualitScale, QuantitScale, is used to define different kinds of measurement or assessment scales used by the security trade-off methods.

A very important class is MethCategory which presents the assumed basic taxonomy of the investigated methods, containing the following subclasses:

- the CostBenMeth class – encompasses the cost-benefit approach methods, including:
  - the CostBenAnalys class – concerns the cost-benefit analysis,
  - the CostEffectAnalys class – is related to the cost-effectiveness analysis,
  - the MultiFacAnalys class – deals with the multi-factor analysis,
- the DecSuppMeth class – is related to the trade-off evaluation and decision-support, including:
  - the AspectOriented class – concerns the aspect-oriented and risk-driven methods,
  - the CautPrecautPrinc class – deals with the methods based on the cautionary and precautionary principles,

  - the DecisAnalSupp class - deals with the decision analysis and decision support methods,
  - the DesignOriented class - concerns the design-oriented methods,
  - the GoalOriented class - deals with the goal-oriented methods,
  - the MissionOriented class - deals with the mission-oriented methods developed in the military sector,
- the RiskAssMeth class - deals with the risk analysis and assessment methods, i.e.:
  - the CmplexRiskAnalys class - is related to the complex risk analysis methods,
  - the ROIbasedAnalys class - is related to the ROI-based (Return on investment) methods,
  - the ROSIbasedAnalys class - deals with the ROSI-based (Return on security investment) methods,
- the OtherMeth class encompasses other approaches, i.e.:
  - the ExpertSysBased class - is related to the expert systems use,
  - the HumFacBased class - deals with the methods based on the human factors models,
  - the InterdepNets class - is related to the interdependency networks for critical trade-offs including hard and soft factors,
  - the OntologyBased class - is related to the ontology-based methods,
  - the ProcessAnalys class - deals with the process analysis methods,
  - the ScenarioBased class - deals with the scenario-based techniques,
  - the SimulGame class - is related to the simulations & gaming,
  - the Technical class - is related to the technical domain (safety) methods adapted to the security applications.

It was assumed that a given method can belong to a few method categories.

The RiskCategory class expresses different kinds of risk considered by the investigated methods. The categories are represented by the subclasses having self-explanatory names: BlackMailing, BusinProcDisrupt, CustomConfidLoss, Epidemy, Harming, HostageTaking, Injuring, KeyPersLoss, LiveLoss, MarkShareLoss, MngmtProcDisrupt, NaturDisaster, Riots, Spionage, Strikes, VitalSuppliesLoss.

The MethDevelOwner class represents the person or the organization who has developed a method or owns it.

The OrganizType class concerns organization types (commercial, public, non-profit, governmental agencies, transnational organizations, etc.) taken into consideration by the methods.

The SecInvArea class deals with the considered investment areas, expresses by the subclasses: Equipment, InfrastrucProt, OperatManag (i.e. operational management), Personnel, Services, StrategyPlan (i.e. development of strategies and plans).

The SecInvType class concerns security investment types (new investment, expansion, modernization, etc.) taken into consideration by the methods.

The SuppTool class points at the supporting tool related to the method. This class needs refinement because currently only the basic information concerning the tool is sampled (name, developer, description, status of development, applications and usability).

The ThreatEscalEffect class expresses different kinds of threats effects considered by the methods (secondary, cascading, escalating, etc).

The TimeHoriz class concerns different time horizons (of the investments and their positive and/or negative impacts) taken into consideration while the given method is used.
The key-importance class, TradeOff, represents different elementary security trade-offs considered by the method. Each of them considers two factors (sometimes groups of factors) from those represented by the TradeOffFactor subclasses: BusinessAcceptance, Convenience, Cost, EnvironAspect, EthicalAspect, LegalStdRestrict, MethodologyAcceptance, PoliticalAspect, Privacy, Prosperity, Security, SocialAceptance, SocialCohesion, TechnologyAcceptance, Transparency. The security factor expressed by the above mentioned Security class is of the key significance for the security trade-off decisions. Please note that the AuxiliaryConcept class is used to arrange different issues concerning the key ontology class, which is the STOMethod class.
The above presented taxonomy has an initial meaning. It is assumed at the beginning of the iterative STMO ontology development process. It will be revised during the knowledge acquisition (investigating details of terms embraced by this ontology) and the validation results (checking if the facilities and features offered by the ontology are useful). The revision, permanent improvement, can be enabled after finishing the first step of the ontology creation iterative process, i.e. after defining a certain number of class properties, some individuals, some queries, etc.
It was assumed that the lowest level classes can have instances (individuals) representing particular application domains, security trade-off methods, applied measures and achieved effects.
The presented there ontology developer's defined class hierarchy is called "an asserted class hierarchy". On this basis, and with the use of the reasoning mechanisms, "an inherited class hierarchy" can be constructed, when needed. It will be used to define best fitted methods for particular application domains.

4.5 Ontology class properties and their restrictions

The classes embraced by the defined hierarchy of classes can have some properties assigned, called slots (or roles). The slots are subject to some general principles. All subclasses of a given class inherit the slots of that class, therefore a slot representing the given class property should be placed on the highest possible level of the class hierarchy. Besides, when a class has multiple superclasses it simply inherits slots from all of them.
There are three kinds of standard slots (Noy, 2001):

- object-type (also called "instance-type") slots; they are used to express "complex properties", i.e. relationships between an individual member of the given class (the object) and other individuals, e.g. when the given individual consists of other individuals or points to other individuals;
- data-type slots; they are used to express "simple properties" or "attributes", i.e. intrinsic or extrinsic properties of the individuals of the most elementary classes; the data type used for this slot can be any of the data types commonly used in the modelling or programming, e.g.: integer, byte, float, time, date, enumeration, string;
- annotation slots; they are used to express the meaning of the given concept, to document different ontology items (concepts, slots, individuals); annotation slots are RDF-based (RDF means Resource Description Framework); the most known

example of this slot is the rdfs:comment slot which gives more explanation of the given ontology item.

An instance-type slot is attached to the classes which are called a domain, while the classes indicated by this slot are called a range. The possible values of the slot can be refined by defining the restrictions (called also "facets") for them. The restriction specifies or limits the set of possible values for the given slot.

The presented there STMO ontology uses all types of slots, however, the chapter is focused on high-importance slots describing key properties of classes. A typical situation deals with building the ontology for the insufficiently known domain. In this case the important issue is, when to use a data-type slot and when an object-type one for some properties. At the beginning the data-type slots can be used. After sampling and analyzing the knowledge, a better knowledge expression will be possible and some data-type slots can be replaced by object-type slots, which allow the better knowledge modelling and retrieving. Similarly to the classes, it was assumed that a slot name is related to its meaning.

With respect to the chapter objectives, the most important is the STOMethod class which represents the investigated methods. Some general-meaning, descriptive slots of the STOMethod have range strings. Other slots of the STOMethod, representing more structured knowledge, where pointing at some other individuals is possible (object-type slots), have a range of appropriate classes. The slot ranges are given in brackets, below. In the validation progress, some data-type slots can be replaced by object-type slots. The STOMethod class slots were organized by thematic groups.

The group of slots expressing the basic method features encompasses:

- the rdfs:comment slot is used as the reference to the source of information about the method,
- the methAcron slot (range: string) presents the used acronym (short name),
- the STOmethodName slot (range: string) presents the full method name,
- the methDevelOwner slot (range: MethDevelOwner) specifies the developer/owner of the method,
- the STOmethodGenDesrcription slot (range: string) contains a short method description,
- the availabTool slot (range: SuppTool class) specifies the tools supporting the given method, as the separate individuals with their own slots,
- the appDomains slot (range: AppDomain class) lists application domains in which the method can be used,
- the secInvesAreas (range: SecInvArea class) specifies the considered investment areas,
- the organizType slot (range: OrganizType class) presents the types of organizations who can use the given method,
- the measurmScale slot (range: MeasureScale class) lists the scales (qualitative, quantitative, monetary) used for the measurements or assessments of the expense values, gained benefits, encountered side effects – related to the trade-off,
- the methCategs slot (range: MethCategory class) specifies categories to which the given method can be classified,
- the riskCategs slot (range: RiskCategory class) lists categories of risk considered by the method,

- the secTradeOffs slot (range: TradeOff class) specifies security trade-off cases considered by the method; each case (the individual) expresses an elementary trade-off issue, e.g. Security-Cost, Security-BussinAccept (i.e.: security vs. business acceptance), Security-Performance (see details below),
- the standardCompliant slot (range: string) specifies main standards with which the method complies,
- the methodOutput slot (range: string) describes how the method results are presented for its user.

The group of slots expressing the investment features considered by the method and applied measures encompasses:

- the expenditureDesc slot (range: string) which generally describes the expense values considered by the method and related to the analyzed trade-off,
- the secMeasures slot (range: SecMeasure class) which lists the possible to use security measures,
- the decisMakingLev slot (range: DecMakingLev class), describing generally considered levels where the security trade-off decisions are undertaken, like: infrastructure management level, strategic level, project level, country level, etc.
- the diffFrmOtherMeasures slot (range: string) which expresses the differences between the proposed security measures and other measures, e.g. governmental, industrial (range: string),
- the secInvesTypes (range: SecInvType class) which specifies investment types possible to consider, such as: new investment, expansion, modernization, etc.,
- the investTimeHor slot (range: TimeHoriz class) which lists the considered time horizons dealing with the investment, such as: 1 Year, 5 Years, etc.
- the investSizeDesc slot (range: string), presenting generally the investment sizes considered by the method,
- the diffFromOtherInvestms slot (range: string), expressing generally specific issues or the differences of the considered security investments from other kinds of investments e.g. safety-, defense-, and business-related investments,
- the no-InvestmConseq slot (range: string), which specifies the method ability to describe the consequences of no investment,
- the organizatReqsDesc slot (range: string), which presents organizational requirements for the effective use of the method.

The group of slots expressing the positive and negative effects of the investment considered by the method encompasses:

- the consideredBenefitDesc slot (range: string), generally describing the benefits considered by the method and related to the analyzed trade-off,
- the midTermBenefs slot (range: Benefit class), listing mid-term benefits possible to gain from the investment, considered by the method,
- the longTermBenefs slot (range: Benefit class), listing long-term benefits possible to gain from the investment, considered by the method,
- the escalEffects slot (range: ThreatEscalEffect) which specifies the threats escalation effects considered by the method, e.g. cascading effects,
- the sideEffects slot (range: MeasSideEffect class) which specifies the side effects related to achieved benefits, considered by the method and related to the analyzed trade-off.

The last group of slots is related to security trade-off method evaluation and includes:

- the statusOfDevelopm (range: string) – specifies the status of the method or tool development (newly created, prototype, matured, etc.)
- the usabilityAssessm slot (range: string) – which characterizes briefly complexity, friendliness, price, cost of analyses, required expertise, etc.,
- the statusOfApplication slot (range: string) – characterizes briefly the current status of applications and gained experiences with the use of the method or tool, e.g.: number of users, organizations, sectors, etc.,
- the ifCombineQualitQuantAppr slot (range: Boolean) – says if the method is able to combine qualitative and quantitative approaches while trade-off,
- the ifMultipleFactors slot (range: Boolean) – says if the method is able to measure or assess multiple effects and/or consider them while trade-off,
- the ifDiffUserRoles slot (range: Boolean) – says if the method supports different roles/groups of roles of users, varied working teams, etc.,
- the strengthsOfMethod slot (range: string) – generally describes the strength of the method considering its applicability conditions,
- the weaknessOfMethod slot (range: string) – generally describes the weakness of the method considering its applicability conditions,
- the whatToImprove (range: string) – generally describes what to improve in the method with respect to its applicability conditions.

Going back to the mentioned TradeOff class which expresses the security trade-off cases considered by method, please note the following slots of the TradeOff class:

- the GenDescripOfSTOcase slot (range: string) – generally describes the considered trade-off decisions, including conflicts, synergies and interdependencies between security and other issues,
- the STOfactor1, and the STOfactor2 (both of the range: TradeOffFactor) – specify two groups of trade-off factors, generally mutually opposing, but the members of the given factor slot are mutually supporting; for the given trade-off problems it will be usually "1factor to 1factor", but the combination "m factors to n factors" is also possible, especially to express more complex cases;
- the STOpairsOfSynergyFactors slot (range: string) – includes comments about the mutual supporting factors, describing their synergies,
- the STOpairsOfOpposingFactors slot (range: string) – includes comments about the opposing or even conflicting pairs of factors,
- the STOinterdependencies slot (range: string) – specifies interdependencies between elements of the considered groups of factors.

Please note that only the main slots were mentioned above, especially the slots related to the investigation of the trade-off method and trade-off concept. In the progress of the method investigation some slots will be refined or substituted by the better matching slots. It is an iterative process based on the sampled knowledge about different security trade-off approaches during the validation.

4.6 Creating individuals – instances of classes and filling in their slots

The next step of the ontology elaboration is to define the individuals, called also class instances. The instances represent class members. Please note that some classes have

instances, some not. General rules of the ontology engineering differ a little from the rules of the object modelling domain. Please note that an instance of a subclass is an instance of a superclass. For the Security Trade-off Methods Ontology the individuals are defined mainly for the classes of the lowest hierarchy level. The main set of individuals with filled-in slots, representing particular methods, is the core element of the STMO related knowledge base.
The ontology is provided by different kinds of the auxiliary individuals necessary at the beginning of the security trade-off method investigation. They represent basic issues used to specify the investigated methods, including predefined values for some issues or patterns, showing how to define other individuals during this investigation.
The STMO ontology creation process will be exemplified using the Protégé Ontology Editor and Knowledge Acquisition System (Protégé, 2008) on a few examples. The Fig. 1 presents one of them dealing with the creation of the **TradeOff** class individuals expressing trade-off cases. It was assumed that the given method is able to include many cases, placed in the **secTradeOffs** slot of the **STOMethod** class individuals. The Protégé tool is provided with the several tabs dealing with the metadata, OWL classes, properties, individuals, forms, queries and other functionalities. Let us consider the tab representing individuals.

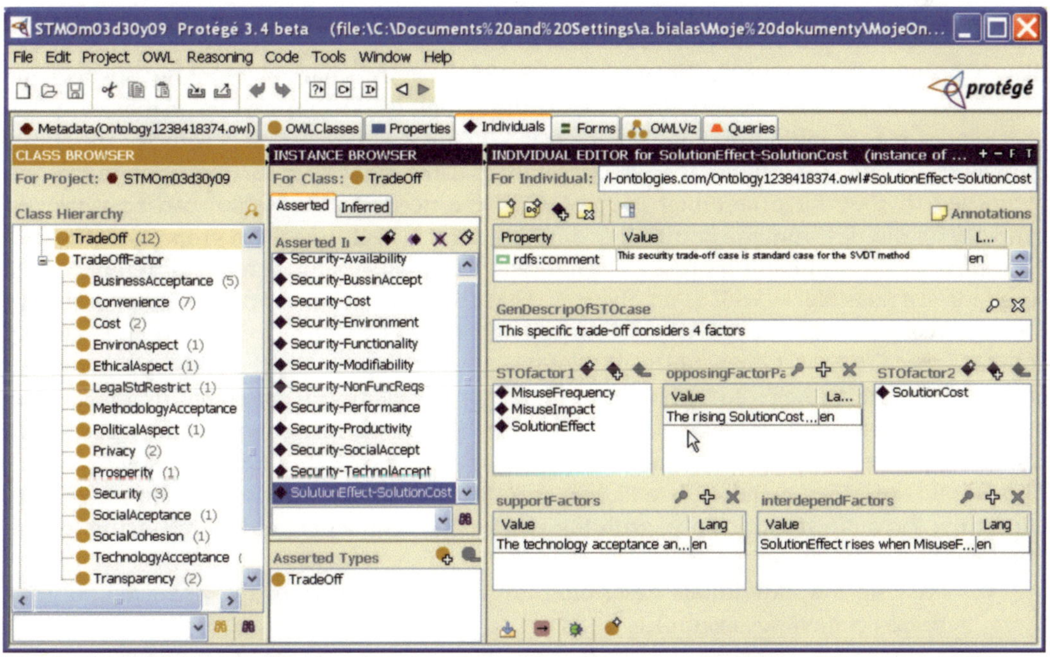

Fig. 1. The STMO individuals related to the trade-off cases in the Protégé (Protégé, 2008)

The left side of the Fig. 1 ("Class Browser") encompassing a part of the STMO ontology class hierarchy and showing some **AuxiliaryConcept** subclasses related to the discussed trade-off cases. The numbers of the defined individuals of the given class are placed next to the class names within the brackets. For the highlighted **TradeOff** class their individuals (marked as rhombuses) are presented within the "Instance Browser" window in the middle: from **Security-Availability** to **SolutionEffect-SolutionCost**, representing particular trade-off cases predefined for different trade-off methods. In the right part of the figure "Individual Editor" shows the highlighted SolutionEffect-SolutionCost case details, expressed by its slots. Please note rdfs:comment and other slots of the TradeOff class, explained at the end of the subsection 4.5. Please note the TradeOffFactor subclasses (on the left side). The combinations of their individuals are used to predefine needed trade-off cases, usually between security and other factors.

The most important individuals that constitute the STMO ontology-related knowledge base are STOMethod class individuals, characterizing particular methods. The ontological representation of the selected methods will be shown in the next subsection.

4.7 Testing and validation of the developed ontology

Similarly to other ontologies, the created STMO ontology should be tested on the fly and validated by the people who can use it. The Protégé environment provides some facilities to support both these activities.

While building an ontology, certain commonly known errors (Noy, 2001) may occur, such as: cycles in the class hierarchy, violation of property constraints, incorrectly defined terms, classes with a single subclass, classes and slots with no definitions, slots with no constraints like value type or cardinality, interval restrictions issuing empty intervals, e.g. when min val > max val was assigned. They can be detected with the use of the Protégé menu functions, like "Checking consistency", "Run ontology tests", or by manual ontology inspections supported by the Protégé built-in visualization tool (OWLViz). While elaborating the ontology, some usability tests can be performed on the fly to early detect some of the above mentioned errors. The ontology developer checks if the right structures of individuals are composed, if they have assumed properties, if the needed information can be retrieved properly by queries from the knowledge database, and if the forms were properly defined.

The ontology development process has a subjective character because many different correct solutions are possible, as well as an objective character because the applied solutions should be objectively correct (Noy, 2001). Please note that usually not all of the possible correct solutions met the expectations of the ontology users. For this reason, the ontology validation is important, which helps to reshape the ontology according the users' requirements. The ontology project ought to be flexible and open to changes. During the ontology validation process the class hierarchy, slots and defined forms are considerably rebuilt on the fly.

The STMO ontology validation encompasses the basic scenarios of the ontology use. Currently, the main scenarios deal with the knowledge acquisition and its retrieving for the ontology testing purpose:

- creating the individuals describing identified properties of the reviewed security trade-off methods examples,
- sampled knowledge retrieval with the use of the Protégé built-in query mechanism.

During the STMO ontology development, the knowledge concerning selected methods is identified, analyzed and placed into the knowledge base. The Examples 1-6 present the first group of methods introduced into the STMO knowledge base.

<u>Example 1:</u> The SecureMark System, ROSI-based, developed by SageSecure, NY, USA (Sonnenreich et al., 2006).

The SecureMark system is the result of the R&D work conducted at the SageSecure, aimed at the security benchmarking method, which gives the "consistently repeatable results that are strongly correlated to financial performance". The variants of the security expenditures are considered, using the Return on Security Investment calculations. The key ROSI parameter, the "Risk exposure", is measured as the productivity loss caused by the security issues. The method is focused on solving everyday security incidents which constitute the significant amount of the aggregated loss. To better assess the security investment two additional well-known factors are used, i.e. NPV (Net Present Value) and IRR (Internal Rate of Return). The method concerns the information security issues and is "almost compliant" (ca. 95%) with ISO17799.

Example 2: The ontology-centred architecture for the technology risk management in the banking industry, developed at the University of Mannheim, Germany (Atkinson et al., 2006).

To foster the technology risk management in the banking sector, an ontological approach is proposed, which is compliant with the Basel II recommendation. The method, based on the ontological model, encompasses processes of the identification, measurement and controlling activities related to the risk self-assessment, loss database creation, model building and regulatory requirements. The ontology encompasses the risk-related issues (i.e. technology, process, human, activity, resource, effects, loss, gain, etc.) with respect to the banking activities (i.e. trading, credit, accounting activities, etc.) influencing the value chain. The identification process (the self-assessment) is questionnaire-based. The risk measurement uses the Monte Carlo simulation algorithms. During the risk controlling process the calculated risk is compared with the real data, including these retrieved from the loss database. The ontology is also used for the above mentioned processes integration and for reasoning. The method is supported by the Java-based tool, encompassing applications for three particular processes, using the common database. The tool is a combination of the enterprise resource planning (ERP) system and the knowledge management system. The former provides monetary data and makes calculations, the latter precisely describes the risk issues.

Example 3: The goal-oriented security trade-off modelling and analysis method, focused on the software development from the University of Toronto, Canada (Elahi & Yu, 2008).

During the software systems development the security or privacy issues should be taken into consideration in the same way as other kinds of requirements, e.g.: functionality, usability and performance. For the given project it is necessary to perform a trade-off analysis issuing the set of the requirements feasible to implement. The presented method is based on a goal-oriented framework for modelling and analyzing security trade-off, integrated with the design framework. The trade-off results can be taken into consideration during architecture design. The trade-off cases are sampled in the knowledge base tool. The first part of the framework is responsible for the security trade-off analyzing in a multi actor environment and with the use of the "i*" notation. This conceptual modelling technique considers three kinds of concepts: explicit goals, actors and security specific concepts (threats, vulnerabilities, risk, etc.). The security goals are usually about conflicts with design objectives derived from the stakeholders' expectations (users, administrators, top managers, customers) and take into consideration other aspects, such as the non-functional requirements, standards, security policies, etc. The designers are the key actors and the other actors compete with them in achieving their particular goals. The second part of the framework is responsible for the requirement engineering issues, and the third is the knowledge base. The framework was used to model the NIST security guidelines and other textbooks. Three validation cases were performed for the framework. The method was implemented in the identity management of an industrial application. The security trade-off analysis procedure and qualitative measurement scale are the key issues of the method.

Example 4: ATAM – Architecture Trade-off Analysis Method, developed in the Software Engineering Institute of the Carnegie Mellon University (CMU-SEI) USA, (Kazman et al., 2000).

Business processes rely on software architectures. They are very complex and their development needs deep analyses and many design trade-offs, particularly those which affect the achievement of quality attributes such as performance, availability, modifiability and security. The ATAM is an evaluation method to analyze if the considered architecture decisions satisfy particular quality goals related to the mentioned attributes and how these goals mutually interact and cause trade-off against each other.

The ATAM provides a framework to model quality attributes and decisions related to them. The introduced quality scenarios express the elementary quality attribute-related requirements, in other words – scenarios express goals. The achievement of these scenarios depends on the chosen tactic. The alternative tactics are allowed. The importance of the given scenario and the difficulties in achieving its goal is assessed by means of a three-level scale: High/Medium/Low. The ATAM is a multi-step process. The architectural approaches are identified after the presentation of the ATAM to the assembled stakeholders, the identification of the business drivers and the description of the proposed architecture (explaining how it addresses the business drivers). Next the "quality attribute utility tree" is generated, which presents "overall goodness" of the system. The system utility is described by the above mentioned quality attributes, including the security attribute. On this basis quality scenarios are specified with their features (stimuli and response, difficulties, importance, etc.) and prioritized. Then the architectural approaches are analyzed. The approaches addressing high-priority factors are analyzed and the architectural risks, sensitivity points, and trade-off points are identified. The risks concern decisions that have not been made during the architecture development or decisions with unclear consequences. The sensitivity points are parameters in the architecture to which some measurable quality attribute is highly correlated with other attributes. The trade-off points are understood as the architecture elements including more than one sensitivity point, where the measurable quality attributes are affected differently by changing that parameter (the increase of one attribute value causes the decrease of the other). Next steps encompass brainstorming, prioritizations of scenarios, and the architecture refinement and reporting with the stakeholders' participation.

The ATAM method is supported by tools, elaborated by different developers. An example of such a tool is ArchKriti – a software architecture-based design and evaluation tool suite (Vallieswaran & Menezes, 2007) which supports the following activities in the architecture-based software development: quality attribute brainstorming, attribute-driven design, architecture evaluation and documentation. Another example is the ATAM Assistant (Lionberger & Zhang, 2007) that is a single application to manage, visualize, and report on all of the artefacts generated during the ATAM process.

Example 5: The integrated Security Verification and security solution Design Trade-off analysis (SVDT) (Houmb et al., 2006).

The work presents the model-driven development method, called SVDT, which is based on the UMLsec notation and the Bayesian Belief Network (BBN) concept. The UMLsec is an

UML extension, introduced by Jürjens, providing a unified approach to security features description during the secure systems development. Established formal rules of security engineering can be encapsulated and hence made available to a wider group of developers and evaluators. In the SVDT, the UMLsec and its supporting tool are used to specify security requirements (project goals) and to verify design alternatives against these requirements. The trade-off decision maker analyzes these alternatives using the ROSI calculation and chooses the best one with respect to the criteria. The trade-off concerns four issues: solution effect, solution cost, misuse frequency and misuse impact. The trade-off input parameters are: security risk acceptance, policies, standards, laws and regulations, priorities, business goals, budget and time to market. The ROSI calculation is based on the Bayesian Belief Network. The SVDT uses the Common Criteria standard for project evaluation on the static level.

Example 6: Mission Oriented Risk and Design Analysis (MORDA), focused on IT military applications, Department of Defense (DoD), USA, (Buckshaw et al., 2007).

MORDA is a top-level information assurance methodology used for critical systems in the military application domain. To evaluate the information system designs, MORDA integrates different approaches: the risk analysis techniques, multiple objective decision analysis models and portfolio analysis techniques. MORDA is a quantitative risk assessment and risk management process. The process helps to allocate the resources encompassed by the information system design and needed for the system operation. This allocation ensures that the information system is operable in a hostile and malicious environment. It has been applied in seven major Department of Defense risk assessment studies, including the assessment of the Global Command and Control System (GCCS). GCCS is a suite of applications residing on the Secret Internet Protocol Router Network, which is a collection of secret LANs connected to the backbone. The important issue for this system is to "determine the optimum of countermeasures to be applied to the system to provide information assurance". The trade-off concerns the security related benefits on one hand and the cost of the applied countermeasures on the other hand. MORDA is based on attack tree models, qualitative/quantitative information assurance models and multiple objective decision analysis models, as well as the previously developed MORA (Mission Oriented Risk Analysis) of the Information Assurance Technical Framework (IATF). Into the mission processes the countermeasures are built in. The countermeasures are elaborated by the Socrates quantitative risk assessment model and tool using the output of "User Mission Support Needs", which is the first of the mission oriented processes. MORDA uses a multiple objective decision analysis and helps to elaborate the adversary attack model (attack tree based), the user model (to maximize the network functionality, interoperability, bandwidth, and easy operation for end users) and system provider model (to maximize the control of evolution path and easy operation for end users and warfighters, to minimize resources and schedule slips, e.g. for testing, fielding, etc.). The considered countermeasure and design options (CDO), e.g. "Install Firewall", "Install VPN", "Auditing" are scored against the likelihood of detection, likelihood of success, adversary resources required and cost (including: the research, procurement, installation and maintenance). Using the Socrates risk analysis all combinations of possible to use CDOs are analyzed, and the best architecture is proposed. It allows to achieve the maximum benefits with respect to the existing constraints (portfolio optimization). The recommended architecture solutions are implemented in the system and maintained. The ontological representation of the MORDA individual is presented in the Fig. 2. Please note a part of the class hierarchy with the highlighted STOmethod (the bottom of the left panel). The Instance Browser window in the middle presents its individuals, i.e. methods that have been identified and introduced into the knowledge base so far. One of them, highlighted, is the MORDA individual. The Individual Editor presents its group of slots expressing the basic method features (about 1/3 of all slots mentioned in the subsection 4.5 above).

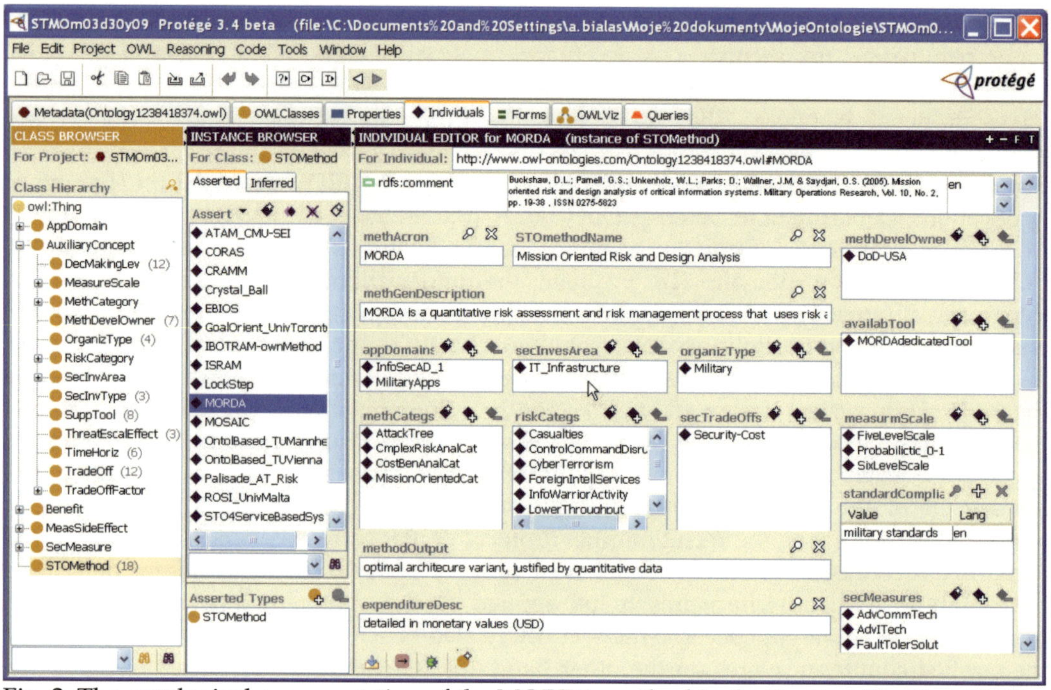

Fig. 2. The ontological representation of the MORDA method in the Protégé (Protégé, 2008)

During the methods investigation, their properties are analyzed and expressed by filling the slots with the auxiliary individuals (object-type slots) or with Boolean, textual descriptors, etc. (for other slots). Some of the auxiliary individuals were predefined at the beginning, some are defined on the fly when needed.

Currently, some other methods are investigated in the same way, concerning well-known methods of the risk management (CORAS, CRAMM, EBIOS, Lockstep, etc.), methods for the service-based systems design (Yau et al., 2007), and, first and foremost, the methods which do not focus on the IT and information security domain only (Crystall Ball, @Risk, MOSAIC).

Example 7: Knowledge retrieving from the STMO knowledge base – a simple example.

The Protégé Ontology Editor and Knowledge Acquisition System has a simple query mechanism built-in (Protégé Query) that can be used iteratively to retrieve knowledge on the defined slots basis. Different working scenarios are possible. The individuals are selected on the slot value basis (any types of slots are allowed). Particular queries can be linked by the OR (see "Match Any" option) or by AND (see "Match All" option) logical operations.

Searching within the results issued by other query is possible too, as well as storing the defined queries.

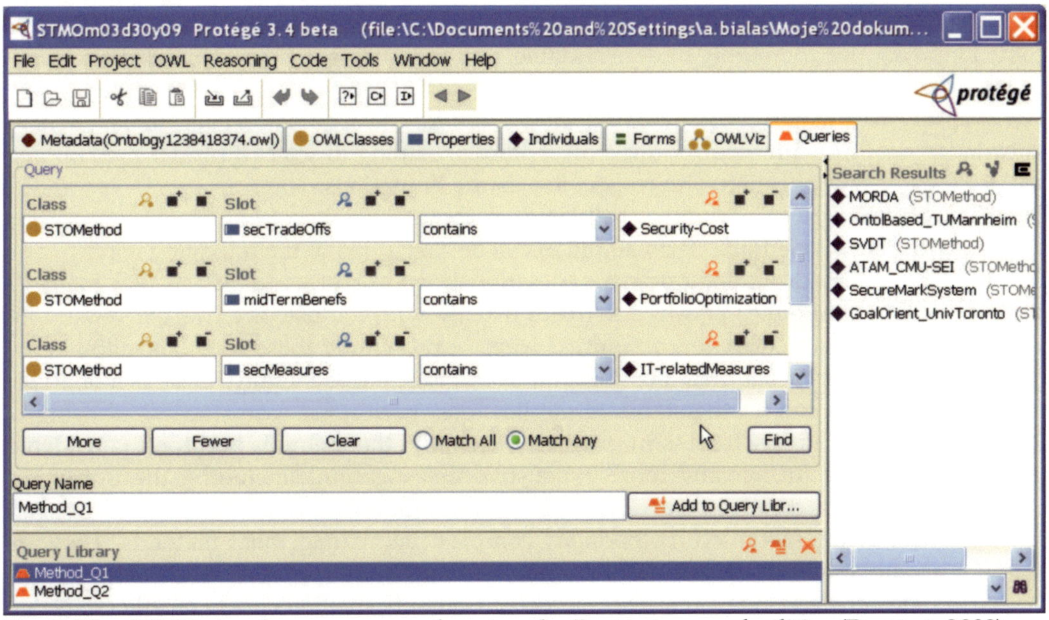

Fig. 3. The STMO simple query example using the Protégé query facilities (Protégé, 2008)

Let us suppose that the knowledge base user wants to find methods on the Security-Cost trade-off decision, implying IT-related measures and allowing the portfolio optimization. For the STOMethod class she/he defines three queries, shown in the Fig. 3. Six matching methods were found. It was done by mistake because the AND/OR condition was not set properly. The user changes the option to "Match All" and, at this moment, only one method, i.e. MORDA was found (not shown), satisfying the query condition.

Currently any queries, based on the existing slots can be defined. The usefulness of this tool will increase when more methods will be analyzed and placed into the knowledge base. Instead of the Protégé Query, a more enhanced query mechanism can be used, allowing to implement the enhanced competency questions.

5. Conclusions

The importance of the security trade-off issue is growing, especially for the organizations representing complex environments with a high risk exposure, having limited resources and complex relations between security and business processes. Usually these organizations need long-term planning to integrate costly and high consequence measures into their business processes. To have at one's disposal a right security trade-off method, supported by an effective tool, is the key issue for many today's organizations irrespective of their domain and character. The selection and use of the right method is difficult and requires specialized knowledge. On one hand, the security knowledge, including the security trade-off related knowledge, is broadly available in different form (reports, books, standards, documentations, software embedded, guidelines) and from different sources (experts, technology providers, researchers, Internet, databases, standard bodies, security promoting organizations, etc.). On the other hand, however, this knowledge is hard to acquire because some terms are not commonly understandable, and sometimes it is hard to extract relevant pieces of knowledge for a given application.

The chapter presents the ontology-based framework for the acquisition and management of knowledge dealing with security trade-off methods, helping to select a proper method and tool for the given application with respect to existing limitations.

The STMO ontology is a prototype, validated on some examples of knowledge acquisition dealing with several methods. The validation can be concluded in the following way:

1. The assumed ontology domain is extremely wide and varied. Particular methods or tools are rather poorly described, usually with the use of terms convenient for their authors. There are no unified ways of presenting these methods, allowing to compare their features, possibilities, usefulness, etc. Generally, there is a shortage of information on the status of applications, performed case studies, allowing to evaluate their usefulness in practice. Generally, the methods and tools considered there need further and more exhaustive investigations, including the use of the particular methods in real environment (case studies).
2. Most of the identified methods are complex risk management methods. They are usually matured, broadly used by professionals and supported by developed tools. There are relatively few true security trade-off methods and, mostly, they are under development. These methods are poorly supported by tools. The security trade-off methods can be considered as the extension of the risk management methods.
3. Most of the security trade-off methods are mixture-mode methods, integrating different approaches, e.g. SVDT uses the UMLsec for the solution variants specification, ROSI scheme for risk assessment, BBN for risk calculation and for elaborating the trade-off decision. For this reason, the given method can belong to several categories.
4. Most methods are related to the information technologies. It seems obvious because these technologies support business processes in other application domains on one hand, and the risk issue is inherent to these technologies on the other hand.
5. The taxonomy of classes and the set of properties, specified at the beginning, were slightly modified during the ontology validation. A serious revision of STMO should be done after acquiring the knowledge on more methods, representing more application domains.

The positive issue is the STMO ontology ability to acquire considerable knowledge from the ontology domain with the use of the recognized tool (Protégé) and standards (OWL-DL). The negative issue is that only several methods and tools were placed into the knowledge base. The knowledge acquisition was much more difficult and laborious than it had been expected. The particular investigated methods and tools are described informally in different, and sometimes incomplete, ways, depending on the author's style and used terms, but the ontology requires uniform, concise knowledge representation.

There is a need to extend the STMO ontology and the related knowledge base by analyzing other methods and application domains, sampling related knowledge to achieve a critical mass of knowledge, allowing effective use of the knowledge base. The future investigation should be focused around some sources of the knowledge concerning the STMO ontology domain, for example:

- the book (Hilson et al, 2007), giving an exhaustive review of methods, focused on varied risk management (RM) issues: Strategic RM, Corporate governance, Financial RM, Business continuity and disaster recovery, Reputational RM, Risk-assessed marketing, Operational RM, Project risk management, Environmental RM, Legal and contract RM, Technical RM, Fraud RM, Counter-terrorism RM;
- the monograph (Graham et al, 2006), focusing on the methods supporting business continuity issues;
- the publication (COSO II, 2004), presenting in details corporate risk management methods and techniques;
- the book (Aven, 2008), reviewing and discussing in details different approaches and applications of risk management;
- the author's book (Bialas, 2007), reviewing different approaches of risk management, focused on IT applications;
- sources of knowledge about methods focused on non-IT application domains;
- project communities, e.g. EU 7th Framework Programme;
- the ENISA Inventory of Risk Management/Risk Assessment Methods and Tools (ENISA, 2009);
- expert communities, e.g. SARMA (Security Analysis and Risk Management Association) community (SARMA, 2009);
- the author's own R&D works focused on the "IBOTRAM - Integrated, Business-Oriented, Two-Stage Risk Analysis Method" and its implementation in business and public organizations; the method is ROI/ROSI-based and supports implementations of the Information Security Management Systems (ISMS), compliant with ISO/IEC 27001 (Bialas, 2007), (Bialas & Lisek, 2007);
- experiences gained by collaborating researchers and the knowledge from many other sources; please note that only (Hilson et al, 2007) enumerates about 20 organizations and 27 standards or best practices dealing with risk management.

Concurrently with the knowledge acquisition, it is necessary to perform some researches, including case studies, focused on the better knowledge understanding and structuring. This will allow to elaborate more enhanced competency questions. Different nuances should be considered, e.g.: between security investments and other kinds of investments (safety, business, defence), understanding of key terms (risk, measure, strategy, benefit, effectiveness, etc.) in different application domains.

Both main objectives of this work mentioned at the beginning of the chapter were fulfilled. The STMO prototype is able to support researchers in conceptualization and knowledge acquisition. The results of their investigations in the realm of security methods and tools can be expressed in a uniform and precise way, i.e. as a knowledge base. Researchers and other interested parties can retrieve and analyze this knowledge. The chapter presents a complete example of the ontology creation process using the basic knowledge engineering principles and the proven tool, open to general use.

6. Acknowledgments

This work was conducted using the Protégé resource, which is supported by the grant LM007885 from the United States National Library of Medicine.

7. References

Atkinson, C.; Cuske, Ch. & Dickopp, T. (2006). Concepts for an Ontology-centric Technology Risk Management Architecture in the Banking Industry, *Proceedings of 10th IEEE International Enterprise Distributed Object Computing Conference Workshops (EDOCW'06)*, pp. 21-29, ISBN: 0-7695-2743-4, Hong Kong, October 2006, IEEE Computer Society

Aven, T. (2008). *Risk Analysis. Assessing uncertainties beyond expected values and probabilities*, Wiley, ISBN: 978-0-470-51736-9, New Jersey

Bialas, A. (2007). *Bezpieczeństwo informacji i usług w nowoczesnej instytucji i firmie*, Wydawnictwa Naukowo-Techniczne, ISBN 978-83-204-3343-2, Warszawa, (*in Polish, English title: „Information and services security within modern organizations and companies" – book published by Scientific and Technical Publishing House, Warsaw*)

Bialas, A. & Lisek K. (2007). Integrated, business-oriented, two-stage risk analysis. *Journal of Information Assurance and Security*, Vol. 2, Issue 3, Atlanta, September 2007 (205-210), ISSN 1554-10, www.dynamicpublishers.com/JIAS

Bialas, A. (2008). Ontology-based Approach to the Common Criteria Compliant IT Security Development, *Proceedings of the 2008 International Conference on Security and Management – SAM'08 (The World Congress In Applied Computing)*, Las Vegas, July 2008, CSREA Press

Bialas, A. (2009). Ontology-based Security Problem Definition and Solution for the Common Criteria Compliant Development Process, *Proceedings of 2009 Fourth International Conference on Dependability of Computer Systems (DepCoS-RELCOMEX 2009)*, Brunow, Poland, June-July 2009, IEEE Computer Society, Los Alamitos, Washington, Tokyo, pp. 3-10, ISBN 978-0-7695-3674-3

Buckshaw, D.L.; Parnell, G.S.; Unkenholz, W.L.; Parks; D.; Wallner, J.M, & Saydjari, O.S. (2005). Mission oriented risk and design analysis of critical information systems. Military Operations Research, Vol. 10, No. 2, pp. 19-38, ISSN 0275-5823

Coras. (2009). *The CORAS Method*, http://coras.sourceforge.net/index.html, accessed March 2009

COSO II. (2004). *Enterprise Risk Management – Integrated Framework: Executive Summary and Framework, Application Techniques*, Vol. I and II, COSO – The Committee of Sponsoring Organizations of the Treadway Commission (Polish edition, 2007)

CSL – Computer Science Laboratory. Security ontologies in OWL. (2008), http://www.csl.sri.com/users/denker/owl-sec/ontologies/, accessed July 2008

DAML Services – Security and privacy. (2008), http://www.daml.org/services/owl-s/security.html, accessed July 2008

Ekelhart, A.; Fenz, S.; Goluch, G. & Weippl, E. (2007a). Ontological Mapping of Common Criteria's Security Assurance Requirements. In: *New Approaches for Security, Privacy and Trust in Complex Environments*, Venter, H; Eloff, M.; Labuschagne, L.; Eloff, J. &

von Solms R., (Eds.), pp. 85-95, Springer, ISBN 978-0-387-72366-2, Boston, http://publik.tuwien.ac.at/files/pub-inf_4689.pdf, accessed March 2009

Ekelhart, A.; Fenz, S.; Goluch, G.; Riedel, B. et al. (2007b). Information Security Fortification by Ontological Mapping of the ISO/IEC 27001 Standard, *Proceedings of the 13th Pacific Rim International Symposium on Dependable Computing*, pp. 381-388, ISBN 0-7695-3054-0, 2007, IEEE Computer Society, Washington DC, USA, http://publik.tuwien.ac.at/files/pub-inf_4689.pdf, accessed March 2009

Ekelhart, A.; Fenz, S.; Klemen, M. & Weippl, E. (2007c). Security Ontologies: Improving Quantitative Risk Analysis. *Proceedings of the 40th Hawaii International Conference on System Sciences (HICSS'07)*, pp. 156-162, ISBN: 0-7695-2755-8, Big Island, Hawaii, 2007, IEEE Computer Society Press

Elahi, G. & Yu, E. (2008). A Goal Oriented Approach for Modeling and Analyzing Security Trade-Offs, *Proceedings of the 26th International Conference on Conceptual Modeling*, pp. 375-390, ISBN 978-3-540-75562-3, Auckland, New Zealand, November 2007. Lecture Notes in Computer Science, Springer Berlin / Heidelberg

ENISA Inventory of Risk Management/Risk Assessment Methods and Tools. (2009). http://www.enisa.europa.eu/rmra/rm_home.html accessed April 2009

Graham, J.; Kaye, D. & Rothstein P.J. (Ed). (2006). *A Risk Management Approach to Business Continuity*, Rothstein Associates Inc., ISBN: 1-931332-36-3, Brookfield, Connecticut

Hilson, D. (Ed). (2007). *The Risk Management Universe – a Guided Tour*, BSI Business Information (BIP 2036), ISBN: 978 0 580 50346, London

Herzog's Security Ontology. (2006). Linköping University, available at (accessed July 2008): http://www.ida.liu.se/~iislab/projects/secont/

Houmb, S.H.; Georg, G.; Jürjens, J. & France, R. (2006). An Integrated Security Verification and Security Solution Design Trade-off Analysis, available at (accessed April 2009): http://mcs.open.ac.uk/jj2924/publications/papers/secse06.pdf

Kazman, R.; Klein, M. & Clements, P. (2000). ATAM: Method for Architecture Evaluation, Technical Report CMU/SEI-2000-TR-004 ESC-TR-2000-004, Carnegie Mellon University, Software Engineering Institute, August 2000

Kim, A.; Luo, J. & Kang, M. (2005). Security Ontology for Annotating Resources, *On the Move to Meaningful Internet Systems 2005: CoopIS, DOA, and ODBASE, Proceedings part II*, pp. 1483-1499, Agia Napa, Cyprus, October - November 2005, LNCS Springer, ISBN 978-3-540-29738-3, Berlin / Heidelberg

Lionberger, B. & Zhang, C. (2007). ATAM Assistant: A Semi-Automated Tool for the Architecture Tradeoff Analysis Method, Proceedings of the Software Engineering and Applications (SEA 2007), Cambridge, USA, November 2007

Lockstep. (2004). *A Guide for Government Agencies Calculating Return on Security Investment*, Government Chief Information Office (GCIO), version 2.0, Lockstep Consulting

Martimiano, L.A.F. & Moreira, E.S. (2005a). Using ontologies to assist security management. *Proceedings of the 8th International Protégé Conference*, ISBN, Madrid, July 2005, http://www.ppgia.pucpr.br/~maziero/pesquisa/ceseg/sbseg06/conteudo/artigos/resumos/19513.pdf, accessed June 2008

Martimiano, L.A.F. & Moreira, E.S. (2005b). An OWL-based Security Incident Ontology. In *Proceedings of the 8th International Protégé Conference*, ISBN, Madrid, July 2005, http://protege.stanford.edu/conference/2005/submissions/posters/poster-martimiano.pdf, accessed June 2008

Noy, N.F. & McGuiness, D.L. (2001). Ontology Development 101: A Guide to Creating Your First Ontology, *Stanford Knowledge Syst. Lab. Tech. Rep. KSL-01-05 and Stanford Medical Informatics Tech. Rep. SMI-2001-0880*, Stanford University, CA. http://www-ksl.stanford.edu/people/dlm/papers/ontology-tutorial-noy-mcguinness-abstract.html, accessed May 2008.

Protégé Ontology Editor and Knowledge Acquisition System, v.3.4. (2008). Stanford University. http://protege.stanford.edu/, accessed May 2008.

REI Ontology Specifications, ver. 2.0. (2008). University of Maryland, available at (accessed May 2008): http://www.cs.umbc.edu/~lkagal1/rei/

SARMA - Security Analysis and Risk Management Association. (2009), http://sarma.org/)

Secure Business, Common Criteria ontology. (2008). available at (accessed October 2008): http://research.securityresearch.at/research/focus/common-criteria-security-assurance/

Sonnenreich, W.; Albanese J. & Stout, B. (2006). Return On Security Investment (ROSI): A Practical Quantitative Model. *Journal of Research and Practice in Information Technology*, Vol. 38, No. 1, February 2006, pp. 55-66, ISSN 1443-458X

Tsoumas, B.; Dritsas, S. & Gritzalis, D. (2005). An Ontology-Based Approach to Information Systems Security Management, *Proceedings of 3rd International Workshop on Mathematical Methods, Models, and Architectures for Computer Network Security*, MMM-ACNS 2005, pp. 151-164, ISBN 978-3-540-29113-8, St. Petersburg, Russia, September 2005, Springer Lecture Notes in Computer Science (LNCS), Volume 3685/2005, Berlin / Heidelberg

Vallieswaran, V. & Menezes B. (2007). ArchKriti: A Software Architecture Based Design and Evaluation Tool Suite, *Proceedings of the International Conference on Information Technology ITNG '07*, pp. 701-706, ISBN:0-7695-2776-0 , Las Vegas, USA, April 2007, IEEE Computer Society

Vorobiev, A. & Bekmamedova, N. (2007). An Ontological Approach Applied to Information Security and Trust, Proceedings of the 18th Australasian Conference on Information Systems, Toowoomba, December 2007, available at (accessed September 2008): http://www.acis2007.usq.edu.au/assets/papers/144.pdf,

Wiki/ontology (2009). http://en.wikipedia.org/wiki/Ontology_(computer_science)

Yau, S.S.; Yan, M. & Huang D. (2007). Design of Service–Based Systems with Adaptive Tradeoff Between Security and Service Delay, *Proceedings of the 4th International Conference on Autonomic and Trusted Computing (ATC)*, pp. 103-113, ISBN 978-3-540-73546-5, Hong Kong, China, July 11-13, 2007. Lecture Notes in Computer Science, Springer Berlin / Heidelberg

Yavagal, D.S.; Lee, S.W.; Ahn, G.J. & Gandhi, R.A. (2005). Common Criteria Requirements Modeling and its Uses for Quality of Information Assurance (QoIA), Proceedings of the 43rd Annual ACM Southeast Conference (ACMSE'05) Vol. 2, pp. 130-135, ISBN:1-59593-059-0, Kennesaw State University Kennesaw, Georgia, ACM New York

4

A Model of Placing Liaisons in the Two Levels of an Organization Structure of a Complete Binary Tree Minimizing Total Path Length

Kiyoshi Sawada
University of Marketing and Distribution Sciences
Japan

1. Introduction

A pyramid organization (Takahashi, 1988) is a formal organization structure which is a hierarchical structure based on the principle of unity of command (Koontz, 1980) that every member except the top in the organization should have a single immediate superior. There exist relations only between each superior and his direct subordinates in the pyramid organization. However, it is desirable to have formed additional relations other than that between each superior and his direct subordinates in advance in case they need communication with other departments in the organization.

The pyramid organization structure can be expressed as a rooted tree, if we let nodes and edges in the rooted tree correspond to members and relations between members in the organization respectively. Then the pyramid organization structure is characterized by the number of subordinates of each member, that is, the number of children of each node and the number of levels in the organization, that is, the height of the rooted tree (Robbins, 2003; Takahara & Mesarovic, 2003). Moreover, the path between a pair of nodes in the rooted tree is equivalent to the route of communication of information between a pair of members in the organization, and adding edges to the rooted tree is equivalent to forming additional relations other than that between each superior and his direct subordinates.

We have proposed some models (Sawada, 2006; Sawada, 2009) of adding relations between members in a pyramid organization structure such that the communication of information between every member in the organization becomes the most efficient. For each model we have obtained a set of additional edges to a complete binary tree minimizing the sum of lengths of shortest paths between every pair of all nodes.

Liaisons (Gittell, 2000; Lievens & Moenaert, 2000) which have roles of coordinating different sections are also placed as a means to become effective in communication of information in an organization. However, it has not been theoretically discussed which members of an organization should form relations to the liaisons.

We have obtained an optimal set for each of the following two models of placing a liaison which forms relations to members of the same level in a pyramid organization structure which is a complete binary tree of height H: (i) a model of adding a node of liaison which gets adjacent to two nodes with the same depth (Sawada, 2008) and (ii) a model of adding a node of liaison which gets adjacent to all nodes with the same depth (Sawada, 2007). A complete binary tree is a rooted tree in which all leaves have the same depth and all internal nodes have two children (Cormen et al., 2001). The depth of a node is the number of edges from the root to the node. Figure 1 shows an example of a complete binary tree of H=5. In Fig. 1 the value of N expresses the depth of each node.

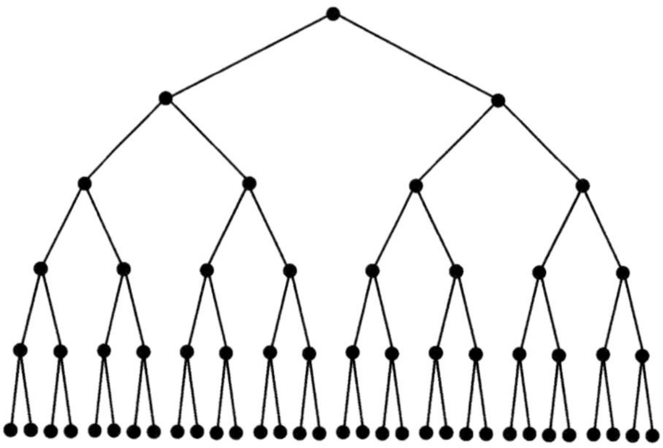

Fig. 1. An example of a complete binary tree of H=5

The above model (ii) corresponds to the formation of additional relations between a liaison and all members in the same level. This model gives us an optimal level when we add relations to the liaison in one level of the organization structure which is a complete binary tree of height H, but this model cannot be applied to placing liaisons in two or more levels. This chapter expands the above model (ii) into the model of placing liaisons in two levels of the organization structure, which is that of adding two nodes of liaisons which get adjacent to all nodes at each depth of two depths in a complete binary tree of height $H(H = 3, 4, \ldots)$.

If $l_{i,j}$ $(= l_{j,i})$ denotes the path length, which is the number of edges in the shortest path from a node v_i to a node v_j $(i, j = 1, 2, ..., 2^{H+1}-1)$ in the complete binary tree of height H, then $\Sigma_{i<j} l_{i,j}$ is the total path length. Furthermore, if $l'_{i,j}$ denotes the path length from v_i to v_j after getting adjacent in the above model, $l_{i,j} - l'_{i,j}$ is called the shortening path length between v_i and v_j, and $\Sigma_{i<j} (l_{i,j} - l'_{i,j})$ is called the *total shortening path length.*

In Section 2 we formulate the total shortening path length when one node of liaison gets adjacent to all nodes with the same depth $M(M = 2, 3, \ldots, H\text{-}1)$ and the other node of liaison gets adjacent to all nodes with the same depth $N(N = M+1, M+2, \ldots, H)$ which is greater than M. In Section 3 we obtain an optimal pair of depth $(M, N)^*$ which maximizes the total shortening path length.

2. Formulation of Total Shortening Path Length

From formulation of shortening path length of adding a node of liaison which gets adjacent to all nodes of the same depth shown in Subsection 2.1, we formulate the total shortening path length when two nodes of liaisons which get adjacent to all nodes of each depth of two depths are added to a complete binary tree in Subsection 2.2. Since we don't consider efficiency of communication of information between the liaisons and the other members, the total shortening path length doesn't include the shortening path length between the nodes of liaisons and nodes in a complete binary tree.

2.1 Placing a Liaison in One Level

This subsection shows formulation of the total shortening path length when one node of liaison gets adjacent to all nodes with the same depth $L(L = 2, 3, \ldots, H)$ in a complete binary tree of height $H(H = 2, 3, \ldots)$.

The sum of shortening path lengths between every pair of nodes whose depths are equal to or greater than L is given by

$$\alpha_H(L) = \{W(H-L)\}^2 2^L \sum_{i=1}^{L-1} i2^i, \tag{1}$$

where $W(h)$ denotes the number of nodes of a complete binary tree of height $h(h=0, 1, 2, \ldots)$.

The sum of shortening path lengths between every pair of nodes whose depths are less than L and those whose depths are equal to or greater than L is given by

$$\beta_H(L) = W(H-L)2^{L+1}\sum_{i=1}^{L-2}(L-i-1)i2^i, \tag{2}$$

and the sum of shortening path lengths between every pair of nodes whose depths are less than L is given by

$$\gamma(L) = 2^L \sum_{i=1}^{L-3}\sum_{j=1}^{i}(i-j+1)j2^j, \tag{3}$$

where we define $\sum_{i=1}^{0} \cdot = 0$, $\sum_{i=1}^{-1} \cdot = 0$.

From these equations, the total shortening path length $\sigma_H(L)$ is given by

$$\sigma_H(L) = \alpha_H(L) + \beta_H(L) + \gamma(L). \tag{4}$$

2.2 Placing Two Liaisons in Two Levels

This subsection shows formulation of the total shortening path length when one node of liaison gets adjacent to all nodes with the same depth $M(M = 2, 3, \ldots, H\text{-}1)$ and the other node of liaison gets adjacent to all nodes with the same depth $N(N = M+1, M+2, \ldots, H)$ which is greater than M in a complete binary tree of height $H(H = 3, 4, \ldots)$.

Let V_1 denote the set of nodes whose depths are less than M. Let V_2 denote the set of nodes whose depths are equal to or greater than M and are less than N. Let V_3 denote the set of nodes whose depths are equal to or greater than N.

The sum of shortening path lengths between every pair of nodes in V_3 is given by

$$A_H(N) = \alpha_H(N) \tag{5}$$

from Eq.(1). The sum of shortening path lengths between every pair of nodes in V_3 and nodes in V_1 and V_2 is given by

$$B_H(N) = \beta_H(N) \tag{6}$$

from Eq.(2). The sum of shortening path lengths between every pair of nodes in V_1 is given by

$$C(M) = \gamma(M) \tag{7}$$

from Eq.(3), and the sum of shortening path lengths between every pair of nodes in V_1 and nodes in V_2 is given by

$$D(M,N) = \beta_{N-1}(M) \tag{8}$$

from Eq.(2). The sum of shortening path lengths between every pair of nodes in V_2 is formulated as follows.
The sum of shortening path lengths between every pair of nodes in each subtree whose root is a node with depth M is given by

$$E(M,N) = \gamma(N-M)2^M \tag{9}$$

from Eq.(3). The sum of shortening path lengths between every pair of nodes in two different subtrees whose roots are nodes with depth M is given by summing up $F(M, N)$ and $G(M, N)$. $F(M, N)$ which is the sum of shortening path lengths by adding edges only between one node of liaison and all nodes with depth M is given by

$$F(M,N) = \alpha_{N-1}(M) \tag{10}$$

from Eq.(1). $G(M, N)$ which is the sum of additional shortening path lengths by adding edges between the other node of liaison and all nodes with depth N after adding edges between one node of liaison and all nodes with depth M is expressed by

$$G(M,N) = \left(2^M - 1\right) \sum_{i=1}^{N-M-2} 2^{N-i} \sum_{j=1}^{N-M-i-1} 2^{N-M-j}(N-M-i-j), \tag{11}$$

where we define $\sum_{i=1}^{0} \cdot = 0, \sum_{i=1}^{-1} \cdot = 0 \cdot$
From these equations, the total shortening path length $S_H(M, N)$ is given by

$$\begin{aligned} S_H(M,N) &= A_H(N)+B_H(N)+C_H(N)+D(M,N)+E(M,N)+F(M,N)+G(M,N) \\ &= \{W(H-N)\}^2 2^N \sum_{i=1}^{N-1} i2^i + W(H-N)2^{N+1}\sum_{i=1}^{N-2}(N-i-1)i2^i \\ &+2^M \sum_{i=1}^{M-3}\sum_{j=1}^{i}(i-j+1)j2^j + W(N-M-1)2^{M+1}\sum_{i=1}^{M-2}(M-i-1)i2^i \\ &+2^N \sum_{i=1}^{N-M-3}\sum_{j=1}^{i}(i-j+1)j2^j + \{W(N-M-1)\}^2 2^M \sum_{i=1}^{M-1} i2^i \\ &+\left(2^M-1\right)\sum_{i=1}^{N-M-2} 2^{N-i}\sum_{j=1}^{N-M-i-1}2^{N-M-j}(N-M-i-j). \end{aligned} \tag{12}$$

Since the number of nodes of a complete binary tree of height h is

$$W(h) = 2^{h+1} - 1, \tag{13}$$

$S_H(M, N)$ of Eq.(12) becomes

$$\begin{aligned} S_H(M,N) &= (N-2)2^{2H+2} + 2^{2H-N+3} - 2^{H+N+3} + (N+1)2^{H+3} + (N-M)2^{N+M+1} \\ &+ (N-M)(N-M-3)2^N + M(M-1)2^M. \end{aligned} \tag{14}$$

3. An Optimal Pair of Depths

This section obtains an optimal pair of depths $(M, N)^*$ by maximizing the total shortening path length $S_H(M, N)$ of Eq.(14).

3.1 An Optimal Depth N^* for a Fixed Value of M

In this subsection, we seek $N = N^*$ which maximizes $R_{H,M}(N) = S_H(M, N)$ for a fixed value of M.

Let $\Delta R_{H,M}(N) \equiv R_{H,M}(N+1) - R_{H,M}(N)$, so that we have

$$\begin{aligned} \Delta R_{H,M}(N) &= \left(4-2^{-N+2}\right)2^{2H} + \left(8-2^{N+3}\right)2^H + (N-M+2)2^{N+M+1} \\ &+ \{(N-M)(N-M+1)-4\}2^N. \end{aligned} \tag{15}$$

for $N = M+1, M+2, ..., H-1$. Let us define x as

$$x = 2^H, \tag{16}$$

then $\Delta R_{H,M}(N)$ in Eq.(15) becomes

$$\begin{aligned} T_{M,N}(x) &= \left(4-2^{-N+2}\right)x^2 + \left(8-2^{N+3}\right)x + (N-M+2)2^{N+M+1} \\ &+ \{(N-M)(N-M+1)-4\}2^N \end{aligned} \tag{17}$$

which is a quadratic function of the continuous variable x. By differentiating $T_{M,N}(x)$ in Eq.(17) with respect to x, we obtain

$$T'_{M,N}(x) = \left(8 - 2^{-N+3}\right)x + 8 - 2^{N+3}. \tag{18}$$

Since $T_{M,N}(x)$ is convex downward from $4 - 2^{-N+2} > 0$, and

$$T_{M,N}(2^{N+1}) = (N-M)2^{N+M+1} + (N-M)(N-M+1)2^{N} + \left(2^{M} - 1\right)2^{N+2} > 0 \tag{19}$$

and

$$T'_{M,N}(2^{N+1}) = 2^{N+3} - 8 > 0, \tag{20}$$

we have $T_{M,N}(x) > 0$ for $x \geq 2^{N+1}$. Hence, we have $\Delta R_{H,M}(N) > 0$ for $H \geq N+1$; that is, $N = M+1, M+2, ..., H-1$.
From the above results, the optimal depth for a fixed value of M is $N^* = H$.

3.2 An Optimal Pair of Depths (*M, N*)*

In this subsection, we seek $(M, N) = (M, N)^*$ which maximizes $S_H(M, N)$ in Eq.(14).
Let $Q_H(M)$ denote the total shortening path length when $N = H$, so that we have

$$\begin{aligned} Q_H(M) &\equiv S_H(M,H) \\ &= (H-4)2^{2H+2} + (H-M)2^{H+M+1} + (H+2)2^{H+3} + (H-M)(H-M-3)2^{H} \\ &\quad + M(M-1)2^{M}. \end{aligned} \tag{21}$$

Let $\Delta Q_H(M) \equiv Q_H(M+1) - Q_H(M)$, so that we have

$$\Delta Q_H(M) = (H-M-2)\left(2^{M} - 1\right)2^{H+1} + M(M+3)2^{M} > 0 \tag{22}$$

for $M = 2, 3, \ldots, H-2$.
From the results in Subsection 3.1 and 3.2, the optimal pair of depths is $(M, N)^* = (H-1, H)$.
Table 1 shows the optimal pairs of depths $(M, N)^*$ and the total shortening path lengths $S_H(M,N)^*$ in the case of $H=3, 4, \ldots, 20$.

4. Conclusions

This study considered obtaining optimal depths of adding nodes of liaisons to a complete binary tree maximizing the total shortening path length which is the sum of shortening lengths of shortest paths between every pair of all nodes in the complete binary tree. This means to obtain optimal levels of placing liaisons to the basic type of a pyramid organization such that the communication of information between every member in the organization becomes the most efficient.

H	$(M, N)^*$	$S_H(M, N)^*$
3	(2, 3)	120
4	(3, 4)	1040
5	(4, 5)	7040
6	(5, 6)	41472
7	(6, 7)	223872
8	(7, 8)	1139456
9	(8, 9)	5563392
10	(9, 10)	26347520
11	(10, 11)	121935872
12	(11, 12)	554323968
13	(12, 13)	2484535296
14	(13, 14)	11009196032
15	(14, 15)	48325754880
16	(15, 16)	210469584896
17	(16, 17)	910568456192
18	(17, 18)	3917087244288
19	(18, 19)	16767719571456
20	(19, 20)	71468617564160

Table 1. Optimal pairs of depths $(M, N)^*$

For the model of adding a node of liaison which gets adjacent to all nodes of the same depth L to a complete binary tree of height H, we had already obtained an optimal depth $L^* = H$ in our paper (Sawada, 2007). This result shows that the most efficient way of adding relations between the liaison and all members in one level is to add relations at the lowest level, irrespective of the number of levels in the organization structure.

This chapter expanded the above model into the model of placing liaisons in two levels of the organization structure, which is that of adding two nodes of liaisons which get adjacent to all nodes at each depth of two depths M and N which is greater than M to a complete binary tree of height H. We obtained an optimal pair of depth $(M, N)^* = (H\text{-}1, H)$ which maximizes the total shortening path length. In the case of $H = 5$ illustrated with the example in Fig. 1 an optimal pair of depths is $(M, N)^* = (4, 5)$. This result means that the most efficient manner of adding relations between two liaisons and all members in each level of two levels is to add relations at the lowest level and the second lowest level, irrespective of the number of levels in the organization structure.

5. References

Cormen, T. H.; Leiserson, C. E.; Rivest, R. L. & Stein, C. (2001). *Introduction to Algorithms*, 2nd Edition, MIT Press

Gittell, J. H. (2000). Organizing work to support relational co-ordination. *International Journal of Human Resource Management*, Vol. 11, pp. 517-539

Koontz, H.; O'Donnell, C. & Weihrich, H. (1980). *Management*, 7th Edition, McGraw-Hill

Lievens, A. & Moenaert, R. K. (2000). Project team communication in financial service innovation. *Journal of Management Studies*, Vol. 37, pp. 733-766

Robbins, S. P. (2003). *Essentials of Organizational Behavior*, 7th Edition, Prentice Hall

Sawada, K. & Wilson, R. (2006). Models of adding relations to an organization structure of a complete *K*-ary tree. *European Journal of Operational Research*, Vol. 174, pp. 1491-1500

Sawada, K. (2007). A model of placing a liaison in the same level of a pyramid organization structure. *Proceedings of 2007 IEEE International Conference on Industrial Engineering and Engineering Management*, pp. 804-806, Singapore

Sawada, K. (2008). Placing a liaison between two members of the same level in an organization structure of a complete binary tree. *Proceedings of the Ninth ACIS International Conference on Software Engineering, Artificial Intelligence, Networking, and Parallel/Distributed Computing*, pp. 69-72, Phuket, Thailand

Sawada, K. (2009). Two models of additional adjacencies between the root and descendants in a complete binary tree minimizing total path length. *IAENG Transactions on Engineering Technologies*, Vol. 1, pp. 244-252

Takahara, Y. & Mesarovic, M. (2003). *Organization Structure: Cybernetic Systems Foundation*, Kluwer Academic/Plenum Publishers

Takahashi, N. (1988). Sequential analysis of organization design: a model and a case of Japanese firms. *European Journal of Operational Research*, Vol. 36, pp. 297-310

Object Tracking under High Correlation for Kalman & $\alpha - \beta$ Filter

D. M. Akbar Hussain and Zaki Ahmed*
Department of Electronic Systems
Esbjerg Institute of Technology
Aalborg University Esbjerg, Denmark
akbar@aaue.dk
* *zaki424@hotmail.com*

Abstract. The investigation presented here compares the advantage of using a Kalman filter as opposed to an $\alpha - \beta$ filter for multi-target tracking systems. The former is often used to speed up the computation time. However, it is shown here that due to the difficulty of data association the benefits are not as great as might be expected when correlation is high. Extensive analyses are performed by selecting various scenarios where the correlation factor affects the performance of $\alpha - \beta$ filter compared with Kalman filter. The research also investigate a new framework of forming a tree clustering scheme to prune false target-measurement pairing introduced when multiple targets are in the same vicinity.

Key words: Filtering, Kalman, $\alpha - \beta$, Filter, Target Tracking, State Estimation.

1. Introduction

During the past two decades the improved technology available for surveillance systems has generated a great deal of interest in algorithms capable of tracking large number of objects using information from one or more sensors like radar, sonar etc. Typical sensor systems, such as radar, obtain data returns corrupted with noise from true targets and possibly from other objects. In general the tracking problem requires processing of incoming data to produce accurate position and velocity estimates [1-3]. There are two types of uncertainties involved with this incoming data, first the position inaccuracy, as the measurements are corrupted by noise, and second the measurement origin since there may be uncertainty as to which measurement originates from which target [4, 5]. These uncertainties lead to a data association problem and the tracking performance depends not only on the measurement noise but also upon the uncertainty in the measurement origin [6-8]. Therefore, in a multi-target environment extensive computation may be required to establish the correspondence between measurements and tracks at each radar scan [9, 10]. After the data association process, tracks are normally updated using either standard Kalman or $\alpha - \beta$ filter [11-13]. Also tracks whose statistics deviate from the assumed model and shown to be following the same target are normally eliminated [14, 15]. Kalman or

$\alpha - \beta$ filters can be ideal choice for a single target case where one noisy measurement is obtained at each radar scan. In the multi-target tracking case, an unknown number of measurements are received at each radar scan and assuming no false measurements, each one has to be associated with an existing or new tracking filter. When the targets are well apart from each other then forming a measurement prediction ellipse around a track to associate the correct measurement with that track is a standard technique [16]. When targets are near to each other, more than one measurement may fall within the prediction ellipse of a filter and prediction ellipses of different filters may interact. The number of measurements accepted by a filter will therefore be quite sensitive in this situation to the accuracy of the prediction ellipse. Several approaches may be used for this situation [17, 18], one of which is called the Track Splitting Filter algorithm (explained later in the text). In this research as mentioned earlier we extend our investigation and introduce a tree based clustering framework to prune the excessive tracks generated at ambiguity time. A typical recursive multi-target tracking system is shown in figure 1. The algorithm is implemented using an AMD Athlon 64, 2.2 GHz microprocessor on a standard PC for convenience. However, real implementation should be on a much powerful processor for example on a DSP for faster computation.

2. Problem Statement

2.1 The Data Association Problem

In a general multiple target tracking situation, as explained in the introduction, a number of measurements from an unknown number of targets are received at each radar scan. Typically the radar sensor measures target position in polar co-ordinates, that is in range r and bearing θ. Measurement inaccuracy can normally be modeled as additive zero-mean uncorrelated Gaussian noise on r and θ, with given variances σ_r^2 and σ_θ^2 respectively. The multiple targets tracking problem requires each measurement received at every radar scan to be associated with an existing or new target track. The associated observations are then incorporated in a state estimation algorithm or initialization procedure to produce updated track position and velocity estimates. Basically there are two fundamental approaches to deal with the data association problem, first there is the deterministic approach in which the most likely of several "candidate" associations are formed and then treated as if they were certain, ignoring the fact that this may not necessarily be true. The results of the deterministic association are then used in a standard state estimation algorithm. The Nearest Neighbour Filter (NNF) and the Track Splitting Filter (TSF) are two common examples of the deterministic approach. The second method is a probabilistic model, based on a Bayesian approach, which computes the probabilities of individual associations and state estimations are obtained with associated probabilities. The multiple Hypothesis Tracking (MHT) approach, where a number of hypotheses are generated and evaluated as more data is received, and the Joint Probabilistic Data Association Filter (JPDAF) are examples of algorithms which use the Bayesian approach. The fundamental difference between the deterministic approach and the Bayesian approach is that the latter explicitly takes into account the uncertainty in the measurement origin. The Bayesian approach is the optimal solution to the data association problem, but it is computationally very expensive. The JPDAF method is a suboptimal modification of the Bayesian approach and is simpler since it does not require storage of information regarding hypotheses at previous time instants.

Here we will be concerned with the implementation of a deterministic approach, the TSF algorithm.

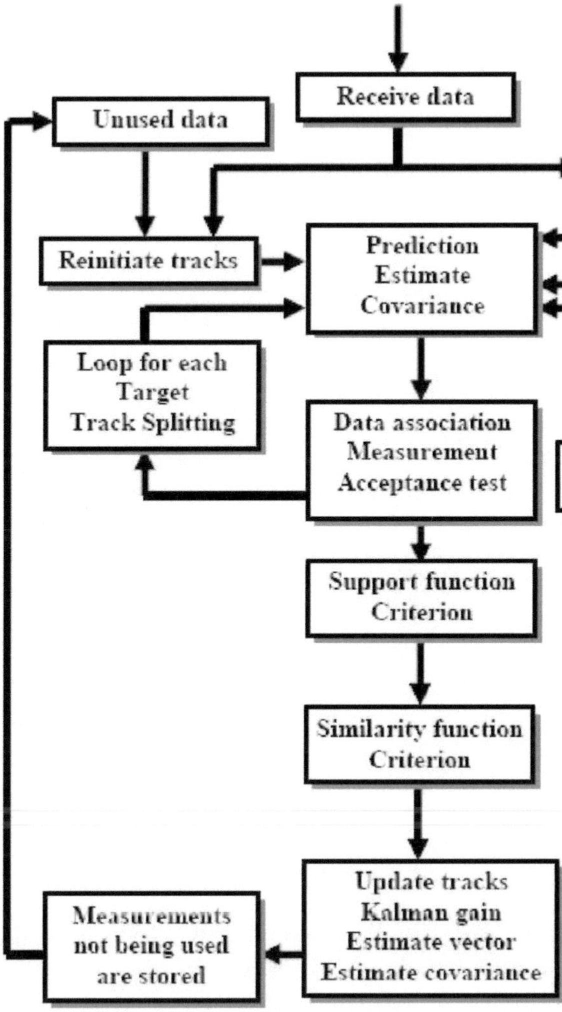

Fig. 1. Recursive Multi-Target Tracking System

2.2 State Estimation

For the estimation of target position and velocity from the track data, it is common to use a recursive Kalman filtering algorithm, [17, 18]. This requires a model for the motion of the target being tracked and one often assumed a constant velocity target with random acceleration description given by;

$$\underline{x}_{n+1} = \mathbf{\Phi}\underline{x}_n + \mathbf{\Gamma}\underline{w}_n \tag{1}$$

and the corresponding measurement $\underline{z}_{n+1}$ is given by

$$\underline{z}_{n+1} = \mathbf{H}\underline{x}_{n+1} + \underline{\nu}_{n+1} \tag{2}$$

The state vector, the state transition matrix, the excitation and the measurement matrix are respectively,

$$\underline{x}_{n+1}^T = (x \;\; \dot{x} \;\; y \;\; \dot{y})_{n+1} \tag{3}$$

$$\mathbf{\Phi} = \begin{bmatrix} 1 & \Delta t & 0 & 0 \\ 0 & 1 & 0 & 0 \\ 0 & 0 & 1 & \Delta t \\ 0 & 0 & 0 & 1 \end{bmatrix} \tag{4}$$

$$\mathbf{\Gamma} = \begin{bmatrix} \Delta t^2/2 & 0 \\ \Delta t & 0 \\ 0 & \Delta t^2/2 \\ 0 & \Delta t \end{bmatrix} \tag{5}$$

$$\mathbf{H} = \begin{bmatrix} 1\,0\,0\,0 \\ 0\,0\,1\,0 \end{bmatrix}. \tag{6}$$

Here Δt is the sampling interval and corresponds to the time interval, assumed uniform, at which radar measurement data is received. The acceleration noise $\underline{w}_n$ is zero mean Gaussian and independent in each Cartesian co-ordinate with covariance $\mathbf{Q}_n$. The measurement noise $\underline{\nu}_n$ is assumed Gaussian with covariance $\mathbf{R}_n$. The Cartesian coordinates of the measurements are obtained from the polar coordinates (r, θ) received by radar through a non-linear transformation.

$$x = r \; Cos \; \theta \tag{7}$$

$$y = r \; Sin \; \theta \tag{8}$$

This transformation results in the measurement errors on the Cartesian coordinates being non-Gaussian distributed, but under the reasonable assumption that the measurement errors on the polar coordinates are small compared with the true target coordinates (r, θ), it can be shown that the Cartesian errors are bivariate Gaussian random variables [19] with zero mean and covariance $\mathbf{R}_n$ given by

$$\mathbf{R}_n = \begin{bmatrix} \sigma_x^2 & \sigma_{xy} \\ \sigma_{xy} & \sigma_y^2 \end{bmatrix} \tag{9}$$

where,

$$\sigma_x^2 = \sigma_r^2 \; Cos^2\theta + \; \sigma_\theta^2 \; r^2 \; Sin^2\theta \tag{10}$$

$$\sigma_y^2 = \sigma_r^2 \; Sin^2\theta + \; \sigma_\theta^2 \; r^2 \; Cos^2\theta \tag{11}$$

$$\sigma_{xy} = 0.5\ (\sigma_r^2 - r^2\ \sigma_\theta^2)\ Sin2\theta \tag{12}$$

Although the analysis in [19] is approximate, it is the only way of avoiding a non-linear tracking filter, because if the measurement errors on the Cartesian coordinates are non-Gaussian distributed the optimum tracking filter in these coordinates is non-linear. On the other hand tracking can be performed in polar coordinates to avoid the correlation introduced by the non-linear transformation but it leads to large dynamic errors when a linear model for target motion is used, even simple constant velocity tracks appear non-linear in polar coordinates and artificial acceleration components are generated. This problem does not arise if tracking is performed in Cartesian coordinates. When the target position measurement errors are correlated, a fourth order full Kalman filter is the optimal tracker in that it minimizes the mean squared error between the estimated and the actual states, and it accounts for the cross-correlation term in the measurement covariance matrix. The standard Kalman filter equations for estimating the position and velocity are;

$$\hat{x}_{n+1/n} = \mathbf{\Phi}\underline{\hat{x}}_n \tag{13}$$

$$\underline{\hat{x}}_{n+1} = \mathbf{\Phi}\underline{\hat{x}}_{n+1/n} + \mathbf{K}_{n+1}\underline{\nu}_{n+1} \tag{14}$$

$$\mathbf{K}_{n+1} = \mathbf{P}_{n+1/n}\mathbf{H}^T\mathbf{B}_{n+1}^{-1} \tag{15}$$

$$\mathbf{P}_{n+1/n} = \mathbf{\Phi}\mathbf{P}_n\mathbf{\Phi}^T + \mathbf{\Gamma}\mathbf{Q}_n\mathbf{\Gamma}^T \tag{16}$$

$$\mathbf{B}_{n+1} = \mathbf{R}_{n+1} + \mathbf{H}\mathbf{P}_{n+1/n}\mathbf{H}^T \tag{17}$$

$$\mathbf{P}_{n+1} = (\mathbf{I} - \mathbf{K}_{n+1}\mathbf{H})\mathbf{P}_{n+1/n} \tag{18}$$

$$\underline{\nu}_{n+1} = \underline{z}_{n+1} - \mathbf{H}\underline{\hat{x}}_{n+1/n} \tag{19}$$

where $\mathbf{\Phi}$ is the assumed target motion model of eqn. 1, $\mathbf{K}_{n+1}$ is the filter gain, $\underline{\nu}_{n+1}$ the innovations, $\mathbf{H}$ is the measurement matrix, $\mathbf{P}_{n+1}$ is the state covariance matrix, $\mathbf{B}_{n+1}$ is the covariance of the innovations, $\mathbf{\Gamma}$ is the excitation matrix, $\mathbf{R}_{n+1}$ the assumed measurement noise covariance matrix, and $\mathbf{Q}_n$ the filter acceleration noise matrix. The measurement noise matrix $\mathbf{R}_n$ and filter acceleration noise matrix $\mathbf{Q}_n$ are parameters which must be estimated in a practical situation. Clearly when $\mathbf{R}_n$ is not diagonal, the recursive updating of the innovation covariance matrix $\mathbf{B}_{n+1}$ and the state covariance matrices $\mathbf{P}_{n+1}$ and $\mathbf{P}_{n+1/n}$ using the above equations introduces off-diagonal terms. When the measurement errors in each co-ordinate are independent that is $\mathbf{R}_n$ is diagonal, the Kalman filter may be decoupled into two optimal tracking filters, known as $\alpha - \beta$ filters [20]. This filter configuration simplifies the computational requirements considerably, because the states relating to each of the two co-ordinates can be estimated independently. The equations for an $\alpha - \beta$ filter to estimate x-position and velocity are;

$$\hat{x}_{n+1} = x_{n+1/n} + \alpha_{n+1}(z_{x_{n+1}} - x_{n+1/n}) \tag{20}$$

$$\hat{\dot{x}}_{n+1} = \dot{x}_{n+1/n} + (\beta_{n+1}/\Delta t)(z_{x_{n+1}} - x_{n+1/n}) \tag{21}$$

Where $x_{n+1/n}$ and $\dot{x}_{n+1/n}$ are the predicted position and velocity respectively, that is $\underline{x}_{n+1/n} = \mathbf{\Phi}\,\hat{\underline{x}}_n$ for the full Kalman filter, and $z_{x_{n+1}}$ is the x-component of the measurement vector $\underline{z}_{n+1}$. The Kalman gain for the $\alpha - \beta$ filter is;

$$\mathbf{K}_{n+1} = (\alpha_{n+1} \quad \beta_{n+1}/\Delta t)^T \tag{22}$$

where α_{n+1} and β_{n+1} are the gain coefficients. The estimation error covariance can be shown to be given by

$$\mathbf{P}_{n+1} = (\sigma_x^2)_{n+1} \begin{bmatrix} \alpha_{n+1} & \beta_{n+1}/\Delta t \\ \beta_{n+1}/\Delta t & \delta_{n+1}/\Delta t^2 \end{bmatrix} \tag{23}$$

Where $(\sigma_x^2)_{n+1}$ is the variance in the error of the $(n+1)^{th}$ x-position measurement. Recurrence relations for α, β and δ can easily be obtained using equations 13 to 19.

3. Track Splitting Algorithm

Tracking of a single target, in the ideal situation where one noisy measurement is obtained at each radar scan, can be achieved using standard Kalman filter techniques. In the multi-target case, an unknown number of measurements are received at each radar scan and, assuming no false measurements, each measurement has to be associated with an existing or new target tracking filter. The standard approach for associating a measurement with an already established track is to form an ellipse or gate, around the predicted position measurement [16] and if a measurement falls inside the ellipse it is normally used to update the track. When targets are near to each other, then more than one measurement may fall within the prediction ellipse of a filter. For example, if n measurements occur inside a prediction ellipse, then the filter branches or splits into n tracking filters. This approach is known as the track splitting algorithm [16]. The multiple target tracking algorithm using a track splitting filter consists of the following three basic modules, track initialization, track continuation and the track pruning as a means of controlling the explosion in the number of tracks due to measurement ambiguity [21].

3.1 Track Initialization

One of the basic requirements for any filtering algorithm is satisfactory "initialization" of the filter that is providing the initial estimate vector and the initial covariance matrix of the estimate vector. The filter initialization becomes more important in the multi-target environment where additional algorithms such as those for data association are involved. The measurement acceptance test, which is an essential part of the algorithm, is also affected by a poor guess for the initialization of the covariance matrix of the estimate. The initial state is usually assumed to be a normally distributed random variable [17] that is;

$$\underline{x}_0 \sim N[\hat{\underline{x}}_{0/0}, \mathbf{P}_{0/0}] \tag{24}$$

The scheme for track initialization is quite simple. A measurement m is considered to be unused if it has not been used to update a track. This measurement is then stored for possible correlation with another measurement n arriving at a later scan, usually the next scan, and if the actual distance between these two measurements m and n is less than a distance threshold $\delta_d(m,n)$ a new track is initialized. A maximum speed V_{max} is assumed for a target, thus the maximum distance that can be traveled in j time step is $V_{max}\ j\ \Delta t$, *where* Δt is the time interval between two scans. The distance measurement noise variance $\sigma_T^2(m,k)$ of measurement m at time k is obtained from the measurement noise variances on the (x, y) coordinates as;

$$\sigma_T^2(m,k) = \sigma_x^2(m,k) + \sigma_y^2(m,k) \tag{25}$$

The distance threshold $\delta_d(m,n)$ between measurements m and n, j time step apart is therefore taken as;

$$\delta_d(m,k) = V_{max}\ j\ \Delta t + \sigma_T(m,k) + \sigma_T(n,k+j) \tag{26}$$

When the above test is satisfied the most recent measurement is taken as the initial track position estimate. The initial velocity of the track is taken by dividing the difference between the two measurements m and n with the time elapsed between the two scans. Thus the x co-ordinate velocity estimate is given by;

$$\hat{\dot{x}}_0 = \frac{z_x(k+j,\ n)\ -\ z_x(k,\ m)}{j\ \Delta t}. \tag{27}$$

The initial velocity estimate for the y co-ordinate can be similarly derived. The choice of the covariance matrix of the estimate should be such that the expected value of the estimation errors achieved by the filter match the filter calculated covariance that is;

$$E[(x_0 - \hat{x}_{0/0})(x_0 - \hat{x}_{0/0})^T] = \mathbf{P}_{0/0} \tag{28}$$

The Kalman gain or the weighting given to the predicted estimate is directly proportional to the covariance of the estimate. This means that an optimistic (very accurate) covariance at the initial stage will produce a low gain with the result that a small weighting is given to incoming measurements, which normally results in large errors in the initial estimates. At the other extreme a very high value of gain may have a bad effect on tracking accuracy since a high weighting is placed on the noisy measurements. The covariance of the measurement noise $\mathbf{R}_n$ can be taken as an initial uncertainty of the target position, thus, supposing the initial covariance matrix for a two dimensional Kalman filter is

$$\mathbf{P}_{0/0} = \begin{bmatrix} \sigma_x^2 \begin{pmatrix} \alpha & \beta/\Delta t \\ \beta/\Delta t & \delta/\Delta t^2 \end{pmatrix} & \sigma_{xy} \begin{pmatrix} \alpha & \beta/\Delta t \\ \beta/\Delta t & \delta/\Delta t^2 \end{pmatrix} \\ \sigma_{xy} \begin{pmatrix} \alpha & \beta/\Delta t \\ \beta/\Delta t & \delta/\Delta t^2 \end{pmatrix} & \sigma_y^2 \begin{pmatrix} \alpha & \beta/\Delta t \\ \beta/\Delta t & \delta/\Delta t^2 \end{pmatrix} \end{bmatrix} \tag{29}$$

where $\alpha = 1$, $\beta = 1$, and $\delta = 2$ are the gain coefficients [22]. For a decoupled $\alpha - \beta$ filter it follows that the above covariance matrix becomes the block diagonal matrix.

3.2 Track Continuation

As shown in figure 1, following the initial track formation incoming observations are considered for the continuation of existing tracks. The continuation procedure consists of prediction, measurement association and state estimation (i.e. updating). At each radar scan, the target position is predicted using eq. 13 and the uncertainty associated (eq. 19) with this is used to place a measurement acceptance ellipse around the predicted position. If the dynamics of the assumed target model is correct then each measurement from that particular target will fall inside the predicted ellipse (measurement acceptance ellipse). However, at times incorrect measurements (that are not original returns from that particular target) may have been used to update the target. In such case the target dynamic does not remain correct and true measurement may fall outside the prediction ellipse. On the other hand, when targets are very close together, more than one measurement may fall within the prediction ellipse of a particular target. Therefore, one has to resolve such situations through various data association techniques [17, 18]. The track splitting filter algorithm is one such technique in which the filter is allowed to split into the total number of measurements inside the ellipse [16]. This approach assumes that all the measurements falling inside the ellipse are equally probable for that particular target; therefore, all of them are used to update its state. Once the filter determines that a measurement has fallen inside its prediction ellipse, it uses a measurement acceptance test and if the test is satisfied then that particular measurement is used for update. The measurement acceptance criterion uses a simple test i.e., if the dimension of the measurement vector $\mathbf{Z}_n$ is M, then the norm $\mathbf{d_n^2}$ of the innovation vector $\underline{\nu}_n$ at scan n for a filter is given by;

$$\mathbf{d_n^2} = \underline{\nu}_\mathbf{n}^\mathbf{T} \mathbf{B_n^{-1}} \underline{\nu}_\mathbf{n} \tag{30}$$

where the M-dimensional Gaussian probability density for the innovation is;

$$f(\underline{\nu}) = \frac{e^{\frac{-d^2}{2}}}{(2\pi)^{\frac{M}{2}} \sqrt{|\mathbf{B_n}|}} \tag{31}$$

with $\mathbf{B_n}$ being the innovations covariance matrix for the specific filter and $|\mathbf{B_n}|$ its determinant. Provided that the filter model for the track dynamics is accurate and that all the measurements used to update the track did indeed originate from one particular target, the quantity $\mathbf{d_n^2}$ is a sum of squares of M-independent zero mean and unit standard deviation Gaussian random variables. Thus $\mathbf{d_n^2}$ will have a χ^2 distribution with M degrees of freedom. The measurement acceptance criterion for a track is thus defined that if $\mathbf{d_n^2}$ is less than a threshold $\mathbf{J}^2$ (with some known probability) then that particular measurement at scan n can be used for update [22].

3.3 Support Function Criterion

A mechanism for restricting the excess tracks that originate from track splitting under measurement ambiguity is needed and one possibility is the use of the track support function. The likelihood function of a track is the measure of the probability of the track accepting a sequence of measurements in n scans. It is given by [16];

$$\Lambda = \prod_{i=1}^{n} f(\underline{\nu}_i) \tag{32}$$

$$= \left(\prod_{i=1}^{n} \frac{1}{(2\pi)^{M/2}\sqrt{|\mathbf{B}|}} \right) \left(e^{-\frac{1}{2}\sum_{i=1}^{n} d_i^2} \right) \tag{33}$$

The natural logarithm of the second part of the above equation is called the modified log-likelihood function (or support function S_n) [17]. The support function S_n is given by;

$$S_n = -\frac{1}{2}\sum_{i=1}^{n} d_i^2 \tag{34}$$

and it can be calculated recursively from

$$S_{n+1} = S_n - \frac{1}{2}\underline{\nu}_{n+1}^T \mathbf{B}_{n+1}^{-1} \underline{\nu}_{n+1} \tag{35}$$

If the support function of a track is smaller than a threshold value, it may not represent a true target in the sense that the measurements it has been using are inconsistent with the assumed target motion. This is used as a criterion in the track-splitting algorithm to terminate a track. The summation of the norm $\mathbf{d_n^2}$ for n scans is χ^2 distributed with N degrees of freedom where $N = n \times M$. Therefore the support function S_n is also χ^2 distributed with N degrees of freedom. If we wish to define a threshold T for a χ^2 distribution so that the probability of the variable exceeding the threshold is P_{rT} then we can either use χ^2 tables or, if the degree of freedom is large, use the approximate relationship [23];

$$T = N + T_g\sqrt{(2N)} \tag{36}$$

which relates the equivalent threshold T_g for a Gaussian distribution of unit variance to that of T for the χ^2 distribution. For example if $N = 30$, $T_g = 2.327$ for a threshold probability of P_{rT} equal to 0.01, and the above formula yields $T = 48.025$ compared with the value 50.892

from the χ^2 table. For the implementation of the support function criterion, assuming that $M = 2$ and thus $N = 2 \times n$, then T'_n the threshold for the support function S_n is given by the following relationship.

$$T_n^{'} = -(n + T_g\sqrt{(n)}) \tag{37}$$

3.4 Similarity Criterion

To further reduce the number of filters obtained when using the track-splitting algorithm the similarity criterion is used to ensure that no more than one filter is tracking the same target [24, 25]. The similarity criterion provides a measure for the nearness of two tracking filter position estimates and if this is below a certain threshold one filter can be eliminated. Any two tracks i and j are deemed to be similar if

$$(\hat{\underline{x}}_i - \hat{\underline{x}}_j)^T \mathbf{P}^{-1} (\hat{\underline{x}}_i - \hat{\underline{x}}_j) \leq D_{th} \tag{38}$$

where $\hat{\underline{x}}_i$ and $\hat{\underline{x}}_j$ are the two filter state estimate vectors. **P** is a weighting matrix chosen to be the sum of the covariance matrices of the two filters with off diagonal elements set to zero and D_{th} is the chosen threshold. As the estimates $\hat{\underline{x}}_i$ and $\hat{\underline{x}}_j$ are correlated **P** will not be the true covariance of $(\hat{\underline{x}}_i - \hat{\underline{x}}_j)$ but in many instances a reasonable estimate. When the two tracks are similar, one obviously wishes to keep the best supported track. The support function of track is proportional to the life of the track; therefore if two tracks with different track life are compared then the track with a longer life may incorrectly be eliminated. To prevent such a situation the support function of a track is normalized where the normalized support function, is [26]

$$S_{normalize} = -\frac{S_n + n}{\sqrt{n}} \tag{39}$$

Similarity pruning as described above may lead to a different elimination of tracks in a multi-target scenario, depending upon the order in which similarity calculations between tracks are made.

3.5 Clustering Scheme

Here we discuss some additional modifications using clustering methods to reduce the number of similarity calculations so that further speed up can be achieved. If targets are far from each other then only one measurement will be accepted by each tracking filter, assuming that there are no false measurements. When track splitting occurs it means that at least two targets are close to each other. At subsequent scans a tree is formed for each target. Only one branch of this tree corresponds to the real target, the others are false tracks and they will usually be eliminated by either the similarity or support function tests.

The similarity test checks the nearness of two tracks so that non-interfering trees cannot be similar to each other. Therefore, only tracks which belong to interfering trees need to be compared to detect similar tracks. Interfering trees can be detected as follows. When a track is initiated it is given a unique number as its identity and when a track splits its identity is passed to all new branches. If any two branches from two different trees have been formed by accepting the same measurements, then it means these trees are interfering with each other. Therefore, the clustering algorithm first finds the branches which have used the same measurements, which are called interfering branches. These branches are placed in different groups (i.e. tracks which have used measurement-0 will be in the first group, those which have used measurement-1 will be in the second group and so on). Then the identities of the tracks in different groups are checked. If there are two tracks in two different groups with the same identity these two groups are merged to form a cluster. This procedure is known as clustering algorithm A. A somewhat similar approach has been investigated in reference [27] to form clusters and distributing them on parallel processing architecture. Now if only the interfering branches are considered instead of interfering trees, then each group becomes a cluster. This approach has been used by Reid [28] to implement his multiple hypotheses tracking algorithm for multiple target tracking. This clustering method has also been implemented and is called clustering algorithm B, results of these two algorithms are discussed in the next section.

4. Analysis

As mentioned earlier, when the track splitting filter algorithm is used, the tracking filter splits into branches which are equal to the number of measurements found within the predicted acceptance ellipse. This means the shape of the measurement ellipse is very important in the case of neighboring or crossing targets. A four crossing target scenario is considered for our investigation as shown in figure 2 for low and high correlation factors of 0.1 and 0.9 respectively. These four targets are moving from a fixed location with same velocity and they cross each other after 30 seconds. The correlation factor is approximately kept constant throughout the run (100 Seconds) by maintaining the relative positions of the target and the platform (sensor is on-board a ship). To obtain the two correlation factors only the initial position of the platform is changed and all other parameters remain the same. The scenario was run with ten different random seeds; table 1 gives the number of average tracks present for the two filters with low and high correlation factors. As anticipated, because of the inferior measurement prediction ellipse, $\alpha - \beta$ filter has considerably more branching near the crossing point (30th seconds) for the high correlation factor. For low correlation the numbers of branches are almost the same. The fact of the matter is, this increased branching requires extra overhead computation for data association and track maintenance. The clustering schemes Algorithm A and B for similarity criterion produced relatively low number of branches because of the more structured and intelligent techniques as shown in table 1. We selected a number of similar scenarios to compare the speed-up between the two filters, the computation ratio for Kalman vis a v $\alpha - \beta$ filter is in the order of 1 to 7 approximately.

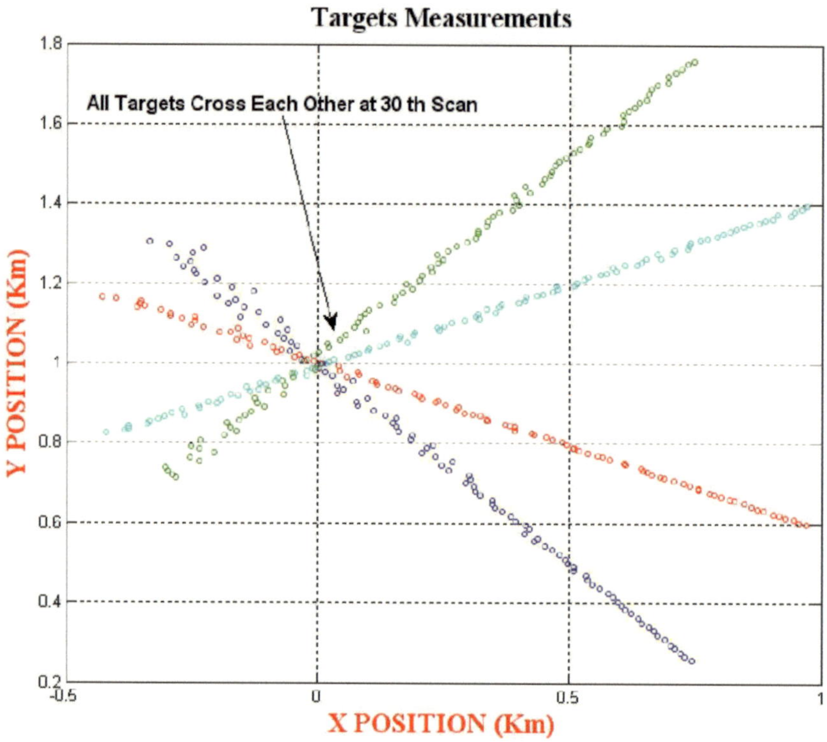

Fig. 2. Crossing Target Scenario

	CORRELATION					
	Kalman Filter		$\alpha - \beta$ Filter		Clustering	
Scan No	Low (0.1)	High (0.9)	Low (0.1)	High (0.9)	A	B
22	4	4	4	4	4	4
23	4	4	4	4	4	5
24	4	4	4	8	6	6
25	4	5	5	10	7	7
26	5	10	6	30	27	29
27	7	24	7	40	32	35
28	12	29	13	51	44	47
29	15	32	18	45	38	40
30	16	28	19	42	38	38
31	16	26	20	42	36	40
32	14	17	19	35	30	31
33	13	12	18	30	27	29
34	10	9	15	22	19	19
35	8	5	10	15	12	11
36	6	4	7	13	10	11
37	4	4	6	12	8	8
38	4	4	5	9	9	8
39	4	4	4	7	7	7
40	4	4	4	4	4	4

Table 1. Average Number of Tracks

Figure 3 shows the average speed-up plotted against various numbers of targets. It can be seen from figure 3 that as the ambiguity increases, the speed-up deteriorates to a ratio of 1 to 3. Therefore, the advantage of using an $\alpha - \beta$ filter under high correlation is not really great. One of the main reasons for excessive branching, in the case of $\alpha - \beta$ filter under high correlation, is due to the shape of the prediction ellipse as shown in figure 4 which is almost like a circle around the predicted position of the track. However, the shape of prediction ellipse in case of Kalman filter is like a true ellipse aligned in the direction of the target heading. For our second part of investigation the scenario geometry was modified and the measurement data was generated corresponding to one of the target before crossing (30th seconds) and the second after the crossing as shown in figure 5, duration of the tracking is 100 seconds. In this investigation we want to find how effective is the support function criterion for the two filters when correlation is high. Tables 2 and 3 show the initial angles when the target starts its motion and the intersection angles when it changes its direction. The correlation ranges during tracking period for these angles are also shown. The idea is to feed different kinds of data to analyze filter's behavior. Both filters Kalman and $\alpha - \beta$ filters were used to track these scenarios for the two values of correlation. Basically each run consists of 10 iterations and a new seed is selected for every iteration. The support function and the measurement acceptance values are obtained during these iterations and finally the average is computed.

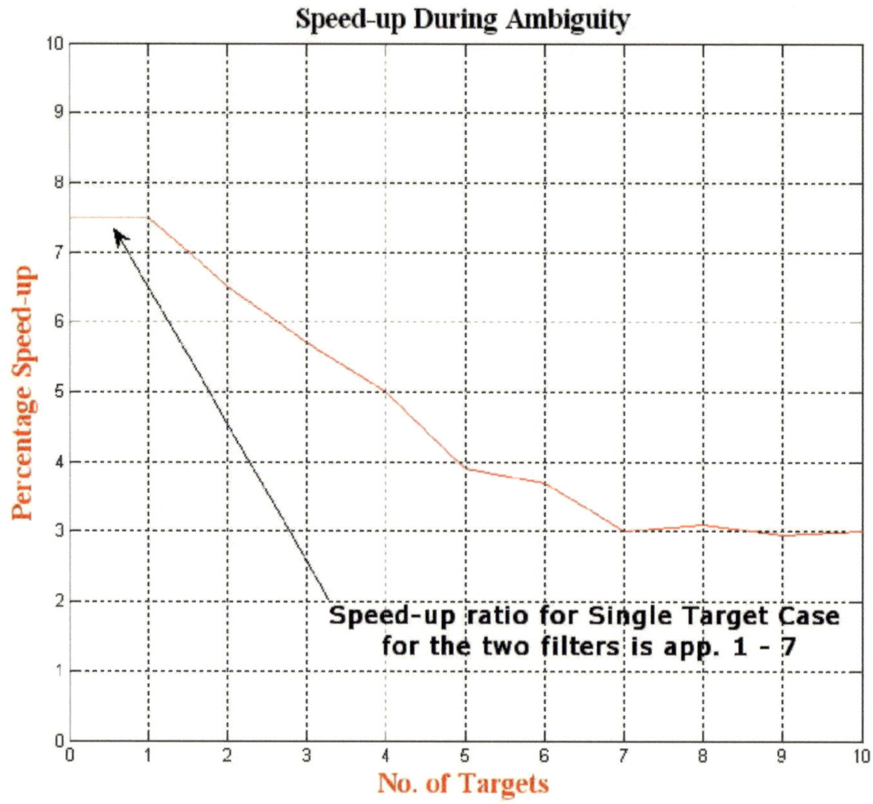

Fig. 3. Kalman & Alpha-Beta Filter Speed-Up Comparison

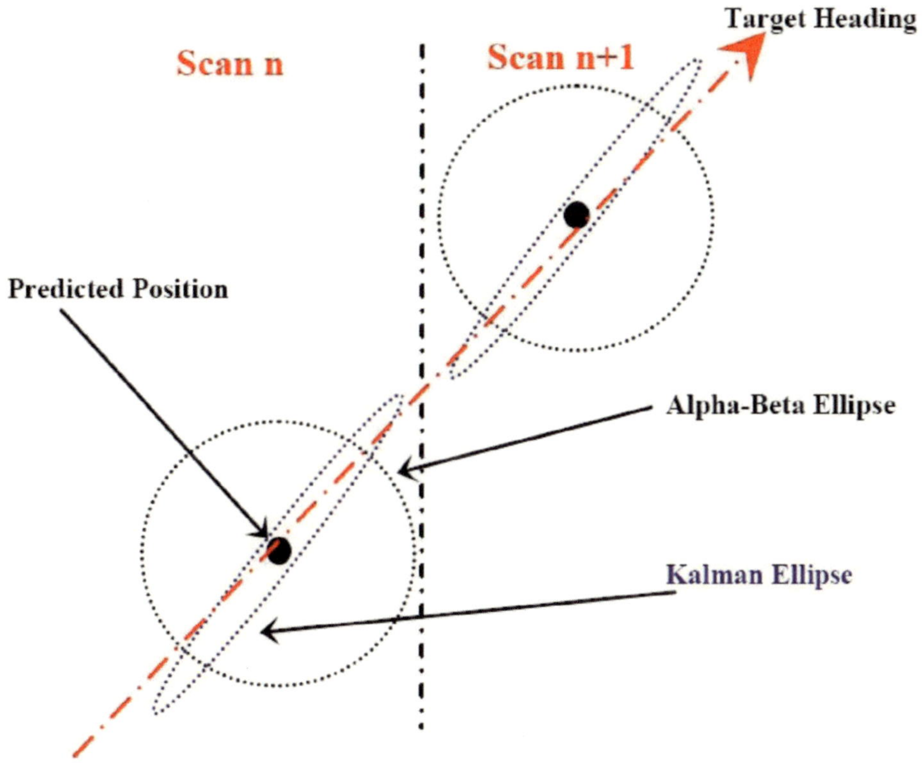

Fig. 4. Prediction Ellipse for Kalman & Alpha-Beta Filter

Figure 6 shows the value of these parameters with low correlation factors corresponding to table 2 and it can be seen that after initial track formation the target is following its path. This actually means that the measurement acceptance criterion remains less than a given probability threshold value, which in our case is 99 %. At the intersection point where a new target appears the track is lost, which should be the case by a tracking filter as the measurement from the second target will fall outside the prediction ellipse. However, in figure 7 where the correlation factor is high (table 3), the behavior of the two filters is totally different. Kalman filter is consistent by losing the track at the intersection point but $\alpha - \beta$ filter kept on tracking the target assuming it is the best supported track.

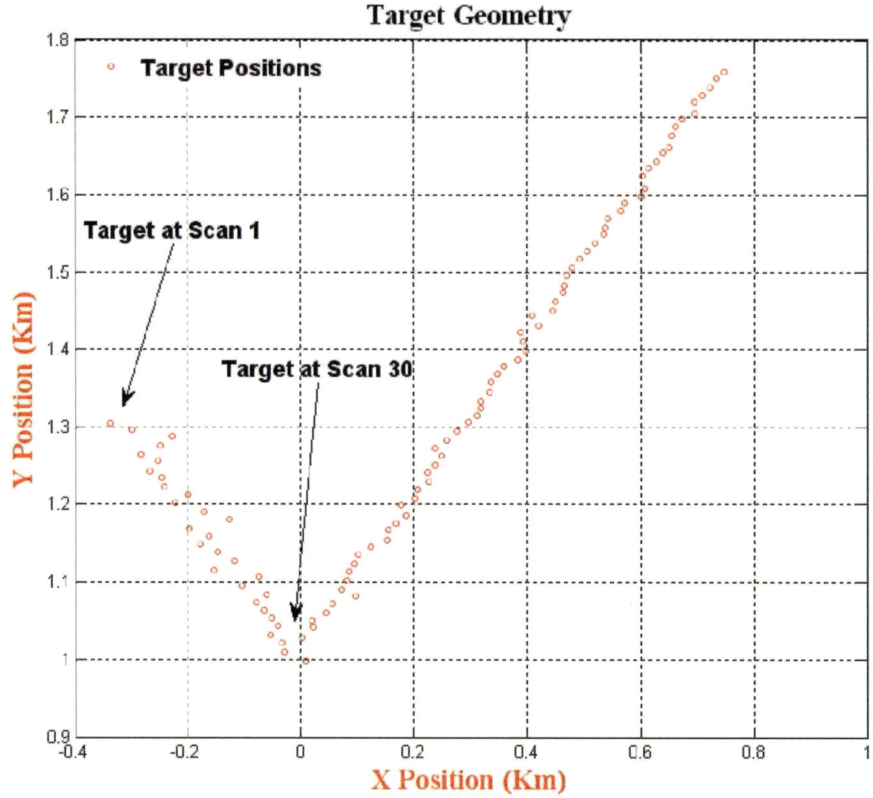

Fig. 5. Scenario Geometry

Scan No	Initial Angle	Intersection Angle	Correlation Range	Average Correlation
1	45°	90°	0.02 - 0.20	0.17
2	90°	135°	0.01 - 0.18	0.05
3	90°	180°	40.02 - 0.50	0.30
4	45°	135°	40.02 - 0.33	0.27

Table 2. Low Correlation

Scan No	Initial Angle	Intersection Angle	Correlation Range	Average Correlation
1	45°	90°	0.90 - 0.99	0.99
2	90°	135°	0.97 - 0.99	0.99
3	90°	180°	0.93 - 0.99	0.99
4	45°	135°	0.98 - 0.99	0.99

Table 3. High Correlation

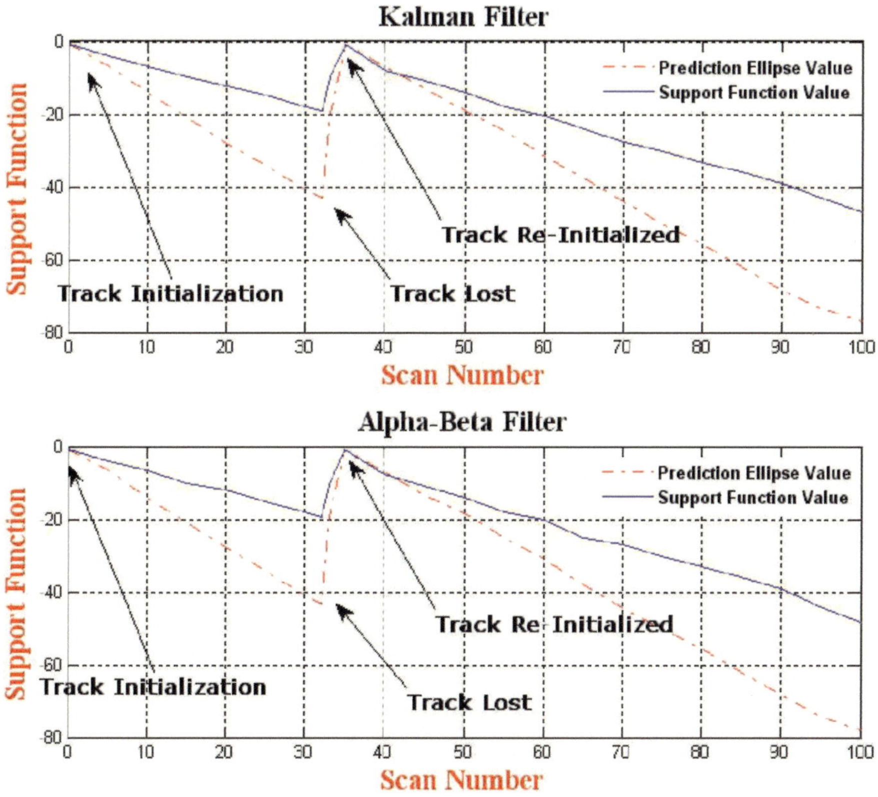

Fig. 6. Low Correlation Behaviour

5. Conclusion

In this paper we have compared the relative merits of the optimal Kalman filter with the sub-optimal $\alpha - \beta$ filter, we introduced tree clustering schemes for pruning the false target-measurement pairing to keep the excessive track explosion under control at the time of ambiguity. The interesting point for investigation is the amount of correlation during tracking period. Much investigation has been carried out in determining the position error accuracy of these two filters that reveals there is not much difference between the two estimates. However, one aspect which has not been given much attention in the past is the shape of the prediction ellipse under different correlation factors. It has been demonstrated by our investigation that in multi-target environments containing neighboring as well as crossing targets, more branching occur in the case of the $\alpha - \beta$ filter due to the shape of the prediction ellipse. It has been shown that in a high correlation scenario, the de-coupled $\alpha - \beta$ filter is more likely to accept unrealistic measurements compared with the Kalman filter. Therefore, the speed of computation when using an $\alpha - \beta$ filter in a multi-target scenario is not high as one would predict from single target considerations. In fact it was found to be only 3 to 4 times faster than a standard Kalman filter for crossing target scenarios containing up to 10 targets. The clustering techniques which are more structured and intelligent therefore, in the case of $\alpha - \beta$ filter less branching is observed, although numbers are not very significant however, the techniques have the premise to produce better results for such scenarios. Further, one important aspect must be kept in mind that number of branches depends on couple of factors, for example the time the target cross each other, their angle of intersection at the time of crossing and the order in which similarity criterion is executed. In future we would like to carry out our research work for more in-depth analyses of these two filters considering the results obtained in our investigation here plus with more realistic scenarios.

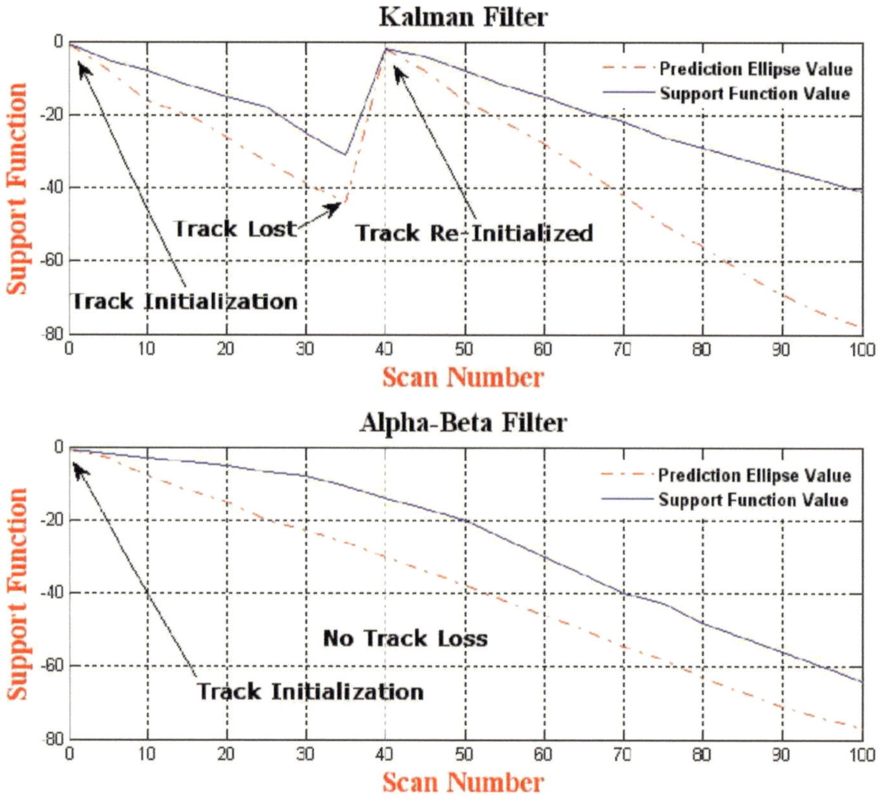

Fig. 7. High Correlation Behaviour

6. References

Glen W. Mabey and Jacob Gunther: A Robust Motion-Estimation Algorithm for Multiple-Target Tracking at Close Proximity Based on Hexagonal Partitioning, July 2003, Proceedings of the IEEE Conference on Advanced Video and Signal Based Surveillance AVSS '03, Publisher: IEEE Computer Society.

David Hall: Lectures in Multi-sensor Data Fusion and Target Tracking, March 2001, Book, Publisher: Artech House, Inc.

Lawrence D. Stone, Thomas L. Corwin, and Carl A. Barlow: Bayesian Multiple Target Tracking, August 1999 Book Publisher: Artech House, Inc.

Peter Nillius, Josephine Sullivan, and Stefan Carlsson: Multi-Target Tracking - Linking Identities using Bayesian Network Inference, June 2006, Proceedings of the 2006 IEEE Computer Society Conference on Computer Vision and Pattern Recognition - Volume 2 CVPR '06, Publisher: IEEE Computer Society.

Ahmet G. Pakfiliz and Murat Efe: Multi-Target Tracking in Clutter with Histogram Probabilistic Multi-Hypothesis Tracker, August 2005, Proceedings of the 18th International Conference on Systems Engineering ICSENG '05, Publisher: IEEE Computer Society.

Junji Satake and Takeshi Shakunaga: Multiple Target Tracking by Appearance-Based Condensation Tracker using Structure Information, August 2004, Proceedings of the Pattern Recognition, 17th International Conference on (ICPR'04) Volume 3 - Volume 03 ICPR '04 , Publisher: IEEE Computer Society.

Hyong-suk Kim, Hong-rak Son, Young-jae Lim and Jae-chul Chung: Target Tracking via Region-Based Confidence Computation with the CNN-UM, December 2002, Proceedings of the Third IEEE Pacific Rim Conference on Multimedia: Advances in Multimedia Information Processing PCM '02, Publisher: Springer-Verlag.

Duncan Smith and Sameer Singh: Approaches to Multi-sensor Data Fusion in Target Tracking, A Survey, December 2006, IEEE Transactions on Knowledge and Data Engineering, Volume 18 Issue 12, Publisher: IEEE Educational Activities Department.

Bum-Jik Lee, Jin-Bae Park and Young-Hoon Joo: IMM Algorithm Using Intelligent Input Estimation for Maneuvering Target Tracking, May 2005, IEICE Transactions on Fundamentals of Electronics, Communications and Computer Sciences, Volume E88-A Issue 5 Publisher: Oxford University Press.

QingE Wu, Tuo Wang, YongXuan Huang and JiSheng Li: Application of Fuzzy Automata on Target Tracking, Proceedings of the Fourth International Conference on Fuzzy Systems and Knowledge Discovery (FSKD 2007) Volume 02, Pages: 437441, 2007, ISBN:0-7695-2874-0.

David Choi and Benjamin Roy: A Generalized Kalman Filter for Fixed Point Approximation and Efficient Temporal-Difference Learning, April 2006 Discrete Event Dynamic Systems, Volume 16 Issue 2, Publisher: Kluwer Academic.

Jon Whittle and Johann Schumann: Automating the implementation of Kalman filter algorithms, December 2004, ACM Transactions on Mathematical Software (TOMS), Volume 30 Issue 4 Publisher: ACM Press.

R. Vasquez and J. Mayora: Estimation of motion and position of a rigid object using a sequence of images (tridimensional Kalman filter approach), April 1991, Proceedings of the 19th annual conference on Computer Science CSC '91 Publisher: ACM Press.

Jae-Chern Yoo and Young-Soo Kim: Alpha-beta-tracking index (?-?-?) tracking filter, January 2003, Signal Processing, Volume 83 Issue 1 Publisher: Elsevier North-Holland, Inc.

P. R. Kalata and K. M. Murphy: Alpha-Beta Target Tracking and Track Rate Variations, Proceedings of the 29th Southeastern Symposium on System Theory (SSST '97) SSST '97, Publisher: IEEE Computer Society.

P. L. Smith and G. Buechler: A branching algorithm for discriminating and tracking multiple objects, IEEE Transactions Automatic Control, Vol. AC-20, February 1975, pp 101-104.

Y. Bar-Shalom and T. E. Fortmann: Tracking and Data Association, Academic Press, Inc. 1988.

S. S. Blackman: Multiple Target Tracking with Radar Applications, Artech House, Inc. 1986.

A. Farina and F. A. Studer: Radar Data Processing Volume 1, Research Studies Press Ltd, 1986.

A. W. Bridgewater: Analysis of second and third order steady state tracking filters, AGARD conference proceedings No. 252, Moterey, CA, Oct. 1978, pp 9-1 to 9-11.

D. P. Atherton, E. Gul, A. Kountzeris and M. Kharbouch: Tracking Multiple Targets using parallel processing ", Proc. IEE, Part D, No. 4, July 1990, pp 225-234.

D. P. Atherton, D. M. Akbar Hussain and E. Gul: Target tracking using transputers as parallel processors, 9th IFAC symposium on identification and system parameter estimation, Budapest Hungary July 1991.

Abramowitz M and Stegun I. A. (Eds): A Handbook of Mathematical Functions, Dover N. Y. 1972.

D. M. Akbar Hussain, David Hicks, Daniel Ortiz-Arroyo, Shaiq A. Haq, Zaki Ahmed: A Case Study: Kalman and Alpha-Beta Computation under High Correlation, published in the proceedings of the IAENG International Conference on Software Engineering, Hong Kong 19 21 March, 2008.

D. M. Akbar Hussain, Zhenyu Yang, Shaiq A Haq, Zaki Ahmed, M. Zafar Ullah Khan: A Novel Technique to Avoid Similarity Criterion Calculations in a MultiProcessor Environment, Springer: Advances and Innovation in System, Computing Science and Software Engineering 2008.

Kharbouch M. M. and D. P. Atherton: A Transputer Implementation for Multiple Target Tracking, Microprocessors and Microsystems, April 1989, Pages: 188 - 194.

E. Gul: An Investigation of Target Tracking on Transputers, D. Phil thesis 1989, University of Sussex, Brighton U.K.

Reid, D. B.: An Algorithm for Tracking Multiple Targets, IEEE Transactions on Automatic Control, Vol. AC-24, pp 843 - 854, December 1979.

6

Numerical Simulation of Converter Fed Squirrel Cage Induction Motors

C. Grabner
Electric Drive Technologies, Austrian Institute of Technology
Giefinggasse 2, 1210 Vienna, Austria

1. Introduction

Electrical drive systems applied for very simple industrial pump, fan or compressor applications require different torque/speed profiles in different operational states (Heintze et al., 1971). This is often realized by robust and reliable converter-fed squirrel cage induction motors as exemplarity depicted in Fig.1.

Fig. 1. Family of variable speed drive systems consisting of induction motors with according power converters

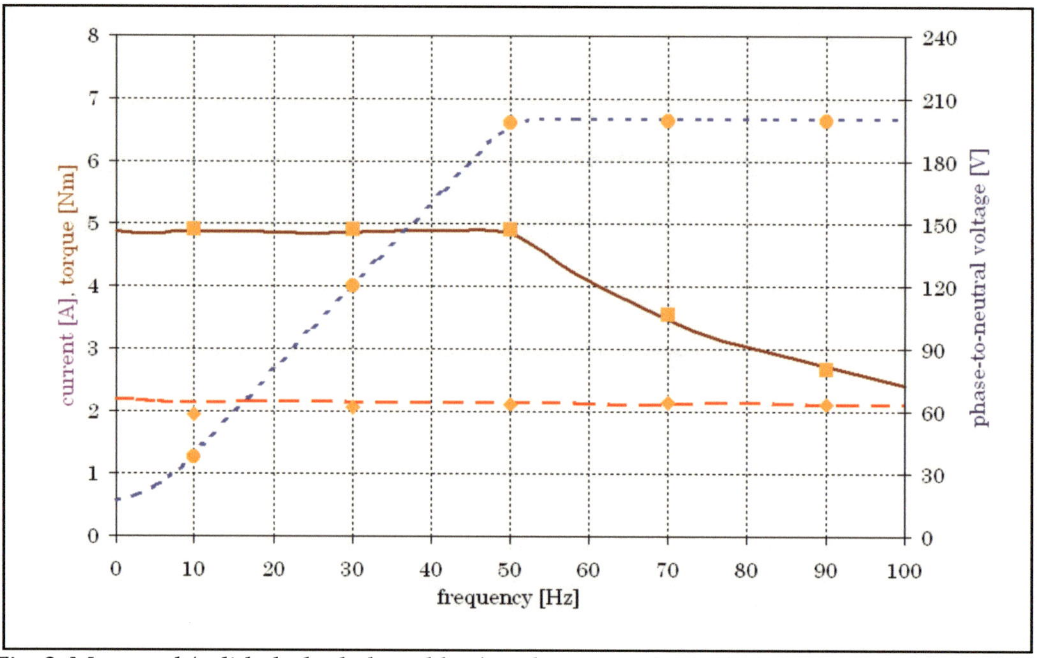

Fig. 2. Measured (solid, dashed, dotted line) and numerical calculated (quadrates, circles) effective voltage (blue), effective current (magenta) and mechanical torque (brown) versus the supply frequency for the steady-state S1-duty

The used V/f control technology needs thereby a voltage magnitude variation in dependency on the drive frequency as it is exemplarily shown in Fig.2. The section with continuously rising effective voltage up to the maximum level of 200 V at 50 Hz permits in the quasi-steady operational state almost a constant mechanical torque of 4.9 Nm, whereas the interval with constant maximal effective voltage magnitude is denoted as field weakening range, characterized with a constant mechanical power output of 770 W.

The desired high quality of the drive system is very sensitive to appearing higher harmonics in the electrical stator current or in the mechanical torque, even from unsuitable machine designs or inappropriate power converter strategies (Lipo et al., 1969; Stuart & Hebbar, 1971).

Such undesired current harmonics in converter driven motors can cause unforeseen losses and lead directly to additional heating effects inside the semiconductors and the winding system (Heimbrock & Seinsch, 2005). Mechanical problems regarding the rotating shaft can in particularly arise whenever frequencies in the generated mechanical torque spectrum coincide with natural resonance frequencies of the rotating shaft (Szabo, 1972).

The application of different commercial calculation tools within the design process of electrical drive systems gains crucial interest in order to overcome such problems. An extended finite element method with directly coupled electrical circuits for instance allows the treatment of the complete drive system in the time-domain. Thereby, the converter topology is included by discrete electronic devices, whereas the induction motor is basically represented by iron laminations, insulation, stator winding and squirrel cage. The procedure overcomes previous insufficiencies and delivers results in dependency on well known control strategies with good accuracy.

2. Converter Topology and Control Unit

The power conversion from the public three-phase ac grid of constant frequency and voltage amplitude into an arbitrary three-phase ac system with variable settings is performed by means of the power converter topology in Fig.3.

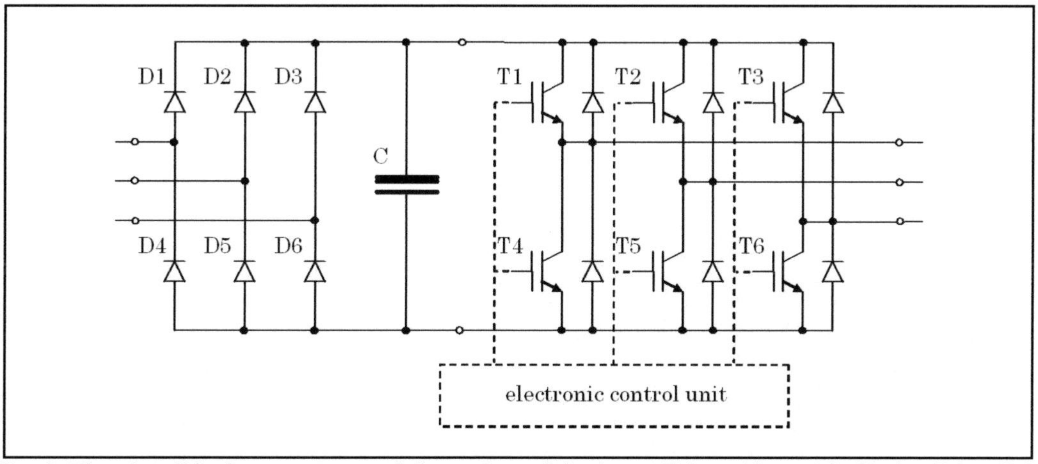

Fig. 3. The simplified converter model consists of the input B6 rectifier with diodes D1 to D6, the dc voltage link, three half-bridges formed by semiconductors T1-T4, T2-T5 and T3-T6 and an electronic control unit

The input ac to dc rectification is done by the diodes D1 to D6. The classical B6-bridge causes thereby an unavoidable voltage ripple. The capacitor smoothes these distinct fluctuations within the dc link level of 565 V, whereas the inductance restricts undesired current peaks during unexpected operational states (Kleinrath, 1980). The conversion of the dc link to three phase output ac power is exclusively performed in the switched mode.

The control unit in Fig.3 has the task to generate different duty cycles for the semiconductor devices T1 to T6. The most widely used method of pulse-width modulation employs carrier modulators in each of the three phases (Buja & Indri, 1977; Kliman & Plunkett, 1979; Murphy & Egan, 1983). A simple realization of the main control part is shown in Fig.4. The according time-dependent signal courses in the control unit are exemplarity depicted in Fig.5 for the maximum output voltage at the frequency of 50 Hz. The phase reference signal with the desired drive frequency 50 Hz is thereby sampled by a single saw-tooth carrier signals with a rate of 2 kHz. The electronic control unit generates signals for the semiconductors whenever the sine-wave and saw-tooth signal have the same value.

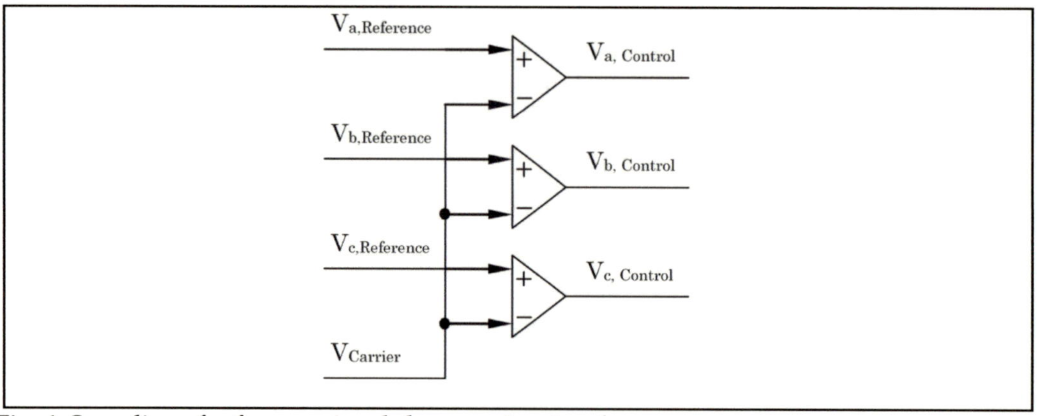

Fig. 4. Sampling of reference signals by a carrier signal

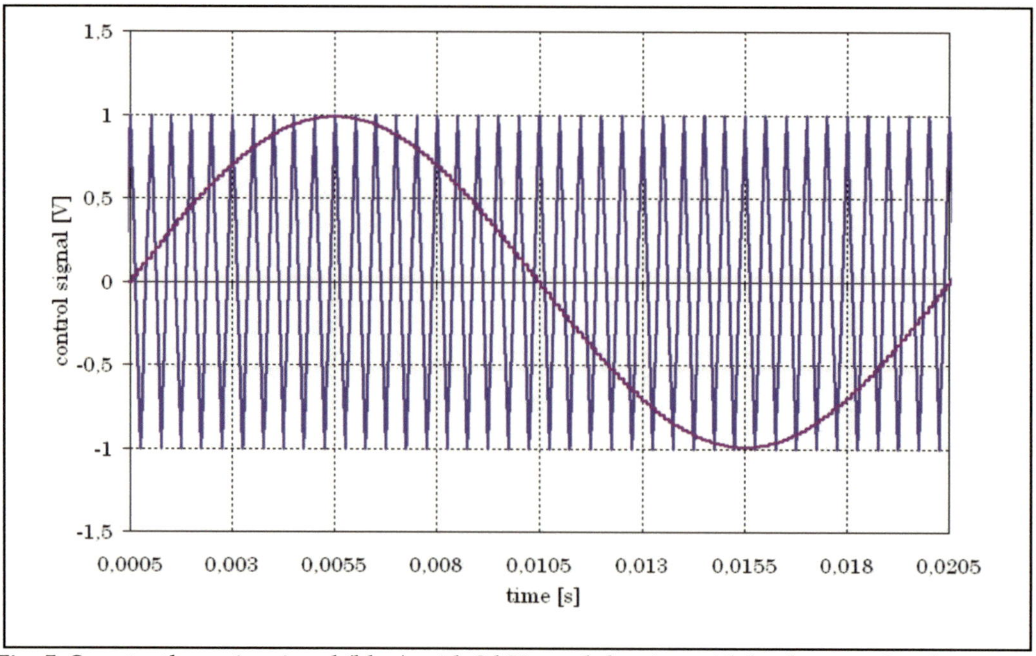

Fig. 5. Saw-tooth carrier signal (blue) with 2 kHz and the sinusoidal reference signal (magenta) with 50 Hz

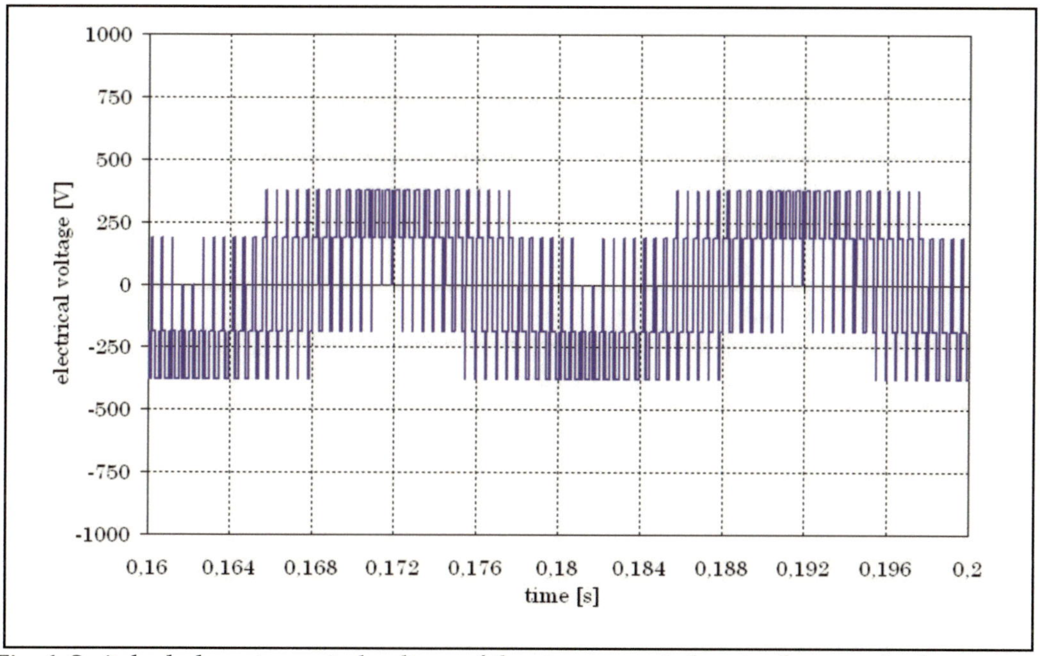

Fig. 6. Switched phase-to-neutral voltage of the star-connected motor for a carrier frequency of 2 kHz

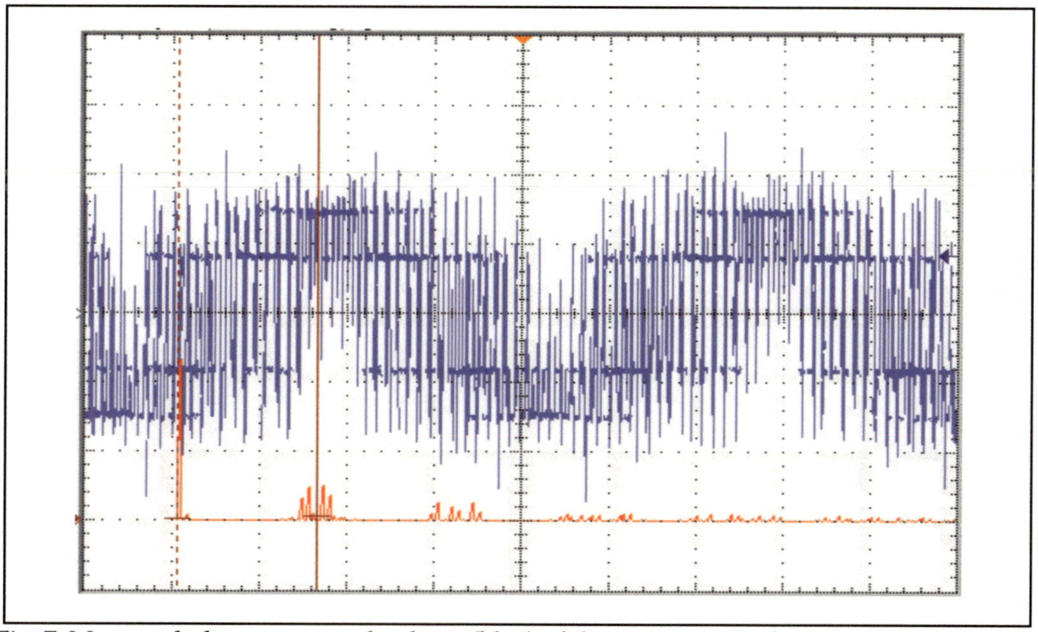

Fig. 7. Measured phase-to-neutral voltage (blue) of the star-connected motor for a carrier frequency of 2 kHz, whereby one division corresponds to 4 ms in the abscissa and 250 V in the ordinate. The Fourier spectrum (red) is based on 140 V per ordinate division

The utilized semiconductors effectuate temporary connections at high repetition rates with short rising times. The generated time-dependent phase-to-neutral output voltage in case of the used control method from Fig.4 shows within the numerical processed course in Fig.6 five distinct voltage levels. The fundamental content of the effective motor voltage is thereby 200 V at 50 Hz, as it was required for that specific steady operational state in Fig.2. The numerical calculation uses idealized switches within the power converter and neglects the motor feed cable in Fig.3.

The measured courses in Fig.7 look slightly different to that in Fig.6 because of the non-ideal effects of the motor feed cable and additionally appearing capacitive influences of the complete stator winding system. Some distinct voltage peaks are obvious in Fig.7 due to voltage reflection at the motor terminals without using additional filters.

3. Field-Circuit Coupling Technique

The local field quantities of the applied 2D finite element algorithm must be coupled to external circuits in order to include the source voltage waveforms of the converter (Silvester, 1995).

The finite element representation of the axially un-skewed stator lamination is exemplarily given in Fig.8. The modelling of the voltage-fed stator winding system in Fig.9 generally demands a distinct number of series connected bars in order to form one single coil. The stator phase resistor and the stator phase inductance in Fig.9 represent the not modelled 3D end-winding effects within the 2D finite element calculation (Salon, 1996). All three stator phases are further star-connected. The supplied voltage at the external terminals in Fig.9 can thereby be arbitrarily varying by time.

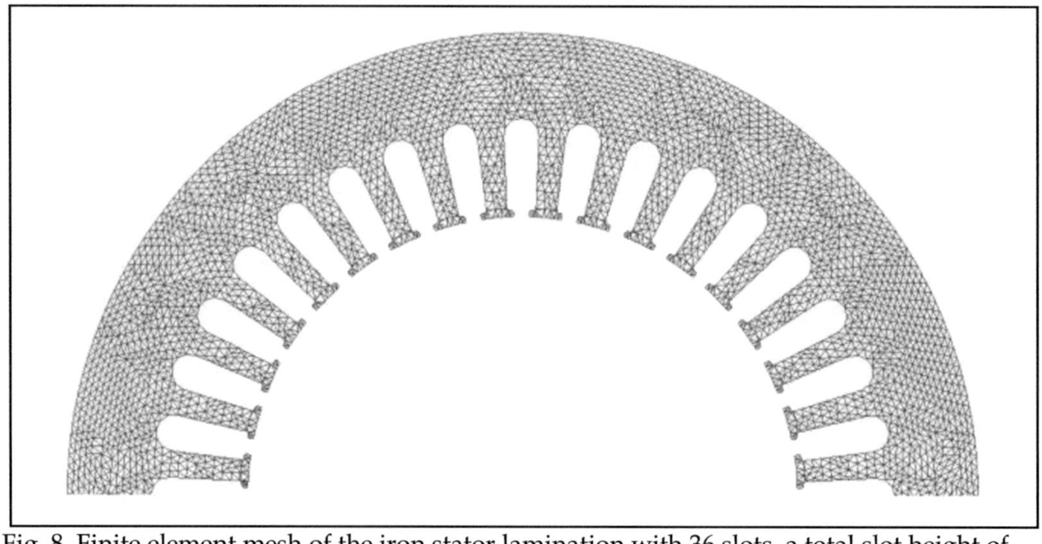

Fig. 8. Finite element mesh of the iron stator lamination with 36 slots, a total slot height of 13mm, an average slot width of 4mm, a stator yoke thickness of 11mm and a bore diameter of 75.5mm

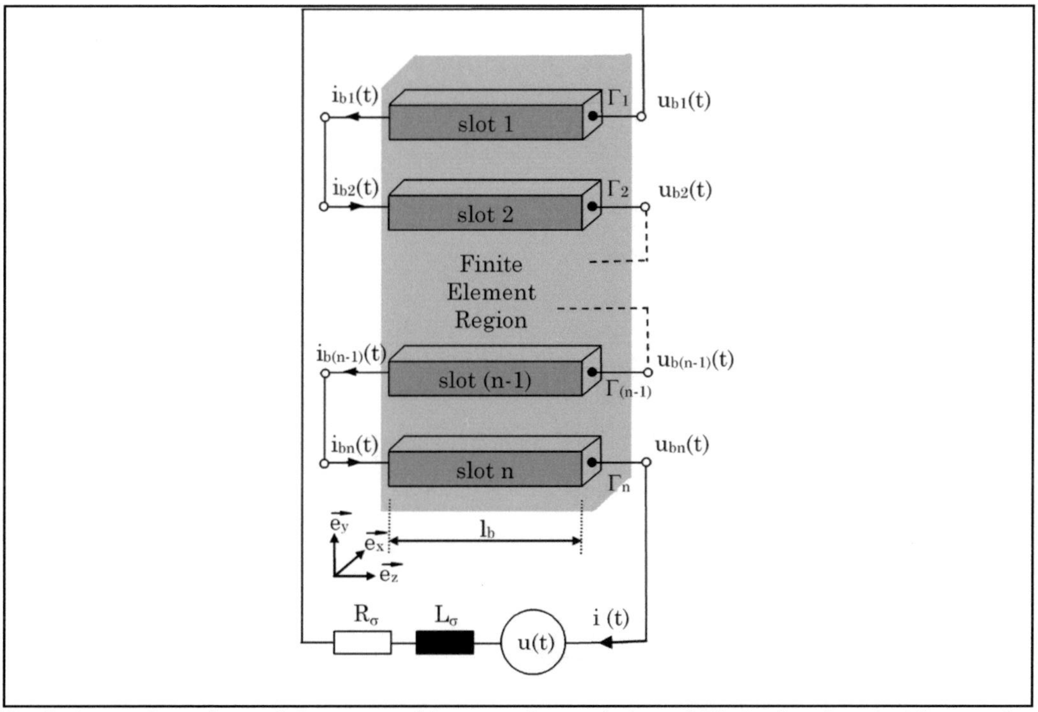

Fig. 9. A number of n-serial connected bars, each consisting of 90 single wires inside one slot, are forming one stator coil with 540 windings inside the plane finite element domain, whereas both external resistive and inductive parameters are representing 3D stator effects

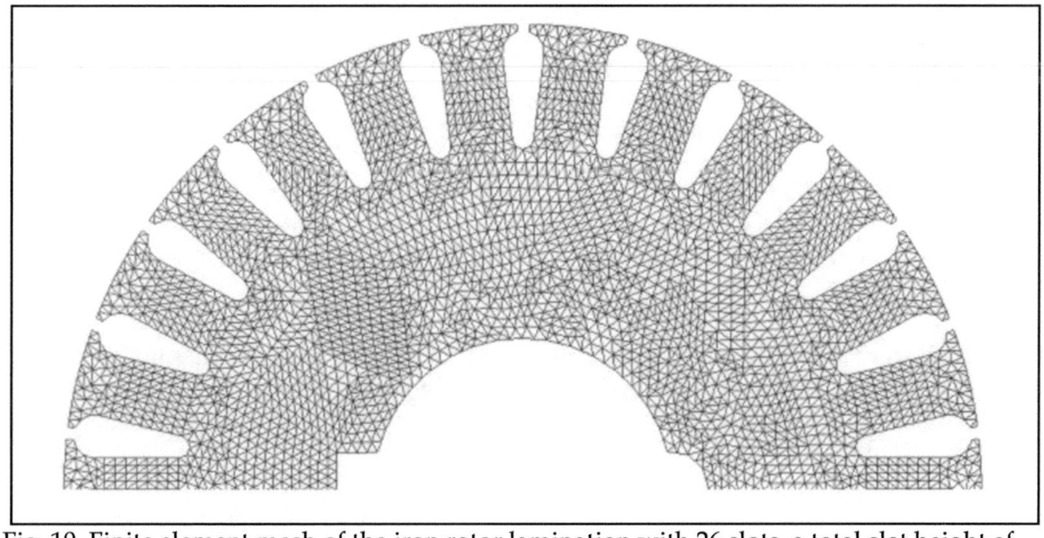

Fig. 10. Finite element mesh of the iron rotor lamination with 26 slots, a total slot height of 9.2mm, an average slot width of 2.6mm, a bore diameter of about 75mm, a rotor yoke thickness of 16mm and a shaft diameter of about 25mm

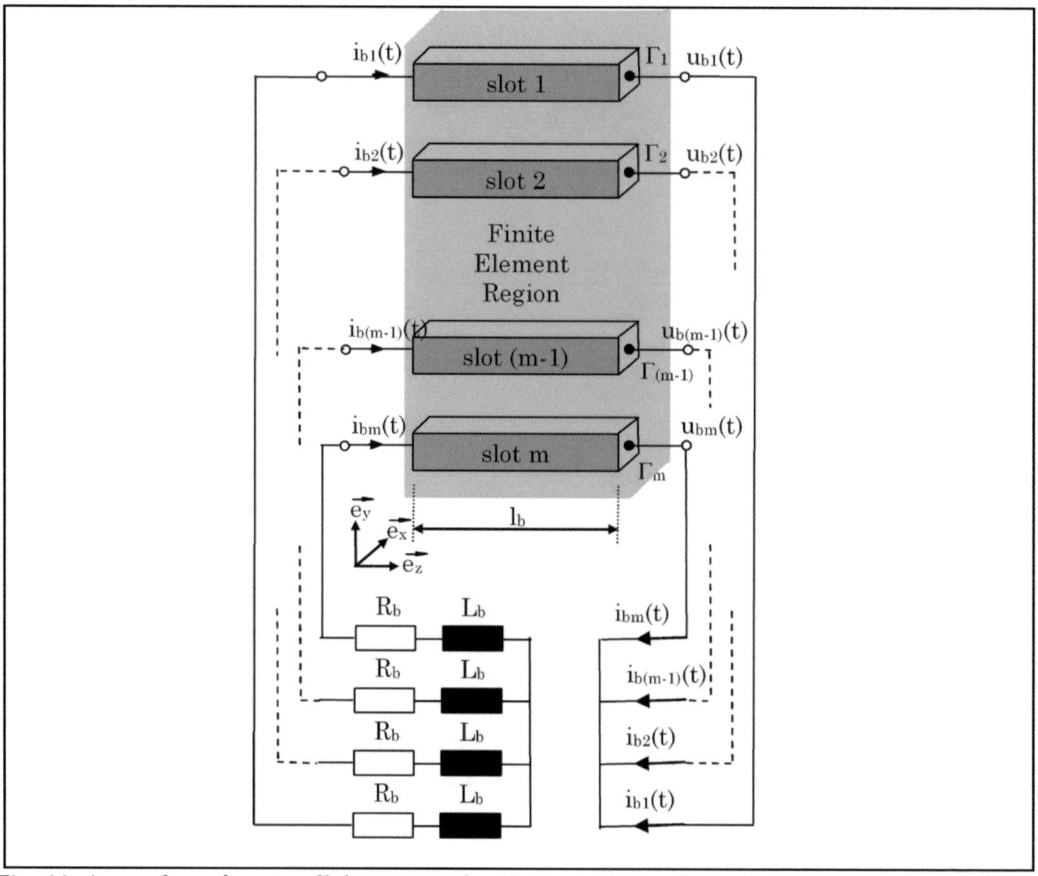

Fig. 11. A number of m-parallel connected coils, consisting of aluminum die casting, built up the squirrel cage rotor inside the plane finite element domain, whereas the external resistive and inductive parameters are implicit representing 3D end-ring effects

The exemplarity depicted time-dependent voltage waveform in Fig.6 is governed by very fast rising/falling voltage flanks, which have to be processed within the coupled numerical finite element analysis. Unfortunately, the chosen time-step for solving such problems is often smaller than 10 ns (Istfan, 1987; Biro et al., 1996).

The used 2D finite element model of the un-skewed rotor depicted in Fig.10 is not suitable to account for 3D end-ring effects. The complete winding schema for the not skewed squirrel cage rotor is shown in Fig.11, whereby the combined parameters approximately take account of 3D influences.

The finite element approach allows the computation of the acting magnetic force on the solid rotor by *virtual motion* as sum over local contributions (DeBortoli, 1992). The rotor moves on stepwise with the aid of the applied *band technique* (Davat et al., 1985). Thus, elements which are situated at these band domain may be deformed during motion since some of their nodes may follow the moving rotor reference frame and some the stationary stator one (Palma, 1989). These element distortions are occurring in dependency on the movement. So, the continuous element distortion enforces a re-meshing of air-gap elements lying on the band.

Due to the non-linear iron material properties, as listed in Table 1, linearization and time-discretization methods are necessary to solve such coupled electromechanical problems in the time domain (Bins et al., 1992; Bathe, 1996; Schwarz, 1984).

B [T]	0	0.4	0.8	1.2	1.6	2.0
H [A/m]	0	140	190	260	1370	20500

Table 1. Non–linear iron magnetization characteristic

4. Electric Input Current and the Mechanical Output Torque

The analysis of the time-dependent courses of the electrical current and the mechanical torque within inverter driven motors in the time-domain is of main importance, because it allows further estimations about additionally heating effects as well as critically resonance frequencies of the rotating shaft.

4.1 Time dependent electrical current courses and their harmonic spectrum

The numerical analysis of the complete voltage-fed drive system with respect to the course depicted in Fig.6 for a carrier frequency of 2 kHz delivers the time-dependent electrical stator current as depicted in Fig.12. The application of the series-expansion

$$i(t) = \sum_{k=1}^{\infty} \hat{I}_k \sin\left(2\pi k f \cdot t + \alpha_k\right) \tag{1}$$

delivers several harmonic components. Thereby, the distinct fundamental component at the frequency of 50 Hz, and additionally the undesired first side pair harmonics at 1950 Hz and 2050 Hz as well as the second side pair harmonics at 3950 Hz and 4050 Hz can be found in the complete spectrum of Fig.13. Higher harmonic contributions show relatively small magnitudes and are therefore only of secondary interest.

The measured electrical current course and the according harmonic analysis are depicted in Fig.14. Not only the comparison of the time-courses with those in Fig.12, even though the harmonic magnitudes received from (1) show a good conformity.

In spite of some differences between the numerical processed voltage shape in Fig.6 and the measured voltage in Fig.7, in particular during the switching on/off state, no significant discrepancy between the numerical calculated and the measured time-dependent current distribution in Fig.12 and Fig.14, respectively, can be found due to the distinct inductive behaviour of the squirrel cage induction motor.

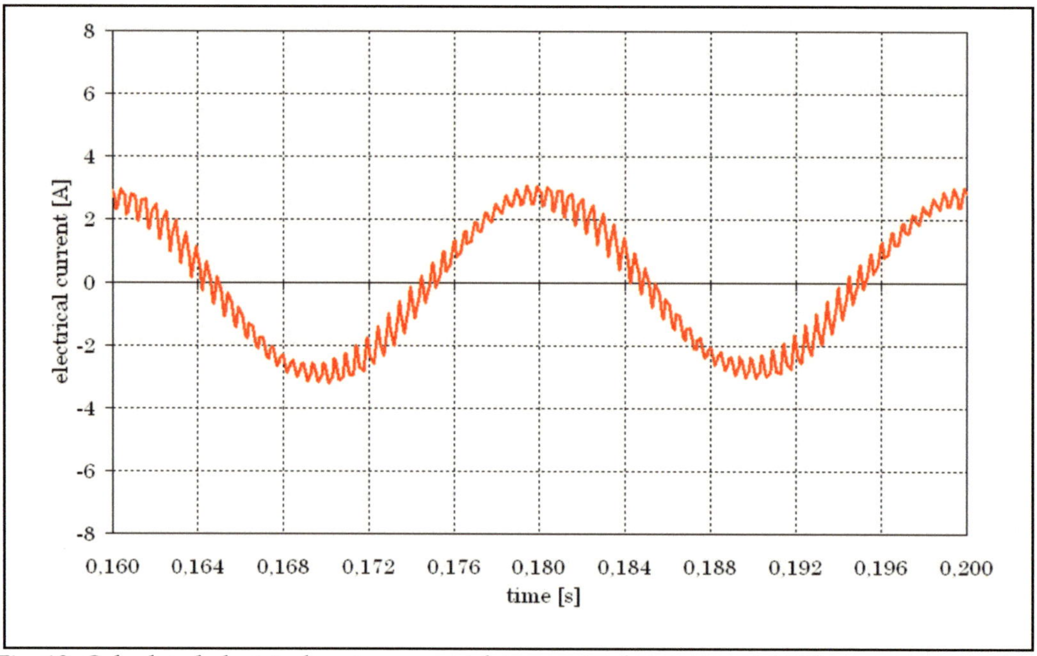

Fig. 12. Calculated electrical motor current for a carrier frequency of 2 kHz

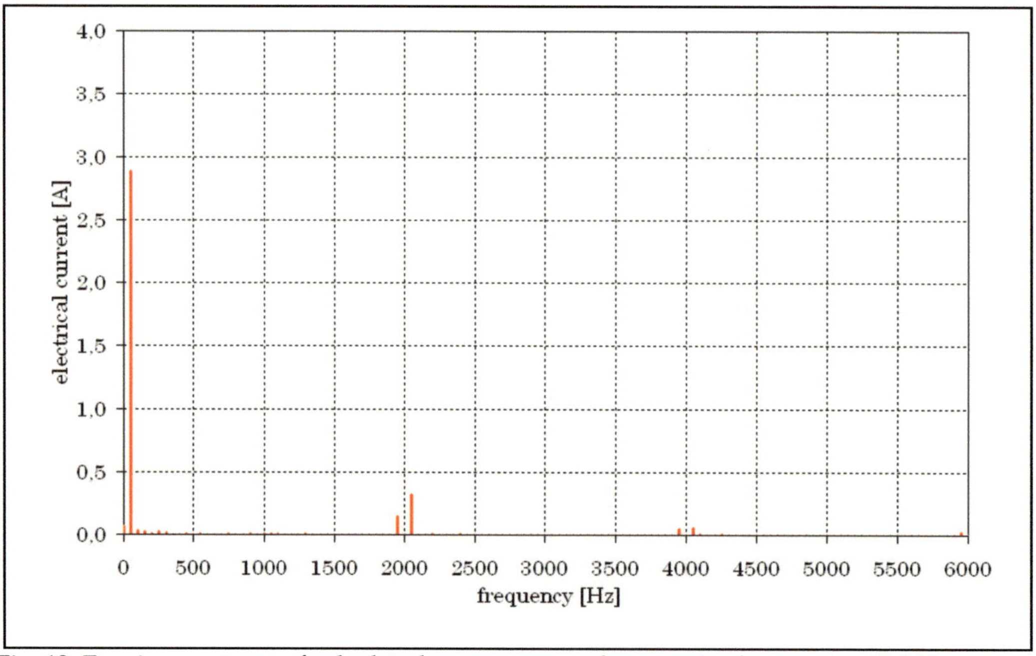

Fig. 13. Fourier spectrum of calculated motor current for a carrier frequency of 2 kHz

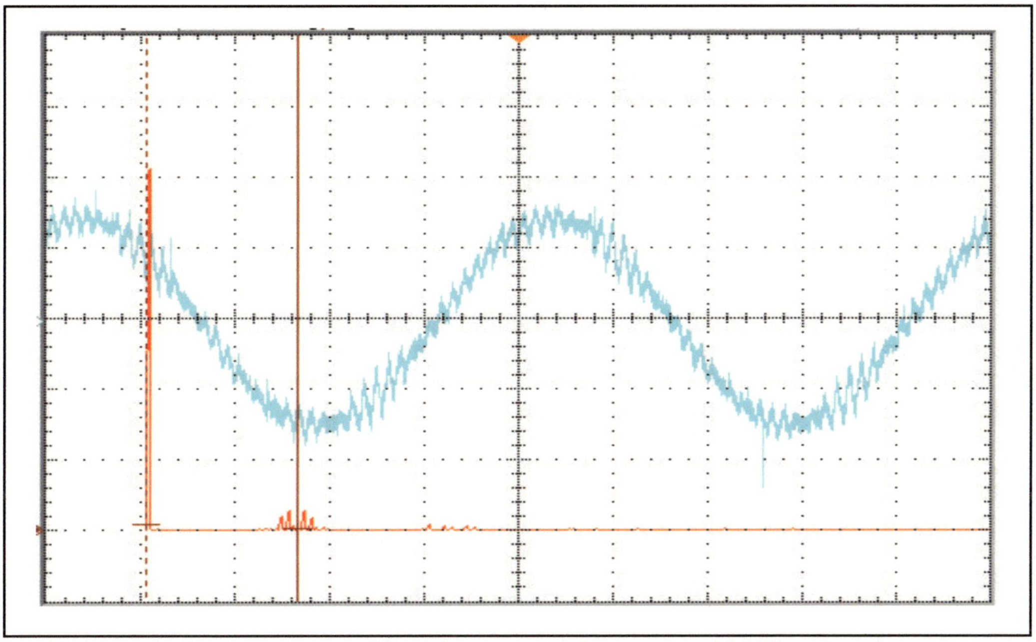

Fig. 14. Measured motor current (blue) for a carrier frequency of 2 kHz, whereby one division corresponds to 4 ms in the abscissa and 2 A in the ordinate. The Fourier spectrum (red) is based on 0.6 A per ordinate division

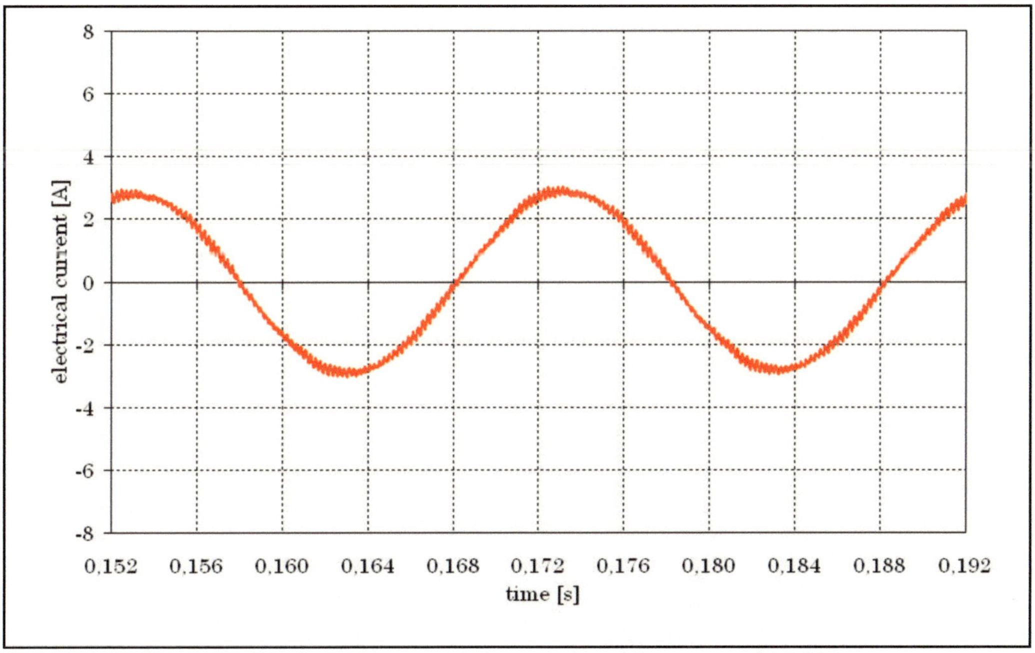

Fig. 15. Calculated electrical motor current for a carrier frequency of 4.5 kHz

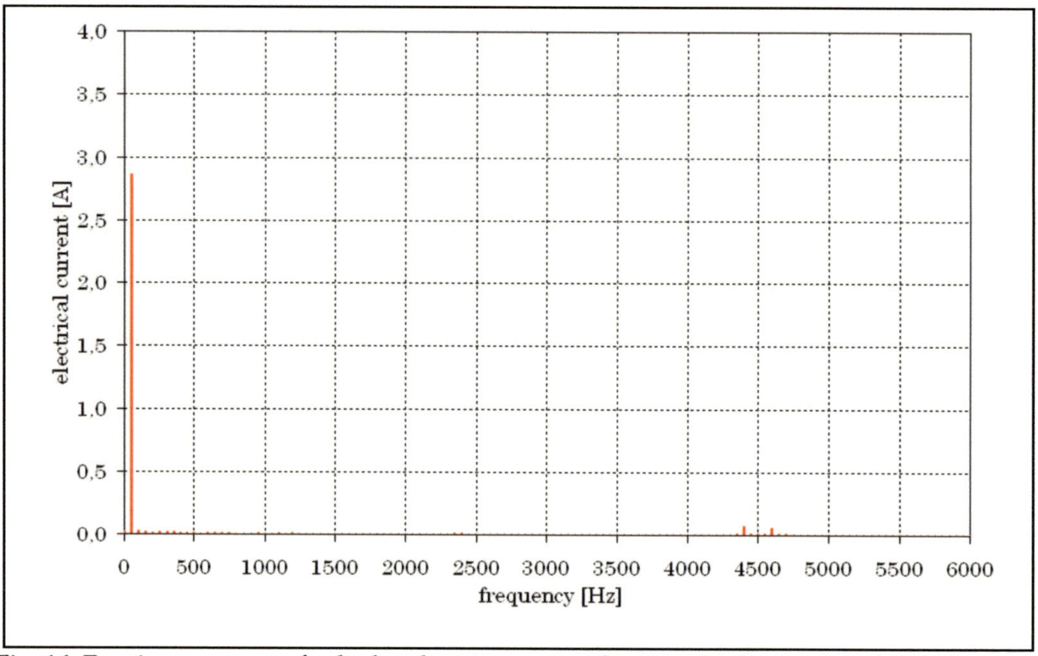

Fig. 16. Fourier spectrum of calculated motor current for a carrier frequency of 4.5 kHz

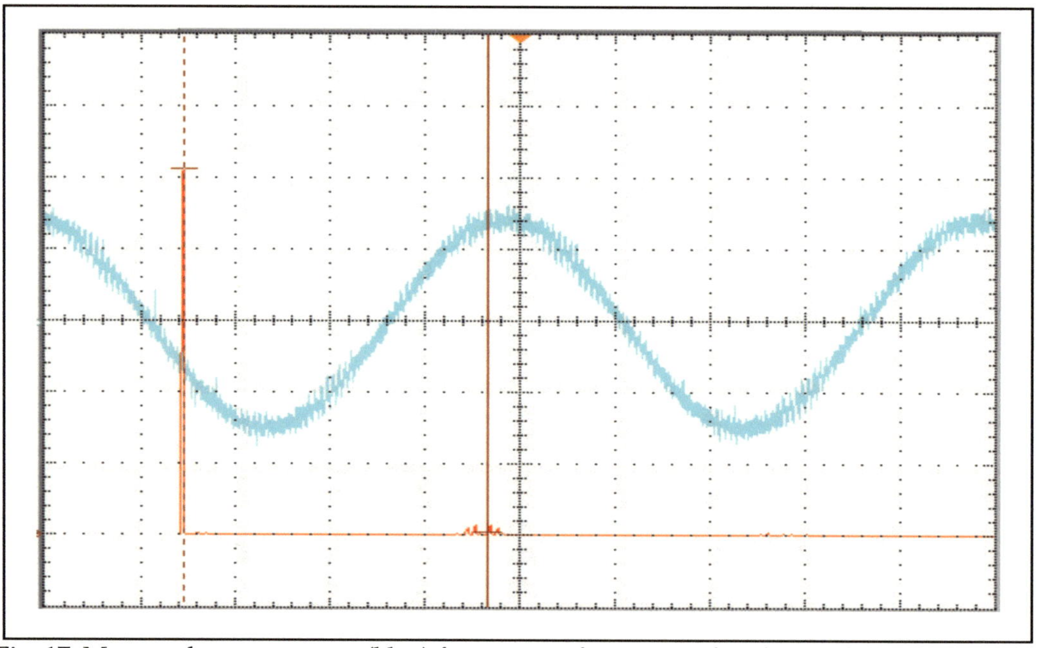

Fig. 17. Measured motor current (blue) for a carrier frequency of 4.5 kHz, whereby one division corresponds to 4 ms in the abscissa and 2 A in the ordinate. The Fourier spectrum (red) is based on 0.6 A per ordinate division

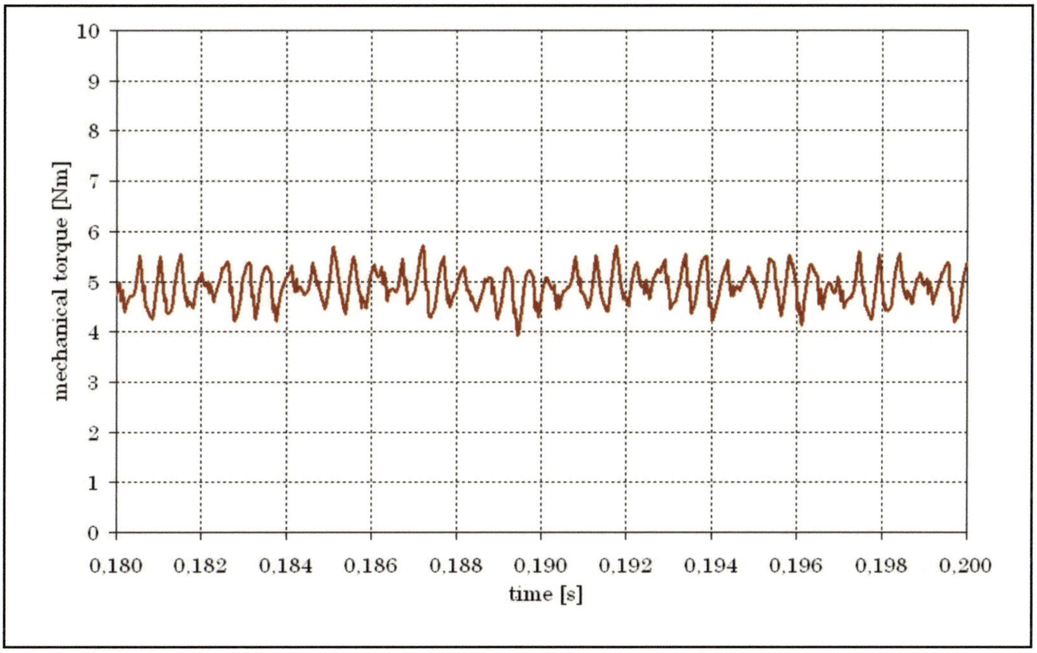

Fig. 18. Calculated mechanical torque for a carrier frequency of 2 kHz

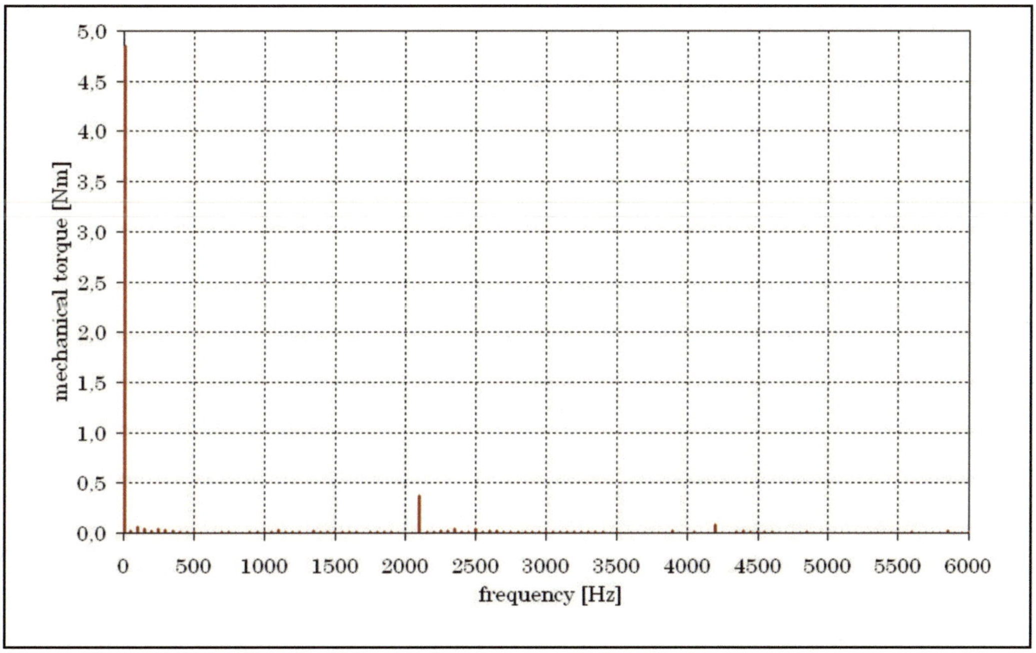

Fig. 19. Fourier spectrum of calculated mechanical torque for a carrier frequency of 2 kHz

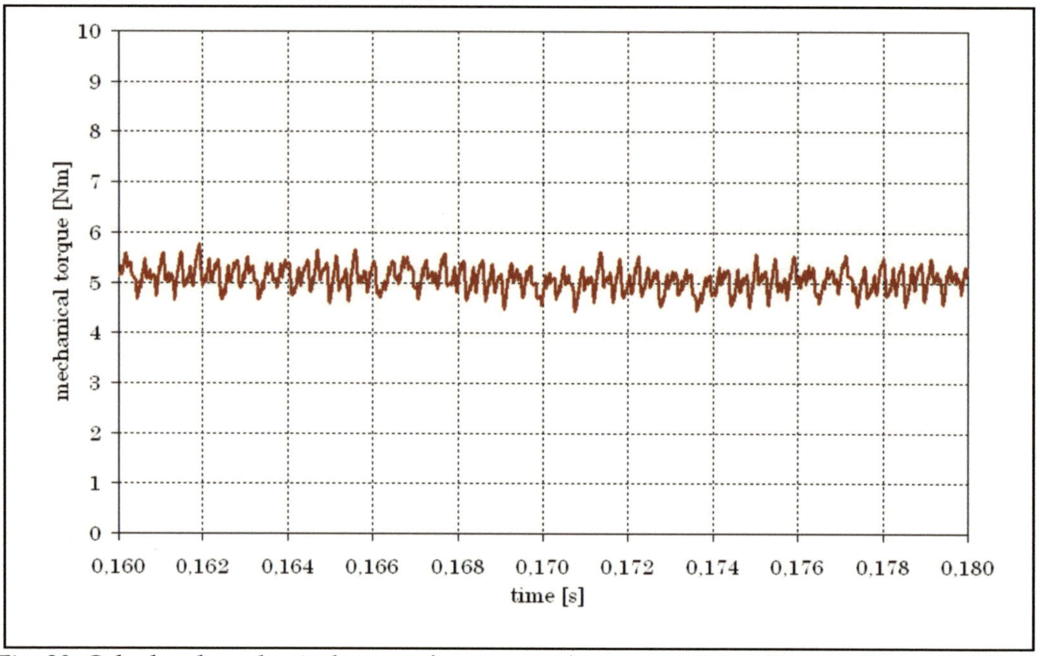

Fig. 20. Calculated mechanical torque for a carrier frequency of 4.5 kHz

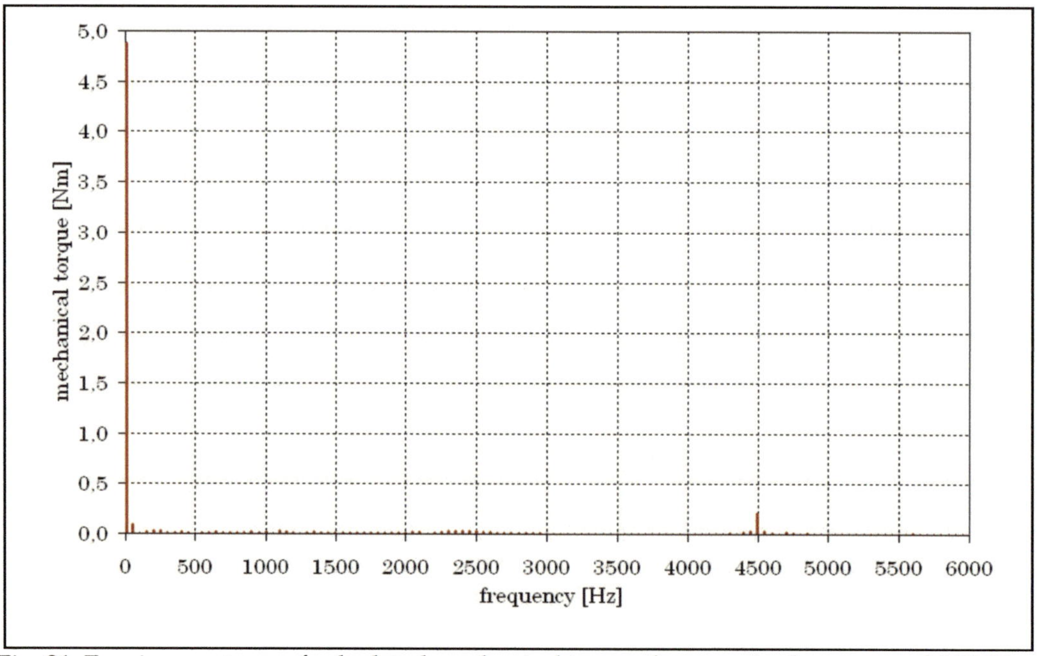

Fig. 21. Fourier spectrum of calculated mechanical torque for a carrier frequency of 4.5 kHz

In order to smooth the overlaid current ripple within the distribution in Fig.12, the first harmonic pair in Fig.13 caused by the carrier frequency of 2 kHz has to be eliminated by increasing the frequency to 4.5 kHz.

The improvement within the electrical current quality is shown in Fig.15. The course is very similar to the desired sinusoidal one. That circumstances are also obvious from the associated spectrum (1) depicted in Fig.16. Beside the desired fundamental component, only a first sideband frequency at 4400 Hz and 4600 Hz exists. From a comparison of the numerical calculated results from Fig.15 and Fig.16 with the measured quantities in Fig.17 it is obvious, that a good agreement could be achieved by the proposed numerical modelling and calculation method.

4.2 Time dependent mechanical torque courses and their harmonic spectrum

The numerical calculated time-dependent mechanical torque is depicted in Fig.18 for a control strategy based on the carrier frequency of 2 kHz. The series-expansion

$$m(t) = \sum_{k=0}^{\infty} \hat{M}_k \sin\left(2\pi k f \cdot t + \beta_k\right) \tag{2}$$

leads to the harmonic torque magnitudes, which are further shown in Fig.19. Beside the desired constant contribution, a very distinct undesired torque fluctuation due to the converter topology of Fig.3 is caused at the frequency of 2100 Hz. Other contributions to the torque ripple are obviously suppressed.

A significant improved spectrum could be achieved by increasing the carrier frequency up to 4.5 kHz. The analysis of the numerical results from Fig.20 in the frequency domain delivers the torque spectrum shown in Fig.21. The previously torque components are shifted to the higher ordinal frequency of 4500 Hz, but the relevant magnitudes are significantly reduced. A comparison of Fig.18 with Fig.20 shows that effect imposingly.

Thus, undesired effects concerning the quality of the true shaft motion of the drive system could be avoided by using higher carrier frequencies within the used power converter.

5. Conclusion

The prediction of undesired current and torque harmonics inside converter-fed induction motors is of crucial interest in order to guarantee a high quality level of the drive system. Thereby, the complex interaction of the converter and the squirrel cage induction motor has to be considered. This is done by using the 2D transient electromagnetic-mechanical finite element method with additionally coupled external circuits. Fortunately, the generated arbitrary time-dependent output voltage waveforms of the converter are directly processed within the non-linear finite element analysis in the time-domain. Effects of minor changes in the mechanical rotor true running due to the torque ripple as well as fluctuations in the electrical current consumption are considered. This kind of *virtual design* delivers a very systematically and deep insight into the interaction of several involved drive components, such as e.g. power converter topology, squirrel cage induction machine and control strategy, within the overall design. Consequently, the method encourages a straightforward and reliable industrial development process of complex electrical drive systems.

6. References

Bathe K.J. (1996). *Finite Element Procedures,* Prentice Hall, New Jersey

Bins K.J., Lawrenson P.J. & Trowbridge C.W. (1992). *The Analytical and Numerical Solution of Electric and Magnetic Fields,* John Wiley & Sons, Chichester

Biro O., Preis K. & Richter K.R. (1996). On the Use of the Magnetic Vector Potential in the Nodal and Edge Finite Element Analysis of 3D Magnetostatic Problems. *IEEE Transactions on Magnetics,* Vol. 32, No. 5.

Buja G.S. & Indri G.B. (1977). Optimal Pulse Width Modulation for Feeding AC Motors. *IEEE Transactions on Industry Applications,* Vol. IA-13, No. 1.

Davat B., Ren Z. & Lajoic-Mazenc M. (1985). The movement in field modeling. *IEEE Transactions on Magnetics,* Vol. 21, No. 6.

DeBortoli M.J. (1992). Extensions to the Finite Element Method for the Electromechanical Analysis of Electrical Machines, *Rensselaer Polytechnic Institute New York,* PhD Thesis.

Heimbrock A. & Seinsch H.O. (2005). Neue Erkenntnisse über Oberschwingungsverluste in Umrichtergespeisten Käfigläufern. *Elektrotechnik und Informationstechnik,* Vol. 122, No. 7.

Heintze K., Tappeiner H. & Weibelzahl M. (1971). Pulswechselrichter zur Drehzahlsteuerung von Asynchronmaschinen. *Siemens Zeitschrift,* Vol.3, No.45.

Istfan B. (1987). Extensions to the Finite Element Method for Nonlinear Magnetic Field Problems, *Rensselaer Polytechnic Institute New York,* PhD Thesis.

Kleinrath H. (1980). *Stromrichtergespeiste Drehfeldmaschinen,* Springer Verlag, Wien

Kliman G.B. & Plunkett A.B. (1979). Development of a Modulation Strategy for a PWM Inverter Drive. *IEEE Transactions on Industry Applications,* Vol. IA-15, No. 1.

Lipo T.A., Krause P.C. & Jordan H.E. (1969). Harmonic Torque and Speed Pulsation in a Rectifier-Inverter Induction Motor Drive. *IEEE Transactions on Power Apparatus and Systems,* Vol. PAS-88, No. 5.

Murphy J.M.D. & Egan M.G. (1983). A Comparison of PWM Strategies for Inverter-Fed Induction Motors. *IEEE Transactions on Industry Applications,* Vol. IA-19, No. 3.

Palma R. (1989). Transient Analysis of Induction Machines using Finite Elements, *Rensselaer Polytechnic Institute New York,* PhD Thesis.

Salon J.S. (1996). *Finite Element Analysis of Electrical Machines,* Cambridge University Press, Cambridge

Schwarz R. (1984). *Methode der Finiten Elemente,* Teubner, Stuttgart

Silvester P.P. (1995). *Finite Elements for Electrical Engineers,* Kluwer Academic Publisher, Boston/London

Stuart D.T. & Hebbar K.M. (1971). Torque Pulsation in Induction Motors with Inverter Drives. *IEEE Transactions on Industry and General Applications,* Vol. GA-7, No. 2.

Szabo I. (1972). *Technische Mechanik,* Springer Verlag, Berlin

RGB Color Analysis for Face Detection

Qieshi Zhang and Jun Zhang
Graduate School of Information, Production and Systems
Waseda University
Kitakyushu, Japan
Q.Zhang@Akane.Waseda.jp
J.Zhang@Akane.Waseda.jp

1. Introduction

1.1 Background

In our daily life, more and more application techniques based on biometrics recognition such as fingerprints, iris pattern and face recognition are developed to secure access control. Along with the development of those techniques, computer control plays an important role in making the biometrics recognition more economically feasible in such developments. Face recognition has gained an immense interest during the last decades with application taken place in many fields such as financial transactions, monitoring system, credit card verification, ATM access, personal PC access, video surveillance, *etc*. For those applications, face detection and tracking are the key processes of face recognition.

1.2 Related Work

In recent surveys on face detection, there are several researches working to solve this problem. Such as Principal Component Analysis (PCA), Neural Networks (NN), Support Vector Machines (SVM), Hough Transform (HT), Geometrical Template Matching (GTM), color analysis *etc*. based methods are used to achieve this application.
For face recognition PCA can be time consuming and this article will give quantitative data for choosing the best platform for implementing this algorithm. El-Bakry & Zhao concentrate on increasing the speed of PCA during the test phase while its performance is the same as conventional implementation. For face detection, the PCA algorithm is applied to check the presence of a face at each pixel position in the input image. This searching problem is realized using cross correlation in the frequency domain. The cross correlation is preformed between the whole input image and the eigen-values. This new idea increases the speed of the detection process compared to normal implementation of PCA algorithm in the spatial domain (El-Bakry & Zhao, 2006).

NN have been used in the field of image processing, it provides an optimistic result in terms of quality of outcome and ease of implementation. NN proved it to be invaluable in applications where a function based model or parametric approach to information processing are difficult to formulate. The description of NN can be summarized as a collection of units that are connected in some pattern to allow communication between the units. These units are referred as neurons or nodes generally. Using NN usually require a large number "face" and "non-face" images to train respectively for getting the network model. Lin *et al.* proposed an approach combing feature-based, knowledge-based and machine learning methods for detecting human faces in color images under different illumination condition, scale, rotation, wearing glasses, *etc.* (Lin *et al.*, 2005).

The method using SVM have attracted much attention recently because it is faster and has demonstrated more excellent results than NN. Jee *et al.* proposed real-time face detection method to detect facial region using skin color and edge information simultaneously in order to complement detect of color information. They using SVM to verifying eye and face candidate o fix the face region (Jee *et al.*, 2004).

The HT transform is a powerful tool to detect the specified geometrical among a cluster of data points. Wu *et al.* use a segment-based stereo vision system to detect the three-Dimension (3-D) feature of objects which include eyes, nose, mouth, *etc.* and use a 3D HT transform to determine the plane containing the rims from the detected 3-D data (Wu *et al.*, 2002).

GTM based methods are incorporated to detect gray faces in real time applications. Face detection methods based on the representation used reveals that detection algorithms using holistic representations have the advantage of finding small faces or faces in low quality images, while those using the geometrical facial features provide a good solution for detecting faces in different poses. A combination of holistic and feature-based approaches is a promising approach to face detection as well as face recognition.

Color analysis based methods have been used and proven to be an effective feature in the applications of face detection and tracking. Although different people have different skin color, several studies have that the major difference lays largely between their intensity rather than their chrominance. Hsu *et al.* proposed a face detection algorithm that is able to handle a wide range of variations in static color images, based on a lighting compensation technique and a nonlinear color transformation. They approach models skin color using a paramedic ellipse in a two-Dimensional (2-D) transformed color space and extracts facial features by constructing feature maps for the eyes, mouth, and face boundary (Hsu *et al.*, 2002). For more effective estimation of the illuminant color, in Do *et al.* proposed method, the pixels in the sclera region of the eyes are first segmented from face images captured under various illuminations. The estimated color from the sclera approximately corresponds to the illuminant color, as the pixel values for sclera region are assumed to be white under the canonical illuminant. The color values of face images are then transformed using a conversion matrix constructed based on the chromaticity values of the estimated and canonical illuminants. Lastly, use the transformed images to detect skin region in HSV color space (Do *et al.*, 2007). Not only this, other color space also have been used to detect pixels as skin region including RGB (Stokman & Gevers, 2007), HSI, YCbCr (Kumar & Bindu, 2006) and YIQ (Dai & Nakano, 1996). Color information is an efficient tool for identifying facial areas and specific facial features if the skin color model can be properly adapted for different lighting environments. However, such skin color models are not effective where the spectrum of the light source varies significantly. In other words, color appearance is often unstable due to changes in both background and foreground lighting. To solve above problems, this chapter analyzes the feature of color instead of using the existing color space and color channel analysis based methods.

1.3 Framework of Proposed Color Feature Analysis based Face Detection Method

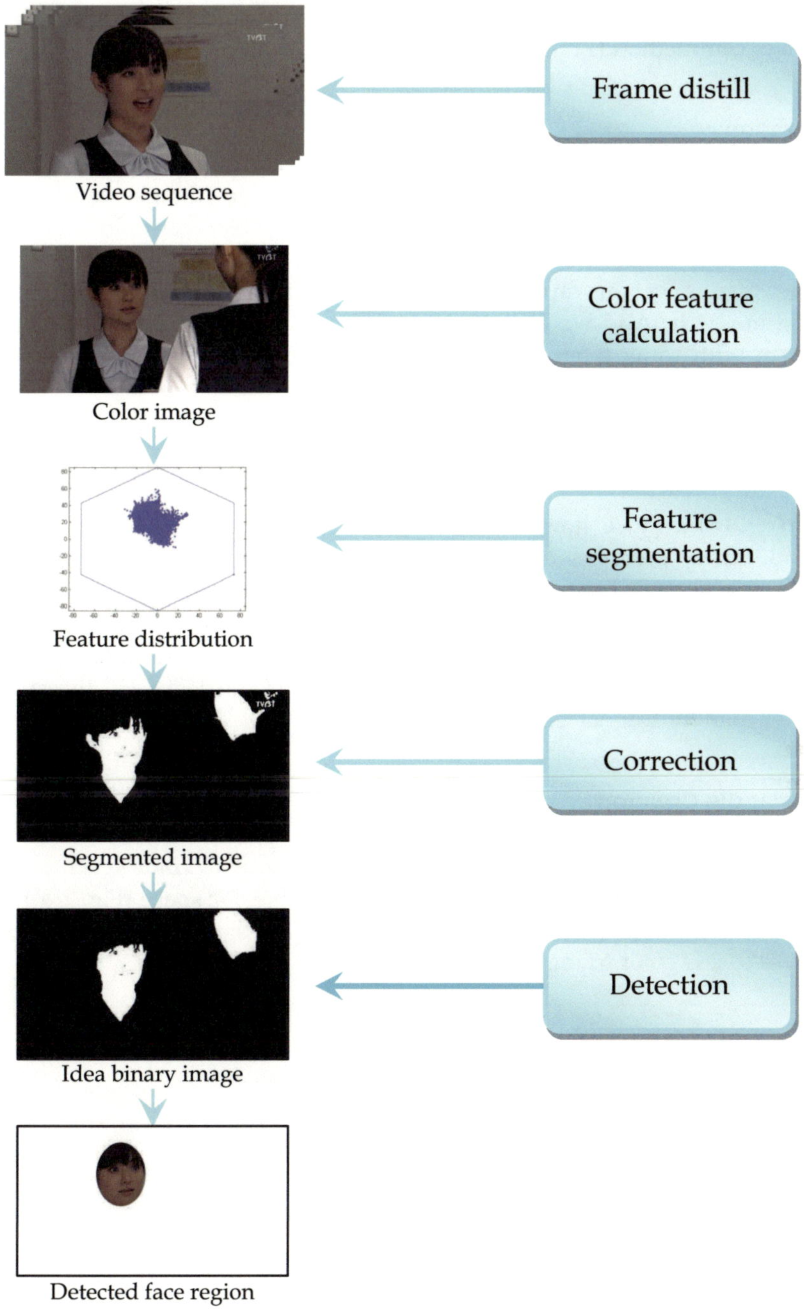

Fig. 1. Framework of proposed method

1.4 Our RGB Color Analysis Model

We have been developed a color analysis model in RGB color space. We propose a color feature detection algorithm based on color centroids analysis for face detection and tracking. The experiments have been made on video sequences with multiple faces in different positions, scales and poses, or the faces appear or disappear from sequence. This chapter is an extension of our method (Zhang *et al.*, 2008).

1.5 Organization

This chapter is composed by five sections. In Section 2, we introduce how to create the Color Centroids Segmentation (CCS) model from created color triangle in detail. Section 3 describes the thresholding algorithm by analyzing the color centroids region. Use CCS model to detect and track face region will introduced in Section 4. Section 5 presents the thresholding results of our approach and gives the comparative results with other thresholding methods. And we also give some detection results of various situations and compare them with some reference methods. In Section 6, we summarize this paper and propose some future works.

2. Color Centroids Segmentation Model

This section will introduce how to create the CCS model and how to use it for color segmentation. Firstly describes how to transform the three components of 3-D RGB color space to 2-D polar coordinate system for creating color triangle. Then calculates the centroids distribution region of all colors and transforms it to histogram for analysis. Finally, analyzes the histogram and gets multi-threshold to segment the centroids region. After these processes, the colors in one image can be divided to 2~7 colors by 2~7 thresholds and the result is better than traditional thresholding methods.

2.1 Color Triangle Creation

In image processing, RGB, YCbCr, HSV, HSI *etc.* color spaces are widely used. These color spaces use three components to reflect different color. *e.g.* RGB color space consists of R, G and B components. This chapter transforms the 3-D RGB color space (Fig. 2(a)) to 2-D polar system as the color triangle (Fig. 2(b)). The following equation shows how to transform from 3-D color cube to 2-D color triangle.

$$\begin{cases} \begin{bmatrix} \varphi_R \\ r_R \end{bmatrix} = \begin{bmatrix} 0 & 0 & 0 \\ 1 & 0 & 0 \end{bmatrix} \begin{bmatrix} R \\ G \\ B \end{bmatrix} + \begin{bmatrix} 90^\circ \\ 0 \end{bmatrix} \\ \begin{bmatrix} \varphi_G \\ r_G \end{bmatrix} = \begin{bmatrix} 0 & 0 & 0 \\ 0 & 1 & 0 \end{bmatrix} \begin{bmatrix} R \\ G \\ B \end{bmatrix} + \begin{bmatrix} 210^\circ \\ 0 \end{bmatrix} \\ \begin{bmatrix} \varphi_B \\ r_B \end{bmatrix} = \begin{bmatrix} 0 & 0 & 0 \\ 0 & 0 & 1 \end{bmatrix} \begin{bmatrix} R \\ G \\ B \end{bmatrix} + \begin{bmatrix} 330^\circ \\ 0 \end{bmatrix} \end{cases} \tag{1}$$

Here R, G and B are the components value of RGB color space, (φ_R, r_R), (φ_G, r_G), (φ_B, r_B), are the coordinate of *R*, G and *B* in polar coordinate system. Color triangle is created by following steps:

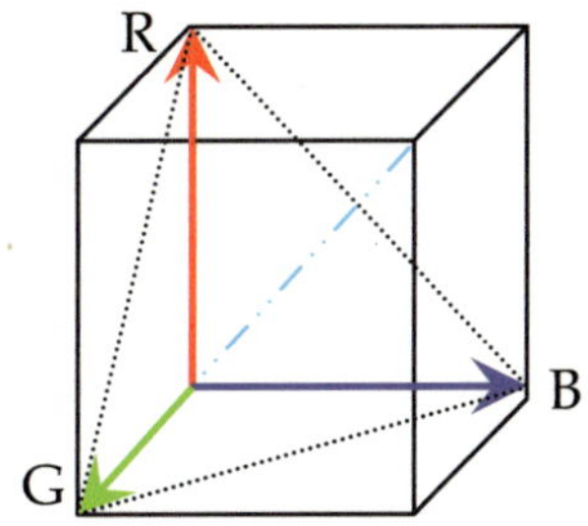

(a) RGB color cube

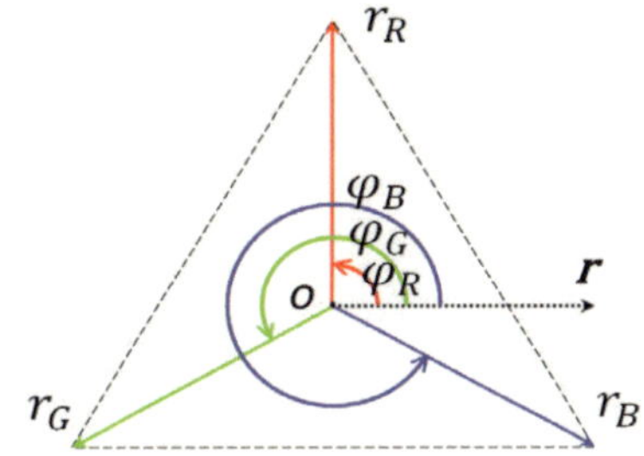

(b) RGB color triangle

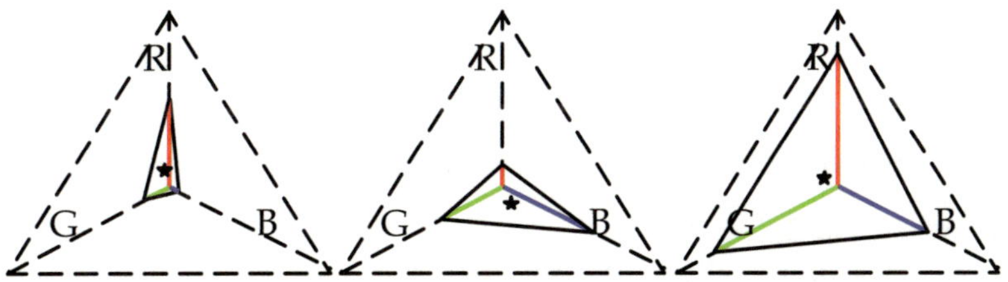

[R,G,B] = [150,25,15] [R,G,B] = [25,91,143] [R,G,B] = [218,200,143]

(c) The example of color triangle shape with different color

Fig. 2. Color triangle model

Step1: Create a standard 2-D polar coordinate system;

Step2: Create three color vectors to reflect *R*, G and *B*, the range of them are [0, 255] and alternation 120° reciprocally as Fig. 2(b) R, G and B radial show;

Step3: Connect the three apexes.

After above processes, the color triangle can be created as Fig. 2(b). For different *R*, G and *B*, the shape of triangle is changeable. For example, Fig. 2(c) show three sets of *R*, G and *B* and their corresponding color triangles. From this example, it can be seen that no matter the *R*, G and *B* values change the main structure is unmodified.

2.2 Centroids Hexagon

Because the direction of *R*, G and *B* vectors are fixed and the value range are [0, 255], different combination of *R*, G and *B* represents different color, and the shape of color triangle is different too. The different shape triangles have different centroids and all centroids result in a hexagon region shown as Fig. 3. This hexagon is divided to 7 regions: *M* (Magenta), *R* (Red), *Y* (Yellow), *G* (Green), *C* (Cyan), *B* (Blue) and *L* (Luminance, achromatic) regions. So we may use seven threshold curves as the separating lines for thresholding.

Observe the relationship between color and its corresponding centroid position of color triangle, we find that if the *R*, *G* and *B* values are close, no matter small or large, it only reflect the luminance information (weak color information). So the centroids of corresponding color triangles will locate in a circular region (L region). And other six color regions reflect the color feature of R, G and B components.

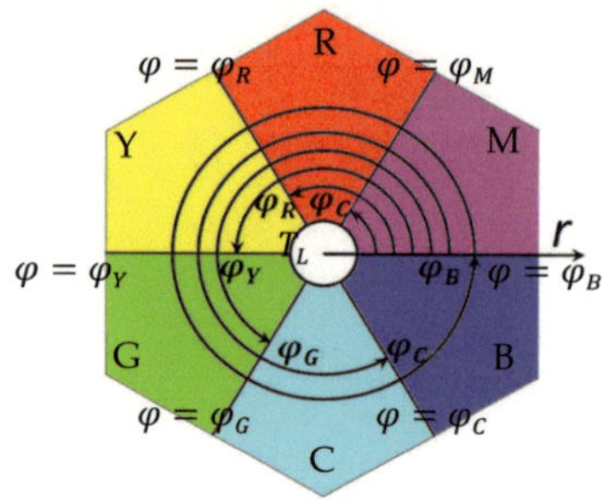

Fig. 3. Color centroids segmentation model

3. Color Centroids Segmentation Model Based Color Segmentation

3.1 Multiple thresholds Selection

Considering the L region usually is not the goal region and the existing method cannot effectively divide white and black region which are noises, cluster them into one region can effectively to overcome the influence from white, black and other achromatic regions. Here we let r_L as the threshold of L region (radius of L region), φ as the angle, the function of threshold curve is:

$$r(\varphi) = T_L, (0° < \varphi \leq 360°) \tag{2}$$

The other six regions which around the L region as following formulas show:

$$\begin{cases} M \text{ Region:} & \varphi_B \leq \varphi \leq \varphi_M, & r_M > r_L \\ R \text{ Region:} & \varphi_M \leq \varphi \leq \varphi_R, & r_R > r_L \\ Y \text{ Region:} & \varphi_R \leq \varphi \leq \varphi_Y, & r_Y > r_L \\ G \text{ Region:} & \varphi_Y \leq \varphi \leq \varphi_G, & r_G > r_L \\ C \text{ Region:} & \varphi_G \leq \varphi \leq \varphi_C, & r_C > r_L \\ B \text{ Region:} & \varphi_C \leq \varphi \leq \varphi_B, & r_B > r_L \end{cases} \tag{3}$$

In formula (3) and (4), r_L, φ_M, φ_R , φ_Y, φ_G, φ_C and φ_B are the thresholds, and the initial value of them is 5, 60°, 120°, 180°, 240°, 300° and 360°.

The seven thresholds can divide all colors in one image into seven clusters and the result is shown in Fig. 4(b). But these thresholds cannot always get ideal result for different image scene. So we propose an automatic threshold selection method to get the suitable threshold for different images.

3.2 Automatic Multi-threshold Acquisition

By observing the distribution of color centroids in hexagon as Fig. 4(d), we can see that the centroid distribution of different color is different, only when the $R = G = B$, the centroids are same and it is the origin of hexagon. The color information is stronger; the centroid is more far away from origin. For example, (R, G, B) = (255, 0, 0) is the pure red color and its centroid is the up peak point in Fig. 3. But threshold curve determination in Fig. 4(d) is not easy. For display the distribution feature more clearly, we transform the centroids hexagon distribution in Polar coordinate system to histogram distribution in Cartesian coordinate system as shown in Fig. 4(e). In the Fig. 4(e), horizontal axis is φ ($\varphi \in (0°, 360°]$), vertical axis is r ($r \in [0, 85]$) and other six vertical color-lines are threshold curves ($\varphi_M, \varphi_R, \varphi_Y, \varphi_G, \varphi_C$ and φ_B).

To segment goal region ideally, the thresholds must be calculated accurately. Because the histogram is not smooth, so we use one-Dimension (1-D) iterative median filter to smooth it for analysis. Through many experiments and observation, we define the adjustment range of threshold curves from left 20° to right 20° and find the left and right valleys respectively in this range by histogram analysis method. For r_L, we define the range from 3 to 15 and calculate the average value of each valley bottom (one color region only calculate one minimum value). After this process, Fig. 4(c) can be got.

(a) Original image (b) Initially segmentation (c) Self-adjusting segmentation

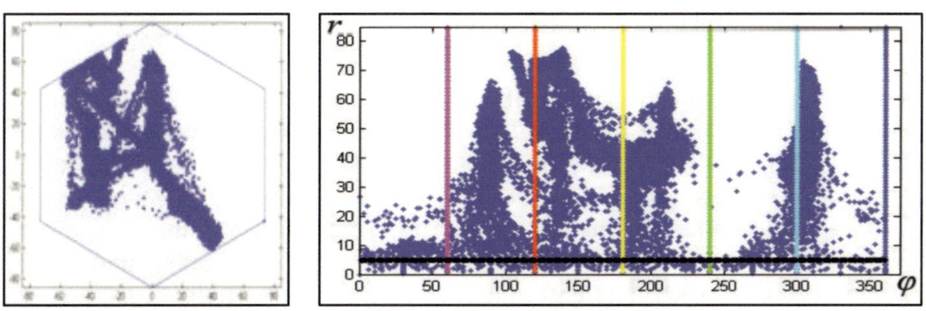

(d) Hexagon distribution (e) Histogram distribution

Fig. 4. Color centroids distribution selection

4. Face Detection and Tracking

4.1 Thresholding

By analyzing the color features introduced above, the thresholding results can be acquired to detect face region in color image.

4.1.1 Color Centroids Segmentation for Thresholding

The CCS can overcome the shortage of existing methods which based on color information, because it can conquer the influences of color and luminance. The proposed method calculates the direction of color and clusters the dark and light region into one cluster which will result in removing some noises. By analyzing many sample color of face region, we find that it always distributes in the range of $50°\sim150°$ and shown in Fig. 5(a). So we only need to calculate the φ'_M, φ'_R and r_L for time saving. The pre-face region:

$$r(\varphi) = r_{Face}, \quad (\varphi \in [\varphi'_M, \varphi'_Y], r \in [r_L, 85]) \tag{4}$$

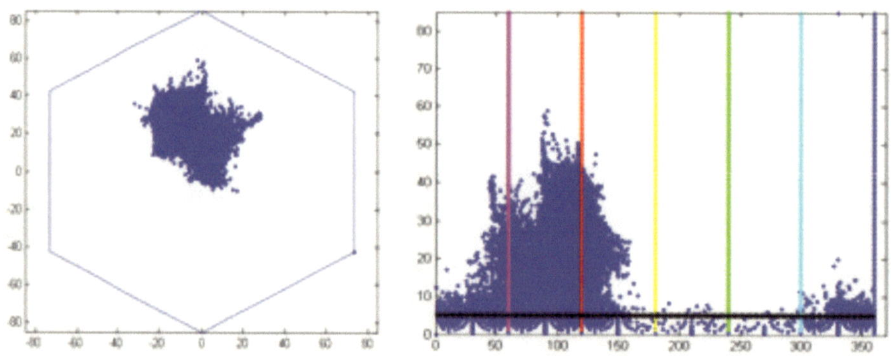

(a) Hexagon distribution (b) Histogram distribution

Fig. 5. Sample face region centrids distribution

Then the method described in Section III is used to select thresholds φ'_M, φ'_R and r_L to get the threshold curves for thresholding. Other thresholds keep invariant as initial values without calculation. By this way, the binary image can be got as Fig. 6(b). From the result we can see that sky, background, white scarf and red cloth region are clustered to black and only the face color similar regions are clustered to white. Through this processing, many noise can be removed, especially the excessive bright, dark and different color regions. But because some color of background and cloth is close to the face region color, it is clustered to pre-face region.

4.1.2 Nonlinear Thresholding for Correction

Despite the CCS thresholding can get better result, but it cannot remove some noises caused by dark color regions. To denoise them, this paper uses the nonlinear thresholding method to correct the binary image acquired by CCS. Considering the gray values of the dark color is lower, apply the nonlinear transform described as equation (5) to transform gray images to divide it into 2 clusters; finally apply inverse transform to get the binary image. Fig. 6(c) is the binary image by nonlinear thresholding.

$$f_{Binary}(x,y) = \frac{\ln[1+255 f_{Original}(x,y)]}{k\ln[1+255]} \tag{5}$$

Where, k is the number of cluster, here k=2. From Fig. 6(c), it can be seen that the background of binary image with white color and scarf region has been clustered to same value with the face region by nonlinear thresholding, so it is hard to separate the face. But this binary image can overcome some shortages of CCS, for example the dark color regions. Sometimes, the centroids of some bright regions are also in the goal region, but in fact they are noise regions. So use formula (6) to correct image processed by the CCS based method with "and operation".

$$f_{Final}(x,y) = f_{CCS}(x,y) \cap f_{Nonliner}(x,y) \tag{6}$$

After this, it will get the ideal result. Fig. 6(d) shows the corrected binary image and from this we can see that have been ignoring many noise.

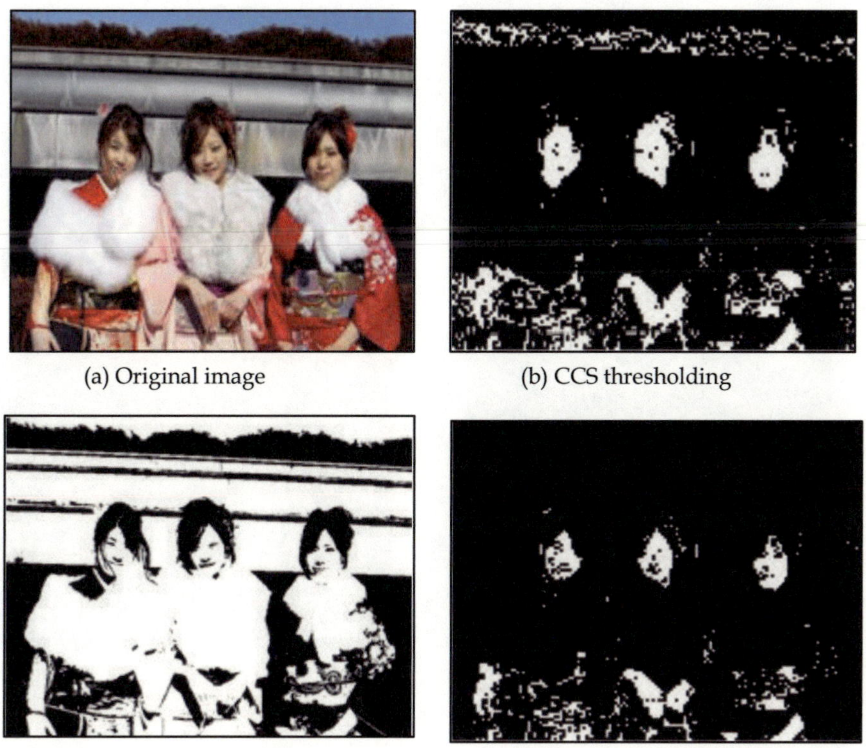

(a) Original image

(b) CCS thresholding

(c) Nonlinear thresholding result

(d) Correction thresholding

Fig. 6. Proposed thresholding method

4.2 Pre-face Region Decision

Once the ideal binary image is got, median filter is used to denoise and show in Fig. 7(b). The white region is the wait-decision region, it maybe include face, hand, skin region and other close color regions (the white region on Fig. 7(b)). Here all wait-decision regions are analyzed in a selection process and some of them will be accepted by the aspect ratio and size.

Accepted by size:
Calculate the average area S_{Ave} of all wait-decision regions; delete the regions whose area is larger than 50% or smaller than 0.25% average area. If the area of face $S_{Face} \in [0.8S_{Ave}, 1.2S_{Ave}]$, it will be accepted as Fig. 7(c).

Accepted by aspect ratio:

$$C = 4\pi S/L^2 \tag{8}$$

Where C aspect ratio, L is the perimeter of boundary and S is the area of wait-decision region. If $C \in [1, 1.7]$, it will be accepted as Fig. 7d).

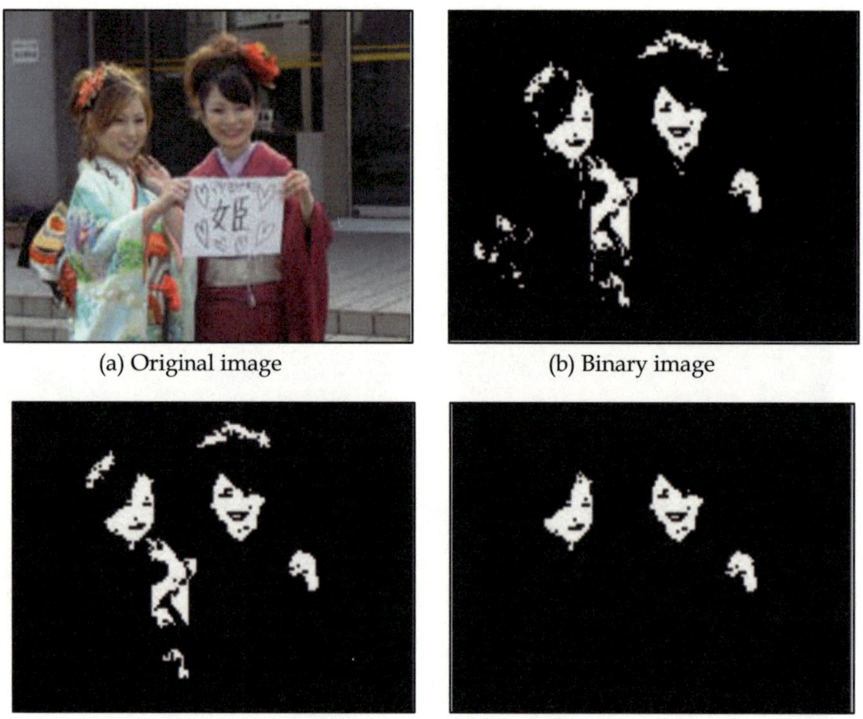

(a) Original image
(b) Binary image
(c) Accepted by size
(d) Accepted by ratio

Fig. 7. Face region decision

4.3 Face Region Tracking

After face region is fixed, it need use a circle to draw it. Here we pass the following steps to achieve this:

Step1: Use the binary face region as the mask to detect the face region from original image. It shows as Fig. 8(a).

Step2: Calculate the width of the detected face region. Then scan from top and bottom to middle line by line respectively. If the total pixels of line are less than half width, it will be deleted as Fig. 8(b).

Step3: After that, calculate the height of Fig. 8(b) and scan from left and right to middle row by row respectively. If the total pixels of row are less than half height, it will be deleted as Fig. 8(c).

Step4: Because of the eyes and mouth region is usually darker than face skin, divide the face region to 16 sub-blocks as Fig. 8(c). Then maximum entropy method is used to thresholding them respectively, shown in Fig. 8(d).

Step5: Remove noise point by median filter and find all pre-eye and pre-mouth regions in the inscribed circle of face region as Fig. 8(e).

Step6: Fix eyes and mouth region by aspect ratio and occupancy as follows:
Aspect ratio: between 0.2 and 1.7.
Occupancy: between 0.5% and 4% of face region.

Step7: Calculate the area centroids of eyes and mouth respectively as the red point in Fig. 8(e).

Step8: Draw a circumcircle (blue circle in Fig. 8(e)) of triangle which is created by the three centroids. Then use concentric circle multiplied by 1.5 to mark face (green circle in Fig. 8(e)).

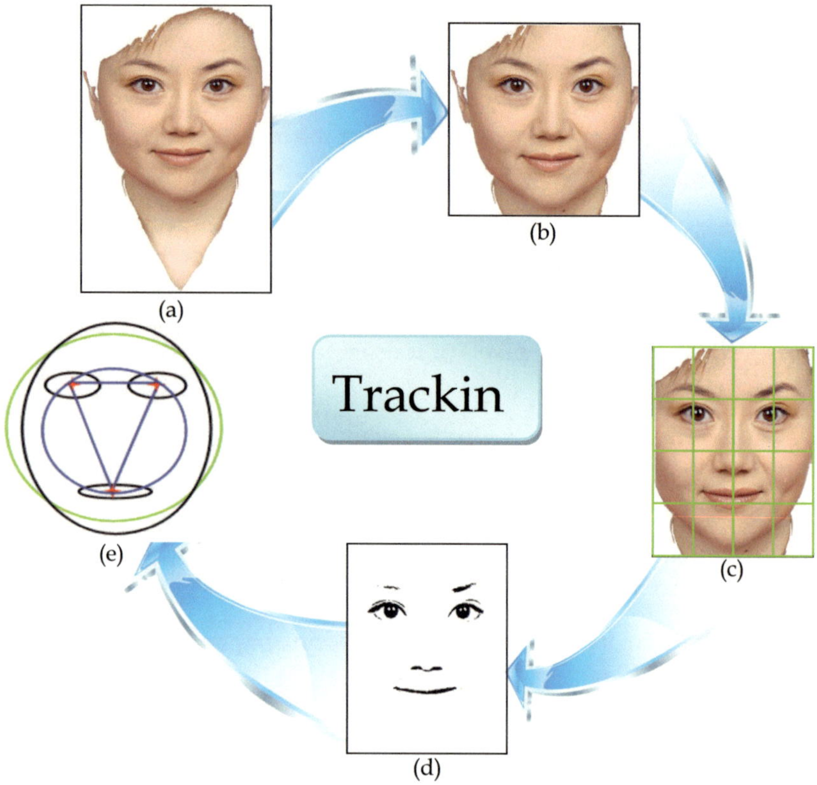

Fig. 8. Face tracking process

5. Experimental Results

All the experiments are achieved using Matlab 7.0 on a Celeron M 1.73GHz platform with 2G memory. And all experiment sample images are searched from internet and reference paper.

5.1 The Result of Proposed Method

5.1.1 Thresholding results and comparison

Fig. 9 shows an example with complex background under outdoor situation, (a) is the original image; (b) is the thresholding result by proposed method; (c)~(f) are different results by traditional thresholding methods. Fig. 9(c) is use the histogram analysis method to get the best result by hand, but it hard to select the white, pink, buff *etc* color region; (d) transform the distributing probability of original gray value to frequency domain for thresholding, by this way it cluster all bright region to one class and cannot separate the color information; (e) adopt the traditional maximum entropy method to calculate the suitable entropy for thresholding and (f) is the result of 1-D Otsu method. Compare those thresholding results, but those methods also cannot select the face region; it can be seeing that the proposed method is better than the others.

(a) Original image

(b) Proposed method

(c) Histogram analysis

(d) Non-linear quantification

(e) Maximum entropy

(f) Otsu thresholding

Fig. 9. Sample image thresholding with different methods

Figure 10(a) is the original image, (b) is the thresholding result by proposed method, (c) is the thresholding result by maximum entropy method, (d) is the thresholding result by histogram analysis method, (e) is the thresholding result by Otsu method, (f)~(i) show the nonlinear thresholding result in every channel of CMKY color space, (j)~(l) show the result of HSV color space, (m)~(o) show RGB color space, (p)~(r) show Lab color space and (s)~(u) show YIQ color space. From the comparison different channel of color space, it only one channel is fit to thresholding, but those channel of color space based method is not good for face detecting. Compare all the thresholding results, the proposed method is better than other thresholding results and color channel based methods.

(a) Original image

(b) Proposed method

(c) Maximum entropy method

(d) Histogram analysis method

(e) Otsu method

(f) C channel of CMYK space

(g) M channel of CMYK space

(h) Y channel of CMYK space

(i) K channel of CMYK space

(j) H channel of HSV space

(k) S channel of HSV space

(l) V channel of HSV space

(m) R channel of RGB space

(n) G channel of RGB space

(o) B channel of RGB space

(p) L channel of Lab space

(q) a channel of Lab space

(r) b channel of Lab space

(s) Y channel of YIQ space (t) I channel of YIQ space (u) Q channel of YIQ space

Fig. 10. Compare with thresholding result in different methods and channel of color space

5.1.2 Face detection results

Fig. 11 is two faces image with outdoor situation. The ideal binary image (Fig. 11(c)) can be got by color feature histogram (Fig. 11(b)) analysis for face detection; (a) shows the original image and the accurately tracking result (green circle). From the Fig. 11(c) we can see that the proposed method can cluster the white scarf, pink cloth, sky, building and other dark region to one cluster. Based this ideal binary image, it will help to face detecting. Fig. 12 and Fig. 13 show the indoor image which contains more than one person under the situation. From Fig. 12(b) and Fig. 13(b), we can see that it is easy to segment the goal color region, the Fig. 12(c) and Fig. 13(c) are binary image and green circles of Fig. 12(a) and Fig. 13(a) are detected result. Usually the light-colored clothing regions have an effect on the thresholding result got by using the method based on luminance or histogram analysis. The results show that the proposed method can overcome those influences. But if the clothing region is connected with the face, the region cannot be detected. To overcome this, it need improve the face detection method to determine the pre-face regions.

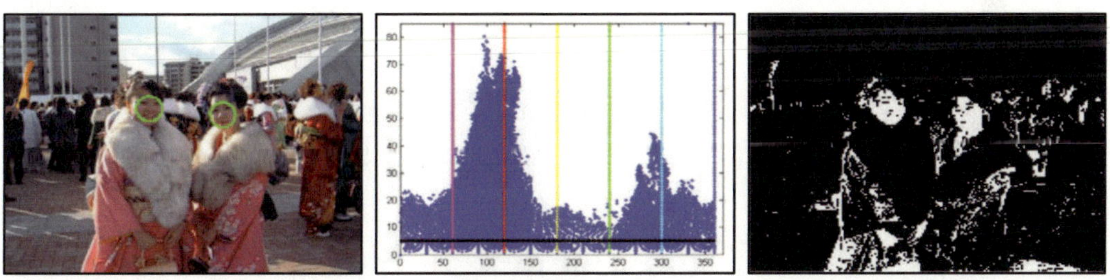

(a) Original image (b) Feature histogram (c) Binary image

Fig. 11. Detection with outdoor condition

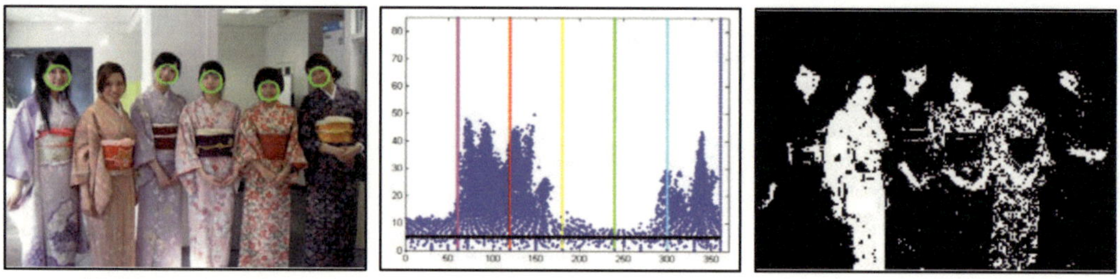

(a) Original image (b) Centroids histogram (c) Binary image

Fig. 12. Detection with indoor condition

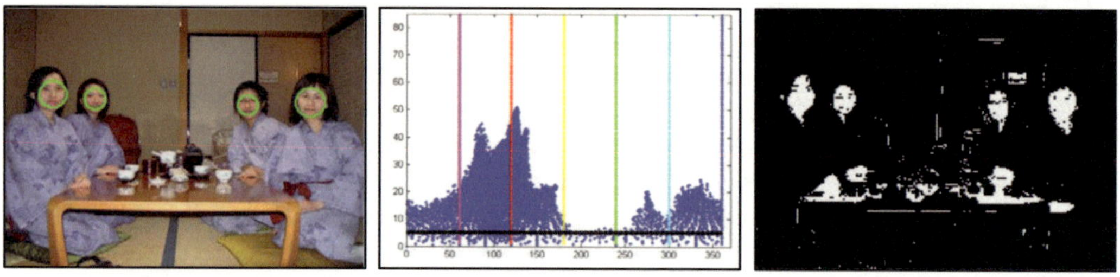

(a) Original image (b) Centroids histogram (c) Binary image

Fig. 13. Detection with sample background

5.2 Comparison with other paper result (Sabeti & Wu, 2007)

Fig. 14 shows a sample image from Sabeti & Wu and (c)~(f) are the results. It is easy to see that Fig. 14(e)(f) are bad thresholding results. (d) is better but include some noise from background. Both (b) and (c) are acceptable results and (b) is better than (c), because (b) lost a small region under left eye. So (c) is the best result in the five methods.

(a) Original image (b) Result of Sabeti & Wu method (c) Proposed

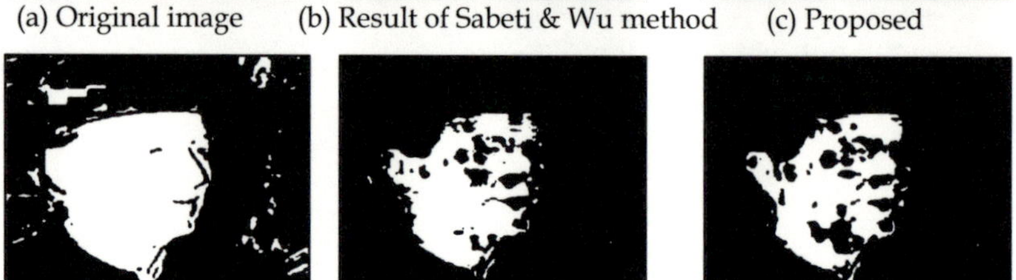

(d) Skin locus (e) Single Gaussian (f) Histogram

Fig. 14. Thresholding result compare with Sabeti & Wu

6. Conclusions and Future Works

We have presented a novel color thresholding method to segment the color image for temporal face detection and tracking as this chapter introduce. The experimental results demonstrate that the proposed method can detect and track faces under various conditions effectively. The proposed method calculates the color centriods distribution which created by color feature of all colors in one image to conquer the disadvantage of color space and gray based methods. After the ideal binary image got, the face can be marked correctly by the proposed tracking method. All experimental results show an excellent performance of the proposed method for different environments such as the change of room, lighting, complex background and color.

In the future, we need to complete the following items to improve the performance of our method further: 1, overcome the change of pose and view point; 2, use motion analysis for effective prediction; 3, integrate the detection and tracking information to make a face model for real-time recognition.

7. References

Jee, H.; Lee, K. & Pan, S. (2004). Eye and Face Detection using SVM, *Proc. of Intelligent Sensors, Sensor Networks and information Processing Conf.*, pp. 577-580, Dec. 2004, Australia

Hsu, R.; Mohamed, A. & Jain, A. (2002). Face Detection in Color Images, *IEEE Trans. on Pattern Analysis and Machine Intelligence*, Vol. 24, No. 5, (May. 2002) pp. 696-706

Do, H.; You, J. & Chien, S. (2007). Skin Color Detection through Estimation and Conversion of Illuminant Color Under Various Illuminations, *IEEE Trans. on Consumer Electronics*, Vol. 53, No. 3, (Aug. 2007) pp. 1103 - 1108

Stokman, H. & Gevers, T. (2007). Selection and Fusion of Color Models for Image Feature Detection, *IEEE Tran. on Pattern Analysis and Machine Intelligence*, Vol. 29, (Mar. 2007) pp. 371-381

Kumar, C. & Bindu, A. (2006). An Efficient Skin Illumination Compensation Model for Efficient Face Detection, *32nd Annual Conf. on IEEE Industrial Electronics*, pp. 3444-3449, Nov. 2006, France

Dai, Y. & Nakano, Y. (1996). Face-Texture Model Based on SGLD and Its Application in Face Detection in a Color Scene, *Pattern Recognition*, Vol. 29, No. 6, (1996) pp. 1007-1017

Lin, H.; Wang, S.; Yen, S. & Kao, Y. (2005). Face Detection Based on Skin Color Segmentation and Neural Network, *Int'l Conf. on Neural Network and Brain*, Vol. 2, pp. 114-1149, Oct. 2005, China

El-Bakry, H. & Zhao, Q. (2006). Fast Neural Implementation of PCA for Face Detection, *Int'l Joint Conf. on Neural Networks*, pp. 806-811, Jul. 2006, Canada

Wu, H.; Yoshikawa, G.; Shioyama, T.; Lao, T. & Kawade, T. (2002). Glasses frame detection with 3D Hough transform, *Proc. of the 16th Int'l Conf. on Pattern Recognition*, Vol. 2, pp. 346 – 349, Aug. 2002, Canada

Zhang, Q.; Kamata, S. & Zhang, J. (2008). Face Detection and Tracking in Color Images Using Color Centroids Segmentation, *2008 IEEE Int'l Conf. on Robotics and Biomimetics*, pp. 1008-1013, Feb. 2009, Thailand

Sabeti, L. & Wu, J. (2007). High-speed Skin Color Segmentation for Real-time Human Tracking, *2007 IEEE Int'l Conf. on Systems, Man and Cybernetics*, pp. 2378- 2382, Oct. 2007, Canada

8

Mind Operator: Zone-Associated Relative Representation

Ching-An Hsiao
University of Tsukuba
Japan

1. Introduction

Since Chinese room argument was presented (Searle, 1980), a wide debate has run to discuss whether a machine could have mind. As Searle clarified, he had no objection to the claims of weak AI, but strong AI – that running the right sort of program necessarily results in a mind. Undoubtedly, the system passes the Turing Test but does not understand anything of its inputs and outputs. Whether there is mind in Chinese room depends on what mind means and whether machine could have human-like minds is not involved here. It is obviously that Searle and his objectors have different point of view on mind, which Wittgenstein clarified as "the picture of world" (Wittgenstein, 1974). Since "What can be said at all can be said clearly" (Wittgenstein, 1922), let's make clear what on earth Chinese room says. Does the man in the room understand Chinese? It is definitely not. Does the whole room understand Chinese? The consensus stops here. Backward one step, we all agree that the whole room acts as it understands Chinese. What causes it? Does a system that has no knowledge of Chinese can operate Chinese rightly? Or can persons operate a car rightly without understanding the whole mechanism of the engine? We should distinguish the knowledge in different level, one is the ontological (or whole) knowledge, the other is part knowledge. Part originates from the whole. For certain application, we only need part knowledge. Return to the Chinese room, how if the master kindly equipped the man with a super Chinese-English dictionary, a hidden book that makes us trapped in controversy? This time, we find clearly that Searle differed from his objectors in whether sub knowledge is equivalent to the whole. Though in this point Searle is right, but because the difference can not be identified by outside observers and understanding can be viewed in different way, we had better to follow Turing's way that "Instead of arguing continually over this point (machine thinking), it is usual to have the polite convention that everyone thinks" (Russell and Norvig, 2003). Final solution deeply depends on what we have mentioned above, i.e., what the mind is and what understanding means.

This chapter approaches mind problem in a new way. Based on latest study to outlier detection and some evidence in psychology and neuroscience, we give a framework to object representation and recognition problem. Because representation is the groundwork for recognition and the proposed representation (ART) has general basis, we call it mind operator. The principle that underlies ART is relativity, which has already made huge success in physics but is still carefully avoided in other fields, being necessary to cause uncertainty. This is right what we need for computing – on probability. Therefore, so-called subjectivity, bridged by ART, gets to connect with the "machines".

2. Intelligence

What's intelligence, or what's artificial intelligence? Historically, there are four categories (Russell and Norvig, 2003): Systems that think like humans, Systems that act like humans, systems that think rationally and systems that act rationally. Because rationality is related to humans, we actually only need the former two: Artificial intelligence is machines that think or act like humans. Another concept concerned is mind, intelligence is not enough for minds. Human beings are unwilling to acknowledge machines being of mind on the main reason that humans keep open to knowledge while machines cannot. Human beings are free to make mistakes and change mind, while machines are preprogrammed thus more seem to be determined forehand. That is to say, human minds are in the process of probability events. The reason that current machine algorithm cannot be treated as human-like algorithm is that machines run definitely in a certain way while human beings do not. What's the special for human beings? Humans comprehend world by constructing relations among related events. Relationship is always experience-concerned, so our cognition is inevitably relative. Relativity is closely relevant to uncertainty. To realize uncertain computing, we can never rely on absolute way. There is an interesting new point of view to probability. Hutter (2005) argued that objective probabilities look somewhat "unscientific", and thus do not exist. It is an outstanding idea, which was supported by recent studies to outlier (Hsiao, et al., 2008; 2009). The studies also indicate how many subjective factors make an object "objective", which implies that relativity is the foundation of uncertainty. Physics tells us that quantum mechanics is truly random. It might be necessary so.

On the other hand, minds have to do with pattern recognition. An important task is to process noise. A good system should be robust to various noises. But in fact, noises are also pattern. The process of pattern recognition is also the process of outlier detection, vice versa.

2.1 Pattern and outlier

"A pattern is essentially an arrangement. It is characterized by the order of the elements of which it is made, rather than by the intrinsic nature of these elements." (Gonzalez and Woods, 2008). Since pattern is a kind of order, outliers can be viewed as disturbers to the order. There are abundant patterns in nature, include noises. Traditional methods preprocess outliers before pattern recognition, which causes solution an ad hoc one. Since there is no general recognition algorithm, way to realize true intelligence is blocked. Reasonable approach is to treat outliers as patterns. Based on this idea, a robust solution was presented recently (Hsiao et al., 2009), where outliers, thus patterns are processed according to the breaking of consistence. Consistence can be viewed as symmetry, so no breaking, no pattern. Here we only give a definition of outlier to show the relation between outlier and patterns.

Definition: An outlier is an observation with a degree greater than a threshold in comparison with other observations referred to or associated with a specified pattern.

Outlier problem can finally be converted to classification of univariate dataset by Expanding Algorithm (Hsiao et al., 2009), which also means that pattern recognition in the end becomes the problem of numbers or the problem of relation of numbers.

2.2 Relativity

Application of relativity in physics is well known by the work of Einstein. General relativity has been accurately tested in the solar system (Hartle, 2003). This theory is currently the most successful gravitational theory, being almost universally accepted and well supported by observations. Besides, relativity also plays a very important role in economics. The influence was mainly exerted by Austrian School, where a subjective theory of value - marginalism was first introduced by Carl Menger (1871). When mensioning value of goods, Menger said, "The measure of value is entirely subjective in nature, and for this reason a goods can have great value to one economizing individual, little value to another and no value at all to a third, depending upon the differences in their requirements and available amounts… Hence not only the nature but also the measure of value is subjective. Goods always have value to certain economizing individuals and this value is also determined only by these individuals". Wittgenstein summed up the nature of relativity by a famous concept "family resemblance" (Wittgenstein, 1953/2001), which was believed to replace the Aristotelian idea of a certain set of attributes being common to all occurrences of a particular class (Osaka et al. 2007). In following section, a model based on relativity is built to describe patterns.

3. Relative Representation and Recognition

3.1 Associated Relative Representation

Recognition implies a match between two entities, and any theory of recognition must specify both the form of representation and the details of the matching process (Edelman, 1999).As brightness, color, texture are all less important than shape, main task of vision is to represent and recognize object's shape. Object recognition includes two categories. One is structure-based (Marr, 1982; Biederman, 1987) and the other is view-based (Poggio and Edelman, 1990; Bulthoff and Edelman, 1992). In contrast, structure based will be more complex to derive, but will provide for less redundant storage (Bruce, 1988). Recent evidence from behavioural (Hummel, 2001; Foster and Gilson, 2002; Stankiewicz, 2002, Haywood, 2003; Thoma et al., 2004) and neuroimaging (Vuilleumier et al., 2002) studies suggests that view-invariant and view-dependent representations do co-exist in the brain with a relative preponderance that may depend on task, context and level of expertise. Thus generic part-based approaches like EBS approach (Martin Juttner, 2007) was presented, which is based on the notion that complex patterns are best encoded in terms of parts and their relations. Furthermore, an abstract framework for learning and recognition of objects was proposed (Wallraven and Bulthoff, 2007). The work was inspired by recent psychophysical results which have shown that object representations in the human brain are inherently spatio-temporal.

Indeed, if removing spatio-temporal relationship, there is nothing in a pattern. Furthermore, view-based or structure-based are not mutually exclusive. In essence, they should be associated with different weighting to become a complete solution. All atom unit (or element) of patterns are all the same. Based on relativity, any pattern should firstly be self-expressed, which leads to the Associated Relative represenTation (ART).

Preliminaries

Let U denote a universe, Δ denote atom unit, and $\Lambda \subseteq U \times U$ denote spatio-temporal relations on U.

An arbitrary pattern $P \subseteq U$, could be expressed by a set of elements $p_1, p_2, \ldots p_m$ with a spatio-temporal structure. Any element p_i may be a Δ or a combined unit by atom units.

Representation

Given a pattern $P\{p_1, p_2, \ldots p_m\}$, which is in n-dimensional timespace, denoted by $\sum_n^m$.

For one kind of tempo-spatial relation, define a set R, denoting relations between any two elements, $R = \{r_1, r_2, \ldots r_\theta\}$, $\theta = m \times (m-1)/2$.

$\forall$ i, j, k ($i \neq j$, $i \neq k$, $j \neq k$, $1 \leq i, j, k \leq m$)

Let p_i and p_j construct a reference system with direction from i to j ($\overrightarrow{ij}$), and p_k be an evaluated element.

Convert the absolute relations to relative relations which could be expressed by a series of scalar quantity, $Q\{q_1, q_2, \ldots\}$. Without loss of generality, we suppose scalar quantity ψ for one spatio-temporal relation.

Let ψ_k^{ij} expresses relative relation of *k* to *i* and *j*, then we can get a matrix for each *i*, *j* or *k*.

We call the following matrix evaluated matrix (E-mat) from the view of *k*, evaluated element;

$$\begin{bmatrix} \psi_k^{11} & \psi_k^{12} & \cdot & \cdot & \psi_k^{1m} \\ \psi_k^{21} & \cdot & \cdot & \cdot & \cdot \\ \cdot & \cdot & \cdot & \cdot & \cdot \\ \cdot & \cdot & \cdot & \cdot & \cdot \\ \psi_k^{m1} & \cdot & \cdot & \cdot & \psi_k^{mm} \end{bmatrix}$$

A random specified value to ψ_k^{ij} when *i*=*j* or *i*=*k* or j=*k*.

and following matrix from-matrix (F-mat) from the view of i; to-matrix (T-mat) from the view of *j*.

F-mat: T-mat:

$$\begin{bmatrix} \psi_1^{i1} & \psi_2^{i1} & . & . & \psi_m^{i1} \\ \psi_1^{i2} & . & . & . & . \\ . & . & . & . & . \\ . & . & . & . & . \\ \psi_1^{im} & . & . & . & \psi_m^{im} \end{bmatrix} \qquad \begin{bmatrix} \psi_1^{1j} & \psi_1^{2j} & . & . & \psi_1^{mj} \\ \psi_2^{1j} & . & . & . & . \\ . & . & . & . & . \\ . & . & . & . & . \\ \psi_m^{1j} & . & . & . & \psi_m^{mj} \end{bmatrix}$$

Three types of matrices can be combined to a whole-matrix (W-mat). In this case, each element p_x ($1 \le x \le m$) is expressed from three aspects, evaluated, from and to. In application, distance and angle can be used for relations. All matrices form reduntant information. The scalar quantity is a kind of code. For a example, to the three apexes of equivalent triangle, we can get a associated code: (1, 60°).

3.2 Zone-Associated Recognition

ART codes the region refer to each element. The scale of region is not limited. If fully chosen, a redundancy holographic information image is coded and no information is lost. The coded list can be used to recognize objects. Usually, region can be limited to a small zone around element, the zone can be treated as a structure. Combine all zones around each element, we get same relative complete representation. Recognition is just a process of comparing to prototypes. Here only full holographic expression is discussed. A possible simple matching algorithm is given as following.

Given a prototype $P(p_1, p_2 \ldots p_m)$, and object $O(o_1, o_2 \ldots o_l)$ in n-dimensional timespace.

1. Choose distance and angle as two associated relations.
2. For any element p_k in P and o_k in O construct two E-mat E_k and $E_{k'}$, whose element is the pair of distance ratio and relative angle like (r_{ij}, θ_{ij}).
3. Define a similar function, $sim(E_k, E_{k'}) \rightarrow [0,1]$, denoted by $sim_{k'}^{k}$.
4. Define max zone match degree $zmd_{k'}^{P} = \max_{k}(sim_{k'}^{k})$
5. Define whole match degree between P and O: $wmd_{O}^{P} = \sum_{k'=1}^{l} w_{k'} \times zmd_{k'}^{P}$, with weighting $w_{k'}$.
6. To multiple prototypes, choose one with max whole match degree as the recognition. Sometimes dual match is needed.
7. To weighting for all possible structure, similar method like tf and idf (Sparck, 1972; Salton and Buckley, 1988) can be adopted, which is experience related. Alternatively, recognition might also be a process of using Markov model.

4. Some evidence

4.1 Visual Illusion

Let's first discuss about the length illusion. In Figure 1a, line a and line b have the same length, but a seems longer than b. The most often cited explanation is that one sees the lines as three dimensional, such as the outgoing and ingoing corners of a room (Gregory, 1968). Segall et al. (1963) argued that the Muller-Lyer illusion would only be perceived by those with experience of a "carpentered environment" containing numerous rectangles, straight lines, and regular corners. People living in Western societies live in a carpentered environment, whereas Zulus living in tribal communities do not. So Rural Zulus did not show the Muller-Lyer illusion, which demonstrates that Muller-Lyer illusion is experience-related and holistic. It means that lines should be represented as a whole with arrows and recognition is view-based, thus is concerned with probability. Such a explanation was also presented recently (Howe and Purves, 2005). All these can be realized well by the method proposed in this chapter.

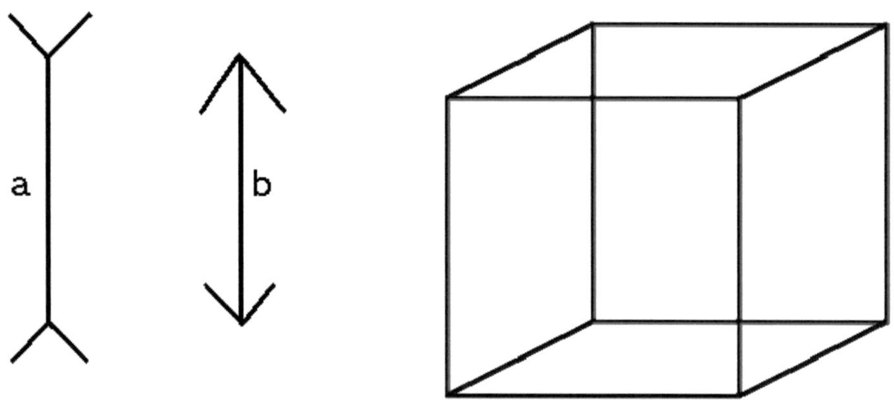

(a) (b)

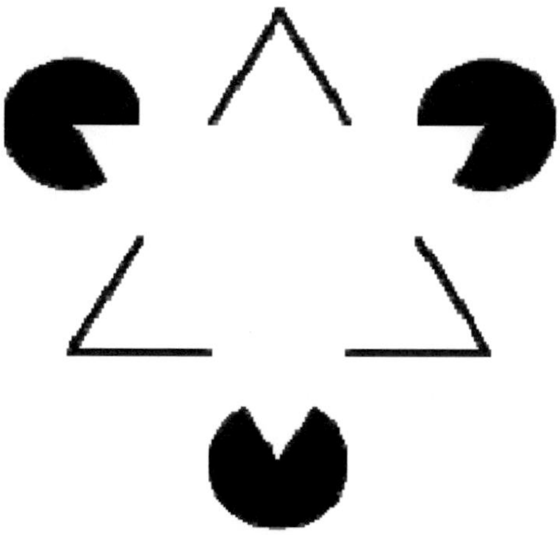

(c)

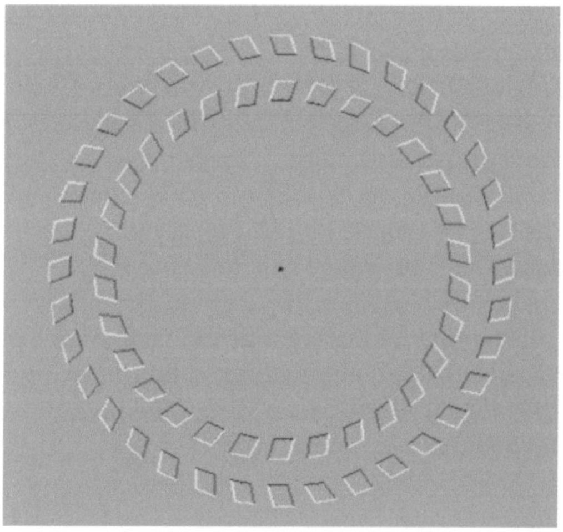

(d)

Fig. 1. Visual illusions. (a) Muller-Lyer Illusion. The left line appears longer than the right one, although they are in fact equal in length (b) The Necker Cube: a wire frame cube with no depth cues (c) Kanizsa's Triangle. In which the eye perceives a white equilateral triangle where none is actually drawn (d) Pinna-Brelstaff Illusion. When observers look close or move away from the image keeping their eyes fixed on the center, the rings appear to rotate in the different directions

The Necker Cube (Figure 1b) is an ambiguous line drawing. It is a wire-frame drawing of a cube in isometric perspective, which means that parallel edges of the cube are drawn as parallel lines in the picture. When two lines cross, the picture does not show which is in front and which is behind. This makes the picture ambiguous; it can be interpreted two different ways. When a person stares at the picture, it will often seem to flip back and forth between the two valid interpretations. The effect is interesting because each part of the picture is ambiguous by itself, yet the human visual system picks an interpretation of each part that makes the whole consistent. The Necker Cube is sometimes used to test computer models of the human visual system to see whether they can arrive at consistent interpretations of the image the same way humans do. Humans do not usually see an inconsistent interpretation of the cube. A cube whose edges cross in an inconsistent way is an example of an impossible object, specifically an impossible cube.

There is evidence that by focusing on different parts of the figure one can force a more stable perception of the cube. The intersection of the two faces that are parallel to the observer forms a rectangle, and the lines that converge on the square form a "y-junction" at the two diagonally opposite sides. If an observer focuses on the upper "y-junction" the lower left face will appear to be in front. The upper right face will appear to be in front if the eyes focus on the lower junction (Einhauser, et al., 2004).

Two important points are concerned with Necker Cube. First, there are two interpretations; second, they cannot be observed at the same time. It shows that matching is necessary entity corresponded and there exists competition, which may be expressed by weighing of zone structure mentioned above with eyes moving.

Figure 1c was introduced by Gaetano Kanizsa (1955). Everyone sees a white triangle in front of the three black disks and inverted triangle. However, the white triangle does not exist. This effect is known as a subjective or illusory contour. Also, the nonexistent white triangle appears to be brighter than the surrounding area, but in fact it has the same brightness as the background. This illusion reveals the importance of subjectivity. Any minds are subjective. There is subjective objectivity, but difficult to make clear objective objectivity. In nature, this illusion reflects furthermore the significance of weighing coefficient, which determines how part can yield the whole.

To Figure 1d, when we stare at the black point and move our head back and forward, we feel rotating. Regardless of the mechanism of this Illusion, it is selected to show that illusive rotation is equivalent to real rotation to mind in case of same representation.

Four visual illusions are given, the phenomena indicates the general existence of relativity in our minds.

4.2 Synesthesia

Next, we discuss an experiment about synesthesia (Ramachandran, 2003), which was said a window into the nature of thought. We are mainly concerned with the mechnism of attention.

To synesthetes, Figure 2a will be like Figure 2b to us, so the triangle formed by 2 will pop-out to them. It shows synesthesia is a genuine sensory. In Figure 3a, if we stare at the small plus sign, we will find that it is easy to discern the number 5 off to one side. But if the 5 is surrounded by other numbers, such as 3's, then we can no longer identify it (Figure 3b). Big surprise is that to two synesthetes, "I cannot see the middle number. It's fuzzy but it looks red, so I guess it must be a 5." How can an "invisible" number produce synesthesia? So it must be visible to color feeling but invisible to shape feeling. This also indicates that reason of unidentification is not because things get fuzzy in the periphery of vision. After all, we could see the 5 perfectly clearly when it wasn't surrounded by 3's. We cannot identify it now because of limited attentive resources. The flanking 3's somehow distract our attention away from the central 5 and prevent us from seeing it. The experiment makes clear the importance of mechanism of attention before representation and recognition.

(a) (b)

Fig. 2. (a) 2's amid 5's (b) 2's pops out for a synesthete

(a) (b)

Fig. 3. (a) a single digit off to one side is easy to see with peripheral vision (b) number 5 is surrounded by others

Another contrast experiment was made in the same paper. When we reduced the contrast between the number and the background, the synesthetic color became weaker until, at low contrast, subjects saw no color at all, even though the number was perfectly visible. That is, whereas the crowding experiment shows that an "invisible" number can elicit color, the contrast experiment conversely indicates that viewing a number does not guarantee seeing a color. They are actually all attention problem that we will mention later.

4.3 Neuroscience

Recently, as the discovery of synchronous oscillation in the visual cortex, some hypothesis and models were presented (Fujii et al, 1996; Watanabe et al, 2001; Zhao et al, 2003). Synchronous oscillation can be thought as a mechanism of attention and could be combined with ZART easily.

Every object is expressed by elements with relations of each other. Each element could be expressed by a matrix, or a series of numbers, which may be the codes being discovered by Lin et al (2006). Combined with פ algorithm (Hsiao et al., 2009), a method can solve outlier problem at the same time when object is identified, ZART might become more robust. There is also evidence for פ algorithm. Recent study also shows that traditional view that figure-ground segregation precedes object recognition may not be right, and though their data cannot determine whether the extra time needed for identification compared to categorization reflects the engagement of a different mechanism or simply a longer engagement of the same mechanism involved in categorization (Kalanit Grill-Spector and Nancy Kanwisher, 2005). They believe it is possible that the initial neuronal responses are sufficient for detection and later neural responses are necessary for identification.

Latest study found that concept and knowledge have its neural encoding in the mouse brain (Lin et al. 2007). From the view of ZART, a concept is something that origins from the common of the same type of objects experienced. In detail, a concept is the common elements and their relations of that type. Undoubtedly, concept can be encoded.

The study presents a feasible model. Our brain may not be complete same as the model, but since what we focus on is to realize mind, we are not required to keep same with the real brain.

5. Natural Classification

As discussed above, attention should be exerted before representation and recognition (mutual case may exist), which is a process of natural classification. An ontological classification method - Expanding Algorithm can be employed to solve this problem. Some applications are accounted as following.

5.1 Cornsweet Illusion

The Cornsweet illusion shown in Figure 4 is an optical illusion that was described in detail by Cornsweet (1970). In the image, the entire region to the right of the "edge" in the middle looks slightly lighter than the area to the left of the edge, but in fact the brightness of both areas is exactly the same, as can be seen by blacking out the region containing the edge. Purves et al. (2002) gave an explanation of this illusion on an empirical basis. In their words, "...[perception] accords not with the features of the retinal stimulus or the properties of the underlying objects, but with what the same or similar stimuli have typically signified in the past".

Fig. 4. Cornsweet illusion. Left part of the picture seems to be darker than the right one. In fact, there have the same brightness.

Explanation based on experience is always effective. While in this case, it is a simple classification problem based on mind, which can be solved easily by Expanding Algorithm. Different values of gray scales could be expressed by one dimensional data sets, major brightness in this image is 173 (0 is black and 255 is white), values of two sides are listed by pixel as a set C{173, 172, 171, 170, 169, 168, 167, 178, 177, 176, 175, 174, 173}. The narrow band from 172 to 167 and 178 to 174 in the middle brings different bright feeling to same most 173s on both sides.

By running Expanding Algorithm to set C, we can divide them into two parts easily. One part is from 173 to 167, 178 to 173 is the other. Though there might be other complicated mechanism in visual system, such division is enough. Mind has to make a distinction, the key is in where. All perceptible things are related to Expanding Algorithm, which is a basis algorithm of mind. There is no absolute division like all 173s should be felt same, it depends.
We consider another example where more than two classes are involved. Used data is Ruspini dataset (Index, 2009).

5.2 Multiple Classes

The Ruspini dataset consists of 75 points (Figure 5) in four groups, which is popular for illustrating clustering techniques (Ruspini, 1970). Clustering is one of the classic problems in machine learning. A popular method is k-means clustering (Lloyd, 1982; Arthur and Vassilvitskii, 2007). Although its simplicity and speed are very appealing in practice, it offers no accuracy guarantee. Furthermore exactly solving the problem is NP-hard (Drineas, et al, 2004). Like k-means, most algorithms use center to represent a cluster, each element is classified according to the distance between it and its closest center. Real case is not always so. According to recent studies (Hsiao et al., 2008; 2009), absolute center is not necessary. "Family resemblance" also demands us to throw away the concept of center (it doesn't mean that center is useless). Based on these theories, a new method is presented to cluster Ruspini data.

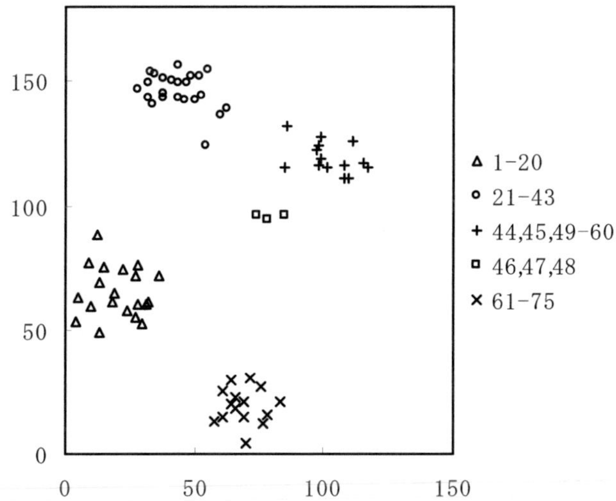

Fig. 5. Ruspini data (five clusters by Oscillator Algorithm)

Given Ruspini data sets D $\{d_1, d_2, \ldots, d_{75}\}$ with each point as a cell.

Oscillator Algorithm:

1. Calculate distances between any two points d_i and d_j.
2. To any point d_i, arrange its distance series (with others) in ascending order.
3. Calculate series of any i by Expanding Algorithm (Safest point is the first one and at least including three points for more than two classes exist). Getting 75 clustering sets.
4. Random choose one point as a seed with firing intensity 1 (others 0).
5. Any partner (clustering member) of the firing cell can receive its stimulus thus begin to fire with same intensity, others receive an identical negative input.
6. Repeat step 5 till all cells keep same or are full charged (include negative charged).
7. To all cells with positive firing, cluster them to one.
8. Choose rest points, repeat from step 4 to step 7.
9. Alternative approach: combine all the results of each cell, determine clusters.

Cluster	Included Elements	Number of elements with right clustering	Silent elements	Probability for right clustering
1	1-20	18	17, 20	90%
2	21-43	21	41, 42	91%
3	44,45,49-60	11	44,45,58	79%
4	46,47,48	2	46	67%
5	61-75	15	-	100%

Table 1. Clustering summarization from the view of each element

Figure 5 shows the clustering condition by Oscillator Algorithm. The data are clustered into five. Considering the small scale of cluster 4 (46-48), we can easily merge it with its nearest neighbor - cluster 3. In that case, result keeps same with the designed. But if there is no extra information or restrict, cluster 4 can also be treated as outlier. Table 1 lists a detailed result by Oscillator Algorithm. Each cell was chosen as seed in turn, two kinds of results were achieved. One matches the result of five clusters, in the other case, cells keep silent, it means corresponding cell had no way to call a resonance. The result appears positive, furthermore, it is totally based on uncertainty- that is what we need for mind.

6. Related Work and Discussion

For object recognition, good method should be robust to noise. Hough Transform is such a technique. Developed by Hough (1962), the transform consists of parameterizing a description of a feature at any given location in the original image's space. A mesh in the space defined by these parameters is then generated, and at each mesh point a value is accumulated, indicating how well an object generated by the parameters defined at that point fits the given image. Mesh points that accumulate relatively larger values then describe features that may be projected back onto the image, fitting to some degree the features actually present in the image. The classical Hough transform was concerned with the identification of lines in the image, later the Hough transform has been extended to identifying positions of arbitrary shapes (Duda and Hart, 1972; Ballard, 1981), called Generalized Hough Transform (GHT).

Although the GHT is optimal for an object that has undergone simple translation, it is far less efficient when an object has also undergone rotation and scaling. Chord-Tangent Transformation (CTT) was thus presented (Dufresne and Dhawan, 1995). The method exploits a simple relationship existed between tangent points and chord lines which allow a transformation which is invariant to rotation, translation and scale. The C-table designed has many similarities to the R-table of the GHT, yet differs in the gradient for index. The GHT uses the absolute gradient of the tangent, while the CCT uses two relative measures of the gradients of a pair of tangents. It is such relativity that guarantees the invariance, which is awfully important in object recognition. In contrast, ART is completed based on relativity.

Another relativity-related tool for object recognition is the shape context (Balongie, et al, 2002), which has been shown to be a powerful one. The shape context is a descriptor to each point in a shape, which captures the distribution of the remaining points relative to it thus offering a globally discriminative characterization. Corresponding points on two similar shapes will have similar shape contexts; the dissimilarity between two shapes is computed as a sum of matching errors between corresponding points, together with a term measuring the magnitude of the aligning transform. The recognition is treated as the problem of finding the stored prototype shape that is maximally similar to that in the image.

ZART has many similarities to the shape context, both have a global descriptor to each point, both try to find corresponding match, both compute dissimilarity between two shapes by a sum of matching errors, both should solve problem of prototype shape. But there exists obvious difference. The shape context is like the original Chinese Room, where many persons do not see mind, while ZART is designed for mind, being of redundant structural knowledge.

Another important technique should be mentioned is AdaBoost, short for Adaptive Boosting, which is formulated by Freund and Schapire (1997). Boosting is a general approach to improve of a given classifier and is one of the most powerful techniques, together with the support vector machines (Theodorideis and Koutroumbas, 2006). The roots of boosting go back to the original work of Viliant and Kearns (Viliant, 1984; Kearns and Viliant, 1994), who posed the question whether a "weak" learning algorithm (i.e., one that performs just slightly better than a random guessing) can be boosted into a strong algorithm with good error performance. The answer is very impressive indeed. The final classifier is obtained as a weighted average of the previously hierarchically designed classifiers. It turned out that given a sufficient number of iterations the classification error of the final combination measured on the training set can become arbitrarily low (Schapire, 1998). Sense of AdaBoost is great: the best is not necessary thus does not exist, there are no magic recipes, and the underlying principle might be relativity. AdaBoost, פּ algorithm and the Chinese Room all imply that syntax is enough for intelligence, does mind really make sense?

Face recognition was thought to be "special" and differ from other object recognition (Farah et al. 1998) in "holistically" (i.e., using relatively less part decomposition than other types of objects). But such distinction does not make significant sense since it is a problem of less and more. Early research by Phodes (1988) indicated that both first (local, i.e. eye, nose, and so on.) and second order features (configurational, i.e. spatial relations among first order features and the position of first order features, along with information about face shape.) were relevant determinants of facial appearance. Up to latest studies, there is no change to it as Khashman (2008) reviewed, "One common concept that is shared by most methods is that the detection of a face requires facial information, which can be obtained locally (using local facial features such as eyes) or globally (using a whole face)". The reason that we use more holistic feature is just that the local one does not work. There is no changeless pattern for mind. Codes are all in ZART, the other work is just mining.

7. Conclusion and Future Work

This chapter proposed a framework to mind problem. A Zone-Associated Relative representation (ZART) was presented for objects. Corresponding method for recognition was also accompanied. Some evidence in psychology and neuroscience was reviewed to support the proposal. Besides, a novel Oscillator Algorithm based on Expanding Algorithm was introduced to simulate the visual mechanism of attention, which is a process pre-head of representation and recognition. Related work has been compared carefully. The whole work was approached from a new one. Algorithms were constructed on uncertainty, which was argued to be necessary to a mind.

Since Feigenbaum formulated the hypothesis about the power of domain-specific knowledge (Feigenbaum, 1977), a great deal of experiments have been done and strongly supported the view. "The power of AI programs to perform at high levels of competence is primarily a function of the program's knowledge of its task domain, and not the program's reasoning processes"(Feigenbaum, 1996). Knowledge-based system is in essence a relative system. The simplest knowledge representation is a kind of rules like the Chinese Room (even the worst knowledge is better than logic), where intelligence appears rather well. But we expect more.

Before we leave the Chinese Room, we have to reach a conclusion. Understanding is to build relations between outside and outside or outside and inside, and mind is to represent and yield understanding. Degree of comprehension is hierarchy of relations. In this way, it is obvious that Searle's Chinese Room is not of "mind" indeed. No representation, no mind.

Very recently, Hamlin et al. (2007) reported that 6- and 10-month-old infants showed crucial social judging skills before they could talk, which does not stem from infants' own experiences with the actors involved. If it is true, we have more to do.

Future work includes further research to ZART and its application in AI, new neural network model and information retrieval. Parallel work includes psychological study to mind.

8. References

Arthur, D. and Vassilvitskii, S. (2007). k-means++ The Advantages of Careful Seeding, *Symposium on Discrete Algorithms (SODA).*

Ballard, D.H. (1981). Generalizing the Hough Transform to Detect Arbitrary Shapes. *Pattern Recognition*, vol. 13, no.2, pp. 111-122.

Belongie, S., Malik, J. and Puzicha, J. (2002). Shape matching and object recognition using shape contexts, *IEEE Transactions on Pattern Analysis and Machine Intelligence*, vol. 24, no. 24.

Biederman, I. (1987) Recognition-by-comonents: a theory of human image understanding. *Psychol Rev*, vol. 94, pp. 115-147.

Bruce, V. (1988). *Recognising Faces*, Lawrence Erlbaum Associates.

Bulthoff, H. H., Edelman, S. (1992). Psychophysical support for a 2-d view inerpolation theory of object recognition. *Proceedings of the National Academy of Science of USA*, vol. 89, pp. 60-64.

Cornsweet T. (1970). *Visual Perception*, Acadamic Press, NewYork.

Drineas, P., Frieze, A., Kannan, R., Vempala, S. and Vinay, V. (2004). Clustering large graphs via the singular value decomposition. *Mach. Learn.*, vol. 56, pp. 9-33.

Duda, R. O. and Hart, P. E. (1972). Use of the hough transformation to detect lines and curves in pictures. *Comm. ACM*, Vol. 15, pp. 11–15.

Dufresne, T. E. and Dhawan, A. P. (1995). Chord-tangent transformation for object recognition, *Pattern Recognition*, vol. 28, no. 9, pp. 1321-1332.

Edelman, S. (1999). *Representation and Recognition in Vision*, MIT Press.

Einhäuser, W., Martin, Kevan A. C. and König, P. (2004). Are switches in perception of the Necker cube related to eye position? *European Journal of Neuroscience*, vol. 20, no. 10, pp. 2811-2818.

Farah, M. J., Wilson, K. D., Drain M. and Tanaka, J. N. (1998). What is "Special" About Face Perception? *Psychological Review*, vol. 105, no.3, pp. 482-498.

Feigenbaum, E. A. (1977). The art of artificial intelligence: themes and case studies of knowledge engineering. *Proceedings of the International Joint Conference on Artificial Intelligence V*, Boston.

Feigenbaum, E. A. (1996). How the "What" Becomes the "How". *Communications of the ACM*, vol. 39, no. 5, pp. 97-104.

Foster, D. H. and Gilson, S. J. (2002). Recognizing novel three-dimensional objects by summing signals from parts and views. *Proc R Soc Lond B*, vol. 269, pp. 1939-1947.

Freund Y., Schapire R.E. (1997). A decision theoretic generalization of on-line learning and an application to boosting, *Journal of Computer and System Sciences*, vol. 55, no. 1, pp. 119-139.

Fujii, H., Ito, H., Aihara, K., Ichinose, N. and Tsukada, M. (1996). Dynamical cell assembly hypothesis — theoretical possibility of spatio-temporal coding in the cortex, *Neural Neworks*, vol.9, no.8, pp. 1303-1350.

Gonzalez, R.C. and Woods, R.E. (2008). *Digital Image Processing*, 3rd , Pearson Prentice Hall.

Gregory, R. L. (1968). Perceptual illusions and brain models. *Proceedings of the Royal Society of London. Series B, Biological Science*, vol. 171, issue 1024, pp. 279–296.

Grill-Spector, K. and Kanwisher, N. (2005). Visual recognition: as soon as you know it is there, you know what it is. *Psychological Science*, vol.16, no. 2, Feb 2005, pp. 152-160.

Hamlin, J. K., Wynn, K. and Bloom,P. (2007). Social evaluation by preverbal infants. *Nature*, Vol 450, Nov 22, 2007.

Hartle, J.B. (2003). *Gravity: An Introduction to Einstein's General Relativity*, Addison Wesley.

Haywood, W. G. (2003). After the viewoint debate: where next in object recognition. *Trends Cogn Sci*, vol. 7, pp 425-427.

Hough, P.V.C. (1962). Method and means for recognizing complex patterns, *U. S. patent 3,069,654*, December 18, 1962.

Howe, C. Q. and Purves, D. (2005). The Muller-Lyer illusion explained by the statistics of image-source relationships. *PNAS*, vol. 102, no. 4, pp. 1234-1239.

Hsiao, C.-A., Chen, H., Furuse, K. and Ohbo, N. (2008). A relative deviation detection for time series data based on Equality, *Proceedings of International Multi-Conference on Engineer and Computer Scientist Vol 1*, pp. 511-516.

Hsiao, C.-A., Chen, H., Furuse, K. and Ohbo, N. (2009). Figure and ground: a complete approach to outlier detection, In: *IAENG Transactions on Engineering Technologies Vol 1*, Ao, S.-L., Chan, A. H.-S., Katagiri, H., Castillo, O. and Xu, L., (Eds.), pp. 70-81, American Institute of Physics, New York.

Hummel, J. E. (2001). Complementary solutions to the binding problem in vision: implications for shape perception and object recognition. *Vis Cogn*, vol. 8, pp. 489-517.

Hutter, M. (2005). *Universal Artificial Intelligence*, Springer.

Index of /~burkardt/f_src/kmeans. (2009), retrieved April 20, 2009, from https://people.sc.fsu.edu/~burkardt/f_src/kmeans/ruspini.txt

Juttner, M. (2007). Part-based strategies for visual categorisation and object recognition, In: *Object Recognition, Attention, and Action*, Osaka, N., Rentschler, I. and Biederman, I., (Eds.), pp. 55-70, Springer, Japan.

Kanizsa, G. (1955), Margini quasi-percettivi in campi con stimolazione omogenea. *Rivista di Psicologia*, vol. 49, no. 1, pp. 7–30.

Kearns M., Valiant L.G. Cryptographic limitations on learning boolean formulae and finite automata. *Journal of the ACM*, vol. 41, no. 1, pp. 67-95.

Khashman, A. (2008). Intelligent Local Face Recognition Recent, in: *Advances in Face Recognition*, Delac, K., Grgic, M. and Bartlett, M. S. (Eds.), In-Teh.

Lin L., Osan, R. And Tsien, J. Z. (2006). Organizing principles of real-time memory encoding: neural clique assemblies and universal neural codes. *TRENDS in Neurosciences*, vol.29, no.1, January 2006.

Lin, L., Chen, G., Kuang, H., Wang, D. And Tsien, J. Z. (2007). Neural encoding of the concept of nest in the mouse brain. *PNAS*, vol. 104, no. 14, April 3, 2007, pp. 6066-6071.

Lloyd, S. P. (1982). Least squares quantization in pcm. *IEEE Transactions on Information Theory*, vol. 28, no. 2, pp. 129-136.

Marr, D. (1982). *Vision*, W.H. Freeman and company, San Francisco.

Menger, C. (1871/1994). *Principles of economics, reprint*, Libertarian Press.

Osaka, N., Rentschler, I. and Biederman, I. (2007). *Object Recognition, Attention, and Action*, Springer

Pinna, B., Brelstaff, G. J. (2000). A new visual illusion of relative motion. *Vision Res* vol. 40, pp. 2091–2096.

Poggio, T., Edelman, S. (1990). A network that learns to recognize 3-dimensional objects. *Nature* vol. 343, pp. 263-266.

Purves, D., Lotto, R.B. and Nundy, S. (2002). Why we see what we do. *American Scientist*, vol. 90, No.3, pp.236-243.

Ramachandran, V. S. and Hubbard, E. M. (2003). Hearing Colors, Tasting Shapes. *Scientific American*, vol 288, Issue 5, pp. 42-49.

Rhodes, G. (1988). Looking at faces: first-order and second-order features as determinates of facial appearance. *Perception*, vol. 17, pp43-63.

Ruspini, E. H. (1970). Numerical methods for fuzzy clustering. *Inform Sci*, vol. 2, pp. 319-350.

Russell, S. and Norvig, P. (2003). *Artificial Intelligence: A Modern Approach*, 2nd, Prentice Hall.

Salton, G. & Buckley, C. (1988). Term-weighting approaches in automatic text retrieval. *Information Processing and Management*, vol. 24, no. 5, pp. 513-523.

Schapire R.E., Freund V., Bartlett P., Lee W.S. (1998). Boosting the margin: A new explanation for the effectiveness of voting methods, *the Annals of Statistics*, vol.26, no.5, pp. 1651-1686.

Searle, J. R. (1980). Minds, Brains, and Programs. *Behavioral and Brain Sciences*, vol. 3, pp. 417-424.

Segall, M. H., Campbell, D. T. and Herskovits, M. J. (1963). Cultural differences in the perception of geometrical illusions. *Science*, vol. 139, pp. 769-771.

Sparck J. K. (1972). A statistical interpretation of term specificity and its application in retrieval. *Journal of Documentation*, vol. 28, no. 1, pp. 11-21.

Stankiewicz, B. J. (2002). Empirical evidence for independent dimensions in the visual representation of three-dimensional shape. *J Exp Psychol Hum*, vol. 28, pp. 913-932.

Theodoridis, S. and Koutroumbas, K. (2006). *Pattern Recognition*, 3rd, Elsevier.

Thoma, V., Hummmel, J. E. and Davidoff, J. (2004). Evidence for holistic representations of ignored images and analytic representations of attended images. *J Exp Psychol Hum* vol. 30, pp. 257-267.

Valiant L.G. (1984). A theory of the learnable. *Communications of the ACM,* vol. 27, no. 11, pp. 1134-1142.

Vuilleumier, P., Henson, R. N., Driver, J. and Dolan, R. J. (2002). Multiple levels of visual object constancy revealed by event-related fMRI of repition priming. *Nat Neurosci* vol. 5, pp. 491-499.

Wallraven, C. and Bulthoff, H. H. (2007). Object Recognition in Humans and Machines, In: *Object Recognition, Attention, and Action,* Osaka, N., Rentschler, I. and Biederman, I., (Eds.), pp. 89-104, Springer, Japan.

Watanabe, M., Nakanishi, K. and Aihara, K. (2001). Solving the binding problem of the brain with bi-directional functional connectivity, *Neural Networks,* vol. 14, issue 4-5, May 2001.

Wittgenstein, L. (1922). *Tractatus Logico-Philosophicus.*

Wittgenstein, L. (1974). *On Certainty,* Blackwell.

Wittgenstein. L. (1953/2001). *Philosophical Investigations,* Blackwell.

Zhao, S., Xiong, X., Yao, G. and Fu, Z. (2003). A computational Model as neurodecoder based on synchronous oscillation in the visual cortex, *Neural Computation* vol. 15, pp. 2399-2418.

9

Adaptive implementation of nonlinear fuzzy image enhancement algorithms in the compressed JPEG images

Camelia Florea, Aurel Vlaicu, Mihaela Gordan and Bogdan Orza
Technical University of Cluj-Napoca
Romania

1. Introduction

With the increasing sizes of high resolution images, their storage and processing directly in the compressed domain has significantly gained importance. Algorithms for compressed domain image processing (Smith, 1993) provide a powerful computational alternative to classical (pixel level) based implementations. While linear algorithms can be applied straightforward to the DCT (Discrete Cosine Transform) encoded JPEG images, this is not the case for non-linear image processing, as for example contrast enhancement algorithms. The implementation of operations involving nonlinear operators is challenging, but not impossible, and when the right combination is found, the processing is much faster, due to the reduced number of coefficients, because the majority of the coefficients in the DCT domain are zero after the quantization.

The field of image processing in the compressed domain is just emerging and the algorithms reported in the literature are mostly based on linear arithmetic operations between pixels. Implementations of image and video sequence processing in the compressed JPEG/MPEG domain are already presented in the literature. Tang (Tang, 2004) defined an algorithm based on the contrast, measured as the ratio of high-frequency content and low-frequency content in the bands of the DCT matrix. In (An et al., 2004) is used the Tang algorithm but each block is enhanced according to its block classification: smooth block or high activity block. A MPEG based image enhancement algorithm for people with low-vision was developed (Kim & Peli, 2003); the contrast enhancement was performed by modifying the quantization matrices for inter and intra frames. Lee (Lee, 2006) uses a basic concept of the Retinex theory for the enhancement of images, directly in the compressed domain.

In recent years, many researchers have applied the fuzzy set theory (Pedrycz & Gomide, 1998; Tizhoosh, 2000; Gonzales, 2008) to develop new techniques for contrast improvement. Fuzzy rule-based contrast enhancement and fuzzy intensification operator, are well-known rather simple approaches with good visual results, but as any fuzzy algorithm, these are by default nonlinear, thus not straightforward applicable on the JPEG bitstream (zig-zag ordered quantized DCT coefficients). Few solutions are reported for this issue, having moderate performances.

This chapter intends to present our approach to a fast and accurate alternative implementation in the compressed domain, for fuzzy image processing algorithms with one or few thresholds as main non-linearity, the other non-linearitys being implementable by classical operations in the compressed domain (as the square in the case of the intensification operator) or not needing an explicit non-linear formulation (as is the case of the fuzzy inference in the Takagi-Sugeno fuzzy systems). The solution proposed here can also be applied to other Takagi-Sugeno fuzzy systems for image processing, or for other types of linguistic modifiers (not only the intensification operator) that one can find useful for image processing. Particularly the strategy is applied on two well-known contrast enhancement methods: the one based on the fuzzy intensification operator, and the fuzzy rule-based contrast enhancement method with a Takagi-Sugeno system. The fuzzy sets parameters are adaptively chosen by analyzing the histogram of the DC coefficients of the compressed blocks as an approximation of the grey level statistics of the image, in order to optimally enhance the image contrast.

The core idea behind the presented strategy refers to the implementation of the brightness threshold comparisons, for which an adaptive solution which takes into account the frequency content of each block in the compress domain JPEG image is suggested. More specifically, this adaptive approach consists in conditionally deciding the need for decompression and pixel level thresholding in a DCT transformed pixel block, only when this is strictly required to preserve accuracy (by a large amount of AC energy of the block). In all the other cases it is enough to compare the DC coefficient (average grey level) value of the block to the equivalent grey level threshold, which is a good estimate of the location of all the pixels brightness versus the threshold. Such an algorithm has been proven (by experiments) to significantly increase the computational efficiency in image processing algorithms applied to a JPEG image (preserving the visual quality of the processing result). The computational efficiency is high since by the strategy, one can avoid the decompression and recompression prior and after the processing. This guarantees the optimal quality at minimum computational cost. The performance of the suggested approach, applied on the 2 fuzzy contrast enhancement methods mentioned above is illustrated in this chapter on several grey scale and color images, and some implementation details are also given. The algorithm is applied only on the luminance component. However, it can be used to enhance color images as well, with no change of the chrominance components (which is a rather common approach in color image enhancement).

2. Fuzzy image enhancement algorithms

Image enhancement involves processing an image in order to make it visually more pleasant to the observers. It is one of the fundamental tasks in image processing. Images have sometimes poor contrast or are blurred. Image enhancement includes a series of different point and spatial operations to improve the contrast, as: piecewise linear grey scale stretching transformation, grey scale clipping, histogram modification/equalization or even highly nonlinear grey scale mappings (Gonzales, 2008).

A particular class of useful techniques in image contrast enhancement is provided by the application of fuzzy sets theory and fuzzy inference systems to this task. The fuzzy sets theory's foundation was set by Prof. Zadeh in 1965 (Zadeh, 1965), followed later on by the fuzzy logic basis, established in 1973; since then, the applications of fuzzy sets theory and fuzzy logic to scientific computing are extremely vast, and still continue to evolve, along with other modern algorithms in the area of soft computing. In short, to underline the essence of "fuzzy thinking", which makes it such an appealing tool for the reformulation and implementation of various data processing algorithms, one can see fuzzy variables, fuzzy logic and fuzzy reasoning as the extension of the crisp (binary) reasoning to the infinite valued logic case, which allows for a mathematical representation of the imprecision and uncertainty in the definition of terms - typical to the human-like thinking - and, dually, for a certain "granularity" in defining otherwise precise terms in a more "approximate", flexible manner. Thus, the fuzzy sets theory and fuzzy logic framework has the main benefit of allowing to still work with a small set of terms, as, e.g.: yes/no answers, true/false evaluations, black/white categorization, but behind each such term, one understand by default (as in the natural language) a certain amount of imprecision, approximation: black is rather "nearly black", not only the black body's black; white is "nearly white", not only pure snow-like white; and, a certain grey can be to some extent, let's say, dark enough to be similar to black, or white enough to be similar to white, or maybe, almost at all black nor white. Of course, for the natural way in which humans express their reasoning and for their interpretation of the observations, there is nothing special in this kind of processing; however the fuzzy mathematical framework is what provides the required foundation to implement this close to human-like thinking in computer programming.

The core concepts behind fuzzy logic and fuzzy reasoning are: the fuzzy set; the operations on fuzzy sets; the fuzzy relations (which are often expressed in the form of fuzzy rules); the fuzzy approximate reasoning. The fuzzy sets, also called linguistic terms, are generalizations of the crisp sets from the classical sets theory, in the sense that they are categorizations of data with associated soft membership degrees having any values between 0 (no membership at all) and 1 (complete membership), showing in fact how much similar is the data to the prototype of the category. One can also see any fuzzy set as a linguistic value for a human-like expressed concept - e.g., in the example above, black; in the human language, black is more than pure perfect black (the dark body's black), as we are all aware of. But even so, we can say that a dark grey satisfies the concept "black" rather than the concept "average grey" or "white", thus, we would assign it some membership degree of, e.g., 0.8 to the fuzzy set "black" and only 0.2 to a fuzzy set representing the concept "average grey". The specification of the memberships of all data range over which the fuzzy set has been defined (according to the type of data we attempt to describe by our sets) gives the most important attribute of a fuzzy set, by which the fuzzy set can be completely described, i.e., *the membership function of the fuzzy set*. Let us denote the set of all data of some given type that we want to describe/analyze by X; this set is usually referred as the *universe of discourse* in fuzzy sets theory. Let us consider that a fuzzy set A should group the data satisfying an approximate concept c_A. Then the definition of this fuzzy set is complete if its membership function, expressed as: $A: X \to [0;1]$, is given.

Various operations can be applied on and between fuzzy sets - most of them being extensions of the crisp sets operations. Some of them, as the complement of a fuzzy set, the intensification, the fuzzification, the power of a fuzzy set, are unary operators (with a single operand). Others, as the union and the intersection of fuzzy sets, are binary or n-ary operators (with two or many operands).

Fuzzy logic, on the other hand, is based on both the concept of fuzzy sets and fuzzy rules. Just as fuzzy sets are generalization of crisp sets, *fuzzy rules* are generalization of the crisp rules employed in classical expert systems. Fuzzy logic theory is employed in the *fuzzy logic systems*, which are the algorithmic representation of fuzzy reasoning based on rules. A fuzzy logic system, also called fuzzy rule-based system or fuzzy inference system, is just a data processing system having on its input - the crisp value of the input (observed) data, and on its output - the value of some output variable, generated as a result of some fuzzy processing, computed through a *fuzzy inference mechanism* (which implements the *approximate reasoning theory*), based on the representation of the input data classes and output data classes as fuzzy sets and on expressing some associations between the input and the output data classes (input and output fuzzy sets) - associations called *fuzzy rules* and expressed as *fuzzy relations*. Several variants of fuzzy logic systems are currently available; among them, the most widely used are the *Mamdani fuzzy inference systems* (characterized by the presence of fuzzy sets over the input and the output data spaces) and the *Takagi-Sugeno fuzzy inference systems* (in which the input data space is described by fuzzy sets, but the output data space is covered by singleton sets - that is, crisp sets containing each a single data value). The Takagi-Sugeno fuzzy systems are especially appealing for their simple forms and the simplicity of the computations required.

Fuzzy sets and fuzzy rule based systems proved to be powerful tools also for several signal and image processing applications, as often reported in the literature since '80s (Tizhoosh, 2000; Bezdek, 1999). Basically, the theoretical fuzzy sets/fuzzy logic framework found on the basis of grey scale processing is the following: the grey level distribution (grey level range) of a digital image can be modeled by a single fuzzy set or by a fuzzy partition, describing linguistically the concept of "bright" or of "degrees of brightness". This is compliant to the human perception of the brightness, and therefore allows an easy formulation (in linguistic terms) of several desired grey scale modification algorithms. Then, by applying some operators on the membership functions associated to these fuzzy sets, or by formulating fuzzy logic rules specifying how the output brightness in some spatial location should depend on the input brightness in the original image (rules that are further incorporated in the knowledge base of an image processing fuzzy inference system), one can achieve different processing of the grey levels in the image (of the grey scale dynamics in the image).

A particularly useful class of such fuzzy image processing methods is that of fuzzy contrast enhancement methods - based on both fuzzy sets theory and fuzzy rules based systems (Pal & King, 1981; Pedrycz, 1998; Tizhoosh, 2000). However, few of these frequently used contrast enhancement methods have presented equivalent implementation in the compressed domain, probably because of their nonlinear nature.

2.1. The fuzzy sets based contrast INT (intensification) algorithm as a grey scale transformation

This method is implemented, in principle, by a very simple operation in the fuzzy sets theory: the intensification operation applied on a fuzzy membership function. In principle, one can represent/model the grey scale of a digital image by a single fuzzy set, describing the linguistic concept of "bright levels": depending on the particular grey level content of each image, more or less of its pixels will have high membership degrees to this fuzzy set. Roughly speaking, if a grey level has a membership less than 0.5 to the "bright levels" set, it is more likely to be dark than bright, whereas in the opposite case it is more likely to be bright than dark. Then, an intensification operator applied on this fuzzy set (Pedrycz &

Gomide, 1998) will increase the membership degrees above 0.5 and decrease the membership degrees below 0.5. If the "intensified" fuzzy set membership function is used in conjunction with the initially defined grey scale to membership function mapping, one can map the newly obtained membership values back to gray levels, and of course for the grey levels that had membership above 0.5 (memberships that are now increased) we will obtain more brighter corresponding grey levels, and the opposite for the memberships below 0.5.
This would naturally lead to contrast improvement; recall that this basic point processing operation aims mainly to maximize (increase) the dynamic range of the image. A higher contrast in an image can be achieved by darkening the gray levels in the lower luminance range (typically under 0.5 on a [0; 1] scale) and brightening the ones in the upper luminance range (Gonzales & Woods, 2008).
In the following, the mathematical formulation of the fuzzy set based contrast intensification operation for image contrast enhancement is briefly summarized. Let us consider a very simple (trapezoidal shaped) fuzzy set membership function for representing the concept of "Bright" grey levels, with the linguistic meaning defined above; this is a typical form in fuzzy image processing algorithms - shown below in Fig.1.a. Let us denote the membership function of this fuzzy set by B: L → [0; 1]. Let $INT(\cdot), INT:[0;1] \rightarrow [0;1]$ be the intensification operator applied to a fuzzy membership function.
Thinking in fuzzy terms, according to the meaning of the "Bright" fuzzy set, the lower the dynamic range of the actually observed image will be, the more the membership degrees different (further apart) from 0 and 1 we will have. Thus, the lower the contrast of the image, the larger will be the fuzziness of the fuzzy set. Therefore, in terms of fuzzy membership degrees, enhancing the contrast would roughly mean to reduce the fuzziness of the set (Pal & King, 1981; Pedrycz, 1998). An easy way to achieve this is to apply the fuzzy intensification operator on the membership function of the fuzzy set introduced above. Then the resulting fuzzy set of reduced fuzziness will have the membership function $B': L \rightarrow [0; 1]$, given by:

$$B'(l) = INT(B(l)) = \begin{cases} 2 \cdot B^2(l), if\ 0 \le B(l) \le 0.5 \\ 1 - 2 \cdot (1 - B(l))^2, if\ 0.5 \le B(l) \le 1 \end{cases} \quad (1)$$

The expression in equation (1) represents a well known operator in the fuzzy sets theory, namely the intensification (INT) operator; when applied on digital images, it has the effect of contrast enhancement.

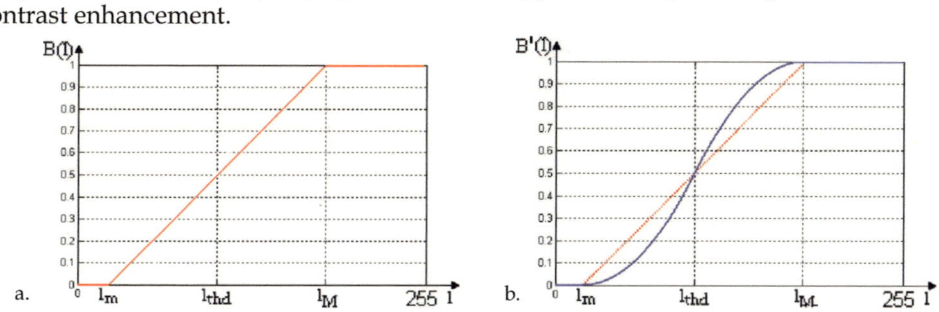

Fig. 1. a. The linear slope; b. The fuzzy intensification operator.

The choice of the fuzzy set membership function B is not unique, and its definition should be done depending on the particular application. However, for general purpose contrast enhancement tasks, a suitable (due to its simplicity) selection would be a piecewise linear shape, in the form presented in Fig.1.a. This is also the case considered in this paper, in order to allow for an efficient implementation in the compressed domain.
For this shape of B, the result of the fuzzy intensification operator would be the membership function B′ shown in Fig.1.b., with less fuzziness than B (or closer to a crisp set than B). The selection of the parameters l_m, l_M, l_{thd} or alternatively, of the slope of B in the range $[l_m; l_M]$ and of the parameter l_{thd} which gives $B(l_{thd}) = 0.5$, should be either set by default to some predefined values (e.g. typically $l_m = 0; l_M = 255; l_{thd} = 128$) or, for better performance, should be selected from the image histogram. In the latter case, the selection is based on the following rules:

- it is reasonable to assume that the value equally plausible to be considered dark and bright (i.e., of 0.5 membership to B) is the median grey level from the histogram;
- the grey level dynamics of the particular image, defined as $[l_{\min}; l_{Max}]$, where $l_{\min}$ = minimum grey level in the histogram and l_{Max} = the maximum grey level in the histogram, should obey the constraints:

$$\begin{aligned} & B(l_{\min}) > 0, \ and \\ & B(l_{Max}) < 1 \end{aligned} , \tag{2}$$

imposed by the fact that the maximum range of fuzzy membership degrees is $[0; 1]$ and that, to guarantee some contrast enhancement especially for narrow histograms, $l_{\min}$ and l_{Max} should not take the extreme membership values 0 and 1, which cannot be modified by the algorithm. In grey level notation terms, the constraint (2) can be rewritten as:

$$\begin{aligned} & l_m \le l_{\min}, \ and \\ & l_M \ge l_{Max} \end{aligned} , \tag{3}$$

We choose in this implementation to keep one constraint to the limit, i.e. either $(l_m = l_{\min} \ and \ l_M \ge l_{Max})$ or $(l_m \le l_{\min} \ and \ l_M = l_{Max})$, whatever of the two can be satisfied for the currently processed image.
Expressing analytically the membership function B from Fig.1.a. as:

$$B(l) = \begin{cases} 0, if \ l \in [0; l_m] \\ a \cdot l + b, if \ l \in [l_m; l_M], \\ 1, if \ l \in [l_M; 255] \end{cases} \tag{4}$$

and taking into account the above rules and constraints, we can express the slope a as:

$$a = \begin{cases} \dfrac{B(l_{thd}) - B(l_m)}{l_{thd} - l_{\min}}, & if \ (l_m = l_{\min} \quad and \ l_M \geq l_{Max}) \\ \dfrac{B(l_M) - B(l_{thd})}{l_{Max} - l_{thd}}, & if \ (l_m \leq l_{\min} \quad and \ l_M = l_{Max}) \end{cases}, \tag{5}$$

which is equivalent to:

$$a = \begin{cases} \dfrac{0.5}{l_{thd} - l_{\min}}, & if \ (l_m = l_{\min} \quad and \ l_M \geq l_{Max}) \\ \dfrac{0.5}{l_{Max} - l_{thd}}, & if \ (l_m \leq l_{\min} \quad and \ l_M = l_{Max}) \end{cases} \Rightarrow a = \frac{0.5}{\max\{(l_{thd} - l_{\min}),(l_{Max} - l_{thd})\}}. \tag{6}$$

The value of the second parameter, *b*, is obtain from $B(l_{thd})$:

$$B(l_{thd}) = 0.5 \Rightarrow a \cdot l_{thd} + b = 0.5 \Rightarrow b = 0.5 - a \cdot l_{thd}. \tag{7}$$

Notice that for the default case, $l_m = 0, l_M = 255, l_{thd} = 128$, the values of *a, b* will be: $a = \frac{1}{255}, b = 0.$

2.2. The fuzzy rule-based contrast enhancement algorithm

Another possible way to express the image contrast enhancement in terms of fuzzy logic is by the means of a Takagi-Sugeno fuzzy rule based system (Gonzalez & Woods, 2008; Tizhoosh, 2000). A common formulation assumes the description of the grey scale of the input image by 3 linguistic terms, denoted by *Dark, Gray* and *Bright.* Typically, the terms *Dark* and *Bright* are represented by trapezoidal-shaped fuzzy membership functions, whereas the term *Gray* is described by a triangular-shaped fuzzy membership function, as illustrated in Fig.2.a. Accordingly, on the universe of discourse of the output variable (i.e., the grey scale of the enhanced image), the other 3 linguistic terms are defined, referred heare as: *Darker, Midgray* and *Brighter.* Since we consider a Takagi-Sugeno fuzzy system, the output fuzzy sets will be fuzzy singleton (or, numerical constants denoted by l_v^d for *Darker*, l_v^g for *Midgray* and l_v^b for *Brighter*), as shown in Fig.2.b. If one denotes the input variable (describing grey levels in the input range) by l, $l \in \{0, 1, ..., 255\}$, and the output variable (describing the gray level in the output image) by l_o, $l_o \in \{0, 1, ..., 255\}$, the fuzzy rule base of the Takagi-Sugeno contrast enhancement fuzzy system comprises the following 3 rules:

R1: IF l is *Dark* THEN l_o is *Darker*
R2: IF l is *Gray* THEN l_o is *Midgray*
R3: IF l is *Bright* THEN l_o is *Brigter,*

or, equivalently,

R1: IF l is *Dark* THEN $l_o = l_o^d$ is *Darker*

R2: IF l is *Gray* THEN $l_o = l_o^g$ is *Midgray*

R3: IF l is *Bright* THEN $l_o = l_o^b$ is *Brigter*

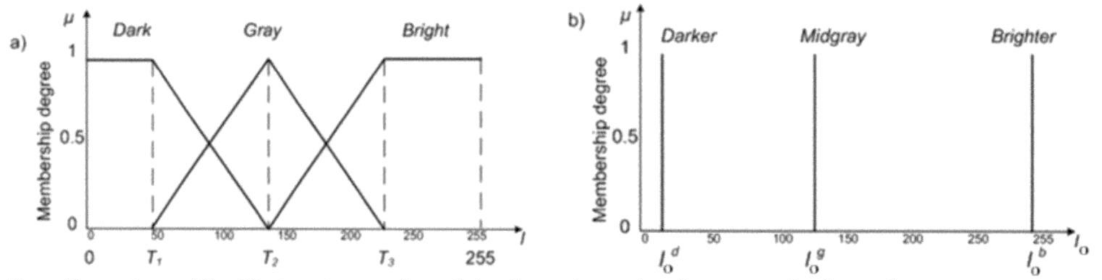

Fig. 2. a. Input, and b. Output membership functions for fuzzy, rule-based contrast enhancement.

Then for any value l^* at the input of our Takagi-Sageno contrast enhancement fuzzy system, in the output image, the corresponding brightness l_o^* is obtained by applying the Takagi-Sugeno fuzzy inference, as:

$$l_o^* = \frac{\mu_{Dark}(l^*) \cdot l_o^d + \mu_{Gray}(l^*) \cdot l_o^g + \mu_{Bright}(l^*) \cdot l_o^b}{\mu_{Dark}(l^*) + \mu_{Gray}(l^*) + \mu_{Bright}(l^*)}, \tag{8}$$

where: $\mu_{Dark}(l^*)$, $\mu_{Gray}(l^*)$, $\mu_{Bright}(l^*)$ denote the membership degrees of the currently processed brightness l^* to the input fuzzy sets *Dark, Gray* and *Bright.*

In the implementation presented here, we assume that the input fuzzy sets form a fuzzy partition of the universe of discourse of l:

$$\mu_{Dark}(l + \mu_{Gray}(l) + \mu_{Bright}(l) = 1 \tag{9}$$

The numerical constants defining output singletons were selected here at: $l_o^d = 1$ (black), $l_o^g = 127$ (gray), $l_o^b = 255$ (white).

For a general computational framework of any of the 3 membership degrees required by equation (8), we propose to represent each of the input fuzzy sets membership functions by a trapezoidal function $f_{tr} : L \rightarrow [0; 1]$, where L is the dynamic grey level range of the image, *L = {0, 1, … , 255}*, represented generically in Fig.3, in analytical form:

$$f_{tr}(a,b,c,d,l)=\begin{cases}0, & if\ l\in[0,a)\\ \dfrac{l-a}{b-a}, & if\ l\in[a,b)\\ 1, & if\ l\in[b,c]\\ \dfrac{-l+d}{d-c}, & if\ l\in(c,d]\\ 0, & if\ l\in(d,255]\end{cases} \quad . \tag{10}$$

With this generic function f_{tr}, any of the 3 membership functions, $\mu_s : L \to [0;1]$, where $s \in \{Dark, Gray, Bright\}$, in Fig.2.a can be expressed, for particular choices of the parameters *a, b, c, d*:

$$\begin{aligned}\mu_{Dark}(l) &= f_{tr}(0,\ 0, T_1, T_2, l)\\ \mu_{Gray}(l) &= f_{tr}(T_1, T_2, T_2, T_3, l)\\ \mu_{Bright}(l) &= f_{tr}(T_2, T_3, 255, 255, l).\end{aligned} \tag{11}$$

The thresholds: T_1, T_2 and T_3 are chosen from the image histogram like the minimum the mean and the maximum gray level values (as suggested in (Gonzales & Woods, 2008) and exemplified in Fig.13.a).

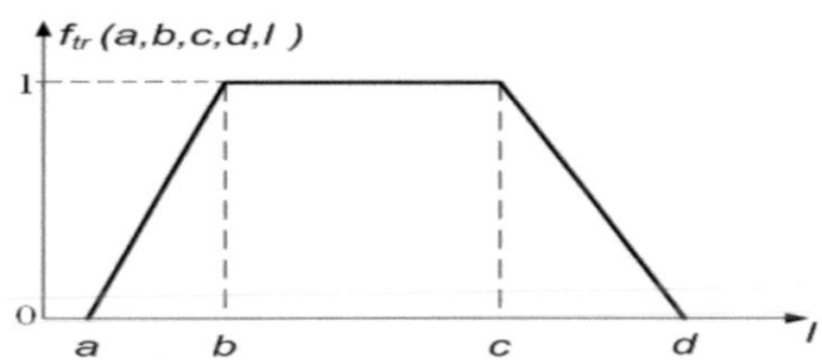

Fig. 3. Function for computing the membership degree on dark, gray and bright.

3. Basis of image processing in the compressed domain

The bitmap format for image storage is seldom used in day-to-day applications; even medical images are stored in JPEG format. This is because of the advantages offered by the JPEG format: little storage capacity needed and better performances in information transmission (via internet). For images stored in JPEG format, it is recommended to process them directly in the compressed domain, in order to reduce the time needed to process data. First, this time economy is related to the fact that it is no longer necessary to decompress the image, to process it at pixel level and to recompress it back; and, second, the image processing in the compressed domain means that there are fewer data to process.
Linear processing can be easily implemented in the compressed domain (Smith & Rowe, 1993; Smith, 1995) because there are no problems to process an image involving linear operations, such as adding a constant, multiplying with a constant, adding of two images, progressive cross fade of two images. The implementation of operations involving nonlinear

operators is challenging, but not impossible, and when the right combination is found, the processing is much faster, due to the reduced number of DCT coefficients.
Further, the basic steps used to compress/decompress the JPEG images will be briefly presented (Smith & Rowe, 1993). The image is first divided into 8x8 blocks, and each 8x8 block is individually processed. A DCT is applied on each block providing the DCT coefficients, which are quantized. Many small coefficients, usually high frequency ones, are quantized to zero. The next step is zig-zag scanning of the DCT matrix, followed by RLE (Run Length Encoding) and entropy coding (Huffman coding). In the decoder, the inverse steps must be computed.
There are two ways to enhance the images which are compressed using JPEG (Fig.4):

(1) the compressed domain processing - no decompression/ recompression, but the enhancement algorithm must be reformulated in the DCT image representation space;

(2) the pixel level processing – enhancement of the image after full decompression, direct manipulation of the pixels is adopted, than recompress the enhanced image;

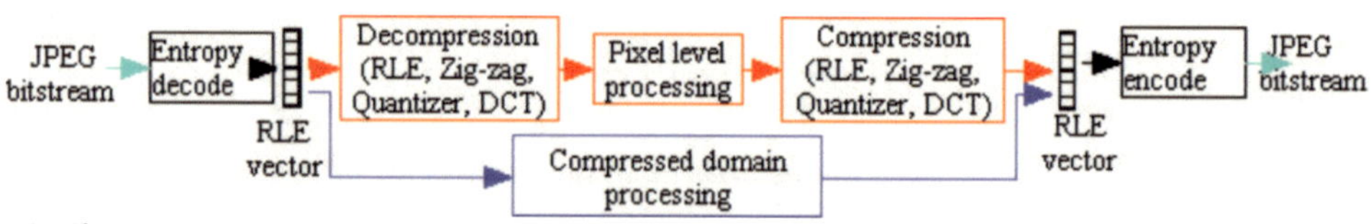

Fig. 4. The two ways to process images compressed JPEG.

For each 8x8 pixels blocks from image, instead of 64 data implied in the pixel level processing, in the compressed domain only a smaller amount of data is processed, because the majority of the coefficients in the DCT domain are zero after the quantization. In our algorithm an adaptive minimal decompression is used: full decompression is no longer needed, but decompression is used for the block having many details, for an improved accuracy of processing.
The following notations will be introduced: considering the original H×W grey level image, divided into 8×8 pixels blocks (as in the typical process of JPEG encoding), we denote any such block of pixels by the matrix $U[8\times 8]$, containing the grey level values of the pixels in the range [0; L], where L is the dynamic grey level range of the image, L = {0, 1, … , 255}: $U=\{u(i,j)\in[0;L], \text{where } i=0,1,\dots,7; j=0,1,\dots,7\}$. Consider $U_{dct}[8\times 8]$ to be the matrix of the zig-zag ordered quantized DCT coefficients of any 8×8 pixels block from the original image U (directly available in the JPEG image coding, as shown in Fig.4), where:

$$U_{dct}=\begin{cases} u_{dct}(0,0)-DC \text{ coefficient,} \\ u_{dct}(i,j)-AC \text{ coefficients, (where } i,j=0,1,\dots,7; \text{with } i\neq j\neq 0) \end{cases} \quad (12)$$

In the JPEG compression steps, prior to applying the DCT on each block, all the luminance values are scaled symmetrically towards 0, from the [0; 255] range to the [-128; 127] range. Since we have in the compressed domain all the gray values scaled symmetrically towards 0, we should express all the terms from classical equations (pixel level algorithms) in terms of these translated grey levels. Note that the DC coefficient will also be scaled towards 0. To differentiate between a grey level l in the original range [0; 255] and its translated version, we will denote the latter by adding the subscript "t", by l_t: $l_t = l - 128 \Rightarrow l = l_t + 128$.

Unlike the basic grey scale transformation formulation of the contrast enhancement, if one aims to obtain the same effect with the general approach presented in Fig.4, the algorithms given in the previous section must be reformulated as a block level processing. Whereas this is not a problem for the linear operations, the nonlinear operations must be carefully addressed.

To compute the membership degrees, we need to perform the operation of adding a constant and multiplying with a constant each pixel brightness value in a DCT block. These imply linear operations. The multiplication with a constant implies multiplying the constant with each coefficient from the DCT matrix, whereas the addition of a constant can be seen as a translation of the average brightness of the block, therefore it will affect only the DC coefficient of the 8×8 pixels block. These two scalar operations needed for the JPEG compressed image processing (Smith 1995), can be performed directly on the U_{dct} matrix by simply changing the values - there is no need to reconstruct the quantized array or even the zig-zag vector. The other operations (linear or nonlinear), needed for the reformulations of the fuzzy algorithms are explained in algorithms description sections.

As mentioned in section above, a reasonable choice for the thresholds values would be from the image histogram. But, in the JPEG compressed domain image representation, the pixel grey levels are not directly available (without decompression). Therefore, one cannot directly compute the grey level histogram for the image and, as such, neither the median grey level. However, what we do have available are the average values of the grey levels in each 8×8 pixels "patch" in the image, given by the DC coefficients of the blocks composing the image. Roughly speaking, if they would be the only ones used to reconstruct the pixel level representation (without any AC information), they would give an approximation of the image, with some block boundary effects/ distortions and some loss of details, but however still preserving the significant visual information. Therefore, the histogram built only from the DC coefficients will have also approximately the same shape as the grey level histogram, built from pixel-level data. This is illustrated in Fig.5.

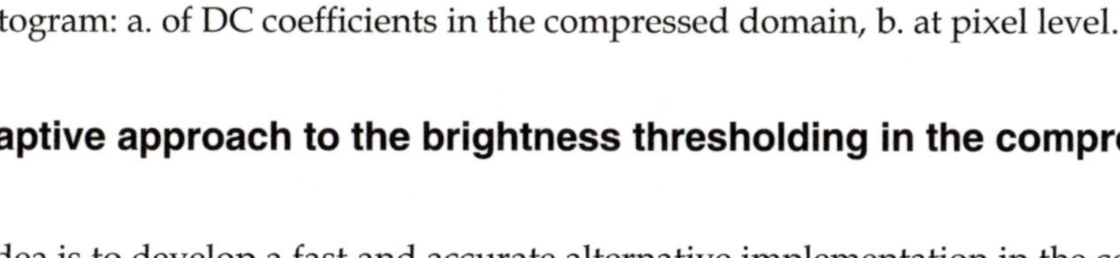

Fig. 5. Histogram: a. of DC coefficients in the compressed domain, b. at pixel level.

4. An adaptive approach to the brightness thresholding in the compressed domain

The core idea is to develop a fast and accurate alternative implementation in the compressed domain, to the classical fuzzy image enhancement algorithms, based on global brightness thresholding, which is usually performed at pixel level. One of the most important difficulties in deriving a compressed domain implementation for these algorithms is the fact that it involves one or two threshold comparison of each grey level to a mean value, which cannot be directly transposed to a processing on the DCT coefficients domain. To this, we developed an adaptive approach, which conditionally decides the need for decompression and pixel level threshold in a DCT transformed pixel block, only when this is strictly required to preserve accuracy (by a large amount of AC energy of the block). In all the other cases it is enough to compare the DC coefficient (average grey level) value of the block to the equivalent grey level threshold, which is a good estimate of the location of all the pixels brightness versus the threshold. Such an algorithm can significantly increase the computational efficiency in image processing algorithms applied to a JPEG image, avoiding compression and decompression prior and after the processing.

The lowest the number of the zero AC coefficients, the more textured is the 8x8 block considered (being proportional to the spatial frequencies in the area). The largest the energy of the AC coefficients, the more significant the luminance changes in the 8x8 pixels area. Large amount of energy usually corresponds to sharp edge and important surface/area discontinuities. Thus in this case, taking into account the average luminance of the area is very likely to produce incorrect thresholding results; such a case should be therefore treated differently than the uniform or almost uniform areas, requiring the block decompression, pixel level processing and compression.

The adaptive algorithm is based on formulating some logical rules to differentiate between the cases presented above and to define the best processing steps according to each situation to maximize the thresholding accuracy while minimizing the computational complexity by processing as few image elements as possible. Based on the DCT coefficients, one can see that the frequency content of each 8x8 block from the image can be estimated, classifying the blocks into:

1) Approximately uniform blocks (of almost uniform luminance) - the energy contained in the AC coefficients is very small.
2) Non-uniform blocks (of significant variable luminance) which could contain:
   a) Only a few details, but significant for the object (for example, horizontal, vertical and oblique edges, like in Fig.6.a)
   b) A large number of significant details for the object (like in the case of a "chess table" image of 8x8 presented in Fig.6.b).

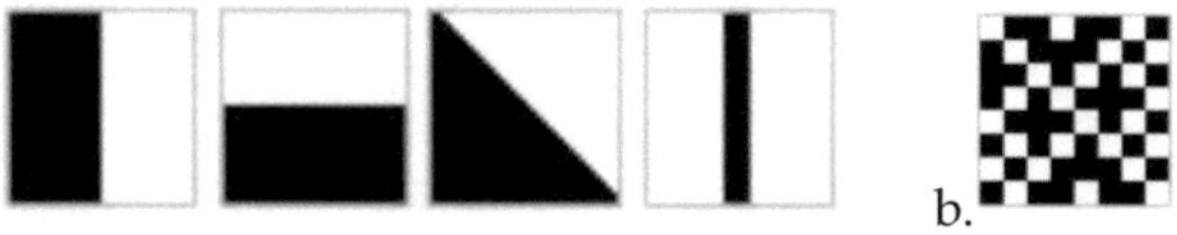

a. b.

Fig. 6. Non-uniform blocks: a. Horizontal, vertical and oblique edges; b. "chess table"

Fuzzy image processing in the compressed domain is not a trivial task, since as it can be seen, if one aims to strictly apply classical algorithms in that form, the comparison would necessarily need the decompression; otherwise one cannot have the grey level value in each of the 64 possible spatial locations, but then we would return to what we aimed to avoid, i.e. full decompression before processing. Fortunately, there are typically many 8×8 pixels blocks in general purpose digital images where the local variation of the brightness is small around the average (i.e., around the DC coefficient of the block). Thus for every such block, it is reasonable to assume that if its average grey level falls on one side of the threshold DC_{thd}, on the same side will be all the individual brightnesses of the pixels in the block.

In the case of 8×8 blocks of pixels exhibiting a large variation of the grey levels around the average brightness value (this is equivalent in the DCT coefficients space to large values of the AC coefficients - which will mean that enough of the 64 pixels of the block have significantly different brightness values than the value of the DC coefficient of the block), performing the comparison with the threshold only on the DC coefficient and using the resulting selected expression of the contrast intensification function for all the 64 pixels in the block can lead to an erroneous processing of the grey levels of the pixels whose grey levels are significantly different from the average brightness value. An example illustrating the processing errors resulting in such a case is presented in Fig.7: notice that for the selected region in Fig.7.b), some of the blocks close to the boundaries of the apple and the tail of the banana, which have a large variance of the grey level, exhibit a much too significant increase of the brightness as compared to the surrounding area of the background. This is due to the incorrect selection of the processing function, determined by the comparison of only the DC coefficient of the block with the threshold DC_{thd}. To avoid the processing errors introduced by the incorrect selection of the grey level enhancement function in the case of the blocks with a highly non-uniform luminance distribution, (large AC energy content), one must perform the decompression of all the blocks containing higher energy factor, and process them at the pixel level (see Fig.7.c.). Even if this reduces to some extent the computational efficiency, as compared to the case of a complete processing in the compressed domain, the loss is not significant, since statistically the number of blocks for which the decompression must be applied is small for most images (i.e., only the blocks exhibiting sharp edges must be decompressed for processing, all the others can be processed completely in the compressed domain), as it can be seen in the experimental part (table 1 and 2). For the 8×8 pixels blocks that are fully decompressed before processing, no rewriting of the contrast intensification algorithm is needed; it is processed at pixel level, using the classical algorithm.

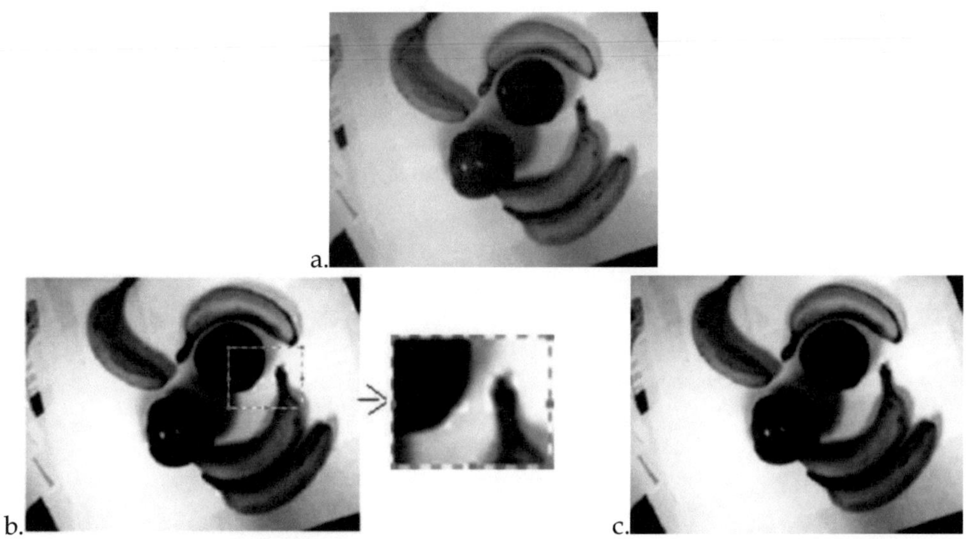

Fig. 7. a. Original image "Banana.jpg"; b. Image processed without consider AC energy content; c. Image processed with adaptive algorithm in the compressed domain.

In the adaptive implementation, the decision whether an 8×8 pixels block needs to be decompressed for applying the enhancement algorithm or not, is done based on estimating its amount of grey level variation versus the average brightness as being proportional to the average AC energy content within the block, amount denoted by E_{AC} and described by the following formula:

$$E_{AC} = \frac{\sum_{i=0}^{7}\sum_{i=0}^{7}\left|U_{dct}(i,j)\right|^2 - U_{dct}^2(0,0)}{63} \tag{13}$$

Then, if the computed estimate of the brightness variation E_{AC} in the currently processed block of 8×8 pixels exceeds a certain threshold, denoted here as e_{thd} (is too large to allow the assumption that the selection of the enhancement function can be done based on the average luminance value $u_{dct}(0,0)$ only), the decision is made to decompress the pixels block and process the grey levels individually, using pixel level equations. Otherwise, the brightness variation within the block is small enough to allow the selection of the processing function based only on the position of $u_{dct}(0,0)$ towards the threshold l_{thd} and do the processing in the compressed domain directly on the U_{dct} matrix, as is describe below (in the next sections).
The e_{thd} value is chosen from the experiments, taking into account the image statistics with respect to the amount and magnitude of image edges (the amount and sharpness of the details within the image). Thus, for images with similar statistics with respect to the frequency content, the same AC energy threshold e_{thd} may be reliably used in the selection of the processing type (with/without decompression). For a given image class, the value e_{thd} providing the best compromise between computational complexity (minimal number of blocks decompressed) and quality of the enhanced image (which, without compromises, should appear visually identical to the image enhanced at pixel level) can be found by examining:

- the plot of the mean square error (MSE) between the enhanced image using our algorithm and the enhanced image using the original algorithm (applied directly at pixel level) for the entire image versus various values of e_{thd}, and
- the plot of the number of blocks decompressed in applying our algorithm, denoted EffBlocks (the estimated efficiency of the adaptive processing method for the compressed domain, evaluated by examining the numbers of blocks processed at pixel level as reported to the total number of 8×8 pixels blocks in the image), versus various values of e_{thd}.

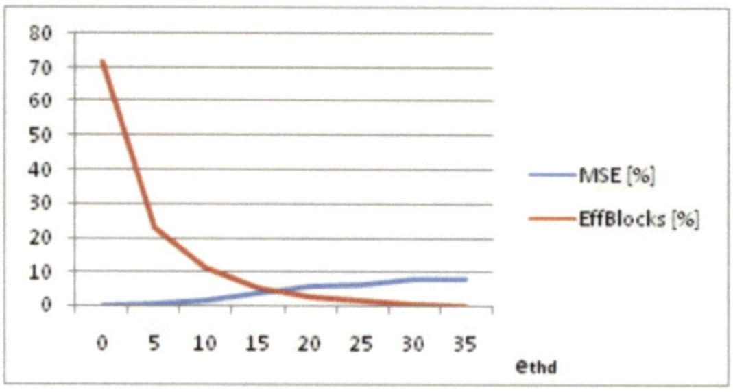

Fig. 8. e_{thd} influence for an image (e.g. Eye.jpg)

Such a pair of plots for the image in Fig.9 is given in Fig.8. Their examination allows us to state that the compromise value of e_{thd} appears at the intersection of the MSE vs. e_{thd} curve and EffBlocks vs. e_{thd} curve. Thus, the optimal threshold should be chosen in the neighborhood of this intersection point, for images with similar grey level distribution statistics.

A very small e_{thd} value will always lead to images of a very good quality, but the number of processed blocks in the compressed domain will be quite small, so the complexity of the computing algorithm is not significantly smaller, compared to the direct processing on the pixel. An appropriate e_{thd} value will lead to the increase of the number of blocks processed in the compressed domain and, in this way, a fast fuzzy algorithm for image enhancement could be obtained.

The adaptive approach to the brightness thresholding in the compressed domain is defined for each 8×8 pixels block of the JPEG image, as follows:

1) Compute the average of AC coefficients energy from DCT block, denoted E_{AC}, using equation (13).
2) If $E_{AC} < e_{thd}$ (where e_{thd} represents the optimal selection threshold between the uniform blocks and the blocks with a significant number of details) => process the block in the compressed domain.
3) Otherwise, if $E_{AC} \geq e_{thd}$ (the block has a significant content of details) => decompress the block and process every pixel from the block separately, using classical equation.

5. A reformulation of the fuzzy contrast enhancement algorithms in the compressed domain

5.1. Contrast enhancement algorithm based on fuzzy INT operator in the compressed domain

Before discussing the implementation of each operation involved by the contrast enhancement with fuzzy INT operator directly in the compressed domain (Florea et al., 2009), we would first like to rewrite the grey level transformation implemented by the algorithm in analytical form as: $f_{\text{int}} : L \to L$, embedding in its form the conversion of the grey levels to fuzzy membership degrees (fuzzification given by B) the INT operator and the conversion of the resulting membership degrees back to gray levels (defuzzification, given by B^{-1}).

Taking into account that, for a given image with the minimum grey level in the histogram $l_{\min}$ and the maximum grey level in the histogram l_{Max}, the previously imposed constraints guarantee that $[l_{\min}, l_{Max}] \subseteq [l_m, l_M]$, the fuzzification is completely described by: $B(l) = a \cdot l + b$, for any l in the image.

Therefore, $B'(l)$ becomes:

$$B'(l) = INT(B(l)) = \begin{cases} 2 \cdot (a \cdot l + b)^2, \text{if } 0 \leq (a \cdot l + b) \leq 0.5 \\ 1 - 2 \cdot (-a \cdot l + 1 - b)^2, \text{if } 0.5 < (a \cdot l + b) \leq 1 \end{cases} \quad (14)$$

This can be written in a form more suitable for the identification of the needed operations, to be performed in the compressed domain as:

$$B'(l) = \begin{cases} 2 \cdot a^2 \cdot l^2 + 4 \cdot a \cdot b \cdot l + 2 \cdot b^2, \text{if } 0 \le (a \cdot l + b) \le 0.5 \\ -2 \cdot a^2 \cdot l^2 + 4 \cdot a \cdot (1-b) \cdot l + 1 - 2 \cdot (1-b)^2, \text{if } 0.5 < (a \cdot l + b) \le 1 \end{cases}. \quad (15)$$

The resulting grey level, $l' = f_{\text{int}}(l) = B^{-1}(B'(l))$, will be:

$$f_{\text{int}}(l) = \frac{B'(l) - b}{a} \Rightarrow$$

$$f_{\text{int}}(l) = \begin{cases} 2 \cdot a \cdot l^2 + 4 \cdot b \cdot l + \dfrac{2 \cdot b^2 - b}{a}, \text{if } 0 \le (a \cdot l + b) \le 0.5 \\ -2 \cdot a \cdot l^2 + 4 \cdot (1-b) \cdot l + \dfrac{1 - 2 \cdot (1-b)^2 - b}{a}, \text{if } 0.5 < (a \cdot l + b) \le 1 \end{cases}. \quad (16)$$

In the following, we describe the implementation of each term from equation (16) in the compressed domain.
Taking into account that, in the compressed domain, prior to applying the DCT based compression of the JPEG algorithm, all the luminance values are scaled to the [-128, 127] range, including the threshold grey level l_{thd}. Consequently, the threshold for the fuzzy algorithm in the compressed domain should change to its equivalent in the range [-128, 127], denoted here by DC_{thd}: $DC_{thd} = l_{thd} - 128$. Note that the resulting DC coefficient (which gives the average brightness in the block and used in our implementation as an estimate for selecting the processing rule) is also scaled towards 0.
Since the value of l_{thd} can be computed from the membership function B as: $a \cdot l_{thd} + b = 0.5 \Rightarrow l_{thd} = \frac{0.5 - b}{a} \Rightarrow l_{thd} - 128 = \frac{0.5 - b}{a} - 128$, the expression of DC_{thd} becomes:

$$DC_{thd} = \frac{0.5 - b}{a} - 128. \quad (17)$$

In the compressed domain all the grey values are scaled symmetrically towards 0, which means, that we should express all the terms in equation (16) in terms of these translated grey levels:

$$l_t = (l - 128) \Rightarrow l = l_t + 128,$$
$$l_t^2 = (l - 128)^2 \Rightarrow l^2 = l_t^2 + 2 \cdot 128 \cdot l_t - 128^2. \quad (18)$$

Replacing the expressions of l and l^2 from equation (18) in equation (16), we will have the following resulting form of the intensification function:

$$f_{\text{int}}(l_t) = \begin{cases} 2 \cdot a \cdot l_t^2 + (4 \cdot a \cdot 128 + 4 \cdot b) \cdot l_t + (2 \cdot a \cdot 128^2 + 4 \cdot b \cdot 128 + \dfrac{2 \cdot b^2 - b}{a} - 128), \\ \quad if\ 0 \le (a \cdot l + b) \le 0.5 \\ -2 \cdot a \cdot l_t^2 + (-4 \cdot a \cdot 128 + 4 \cdot (1-b)) \cdot l_t + (-2 \cdot a \cdot 128^2 + 4 \cdot (1-b) \cdot 128 + \\ \quad + \dfrac{1 - 2 \cdot (1-b)^2 - b}{a} - 128), \quad if\ 0.5 < (a \cdot l + b) \le 1 \end{cases} \quad (19)$$

In order to implement the fuzzy algorithm in the compressed domain, linear operations and nonlinear operations are necessary. The linear operation needed are adding and multiplying a constant to each pixel brightness in an image block. But also, the square of an image is needed (equivalent to l_t^2), which is a nonlinear operation. It can be obtained using the multiplication algorithm of two images, in the compressed domain, developed by B. Smith (Smith & Rowe, 1993). In order to apply the contrast enhancement algorithm described above, we need to compute the square of each pixel luminance in the 8×8 block, in the compressed domain. That is, we should obtain the DCT of the 8×8 block of squared luminance. We denote this DCT matrix by $U_{dct,sq}[8 \times 8]$. According to (Smith & Rowe, 1993), $U_{dct,sq}$ can be obtaining from U_{dct} as follows:

$$\begin{aligned} u_{dct,sq}(x_1, x_2) &= \frac{1}{4 \cdot Q(x_1, x_2)} \sum_i \sum_j C(i, x_1) \cdot C(j, x_2) \cdot [u(i,j)]^2 = \\ &= \sum_{y_1, y_2, w_1, w_2} u_{dct}(y_1, y_2) \cdot u_{dct}(w_1, w_2) \cdot W_Q(y_1, y_2, w_1, w_2, x_1, x_2) \end{aligned}, \quad (20)$$

$$\text{where: } W_Q(y_1, y_2, w_1, w_2, x_1, x_2) = \frac{Q(y_1, y_2) \cdot Q(w_1, w_2)}{256 \cdot 64 \cdot Q(x_1, x_2)} \cdot W(x_1, y_1, w_1) \cdot W(x_2, y_2, w_2)$$

$$\text{with: } W(x, y, w) = \sum_i C(i, x) \cdot C(i, y) \cdot C(i, w);$$

$$C(i, x) = A(x) \cdot \cos \frac{(2 \cdot i + 1) \cdot x \cdot \pi}{16}; \quad A(x) = \begin{cases} \dfrac{1}{\sqrt{2}}, for\ x = 0 \\ 1, for\ x \ne 0 \end{cases}.$$

We can efficiently compute this sum by noticing several facts: firstly, that for compressed images, most of the coefficients in the matrix U_{dct} are zero and, secondly, that in the function $W_Q(y_1, y_2, w_1, w_2, x_1, x_2)$, only about 4 percents of the terms are non-zero.

The reformulation in the compressed domain for the classical fuzzy image enhancement algorithm using INT operator, expressed in equation (1), can be described by the following equations:

$$\begin{aligned} U_{dct,INT} &= k_1 \cdot U_{dct,sq} + k_2 \cdot U_{dct} \\ u_{dct,INT}(0,0) &= u_{dct,INT}(0,0) + k_3 \end{aligned}, \quad (21)$$

where k_1, k_2 and k_3 are real-valued constants defined by:

$$\text{if} \quad u_{dct}(0,0) < DC_{thd} \Rightarrow \begin{cases} k_1 = 2 \cdot a; \\ k_2 = 4 \cdot a \cdot 128 + 4 \cdot b; \\ k_3 = 2 \cdot a \cdot 128^2 + 4 \cdot b \cdot 128 + \dfrac{2 \cdot b^2 - b}{a} - 128 \end{cases}$$

$$\text{if} \quad u_{dct}(0,0) \geq DC_{thd} \Rightarrow \begin{cases} k_1 = -2 \cdot a; \\ k_2 = -4 \cdot a \cdot 128 + 4 \cdot (1-b); \\ k_3 = -2 \cdot a \cdot 128^2 + 4 \cdot (1-b) \cdot 128 + \dfrac{1 - 2 \cdot (1-b)^2 - b}{a} - 128 \end{cases} \quad (22)$$

Notice that: $u_{dct}(0,0)$ is the corresponding DC coefficient of the 8x8 pixels block of the matrix U, and $u_{dct,INT}(0,0)$ is the DC coefficient of the enhanced matrix, obtained using our algorithm.

There are typically many 8×8 pixels blocks in general purpose digital images where the local variation of the brightness is small around the average (i.e., around the DC coefficient of the block). Thus for every such block, it is reasonable to assume that if its average grey level falls on one side of the threshold DC_{thd}, on the same side will be all the individual brightnesses of the pixels in the block. This assumption will not hold in only one case, but the namely, when although the individual pixels brightnessses are close to the average (DC) value, then DC value is itself very near to the threshold DC_{thd}. However, in this case, as presented in Fig.1.b, the change of the membership degree will only very slightly affect the brightness, and as such, the error that can appear by selecting, for some of the pixels, the wrong equation for processing will be visually not noticeable. The adaptive implementation was applied: for any such blocks (described above) the processing is performed directly in the compressed domain using the equation (21), but, the blocks with high energy contents will be decompressed and pixel level processed using the equation (1).
The software implementation was done using the C++ programming language. A set of different images, with different dimensions, content, details content, contrast and medium luminance has been chosen for implementation. The performance of the algorithm has been examined, with respect to: MSE, and EffBlocks.
When we have a dark/bright image and we want to enhance it, if we define the fuzzy set membership function B with the default value of the parameter l_{thd} (i.e., 128), the image will be more dark/bright, but if we define the membership function using for l_{thd} the median value selected from the histogram of the DC coefficients, the image will be correctly enhanced.
Results of enhanced images using the fuzzy contrast enhancement algorithm, using INT operator directly in the compressed domain, are presented in the next figures:

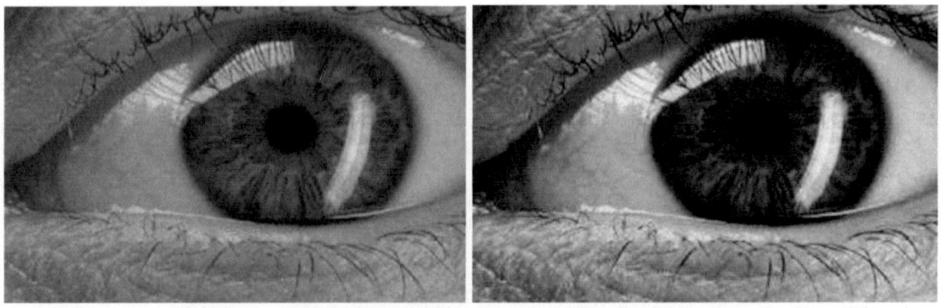

Fig. 9. Original image Eye.jpg and enhanced image using the proposed algorithm.

a. 

b.  c. 

Fig. 10. a. Original image Cars.jpg; b. Enhanced image using the default value for the parameter l_{thd} of the fuzzy set B, l_{thd}=128; c. Enhanced image using the proposed algorithm, with the value l_{thd} adaptively selected from the histogram of the DC coefficients;

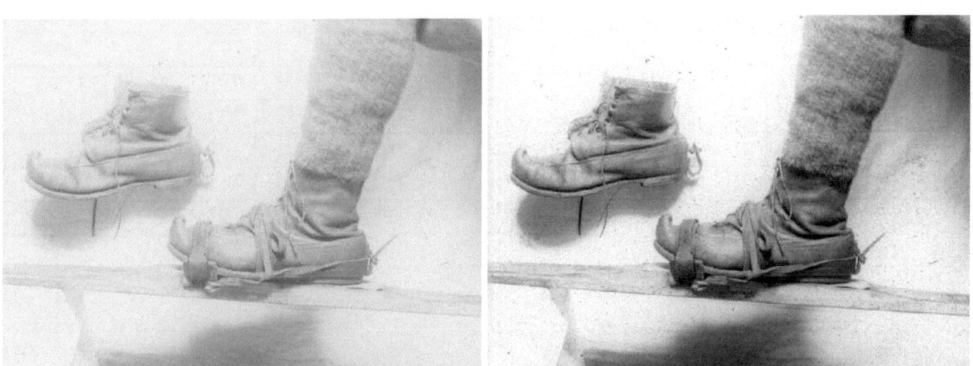

Fig. 11. Original image oldPicture.jpg and enhanced image using the proposed algorithm;

Fig. 12. Original image Keyboard.jpg and enhanced image using the proposed algorithm;

Image name	e_{thd}	l_{thd}	*Number of blocks processed at pixel level*	*Total number of blocks 8x8*	*EffBlocks [%]*	*MSE [%]*
banana.jpg	10	157	147	1344	10.938	0.223
eye.jpg	10	117	104	912	11.404	1.714
medical1.jpg	20	97	49	1768	2.771	0.641
medical2.jpg	20	90	67	1976	3.391	0.7259
medical3.jpg	20	52	235	1440	16.319	8.272
biopsi1	10	98	0	1200	0.000	0.0082
biopsi2	20	85	34	1200	2.833	0.074
lisa.jpg	10	88	70	1000	7.000	0.262
cars.jpg	15	161	25	1200	2.083	1.059
keyboard.jpg	15	34	2	4800	0.042	0.172
oldPicture1.jpg	10	207	174	4800	3.625	0.11
oldPictGirl.jpg	15	117	63	3136	2.009	1.125
photoInside.jpg	15	99	39	4800	0.813	0.831
seaLion.jpg	15	55	46	4800	0.958	0.177
barber.jpg	15	114	147	1520	9.671	2.918
nature.jpg	10	117	31	1728	1.794	2.89
lena.jpg	10	118	407	4096	9.937	0.6
mouse.jpg	20	51	47	1000	4.700	0.06
wom1.jpg	10	107	4	1024	0.391	0.66
sap1.jpg	20	83	31	784	3.954	2.334
fingerPrint.jpg	10	117	118	2016	5.853	0.824
jacob_strand.jpg	15	156	16	1200	1.333	0.541

Table 1. Results for different values e_{thd}

5.2. The reformulation of the fuzzy rule-based algorithm in the compressed domain

To compute the membership degrees for the fuzzy rule-based contrast enhancement algorithm in the compressed domain (Popa et al., 2008), we need to perform the operation of adding a constant and multiplying with a constant each pixel brightness value in a DCT block. These are linear operation.

Let denote with $K_s[1\times 2]$ $(s \in \{Dark, Gray, Bright\})$ the line vector of two constants (necessary for adding and multiplying the zig-zag ordered quatezed DCT coefficients) needed to compute the membership degrees in the compressed domain using the trapezoidal function:

$$K_s = [k_1^s, k_2^s] = f_{tr}^{DCT}(a,b,c,d,u_{dct}(0,0)) = \begin{cases} [0 \quad 0], & if \quad u_{dct}(0,0) \in [-128, a-128) \\ \left[\dfrac{1}{b-a} \quad \dfrac{128-a}{b-a}\right], & if \quad u_{dct}(0,0) \in [a-128, b-128) \\ [1 \quad 1], & if \quad u_{dct}(0,0) \in [b-128, c-128) \\ \left[\dfrac{-1}{d-c} \quad \dfrac{-128+d}{d-c}\right], & if \quad u_{dct}(0,0) \in [c-128, d-128) \\ [0 \quad 0], & if \quad u_{dct}(0,0) \in [d-128, 128) \end{cases} \quad (23)$$

Therefore, we will have:

$$\begin{aligned} K_{Dark} &= [k_1^{Dark}, k_2^{Dark}] = f_{tr}^{DCT}(0,0,T_1,T_2,u_{dct}(0,0)) \\ K_{Gray} &= [k_1^{Gray}, k_2^{Gray}] = f_{tr}^{DCT}(T_1,T_2,T_2,T_3,u_{dct}(0,0)) \\ K_{Bright} &= [k_1^{Bright}, k_2^{Bright}] = f_{tr}^{DCT}(T_2,T_3,255,255,u_{dct}(0,0)) \end{aligned} \quad (24)$$

Notice that: $u_{dct}(0,0)$ is the corresponding DC coefficient of the 8×8 pixels block of the matrix U.

Differently from the contrast enhancement using the INT operator, the fuzzy algorithm Takagi-Sugeno implies the comparison with more than one threshold, which is much more difficult. For each of the 8×8 pixels blocks the comparison with the thresholds in the compressed domain is done on the DC coefficient only, since it is reasonable to assume that a block level classification is likely to correctly place all the pixels in the block on the correct subrange of the membership function (where it is piece wise linear). This is valid for the blocks with moderate frequency content.

Once we have established in this fashion, for a certain pixels block, which of the 5 cases given by equation (23) seems more suitable to apply for all grey levels in the block, we directly compute the 3 vectors K_s $(s \in \{Dark, Gray, Bright\})$, which will be used to compute the 3 membership degrees of each pixel in the block to the fuzzy sets *Dark, Gray* and *Bright* in a single step for the entire block, using a matrix-vector formulation.

If one denotes by $D^s[8\times8]$, $\forall\, s\in\{Dark,\ \ Gray, Bright\}$, the matrices of membership degrees of the 64 grey levels in the 8×8 pixels block to the 3 input fuzzy sets, then any element in D^s is given by: $d^s(i,j)=\mu_s(u(i,j)), \forall\, i,j=0,1,...,7$.
Furthermore, for all the elements in the block, the function μ_s is assumed to have the same linear form, generally speaking, $\mu_s(u(i,j))=c_m\cdot u(i,j)+c_a$, with: c_m, c_a scalar constants for the multiplication and addition. So,

$$d^s(i,j)=c_m\cdot u(i,j)+c_a, \forall\, i,j=0,1,...,7. \tag{25}$$

where: $C_a[8\times8], c_a(i,j)=c_a, \forall\, i,j=0,1,...,7$.

Applying a DCT, quantization, zig-zag scanning on both sides of the equation (25), and denoting the resulting vector obtained from D^s by $D^s_{dct}[1\times2N]$, one gets its form as:

$$D^s_{dct}=c_m\cdot U_{dct}+C_a^{dct}, \tag{26}$$

where using the notations in equation (23):

- $C_a^{dct}[1\times2N]$, $\quad C_a^{dct}=[k_2^s\ 0\ 0\ ...\ 0]$, and
- $c_m=k_1^s$, computed previously.

The fuzzy rule-based contrast enhancement algorithm, from equation (8) taking in account the equation (9), reformulated in the compressed domain as a block level processing, can be described by the following formula (we denote the DCT matrix for the 8×8 enhanced block from the image with the $U_{dct,Int}[1\times128]$):

$$U_{dct,Int}=D^{Dark}_{dct}\cdot(l_o^d-128)+D^{Gray}_{dct}\cdot(l_o^g-128)+D^{Bright}_{dct}\cdot(l_o^b-128). \tag{27}$$

The adaptive implementation was used for processing: the decompression was performed for the blocks with high energy and pixel level processed using the equation (8); for the blocks with uniform variances the processing is done directly in the compressed domain, using the equation (27).
We can see in the experimental results that the visual effect is more powerful using Takagi-Sugeno fuzzy algorithm comparing with results obtained using INT operator for contrast enhancement. The problem in Takagi-Sugeno algorithm was that we have two thresholds and this leads to a bigger e_{thd} value (for not having block artifacts), which means more blocks decompressed. But, how is shown in Table 2, the *EffBlocks* is still less than 20% (blocks decompressed and processed at pixel level).
The algorithm was tested on different images having different statistics, with different contrast factors and different average luminance, collected from different sources. The experimental results show a much better computational efficiency, compared to the standard processing method, which needs a total decompression of the image.

Results of enhanced images using the adaptive algorithm are presented in next figures: 14, 15, 16, 17 below. In Fig.14 we have the original image *frog.jpg* with the histogram from Fig.13.a and the enhanced image with the histogram in Fig.13.b.

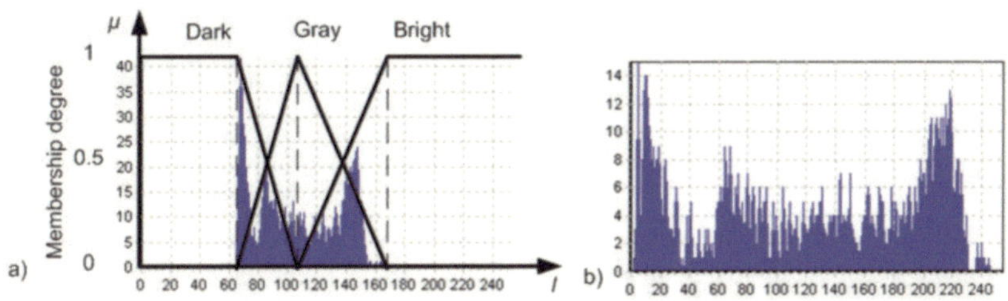

Fig. 13. a. Input membership function superimposed on the DC histogram of *frog.jpg*;
b. DC histogram of *frog.jpg* after fuzzy contrast enhancement.

Fig. 14. Original and enhanced image *frog.jpg*

Fig. 15. Original and enhanced image *keyboard.jpg*

Fig. 16. Original and enhanced image *Cars.jpg*

Fig. 17. Original and enhanced image *Monarch.jpg*

Image	e_{thd}	T_1	T_2	T_3	**EffBlocks [%]**	**MSE**
frog.jpg	5	66	104	166	20	1.9
woman.jpg	5	78	141	191	15	0.44
Lena.jpg	5	33	126	223	20.1	0.004
Lena.jpg	10	33	126	223	15.03	0.005
Lena.jpg	20	33	126	223	10.41	0.02
keyboard.jpg	10	0	34	78	16.02	0.01
eye.jpg	10	3	117	199	14.6	1.78
medical.jpg	10	5	90	208	10.07	0.93
butterfly.jpg	10	32	117	207	10.58	0.011
cars.jpg	5	106	161	200	8.16	0.5
bee.jpg	10	7	170	48	15.4	0.55
fingerPrint.jpg	10	45	117	190	18	0.29
children.jpg	10	60	128	228	13.1	0.28
monarch.jpg	10	29	101	223	16.15	0.63
lisa.jpg	10	33	88	223	14.9	1.5
girl.jpg	10	76	104	174	7.24	2.1

Table 2. Results for different values e_{thd}

6. Conclusion

An adaptive approach for image enhancement using fuzzy sets theory and fuzzy logic, in the class of digital image processing in the compressed domain, is presented in this chapter. Fuzzy rule-based contrast enhancement and fuzzy intensification operator are by default nonlinear, with one or few threshold comparisons as main nonlinearity; they are not straightforward applicable on the JPEG bitstream. We have presented a strategy for implementation of the brightness thresholding, for which an adaptive solution which takes into account the frequency content of each block in the JPEG compress domain is suggested.
To obtain the best enhancement possible with these approaches, we chose to use, in the grey levels fuzzification step of the methods, a parameterized membership function, with the parameters adapted to the grey level statistics in the image. The selection of the fuzzy set membership function parameters was done directly in the compressed domain, using the histogram of the DC coefficients of the compressed blocks as an approximation of the grey level statistics of the image. The algorithm was tested on different images having different statistics, with different contrast factors and different average luminances. The algorithms are applied only on the luminance component, but they can be applied for color image enhancement as well, with no change of the chrominance components. The experimental results show a better computational efficiency, compared to the standard processing method (which needs a total decompression of the image), practically at no processing error as compared to the reference algorithm (i.e., the same fuzzy image enhancement algorithm formulated at pixel level).
We also provide a principled formulation of a procedure to select the optimal value of the threshold for the AC energy content of each block, in order to guarantee the best possible computational efficiency with no visually noticeable processing error; embedding this principle in a fully automatic procedure and its verification for several types of images will make the object of our future work.

7. References

Agaian, S.S.; Silver, B.; Panetta, K.A. (2007). Transform Coefficient Histogram-Based Image Enhancement Algorithms Using Contrast Entropy, *IEEE Transactions On Image Processing*, Vol. 16, No. 3, March 2007, pp.741-758.

An, K.; Ni, Q.; Sun, J. (2004). A contrast enhancement method for compressed images, IEICE Electronic Express Vol. 1, No. 18, pp. 582-587.

Bezdek, J.C.; Keller, J.M.; Krishnapuram, R.; Pal, N.R. (1999). *Fuzzy Models and Algorithms for Pattern Recognition and Image Processing*, Boston.

Florea, C.; Vlaicu, A.; Gordan, M.; Orza, B.; (2009). Fuzzy intensification operator based contrast enhancement in the compressed domain, *Applied Soft Computing*, Elsevier, ISSN: 1568-4946.

Gonzales, R.C.; Woods R.E, (2008). *Digital Image Processing, 3rd edition*, Prentice Hall, ISBN 9780131687288, United States.

Gunturk, B.K.; Altunbasak, Y. (2002). Multiframe Resolution-Enhancement Methods for Compressed Video, *Signal Processing Letters*, IEEE, Vol. 9, No. 6, pp. 170-174.

Kim, J.; Peli, E. (2003). MPEG based image enhancement for people with low vision, Soc *for Information Display, Digest of Technical Papers*, pp. 1156-1159.

Mezaris, V.; Kompatsiaris, I.; Kokkinou, E.; Strintzis, M.G. (2003). Real-time compressed-domain spatiotemporal video segmentation, *Proceedings.of Third International Workshop on Content-Based Multimedia Indexing*, France, 2003, pp. 373-380.

Pal, S.K.; King, R.A. (1981). Image Enhancement Using Smoothing with Fuzzy Sets, *IEEE Transaction Systems Man Cybernet,* Vol. SMC-11, No. 7, pp. 494-501.

Popa, C.; Gordan, M.; Vlaicu, A.; Orza, B.; Oltean, G. (2008). Computationally efficient algorithm for fuzzy rule-based enhancement on JPEG compressed color images, *Transactions on Signal Processing,* WSEAS, Vol. 4, No.5, May 2008, pp. 310 - 319, ISSN: 1790-5052.

Pedrycz, W.; Gomide, F. (1998). An Introduction to Fuzzy Sets: Analysis and Design, *The MIT Press,* 1998.

Sangkeun, L. (2006). Content-based image enhancement in the compressed domain based on multi-scale alpha-rooting algorithm, *Pattern Recognition Letters,* Vol. 27, No. 10, 15 July 2006, pp. 1054-1066.

Smith, B.C.; Rowe, L.A. (1993). A New Family of Algorithms for Manipulating Compressed Images, *IEEE Computer Graphics and Applications,* vol.13, (no.5), pp: 34-42, Sept. 1993.

Smith, B.C. (1995). A survey of compressed domain processing techniques, *Proceedings of NSF Workshop on Reconnecting Science and Humanities in Digital Libraries,* Oct. 1995.

Smith, B.C.; Rowe, L.A. (1996). Compressed Domain Processing of JPEG-encoded Images, *Real-Time Imaging Journal,* Vol. 2, July, pp 3-17.

Tang, J. (2004). A contrast based image fusion technique in the DCT domain, *Digital Signal Processing,* Vol. 14, No. 3, pp. 218-226.

Tang, J.; Peli, E.; Acton, S. (2003). Image enhancement using a contrast measure in the compressed domain, *Signal Processing Letters,* IEEE, Vol. 10, No. 10, Oct. 2003, pp. 289 - 292.

Tizhoosh, H.R. (2000). Fuzzy Image Enhancement: An Overview, In: Kerre, E., Nachtegael, M. (Eds.): "Fuzzy Techniques in Image Processing", *Studies in Fuzziness and Soft Computing,* Springer, pp. 137-171, ISBN: 3-7908-1304-4.

Triantafyllidis, G.A.; Varnuska, M.; Sampson, D. ; Tzovaras, D. ; Strintzis, M.G. (2003). An efficient algorithm for the enhancement of JPEG-coded images, *Computers and Graphics,* Vol. 27, No. 4, August 2003, pp. 529-534, Publisher: Elsevier.

Zadeh, L.A. (1965). Fuzzy sets, *Information and Control,* Vol. 8, No. 3, pp. 338-353.

10

Estimation of Per Unit Length Parameters of Multiconductor Lines by the Method of Rectangular Subareas

Saswati Ghosh and Ajay Chakrabarty
Kalpana Chawla Space Technology Cell, Dept. of E & ECE, Indian Institute of Technology, Kharagpur-721302 India

1. Introduction

The high operating frequency and small dimensions of modern electronic systems causes strong electromagnetic interaction within electronic circuits. The accurate evaluation of the per unit length capacitance and inductance of multiconducting lines and PCB lands is an important step in the design and packaging of these high frequency electronic circuits. Considerable work was already performed by other researchers on the development of different wideband microstrip interconnects and determination of capacitance of microstrip transmission lines (Ruehli and Bernnan, 1973), (Rao et al., 1979), (Ponnapalli et al., 1993). In the work of Ruehli and Brennan, the basic equations for the potential coefficients of rectangular conducting element were derived and used for the evaluation of capacitance of square plate, cube via Method of Moments (Ruehli and Bernnan, 1973). However, the resulting equations for the potential coefficients are found to be complicated and also these were mainly used for two / three dimensional bodies with square / rectangular surfaces. The Method of Moments analysis with triangular and square subsections for the evaluation of capacitance of arbitrary-shaped conducting surface is available in other literatures (Rao et al., 1979), (Harrington, 1985), (Ponnapalli et al., 1993). Harrington evaluated data on the capacitance of a square conducting plate employing square subdomain regions, but did not present clearly the exact formulas of the matrix elements for the evaluation of capacitance (Harrington, 1985). The triangular subdomains have been used for more complex surfaces by Rao et al (Rao et al., 1979). Also some interesting work on capacitance evaluation of square, cube etc. using method of subareas was developed in Matlab by Bai (Bai and Lonngren, 2002, 2004). However the authors had not noticed any work on the evaluation of per unit length parameters of multiconductor lines with a more generalized and simple elemental shape which can be used for any planar surface and can be extended for three dimensional lines. In the present work, the per unit length parameters of multiconductor lines are evaluated using Method of Moments and rectangular subdomain modeling. The rectangular subsection is chosen because of its ability to conform easily to any geometrical surface or shape and at the same time to maintain the simplicity of approach compared to the triangular patch modelling. The exact formulation for the evaluation of the impedance matrix for rectangular subdomain is determined. The Method of Moments with Pulse basis function and Point Matching is used to evaluate the charge distribution and hence the capacitance and inductance of multiconducting bodies. The capacitances of different conducting structures such as square plates, circular disc are compared with other available data in literature (Harrington, 1985), (Higgins and Reitan, 1957), (Nishiyama and M. Nakamura, 1992). Next the same method is extended for multiconducting bodies e.g. parallel rectangular plates, parallel circular discs and later for three dimensional structures e.g. circular coaxial conducting structures. The per unit length capacitance and inductance of circular coaxial structures is presented and compared with the analytical results.

2. Theory

We consider a perfectly conducting surface is charged to a potential V. The unknown surface charge density distribution σ (r′) can be determined by solving the following integral equation (Harrington, 1985)

$$V = \iint_S \frac{\sigma(r')}{4\pi\varepsilon|r - r'|} ds' \tag{1}$$

Here r and r' are the position vectors corresponding to observation and charge source points respectively, ds' is an element of surface S and ε is the permittivity of free space. The conducting bodies are approximated by planar rectangular subdomains (Figure 1). The Method of Moments with pulse basis function and point matching is then used to determine the approximate charge distribution (Harrington, 1985). On each subdomain, a pulse expansion function Pn(r) is chosen such that Pn(r) is equal to 1 when r is in the n-th rectangle and Pn(r) is equal to 0 when r is not in the n-th rectangle. With the above definition of expansion function, the charge density, $\sigma(r')$ may be approximated as follows

$$\sigma(r') = \sum_{n=1}^{N} \sigma_n P_n(r') \quad where \quad P_n = \begin{matrix} 1 & for\ n-th\ subsection \\ 0 & elsewhere \end{matrix} \tag{2}$$

Here N is the number of rectangles modelling the surface and σ_n's are the unknown weights (charge density).

Substitution of charge expansion (2) in (1) and point matching the resulting functional equation, yields an N x N system of linear equations which may be written in the following form

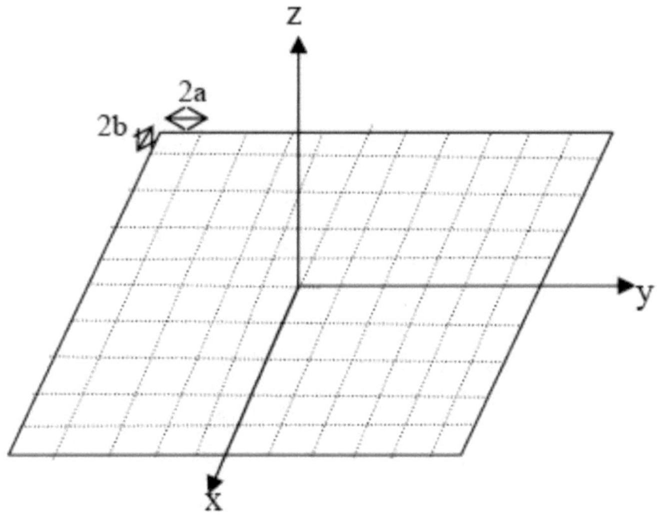

Fig. 1. Square plate divided into rectangular subsections.

$$[V] = [K][Q] \tag{3}$$

Here [K] is an N × N matrix and [Q] and [V] are column vectors of length N. The elements of [K], [Q] and [V] are given as follows

$$K_{mn} = \iint_{rectangle} \frac{1}{4\pi\varepsilon |r_m - r'|} dA' \tag{4}$$

$Q_n = \sigma_n$ =unknown charge density in subdomain n
$V_n = V$
r_m denotes the position vector of the center of the mth rectangle. A' is the area of the source rectangle.

$$|r_m - r'| = \sqrt{(x_m - x')^2 + (y_m - y')^2}$$

Here we have considered the conducting surface at z=0 plane.

Since the numerical formulation of (1) via the Method of Moments is well-known [4], we consider only the evaluation of the element of the moment matrix as given by equation (4). Each element of the matrix corresponds to the potential at some point in space, r = (x, y, z), due to a rectangular patch of surface charge of unit charge density. In general, the patch is arbitrarily positioned and oriented in space.

The integration of equation (4) is quite tedious, but the final result is relatively simple (Ghosh and Chakrabarty, 2006).

For the diagonal elements of the matrix, the integration is evaluated as follows

$$K_{nn} = \frac{1}{\pi\varepsilon}\left(a\,ln\left(\frac{b}{a} + \sqrt{\frac{b^2}{a^2}+1} \right) + b\,ln\left(\frac{a}{b} + \sqrt{\frac{a^2}{b^2}+1} \right)\right) \tag{5}$$

Here 2a and 2b are the sides of each rectangular subsection.
Using the standard integral formula the non-diagonal elements are evaluated as follows

$$K_{mn} = \frac{1}{4\pi\varepsilon}\left(\begin{array}{l} -\left[|x_m - x'|\, ln \dfrac{(|y_m - y_n + b| + \sqrt{(x_m - x')^2 + (y_m - y_n + b)^2})}{(|y_m - y_n - b| + \sqrt{(x_m - x')^2 + (y_m - y_n - b)^2})} \right]_{x_n - a}^{x_n + a} \\ -\left[|y_m - y'|\, ln \dfrac{(|x_m - x_n + a| + \sqrt{(y_m - y')^2 + (x_m - x_n + a)^2})}{(|x_m - x_n - a| + \sqrt{(y_m - y')^2 + (x_m - x_n - a)^2})} \right]_{y_n - b}^{y_n + b} \end{array} \right) \tag{6}$$

Here the source point is (x_n , y_n) and the field point is (x_m , y_m). The x′ and y′ of equation (6) are replaced by their respective limits. Solution of the matrix equation (3) yields values for the surface charge density at the centres of the subdomains. The capacitance, C, of the conducting surface is obtained from the following equation

$$C = Q/V = \frac{1}{V}\sum_{n=1}^{N} \sigma_n A_n \tag{7}$$

Here N is the total number of rectangular subsections.
The same method for a single conductor is extended for evaluating the capacitance of multiconducting bodies.

We consider two parallel rectangular conducting plates (2Lx2W) each divided into equal number of subsections (Figure 2).

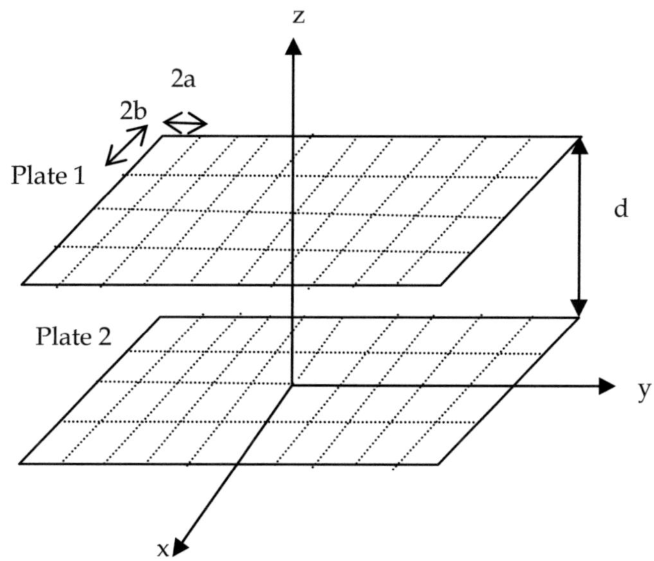

Fig. 2. Parallel plate divided into rectangular subsections.

The simplified formula achieved is as follows

$$V=\sum_{n=1}^{N} K_{mn}\sigma_n$$
$$\text{where } K_{mn}=\frac{1}{4\pi\varepsilon}\int_{x_n-a}^{x_n+a} dx' \int_{y_n-b}^{y_n+b} \frac{dy'}{\sqrt{(x_m-x')^2+(y_m-y')^2+(z_m-z')^2}} \tag{8}$$

In matrix form, equation (8) can be written as follows

$$[K_{mn}][\sigma_n]=[V_n] \tag{9}$$

Here

$$[K_{mn}]=\begin{bmatrix}\left[K_{mn}^{11}\right] & \left[K_{mn}^{12}\right]\\ \left[K_{mn}^{21}\right] & \left[K_{mn}^{22}\right]\end{bmatrix}; \qquad [V_n]=\begin{bmatrix}\left[V_n^{1}\right]\\ \left[V_n^{2}\right]\end{bmatrix}$$

The diagonal sub matrices represent the effect of the plate itself and the non diagonal sub matrices represent the mutual interaction between the plates.

The elements of the diagonal matrix remain same as the single element case. The elements of the non-diagonal matrix are evaluated following the same method. The diagonal and non-diagonal elements of the matrix is evaluated as follows

$$K_{nn}^{12}=K_{nn}^{21}$$
$$=\frac{1}{\pi\varepsilon}\left(a\ ln\frac{b+\sqrt{a^2+b^2+d^2}}{\sqrt{a^2+d^2}}+b\ ln\frac{a+\sqrt{a^2+b^2+d^2}}{\sqrt{b^2+d^2}}\right)$$
$$+\frac{2d}{\pi\varepsilon}\left(tan^{-1}\left(\frac{\sqrt{b^2+d^2}+b}{d}tan\left(\frac{1}{2}tan^{-1}\frac{a}{\sqrt{b^2+d^2}}\right)-\frac{1}{2}tan^{-1}\frac{a}{d}\right)\right) \quad (10)$$

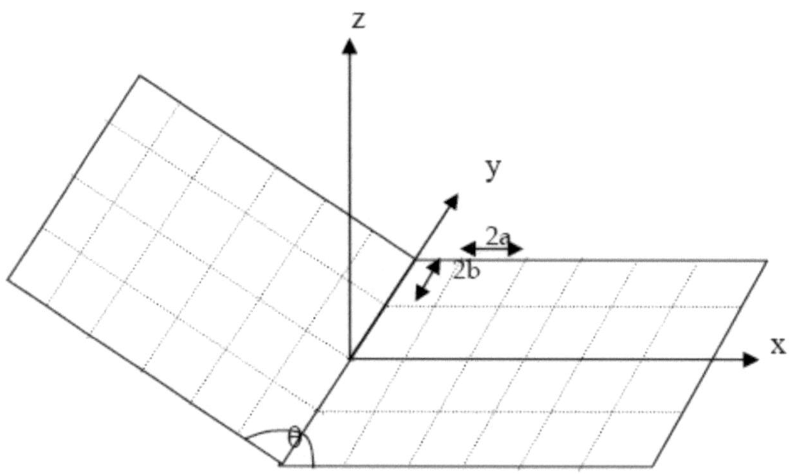

Fig. 3. Inclined plate divided into rectangular subsections.

$$K_{mn}^{12} = K^{21}_{mn}$$

$$= \frac{1}{4\pi\varepsilon}\left(\begin{array}{l} |x_m - x_n + a| \ ln\dfrac{\left(|y_m - y_n + b| + \sqrt{(x_m - x_n + a)^2 + (y_m - y_n + b)^2 + d^2}\right)}{\left(|y_m - y_n - b| + \sqrt{(x_m - x_n + a)^2 + (y_m - y_n - b)^2 + d^2}\right)} \\ - |x_m - x_n - a| \ ln\dfrac{\left(|y_m - y_n + b| + \sqrt{(x_m - x_n - a)^2 + (y_m - y_n + b)^2 + d^2}\right)}{\left(|y_m - y_n - b| + \sqrt{(x_m - x_n - a)^2 + (y_m - y_n - b)^2 + d^2}\right)} \\ - |y_m - y_n + b| \ ln\dfrac{\left(|x_m - x_n - a| + \sqrt{(x_m - x_n - a)^2 + (y_m - y_n + b)^2 + d^2}\right)}{\left(|x_m - x_n + a| + \sqrt{(x_m - x_n + a)^2 + (y_m - y_n + b)^2 + d^2}\right)} \\ + |y_m - y_n - b| \ ln\dfrac{\left(|x_m - x_n + a| + \sqrt{(x_m - x_n + a)^2 + (y_m - y_n - b)^2 + d^2}\right)}{\left(|x_m - x_n - a| + \sqrt{(x_m - x_n - a)^2 + (y_m - y_n - b)^2 + d^2}\right)} \end{array}\right)$$

$$+ \frac{d}{2\pi\varepsilon}\left(\begin{array}{l} tan^{-1}\left(\dfrac{\sqrt{(y_m - y_n + b)^2 + d^2} + |y_m - y_n + b|}{d} tan\left(\dfrac{1}{2} tan^{-1}\dfrac{|x_m - x_n + a|}{\sqrt{(y_m - y_n + b)^2 + d^2}}\right)\right) \\ - tan^{-1}\left(\dfrac{\sqrt{(y_m - y_n - b)^2 + d^2} + |y_m - y_n - b|}{d} tan\left(\dfrac{1}{2} tan^{-1}\dfrac{|x_m - x_n + a|}{\sqrt{(y_m - y_n - b)^2 + d^2}}\right)\right) \\ - tan^{-1}\left(\dfrac{\sqrt{(y_m - y_n + b)^2 + d^2} + |y_m - y_n + b|}{d} tan\left(\dfrac{1}{2} tan^{-1}\dfrac{|x_m - x_n - a|}{\sqrt{(y_m - y_n + b)^2 + d^2}}\right)\right) \\ + tan^{-1}\left(\dfrac{\sqrt{(y_m - y_n - b)^2 + d^2} + |y_m - y_n - b|}{d} tan\left(\dfrac{1}{2} tan^{-1}\dfrac{|x_m - x_n - a|}{\sqrt{(y_m - y_n - b)^2 + d^2}}\right)\right) \end{array}\right) \quad (11)$$

Similarly the exact expression for the elements of the non-diagonal sub matrices can be evaluated for two inclined plates (Figure 3). In this case, the expressions for the non diagonal elements remain almost same as for parallel plates, the only difference is that the value of d does not remain constant – it varies with the positions of the subsections.

For multiconductor lines surrounded by homogeneous medium the inductance of the line is evaluated from the following relation

$$C = \mu\varepsilon L^{-1} \quad (12)$$

The surrounding medium is characterized by μ and ε.
The characteristic impedance can be found out using the simple formula Z=1/vC where v=$3x10^8$ *m/sec*

3. Results and Discussions

A computer program based on the preceding formulation has been developed to determine the charge distribution and hence the capacitance of arbitrary shaped multiconducting bodies. The capacitance of different conducting surfaces e.g. rectangular plate, square plate, circular disc have been calculated (Figure 4 – 6). The capacitance data for a square and rectangular plate agrees with the available data in literature (Harrington, 1985; Higgins and Reitan, 1957; Nishiyama and M. Nakamura, 1992; Hariharan et al., 1998; Goto et al., 1992). Also the result for a circular disc (radius=1m, N=24, capacitance=68.36 pF) matches with the value available in literature (Nishiyama and M. Nakamura, 1992). Next the same method has been extended for the evaluation of per unit length parameters of multiconducting bodies e.g. parallel rectangular and circular plates, co-axial conductors with circular cross-section. The per-unit-length parameters for parallel square conductors, circular discs and co-axial conductors are presented and compared with other available data in Table 1 - 3.

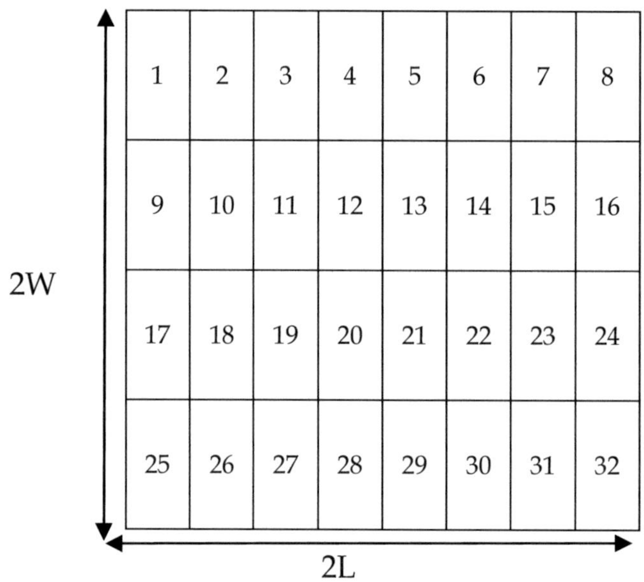

Fig. 4. Square plate (2L=1m; 2w=1m; V=1 volt) divided into N=32 subsections. Capacitance=38.69 pF.

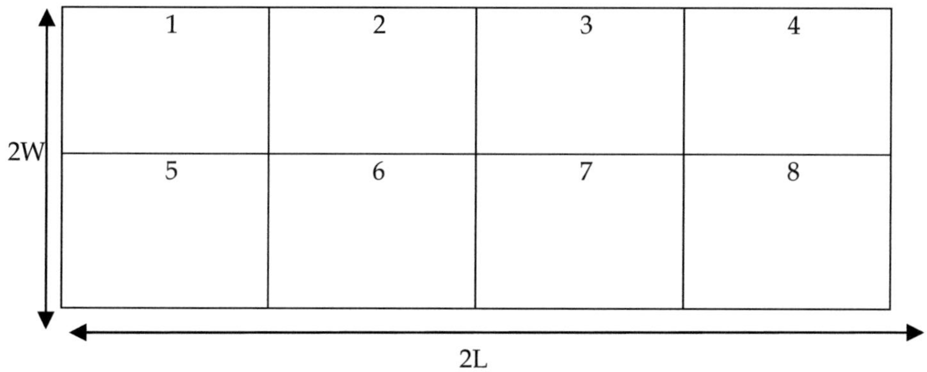

Fig. 5. Rectangular plate (2L=4m; 2w=1m; V=1 volt) divided into 4x2 subsections Capacitance=54.73 pF.

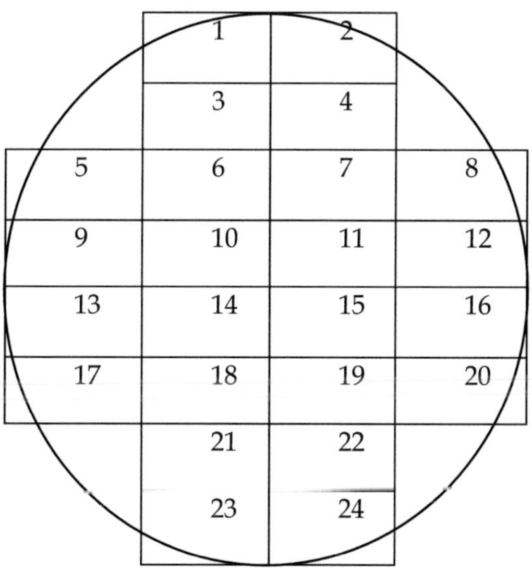

Fig. 6. Circular disc (radius=1m, N=24). Capacitance=68.36 pF agrees withthe value in literature =70.73 pF [9].

For circular coaxial conductor, each circular cylinder is replaced by a cylinder with octagonal structure of surface area equal to that of the circular cylinder (Figure 7). Each side of the octagonal cylinder is divided into rectangular subsections. For co-axial conductors of finite length, there is appreciable fringing effect. The per unit length capacitance of the circular coaxial line is found by evaluating the capacitance of various lengths and then subtracting the part due to the fringing effect. Also the characteristic impedance of the coaxial conductor is evaluated and compared with the analytical value (Figure 8).

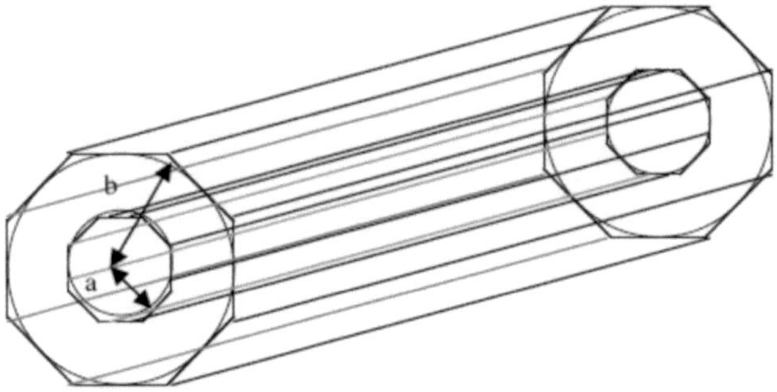

Fig. 7. Circular coaxial conductor approximated with octagonal cross-sectional coaxial structure.

d/2L	Capacitance in pF (calculated)	Capacitance in pF ($C_0=\varepsilon A/d$)	C/C_0	C/C_0 (Harrington, 1985)
0.01	904.48	884.14	1.023	1.024
0.025	378.43	353.67	1.07	1.05
0.05	203.35	176.83	1.15	1.15
0.10	105.92	88.41	1.198	1.2

Table 1. Capacitance of parallel square conducting plate (length=width=2L=1 m)

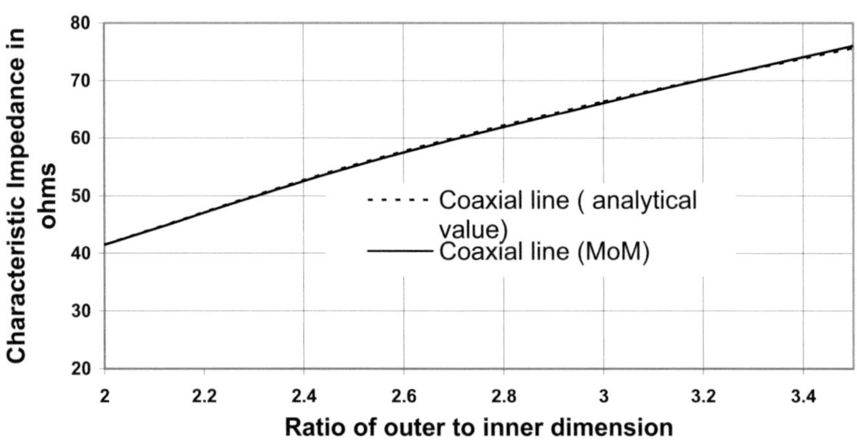

Fig. 8. Plot of the characteristic impedance versus ratio of outer to inner dimension of circular coaxial line.

d in meter	Capacitance in pF (MoM)	Capacitance in pF using analytical formula ($C_0=\varepsilon\pi r^2/d$)	C/C_0	C/C_0 (Jordan and Balmain, 1971)
0.02	1405.86	1388.8	1.015	
0.03	981.16	925.92	1.0597	1.062
0.05	617.64	555.56	1.11	
0.07	471.5	396.82	1.18	

Table 2. Capacitance of parallel circular conducting plates (radius=1m)

Ratio of outer to inner dimension	Capacitance in pF (including fringing effect)		Capacitance / unit length in pF/meter	Analytical value $C=2\pi\varepsilon/\ln(b/a)$ pF/meter	Inductance / unit length in μH / m
	Length =1m	Length =2 m			
2	109.44	189.75	80.21	80.15	0.1386

Table 3. Capacitance and inductance of circular coaxial lines (radius=1m)

4. Conclusion

A simple and efficient numerical procedure based on Method of Moments is presented for the evaluation of the per-unit length parameters of multiconducting bodies. The conducting structure is divided into rectangular sub areas. The data for capacitance of different planar and non-planar conducting structures show well agreement with their analytical value. This method can be used for the determination of equivalent circuit models of multiconductor or multiwire arrangements used in electronic systems.

5. References

Albert E. Ruehli, Pierce A. Bernnan, Efficient Capacitance Calculations for Three-Dimensional Multiconductor Systems, *IEEE Transactions on Microwave Theory and Techniques*, Vol. MTT-21, No. 2, February 1973.

E. Goto, Y. shi and N. Yoshida, Extrapolated Surface Charge method for Capacity Calculation of Polygons and Polyhedra, *Journal of Computational Physics,* Vol. 100, 1992.

Er-Wei Bai, Karl E. Lonngren, Capacitors and the method of moments, *Journal of Computers and Electrical Engineering*, Elsevier Publishers, Vol. 30 (2004) 223–229.

Er-Wei Bai, Karl E. Lonngren, On the capacitance of a cube, *Journal of Computers and Electrical Engineering,* Elsevier Publishers, Vol. 28 (2002) 317–321.

E. C. Jordan, K. G. Balmain, *Electromagnetic Waves and Radiating Systems*, Prentice Hall of India Private Limited, New Delhi, 1971.

N. Nishiyama and M. Nakamura, Capacitance of Disk Capacitors by the Boundary Element Method, *Proceedings of First European Conference on Numerical Methods in Engineering*, September 1992.

R. F. Harrington, Field Computation by Moment Method, Krieger Publishing Company, Florida, 1985.

Sadasiva M. Rao, Allen W. Glisson, Donald R. Wilton, B. Sarma Vidula, A Simple Numerical Solution Procedure for Statics Problems Involving Arbitrary-Shaped Surfaces, *IEEE Transactions on Antennas and Propagation*, Vol. AP-27, No. 5, September 1979.

S. Ghosh and A. Chakrabarty, Capacitance evaluation of Arbitrary-shaped Multiconducting Bodies using Rectangular Subareas, *Journal of Electromagnetic Waves and Applications*, Vol. 20, No. 14, pp. 2091-2102, 2006.

S. Ghosh and A. Chakrabarty, Estimation of Capacitance of Different Conducting Bodies by the Method of Rectangular Subareas, *Journal of Electrostatics, Elsevier Publication*, Vol. 66, Issues 3-4, March 2008, Pages 142 - 146.

Saila Ponnapalli, Alina Deutsch, Robert Bertin, A Package Analysis Tool Based on a Method of Moments Surface Formulation, *IEEE Transactions on Components, Hybrids, and Manufacturing Technology*, Vol. 16, No. 8, December 1993.

T. J. Higgins and D. K. Reitan, Accurate Determination of the Capacitance of a Thin Rectangular Plate, *AIEE Transactions* Vol.75, part-1, January 1957.

V. K. Hariharan, S. V. K. Shastry, Ajay Chakrabarty and V. R. Katti, Free Space Capacitance of Conducting Surfaces, *Journal of Spacecraft Technology*, Vol. 8, No. 1, pp. 61-73, January 1998.

11

Alternative analytical method used in calculus of hyper static mechanical systems, in plotting the distribution of shear force, bending moment, displacements and rotations of section beam

Cornel MARIN[1], Viviana FILIP[2] and Alexandru MARIN[3]

Abstract. The actual graphical methods used by engineers when plotting the stress distributions are based on integrating the differential equations of stresses for each beam segment. The resulting integration constants are obtained by imposing boundary conditions for each beam segment. This alternative proposed analytical method uses the *MATHCAD step function* $\Phi(x\text{-}a)$ which introduces a friendly analytical form of the shear force, bending moment, rotation (slope) cross-section and displacement expressions. The calculus of *hyper static mechanical systems* using the step function and matrix expression of equations and also the constructive optimization of structures is thus easier to be performed using this method. The traditional methods use integral expressions which are solved by means of numerical methods. The practical application presented in this chapter is representative for o large area of mechanical engineering.

Keywords: MATHCAD step function, hyper static mechanical systems

1. Expression of cross sectional and deflections founctions

In this chapter we will present the expressions of the cross sectional functions for the shear force $T_z(x)$, bending moment $M_{iy}(x)$, transversal section rotations $\varphi_y(x)$ and displacement section $w(x)$, using the MATHCAD step function $\Phi(x\text{-}a)$ [1], [2], [3], [4] .The step function $\Phi(x\text{-}a)$ in MATHCAD have the well-known form:

$$\Phi(x-a)=\begin{cases}0 & if \quad x<a\\ 1 & if \quad x\geq a\end{cases} \tag{1}$$

[1] VALAHIA University Targoviste, Romania, e-mail: cor_marin@yahoo.com
[2] VALAHIA University Targoviste, Romania, e-mail: v_filip@yahoo.com
[3] Technical University of Constructions Bucharest, Romania, e-mail: adu_de@yahoo.com

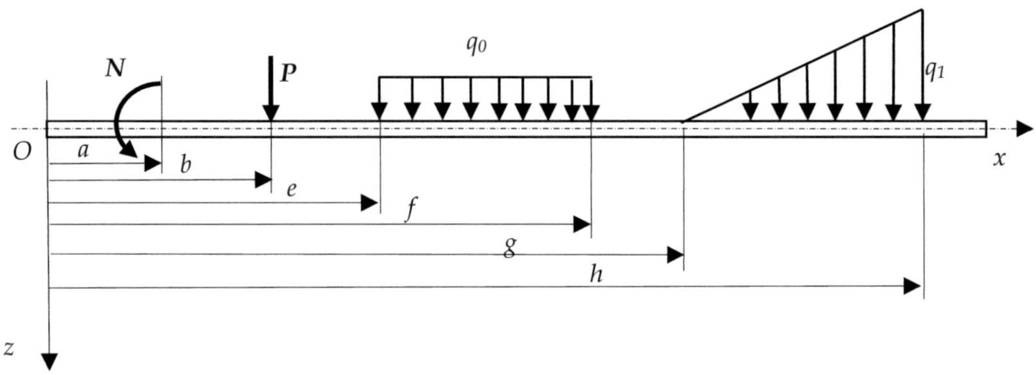

Fig. 1. The Beam model loaded with 4 different loading types

One considers a beam subjected to bending. The beam is characterized by length L and constant bending stiffness EI_y. There are 4 different load types [1], [2], [3], [4], presented in fig. 1:

- The bending moment N, placed at distance a from the left end of the beam;
- The concentrated force P, placed at distance b from the left end of the beam;
- The uniform distributed load q_0 which acts on a beam segment delimitated by the distances e and f from the left end of the beam;
- The linear distributed load $q(x) = q_1 \dfrac{x-g}{h-g}$, $x \in [g, h]$ which acts on a beam segment delimitated by the distances g and h from the left end of the beam.
-

The **analytical expressions for the cross sectional resultants** considering the one loading types from figure 1, written using the step function Φ are:
For the bending moment N:

$$M_i(x) = -N \cdot \Phi(x-a) \tag{2}$$

The bending cross sectional resultant diagram is represented using MATHCAD software in figure 2.

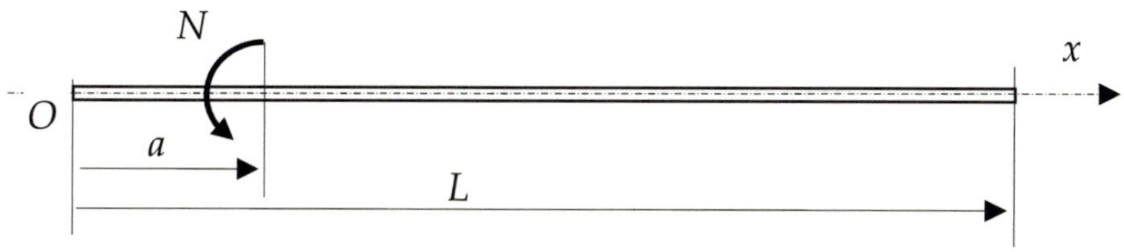

N := 5 a := 2 L := 10 Axa (x) := 0 Mi (x) := − N·Φ (x − a)

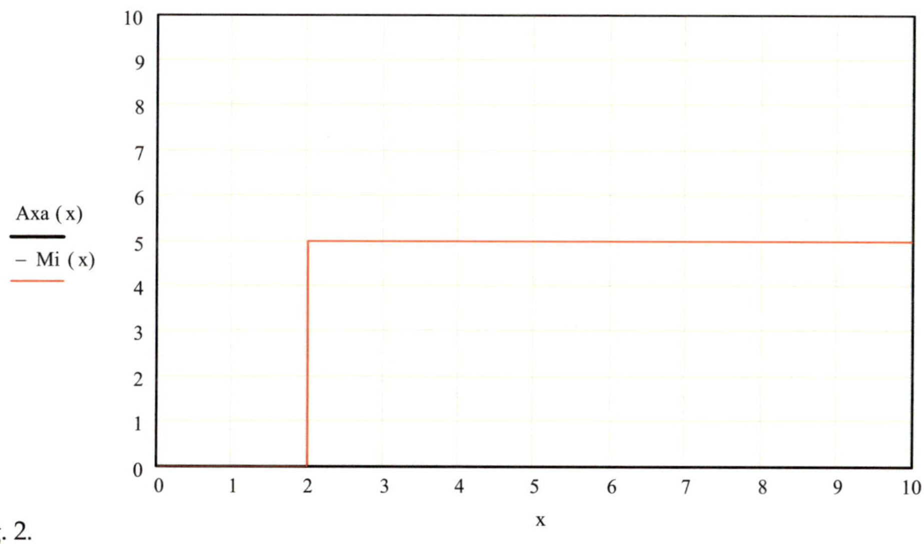

Fig. 2.

For the concentrated force P:

$$T(x) = -P \cdot \Phi(x-b);$$
$$M_i(x) = -P \cdot \Phi(x-b) \cdot (x-b) \tag{3}$$

The bending and shear cross sectional resultants diagrams for this case is represented using MATHCAD software in figure 3.

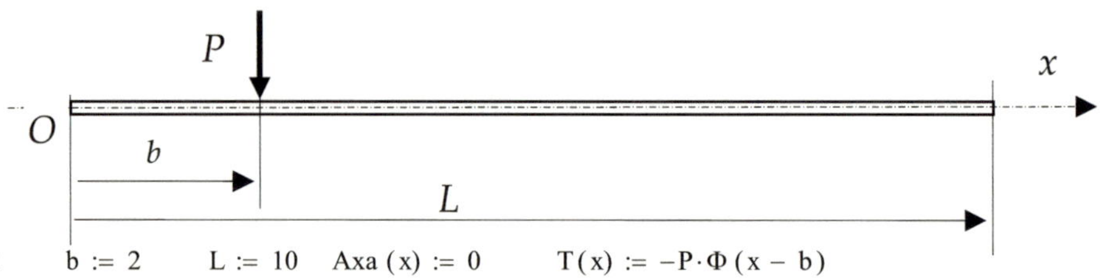

P := 2 b := 2 L := 10 Axa (x) := 0 T(x) := −P·Φ (x − b)

Mi (x) := −P·Φ (x − b)(x − b)

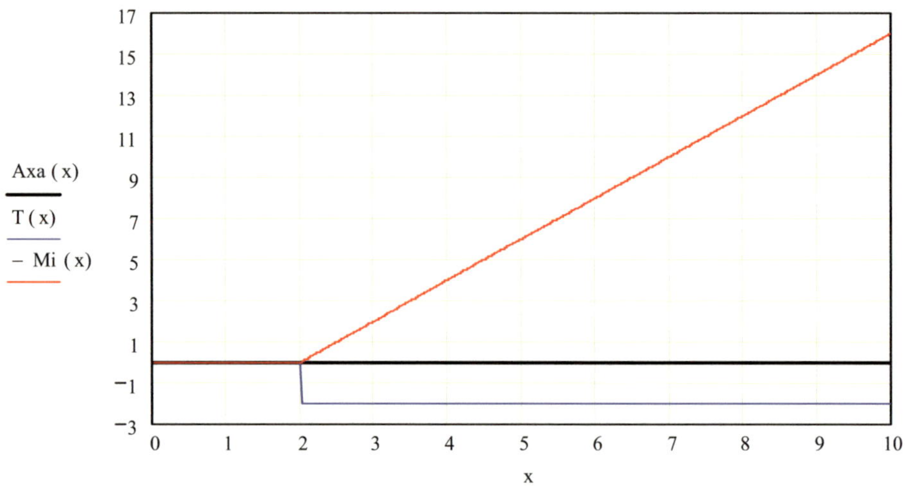

Fig. 3.

For the uniform distributed load $q(x) = q_0$, $x \in [e, f]$:

$$T(x) = -q_0 \cdot \Phi(x-e) \cdot (x-e) + q_0 \cdot \Phi(x-f) \cdot (x-f);$$
$$M_i(x) = -\frac{q_0}{2} \cdot \Phi(x-e) \cdot (x-e)^2 + \frac{q_0}{2} \cdot \Phi(x-f) \cdot (x-f)^2; \tag{4}$$

The bending and shear cross sectional resultants diagrams for this case is represented using MATHCAD software in figure 4.

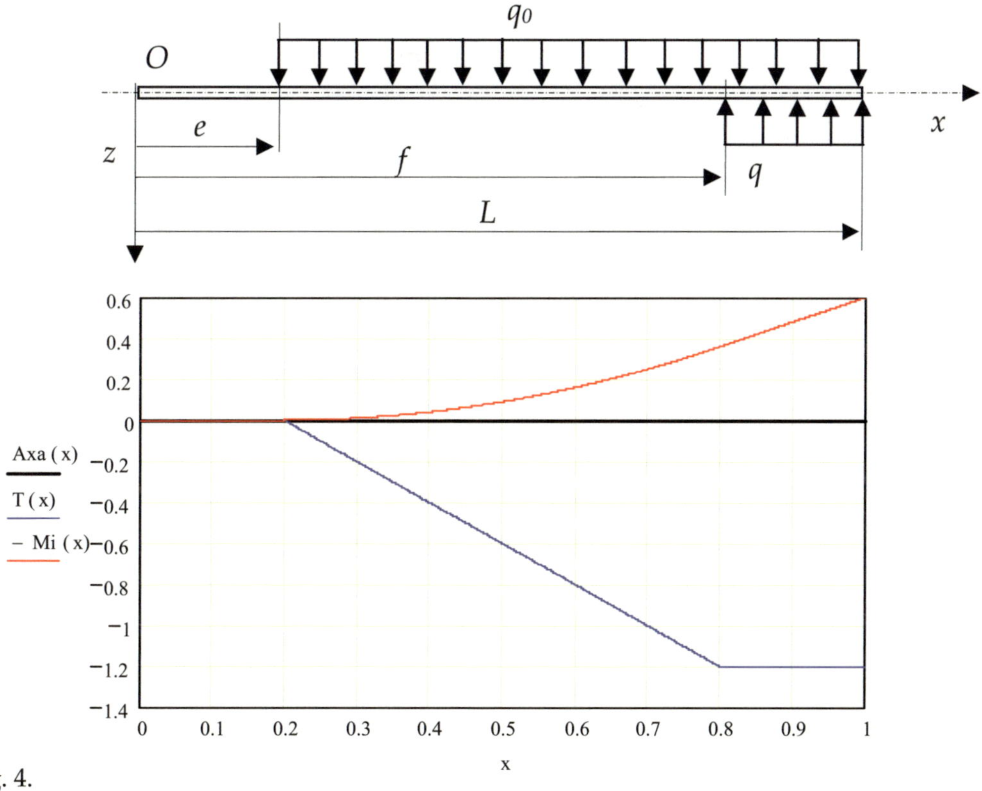

Fig. 4.

For the linear distributed load $q(x) = q_1 \dfrac{x-g}{h-g}, \quad x \in [g, h]$ (fig.5.)

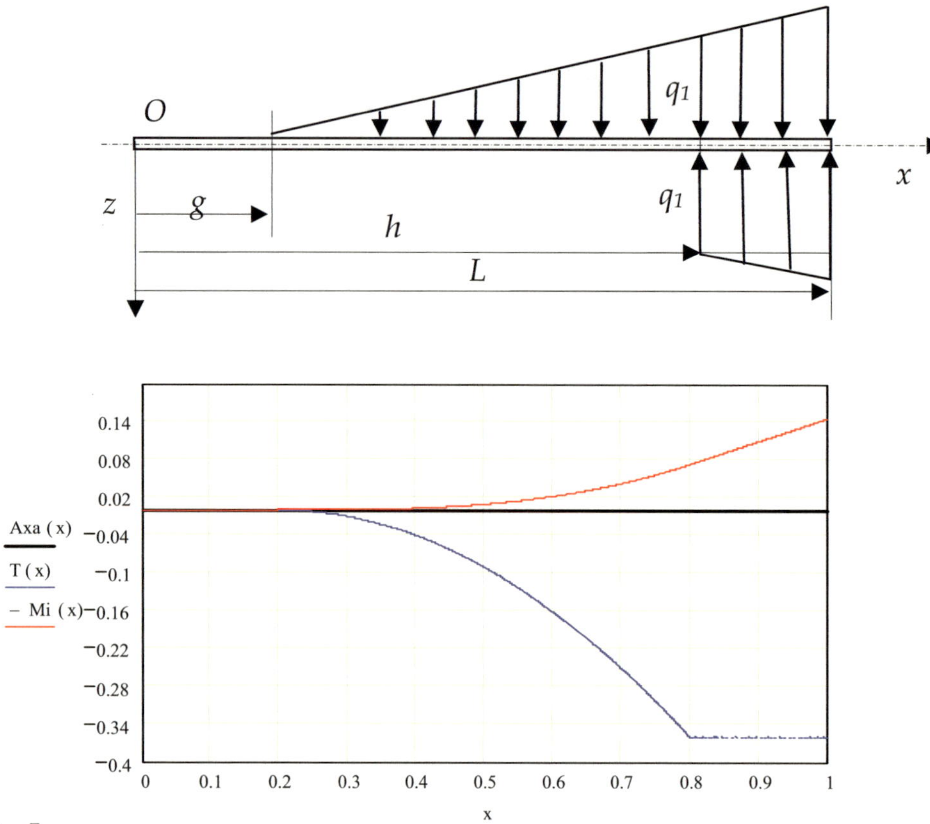

Fig. 5.

The analytical expressions for the cross sectional resultant is obtained:

$$T(x) = -\frac{q_1}{2(h-g)} \cdot \Phi(x-g) \cdot (x-g)^2 + q_1 \cdot \Phi(x-h) \cdot (x-h) + \frac{q_1}{2(h-g)} \cdot \Phi(x-h) \cdot (x-h)^2;$$

$$M_i(x) = -\frac{q_1}{6(h-g)} \cdot \Phi(x-g) \cdot (x-g)^3 + \frac{q_1}{2} \cdot \Phi(x-h) \cdot (x-h)^2 + \frac{q_1}{6(h-g)} \cdot \Phi(x-h) \cdot (x-h)^3; \tag{5}$$

The bending and shear cross sectional resultants diagrams for this case is represented using MATHCAD software in figure 5.

If the beam is subjected simultaneous of the four types of load above, the analytical expressions of cross sectional are obtained using the principle of superposition effects:

- *For shear force:*

$$T_z(x) = -P \cdot \Phi(x-b) - q_0 \cdot (x-e) \cdot \Phi(x-e) + q_0 \cdot (x-f) \cdot \Phi(x-f) - \\ -q_1 \cdot \frac{(x-g)^2}{2(h-g)} \cdot \Phi(x-g) + q_1 \cdot (x-h) \cdot \Phi(x-h) + q_1 \cdot \frac{(x-h)^2}{2(h-g)} \cdot \Phi(x-h); \tag{6}$$

▪*For bending moment:*

$$
\begin{aligned}
&M_{iy}(x)=-N\cdot\Phi(x-a)-P\cdot(x-b)\cdot\Phi(x-b)-\\
&-q_0\cdot\frac{(x-e)^2}{2}\cdot\Phi(x-e)+q_0\cdot\frac{(x-f)^2}{2}\cdot\Phi(x-f)-\\
&-q_1\cdot\frac{(x-g)^3}{6(h-g)}\cdot\Phi(x-g)+q_1\cdot\frac{(x-h)^2}{2}\cdot\Phi(x-h)+q_1\cdot\frac{(x-h)^3}{6(h-g)}\cdot\Phi(x-h);
\end{aligned}
\tag{7}
$$

The differential equation of displacements $w(x)$ corresponding to a cross-section is [1]:

$$
\frac{d^2w}{dx^2}=-\frac{M_{iy}(x)}{EI_y}
\tag{8}
$$

Integrating twice the differential equation (2), one obtains the function of cross-sectional rotations $\varphi_y(x)$ and displacement $w(x)$:

$$
\begin{aligned}
&\varphi_y(x)=\frac{dw}{dx}=\varphi_0-\int_0^x\frac{M_{iy}(s)}{EI_y}ds\\
&w(x)=w_0+\varphi_0\cdot x-\int_0^x\int_0^t\left(\frac{M_{iy}(s)}{EI_y}ds\right)dt
\end{aligned}
\tag{9}
$$

If the beam is subjected simultaneous of the four types of load above, the analytical expressions for the function of cross-sectional rotations $\varphi_y(x)$ and displacement $w(x)$ obtained using relation (9) are written:

$$
\begin{aligned}
EI_y\varphi_y(x)=&EI_y\varphi_0+N\cdot(x-a)\cdot\Phi(x-a)+P\cdot\frac{(x-b)^2}{2}\cdot\Phi(x-b)+\\
&+q_0\cdot\frac{(x-e)^3}{6}\cdot\Phi(x-e)-q_0\cdot\frac{(x-f)^3}{6}\cdot\Phi(x-f)+\\
&+q_1\cdot\frac{(x-g)^4}{24(h-g)}\cdot\Phi(x-g)-q_1\cdot\frac{(x-h)^3}{6}\cdot\Phi(x-h)-q_1\cdot\frac{(x-h)^4}{24(h-g)}\cdot\Phi(x-h);
\end{aligned}
\tag{10}
$$

$$
\begin{aligned}
EI_yw(x)=&EI_yw_0+EI_y\varphi_0\cdot x+N\cdot\frac{(x-a)^2}{2}\cdot\Phi(x-a)+P\cdot\frac{(x-b)^3}{6}\cdot\Phi(x-b)+\\
&+q_0\cdot\frac{(x-e)^4}{24}\cdot\Phi(x-e)-q_0\cdot\frac{(x-f)^4}{24}\cdot\Phi(x-f)+\\
&+q_1\cdot\frac{(x-g)^5}{120(h-g)}\cdot\Phi(x-g)-q_1\cdot\frac{(x-h)^4}{24}\cdot\Phi(x-h)-q_1\cdot\frac{(x-h)^5}{120(h-g)}\cdot\Phi(x-h);
\end{aligned}
\tag{11}
$$

2. Numerical application for computing diagrams

Application 1. Beam supported by 2 rigid bearings (statically determined structure)

One considers a beam supported by two bearings. The length of the beam is *10a* and the flexural stiffness *EI* constant along its entire length. The beam is loaded with two uniformly distributed loads q_0 , a linearly distributed load $0 - q_1$ and a force couple (moment) $N=qa^2$, as shown in figure 6. One should determine the analytical expressions of the shear force *T(x)* and bending moment *M(x)*, cross-sectional rotations $\varphi(x)$ and displacements *w(x)* and plot the variation diagrams along the beam's length using the step function Φ(x-a) from MATHCAD.
Particular values: $q_0=q$, $q_1=2q$; q=1kN/m, a=1m and EI=1000 kNm².

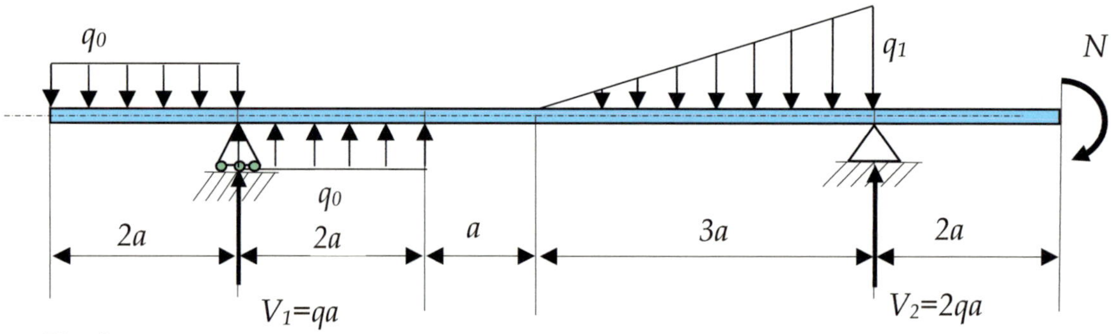

Fig. 6.

For the statically determined system one will first determine the reaction forces V_1 and V_2 using the equilibrium equations from the Mechanics of Solids:

$$\sum M_{1y} = 0 \Rightarrow \quad V_2 \cdot 6a + q_0 \cdot 2a \cdot a + q_0 \cdot 2a \cdot a - \frac{1}{2} q_1 \cdot 3a \cdot 5a - N = 0 \Rightarrow \; V_2 = 2qa$$

$$\sum M_{2y} = 0 \Rightarrow \quad V_1 \cdot 6a - q_0 \cdot 2a \cdot 7a + q_0 \cdot 2a \cdot 5a - \frac{1}{2} q_1 \cdot 3a \cdot a + N = 0 \Rightarrow \; V_1 = qa \tag{12}$$

The analytical expressions of the shear force T(x) and bending moment M(x) will be determined using the *principle of effects superposition*, considering the corresponding analytical expressions of the moment *N*, reaction forces V_1, V_2, uniformly distributed loads q_0 and linearly distributed loads $0\text{-}q_1$:

$$T(x) = V_1 \cdot \Phi(x-2a) + V_2 \cdot \Phi(x-8a) -$$
$$-q_0 \cdot \Phi(x) \cdot x + q_0 \cdot \Phi(x-2a) \cdot (x-2a) + q_0 \cdot \Phi(x-2a) \cdot (x-2a) - q_0 \cdot \Phi(x-4a) \cdot (x-4a) -$$
$$-\frac{q_1}{2 \cdot 3a} \cdot \Phi(x-5a) \cdot (x-5a)^2 + q_1 \cdot \Phi(x-8a) \cdot (x-8a) + \frac{q_1}{2 \cdot 3a} \cdot \Phi(x-8a) \cdot (x-8a)^2.$$

$$M_i(x) = N \cdot \Phi(x-10a) + V_1 \cdot \Phi(x-2a)(x-2a) + V_2 \cdot \Phi(x-8a)(x-8a) -$$
$$-\frac{q_0}{2} \cdot \Phi(x) \cdot x^2 + \frac{q_0}{2} \cdot \Phi(x-2a) \cdot (x-2a)^2 + \frac{q_0}{2} \cdot \Phi(x-2a) \cdot (x-2a)^2 - \frac{q_0}{2} \cdot \Phi(x-4a) \cdot (x-4a)^2 -$$
$$-\frac{q_1}{6 \cdot 3a} \cdot \Phi(x-5a) \cdot (x-5a)^3 + \frac{q_1}{2} \cdot \Phi(x-8a) \cdot (x-8a)^2 + \frac{q_1}{6 \cdot 3a} \cdot \Phi(x-8a) \cdot (x-8a)^3$$

(13)

The analytical expressions of the cross-sectional rotations $\varphi(x)$ will be determined using the *principle of effects superposition*, considering the general relations (10) for the 4 types of loads:

$$EI_y\varphi(x) = EI_y\varphi_0 - N \cdot \Phi(x-10a) \cdot (x-10a) - V_1 \cdot \Phi(x-2a)\frac{(x-2a)^2}{2} - V_2 \cdot \Phi(x-8a)\frac{(x-8a)^2}{2} +$$
$$+q_0 \cdot \Phi(x) \cdot \frac{x^3}{6} - q_0 \cdot \Phi(x-2a) \cdot \frac{(x-2a)^3}{6} - q_0 \cdot \Phi(x-2a) \cdot \frac{(x-2a)^3}{6} + q_0 \cdot \Phi(x-4a) \cdot \frac{(x-4a)^3}{6} +$$
$$+\frac{q_1}{3a} \cdot \Phi(x-5a) \cdot \frac{(x-5a)^4}{24} - \frac{q_1}{3a} \cdot \Phi(x-8a) \cdot \frac{(x-8a)^4}{24} - q_1 \cdot \Phi(x-8a) \cdot \frac{(x-8a)^3}{6}$$

(14)

The analytical expressions of the cross-sectional displacements $w(x)$ will be determined using the *principle of effects superposition*, considering the general relations (11) for the 4 types of loads:

$$EI_yw(x) = EI_yw_0 + EI_y\varphi_0 \cdot x - N \cdot \Phi(x-10a)\frac{(x-10a)^2}{2} - V_1 \cdot \Phi(x-2a)\frac{(x-2a)^3}{6} - V_2 \cdot \Phi(x-8a)\frac{(x-8a)^3}{6} +$$
$$+q_0 \cdot \Phi(x) \cdot \frac{x^4}{24} - q_0 \cdot \Phi(x-2a) \cdot \frac{(x-2a)^4}{24} - q_0 \cdot \Phi(x-2a) \cdot \frac{(x-2a)^4}{24} + q_0 \cdot \Phi(x-4a) \cdot \frac{(x-4a)^4}{24} +$$
$$+\frac{q_1}{3a} \cdot \Phi(x-5a) \cdot \frac{(x-5a)^5}{120} - \frac{q_1}{3a} \cdot \Phi(x-8a) \cdot \frac{(x-8a)^5}{120} - q_1 \cdot \Phi(x-8a) \cdot \frac{(x-8a)^4}{24}$$

(15)

The integration constants EI_yw_0 and *$EI_y\varphi_0$* will be determined for the displacements' conditions imposed in the supports:

$$\begin{cases} EI_yw(2a) = EI_yw_0 + EI_y\varphi_0 \cdot 2a + W(2a) = 0 \\ EI_yw(8a) = EI_yw_0 + EI_y\varphi_0 \cdot 8a + W(8a) = 0 \end{cases} \Rightarrow \begin{cases} EI_y\varphi_0 = \frac{1}{6a}[W(2a) - W(8a)] \\ EI_yw_0 = \frac{1}{3}[W(8a) - 4 \cdot W(2a)] \end{cases}$$

(16)

The shear forces $T(x)$ and bending moments $M_i(x)$ diagrams are shown in figure 7. In figure 8 one plotted the deflection function $EIW(x)$ and the rotation one $EIF(x)$, for the particular numerical data.

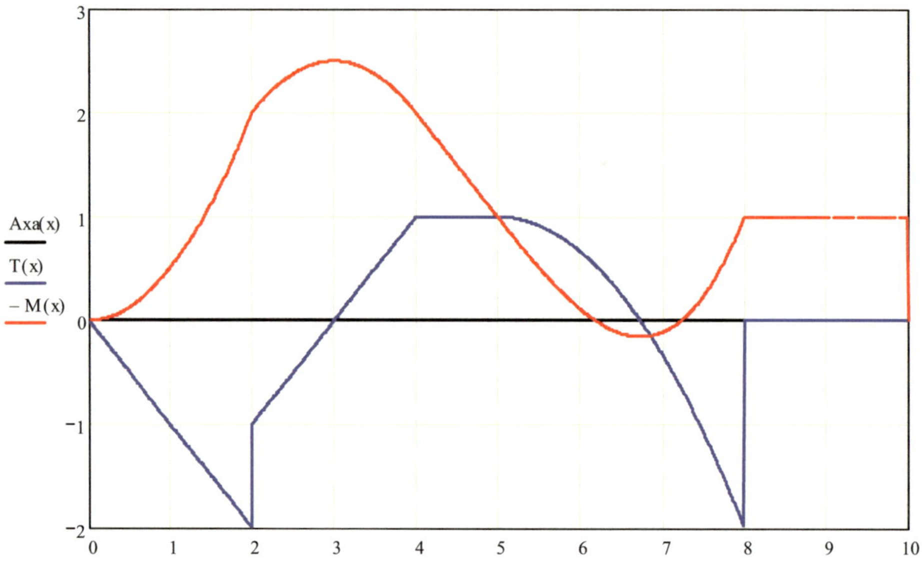

Fig. 7. Shear force T and bending moment M_i diagrams

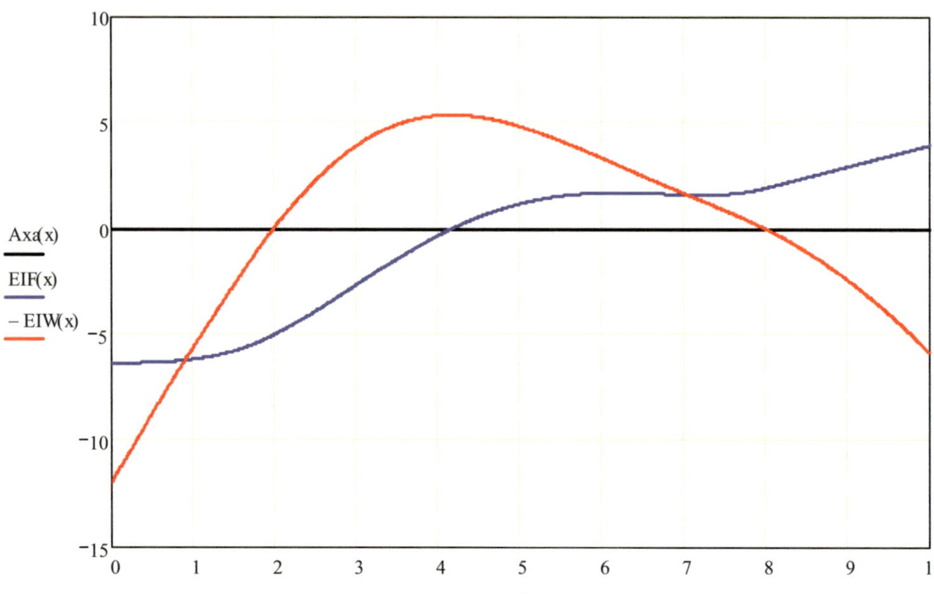

Fig. 8. Cross-sectional deflection $EIw(x)$ and rotation $EI\varphi(x)$ diagrams

Application 2: Continuous beam supported by 4 uneven rigid bearings (statically undetermined system)

One considers the continuous beam *OA* supported by 4 stiff bearings, having different levels with respect to the beam's axis: $w_1=0$, $w_2\neq0$, $w_3\neq0$, $w_4=0$. The beam has a constant bending stiffness *EI*, along its whole length. The beam's exterior loading is known: *N*, *P*, q_0 and q_1. The support reactions V_1, V_2, V_3 and V_4 are unknown (fig.9). Particular values: $q_0=1kN/m$; $a=1m$; $EI=1000\ kNm^3$; $w_2=0{,}001\ m$; $w_3=0{,}003\ m$; $r_1=2a$; $r_2=3a$; $r_3=7a$; $r_4=10a$; $w_1=w_4=0$

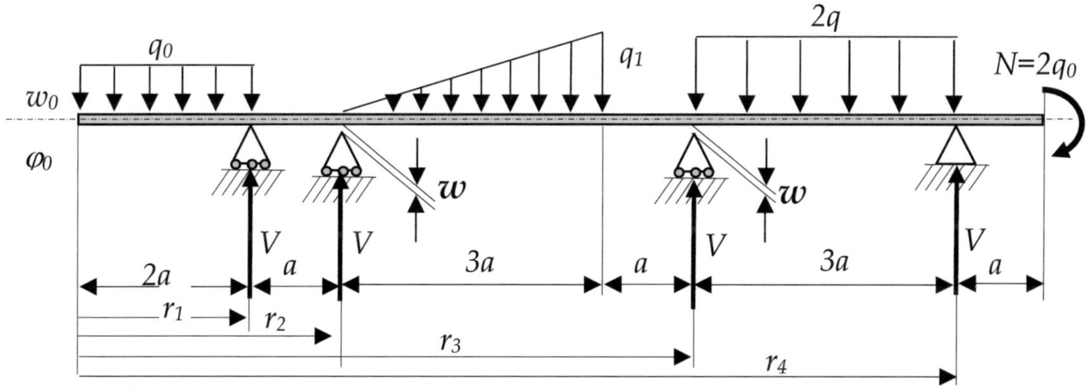

Fig. 9.

In order to compute the values of the unknown reaction forces V_1, V_2, V_3 şi V_4 one uses the two equations of equilibrium from Mechanics:

$$\sum F_{zs}\downarrow = V_1+V_2+V_3+V_4$$
$$\sum \overleftarrow{M}_{4s} = V_1(r_4-r_1)+V_2(r_4-r_2)+V_3(r_4-r_3) \qquad (17)$$

where: $\sum F_{zs}\downarrow$ is the sum of exterior forces on *Oz* axis;

$\sum \overleftarrow{M}_{4s}$ the sum of moments and exterior force couples with respect to the *Oy* axis through point 4.

The third and the fourth equations will result by replacing the origin parameters (w_0 and φ_0) in the displacement equations from the supports:

$$\begin{cases} w_0+\varphi_0\cdot r_1+\dfrac{1}{EI}W(r_1)=w_1 \\ w_0+\varphi_0\cdot r_2+\dfrac{1}{EI}W(r_2)=w_2 \end{cases} \qquad \begin{cases} w_0+\varphi_0\cdot r_3+\dfrac{1}{EI}W(r_3)=w_3 \\ w_0+\varphi_0\cdot r_4+\dfrac{1}{EI}W(r_4)=w_4 \end{cases} \qquad (18)$$

where *W(x)* is the second integral of the bending efforts with changed sign for the four types of known efforts as well as for the unknown reaction forces V_1, V_2, V_3 and V_4 (fig.9.):

$$W(x)=-\frac{N}{2}\cdot\Phi(x-11a)\cdot(x-11a)^2-\frac{V_1}{6}\cdot\Phi(x-2a)\cdot(x-2a)^3-\frac{V_2}{6}\cdot\Phi(x-3a)\cdot(x-3a)^3-$$
$$-\frac{V_3}{6}\cdot\Phi(x-7a)\cdot(x-7a)^3-\frac{V_4}{6}\cdot\Phi(x-10a)\cdot(x-10a)^3-\frac{q_0}{24}\cdot\Phi(x)\cdot x^4-\frac{q_0}{24}\cdot\Phi(x-2a)\cdot(x-2a)^4+$$
$$+\frac{q_1}{120\cdot 3a}\cdot\Phi(x-3a)\cdot(x-3a)^5-\frac{q_1}{24}\cdot\Phi(x-6a)\cdot(x-6a)^4-\frac{q_1}{120\cdot 3a}\cdot\Phi(x-6a)\cdot(x-6a)^5+$$
$$+\frac{q_0}{24}\cdot\Phi(x-7a)\cdot(x-7a)^4-\frac{q_0}{24}\cdot\Phi(x-10a)\cdot(x-10a)^4 \tag{19}$$

Replacing w_0 and φ_0 in the first and last couple of equations (18) one obtains two equations:

$$\frac{W(r_2)-W(r_1)}{r_2-r_1}-EI\frac{w_2-w_1}{r_2-r_1}=\frac{W(r_3)-W(r_2)}{r_3-r_2}-EI\frac{w_3-w_2}{r_3-r_2}$$
$$\frac{W(r_3)-W(r_2)}{r_3-r_2}-EI\frac{w_3-w_2}{r_3-r_2}=\frac{W(r_4)-W(r_3)}{r_4-r_3}-EI\frac{w_4-w_3}{r_4-r_3} \tag{20}$$

Denotes with $Ws(x)$ the second integral of the bending efforts with changed sign written *only for known exterior loads*:

$$Ws(x)=-N\cdot\Phi(x-11a)\cdot\frac{(x-11a)^2}{2}+q_0\cdot\Phi(x)\cdot\frac{(x)^4}{24}-q_0\cdot\Phi(x-2a)\cdot\frac{(x-2a)^4}{24}+$$
$$+q_1\cdot\Phi(x-3a)\cdot\frac{(x-3a)^5}{120(3a)}-q_1\cdot\Phi(x-6a)\cdot\frac{(x-6a)^4}{24}-q_1\cdot\Phi(x-6a)\cdot\frac{(x-6a)^5}{120(3a)}+$$
$$+2q_0\cdot\Phi(x-7a)\cdot\frac{(x-7a)^4}{24}-2q_0\cdot\Phi(x-10a)\cdot\frac{(x-10a)^4}{24} \tag{21}$$

Notate : $Ws(r_1)=W_{s1};\ Ws(r_2)=W_{s2};\ Ws(r_3)=W_{s3},$ *and so on.*

$$k_1(x)=\Phi(x-r_1)\cdot\frac{(x-r_1)^3}{6};\quad k_2(x)=\Phi(x-r_2)\cdot\frac{(x-r_2)^3}{6};$$
$$k_3(x)=\Phi(x-r_3)\cdot\frac{(x-r_3)^3}{6};\quad k_4(x)=\Phi(x-r_4)\cdot\frac{(x-r_4)^3}{6}; \tag{22}$$

Notate : $k_1(r_1)=k_{11};\ k_1(r_2)=k_{12};\ k_2(r_1)=k_{21},$ *and so on.*

Isolating the unknowns V_1, V_2, V_3 and V_4 from equations (20) one obtains the third and the fourth equations:

$$\begin{cases} V_1\cdot\left(\frac{k_{11}-k_{12}}{d_{12}}-\frac{k_{12}-k_{13}}{d_{23}}\right)+V_2\cdot\left(\frac{k_{21}-k_{22}}{d_{12}}-\frac{k_{21}-k_{23}}{d_{23}}\right)+V_3\cdot\left(\frac{k_{31}-k_{32}}{d_{12}}-\frac{k_{32}-k_{33}}{d_{23}}\right)= \\ \qquad =\frac{W_{s1}-W_{s2}}{r_2-r_1}-\frac{W_{s2}-W_{s3}}{r_3-r_2}-EI\frac{w_1-w_2}{r_2-r_1}+EI\frac{w_2-w_3}{r_3-r_2} \\ V_1\cdot\left(\frac{k_{12}-k_{13}}{d_{23}}-\frac{k_{12}-k_{13}}{d_{34}}\right)+V_2\cdot\left(\frac{k_{22}-k_{23}}{d_{23}}-\frac{k_{23}-k_{24}}{d_{34}}\right)+V_3\cdot\left(\frac{k_{32}-k_{33}}{d_{23}}-\frac{k_{33}-k_{34}}{d_{34}}\right)+ \\ +V_4\cdot\left(\frac{k_{42}-k_{43}}{d_{23}}-\frac{k_{42}-k_{43}}{d_{34}}\right)=\frac{W_{s2}-W_{s3}}{r_3-r_2}-\frac{W_{s3}-W_{s4}}{r_4-r_3}-EI\frac{w_2-w_3}{r_3-r_2}+EI\frac{w_3-w_4}{r_4-r_3} \end{cases} \tag{23}$$

The equations (17) and (22) are written in matrix form as it follows:

$$\begin{bmatrix} 1 & 1 & 1 & 1 \\ r_4-r_1 & r_4-r_2 & r_4-r_3 & 0 \\ \frac{k_{11}-k_{12}}{r_2-r_1}-\frac{k_{12}-k_{13}}{r_3-r_2} & \frac{k_{21}-k_{22}}{r_2-r_1}-\frac{k_{22}-k_{23}}{r_3-r_2} & \frac{k_{31}-k_{32}}{r_2-r_1}-\frac{k_{32}-k_{33}}{r_3-r_2} & 0 \\ \frac{k_{12}-k_{13}}{r_3-r_2}-\frac{k_{13}-k_{14}}{r_4-r_3} & \frac{k_{22}-k_{23}}{r_3-r_2}-\frac{k_{23}-k_{24}}{r_4-r_3} & \frac{k_{32}-k_{33}}{r_3-r_2}-\frac{k_{33}-k_{34}}{r_4-r_3} & \frac{k_{42}-k_{43}}{r_3-r_2}-\frac{k_{43}-k_{44}}{r_4-r_3} \end{bmatrix}\begin{Bmatrix} V_1 \\ V_2 \\ V_3 \\ V_4 \end{Bmatrix}=$$

$$=\begin{Bmatrix} \sum F_{zs}\downarrow \\ \sum \overleftarrow{M}_{4s} \\ \frac{W_{s1}-W_{s2}}{r_2-r_1}-\frac{W_{s2}-W_{s3}}{r_3-r_2}-EI\frac{w_1-w_2}{r_2-r_1}+EI\frac{w_2-w_3}{r_3-r_2} \\ \frac{W_{s2}-W_{s3}}{r_3-r_2}-\frac{W_{s3}-W_{s4}}{r_4-r_3}-EI\frac{w_2-w_3}{r_3-r_2}+EI\frac{w_3-w_4}{r_4-r_3} \end{Bmatrix} \tag{24}$$

If one introduces the particular numerical data and the matrix equation (23) in MATHCAD, the following values of the reaction forces will yield:

$$\begin{pmatrix} \mathrm{V1} \\ \mathrm{V2} \\ \mathrm{V3} \\ \mathrm{V4} \end{pmatrix}=\begin{pmatrix} 3.550 \\ -0.225 \\ 4.392 \\ 3.283 \end{pmatrix} \tag{25}$$

The particular expressions of the shear force and bending moment are:

$$\begin{aligned}T(x)=&V_1\cdot\Phi(x-2a)+V_2\cdot\Phi(x-3a)+V_3\cdot\Phi(x-7a)+V_4\cdot\Phi(x-10a)-\\&-q_0\cdot\Phi(x)\cdot x+q_0\cdot\Phi(x-2a)\cdot(x-2a)-\\&-\frac{q_1}{2\cdot 3a}\cdot\Phi(x-3a)\cdot(x-3a)^2+q_1\cdot\Phi(x-6a)\cdot(x-6a)+\frac{q_1}{2\cdot 3a}\cdot\Phi(x-6a)\cdot(x-6a)^2-\\&-q_0\cdot\Phi(x-7a)\cdot(x-7a)+q_0\cdot\Phi(x-10a)\cdot(x-10a)\end{aligned} \tag{26}$$

$$\begin{aligned}M(x)=&N\cdot\Phi(x-11a)+V_1\cdot\Phi(x-2a)\cdot(x-2a)+V_2\cdot\Phi(x-3a)\cdot(x-3a)+\\&+V_3\cdot\Phi(x-7a)\cdot(x-7a)+V_4\cdot\Phi(x-10a)\cdot(x-10a)-\\&-\frac{q_0}{2}\cdot\Phi(x)\cdot x^2+\frac{q_0}{2}\cdot\Phi(x-2a)\cdot(x-2a)^2+\\&-\frac{q_1}{6\cdot 3a}\cdot\Phi(x-3a)\cdot(x-3a)^3+\frac{q_1}{2}\cdot\Phi(x-6a)\cdot(x-6a)^2+\frac{q_1}{6\cdot 3a}\cdot\Phi(x-6a)\cdot(x-6a)^3-\\&-\frac{q_0}{2}\cdot\Phi(x-7a)\cdot(x-7a)^2+\frac{q_0}{2}\cdot\Phi(x-10a)\cdot(x-10a)^2\end{aligned} \tag{27}$$

The particular expression of the cross-sectional rotation is written:

$$\begin{aligned}&EI_y\varphi(x)=EI_y\varphi_0+F(x);\\&F(x)=-N\cdot\Phi(x-11a)\cdot(x-11a)-\frac{V_1}{2}\cdot\Phi(x-2a)\cdot(x-2a)^2-\frac{V_2}{2}\cdot\Phi(x-3a)\cdot(x-3a)^2-\\&\quad-\frac{V_3}{2}\cdot\Phi(x-7a)\cdot(x-7a)^2-\frac{V_4}{2}\cdot\Phi(x-10a)\cdot(x-10a)^2-\\&\quad+\frac{q_0}{6}\cdot\Phi(x)\cdot x^3-\frac{q_0}{6}\cdot\Phi(x-2a)\cdot(x-2a)^3-\\&\quad+\frac{2q}{24\cdot 3a}\cdot\Phi(x-3a)\cdot(x-3a)^4-\frac{2q_0}{6}\cdot\Phi(x-6a)\cdot(x-6a)^3-\frac{2q_0}{24\cdot 3a}\cdot\Phi(x-6a)\cdot(x-6a)^4+\\&\quad+\frac{q_0}{6}\cdot\Phi(x-7a)\cdot(x-7a)^3-\frac{q_0}{6}\cdot\Phi(x-10a)\cdot(x-10a)^3\end{aligned} \tag{28}$$

The particular expression of the cross-sectional displacement is:

$$EI_y w(x) = EI_y w_0 + EI_y \varphi_0 \cdot x + W(x)$$

$$\begin{aligned} W(x) = &-\frac{N}{2}\cdot\Phi(x-11a)\cdot(x-11a)^2 - \frac{V_1}{6}\cdot\Phi(x-2a)\cdot(x-2a)^3 - \frac{V_2}{6}\cdot\Phi(x-3a)\cdot(x-3a)^3 - \\ &-\frac{V_3}{6}\cdot\Phi(x-7a)\cdot(x-7a)^3 - \frac{V_4}{6}\cdot\Phi(x-10a)\cdot(x-10a)^3 - \\ &+\frac{q_0}{24}\cdot\Phi(x)\cdot x^4 - \frac{q_0}{24}\cdot\Phi(x-2a)\cdot(x-2a)^4 + \\ &+\frac{q_1}{120\cdot 3a}\cdot\Phi(x-3a)\cdot(x-3a)^5 - \frac{q_1}{24}\cdot\Phi(x-6a)\cdot(x-6a)^4 - \frac{q_1}{120\cdot 3a}\cdot\Phi(x-6a)\cdot(x-6a)^5 + \\ &+\frac{q_0}{24}\cdot\Phi(x-7a)\cdot(x-7a)^4 - \frac{q_0}{24}\cdot\Phi(x-10a)\cdot(x-10a)^4 \end{aligned} \quad (29)$$

$EI_y w_0$ and $EI_y \varphi_0$ integration constants, corresponding to the origin parameters will be determined for the zero displacement conditions from supports 1 and 4:

$$\begin{cases} EI_y w(2a) = EI_y w_0 + EI_y \varphi_0 \cdot 2a + W(2a) = 0 \\ EI_y w(10a) = EI_y w_0 + EI_y \varphi_0 \cdot 10a + W(10a) = 0 \end{cases} \qquad \begin{cases} EI_y \varphi_0 = \frac{1}{8a}[W(2a) - W(10a)] \\ EI_y w_0 = \frac{1}{4}[W(10a) - 5\cdot W(2a)] \end{cases} \quad (30)$$

The shear force $T(x)$ and bending moment $M_i(x)$ variation diagrams are shown in fig 10.

In figure 11 one plotted the deflection function *EIW(x)* and the rotation one *EIF(x)*, for the particular numerical data

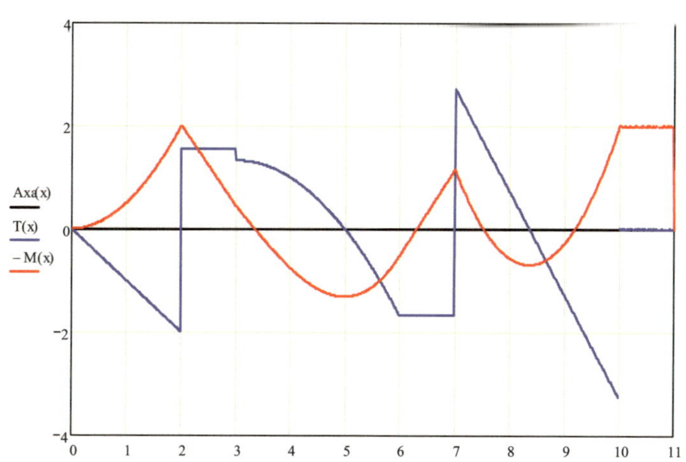

Fig. 10. Shear force *T* and bending moment M_i diagrams

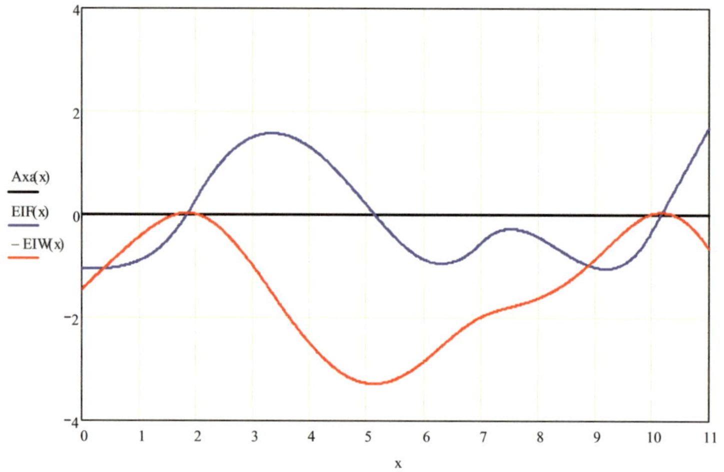

Fig. 11. Cross-sectional deflection $EIw(x)$ and rotation $EI\varphi(x)$ diagrams

In the particular case when all the supports are placed at the same level, the change will occur in $w_2=w_3=0$ in the MATHCAD sequence and the following results will be obtained for the reaction forces:

$$\begin{pmatrix} V1 \\ V2 \\ V3 \\ V4 \end{pmatrix} = \begin{pmatrix} 3.219 \\ 0.114 \\ 4.483 \\ 3.184 \end{pmatrix} \tag{31}$$

The shear force $T(x)$ and bending moment $M_i(x)$ variation diagrams are shown in fig 12.
In figure 13 one plotted the deflection function $EIW(x)$ and the rotation one $EIF(x)$, for the particular numerical data.

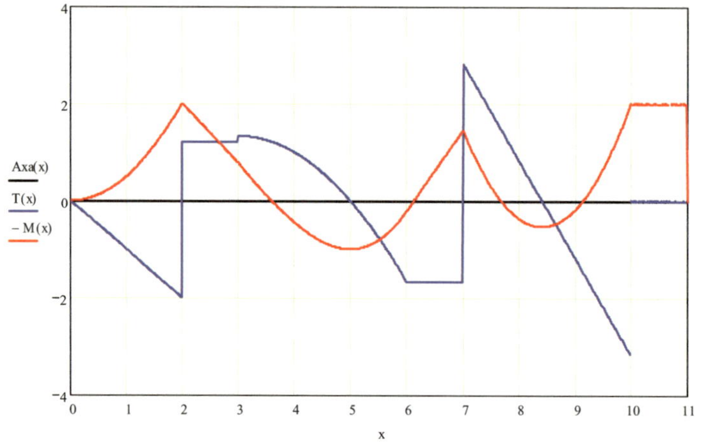

Fig. 12. Shear force T and bending moment M_i diagrams

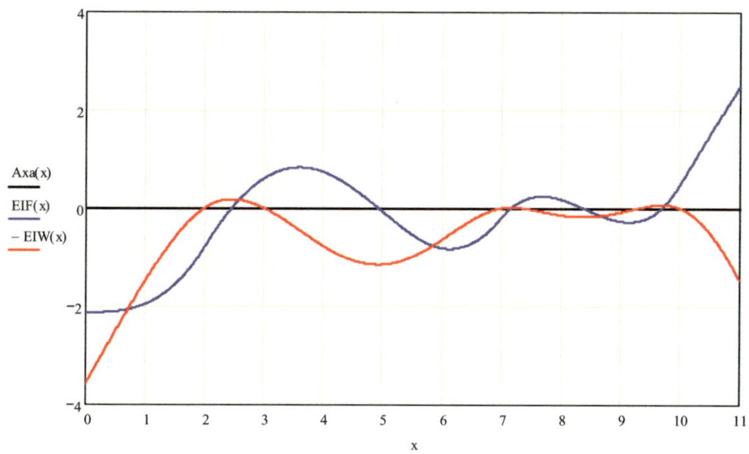

Fig. 13. Cross-sectional deflection $EIw(x)$ and rotation $EI\varphi(x)$ diagrams

Application 3: Continuous beam supported by 7 elastic bearings (statically undetermined system)

One considers a continuous beam *OA* supported by 7 level equidistant linear elastic bearings (having the same stiffness *k*). The beam has a constant flexural stiffness *EI* and it is subjected to the action of a load *P* as shown in figure 14. One should determine the reaction forces V_1, V_2, ... V_7 and plot the shear force $T(x)$ and bending moment $M(x)$, cross-sectional rotations $\varphi(x)$ and displacements $w(x)$ variation diagrams, as a function of the stiffness *k* of the elastic elements. Numerical input data: $EI = 2\ kN/m^2$; $r_1=1\ m$; $r_2=2\ m$; $r_3=3\ m$; $r_4=4\ m$; $r_5=5\ m$; $r_6=6$; $r_7=7\ m$; $d=4\ m$; $P=10\ kN$; springs' stiffness particular cases: $k_1=100\ kN/m$; $k_2=10\ kN/m$; $k_3=1\ kN/m$.
In order to determine the reactions V_1, V_2, ... V_7 one will use the two equilibrium equations from Mechanics of Solids:

$$\sum F_{zs} \downarrow = V_1 + V_2 + V_3 + V_4 + V_5 + V_6 + V_7$$
$$\sum \overleftarrow{M}_{7s} = V_1 \cdot (r_7 - r_1) + V_2 \cdot (r_7 - r_2) + V_3 \cdot (r_7 - r_3) + V_4 \cdot (r_7 - r_4) + V_5 \cdot (r_7 - r_5) + V_6 \cdot (r_7 - r_6) \tag{32}$$

where: $\sum F_{zs} \downarrow = P$ is the sum of exterior forces along the *Oz* axis;

$\sum \overleftarrow{M}_{7s} = P(r_7 - d)$ - is the sum of exterior moments around the *Oy* axis, passing through support 7.

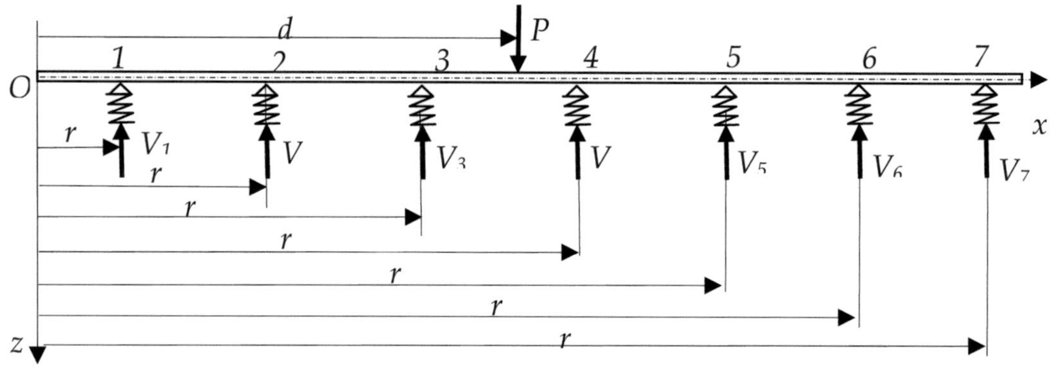

Fig. 14.

In order to obtain the **3 Displacements Equation** one will write the displacements corresponding to 3 beam sections denoted by i, j and k as in figure 15 ($x_j = x_i + L_i$; $x_k = x_i + L_i + L_j$), according to the general relations (11):

$$\begin{cases} EI \cdot w_i = EI \cdot w_0 + EI\varphi_0 \cdot x_i + W(x_i) & \mid L_j \\ EI \cdot w_j = EI \cdot w_0 + EI\varphi_0 \cdot x_j + W(x_j) & \mid -(L_i + L_j) \\ EI \cdot w_k = EI \cdot w_0 + EI\varphi_0 \cdot x_k + W(x_k) & \mid L_i \end{cases} \tag{33}$$

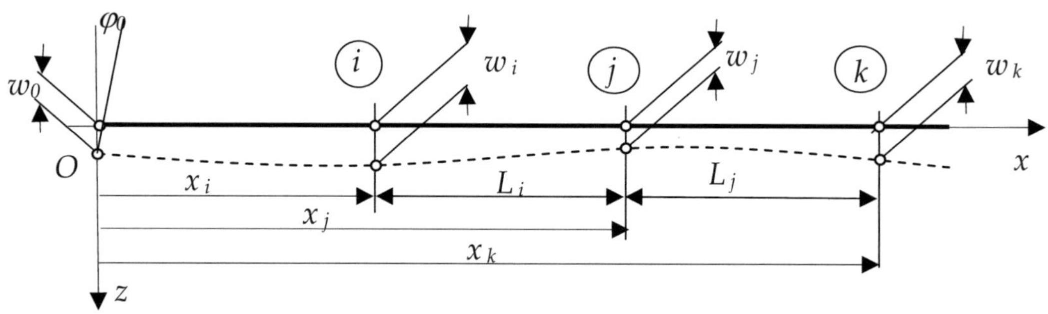

Fig. 15.

If one multiplies the first equation with L_j, the second one with $(- L_i - L_j)$, the third one with L_i and if one adds up the obtained expressions, by eliminating the origin parameters one will obtain the **3 Displacements Equation:**

$$EI\left[w_i L_j - w_j(L_j + L_i) + w_k L_i\right] = W(x_i)L_j - W(x_j)(L_j + L_i) + W(x_k)L_i \tag{34}$$

The other five equations required to solve the statically undetermined system form fig. 14 can be obtained using the **3 Displacements Equation** for 5 sets of 3 consecutive supports, as it follows:

$$
\begin{aligned}
&1-2-3: \quad EI[w_1(r_3-r_2)-w_2(r_3-r_1)+w_3(r_2-r_1)]=[W(r_1)\cdot(r_3-r_2)-W(r_2)\cdot(r_3-r_1)+W(r_3)\cdot(r_2-r_1)]\\
&2-3-4: \quad EI[w_2(r_4-r_3)-w_3(r_4-r_2)+w_4(r_3-r_2)]=[W(r_2)\cdot(r_4-r_3)-W(r_3)\cdot(r_4-r_2)+W(r_4)\cdot(r_3-r_2)]\\
&3-4-5: \quad EI[w_3(r_5-r_4)-w_4(r_5-r_3)+w_5(r_4-r_3)]=[W(r_3)\cdot(r_5-r_4)-W(r_4)\cdot(r_5-r_3)+W(r_5)\cdot(r_4-r_3)]\\
&4-5-6: \quad EI[w_4(r_6-r_5)-w_5(r_6-r_4)+w_6(r_5-r_4)]=[W(r_4)\cdot(r_6-r_5)-W(r_5)\cdot(r_6-r_4)+W(r_6)\cdot(r_5-r_4)]\\
&5-6-7: \quad EI[w_5(r_7-r_6)-w_6(r_7-r_5)+w_7(r_6-r_5)]=[W(r_5)\cdot(r_7-r_6)-W(r_6)\cdot(r_7-r_5)+W(r_7)\cdot(r_6-r_5)]
\end{aligned}
\tag{35}
$$

where $W(x)$ has the particular shape:

$$
\begin{aligned}
W(x)=P\cdot\Phi(x-d)\cdot\frac{(x-d)^3}{6}-V_1\cdot\Phi(x-r_1)\cdot\frac{(x-r_1)^3}{6}-V_2\cdot\Phi(x-r_2)\cdot\frac{(x-r_2)^3}{6}-V_3\cdot\Phi(x-r_3)\cdot\frac{(x-r_3)^3}{6}-\\
-V_4\cdot\Phi(x-r_4)\cdot\frac{(x-r_4)^3}{6}-V_5\cdot\Phi(x-r_5)\cdot\frac{(x-r_5)^3}{6}-V_6\cdot\Phi(x-r_6)\cdot\frac{(x-r_6)^3}{6}-V_7\cdot\Phi(x-r_7)\cdot\frac{(x-r_7)^3}{6}
\end{aligned}
\tag{36}
$$

The displacements w_1, w_2, .. w_5 are linear functions of V_1, V_2, … V_7, as it follows:

$$
w_1=\frac{V_1}{k};\quad w_2=\frac{V_2}{k};\quad w_3=\frac{V_3}{k};\quad w_4=\frac{V_4}{k};\quad w_5=\frac{V_5}{k};\quad w_6=\frac{V_6}{k};\quad w_7=\frac{V_7}{k}
$$

The step functions in $W(x)$ will be denoted like:

$$
\begin{aligned}
&k_P(x)=\Phi(x-d)\cdot\frac{(x-d)^3}{6}; \quad k_1(x)=\Phi(x-r_1)\cdot\frac{(x-r_1)^3}{6};\\
&k_2(x)=\Phi(x-r_2)\cdot\frac{(x-r_2)^3}{6}; \quad k_3(x)=\Phi(x-r_3)\cdot\frac{(x-r_3)^3}{6};\\
&k_4(x)=\Phi(x-r_4)\cdot\frac{(x-r_4)^3}{6}; \quad k_5(x)=\Phi(x-r_5)\cdot\frac{(x-r_5)^3}{6};\\
&k_6(x)=\Phi(x-r_6)\cdot\frac{(x-r_6)^3}{6}; \quad k_7(x)=\Phi(x-r_7)\cdot\frac{(x-r_7)^3}{6}
\end{aligned}
\tag{37}
$$

One will denote the values of $k_i(x)$ functions given by (34) in the beam's supports as it follows:

$$k_P(r_1)=k_{P1};\quad k_1(r_1)=k_{11};\; k_2(r_1)=k_{21};\; k_3(r_1)=k_{31};\; k_4(r_1)=k_{41};\; \ldots.$$
$$k_P(r_2)=k_{P2};\quad k_1(r_2)=k_{12};\; k_2(r_2)=k_{22};\; k_3(r_2)=k_{32};\; k_4(r_2)=k_{42};\; \ldots. \quad (38)$$
$$\textit{One will denote}: \quad EI/k=\beta$$

After introducing the functions $W(r_i)$ in equations (32) and separating the unknown values $V_1, V_2, \ldots V_7$, one obtains:

$$\begin{aligned}
&V_1\cdot(k_{11}d_{32}-k_{12}d_{31}+k_{13}d_{21}+\beta\cdot d_{32})+V_2\cdot(k_{21}d_{32}-k_{22}d_{31}+k_{23}d_{21}-\beta\cdot d_{31})+\\
&+V_3\cdot(k_{31}d_{32}-k_{32}d_{31}+k_{33}d_{21}+\beta\cdot d_{21})+V_4\cdot(k_{41}d_{32}-k_{42}d_{31}+k_{43}d_{21})+V_5\cdot(k_{51}d_{32}-k_{52}d_{31}+k_{53}d_{21})+\\
&+V_6\cdot(k_{61}d_{32}-k_{62}d_{31}+k_{63}d_{21})+V_7\cdot(k_{71}d_{32}-k_{72}d_{31}+k_{73}d_{21})=P\cdot(k_{P1}d_{32}-k_{P2}d_{31}+k_{P3}d_{21})\\
&V_1\cdot(k_{12}d_{43}-k_{13}d_{42}+k_{14}d_{32})+V_2\cdot(k_{22}d_{43}-k_{23}d_{42}+k_{24}d_{32}+\beta\cdot d_{43})+V_3\cdot(k_{32}d_{43}-k_{33}d_{42}+k_{34}d_{32}-\beta\cdot d_{42})+\\
&+V_4\cdot(k_{42}d_{43}-k_{43}d_{42}+k_{44}d_{32}+\beta\cdot d_{32})+V_5\cdot(k_{52}d_{43}-k_{53}d_{42}+k_{54}d_{32})+\\
&+V_6\cdot(k_{62}d_{43}-k_{63}d_{42}+k_{64}d_{32})+V_7\cdot(k_{72}d_{43}-k_{73}d_{42}+k_{74}d_{32})=P\cdot(k_{P2}d_{43}-k_{P3}d_{42}+k_{P4}d_{32})\\
&V_1\cdot(k_{13}d_{54}-k_{14}d_{53}+k_{15}d_{43})+V_2\cdot(k_{23}d_{54}-k_{24}d_{53}+k_{25}d_{43})+V_3\cdot(k_{33}d_{54}-k_{34}d_{53}+k_{35}d_{43}+\beta\cdot d_{54})+\\
&+V_4\cdot(k_{43}d_{54}-k_{44}d_{53}+k_{45}d_{43}-\beta\cdot d_{53})+V_5\cdot(k_{53}d_{54}-k_{54}d_{53}+k_{55}d_{43}+\beta\cdot d_{43})+\\
&+V_6\cdot(k_{63}d_{54}-k_{64}d_{53}+k_{65}d_{43})+V_7\cdot(k_{73}d_{54}-k_{74}d_{53}+k_{75}d_{43})=P\cdot(k_{P3}d_{54}-k_{P4}d_{53}+k_{P5}d_{43})
\end{aligned} \quad (39)$$

$$\begin{aligned}
&V_1\cdot(k_{14}d_{65}-k_{15}d_{64}+k_{16}d_{54})+V_2\cdot(k_{24}d_{65}-k_{25}d_{64}+k_{26}d_{54})+V_3\cdot(k_{34}d_{65}-k_{35}d_{64}+k_{36}d_{54})+\\
&+V_4\cdot(k_{44}d_{65}-k_{45}d_{64}+k_{46}d_{54}+\beta\cdot d_{65})+V_5\cdot(k_{54}d_{65}-k_{55}d_{64}+k_{56}d_{54}-\beta\cdot d_{64})+\\
&+V_6\cdot(k_{64}d_{65}-k_{65}d_{64}+k_{66}d_{54}+\beta\cdot d_{65})+V_7\cdot(k_{74}d_{65}-k_{75}d_{64}+k_{76}d_{54})=P\cdot(k_{P4}d_{65}-k_{P5}d_{64}+k_{P6}d_{54})\\
&V_1\cdot(k_{15}d_{76}-k_{16}d_{75}+k_{17}d_{65})+V_2\cdot(k_{25}d_{76}-k_{26}d_{75}+k_{27}d_{65})+V_3\cdot(k_{35}d_{76}-k_{36}d_{75}+k_{37}d_{65})+\\
&+V_4\cdot(k_{45}d_{76}-k_{46}d_{75}+k_{47}d_{65})+V_5\cdot(k_{55}d_{76}-k_{56}d_{75}+k_{57}d_{65}+\beta\cdot d_{76})+\\
&+V_6\cdot(k_{65}d_{76}-k_{66}d_{75}+k_{67}d_{65}-\beta\cdot d_{75})+V_7\cdot(k_{75}d_{76}-k_{76}d_{75}+k_{77}d_{65}+\beta\cdot d_{65})=P\cdot(k_{P5}d_{76}-k_{P6}d_{75}+k_{P7}d_{65})
\end{aligned}$$

Equations (32) and (39) will have the matrix shape:

$$\mathbf{A}\cdot\mathbf{B}=\mathbf{X} \quad (40)$$

Case a. for $k_1=1\ kN/m$, the matrices **A** and **B** have the particular shape:

$$A=\begin{pmatrix}
1 & 1 & 1 & 1 & 1 & 1 & 1\\
6 & 5 & 4 & 3 & 2 & 1 & 0\\
3 & -3.833 & 2 & 0 & 0 & 0 & 0\\
2 & 3 & -3.833 & 2 & 0 & 0 & 0\\
3 & 2 & 3 & -3.833 & 2 & 0 & 0\\
4 & 3 & 2 & 3 & -3.833 & 2 & 0\\
5 & 4 & 3 & 2 & 3 & -3.833 & 2
\end{pmatrix}
\qquad
B=\begin{pmatrix}10\\30\\0\\0\\1.667\\10\\20\end{pmatrix}$$

Solving this matrix equation in MATHCAD, one obtains the reaction forces for this particular case:

$$X := \mathrm{lsolve}(A, B) \qquad X = \begin{pmatrix} -0.194 \\ 1.131 \\ 2.458 \\ 3.21 \\ 2.458 \\ 1.131 \\ -0.194 \end{pmatrix} \qquad \begin{pmatrix} V1 \\ V2 \\ V3 \\ V4 \\ V5 \\ V6 \\ V7 \end{pmatrix} := X$$

The analytical expressions of the shear force $T_z(x)$ and bending moment $M_{iy}(x)$ determined using the step function Φ are:

$$\begin{aligned} T_z(x) &= V_1 \cdot \Phi(x-r_1) + V_2 \cdot \Phi(x-r_2) + V_3 \cdot \Phi(x-r_3) + V_4 \cdot \Phi(x-r_4) + \\ &+ V_5 \cdot \Phi(x-r_5) + V_6 \cdot \Phi(x-r_6) + V_7 \cdot \Phi(x-r_7) - P \cdot \Phi(x-d) \\ M_{iy}(x) &= V_1 \cdot (x-r_1) \cdot \Phi(x-r_1) + V_2 \cdot (x-r_2) \cdot \Phi(x-r_2) + V_3 \cdot (x-r_3) \cdot \Phi(x-r_3) + V_4 \cdot (x-r_4) \cdot \Phi(x-r_4) + \\ &+ V_5 \cdot (x-r_5) \cdot \Phi(x-r_5) + V_6 \cdot (x-r_6) \cdot \Phi(x-r_6) + V_7 \cdot (x-r_7) \cdot \Phi(x-r_7) - P \cdot (x-d) \cdot \Phi(x-d) \end{aligned} \tag{43}$$

The shear force $T(x)$ and bending moment $M_i(x)$ diagrams for this case are shown in figure 16.

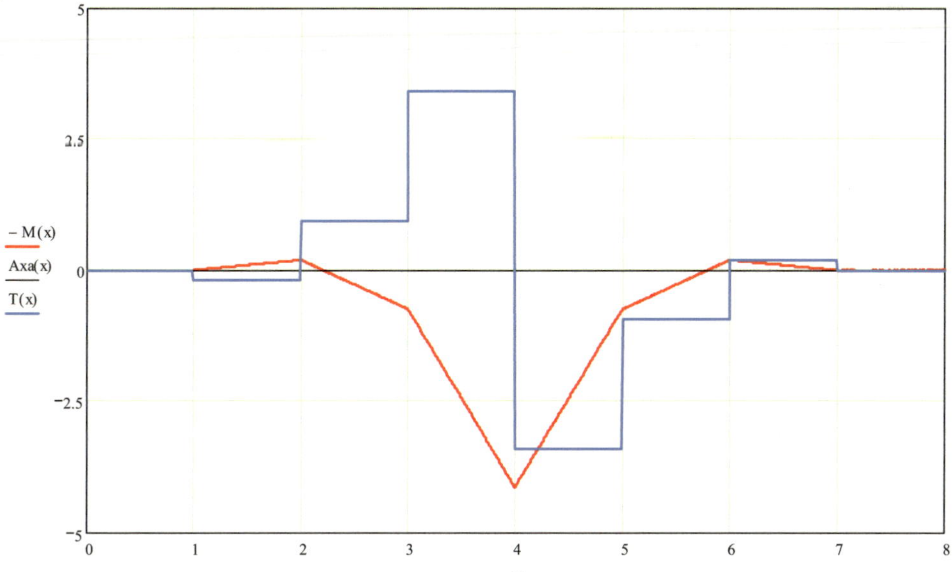

Fig. 16. $T_z(x)$ and $M_{iy}(x)$ diagrams for $k=1$ kN/m T_{max} =3,395 kN ; M_{max} =4,138 kNm

Case b. for k_2=*10 kN/m* the matrices **A** and **B** have the particular shape:

$$A = \begin{pmatrix} 1 & 1 & 1 & 1 & 1 & 1 & 1 \\ 6 & 5 & 4 & 3 & 2 & 1 & 0 \\ 1.2 & -0.233 & 0.2 & 0 & 0 & 0 & 0 \\ 2 & 1.2 & -0.233 & 0.2 & 0 & 0 & 0 \\ 3 & 2 & 1.2 & -0.233 & 0.2 & 0 & 0 \\ 4 & 3 & 2 & 1.2 & -0.233 & 0.2 & 0 \\ 5 & 4 & 3 & 2 & 1.2 & -0.233 & 0.2 \end{pmatrix} \quad B = \begin{pmatrix} 10 \\ 30 \\ 0 \\ 0 \\ 1.667 \\ 10 \\ 20 \end{pmatrix} \tag{44}$$

Solving this matrix equation in MATHCAD one obtains the reaction forces for this particular case:

$$X := \text{lsolve}(A, B) \qquad X = \begin{pmatrix} -0.373 \\ 0.24 \\ 2.519 \\ 5.229 \\ 2.519 \\ 0.24 \\ -0.373 \end{pmatrix} \qquad \begin{pmatrix} V1 \\ V2 \\ V3 \\ V4 \\ V5 \\ V6 \\ V7 \end{pmatrix} := X \tag{45}$$

The shear force *T(x)* and bending moment $M_i(x)$ diagrams for this case are shown in figure 17.

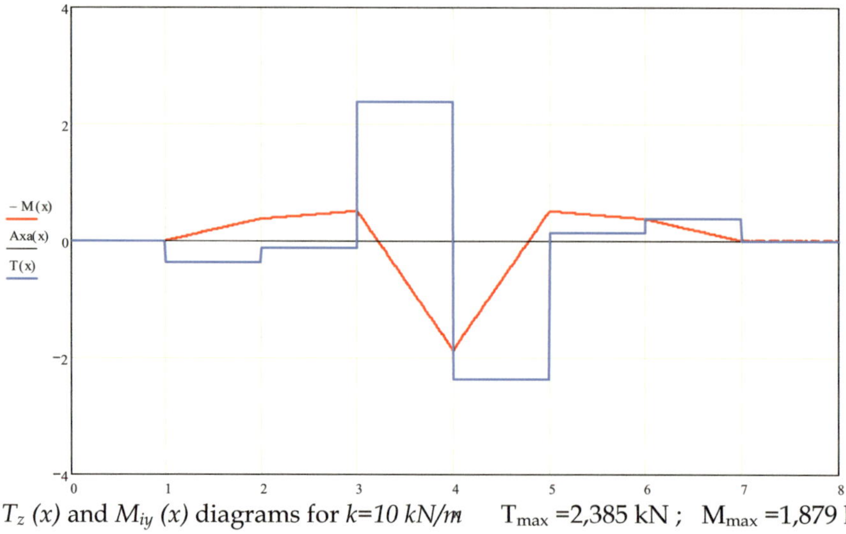

Fig. 17. T_z *(x)* and M_{iy} *(x)* diagrams for *k=10 kN/m* T_{max} =2,385 kN ; M_{max} =1,879 kNm

Case c. For k_2=*100 kN/m* the matrices **A** and **B** have the particular shape:

$$A = \begin{pmatrix} 1 & 1 & 1 & 1 & 1 & 1 & 1 \\ 6 & 5 & 4 & 3 & 2 & 1 & 0 \\ 1.02 & 0.127 & 0.02 & 0 & 0 & 0 & 0 \\ 2 & 1.02 & 0.127 & 0.02 & 0 & 0 & 0 \\ 3 & 2 & 1.02 & 0.127 & 0.02 & 0 & 0 \\ 4 & 3 & 2 & 1.02 & 0.127 & 0.02 & 0 \\ 5 & 4 & 3 & 2 & 1.02 & 0.127 & 0.02 \end{pmatrix} \qquad B = \begin{pmatrix} 10 \\ 30 \\ 0 \\ 0 \\ 1.667 \\ 10 \\ 20 \end{pmatrix} \tag{46}$$

Solving this matrix equation in MATHCAD one obtains the reaction forces for this particular case:

$$X := \text{lsolve}(A,B) \qquad X = \begin{pmatrix} 0.02 \\ -0.351 \\ 1.22 \\ 8.224 \\ 1.22 \\ -0.351 \\ 0.02 \end{pmatrix} \qquad \begin{pmatrix} V1 \\ V2 \\ V3 \\ V4 \\ V5 \\ V6 \\ V7 \end{pmatrix} := X \tag{47}$$

The shear force $T(x)$ and bending moment $M_i(x)$ diagrams for this case are shown in figure 18.

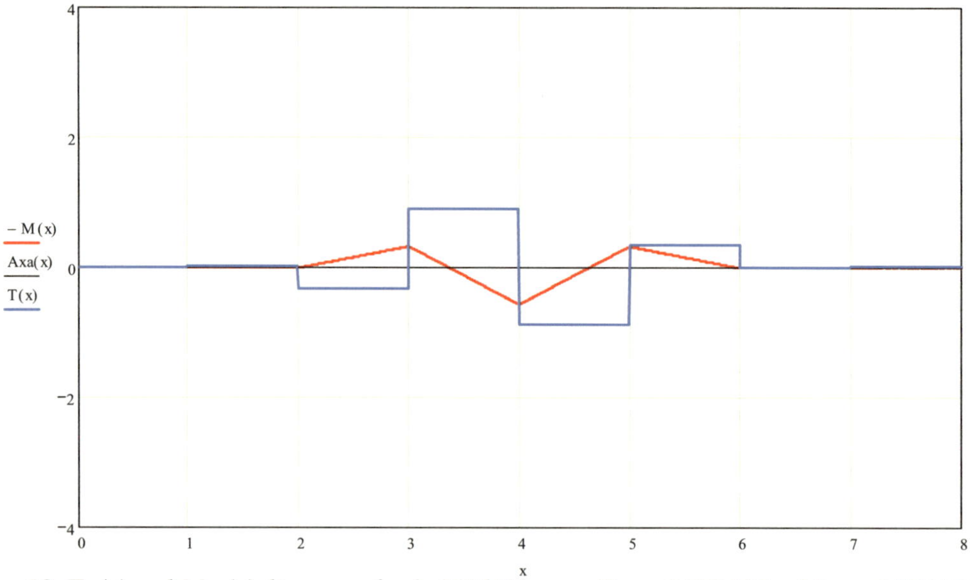

Fig. 18. T_z (x) and M_{iy} (x) diagrams for $k=100$ kN/m T_{max} =0,888 kN ; M_{max} =0,576 kNm

3. Conclusions

- This is a method of expressing the variation of the shear force $T_z(x)$, bending moment $M_{iy}(x)$, transversal cross-section rotations $\varphi_y(x)$ and displacements $w(x)$ using the MATHCAD step function $\Phi(x\text{-}a)$ in a more compact form than the traditional methods;
- The above shown method has a high degree of generality. One can use it to determine the reactions in the *N* (rigid or elastic) supports (equidistant or randomly placed) of a continuous beam. Thus one can better assimilate the results of the Winkler Method for a continuous perfect elastic space with the results obtained for a discrete elastic space.
- Figures 16, 17 and 18 show that increasing the stiffness of the elastic elements leads to an increase of the elastic supports load in the central part of the beam (*3,21kN* ↑ *8.224 kN*) and a decrease of the maximum bending moments (*4,138kNm* ↓ *0,576 kNm*); on the other hand, when decreasing the elastic elements' stiffness, a decrease of the central supports load and maximum bending moments occurs.
- Considering the fact that the step function method uses simple operation expressions, the numerical applications are being solved fast with a minimum number of computational cycles. The traditional methods use integral expressions which are solved by means of numerical methods. These methods imply a large number of computational cycles, which will cause slower obtained results;

4. References

Cornel MARIN, Alexandru MARIN - *Metoda analitica pentru trasarea diagramelor de eforturi în barele drepte.* Sesiunea de comunicări ştiinţifice SIMEC 2006, UTCB Bucuresti, Facultatea de Utilaj Tehnologic, 31 martie 2006, pp.81-86

Cornel MARIN, Alexandru MARIN - *Metoda analitica pentru calculul deplasărilor şi rotiriulor barelor drepte supuse la încovoiere.* Sesiunea de comunicări ştiinţifice SIMEC 2006, UTCB Bucuresti, Facultatea de Utilaj Tehnologic, 31 martie 2006, pp.87-92

Cornel MARIN, Alexandru MARIN - *O metodă analitica pentru rezolvarea sistemelor static nedeterminate de tipul grinzilor continue pe mai multe reazeme punctuale rigide la acelaşi nivel* Sesiunea de comunicări ştiinţifice a UTCB, Facultatea de Utilaj Tehnologic - SIMEC 2007.

Cornel MARIN, Alexandru MARIN - *Calculul grinzilor continue situate pe reazeme elastice la acelaşi nivel, considerând terenul de sub reazeme ca un mediu perfect elastic* Sesiunea de comunicări ştiinţifice a UTCB, Facultatea de Utilaj Tehnologic - SIMEC 2007.

Cornel Marin, Viviana Filip, Alexandru Marin - *Analytical Method Used for Plotting the Shear Force and Bending Moment Diagrams, Translations and Rotations Distributions on Beams Subjected to Bending,* International MultiConference of Engineers and Computer Scientists ICMES 2008, Hong Kong, 19-21 March 2008. Lecture Notes IMECS 2008, Volume II, ISBN 978-988-17012-1-3, pp 1629-1633

Marin Cornel, Hadar Anton, Marin Alexandru, *Step Function Method Used in Calculating Continuous Footing Foundation Placed of Elastic and Discrete Soil* - Annals of DAAAM for 2008, ISSN 1726-9679, ISBN 978-3-901 509-68-1, pp.0793-0794.

Cornel MARIN, Nicolae POPA, Elena DINU, *Grinzi continue situate pe 7 reazeme elastice la acelaşi nivel pe un mediu discret perfect elastic,* Sesiunea de comunicări ştiinţifice a studenţilor FIMMR Târgovişte, iunie 2008.

Cornel MARIN - *Simularea încărcarii unui pod elsatic situat pe şapte reazeme elastice proporţionale.* Al VI lea Simpozion Naţional de Mecatronica, Microtehnologii şi Materiale Noi, 7 noiembrie 2008, Târgovişte.

Cornel MARIN - *Rezistenţa materialelor şi elemente de Teoria elasticităţii,* Editura Bibliotheca, Târgovişte 2006, ISBN (10) 973-721-198-8, ISBN (13) 973-973-721-198-1;

Cornel MARIN - *Aplicaţii ale Teoriei elasticităţii şi plasticităţii în inginerie,* Editura Bibliotheca, Târgovişte 2007, ISBN 978-973-712-297-1.

Cornel Marin, Viviana Filip, Alexandru Marin, IAENG TRANSACTIONS ON ENGINEERING TECHNOLOGIES VOLUME I –Ch. ICINDE_23: Alternative analytical method used in plotting the shear force and bending moment diagrams, displacements and rotations distributions for beams subjected to bending, America Institute of Physics, USA 2009, ISBN: 978-0-7354-0622-3.

Learning distributed selective attention strategies with the Sigma-if neural network

Maciej Huk
Wroclaw University of Technology
Poland

1. Introduction

Selective attention systems are found to be very interesting as well from theoretical point of view, as also as useful tools for many practical applications, such as analysis of large data sets, real time route planning for autonomic robots in dynamical environments, and dispersed sensor networks control. However up to date models of biological selective attention systems and other methods that realise similar functionalities still have some drawbacks. Decision trees are easy to analyse by humans, but once created are hard to adapt to the changes in the system environment. They are also not resistant to damages in their rigid logical structure as well as in the hardware that executes them. The next example - statistical feature selection algorithms create solutions that use globally suboptimal feature sets, but in general they are not optimal from the point of view of single input vectors, and those algorithms are hard to apply in fast changing environments. This is why biologically founded neuronal selective attention systems seem to offer better properties for many possible applications. They have distributed nature and in the effect are more damage resistant than centralised models. They are also easy to adapt to the changing environment conditions, and were tested and selected by nature as simple, cheap and scalable solutions. The only problem with neuronal selective attention systems is that their existing models implement artificial, centralised attention directing algorithms and in the effect they do not offer functionalities observed in the nature. This is why there is still a need for analysing properties of natural selective attention mechanisms, as well as for further exploration of possible models of biological neuronal selective attention systems.

2. Sources and properties of natural selective attention systems

In the nature selective attention is a mechanism that gives a living organism the possibility to extract from the incoming information a part that is most important at a given moment and that should be processed in detail (Broadbent, 1982; Treisman, 1960). This mechanism is necessary to avoid wrong or delayed decisions and reactions, due to limited processing capabilities of the typical nerve system which does not allow rapid analysis of the whole visual and other senses scene (Tsotsos et al., 2001; VanRullen & Koch, 2003). So selective attention can be viewed as a strategy of dynamical input space selection for gaining predefined goals by an organism interacting with a very complicated environment.

It is easy to search for selective attention manifestations during animal life-threatening situations. When fast conditioned and unconditioned reflex start to rule over animal behavior, often some important signals from one given sense cause that other signals or signals from other senses are left almost completely unprocessed. A good example here is a very hungry sparrow that observe something to eat and suddenly hears sound of an eagle – in most cases at this very moment signals about food in front of the eyes as well as signals about hunger automatically became not important for the little bird and do not affect its decisions – it starts to run away. What is also interesting, such behaviour happens sometimes even if the little bird is young and has never heard the eagle before. This is because some very important strategies of senses and signals prioritisation can be those that were developed by evolution and in such cases are already hard-coded in the nervous system of the animal (Tinbergen, 1951; Dole, 2008).

Above simple example suggests basic properties of selective attention mechanisms. They are simple, process information very fast and most probably have direct access to signals form sensors. What's more – they seem to function as independent subsystems and can have great influence on decisions and behaviour of an animal. It can also be seen, that once developed, selective attention strategy can help its user to reduce time from signal arrival to target decision or reaction, to reduce information acquisition and processing costs, e.g. in terms of energy. But there is more – it can help to gain better decisions – especially in multi-criteria optimisation problems, by reducing them to simpler ones with use of historical knowledge encoded in used selective attention strategy.

It would be a great advantage to use such systems as tools in science and industry. Applications range here is very wide – from data mining and picture recognition, through robot control and advisory systems (e.g. medical, financial) to strategic planning and autonomous target selection and tracking. It would be also a new opportunity to study psychophysiology of human perception, development of artificial senses and artificial agents that mimic human behaviour. In theory the key to such an interesting and very useful functionality seems to be simple - a generation and use of a set of rules that for every possible situation define parts of perception space (fields of attention) that should be observed and processed with highest, medium or lowest priority (Tsal, 1983, Tsotsos et al., 2001, Claus et al., 2004). But in practice to develop such systems and to see selective attention phenomenon in greater detail one should familiarize himself with a key observations of selective attention mechanisms in humans and other primates.

Among observations of selective attention in humans the most widely known are early experiments of Cherry, Gray and Treisman on such called "cocktail party problem". They have shown that even in crowded and noisy party room, people can effectively discuss in pairs by passing over the global noise, and – in the same time – can react on some keywords (e.g. their name, surname) even if those words were told in the opposite side of the room (Cherry, 1953; Gray & Wedderburn, 1960; Treisman, 1960). This gives a suggestion that we use some kind of automated processes that are specialised in filtering out unimportant information. Properties of those processes were further examined by Deutsch, Lewis and Spelke in experiments on dichotic listening (Deutsch & Deutsch, 1963; Lewis, 1970; Spelke et al., 1976). They have shown that all signals reaching our perceptual system, at first undergo non-conscious, automatic semantic preprocessing.

Nature of this semantic preprocessing was later partially uncovered in experiments on human analysis of words (Neely, 1977; Grosjean, 1980; Marslen-Wilson & Tyler, 1980) and sentences (Swinney, 1979; Swinney, 1982; Pynte et al., 1984). Measurements of the time of understanding and reaction on heard words have shown that the process of understanding of their meaning lasts for about 200ms from the beginning of signals arrival. In this time usually are received only two first phonemes of the word, but it allows for significant automatic reduction of the number of word's potential meanings (in English language first phoneme in average reduces that number to 1033 and the second phoneme to 87 meanings (Kucera & Francis, 1967)). It should be also noticed that in such a short time the signals can be processed only by two or three subsequent layers of human brain neurons. Thus such structures most probably act as information context selection subsystems, and quickly activate synaptic paths to parts of the human neural system, that are semantically connected with just processed signals and do the final part of those signals interpretation (LaBerge, 1990). Those findings coincide with previous results of Spelke and Shiffrin, that show that automated processing is very flexible, and can be significantly modified by training in a short period of time (about six weeks) (Spelke et al., 1976; Shiffrin & Schneider, 1977). Their experiments concerned a task of writing some phrases and reading other phrases in the same time. While before the training it was hard enough to disturb processing of other signals, that after the training, doing the same was easy and almost automatic, and saved resources could be used to realise other tasks.

But one may ask - what is the main, most crucial physical or statistical effect that makes selective attention to appear and function so well? The answer is not simple and most probably we currently know only a half of the truth. What we know, is that there is no central, specialised part of a brain that govern our attention (Allport et al., 1972). Also simple biological neural networks that somehow learn how to direct our attention, seem not to have any special neurons or uncommon architectures of interconnections between them. Thus basic mechanism of selective attention emerge invisibly somewhere between levels of single neurons and simple neural network. While it is hard to analyse the way neural network process information, nature gives us a unique chance to observe the way we direct our visual attention by moving our eyes. The most important achievement in this field is an identification of the role of saccadic eyes movements in picture recognition and objects tracking (Noton & Stark, 1971; Findlay, 1982; Chelazzi et al., 1993; Schall & Hannes, 1993). For every scene eyes control subsystem learns to quickly direct gaze to the most important scene elements, by following a unique directed scan path, that defines number, locations and sequence of picture points to be analysed. This seem to be the central mechanism of natural selective attention systems, because an element of automatic, cyclic selection of regions of attention, guided by previously learned scan paths, was found to be common for almost all input channels of human brain (Tsal, 1983; Kastner et al., 1998). Unfortunately we still don't know exactly how biological neural networks develop and realise selective attention mechanisms and how to mimic this functionality.

3. Towards neuronal models of selective attention

Promising prospects of the use of human-like artificial selective attention systems made many authors to look for precise theoretical description of this phenomenon. But it took almost seventy years from the moment of writing down the first definition of selective attention by sir William James in 1890, to the formulation of the first models. Unfortunately those first attempts to model selective attention, such as Broadbent's bottleneck theory (Broadbent, 1958), Treisman's two step filtering (Gray & Wedderburn, 1960; Treisman, 1964) and Kahneman's centralised attention resource model (Kahneman, 1973) were too general and too imprecise (not to say completely not true) to stand the tests of further experiments. After those first steps, proposed models evolved it the direction of more and more specialised ones, such as Allport's multiple resource capacity, that captured distributed nature of selective attention processes, and Posner's late selection model, that described the role of non conscious, automatic semantic preprocessing observed by Deutsch, Neely and Swinney.

But the first groups of models that could have been used in practice emerged as the realisations of Noton and Stark scan path theory — those were so called neuronal hierarhical routing and shifting circuits models. Their authors assumed that to realise dynamic changes of region of interest, neural networks should be governed by specialised external element that uses predefined algorithm of selection of inputs to activate (Koch & Ullman, 1985; Anderson & Van Essen, 1987; Olshausen et al., 1993) or various artificial mechanisms for dynamic network architecture changes (Niebur et al., 1993; Tsotsos et al., 1995; Houghton & Tipper, 1996; Pelc, 1998), which in fact also were realisations of some constant embedded strategies of selective attention. This was not correct in the light of neurobiological observations and earlier experimental proofs for distributed nature of selective attention, but it allowed producing specialised tools that were useful in tasks such as face recognition, objects tracking or even pointing interesting objects for observation by cosmic probes (Yamada & Cottrell, 1995; Rybak et al., 1998; Hager & Toyama, 1999; Privitera et al., 2000).

As those models were not universal solutions of the problem of building neural selective attention systems, were very complicated and neurobiologically unfounded (Privitera & Stark, 2000; Eckstein et al., 2001; Clauss et al., 2004), this gave a strong impulse to further searching for basic attention mechanisms on the level of single synapses and neurons (Lee, 2000; VanRullen, 2003; Renninger, 2004). The basic paradigm of this direction of research is that selective attention at higher levels of brain structure organization emerges as an effect of synergy between elementary structures at lower levels. Thus the attention of researchers was concentrated on exploring new artificial neurons models - especially those, that allow interactions or other dependencies between signals arriving to neuron's inputs.

To achieve that, one had to consider input signals aggregation methods other than simple weighted sum of input values known from perceptron neuron model. This is due to the fact, that aggregation function is the only one part of neuron transmit function that has full access to all information that is available through neuron's inputs - and after the aggregation process most of the information about the sources of particular signals and dependencies between them is lost. It would also provide a way to search not only for models that take into consideration dependencies between signals from distinct inputs, but also that allow in some situations the reduction of the number of signals read in for processing. For those reasons, a set of appropriate neuron models was proposed, along with definitions of two basic types of aggregation functions. First family of those aggregation functions incorporate so called higher order neuron models, and the second family - nonlinear neuron models.

3.1 Higher order polynomial aggregation functions

Higher order neuron models extend simple weighted sum aggregation schema by adding into it also higher order terms. In general such solutions are variations of polynomial aggregation function:

$$\varphi_{Poly}(\mathbf{x},\mathbf{w}) = w_0 + \sum_{i=1}^{N} w_i x_i + \sum_{i,j=1}^{N} w_{ij} x_i x_j + \ldots + \sum_{i,j,..,k=1}^{N} w_{ij\ldots k} x_i x_j \cdots x_k \quad (1)$$

in which **x** and **w** are input and weights vectors (respectively of dimension N and N+1). They include all or only chosen terms of the right side of this expression. Such extension of aggregation function form, not only increases information capacity of resulting neural networks (Cover, 1965; Venkatesh & Baldi 1991), but also their ability of learning of geometrically invariant properties of input patterns (Giles & Maxwell, 1987; Perantonis & Lisboa, 1992). Unfortunately with the increasing number of neuron's inputs, this leads to the phenomenon of exponential explosion of the number of higher order terms. But in practice, when it is necessary to implement some particular function, usually only few high order terms are required (Redding et al., 1993). This can prevent exponential explosion of aggregation function complexity, and is the key to the effectiveness and practical use, of such standard examples of the higher order aggregation functions as the Sigma-Pi (sum of products) and the Clusteron (Mel, 1990; Mel, 1992):

$$\phi_{Sigma-Pi}(\mathbf{x},\mathbf{w}) = w_0 + \sum_{i=1}^{d}\left(w_i \prod_{k\in R_i} x_k \right). \quad (2)$$

It can be seen that aggregation function of Sigma-Pi neuron defines a set of d input connections clusters R_i within which connections collectively build up an importance of incoming signals group by multiplying them with each other. In this model, low value of only one input signal in the group can block signals from all other inputs in a cluster. This simple conditional behavior of aggregation function generates interesting properties of Sigma-Pi neural networks (Neville & Eldridge, 2002; Weber & Wermter, 2007), but in general it is hard to optimally define inputs clusters and collective blocking of the whole clusters seems to be too rigorous. This is why Clusteron aggregation function was made to almost automatically define clusters of neighbouring inputs (one has only to specify radius r of all the clusters), and independently consider mutual dependencies between signals from each pair of inputs in a given cluster:

$$\phi_{Clusteron}(\mathbf{x},\mathbf{w},r) = w_0 + \sum_{i=1}^{N}\left(w_i x_i \sum_{k=i-r}^{i+r} w_k x_k \right). \quad (3)$$

Nevertheless, those improvements don't outdate the question, if chosen or predefined clusters of connections are in the given situation optimal or even suboptimal. In the effect in the literature exist also a set of slightly different solutions that do not use the concept of input connections clusters. In their case the only mechanism that allows taking into account interconnection dependencies is defined by chosen, simple higher order polynomial terms. Good examples of those are Compensatory aggregation function (Sinha et al., 2001):

$$\varphi_{Compensatory}(\mathbf{x},\mathbf{w},\mathbf{w}') = w_0 + \sum_{i=1}^{N} w_i x_i + 0.5 \sum_{j=1}^{M} \sum_{\substack{i=1 \\ i \neq j}}^{N} w'_i w'_j x_i x_j \,, \qquad (4)$$

as well as aggregation functions of the Quadratic neuron:

$$\varphi_{Quadratic}(\mathbf{x},\mathbf{w}) = w_0 + \sum_{i=1}^{N} \sum_{j=i}^{N} x_i x_j w_{ij} \,, \qquad (5)$$

and the Cubic neuron (Bukovsky et al., 2007):

$$\varphi_{Cubic}(\mathbf{x},\mathbf{w}) = w_0 + \sum_{i=1}^{N} \sum_{j=i}^{N} \sum_{k=j}^{N} x_i x_j x_k w_{ijk} \,. \qquad (6)$$

Their simplicity makes them easier to apply than Sigma-Pi or Clusteron function, and they still mimic some aspects of selective attention (Gupta, 2008). But in practice it is unanswered fundamental question if chosen subset of higher order terms is a best one for solving a given problem.

3.2 Nonlinear neural aggregation functions

As polynomial aggregation functions do not solve all the problems with modeling low-level selective attention, there also exists a parallel research on different, nonlinear aggregation methods. The main idea of those solutions is to model nonlinear aspects of input signals accumulation observed in biological neurons (Anderson et al., 1985; Karlholm, 1993; Stuart & Spruston, 1998; Larkum et al., 1999; Körding & König, 2001), with the use of operations other than signals multiplication. In the effect selective attention behaviour could be generated also in the situations when all neuron's input signals values are definitely non zero.

The first widely known nonlinear aggregation function was proposed with a neuron model called the product unit (Durbin & Rumelhart, 1990):

$$\varphi_{PU}(\mathbf{x},\mathbf{w}) = w_0 + \prod_{i=1}^{N} w_i^{x_i} \,. \qquad (7)$$

It uses nonlinearity of the exponential function, but still the dependencies between input signals are generated through multiplication of the terms connected with particular input connections. Many authors reported usefulness and interesting theoretical properties of the product unit model and it is still an object of a research (Leernik, 1995; Schmidt, 2002; Martínez-Estudillo et al., 2008).

Another essential example and the first attempt to build a strictly non multiplicative, nonlinear aggregation function is the Spratling-Hayes function (Spratling & Hayes, 2000):

$$\varphi_{SH}(\mathbf{x},\mathbf{w},\mathbf{c},\kappa)=w_0+\sum_{i=1}^{N}w_i\min\left(\frac{x_1+\kappa}{c_{i,1}},\frac{x_2+\kappa}{c_{i,2}},\ldots,\frac{x_{i-1}+\kappa}{c_{i,i-1}},x_i,\frac{x_{i+1}+\kappa}{c_{i,i+1}},\ldots,\frac{x_N+\kappa}{c_{i,N}}\right). \quad (8)$$

In its case nonlinearity as well as dependencies between neuron's input connections are induced by the minimum function. This solution uses also a matrix $\boldsymbol{c}$, which elements define a ratio of mutual dependence between each two input connections, and a parameter κ that determines a threshold of signals values difference, below which dependence between two given connections is not considered.

As it is hard to choose most representative subset of aggregation functions proposed up to date, let that the last presented nonlinear solution will be very interesting aggregation function of generalised-mean neuron model (Yadav et al., 2004):

$$\varphi_{GMN}(\mathbf{x},\mathbf{w})=\left(w_0+\sum_{i=1}^{N}w_i x_i^r\right)^{1/r}. \quad (9)$$

The behaviour of this function is highly dependent on the value of single continuous parameter r. When r is equal one, resulting function is identical to the perceptron's aggregation function. When r is greater than one, no connection influences the other, and when r is greater than zero and less than one, GMN function can include various higher order terms (e.g. for r=1/2). Such flexibility makes that function applicable in many problems (Yadav et al., 2006), but there is no explicit rule describing how to properly choose value of the r parameter for a given problem.

3.3 Remarks and further directions of research

Above examples of polynomial and nonlinear aggregation functions present proposed up to date basic schemes of mimicking biological low-level selective attention systems. Resulting models of artificial neurons during input signals processing can take advantage of additional information about mutual dependencies between signals from different input connections. Additional nonlinearities, after proper selection of model's parameters values, allow also effective directing of an attention to the most important elements of input data. But they all also have one common fundamental disadvantage - in every situation they require reading in of all input signals, regardless of their importance. Thus their selective attention abilities are very limited when compared to properties of natural systems.

In theory for above functions can exist additional mechanism that in some situations would prevent reading in unimportant information. If the aggregation function would include higher order terms and input signals from different inputs would be read in and analysed in many steps, similarly as in the Stark's scan path model, a zero valued signal could be information that signals from some other input connections can be left unread. But in practice results of such a solution would strongly depend on the order of input signals analysis. It is interesting that similar effects are detected in nature — observations of neurobiologists show that biological neurons are asynchronous in nature, and that their behaviour depend on the order in which input signals reach the neuron. An example of biologically founded asynchronous neurons models are integrate and fire neurons, that process information coded in the time domain (e.g. with use of frequency modulation) -

their most important property is ability to mimic capacitive character of signals accumulation process (Stein, 1967; Maass, 1997; Burkitt & Clark, 1999; Quiles et al., 2008).
Unfortunately artificial asynchronous neuron networks also do not show attentional properties observed in the nature. This is due to the fact, that asynchronous, continuous accumulation of input signals, neglect the information about that, from which neuron's inputs come the signals which influenced neuron's actual activation potential. This make it impossible to realise selective attention in the form other than making neuron's output value dependant from only most intense stimuli and regardless of their meaning.
As both synchronous and asynchronous neuron signals aggregation schemes don't provide general and precise models of selective attention, it seem to be plausible to search for hybrid solutions that are both synchronous, and read in and analyse signals in a step by step manner. This research direction finds strong support in recent observations that link selective attention of biological systems with synchronisation processes in asynchronous neural networks (Wróbel, 2000; Niebur et al., 2002; Grammont & Riehle, 2003; Gross et al., 2004; Usher, 2006). Further parts of this chapter will describe a proposition of artificial neuron model that try to fulfil mentioned requirements, and realise low-level selective attention by conforming to the Noton & Stark scan path theory.

4. Synchronous, conditional signals aggregation as a key to distributed selective attention

Analysis of the properties of aggregation functions presented in the previous subchapters leads to the conclusion that up to date neuronal models of low-level selective attention can be enriched by using synchronous data processing along with input connections grouping and stepwise conditional input signals accumulation. As even simple perceptron neuron model is synchronous in nature – all its input signals are treated like if were received in the same time – it should be possible to extend its attention directing abilities by dividing its input connections into groups, defining proper sequence in which signals from different groups should be read in and processed, and specifying a condition that stops signals aggregation when is met. In general this is a very difficult task, especially finding input's grouping and sequence of input signals processing proper for a given task. But, as it will be shown in further sections, with additional assumptions on the inputs grouping algorithm and the form of scan path used to analyse them, the problem can be essentially reduced and effectively solved. In the effect, proposed synchronous conditional aggregation strategy and resulting neuron models can be easily used as one-to-one nodes replacement in widely used fully connected, multilayer perceptron neural networks. A basic but legible example of such a solution is Sigma-if neuron along with Sigma-if neural network(Huk, 2004; Huk, 2007).

4.1 The Sigma-if neuron

The Sigma-if neuron, in contrast to a typical perceptron neuron, aggregates input signals for the given data vector $\mathbf{x}=[x_1,x_2,..,x_N]$ not in one but in a series of given *K* steps according to the corresponding state graph. Its input connections are divided into *K* discrete subsets during the training process. Subsequently, when the neuron's aggregation function value is computed, in every *k*-th step of this process, the subset of input signals X_k is taken from the environment and processed to determine the current value of the partial activation level

φ_k of the neuron. The process continues until the value of φ_k exceeds a given aggregation threshold φ^*. When that condition is met, signals which were not analysed are ignored, and φ_k is considered the input value for the neuron's activation function *F*. As a result, signal level information coding and even the use of a non-local activation function (e.g. sigmoid) do not degrade the neuron's selective attention abilities. A sample scheme of a state graph for a Sigma-if neuron is presented in Fig. 1.

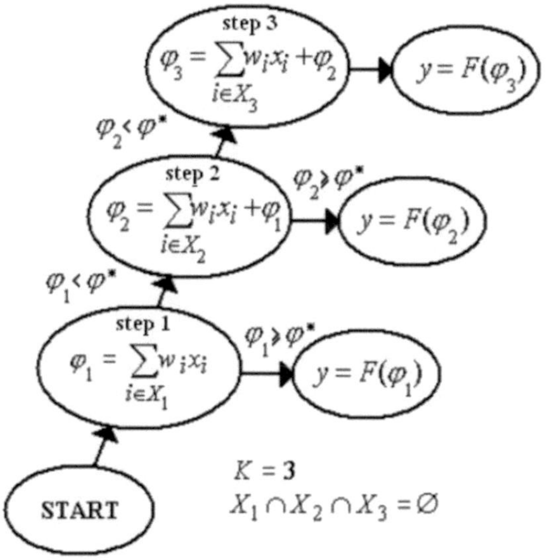

Fig. 1. Sample process of a three-step input signal aggregation in the Sigma-if neuron

Formally speaking, *N* dendrites of the Sigma-if neuron are divided into *K* distinct groups, by complementing each *i*-th input connection with an additional integer parameter $\theta_i \in \{0,..,K-1\}$, determining membership in one of the groups. This allows us to divide the process of signal accumulation into *K* steps, where *K* is a function of the neuron's grouping vector $\boldsymbol{\theta}^T=[\theta_1,\theta_2,..,\theta_N]$:

$$K(\boldsymbol{\theta}) = \max_{i=1}^{N} \theta_i . \tag{10}$$

During each step *k* (from 0 to *K*-1), the neuron accumulates data belonging to one selected group, such that

$$\theta_i = k. \tag{11}$$

Within each *k*-th group, partial activation $\Delta\varphi_k$ is determined as a weighted sum of input signals and the appropriate Kronecker's delta:

$$\Delta\varphi_k(\boldsymbol{w},\boldsymbol{x},\boldsymbol{\theta}) = \sum_{i=1}^{N} w_i\, x_i \delta(k,\theta_i), \tag{12}$$

where w_i and x_i are coefficients of the neuron's weight vector $\boldsymbol{w}$ and an input vector $\mathbf{x}$. This process is repeated until the actual activation φ_k derived from respective inputs groups exceeds a preselected aggregation threshold φ^*. It can be described by the following recursive formula (vectors $\boldsymbol{w}$, $\boldsymbol{x}$ and $\boldsymbol{\theta}$ are omitted for clarity):

$$\varphi_k = \begin{cases} \Delta\varphi_k \cdot H(\varphi^* - \varphi_{k-1}) + \varphi_{k-1} & : k \geq 0 \\ 0 & : k < 0 \end{cases}, \tag{13}$$

where $\boldsymbol{H}$ is Heaviside step function. This sum is then treated as the neuronal activation value. The input from remaining (heretofore unconsidered) groups is neglected. Thus, the proposed form of the aggregation function $\varphi_{Sigma\text{-}if}$ is:

$$\varphi_{Sigma-if}(\boldsymbol{w},\boldsymbol{x},\boldsymbol{\theta}) = \varphi_K(\boldsymbol{w},\boldsymbol{x},\boldsymbol{\theta}). \tag{14}$$

In the final stages of determining the output value $\boldsymbol{Y}$ of the neuron, function (14) serves as a parameter of the nonlinear threshold (e.g. sigmoidal) function $\boldsymbol{F}$:

$$Y(\boldsymbol{w},\boldsymbol{x},\boldsymbol{\theta}) = F(\varphi_{Sigma-if}(\boldsymbol{w},\boldsymbol{x},\boldsymbol{\theta})). \tag{15}$$

The described model assumes that the state graph used during signal aggregation is always a simple directed path of non-terminal nodes corresponding with the neural activation accumulation procedure. In a general case, the Sigma-if neuron, besides the weights vector $\boldsymbol{w}$, includes one continuous valued parameter for aggregation threshold φ^*, and an additional connections grouping vector $\boldsymbol{\theta}$ with only one nominal valued coefficient for each neuronal input connection.

It is easy to find, that if all coefficients of grouping vector have the same value (what means that all input connections belong to the same group), the functionality of Sigma-if neuron is equivalent to the functioning of the perceptron. Similar effect appears also in the case when there are many different groups and after aggregation of all $\Delta\varphi$ the total activation is not grater than threshold value φ^*, or is greater than φ^* just after adding $\Delta\varphi_K$. But it is much more interesting how Sigma-if neurons function, when for given input values:

$$\underset{k^*<K}{\exists} : \varphi_{k^*}(\boldsymbol{w},\boldsymbol{x},\boldsymbol{\theta}) >= \varphi^*. \tag{16}$$

This corresponds to the case, when due to suitable selection of $\boldsymbol{w}$ and $\boldsymbol{\theta}$ vectors, for a given input vector Sigma-if neuron reads in and analyse only a part of available input signals. The value k^* defines the number of inputs groups, which are used to determine the activation of the neuron.

It also is important to notice, that assumption that introduced value k^* is known for every input vector, helps to avoid recursive formula (13) and to write that:

$$\varphi_{Sigma-if}(\mathbf{w},\mathbf{x},\boldsymbol{\theta}) = \sum_{k=1}^{k^*} \Delta\varphi_k(\mathbf{w},\mathbf{x},\boldsymbol{\theta}) = \sum_{k=1}^{k^*}\sum_{i=1}^{N} w_i\, x_i \delta(k,\theta_i). \tag{17}$$

Above form of proposed aggregation function reflects actual simplicity of the conditional inputs accumulation method, and is more suitable to use in practice and in theoretical considerations than its recursive equivalent. However it should be remembered, that in practice k^* value remains unknown, until the end of calculation of Sigma-if neuron activation.

4.2 Sigma-if network architecture and training

Proposed Sigma-if neurons can be used to build a simple model called Sigma-if neural network, which possess selective attention abilities. The proposed neural network is a generalisation of synchronous, three layer, fully connected perceptron neural network (MLP), in which hidden perceptron neurons were changed to the Sigma-if neurons. Such a neural network does not need separate centralised attention guidance module. This is because its ability to realise selective attention functionality emerges as an effect of synergy between its hidden Sigma-if neurons.

In this place it is good to ask, how described properties of Sigma-if network can be achieved? It is easy to see, that in comparison to MLP neural network training, searching for an optimal set of Sigma-if network parameters would be very computationally challenging, due to the non-continuous character of Sigma-if neuron grouping vector. The answer to this general question is that while we don't know quick and effective method for global searching for optimal Sigma-if network weights and grouping vectors, the problem should be reduced to a simpler one.

The proposed solution assumes that at each Sigma-if neuron, coefficients of the grouping vector $\boldsymbol{\theta}$ are in fact direct functions of weight vector w. In this work, the grouping vector computation procedure (as well as the predefined value of the aggregation threshold φ^*) is common for all Sigma if neurons. It simply divides input connections into a given number of groups of similar sizes, according to "the greater the connection weight, the smaller the connection group number" principle. Such a search problem reduction leads to very interesting results, and allows practical elimination of the additional $\boldsymbol{\theta}$ vectors after the end of neural network training process. However, during further analysis of the general Sigma-if model, it is still very helpful to use the grouping vector concept.

As a result, network connection weights are established by the well known error backpropagation algorithm, but for every ω training epoch, actual grouping vectors are computed. This reflects the application of the self-consistency idea widely used in physics. According to this idea, two sets of mutually dependent parameters of a system converge to the optimum, during repeated forcing known directions of improvement at parameters values of at least one of those sets (Kohn & Sham, 1965; Mannheim, 1975; Noyh et al., 1991; Fonseca et al., 1998, Raczkowski et al., 2001). During the training, this method allows also regulation of ratio of mutual dependency between neurons weights and grouping vectors, by setting the number of training epochs ω, after which actualisation of the grouping

vector takes place. It is interesting, when ω tends to infinity, described training algorithm tends to be identical to oryginal backpropagation method.
The last element needed to carry out described backpropagation process, is an information about that how proposed conditional aggregation function of the Sigma-if neuron changes methods of calculating errors and delta rule values for each layer of Sigma-if neural network. Fortunately it is easy to show, that when the Sigma-if aggregation method φ is given by expression (17), the output error $\delta_j^{m\mu}$ of j-th neuron in m-th hidden layer of Sigma-if neurons for the input vector of number μ is given by the following equation:

$$\delta_j^{m\mu} = F'(\varphi_j^{m\mu}) \sum_{l=1}^{n_{m+1}} \delta_l^{(m+1)\mu} w_{l,j}^{m+1} H(k_l^{*(m+1)\mu} - \theta_{l,j}^{m+1}), \tag{18}$$

where n_{m+1} is the number of neurons in m+1 neurons layer, F is neuron's activation function and H is a two-valued Heaviside unit step function. Presented equation is different from analogous expression for the perceptron network only by Heaviside step function. This change causes that when some of neuron's input connections are not used during calculation of its activation, they do not influence neuron's output error, even when their weights and input signals are nonzero.
In turn, by using equation (18), the value of general delta rule $\Delta w_{ji}^{m\mu}$ used to update weight of the connection, between j-th neuron in m-th neuron layer and i-th neuron in m-1 layer, can be defined as:

$$\Delta w_{ji}^{m\mu} = \eta \delta_j^{m\mu} u_i^{(m-1)\mu} H(k_j^{*m\mu} - \theta_{j,i}^{m}), \tag{19}$$

where η is a learning coefficient and $u_i^{(m-1)\mu}$ is an output value of i-th neuron in m-1 network layer for given input vector μ. Repeated appearance of Heaviside function is here natural for backpropagation algorithm – while connections not active during input signals aggregation do not influence neuron's error, thus their weights should not be updated.
At the end of this section it is also important to notice, that the procedure of grouping vector modification according to weights values is run only after the phase of connections weights update. Thus, while we do not want to determine Sigma-if neural network behaviour just after random initialisation of neurons connections weights, at the beginning of the training process Sigma-if neurons are reduced to perceptron neurons by setting all coefficients of their grouping vectors to 1.

5. Properties of the Sigma-if model

The conditional aggregation method of the Sigma-if neuron can be considered also from the perspective of its decision space characteristics. In particular it is interesting how its form evolves during single input values aggregation. Before outputting a selected value, Sigma-if neuron can consider multiple hypotheses involving its input signals. Speaking in formal terms, a trained neuron before output value calculation can do many attempts to partition the data space with hypersurfaces using an increasing number of dimensions, where the maximal number of attempts is determined by the number of its input groups K. In the effect, the final dimensionality of Sigma-if neuron decision space is known just after determination of its total activation value, and effective form of its decision borders is a composition of individual hypersurfaces in appropriate variables value ranges, that with respect to the order of signals aggregation. This capability significantly extends the classification potential of neural processing units, and introduces neuron's selective attention behaviours.

Experience dictates that a single Sigma-if neuron, unlike the perceptron neuron, is capable of solving linearly non-separable problems, despite using a linear or sigmoid non-local threshold function. The simplest example of such an approach is a two-input Sigma-if neuron, which, provided both dendrites belong to different input groups, can implement a function defined by expression (20):

$$D_{LNS}(x_1,x_2) = \begin{cases} 0 : (x_1,x_2) \in \{(0,0),(0.8,0.8)\} \\ 1 : (x_1,x_2) \in \{(0,1),(1,0)\} \end{cases}. \tag{20}$$

Let's now assume that components of the grouping vector θ_1 and θ_2 connected adequately with input connections x_1 and x_2 are not equal – e.g. that θ_1 is less than θ_2. Then neuron's input x_2 is read in only when partial neuron activation $\Delta\varphi_1$ (equal to the product of w_1 and x_1) is lesser than activation threshold φ^*. This allows a division of input signals classification process into two stages. In the first phase, aggregation method considers only input space dimension connected with variable x_1, and all input vectors are perceived by neuron as adequate projections to a one dimensional subspace defined by axis X_1. Adequately, connection weight w_1 and aggregation threshold φ^* define a boundary line that separates region of the full decision space, which analysis is based only on signals from input x_1, from the region for which neuron's output value is calculated in the second aggregation phase with use of all input signals. However in the one dimension this border is reduced to the point, in the given example defined as:

$$c^* = \frac{\varphi^*}{w_1}, \tag{21}$$

that after considering also the second input variable – that is in the full decision space – it has the form of a straight line that passes through the point c^*, and is perpendicular to the axis X_1 (in general case this is a hyperplane).

With a fixed value of threshold φ^*, proper selection of w_1 allows such division of decision space that breaks linearly non-separable problem into two subproblems that are linearly separable. Since both partial problems are being solved in subspaces of different number of dimensions, it should be remembered that each of the subproblems should have to be linearly separable only in the subspace it is associated with. In the given example, the partial problem that is solved only with use of variable x_1 thus must be linearly separable in one dimensional space. As it is shown on the Fig. 2, in a solved problem this condition can be met.

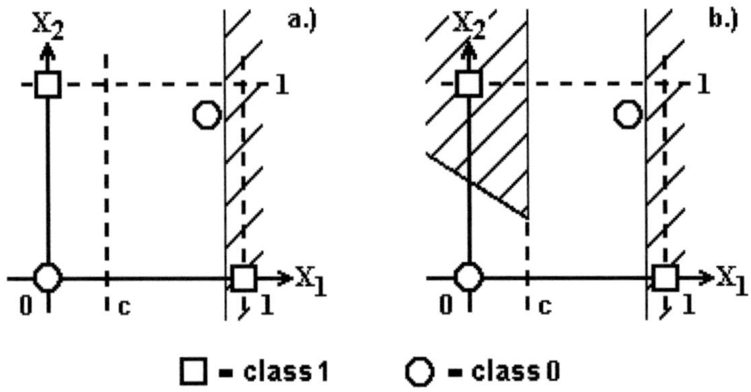

Fig. 2. Phases of two-input Sigma-if neuron decision space evolution, during step-by-step accumulation of input signals (θ^T=[1; 2], w^T=[1,3; 2,5], φ^*=0,4). a.) division into two subproblems and solution of the one dimensional problem, b.) composition of decision regions of the first and the second phase

During analysis of the above illustration it should be remembered, that in case of Sigma-if neuron, the final shape of decision borders is also determined by bipolar, sigmoidal activation function and necessity of neuron output values discretization. In the given example, neuron output values that were less or equal 0.5 were treated as class 0, and other values were associated with class 1. Results for chosen input vectors are presented in table 1.

Nr	Input vector (x_1, x_2)	Number of used input values	Total neuron activation	Output value Y	Class
1	(0; 0)	2	0,00	0,00	0
2	(0; 1)	2	2,50	0,85	1
3	(1; 0)	1	1,30	0,57	1
4	(0,8; 0,8)	1	1,04	0,48	0

Table 1. Numerical quantities depicting classification of chosen input vectors by Sigma-if neuron ($\boldsymbol{\theta}^T$=[1; 2], w^T=[1,3; 2,5], φ^*=0,4)

On the basis of above analysis, it is easy to point an example of the problem, which is not solvable by single Sigma-if neuron. While sometimes it is not possible to fulfil the criteria of linear separability for all partial problems produced by step-by-step input signals aggregation, proposed solution fails for the original XOR problem. In this case each straight line perpendicular to one of the dimensions of the data space and passing though a selected point of input data belonging to class C, also necessarily contains a point from a class different than C, making it impossible to discern between both points through the use of straight lines perpendicular to data space versors. Such problems may, however, be attacked through rotating the entire coordinate system by a given acute angle - a transformation, which enables the Sigma-if neuron to properly classify points defining the XOR function. It is also worth to mention, that Sigma-if neuron is also capable of solving AND and OR problems (Huk, 2006).

6. Experimental verification of Sigma-if model properties

Above theoretical analysis of the Sigma-if neuron and its conditional aggregation function, was extended and verified by examination of the whole Sigma-if network properties in practical applications, on the example tasks of classification of the UCI Machine Learning benchmark problems. During examination, simulated Sigma-if neural networks were compared to MLP networks with the same architectures. All networks were fully connected and had one hidden layer with the number of neurons for which the MLP network in preliminary tests gained highest test data classification accuracy. Numbers of inputs groups K and aggregation threshold φ^* values of all hidden Sigma-if neurons in the given network were equal. As the sigmoidal perceptron is a special case of a Sigma-if neuron, MLP networks were in fact simulated by Sigma-if networks with the number of inputs groups K of all Sigma-if neurons set to one. In all cases, standard input signal coding was used, and answers of the network were computed in the winner-takes-all manner.

Along with classification accuracies u for training and γ for test data, properties such as neural network data processing time τ, as well as hidden connections and network input activity (designated *hca* and *nia* respectively) were considered. The data processing time τ for all trained networks was measured to check relative data processing costs for MLP and Sigma-if networks. Regardless of the very precise time measurement procedure used, actual timings on other hardware setups may vary considerably. Hidden connection activity *hca* and network input activity *nia* were used to representing the percentage ratio of the number of hidden and input connections used during data processing, compared to all of the network's hidden and input connections respectively. These parameters allowed check if hidden Sigma-if neurons use their selective attention ability in practice. For the completeness of analysis, for each given problem and trained network, the percent of all inputs used to classify all test vectors *niu* was calculated. This procedure was important in order to determine if selective attention functionality is also realised at the level of the whole Sigma−if network. All measured values were calculated as averaged outcomes of ten independent 10-fold cross validations.

The experiments were divided into two groups: examination of Sigma-if network classification properties and verification of the hypotheses that Sigma-if networks realise selective attention at the level of single neurons and of the whole network. In both cases all of the considered properties were analysed in relation to the number of Sigma-if neuron inputs groups K. This was because the K value has the highest influence on the properties of the proposed network. Other parameters, such as the aggregation threshold φ^* and the grouping vector actualisation interval ω, were set to 0.6 and 25 respectively, following preliminary tests.

The obtained results indicate that increasing the number of Sigma-if neuron input groups K to more than one, results in an increase of test data classification accuracy γ as well as in simultaneous decrease of data processing time τ. The drawback here is a decrease of training data classification accuracy u. Typical examples of such a dependencies can be observed for the HeartC and Wine problems, which are presented in Fig. 3 and Fig. 4 (as the number of input connections groups K is discrete, values on presented figures are connected only to ease analysis of the results).

The observed decrease in training data classification accuracy u for the HeartC problem was caused by to the fact that it is harder to learn when the neuron's input space is changed every ω epoch. However, and more importantly, the obtained increase in test data classification accuracy γ is a result of rejecting redundant or noisy signals from processed data and the consequence of effective reduction of problem dimensionality. This thesis is confirmed by the observed simultaneous decrease in data processing time τ. Reduction of τ can only be caused by reduction of the network's hidden and input connections activities. However, regardless of the reasons, these results show that the Sigma-if neural network can have better classification properties than MLP.

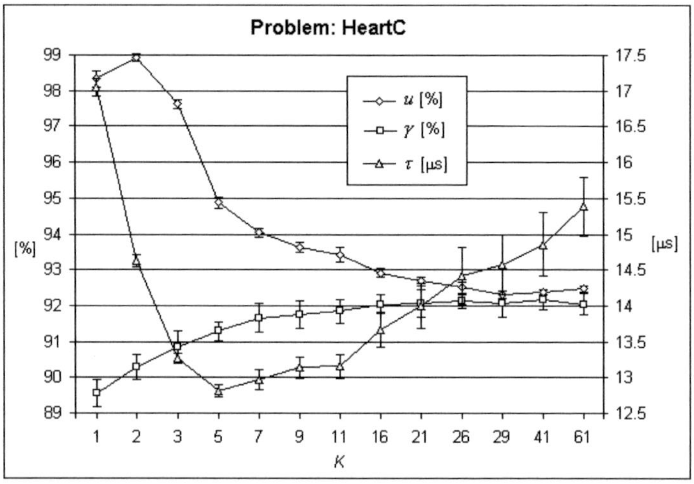

Fig. 3. The time of Sigma-if network output signal generation τ, the classification accuracy of training u and test γ data for the HeartC problem versus the number of hidden neuron input connections groups K (networks architecture: 28 inputs, 10 hidden neurons, 5 outputs)

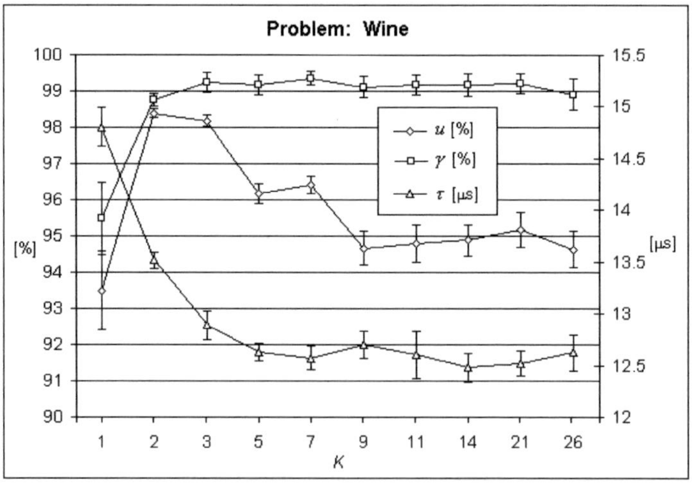

Fig. 4. The time of Sigma-if network output signal generation τ, the classification accuracy of training u and test γ data for the Wine problem versus the number of hidden neuron input connections groups K (networks architecture: 13 inputs, 10 hidden neurons, 3 outputs)

The visible increase of HeartC data processing time τ for K greater than 7 inputs groups is the effect of a linear increase of time cost, connected with the existence of additional instructions for grouping vector $\boldsymbol{\theta}$ information processing. This factor can be easily seen for the number of groups K greater than the given number of network inputs. Without it, data processing time would semi-logarithmically decrease with rising K, similarly as in the case of Wine problem, for which low number of network inputs and connections between hidden and input layer, make this effect negligible. This indicates the character of the changes of Sigma-if network hidden *hca* and input connection activities *nia* as a function of K, which can be observed in Fig. 5 (for the Sonar problem) and in Fig. 6 (for the Votes problem).

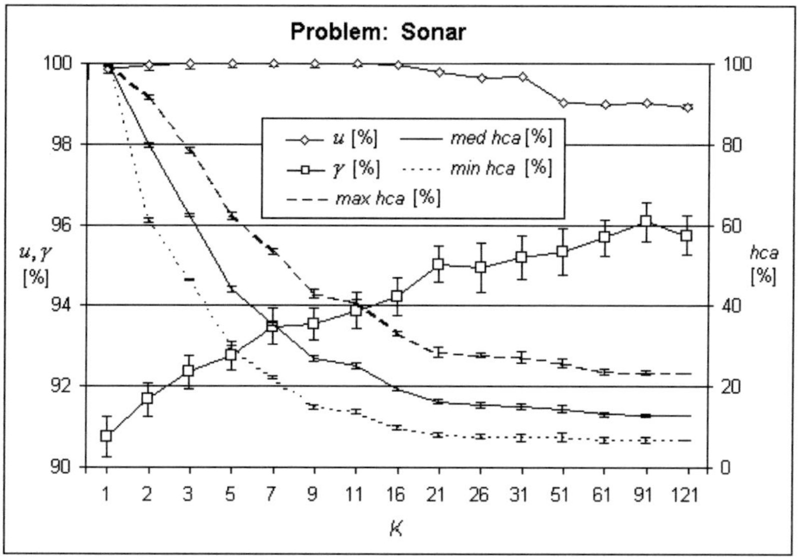

Fig. 5. The Sigma-if network hidden connection activity *hca*, the classification accuracy of training u and test γ data for the Sonar problem versus the number of hidden neuron input connections groups K (network architecture: 60 inputs, 30 hidden neurons, 2 outputs)

It can be easily seen that in the case of the Sonar problem the increase in K causes an increase of the test data classification accuracy, with a corresponding slight decrease of the training data classification accuracy. These changes are accompanied with a much stronger reduction of hidden connection activities. The shape of the *hca*(K) function confirms earlier conclusions that the data processing time reduction is connected with Sigma-if neurons' selective attention abilities. All this is clear evidence that Sigma-if neurons use selective attention, and that this can reduce the generalization error level as well as data processing costs. But results for the Wine problem show that these savings are not always gained for the price of lowering training data accuracy (Fig. 4).

The last example concerns how selective attention abilities manifest themselves on the level of the whole Sigma-if network. The analysis of results for the Votes problem (Fig. 6) shows that when a significant decrease of network input activity *nia* occurs, one can expect a simultaneous reduction in the number of Sigma-if network inputs used to classify data (*niu*) without a notable decrease of classification accuracy in comparison to the MLP network.

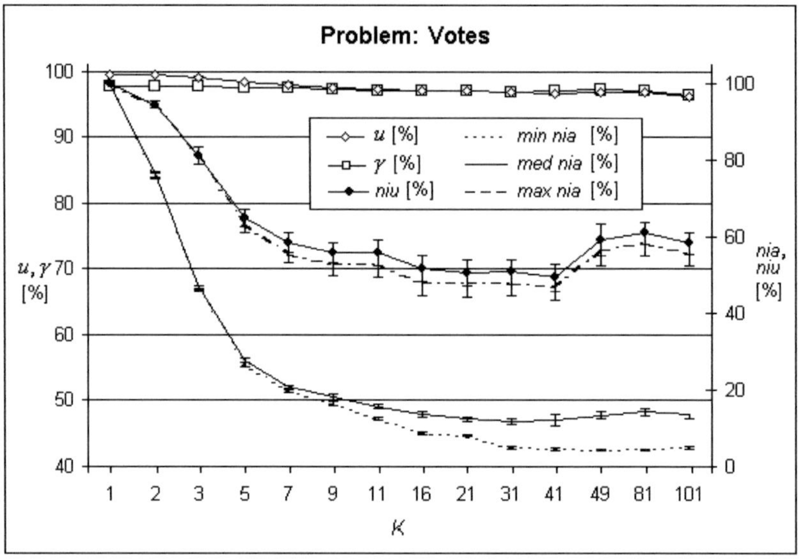

Fig. 6. The Sigma-if network input activity *nia*, the number of network input used *niu*, and the classification accuracy of training *u* and test γ data for the Votes problem versus the number of hidden neuron input connections groups *K* (network architecture: 48 inputs, 2 hidden neurons, 2 outputs)

While the Sigma-if network has no specialised or separate attention guiding unit, all such activities can emerge only as the effect of synergy between individual neurons. Thus, the observed selective attention behaviour of the proposed network, treated as a black box, is a significant indication that the Sigma-if model effectively mimics basic aspects of low level attentional processes observed in nature. This can, in turn, make the model an interesting tool for feature selection and other data processing purposes.

7. Conclusion

In this chapter, a novel computational model of distributed neuronal selective attention, based on the scan-path theory and up-to-date findings of neurobiologists, has been presented. In described solution, attention is conceived by new, synchronous, sequential and conditional input signals aggregation function of an artificial neuron. While the resulting Sigma-if network has no specialised or separate attention guiding unit, selective attention emerges at the level of the whole neuronal network as an effect of synergy among the network's hidden neurons.

Introduced idea allowed construction of the whole attentional classification neuronal system along with efficient Sigma-if network training method that is combination of gradient backpropagation algorithm and self-consistency paradigm. Thanks to this, a series of experiments have been conducted with the use of benchmark problems, to test basic properties of Sigma-if network. The model's selective attention ability for medium-size test problems manifests itself in an increase of classification accuracy and in a simultaneous decrease of data processing costs. Observed reduction of the number of network inputs used

to classify data shows the possibility of further reduction of data acuqisition costs, during as well as after the network training process.
The Sigma-if selective attention feature also introduces new possibilities in the area of analysing the network decision process via its inputs activity interpretation. This can point at features of given data sets that are most important for classification, and help to identify features that are irrelevant, redundant or contaminated by noise. All this makes the Sigma-if neural network a very useful tool for the data acquisition and analysis domain. As proposed Sigma-if network training method allow automatic construction of selective attention strategies, proposed model can be also a very promising solution for applications such as remote sensing in dispersed sensor networks as well as automatic robot navigation and control.
In fact the Sigma-if neuron is very simple and differs in much details from biological neurons. But from theoretical point of view it can be also treated as an interesting model of low-level human selective attention. In this light it is astonishing that for many of mid-sized benchmark classification problems Sigma-if network gained the best and the quickest classification results, when number of input connections groups was set between 3 and 11. This is because it seems to correlate with real life observations of the maximum number of seven information groups (e.g. displayed on a poster) that average human brain finds easy to analyse. But this should be treated only as a kind of intuition not a strict result.
Due to a very interesting theoretical and practical properties, proposed Sigma-if model should be further tested as well on benchmark as also on real-life data. Also the whole idea of synchronised conditional signals aggregation should be further explored, as other aggregation functions than the one presented in this chapter can be proposed. All this makes a wide and promising direction of research on the neuronal selective attention models, and in this time it is a subject of continuous investigation.

8. References

Allport, D.A.; Antonis, B. & Reynolds, P. (1972). On the division of attention: a disproof of the single channel hypothesis, *Quarterly Journal of Experimental Psychology*, Vol. 24, pp. 225-235

Anderson, R.A.; Essich, G.K. & Siegal, R.M. (1985). Encoding of spatial location by posterior parietal neurons, Science, Vol. 230, pp. 456–458

Anderson, C. & Van Essen, D. (1987). Shifter Circuits: a computational strategy for dynamic aspects of visual processing, *Proceedings of National Academy of Sciences*, USA 84, pp. 6297-6301

Baldassi, S. & Verghese, P. (2002). Comparing integration rules in visual search, *Journal of Vision*, Vol. 2, pp. 559-570

Broadbent, D.E. (1982). Task combination and selective intake of information. *Acta Psychologica*, Vol. 50, pp. 253-290, 0001-6918

Bryden, M.P. (1971). Attentional strategies and short-term memory in dichotic listening, *Cognitive Psychology*, Vol. 2, pp. 99-116.

Bukovsky, I.; Zeng-Guang Hou; Bila, J. & Gupta, M.M. (2007) Foundation of Notation and Classification of Nonconventional Static and Dynamic Neural Units, *Proceedings of 6th IEEE International Conference on Cognitive Informatics*, pp. 401-407, 978-1-4244-1328-7

Burkitt, A.N. & Clark, G.M. (1999). Analysis of integrate-and-fire neurons: synchronization of synaptic input and spike output, *Neural Computation*, Vol. 11, No. 4, pp. 871-901, 0899-7667

Chelazzi, L.; Miller, E.; Duncan, J. & Desimone, R. (1993). A Neural Basis for Visual Search in Inferior Temporal Cortex, *Nature*, Vol. 363, pp. 345-347, 0028-0836

Cherry, E.C. (1953). Some experiments on the recognition of speech, with one and with two ears, *Journal of the Acoustical Society of America*, Vol. 25, No. 5, pp. 975-979, 0001-4966

Clauss, M.; Bayerl, P. & Neumann, H. (2004). Evaluation of regions-of-interest based attention algorithms using a probabilistic measure, *Proceedings of the 5th. Workshop Dynamic Perception 2004*, pp. 227-232, 3-89838-059-9, Germany, IOS Press, Tübingen

Cover, T.M. (1965). Geometrical and Statistical Properties of Systems of Linear Inequalities with Applications in Pattern Recognition, *IEEE Transactions on Electronic Computers*, Vol. EC-14, No. 3, June 1965, pp. 326-334, 0367-7508

Deutsch, J. & Deutsch, D. (1963). Attention: Some theoretical considerations, *Psychological Review*, Vol. 70, No.1, pp. 80-90

Dole, G.H. (2008). The Philosophy of Creation, Elsevier Science Publishers B.V., 0559702159, Amsterdam

Durbin, R. & Rumelhart, D.E. (1990). Product units: A computationally powerful and biologically plausible extension to backpropagation networks, *Neural Computation*, Vol. 1, No. 1, pp. 133-142, 0899-7667

Eckstein, M.P.; Beutter, B.R. & Stone, L.S. (2001). Quantifying the performance limits of human saccadic targeting in visual search, *Perception*, Vol. 30, pp. 1389-1401, 0301-0066

Findlay, J.M. (1982). Global visual processing for saccadic eye movements, *Vision Research*, Vol. 22, pp. 1033-1046, 0042-6989

Fonseca, L.R.C.; Jimenez, J.L.; Leburton, J.P. & Martin R.M. (1998). Self-consistent calculation of the electronic structure and electron-electron interaction in self-assembled InAs-GaAs quantum dot structures, *Physical Review B*, Vol. 57, pp. 4017-4026

Giles, C.L. & Maxwell, T. (1994). Learning, Invariance, and Generalization in High Order Neural Networks, *Applied Optics*, Vol. 26, No. 23, pp. 4972-4978, 0003-6935

Grammont, F. & Riehle, A. (2003). Spike synchronization and firing rate in a population of motor cortical neurons in relation to movement direction and reaction time, *Biological cybernetics*, Vol. 88, No. 5, pp. 360-373, 0340-1200

Gray, J. & Wedderburn A. (1960). Grouping strategies with simultaneous stimuli, *Quarterly Journal of Experimental Psychology*, Vol. 12, pp. 180-184, 1747-0218

Grosjean, F. (1980). Spoken word recognition processes and the gating paradigm, *Perception and Psychophysics*, Vol. 28, No. 4, pp. 267-283, 0031-5117

Gross, J.; Schmitz, F.; Schnitzler, I.; Kessler, K.; Shapiro, K. & Hommel, B. (2004). Modulation of long-range neural synchrony reflects temporal limitations of visual attention in humans. *Proceedings of the National Academy of Sciences of the United States of America*, Vol. 101, No. 35, August 2004, pp. 13050–13055, 0027-8424

Gupta, M.M. (2008). Correlative type higher-order neural units with applications, *Proceedings of the IEEE International Conference on Automation and Logistics 2008*, September 2008, pp. 15-718, 978-1-4244-2502-0, Quingdao, China

Hager, G. & Toyama, K. (1999). Incremental focus of attention for robust visual tracking, *International Journal of Computer Vision*, Vol. 35, No. 1, pp. 45-63

Houghton, G. & Tipper, S.P. (1996). Inhibitory Mechanisms of Neural and Cognitive Control: Applications to Selective Attention and Sequential Action, *Brain and Cognition*, Vol. 30, pp. 20-43

Huk, M. (2004). The Sigma-if neural network as a method of dynamic selection of decision subspaces for medical reasoning systems, *Journal of Medical Informatics and Technologies*, Vol. 7, October 2004, pp. KB-65-73, 1642-6037

Huk, M. (2006). Sigma-if neural network as a use of selective attention technique in classification and knowledge discovery problems solving, *Annales UMCS Informatica AI*, Szczygieł R., Mikołajczak P., Budzyński M., Kamiński W.A., Sielanko J., Złotkiewicz E. (Ed.), Vol 5., No. 2, pp. 121-131, 1732-1360

Huk, M. (2007). Manifestation of selective attention in Sigma-if neural network, *Proceedings of the International Multiconference on Computer Science and Information Technology IMCSIT/AAIA'07, 2nd International Symposium Advances in Artificial Intelligence and Applications*, Vol. 2, October 2007, pp. 225-236, 1896-7094

Kahneman, D. (1973). Attention and Effort, Englewood Cliffs, New Jersey, Prentice-Hall

Karlholm, J.M. (1993) Associative memories with short-range, higher order couplings, Neural Networks, Vol. 6, pp. 409–421

Kastner, S.; De Weerd, P.; Desimone, R. & Ungerleider, L. (1998). Mechanisms of Directed Attention in the Human Extrastriate Cortex as Revealed by Functional MRI, *Science*, Vol. 282, pp. 108–111, 0036-8075

Koch, C. & Ullman, S. (1985). Shifts in selective visual attention: towards the underlying neural circuitry, *Human Neurobiology*, Vol. 4, pp. 219–227

Kohn W. & Sham LJ. (1965). Self-Consistent Equations Including Exchange and Correlation Effects, *Physical Review*, Vol. 140, pp. A1133-A1138

Körding, K.P. & König, P. (2001) Neurons with two sites of synaptic integration learn invariant representations, Neural Computation, Vol. 13, No. 12, pp. 2823-2849, 0899-7667

Kucera, H. & Francis, W.M. (1967). *Computational analysis of present-day American English,* Brown University Press

LaBerge, D. (1990). Thalamic and cortical mechanisms of attention suggested by recent positron emission tomographic experiments, *Journal of Cognitive Neuroscience*, Vol. 2, pp. 358-372, 0898-929X

Larkum, M.E.; Zhu, J.J. & Sakmann, B. (1999) A new cellular mechanism for coupling inputs arriving at different cortical layers, Nature, Vol. 398, pp. 338–41, 0028-0836

Lee, Y. (2000). An information-theoretic framework for understanding saccadic behaviors. *Advances in Neural Processing Systems*, Vol. 12, pp. 834-840

Leerink, L.R.; Giles, C.L.; Horne, B.G.& Jabri, M.A. (1995). Learning with Product Units, *Advances in Neural Information Processing Systems 7*, Tesauro, G.; Touretzky, D.; Leen T. (Ed.), pp. 537-544, MIT Press

Lewis, J.L. (1970). Semantic processing of unattended messages using dichotic listening. *Journal of Experimental Psychology*, Vol. 85, pp. 220-227

Maass, W. (1997). Networks of spiking neurons: the third generation of neural network models, *Neural Networks*, Vol. 10, No. 9, pp. 1659-1671

Marslen-Wilson, W.D. & Tyler, L.K. (1980). The temporal structure of spoken language understanding, *Cognition*, Vol. 8, pp. 1-71

Martínez-Estudillo, C.; Hervás-Martínez, P.A.; Gutiérrez, & A.C. Martínez-Estudillo, Evolutionary product-unit neural networks classifiers, *Neurocomputing, Life System Modelling, Simulation, and Bio-inspired Computing (LSMS 2007)*, Vol. 72, No. 1-3, December 2008, pp. 548-561,

Mel, B.W. (1999). Why have dendrites? A computational perspective, *Dendrities*, Stuart G., Hausser M., pp. 271-289, Oxford University Press

Mel, B. W. (1992). The clusteron: toward a simple abstraction for a complex neuron, *Advances in Neural Information Processing Systems*, Vol. 4, pp. 35–42, Morgan Kaufmann

Mel, B. W. (1990). The sigma-pi column: a model of associative learning in cerebral cortex. *Technical Report CNS Memo 6, Computation and Neural Systems Program*, California Institute of Technology

Mannheim, P.D. (1975). Dynamical symmetry breaking as a bootstrap, *Physical Review D*, Vol. 12, p. 1772-1793

Neely, J.H. (1977). Semantic priming and retrieval from lexical memory: Roles of inhibitionless spreading activation and limited capacity attention, *Journal of Experimental Psychology: General*, Vol. 106, pp. 226-254, 0096-3445

Neville, R. S.; S. (2002). Eldridge, Transformations of sigma-pi nets: obtaining reflected functions by reflecting weight matrices, *Neural Networks*, Vol. 15, No. 3, pp.: 375-393, 0893-6080, Elsevier Science Ltd. Oxford, UK

Niebur, E.; Hsiao, S.S. & Johnson, K.O. (2002). Synchrony: a neuronal mechanism for attentional selection?, *Current Opinion in Neurobiology*, Vol. 12, No. 2, April 2002, pp. 190-194, 0959-4388.

Niebur E.; Koch C. & Rosin C. (1993). An oscillation-based model for the neural basis of attention. *Vision Research*, Vol. 33, pp. 2789-2802

Noh, T.W.; Song, P.H. & Sievers, A.J. (1991). Self-consistency conditions for the effective-medium approximation in composite materials, *Physical Review B*, Vol. 44, No. 11, pp. 5459-5464,

Noton D. & Stark L. (1971). Scanpaths in Saccadic Eye Movements While Viewing and Recognizing Patterns, *Vision Research*, Vol. 11, pp. 929-942, 00426989

Olshausen B.; Anderson C. & Van Essen, D. (1993). A Neurobiological Model of Visual Attention and Invariant Pattern Recognition based on Dynamic Routing of Information, *The Journal of Neuroscience*, Vol. 13, pp. 4700-4719

Pelc, T. (1998). A formal model of an artificial neural network used to store and recognize the semantics of some sentences of natural language, *Proceedings of the Fifth International Conference on Neural Information Processing ICONIP'98*, pp. 21-23, 9789051994636, October 1998, IOA Press

Perantonis, S.J. & Lisboa, P.J. (1992). Translation, rotation, and scale invariant pattern recognition by high-order neural networks and moment classifiers, *IEEE Trans.Neural Networks*, Vol. 3, pp. 241–251

Privitera, C.M.; Azzariti, M. & Stark, L.W. (2000). Locating regions-of-interest for the Mars Rover expedition, *Journal of Remote Sensing*, Vol. 21, No. 17, pp. 3327-3347

Privitera, C. & Stark, L.W. (2000). Algorithms for Defining Visual Region-of-Interest: Comparison with Eye Fixations, *IEEE Transactions on Pattern Analysis and Machine Intelligence*, Vol. 22, No. 9, pp. 970-982

Pynte, J.; Do, P. & Scampa, P. (1984). Lexical decisions during the reading of sentences containing polysemous words, In: *Preparatory States and Processes*, S. Kornblum, J. Requin (Ed.), Hillsdale NJ, Erlbaum

Quiles, M.G., Breve F., Romero R.A.F., Zhao L. (2008). Visual Selection with Feature Contrast-Based Inhibition in a Network of Integrate and Fire Neurons, Fourth International Conference on Natural Computation, ICNC 2008, Vol. 3, pp. 601-605, 978-0-7695-3304-9

Raczkowski, D.; Canning, A. & Wang, L.W. (2001). Thomas-Fermi charge mixing for obtaining self-consistency in density functional calculations, *Physical Review B*, Vol. 64, No. 12, pp. 121101-121105

Redding, N.J.; Kowalczyk, A. & Downs, T. (1993). Constructive higher order network algorithm that is polynomial time, *Neural Networks*, Vol. 6, pp. 997-1010

Renninger, M. (2004). Sequential information maximization can explain eye movements in an object learning task, *Journal of Vision*, Vol. 4, No. 8, pp. 744a

Rybak, I.A.; Gusakova, V.I.; Golovan, A.V.; Podladchikova, L.N.& Shevtsova, N.A. (1998). A model of attention-guided visual perception and recognition, *Vision Research*, Vol. 38, pp. 2387-2400

Schall, J.& Hanes, D. (1993). Neural Basis of Saccade Target Selection in Frontal Eye Field during Visual Search, *Nature*, Vol. 366, pp. 467–469, 0028-0836

Schmitt, M. (2002). On the Complexity of Computing and Learning with Multiplicative Neural Networks, *Neural Computation*, Vol. 14, No. 2, pp. 241-301

Schmitt, M. (2000). VC dimension bounds for product unit networks, *Proceedings of the IEEE-INNS-ENNS International Joint Conference on*, Vol. 4, pp. 165-170

Shiffrin, R.M. & Schneider, W. (1997). Controlled and automatic human information processing: Perceptual learning, automatic attending and a general theory, *Psychological Review*, Vol. 84, pp. 127-190

Sinha, M.; Gupta, M.M. & Nikiforuk, P.N. (2001). A compensatory wavelet neuron model, *Proceedings of IFSA World Congress and 20th NAFIPS International Conference*, Vol. 3, July 2001, pp. 1372-1377

Spelke, E.; Hirst, W. & Neisser, U. (1976). Skills of divided attention, *Cognition*, Vol. 4, pp. 215-230

Sperling, G.A. (1984). A unified theory of attention and signal detection, In *Varieties of attention*, Parasurmaman R., Davies D.R. (Ed.), pp. 103-181. New York: Academic Press

Spratling, M.W. & Hayes, G. (2000). Learning Synaptic Clusters for Nonlinear Dendritic Processing, *Neural Processing Letters*, Vol. 11, No. 1, pp. 17-27

Stein R.B. (1967). The information capacity of nerve cells using a frequency code, *Biophysical Journal*, Vol. 7, pp. 797-826

Stuart, G.J. & Spruston, N. (1998) Determinants of voltage attenuation in neocortical pyramidal neuron dendrites, The Journal of Neuroscience, Vol. 18, pp. 3501–3510

Swinney, D.A. (1979). Lexical access during sentence comprehension: (Re) consideration of context effects, *Journal of Verbal Learning and Verbal Behaviour*, Vol. 18, pp. 645-659

Swinney, D.A. (1982). The structure and time-course of information interaction during speech comprehension: Lexical segmentation, access, and interpretation, In *Perspectives on Mental Representation*, J. Mehler, E.C.T. Walker & M. Garrett (Ed.), Hillsdale, NJ: Erlbaum

Tinbergen, N. (1951). *The Study of Instinct*, Oxford: Clarendon Press, Oxford

Treisman, A. M. (1964). Selective attention in man. British Medical Bulletin, Vol. 20, pp. 12-16

Treisman, A.M. (1960). Contextual cues in selective listening. *Quarterly Journal of Experimental Psychology*, Vol. 12, pp. 242-248, 1037-1054.

Tsal, Y. (1983). Movements of attention across the visual field, *Journal of Experimental Psychology: Human Perception and Performance*, Vol. 9, No 4., pp. 523-530, 0096-1523

Tsotsos, J.K.; Culhane, S. & Cutzu, F. (2001). From foundational principles to a hierarchical selection circuit for attention, In: *Visual Attention and Cortical Circuits*, Braun J, Koch C, Davis J. (Ed.), pp. 285-306, MIT Press, 02620-24934, Cambridge, MA,

Tsotsos, J.K.; Culhane, S.; Wai, W.; Lai, Y.; Davis, N.& Nuflo, F. (1995). Modeling visual attention via selective tuning, *Artificial Intelligence*, Vol. 78, No. 1-2, pp. 507-547

Usher, M. (2006). What has been learned from computational models of attention, *Neural Networks, Special Issue: Brain and Attention*, Vol.19, No.9, November 2006, pp. 1440-1442, 0893-6080

van den Bergh, F. & Engelbrecht, A.P. (2001). Training product unit networks using cooperative particle swarm optimisers, *Proceedings of International Joint Conference on Neural Networks*, Vol. 1, pp. 126–131, Washington DC, USA

VanRullen, R. & Koch, C. (2003). Visual Selective Behavior can be Triggered by a Feedforward Process, *Journal of Cognitive Neuroscience*, Vol. 15, No. 2, pp. 209-217, 0898-929X

VanRullen, R.; Reddy, L. &. Koch, C. (2004). Visual search and dual-tasks reveal two distinct attentional resources, *Journal of Cognitive Neuroscience*, Vol. 16, No. 1, pp. 4-14

Venkatesh, S.S. & Baldi, P. (1991). Programmed interactions in higher order neural networks: maximal capacity, *Journal of Complexity*, Vol. 7, pp. 316-337

Weber, C. & Wermter, S. (2007), A self-organizing map of sigma-pi units, *Neurocomputing*, Vol. 70, No. 13-15, August 2007, pp. 2552-2560, 0925-2312

Wright, R.D., & Ward, L.M. (2008). *Orienting of Attention*, Oxford University Press

Wróbel, A. (2000). Beta activity: a carrier for visual attention, *Acta neurobiologiae experimentalis*, Vol. 60, No. 2, pp. 247-260, 0065-1400, Warsaw

Yadav, R.N.; Kalra, P.K. & John, J. (2006). Neural network learning with generalized-mean based neuron model, *Soft Computing – A Fusion of Foundations, Methodologies and Applications*, Vol. 10, No. 3, February 2006, pp. 257-263, 1432-7643, Springer Berlin / Heidelberg

Yadav, R.N.; Kumar, N.; Kalra, P.K. & John, J. (2004). Multi-layer neural networks using generalized-mean neuron model, *Proceedings of IEEE International Symposium on Communications and Information Technology ISCIT 2004*, Vol. 1, Issue, October 2004, pp. 93 - 97

Yang, H. & Guest, C.C. (1990). High order neural networks with reduced numbers of interconnectionweights, *Proceedings of IJCNN International Joint Conference on Neural Networks*, Vol. 3, June 1990, pp. 281–286

Yamada, K. & Cottrell, G.W. (1995). A model of scan paths applied to face recognition, Procedings of 17th Ann. Cognitive Science Conference, pp.55-60, Pittsburgh

13

Numerical Integration Tools in Material Point Relative Motion Dynamics

Viviana Filip, Cornel Marin and Alexandru Marin

Abstract
The authors have proposed to show the advantages of different specialized software that can used in solving the algebraic and transcendental differential equations applied in mechanics, as applications of material point relative motion dynamics.

Keywords: differential equations, motion dynamics, approximate numerical solution, specialized software.

1. INTRODUCTION

The relative motion of the material point can be described with relation [5]:

$$m\,\vec{a}_r = \vec{F} + \vec{F}_{Cor} + \vec{F}_t \tag{1}$$

where:
m is the material point mass
$\vec{a}_r$ is the relative acceleration
$\vec{F}$ is the exterior force resultant
$\vec{F}_{Cor}$ is the Coriolis force
$\vec{F}_t$ is the transport force

The equation (1) can be expressed by a differential equation at limit, like this:

$$\frac{d^2\vec{y}}{d\,t^2} = f(\vec{y}, \frac{d\,\vec{y}}{d\,t}, t) \tag{2}$$

The initial conditions are:

$$\vec{y}(0) = \vec{y}_0 \text{ and } \frac{d\,\vec{y}(0)}{d\,t} = \vec{v}_0 \tag{3}$$

The relations (2) and (3) represent a differential equation of order two with initial conditions[1].

2. THE CALCULATION METHODS

The determination of numerical solution using the Euler method:
A differential equation of order n with initial conditions can be transformed in a system of n differential equations of first order by introducing n-1 auxiliary variables for the n-1 derivates (in our example n=2).
This can be expressed in a matriceal form:

$$\vec{Y} = \begin{bmatrix} \vec{y} \\ \vec{y}' \end{bmatrix}, \quad \frac{d\,\vec{Y}}{d\,t} = \vec{F}(t,\vec{Y}), \quad \vec{Y}(t_0) = \begin{bmatrix} \vec{y}'_0 \\ \vec{y}_0 \end{bmatrix} \tag{4}$$

where:

$$\vec{F}(t,\vec{Y}) = \begin{bmatrix} \vec{f}(t,\vec{y},\vec{y}') \\ \vec{y}' \end{bmatrix} \tag{5}$$

The simplest method for solving these equations is the Euler method, where, to approximate the y variable at moment t+dt, it is used the Taylor series development until the first derivative:

$$\vec{y}(t+dt) \approx \vec{y}(t) + \frac{d\,\vec{y}(t)}{d\,t} = \vec{y}(t) + \vec{f}(t,\vec{y}(t)) \tag{6}$$

Any time there is this kind of problem, there must begin from an initial value of time t_0, it is used a very small step dt, until it is obtained an approximate solution for equation with initial conditions.
The Euler method is very slow and it is necessary a very small time step dt to obtain good results, but it is typical for usual methods, like Runge-Kutta method.
The determination of numerical solution using the Runge-Kutta method:
The approximate solution y_{i+1} for equation (4) in next point $t_{i+1}=t_i+h$, is calculation with relation [4]:

$$\begin{gathered} y_{i+1} = y_i + \Delta y_i \\ \Delta y_i = \frac{1}{6}\left[K_1^{(i)} + 2K_2^{(i)} + 2K_3^{(i)} + K_4^{(i)}\right] \end{gathered} \tag{7}$$

where:

$$\begin{aligned} &K_1^{(i)} = h \cdot f(t_i, y_i) \\ &K_2^{(i)} = h \cdot f(t_i + \frac{1}{2}h, y_i + \frac{1}{2}K_1^{(i)}) \\ &K_3^{(i)} = h \cdot f(t_i + \frac{1}{2}h, y_i + \frac{1}{2}K_2^{(i)}) \\ &K_4^{(i)} = h \cdot f(t_i + h, y_i + K_3^{(i)}) \\ &i = 1,2,3... \end{aligned} \tag{8}$$

3. THE SOLUTION OF DIFFERENTIAL EQUATION OF SECOND ORDER USING SPECIALIZED SOFTWARE

3.1. Application I:

It is considered a semicircular tube of R radius [8], which rotates with constant angular velocity $\dot{\theta}$ around the fixed axis presented in Figure 1. Inside the tube there is a material point of mass m that rotates with angular velocity $\dot{\varphi}$ around the center A of the semicircle. The authors proposed to determine the graphical representation of the relative motion $\varphi = \varphi(t)$ function, for t between t_i and t_f.

It is considered the following case: R = 1 m, θ (t)=2 t, $\varphi(0) = 0$, $\varphi'(0) = 1$, m = 0,01 kg, t_i = 0, t_f = 2 s.

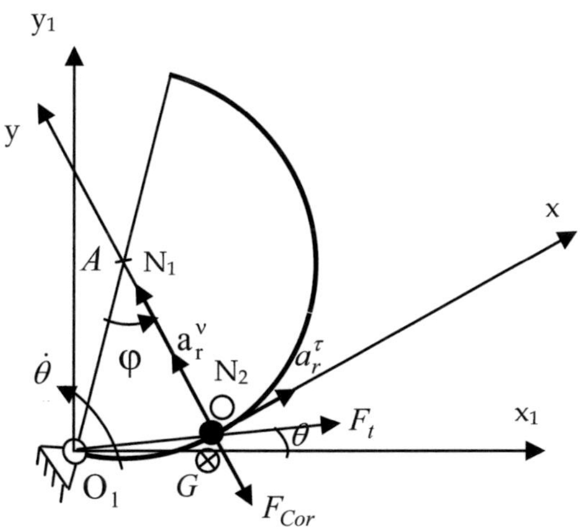

Fig. 1.

N1 and N2 are the reactions of the tube against the material point.
It is projected the motion equation (1) on the x axis:

$$m\,\ddot{\varphi}\,R = 2\,m\,\dot{\theta}^2\,R\,sin\frac{\varphi}{2}\,cos\frac{\varphi}{2} \tag{9}$$

It is projected the motion equation (1) on the y axis:

$$m\,\dot{\varphi}^2\,R = N_1 - m\,\dot{\theta}^2\,2\,R\,sin^2\frac{\varphi}{2} - m\,2\,\dot{\theta}\,\dot{\varphi}\,R \tag{10}$$

It is projected the motion equation (1) on the z axis:

$$N_2 = m\,g \tag{11}$$

3.1.1. The solution obtained using Mathematica

In order to determine the graphical representation for $\varphi = \varphi(t)$ it will be solved the differential equation of second order, using the Mathematica software.
It was run this program for equation (9):

```
a = NDSolve[{fi''[t] * 1 == 2^2 * Sin[fi[t]], fi[0] == 1, fi'[0] == 0}, fi[t], {t, 0, 2}]
```
(12)

and it was obtained the following results:

```
{{fi[t] → InterpolatingFunction[{{0., 2.}}, <>][t]}}
```

After the graphical construction command

```
Plot[fi[t] /. a, {t, 0, 2}]
```
(13)

it was obtained the curve presented in Figure 2:

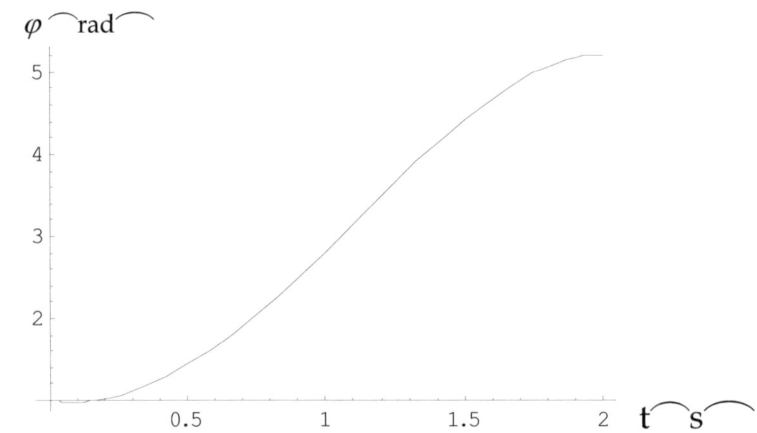

Fig. 2.

3.1.2. The solution obtained using Mathcad

The differential equation (2) that must be solved is:

$$\frac{d^2}{dt^2}\phi(t) = 4\sin(\phi(t)) \tag{14}$$

with the initial conditions:

$$\begin{bmatrix} \phi_0(0) \\ \phi_1(0) \end{bmatrix} = \begin{bmatrix} 1 \\ 0 \end{bmatrix} \tag{15}$$

It was defined the initial conditions vector:

$$ic := \begin{bmatrix} 1 \\ 0 \end{bmatrix} \tag{16}$$

It was defined the time period against it will be represented the $\varphi = \varphi(t)$ function, and the number of iteration (N):

$$t_0 := 0 \quad t_1 := 2$$
$$N := 10 \tag{17}$$

The Mathcad software needs to transform the differential equation of second order (2), in a two differential equations of first ordered system, as following:

$$\phi_0(t) = \phi(t) \qquad \phi_1(t) = \frac{d}{dt}\phi_0(t)$$
$$D(t,\Phi) := \begin{bmatrix} \Phi_1 \\ 4\sin(\Phi_0) \end{bmatrix} \tag{18}$$

The command:

$$S := \text{rkfixed}(ic, t_0, t_1, N, D) \tag{19}$$

will solve the differential equations system.
In order to construct the graphical representation, it was assigned:

$$t := S^{<0>} \quad \phi(t) := S^{<1>} \tag{20}$$

After the running of the program it was obtained the curve presented in Figure 3:

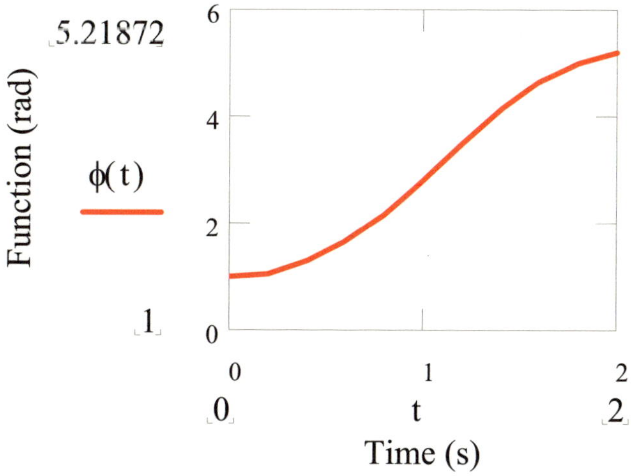

Fig. 3.

3.2. Application II:

One considers the following problem [3]:

Inside a tube OA, a material point M of mass m slides with friction (Fig.4). In the same time, the tube is rotating with the angular velocity ω, around a vertical axis which intersects its ends.

In this example, the absolute and relative motion of the material point will be studied considering the following cases:

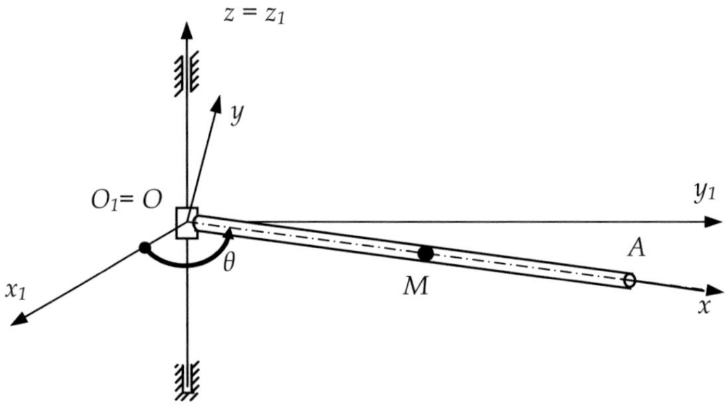

Fig. 4.

Case I: $F_r = k\,f(\dot{x})$

a) $\dot{x} < 1$ m/s, Fr = k $\dot{x}$, k=12.5 kg/s

b) 1 m/s < $\dot{x}$ *< 250 m/s,* $F_r = k\,\dot{x}^2$*, k=12.5 kg/m*

c) 250 m/s< $\dot{x}$ *<300 m/s,* $F_r = k\,\dot{x}^3$*, k=0.05 kg·s/m²*

Case II: $F_r = \mu\sqrt{N_1^2 + N_2^2}$

where

- F_r is the resistant force which acts on the material point;
- k is a constant which depends on the domains of material point velocity values;
- μ is the friction coefficient between the material point and the tube's wall;
- N_1 , N_2 are the normal reactions of the tube's wall on the material point.

In order to be able to compare the motion of the point in the two cases, using numerical methods, the following particular situations will be considered:

$m = 0{,}2\ kg$, $OA = 250\ m$, $\omega = 8\ rad/s$.

One considers the fixed reference frame $x_1y_1z_1$ and the moving reference frame, bonded to the tube. The differential equation of the material point motion is:

$$m\vec{a}_r = \vec{F}_r + \vec{G} + \vec{N}_1 + \vec{N}_2 + \vec{F}_t + \vec{F}_C \tag{21}$$

where G is the weight of the material point and F_t, respectively F_C are the transport and Coriolis forces which act on the material point (Fig. 5). The terms of the equation (21) have the following expressions (22) and (23).

$$\begin{aligned} m\,\overrightarrow{a_r} &= m\,\ddot{x}\,\dot{i}, \ \overrightarrow{F_r} = -k\,f(\dot{x})\,\dot{i}, \\ \vec{G} &= -m\,g\,\vec{k}, \ \overrightarrow{N_1} = N_1\,\vec{j} \end{aligned} \tag{22}$$

$$\begin{aligned} \overrightarrow{N}_2 &= N_2\,\vec{k} \\ \overrightarrow{F_C} &= -2\,m\,\omega\,\dot{x}\,\vec{j}, \ \overrightarrow{F_t} = m\,\omega^2\,x\,\dot{i} \end{aligned} \tag{23}$$

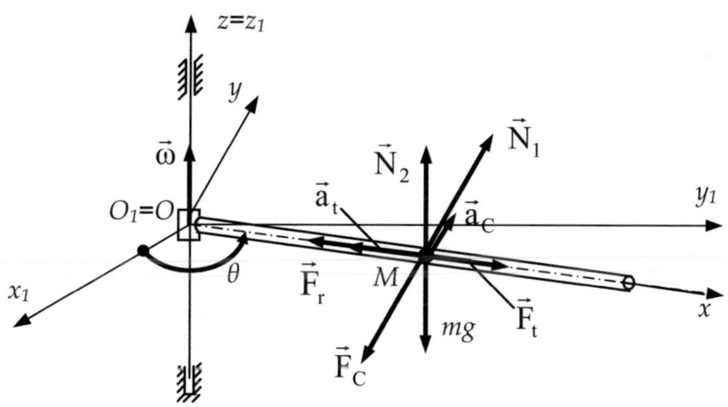

Fig. 5.

Case I a)

In the case of velocity values in the domain *[0,1] m/s*, the resistant force F_r is proportional to the velocity: $F_r = k\,\dot{x}$, where $k = 12{,}5$ *kg/s*.

If one projects the equation (21) on the *x* axis of the moving reference system, one obtains:

$$m\,\ddot{x} = -k\,\dot{x} + m\,x\,\omega^2 \tag{24}$$

The solution of this equation is given by relation (25).

$$x[t] = C_1\, e^{\frac{t\left(-k_1-\sqrt{k_1^2+4m^2\omega^2}\right)}{2m}} + C_2\, e^{\frac{t\left(-k_1+\sqrt{k_1^2+4m^2\omega^2}\right)}{2m}} \tag{25}$$

where C_1 and C_2 are the integration constants.
Considering the particular numerical data and the initial conditions $x[0] = 0{,}25\ m$, $\dot{x}[0] = 0\ m/s$, one obtains the solution (26), plotted in Fig.6 .

$$x[t] = 0{,}00390507\, e^{-63{,}5078\, t} + 0{,}46095\, e^{1{,}00775\, t} \tag{26}$$

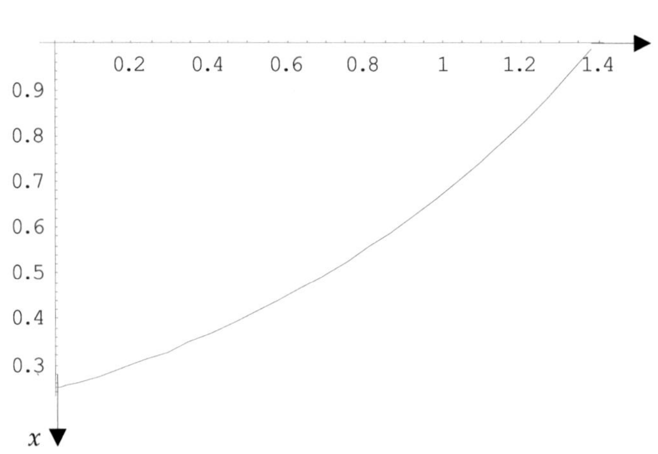

Fig. 6.

Considering that the tube's law of the motion is $\theta(t) = 8\ t$, the parametric equations of the material point with respect to the fixed reference system are:

$$\begin{aligned} x_1[t] = x[t] \cos 8t &= (0.00390507\, e^{-63..5078\ t} + \\ &+ 0.246095\, e^{1.00775\ t}) \cos 8t \\ y_1[t] = x[t] \sin 8t &= (0.00390507\, e^{-63..5078\ t} + \\ &+ 0.246095\, e^{1.00775\ t}) \sin 8t \end{aligned} \tag{27}$$

The trajectory of the material point for the time $[0,1.38]s$ can be seen in Fig. 7.
At moment $t = 1{,}38\ s$, the velocity value reaches $\dot{x} = 1\ m/s$, so the material point enters the velocity domain where the resistant force is proportional to the squared velocity.
At instant $t = 1{,}38\ s$, the material point has the coordinate $x = 0{,}98\ m$. Due to the fact that the point is now in the velocity domain $[1,\ 250]\ m/s$, the resistant force has the expression $F_r = k\,\dot{x}^2$, where $k = 12{,}5 kg/m$.

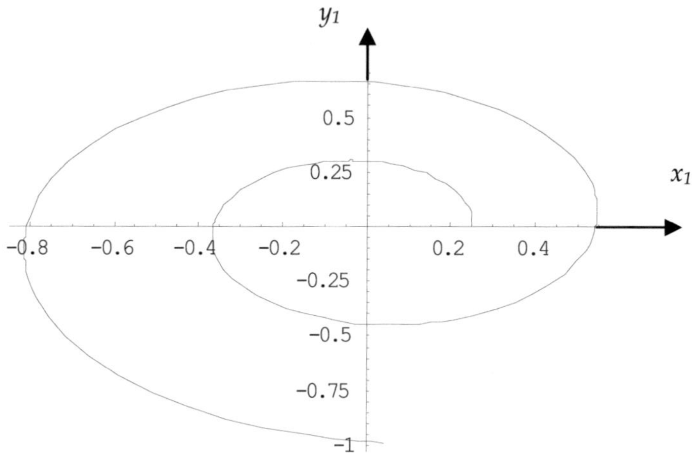

Fig. 7.

Case I b)

The projection of the motion equation (21) on the x axis of the mobile reference system is:

$$m\ddot{x} + k\dot{x}^2 - mx\omega^2 = 0 \tag{28}$$

This equation is solved for the following initial conditions: *x[1,38]* = *0,98 m*, $\dot{x}[1,38] = 1\ m/s$.

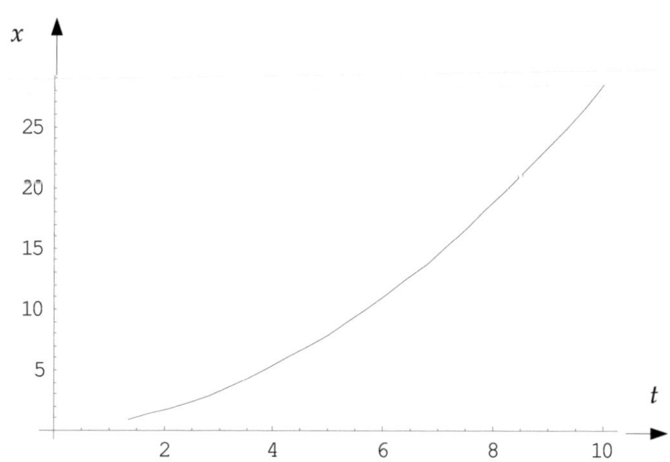

Fig. 8.

Due to the non-linearity of this differential equation, the solution may be obtained only by advanced numerical methods. An analytical solution is not available, just a numerical one can be obtained. This solution's graph is plotted in Fig. 8.
This numerical solution may be approximated using interpolation methods on the polynomial function shown by relation (29).

$$\begin{aligned} x = & 0.98+(1.14516+(0.263249+(-0.00200546+ \\ & 0.000765443+(-0.000579773+0.000311021(-0.0001123+ \\ & (0.0000299515+(6.30748\times10^{-6}+1.10011\times10^{-6} \\ & (-9+t))(-8+t))(-7+t))(-6+t))(-5+t)) \\ & (-4+t))(-3+t))(-2.5+t))(-2+t))(-1.38+t)) \end{aligned} \tag{29}$$

At instant t = *12.5218 s*, the material point's velocity reaches the value $\dot{x} = 250\ m/s$ which is in another domain of values. In this domain the resistant force is proportional with the velocity's power of 3.
Considering the parametric equations of the material point with respect to the fixed reference frame, the trajectory of the material point in the time span [1.38,12.5218] s can be plotted in Fig.9.

Case I c)

At instant t = *12.5218 s*, the material point ahs the coordinate x = *182.713 m*. The resistant force has now the following expression $F_r = k\ \dot{x}^3$, where k = *0,05 kg s / m²*.

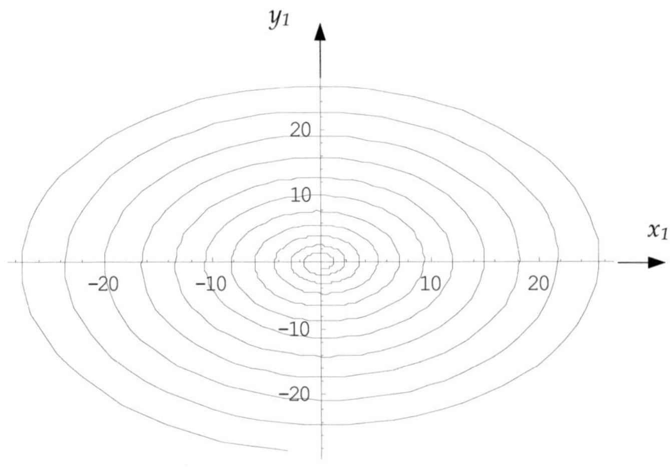

Fig. 9.

The projection of the motion equation (21) on the x axis of the moving reference frame will be:

$$m\ddot{x} + k_3\,\dot{x}^3 - m\,x\,\omega^2 = 0 \tag{30}$$

This equation is solved considering the initial conditions *x[12.5218]=182.713m*, $\dot{x}[12.5218] = 250\,m/s$

The obtained numerical solution is plotted in Figure 10.

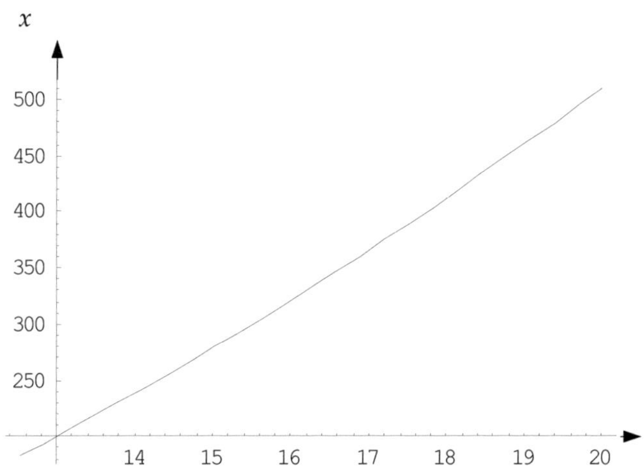

Fig. 10.

The numerical solution can be approximated with the polynomial relation (31):

$$\begin{aligned} x &= 182.713 + (36.7001 + (1.06405 + (0.0082531 + \\ &(-0.00769165 + (0.00186645 + (-0.00034831 + \\ &(0.0000550529 - 7.7067\times10^{-6}(-19+t)) \\ &(-18+t))\,(-17+t))(-16+t))\,(-15+t)) \\ &(-14+t))\,(-13+t))\,(-12.5+t)) \end{aligned} \tag{31}$$

At instant t = *26.46 s*, the material point leaves the tube.
Taking into account the parametric equations of the material point with respect to the fixed reference frame, the trajectory of the point in the time span [12.5218, 26.46] will be Figure 11.

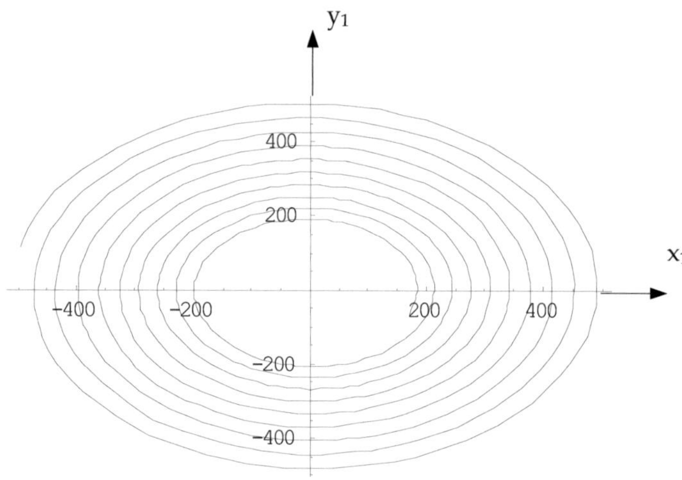

Fig. 11.

Case II

One considers the case when the resistant force which acts on the material point is a Coulombian force $F_r = \mu\sqrt{N_1^2 + N_2^2}$.

The projections of the motion equation (21) on the axis of the moving reference system are:

$$\begin{cases} m\ddot{x} = -\mu\sqrt{N_1^2 + N_2^2} + m x \omega^2 \\ N_1 = 2m\omega\dot{x} \\ N_2 = G \end{cases} \tag{32}$$

This leads to the differential equation of motion on the x axis:

$$m\ddot{x} + \mu\sqrt{(2m\omega\dot{x})^2 + (m g)^2} - m x \omega^2 = 0 \tag{33}$$

Solving this equation with the initial conditions $x[0] = 0.25\ m,\ \dot{x}[0] = 0\,m/s$ one obtains the numerical solution plotted by Figure 12.

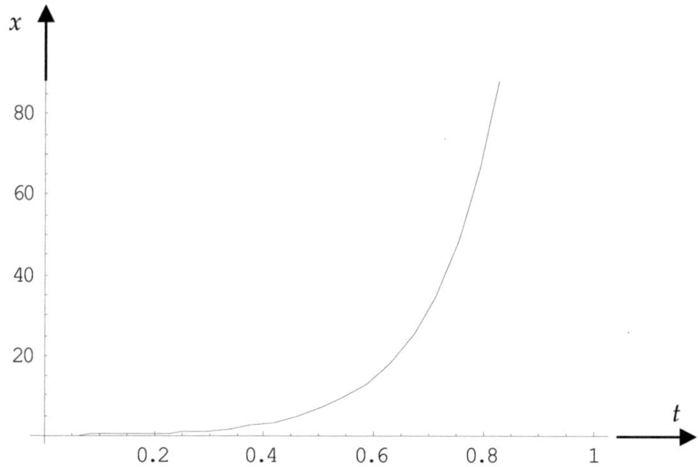

Fig. 12.

The material point exists the tube at instant t = *0,955 s* and up to this point the numerical solution may be approximated by the polynomial relation (34).

$$x = 0.25+(1.945+ (24.6484 + (392.125+ (-462.338 +5874.51 (-0.8 +t))(-0.6 + t)) (-0.4+t)) (-0.2 + t))t \tag{34}$$

Considering the parametric equations of the material point with respect to the fixed reference frame the trajectory of the point for the time span [0, 0.955] s, has the shape shown by Figure 13:

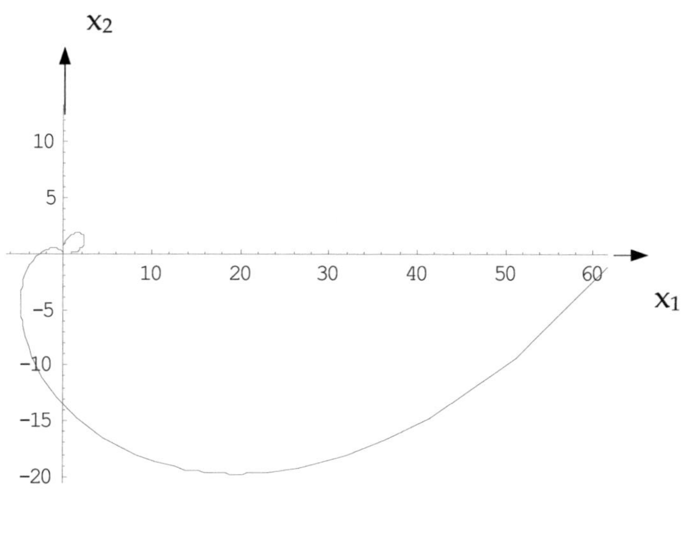

Fig. 13.

4. CONCLUSIONS

4.1. Conclusions about Application I:

In Mathematica and Mathcad, it is not necessary that user ask the program to display the φ values at different time moments between 0 and 2 seconds, in order to construct the graphical representation.
In Mathematica it is not necessary to specify the time step for interpolation, while in Mathcad, the step must be specified.
The NDSolve function from Mathematica has implemented the algorithm for solving the differential equations of first and superior order, when it is known the initial values. Mathematica is an algebraic instrument that can automatically convert any differential equation of superior order with initial conditions to a first ordered differential equation and can determine the numerical solution.
When using Mathcad, the user must make this conversion from superior to first order equation.
The time necessary for solving the equation is smaller when using Mathematica, due to the great number of input data required by the Mathcad.
The disadvantage of Mathematica and Mathcad is the necessity for user to learn the syntax for the specific function.
The advantage for Mathcad and Mathematica is the greater number of mathematical problems that can be solved.
Mathcad has developed a graphical user interface that makes this program very user friendly, despite the great level of complexity of the problems that can be solved using it.
The authors recommend Mathematica for solvers that use frequently the numerical methods due to the reduced time required for solving.
For these who are not interested in learning the syntax of specific functions, the authors recommend Mathcad due to the user friendly interface, which makes it easy to use.

4.2. Conclusions about Application II:

In the given conditions from case I a), the differential equation is linear and admits an analytical solution. The other cases though exhibit non-linear equations with numerical solutions that can be reached only by means of advanced mathematical software. They can be approximated by polynomial functions using interpolation methods.
The contribution of this paper is the study of the material point relative motion dynamics by using the advanced mathematical techniques. This advances techniques allow the trajectory determination, the numerical solutions determination, the motion significant moments calculation.

5. References

Branzanescu, V., Stanasila, O. "Matematici speciale", Ed. All, Bucharest, 1994

Deciu, E., Radoi M., "Mecanica", Ed. Didactica si Pedagogica, R.A., Bucuresti, 1993, pag. 334

Filip, V., Marin C., Marin A, "Advanced Mathematical Model of the Material Point Relative Motion Dynamics", International Multiconference of Engineers and Computer Scientists, 19-21 March 2008, Hong Kong, China, IMECS Proceeding, Volume II, p. 1634-1637, ISBN 978-988-98671-8-8

Micula, G., Pavel, P."Ecuatii diferentiale si integrale prin probleme si exercitii", Ed. Dacia, Oradea, 1989

Rosca, I.: "Mecanica pentru ingineri", MatrixRom, Bucharest, 1998

Zaharia, S., Filip V., Mateoiu C., "e-Mechanics", 5th International Conference on Information Technology Based Higher Education and Training: ITHET '04", Proceedings, IEEE Catalog Number 04EX898C, p. 674-676, ISBN 0-7803-8597-7, 2004, Istanbul, Turkey

Zaharia, S. and other, "Teorie si probleme de mecanica - Teste de Statica si Cinematica", JIF, Bucharest 1996

Zaharia S., Filip V., Tache C. "Some aspects regarding the use of specialized software for numerical integration in solid mechanics applications", Iasi Polytechnic Institute Bulletin, published by "Gheorghe Asachi" University, tomul XLVII (LI), Supliment 2001, p. 97-105

Software Mathematica – Release notes

Software Mathcad – Release notes

14

Slicing techniques to derive the User Interface Abstract Model

Daniela da Cruz and Pedro Rangel Henriques
University of Minho - Department of Computer Science Campus de Gualtar, 4715-057, Braga, Portugal
Email: {danieladacruz,prh} @di.uminho.pt

1. Introduction

To assess a given software application, it is necessary to verify how it complies with the problem requirements and to measure its usability (efficiency, and degree of user satisfaction). To do this, it is necessary a deep analysis to the application code, to understand both the business core and the interface layers. In this chapter we focus on the analysis of the interface layer for the reason that the design of a user interface affects the amount of effort the user must expend to provide input for the system, to interpret the output of the system, and to learn how to use the application.

Interfaces are often difficult to understand and use. In many cases, end-users have problems in identifying all the functionality provided by the application, or in understanding how to reach the operations supported.

While in small user interfaces it is possible to guarantee the correctness, the quality of large and complex user interfaces is hard to assure. As the correctness of the user interface is essential to the correct execution of the overall software, we must guarantee that our software has this characteristic. This becomes more difficult when a graphical user interface is used. However, as Graphical User Interface (GUI) offers the possibility to interact with a computer using graphical images (special graphical element devices called 'widgets') along with text to represent the information and actions usually performed through direct manipulation of the graphical elements.

In this context of understanding and assessing applications with GUIs, we discuss the application of *slicing* to the reverse engineering of user interfaces. The tools so far developed are capable of deriving *user interface abstract models* for interactive applications, enabling us to reason about the design of the system.

As wxHaskell and Swing became the most famous graphic toolkits to build Graphical User Interfaces for Haskell and Java, respectively, we investigate slicing techniques specialized for wxHaskell/Swing modules.

In order to extract the user interface model from a Haskell/Java application we need to construct a slicing function that isolates the wxHaskell/Swing subprogram from the entire program. At a first glance, the obvious and easiest way is to define a recursive function to traverse the Abstract Syntax Tree (AST) of the program and return the wxHaskell/Swing sub-tree. However, that approach forces the analyst to have knowledge of the full grammar of the *host language* (Haskell/Java) and to write a complex and long set of mutually recursive functions. *Strategic programming* allows us to use a set of *generic tree-walker functions (visitors)* that visit any AST using different traversal strategies. As *visitor* parameter we pass the *slicing criterion.* This criterion is an evolution of the original one: we do not have a point (line) on the program, and the set of variables consists in a set of "widget" class. Thus, the analyst only needs to focus on the nodes interesting for the specific task. In fact, the analyst does not need to have a full knowledge of the grammar, but only of those parts he is interested in.

Besides the Introduction and the Conclusion, this chapter is divided into the following sections: section 2, where we briefly define the basic concepts on static slicing; section 3, devoted to a short review of UI models; section 4, containing pointers to related work on recovering UI models, and an introduction to our slicing-based approach; section 5, where we present the first case study (Slicing wxHaskell); and section 6, where we present the second case study (Slicing Swing).

2. Slicing

Program Slicing, in its original version, is a decomposition technique that extracts from a program the statements relevant to a particular computation. A *program slice* consists of the parts of a program that potentially affect the values computed at some point of interest referred to as a *slicing criterion.*

Definition 1 *A* static slicing criterion *of a program P consists of a pair* $C = (p, V_s)$, *where p is a statement in P and* V_s *is a subset of the variables in P.*

A slicing criterion $C = (p, V_s)$ determines a projection function which selects from any state trajectory only the ordered pairs starting with *p* and restricts the variable-to-value mapping function σ to only the variables in Vs.

Definition 2 *Let* $C = (p, V_s)$ *be a static slicing criterion of a program P and* $T =< (p_1, \sigma_1), (p_2, \sigma_2), \ldots (p_k, \sigma_k) >$ *a state trajectory of P on input I.* $\forall i, 1 \leq i \leq k$, *the projection of a pair w.r.t. the criterion C is defined as follows:*

$$Proj'_C(p_i, \sigma_i) = \begin{cases} \epsilon & if\ p_i \neq p \\ < (p_i, \sigma_i | V_s) > & if\ p_i = p \end{cases}$$

where $\sigma_i | V_s$ *is* σ_i *restricted to the domain* V_s, *and* ϵ *is the empty string.*

Definition 3 *The projection of a trajectory T w.r.t. a slicing criterion C is defined as the concatenation of the result of the application of the projection function* $Proj'_C(p_i, \sigma_i)$ *for each pair of the trajectory:*

$$Proj_C(T) = Proj'_C(p_1, \sigma_1) \ldots Proj'_C(p_k, \sigma_k)$$

Definition 4 *A* static slice *of a program P on a static slicing criterion C = (p, V_s) is any syntactically correct and executable program P′ that is obtained from P by deleting zero or more statements, such that whenever P halts, on an arbitrary input I, with state trajectory T, then P′ halts, on the same input I, with the trajectory T′, and $Proj_C(T) = Proj_C(T')$.*

The task of computing program slices is called *program slicing.*
Weiser defined a program slice *S* as a reduced, *executable program* obtained from a program *P* removing statements, such that *S* preserves the original behavior of the program with respect to a subset of variables of interest and at a given program point.
Executable means that the slice is not only a closure of statements, but also can be compiled and run. *Non-executable* slices are often smaller and thus more helpful in program comprehension. The slices mentioned so far are computed by gathering statements and control predicates by way of a *backward traversal* of the program, starting at the slicing criterion. Therefore, these slices are referred to as *backward slices* [Tip95]. In [BC85], Bergeretti et al were the first to define a notion of a forward slice. A *forward slice* is a kind of ripple effect analysis, this is, it consists of all statements and control predicates dependent on the slicing criterion. A statement is dependent of the slicing criterion if the values computed at that statement depend on the values computed at the slicing criterion, or if the values computed at the slicing criterion determine if the statement under consideration is executed or not.
Both classes of slice *(backward* and *forward)* hereafter considered are forms of *static* slices. *Static* means that only statically available information is used for computing slices, this is, all possible executions of the program are taken into account; no specific input I is taken into account. Since the original version proposed by Weiser [Wei81], various different notions of program slicing, which are not static, have been proposed, as well as a number of methods to compute slices. The main reason for this diversity is the fact that different applications require different slice properties.

3. User Interface Models

A Graphical User Interface (GUI) system is a visual tool for users to operate computer applications. A GUI assists the user in reducing the effort and time required to remember all the functionality and the complex command language of real computer applications. It can provide the user with a certain degree of guidance to do the next operation in a safer mode (avoiding errors). For example, *disabling some buttons after a user operation;* this way, the interface allows the user to handle problems directly, forcing him to operate in the correct way. A wizard is a good example of an artifact to guide users' operations.
It is widely recognized that designing a GUI system is a very hard task. Myers [Mye93] enumerated several reasons why the conception of a GUI system is so demanding: designers have difficulty learning the user's tasks; the tasks and domains are intrinsically complex; there are many different design aspects that must be combined and balanced (graphic design, technical writing, and so on); iterative design is cumbersome; and the existing theories and guidelines are not sufficient.

To overcome this problem, some researchers are starting to use formal modeling to design and test GUI systems. Formal models should be used to improve the communication

between designer and implementer, and to analyze system properties and behavior specifying rigorously its data-structures and dynamics.
Some formal models for GUIs have been proposed [MPS00, Too90]. They mostly model the actions of the GUIs internal objects. Analysts can use models of different (complementary) kinds to describe the system to be designed. These kinds include, but are not be limited to *task models, user models* and *interaction models.*
Interaction models can offer information about the interface elements, and the man-machine interaction.
The traditional approach, to capture the interaction model, in UML (Unified Modeling Language) is object-oriented. Designers identify the objects of the proposed interactive system and then analyze the activities of these objects. According to this approach, GUI models are based on *production systems,* i.e., a collection of *condition-reaction rules,* where conditions (patterns) capture events and reaction determine the actions triggered by the events.
Another approach is the Abstract State Machine (abbreviated as ASM) paradigm, introduced by Yuri Gurevich in 1988 [Gur88]. This approach offers a framework for high-level system design and analysis. It has been proved that ASM methodologies are practical in modeling and analyzing different sizes of systems, from small to complex.
ASMs are both abstract and executable, and have precise semantics. Their abstract nature allows the system designer to focus on system concepts and not to be disturbed by the details. ASMs can specify a system at different abstraction levels. The system designer can refine the system from a more abstract level to a less abstract level by providing more details and making more design decisions. ASM can be used to specify new systems to be developed, or used to validate old ones. Many Researchers have successfully validated existing systems, such as Java [SSB01], with ASM methodology. A basic Abstract State Machine (ASM) is defined as a set of transition rules of the form

if **Condition** *then* **Updates**

which specify the transition between two abstract states. The execution of an ASM machine is an update process. Starting from a given state, the values of finite-function (that maps parameters to their actual values) update in parallel to new values, according to rules specified by the ASM. If the updates of these functions are consistent, then a new state is achieved.

4. Recovering User Interface Models

In the area of Software Maintenance, understanding existing software systems is a basilar activity. For that purpose, static and dynamic identification of software artifacts and their relations is crucial. Static information describes the structure of the software as it is written in the source code, while Dynamic information describes its run-time behavior. The Dynamic data analysis also produces information about sequential event trace or concurrent behavior, code coverage, memory management, etc. Static approach to code analysis is supported by parsing technology. Within the dynamic approach, it is usual to run the interactive system and automatically record its state and events. Chava [KCK99] is a system that analyzes and tracks changes in Java applets. The tool extracts, from the applet code to a relational database, information about classes, methods, fields and their relationships. Rigi [MK88] has been used for static reverse engineering. The extracted static information of Java software is viewed as directed graphs. The static dependency graph contains approximately the same information as a class diagram. In Rigi, classes and interfaces have their own node types. Methods, constructors, static initialization blocks, and variables inside a class in the UML class diagram are shown as nodes that are connected with a *contains* arc from the class node in Rigi.

Another alternative is the use of dynamic analysis.

Memon et al. [MBN03] describes *GUI Ripping,* a dynamic process where the software's GUI is automatically *traversed* by opening all its windows and extracting all their widgets (GUI objects), properties, and values. The extracted information is then verified by the test designer and used to automatically generate test cases.

Chen et al. [CS01] propose a visual environment for manipulating test specifications of GUI-based applications in Java, using the internal representation of a test specification. This prototype let users graphically manipulate the test specification given in the form of a Finite State Machine. Shimba prototype [SKM01], a reverse engineering environment, uses Rigi and SCED to analyze, visualize, and explore the static and dynamic aspects of the subject system. The static software artifacts and their dependencies are extracted from Java byte code and shown as directed graphs. The static dependency graphs of a subject system can be annotated with attributes, such as software quality measures, and then be analyzed and visualized using scripts through the end-user programmable interface. In our case we just use a static analysis. In fact, we reverse the code concerned with the graphical user interface and extract its abstract model. We are more interested in models that reflect the interaction created by the user interface, than the actual behavior of the underlaying software implementing it. In order to extract such model, we need to construct a function that isolates, from the entire program, the part respecting to the GUI component. At a first glance, the obvious and easiest way is to define a recursive function to traverse the Abstract Syntax Tree (AST) of the program and return the GUI sub-tree. However, that approach forces the programmer to have knowledge of the full grammar and to write a complex and long set of mutually recursive functions.

So, the solution is the use of slicing techniques [Tip95, XQZ+05]. Using slicing techniques, we are able to focus only on the parts that we are interested in (GUI component). For that purpose, we adapt the definition of the traditional static slicing criterion to deal with GUI components.

Definition 5 (GUI slicing criterion) *Let $\mathcal{L}$ be the subset of a programming language for the GUI definition, and W be the alphabet of that language (the set of GUI widgets – button, checkbox, etc). A* GUI slicing criterion *of a program P consists in W.*

As can be deduced from the definition, the traditional statement p is replaced by a set of statements contained in W and no variables are specified.

In the next two sections, we present two case-studies where we apply these slicing techniques. In the first case-study ($\mathcal{L}$ = wxHaskell, W = *{button, radioButton, frame...}* we make use of strategic programming to extract such widgets, while in the second case-study ($\mathcal{L}$ = Swing, W = *{ J Button, JCheckButton, JMenuBar,... }* we make use of visitor patterns over the AST.

5. Case Study I — Slicing wxHaskell

In order to extract the user interface model from a Haskell program we need to construct a slicing function that isolates the wxHaskell subprogram from the entire program. Strategic programming allows us to use a set of generic tree-walker functions that visit any AST using different traversal strategies (e.g. top-down, bottom-up...). So, we decided to follow this strategic approach. Thus, the programmer only needs to focus on the nodes interesting for the specific task. In fact, the programmer does not need to have a full knowledge of the grammar, but only the vocabulary of the GUI language. In this case-study we will use the Strafunski library: a Haskell library for generic programming and language processing.

5.1 A closer look into wxHaskell

The most usual class ofuserinterfaces are hierarchical graphical front-ends (the upperlayer) ofsoftware systems. These user interfaces produce deterministic graphical output from user input and system events. A graphical user interface (GUI) contains graphical widgets (each one with a fixed set of properties). At any time during the execution of the GUI these properties have discrete values: the set of which compose the state of the GUI.

To understand this layer of software systems and slice the user interface component in Haskell programs, it is necessary to know how the nodes of the GUI can be identified in the program tree. With that goal in mind, we introduce in this subsection wxHaskell.

wxHaskell is a graphical user interface (GUI) library for Haskell that is built over wxWidgets: an industrial GUI library for C++ that has been ported to all major platforms [Lei04]. The wxHaskell library imposes a strong typing discipline on the wxWidgets library. This means that the type checker will reject programs with illegal operations on widgets. Also, the memory management is fully automatic, with the provision that programmers are able to manually manage certain external resources like font descriptors or large bitmaps. The library also checks for NULL pointers, raising a Haskell exception instead of triggering a segmentation fault.

A graphical wxHaskell program is initialized with the `start` function, that registers the application with the graphical subsystem and starts an event loop.

```
main = start gui
```

The argument of `start` is an `IO` value that is invoked at the initialization event. This computation should create the initial interface and install further event handlers. While the event loop is active, Haskell is only invoked via these event handlers. The GUI is described by the following functions.

```
frame   :: [Prop   (Frame   ())]    -> IO   (Frame   ())
button  :: Window a ->  [Prop  (Button  ())] -> IO  (Button ())

text    :: Attr  (Window a)  String
layout  :: Attr  (Frame a)   Layout

(:=)    :: Attr w a -> a -> Prop w
set     :: w -> [Prop w]  -> IO  ()

command :: Event   (Control a)   (IO ())
on      :: Event w a -> Attr w a

widget  :: Window a -> Layout
```

The types `Frame` and `Button` denote graphical objects. These objects can have properties. When an object is created we can supply an initial list of properties but we can also set them later using set. Properties are created by combining attributes with values. Examples of attributes are `text` and `layout`. An attribute of type `Attr w a` is applied to objects of type `w` and values of type `a`. Events are special attributes. An event of type `Event w a` can be transformed into an attribute `Attr w a` using `on` function. The value of an event attribute is normally an IO action that is executed when the event happens.
Since wxHaskell is based on an object-oriented framework, it also encodes inheritance. The extra type parameter of objects encodes the inheritance relationship. When the parameter of an object is `unit()`, it denotes an object of that exact class. When the parameter is a type variable `a`, it denotes any object that is instance of that class.
In this subsection we introduce a simple example that will be used throughout the section to illustrate the steps of the method under discussion to extract the *abstract user interface model.* In subsection 5.6 we present a more complex example.
Let us consider this first example (Prg-ExeHs1):

```
gui :: IO  ()
gui =
  do f     <- frame  [text  := "A demo of slicing"]
     label    <- staticText f  [text   := "WAPL07!"]
     ok <- button f  [text   := "Ok"]
     cancel <- button f  [text   := "Cancel"]
     set ok      [  on command:= infoDialog f "Simple widget"  "Hello"]
     set cancel [on command := close f ]
     set f      [layout := column 17 [floatCenter $ row 8 [widget label],
                                      floatCenter $ row 12[widget ok, widget can]
                ]
```

Fig. 1. Interface of Prg-ExeHs1 (written in wxHaskell)

The frame `f` creates a top level window frame, with the text "A demo of slicing" in the title bar. Inside the frame, we create a text label and two buttons. The expression `on command` designates the event handler that is called when a button is pressed. The `cancel` button closes the frame, which terminates the application, and the `ok` button open a new widget with the info "Slicing Haskell" (Figure 1).

In order to define the slicing functions, we defined a small set of abstract operations to describe the interactions between the user and the system. These are the abstractions that we look for:

- User selection: any choice that the user can make between several different options, such as command menu;
- User action: an action that is performed as the result of user input or user selection;
- System Output: any communication from the application to the user, such as a user dialogue-box.

5.2 Strafunski at a glance

Strafunski is a library for generic programming with strategies [LV02]. The basic idea of the Strafun-ski-style of generic programming is to view traversals as a kind of generic functions that can traverse into terms while mixing uniform and type-specific behavior. Strafunski supports 'strategic programming' via the library *StrategyLib* of reusable strategy combinators, and the *DrIFT* generator for supportive code for user-supplied Haskell datatypes.

There are two kinds of strategies (composed via function combinators):

- The *type preservation* (TP m) where the result of a strategy application to a term of type `t` is of type `m t` – deal with transformations.
- The *type-unifying* (TU m a) where the result of strategy application is always of type m a regardless of the type of the input term – deal with analysis.

These contracts are expressed by the types of the corresponding combinators applyTP and applyTU for strategy application (see primitive strategy combinator below). In both cases, m is a monad parameter to deal with effects in strategies such as state passing or non-determinism. Some of the primitive strategic combinators are [LV02, LV03]:

- **Strategy application**

```
applyTP :: (Monad m;Term t ) ⇒ TP m → t → m t
applyTU :: (Monad m;Term t ) ⇒ TU ma → t → m a
```

- **Traversal combinators**

```
allTP ::  Monad m ⇒ TP m → TP m
oneTP ::  MonadPlus m ⇒ TP m → TP m
allTU ::  (Monad m; Monoid a) ⇒ TU m a → TU m a
oneTU ::  MonadPlus m ⇒ TU m a → TU m a
```

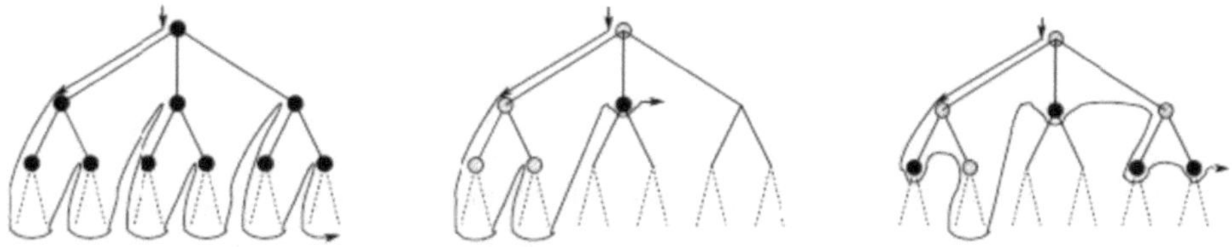

Fig. 2. Full traversal, Single-hit traversal and Cut-off traversal in Strafunski

To do the traversals, we emphasize the 3 types of traversals available in Strafunski: the full traversals; the single-hit traversals and cut-off traversals (see Figure 2).

- **Full traversal:** Traverses the AST in a top-down fashion;
- **Single-hit traversal:** Traverses the AST at most once;
- **Cut-off traversal:** Traverses the AST cutting off below nodes where the strategy succeeds.

The originality of strategic programming arises from the following concepts: update strategies by type-specific cases (denoted by adhocTP and adhocTU); one-layer traversal that acts on immediate sub-terms (e.g., allTU for reduction).

Using strategy update, ingredients for actual traversals can be composed. Using one layer traversal combinators, all kinds of traversal schemes can be assembled as recursive functions. The advantage of using Strafunski in this kind of problem is that programmer does not need to know full grammar of the language but just a subset: the wxHaskell sub-language.

Combining the knowledge in strategic programming with wxHaskell, we must analyze which parts of wxHaskell we are interested in. Once it is in *data entities, actions* and *relationships* that we are interested in we must consider (from GUI library of wxHaskell referred in subsection 5.1) the functions: `on` and `command`.

5.3 Building the AST

Chosen the abstractions that we need to look for in an Haskell/wxHaskell program, in order to discover the relations between the different widgets of the application, we need to identify: *data entities* and *actions* that are involved in the user interface; and the *relationships* between components. To extract this abstract model we need to built the AST in order to isolate a wxHaskell sub-program from the whole Haskell program.

To do this, we use the libraries Language.Haskell.Parser and Language.Haskell.Syntax.

```
module Main  (main)  where

import Language.Haskell.Parser
import Language.Haskell.Syntax

main = interact $ \s -> case parseModule s of
        ParseFailed loc str -> "Error: " ++
                                show loc
        ParseOk m -> show m
```

When applying the parser module defined above to any Haskell program, the result is an object of type in Haskell(HsModule), defined in the Syntax library as:

```
data HsModule
= HsModule
        SrcLoc  Module  (Maybe  [HsExportSpec])  [HsImportDecl]  [HsDecl]
```

where:

- SrcLoc – line/column where appears the definition of module;
- Module – name of module;
- Maybe [HsExportSpec] – a list of possible exports;
- HsImportDecl – a list of imports;
- HsDecl – a list of the declarations.

Using the parser module defined above, the partial result of parsing the program listed in subsection 5.1 (Prg-ExeHsl) is the abstract syntax tree (AST) shown in Figure 3.

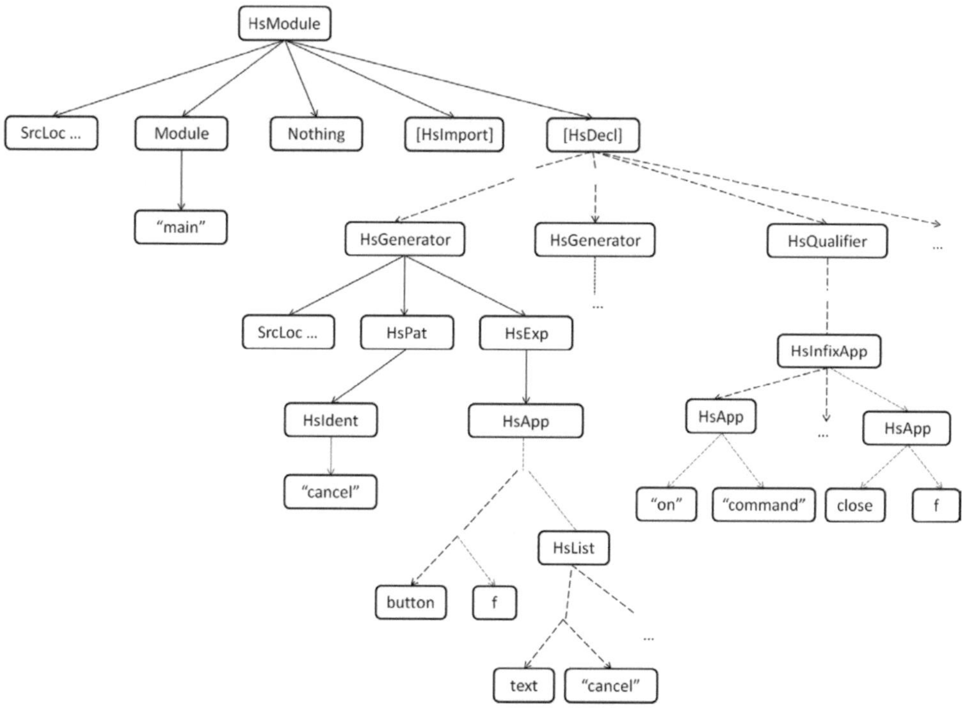

Fig. 3. AST corresponding to Prg-ExeHs1 (partial representation)

5.4 Slicing Haskell with Strafunski

Built the AST, the next step is isolate the wxHaskell sub-trees from the whole Haskell tree. As referred previously, the definition of a recursive function to traverses the AST implies a full knowledge of the grammar by the programmer and leads to a complex, long and inefficient recursive function. To overcome these disadvantages, we followed the strategic programming approach. Strategic programming is a generic programming idiom for processing compound data such as terms and object structures. Strategic programming was initiated in the setting of term rewriting [LVV03, VeABT99], but has been transposed to other programming paradigms, most notably functional and object-oriented programming. With strategic programming, one gains full control over the application of basic actions, most notably full traversal control. Using a combinator style, traversal schemes can be defined, and actual traversals are obtained by passing the problem-specific ingredients as parameters to suitable schemes.

In this style of programming, there is a set of generic traversal functions that traverse any AST. These strategic functions can traverse into heterogeneous data structures while mixing uniform and type-specific behavior [LVV02].

Once Haskell **is not** a generic programming language, generic programming with function strategies in Haskell relies in a class – *Term* – that captures the original contributions of "strategic polymorphism". So, the Haskell combinator library for generic programming used here to do the job is *StrategyLib* that is part of Strafunski, introduced in next subsection.

5.4.1 Pruning the AST

Having the knowledge of the AST in Figure 3, we are able to define a strategic function that given the complete AST extracts the widgets and its attributes present in the source program. Analyzing this AST we conclude that it is the list of declarations that will help us to identify the *data entities,* the *actions* and the *relationships* between them.
To understand the strategy adopted under Strafunski library, let us consider the following fragment of the example given in subsection 5.1:

```
cancel <- button f [text := "Cancel"]
set cancel  [on command := close f ]
```

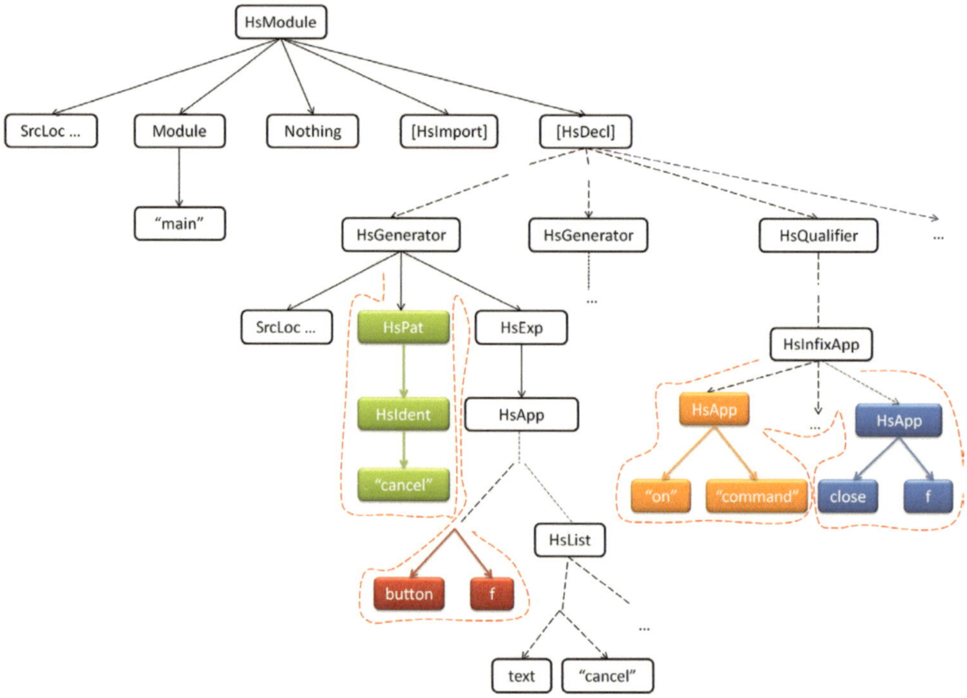

Fig. 4. Pruning the AST of Figure 3 (Prg-ExeHsl)

Analyzing the fragment of the AST in Figure 4 and the Haskell syntax[HJW+ 92] we include that:

- All nodes of type `HsGenerator` appears in the context of `HsPatBind`[1], more precisely in context of `HsRhs` under `HsPatBind` constructor.
- In context of the first `HsGenerator` we obtain information about the declared components in source program. At this point we can infer the source node (`f` – red color) and the action to take (`cancel` – green color) that will guide us to the target node in case of the component be supplied by an action.

1 In *Syntax* library, is defined by: `HsPatBind SrcLoc HsPat HsRhs [HsDecl].`

In Figure 4, the `cancel` component is a `button` and is built under the component `f` – the main window.

- In context of the node `HsQualifier` we can infer the components that have any action (orange color) and where this action lead us (blue color) – target node.

Inferred the needed information, in order to prune the required nodes from whole tree and collect the correct information we use a strategy *top-down* with *full* traversal (`full_td` in Strafunski – it performs a full traversal, i.e. it visits every subterm, in a top-down fashion). Hence we are under a type analyze and not a type transformation we use a strategy *type unification* (`applyTU` in Strafunski). The first two strategic functions in Strafunski defined were to filter from the AST the nodes of type `HsGenerator` and of type `HsQualifier` (to makes easier the understanding of the fragments of code that we expose in this section, we will simplify its description).

```
extractHsGenerator = applyTU  (full_td stepl)
  where
   stepl = constTU  []  'adhocTU' generators  'adhocTU' patBind
   patBind    (HsPatBind _ _ (HsUnGuardedRhs   (HsDo stmtsN)) _)
                                  = extractHsGenerator stmtsN
   generators (HsGenerator srcloc hspat hsexp) = return [HsGenerator srcloc
               hspat hsexp]
```

```
extractHsQualifier = applyTU  (full_td step2)
  where
   step2 = constTU  []  'adhocTU' qualifiers  'adhocTU' patBind
   patBind    (HsPatBind _ _ (HsUnGuardedRhs  (HsDo stmtsN)) _)
                                    = extractHsQualifier stmtsN
qualifiers  (HsQualifier hsexp)     = return  [HsQualifier hsexp]
```

Explaining the functional strategy above: the generic behavior of `constTU` is to return an empty list; and `adhocTU` updates strategies by type-specific cases. While we not found in the AST any node of type `HsGenerator` we continues exploring the tree using the auxiliar function `patBind`, to guarantee that we are in the context of a `HsPatBind`.

The result of pruning the AST, obtained in the previous phase, with this strategic function is a list of statements of type `HsGenerator` .

Still considering the first program example, Prg-ExeHsl, of the subsection 5.1 and the AST in Figure 3 (subsection 5.3), applying the `extractHsGenerator` strategic function, we obtain the result shown in Figure 5.

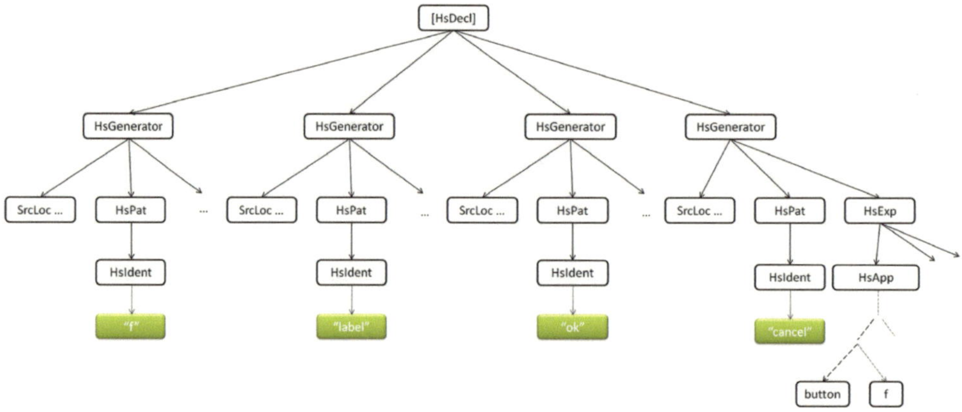

Fig. 5. Widgets identified on the AST of Prg-ExeHs1

We obtain a list with 4 elements, corresponding to each component declared on source program (`f ,label, ok` and `cancel`). Analyzing the type of component (button, staticText, f,...) we filter which components can have an event.

5.5 Building and exploring Widget Dependency Graph

Built the AST and identified the *data entities, actions* and *relationships* between them, we are able to build the dependency graph of a given program.

A program dependence graph combined with operations such as program slicing, can provide the basis for powerful programming tools that could help solving some software-engineering problems such as: understanding what an existing program does and how it works; understanding the differences between several versions of a program; and creating new programs by combining pieces of old programs [HR92]. In fact, the dependence-graph representation of programs can be used to [Gra09]:

- Anomaly detection. The dependence graphs can be used to discover if control flow of program is the expected (this is, if user interface was built correctly);
- Feature extraction. Implementations of different program features are often interwoven;
- Design and architecture recovery. The structure of complex interfaces can be explored by analysis of control and flow dependencies.
- Optimization. Slicing a class library from the client's uses can eliminate both dead code and dead instance variables.

The graph we intend to build is a graph where the nodes will be possible states of a graphical user interface provided by attributes; the connections between these nodes will be the actions between them. With the list of components declared in a program obtained with `extractHsGenerator` and its attributes (actions and its result) with `extract-HsQualifier,` we are able to extract the information about the source/target node and the connection *(action* taken) between them. This is, from the list of statements of `HsGenerator` and `HsQualifier,` we want extract triples in the form: `(from,action,to).`

Still in a functional strategy, we will use **Strafunski** to extract this information from the list obtained at previous phase.
To reach this goal, we develop 3 functional strategies:

- To extract the source node we explore the information from the first expression in context of a `HsApp`, exploring until we found a node with type `HsVar`:

```
extractSourceNode = applyTU  (full_td step3)

   where step3 = constTU  []  'adhocTU' giveHsG adhocTU'
giveSourceWidget
     giveHsG (HsGenerator x y (HsApp expl _)) = extractSourceNode expl
     giveSourceWidget  (HsVar node) = return  [node]
```

- To extract the action: analyzing the AST referred at previous subsection, the name of the widget appears in the context of a `HsApp;` more precisely, in context of the first `HsVar.`

```
extractAction = applyTU   (full_td step4)

 where step4 = constTU [] 'adhocTU' giveName 'adhocTU' extractApp
   giveName (HsGenerator x y (HsApp expl _)) = extractAction expl
   giveApp  (HsApp  (HsVar x)  (HsVar y))  = return  [HsVar x]
```

- To extract the target node (in case of having action) we prune the node that appears in the context of a `HsQualifier.` And we explore until we find a node of type `HsInfixApp` but returning the right side of the expression.

```
extractTargetNode = applyTU  (full_td step5)

    where step5 = constTU  []   'adhocTU' giveHsQ  'adhocTU'
giveInfApp
      giveHsQ  (HsQualifier expr)             = extractTargetNode expr
      giveInfApp  (HsInfixApp expl op exp2)  = return  [exp2]
```

The widget dependency graph obtained is shown in Figure 6.
The green state represents the initial state and the red one represents the final state.

5.6 A more complex example

In this subsection we present a more complex example (Prg-ExeHs2) than the one introduced in subsection 5.1 (Prg-ExeHs1). Due to space limitations we will not discuss, neither the program, nor the slicing process, in detail.

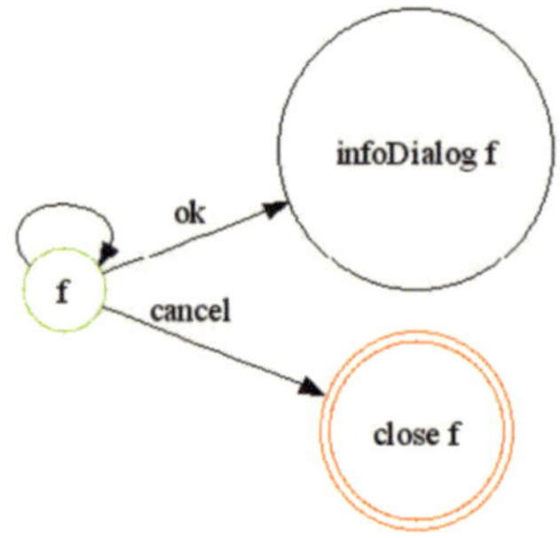

Fig. 6. Widget Dependency Graph for Prg-ExeHsl

So we briefly present (in Figure 7) the interface of program Prg-ExeHs2 exhibiting two screenshots of the main window. This main window is composed of 4 tablets, 2 of them (the first 2) being displayed in Figure 7.

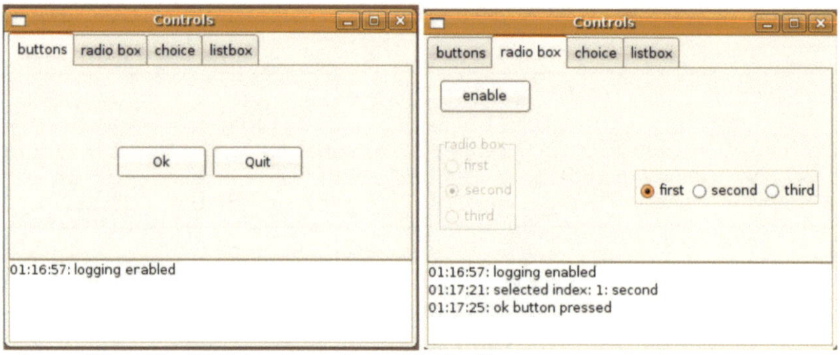

Fig. 7. Interface of Prg-ExeHs2 (written in wxHaskell)

Each tablet provides a set of components that the user can choose to build up his interface. Although not a huge example, it is a rich one, that focus on different components and different actions. Submitting the source program to the strategic slicing tool, described in this section, produces the widget dependency graph shown in Figure 8.

6 Case Study II — Slicing Swing

In order to extract the user interface model from a Java program we need to construct a slicing function that isolates the Swing subprogram from the entire program. Visitor patterns allow us to use a set of tree-walker functions that visit an AST. Thus, the programmer only needs to focus on the nodes interesting for the specific task. In fact, the programmer does not need to have a full knowledge of the grammar, but only the vocabulary of the GUI language.

6.1 A closer look into Swing

Swing is a widget toolkit for Java. It is part of Sun Microsystems' Java Foundation Classes (JFC) – an API for providing a graphical user interface (GUI) for Java programs.
Swing component set was originally created because the basic Abstract Window Toolkit (AWT) components that came with the original version of the Java libraries were insufficient for real-world forms-based applications. All the basic components were there, but the existent set was too small and too restrictive. The Swing components support all the capabilities of the original set and offer a whole lot more besides [Zuk05, WCHZ04].

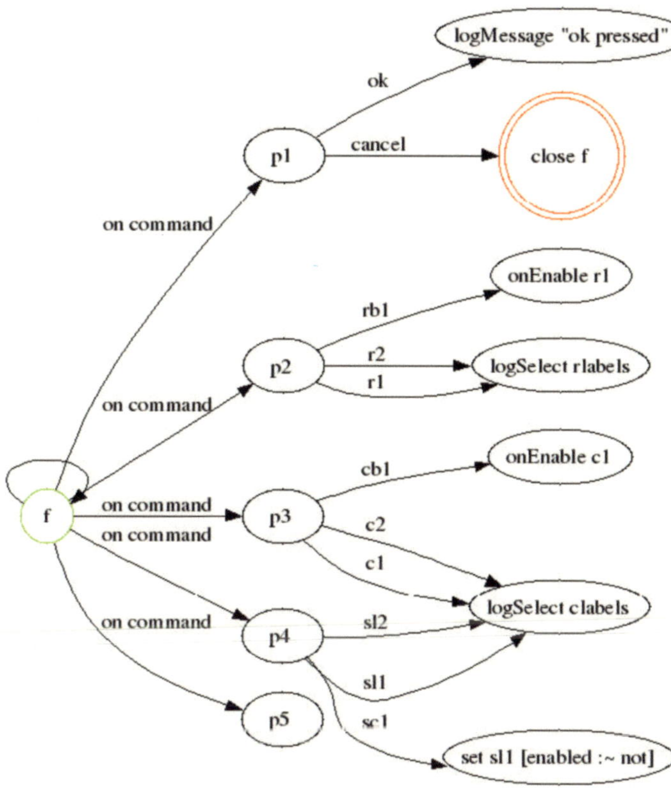

Fig. 8. Widget Dependence Graph for Prg-ExeHs2

The basic distinction between the Swing and equivalent AWT component is, in most cases, the Swing component class names begin with *J* and the AWT ones do not. For instance, the Swings `JButton` is a replacement for the AWT `Button`.
In addition to replacing each of the basic components, the Swing component set has a replacement for the higher-level window objects (e.g. the Swing `JApplet` is a replacement for the AWT `Applet)`. Essentially, Swing was developed to provide a more sophisticated set of GUI components than the earlier AWT. Swing provides a native look and feel that emulates the look and feel of several platforms, and also supports a pluggable look and feel that allows applications to have a look and feel unrelated to the underlying platform.
The Swing library makes heavy use of the Model-View-Controller (MVC) software design pattern, which conceptually decouples the data being viewed from the user interface

controls through which it is viewed. Because of this, most Swing components have associated models (which are specified in terms of Java interfaces), and the programmer can use various default implementations or provide their own. The framework provides default implementations of model interfaces for all of its concrete components. Typically, Swing component model objects are responsible for providing a concise interface defining events fired, and accessible properties for the (conceptual) data model for use by the associated `JComponent`. Given that the overall MVC pattern is a loosely-coupled collaborative object relationship pattern, the model provides the programmatic means for attaching event listeners to the data model object. Typically, these events are model centric (ex: a "row inserted" event in a table model) and are mapped by the `JComponent` specialization into a meaningful event for the GUI component. A distinction of Swing, as a GUI framework, is in its reliance on programmatically-rendered GUI controls (as opposed to the use of the native host operating system's GUI controls). Some of the characteristics that make Swing so appealing are: platform independence; extensibility; component-oriented; customizable; configurable; lightweight user interface; and loosely-coupled/MVC. In this subsection we introduce a simple example (named Prg-ExeSw1) that will be used throughout the rest of this case study to illustrate the steps of the method under discussion to extract the abstract user interface model.

```
import javax.swing.JButton;
import javax.swing.JFrame;
import javax.swing.JLabel;
import javax.swing.JTextField;
import javax.swing.JPanel;

public class SwingExample extends JFrame {

   private JButton button1;
   private JLabel label1;
   private JTextField textFld1;
   private JPanel  jPanel1;

   public SwingExample()    {
       initComponents();
   }

   private void initComponents()   {
       jPanel1 = new javax.swing.JPanel();
       textFld1 = new javax.swing.JTextField();
       button1 = new javax.swing.JButton();
       label1 = new javax.swing.JLabel();

setDefaultCloseOperation(javax.swing.WindowConstants.EXIT_ON_CLOSE);

textFld1.setText("Text Example");

   javax.swing.GroupLayout  jPanel1Layout = new GroupLayout(jPanel1);
   jPanel1.setLayout(jPanel1Layout);
   jPanel1Layout.setHorizontalGroup(
       jPanel1Layout.createParallelGroup(GroupLayout.Alignment.LEADING)
      .addGroup(GroupLayout.Alignment.TRAILING,
               jPanel1Layout.createSequentialGroup()
          .addContainerGap(91,  Short.MAX_VALUE)
          .addComponent(textFld11,   GroupLayout.PREFERRED_SIZE,  189,
                                     GroupLayout.PREFERRED_SIZE)
          .addGap(96,   96,   96))
   );

   button1.setText("Press the Button1");
   button1.addActionListener(new java.awt.event.ActionListener()    {
       public void actionPerformed(java.awt.event.ActionEvent evt)    {
           button1ActionPerformed(evt);
       }
   });
   ....
   }
   public static void main(String[]   args)  {
       java.awt.EventQueue.invokeLater(new Runnable()    {
           public void run()    {
               new SwingExample().setVisible(true);
           }
       });
   }
```

The types `JFrame`, `JLabel` and `JButton` denote graphical objects that becomes accessible through the `import` declaration explicit in the first three lines of the above program. Figure 9 depicts the interface of program example Prg-ExeSw1.

As can be observed in the source code above, the components are added to a panel through the method call `addComponent`. Also, events are added to buttons through the method call `addActionListener`. Each time, the user press a button, a message will be displayed in the text field.

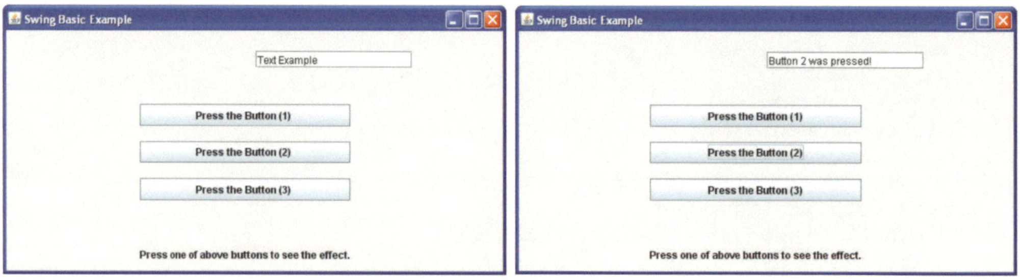

Fig. 9. Interface of Prg-ExeSw1 (written in Swing)

6.2 A closer look into Abstract Syntax Tree

The Abstract Syntax Tree [Ecl09], AST by short, is the way how Eclipse[2] looks at Java source code: every Java source file is entirely represented as tree of AST nodes. These nodes are all subclasses of `ASTNode`. Every subclass is specialized for an element of the Java Programming Language. E.g. there are nodes for method declarations (`Method-Declaration`), variable declaration (`VariableDeclarationFragment`), assignments and so on. A `SimpleName` is any string of Java source that is not a keyword, a Boolean literal (true or false) or the null literal. An AST is created by parsing the Java code. This is done using the `ASTParser`. It processes whole Java files as well as portions of Java code. In the example below the method `parse(ICompilationUnit unit)` parses the source code stored in the file that `unit` points to (a `ICompilationUnit` corresponds to a Java source file).

```
protected CompilationUnit parse(ICompilationUnit unit)    {
    ASTParser parser = ASTParser.newParser(AST.JLS3);
    parser.setKind(ASTParser.K_COMPILATION_UNIT);
    parser.setSource(unit);
    parser.setResolveBindings(true);
    return  (CompilationUnit)  parser.createAST(null);    // parse
}
```

However, even the simplest Java program results in a quite complex tree. Consequently, to find out a specific node in its AST can be a hard task. If we intend to get the `MethodInvocation`, scanning all the levels is a possible, but not the most convenient solution.

---

2 Eclipse is a Trademark of Eclipse Foundation – http://www.eclipse.org

There is a better solution: every **ASTNode** allows querying for a child node by using a visitor (visitor pattern []). In the class `ASTVisitor`, we find for every subclass of `ASTNode` two methods, one called `visit()`, and other called `endVisit()`. Further, the `ASTVisitor` declares these two methods: `preVisit(ASTNode node)` and `postVisit(ASTNode node)`.

The subclass of`ASTVisitor` is passed to any node ofthe AST. The AST will recursively step through the tree, calling the mentioned methods of the visitor for every AST node in this order. In the case of a `MethodInvocation`, we will obtain:

- `preVisit(ASTNode node)`
- `visit(MethodInvocation node)`
- ... now the children of the method invocation are recursively processed if visit returns true
- `endVisit(MethodInvocation node)`
- `postVisit(ASTNode node)`

If `false` is returned from `visit()`, the subtree of the visited node will not be considered. This is to ignore parts of the AST.

There is another subclass of the `ASTVisitor` that can be used, amongst other things, to collect all local variable declarations of a compilation unit – the `LocalVariable-Detector` subclass. Every subclass of `ASTNode` contains specific information for the Java element it represents. For instance, a `MethodDeclaration` will contain information about the name, return type, parameters, etc. The information of a node is referred as structural properties. The structural properties are grouped into three different kinds:

- Properties that hold simple values;
- Properties which contain a single child AST node; and
- Properties which contain a list of child AST nodes.

A typical workflow of an application using AST looks like the one in Figure 10[3].

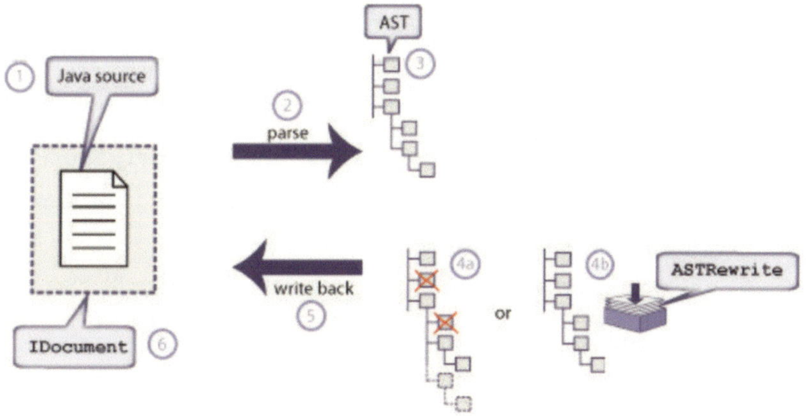

Fig. 10. Workflow of an application using AST

[3] Figure retrieved from [Ecl09]

As can be deduced from Figure 10, the AST allows to apply changes to the abstract syntax tree and reflect them over the source code. The AST have also a mechanism of error recovering. More information about these features can be found in [Ecl09], but as they are not needed for this case study are not detailed.

6.3 Slicing Swing with AST

As the Swing component set is too big to explore, we decide to restrict to a small subset. Therefore, in a first phase we only try to find components of type `JButton` with a specific behavior `(Click)`. Latter, we expand the subset to include other common components like `JMenuBar`, `JMenu`, `JMenuItem`, `JTabbedPane JSpinner`, and `JCheckBox`.
As we are interested to recover the abstract model of the GUI under consideration, we need to start the components that have some behavior `(Click, Mouse_Over,` and so one).
In Java, how we implement event handling depends on the type of button we use and how we use it. Generally, we implement an *action listener,* which is notified every time the user clicks the button. For check boxes we usually use an *item listener,* which is notified when the check box is selected or deselected.
Action listeners are probably the easiest and most common event handlers to implement. We implement an action listener to define what should be done when an user performs certain operation. An action event occurs, whenever an action is performed by the user.
Usually, to write an *Action Listener,* the following steps are given[4]:

1. Declare an eventhandlerclass and specify thatthe class eitherimplements an `Action-Listener` interface or extends a class that implements an `ActionListener` interface. For example:

```
public class MyClass implements ActionListener  {
```

2. Register an instance of the event handler class as a listener on one or more components. For example:

```
buttonl.addActionListener(instanceOfMyClass);
```

3. Include code that implements the methods in listener interface. For example:

```
public void actionPerformed(ActionEvent e)   {
   ...//code that reacts to the action...
}
```

From this information, we conclude that we need to perform two traversals to extract information about `JButtons` that belongs to the program under analysis as well as its associated behavior. The first traversal is responsible to find all instances of the `JButton` class (identical to the extraction of the identifiers table from a program); and the second

---

[4] Information retrieved from http://java.sun.com/docs/books/tutorial/uiswing/events/actionlistener.html.

traversal is responsible to find, for each `JButton` find in the first phase, its associated `actionPerformed` event.

Another alternative to this two-traversal algorithm is to perform all in one step (in the same traversal collect all instances of the `JButton` class and its associated actions). But, due to questions of clearness, we decide to perform two traversals as described above.

This two traversals are implements using the `public boolean visit(T n)` and `public boolean endVisit(T n)` methods referred previously. Recall that the method `visit` is executed during the visit done at each node and returns `true` only if its children should to be visited. The method `endVisit` is invoked after the visit of the children nodes is finished. This is, the method is invoked only in case of the method `visit` return `true`.

Both methods `visit` and `endVisit` has a parameter a node of type `T`, pointing that they can receive any kind of `ASTNode (MethodInvocation, MethodDeclaration, VariableDeclarator Fragment,` and so on).

To perform the first visit (collect all instances of `JButton)` we implement an instance of the class `ASTVisitor`, named `ASTFindJButtons`. This class is responsible for visit all nodes that corresponds to variables declarations (with `VariableDeclarationFragment` type – Figure 11) and collect them in an hashtable.

This `VariableDeclarationFragment` node type is used in field declarations, local variable declarations, and `for` statement initializers.

After perform the first traversal and collected all buttons in an hashtable, it is time to perform the second traversal. Hence we are interested in find all `Actions`, all we need is to find all nodes in the AST that match the `MethodInvocation` node type (Figure 12) and if is invoked by a button collected in the first phase. To perform this traversal, we extend again the class `ASTVisitor` within a class called `ASTFindActions`.

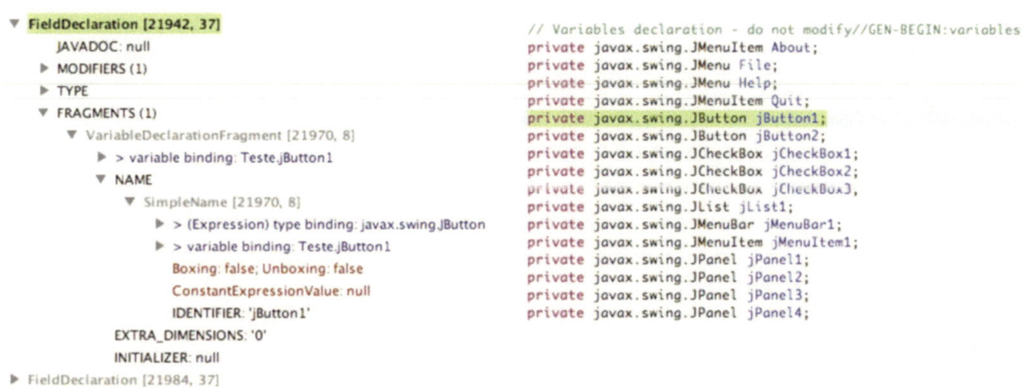

Fig. 11. `VariableDeclarationFragment` node

Fig. 12. `MethodInvocation` node

6.4 Building and exploring Widget Dependency Graph

In this subsection we briefly explain how is built the dependency graph.

As referred previously in subsection 5.5, the graph we intend to build is a graph where the nodes are possible states of a graphical user interface provided by attributes; and the connections between these nodes will be the actions between them.

To extract this information needed to build the graph we use the data structure (a `hashmap)` to collect such information. In the first traversal, the graphical components (buttons, menus, etc) are collected. In the second traversal, the actions associated with the graphical components collected in the first phase are also retrieved. And, to connect each one of the components to each other, a third traversal is performed in order to detect the parent-child relations among them (using the `addComponent` method to collect such data).

In order to make easier the comprehension of the model obtained, two kinds of arrows were used: a thin arrow is used to describe the relation *the component X is contained on component Y*; and a dashed arrow is used to describe the relation *the method A is invoked when the event alpha occurs over the component Z*.

After that, a widget dependence graph is built using this information. For the example present in subsection 6.1 (Prg-ExeHsl), the result of this traversal is depicted in Figure 13.

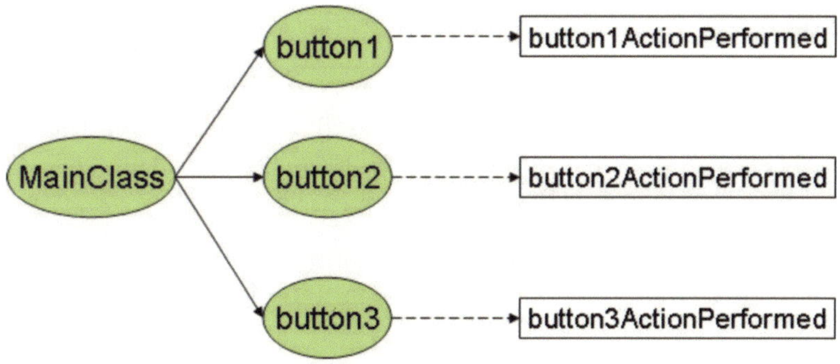

Fig. 13. Widget Dependence Graph for Prg-ExeSw1

6.5 A more complex example

In this subsection we present a more complex example (Prg-ExeSw2) than the first one introduced in subsection 6.1 (Prg-ExeSw1); Prg-ExeSw2 is similar to the one introduced in section 5.1 (see Figure 14). Due to space limitations we will not discuss, neither the program, nor the slicing process, in detail. So we briefly present the application interface showing, in Figure 14, two screenshots of its main window that is divided into 4 parts (tablets).

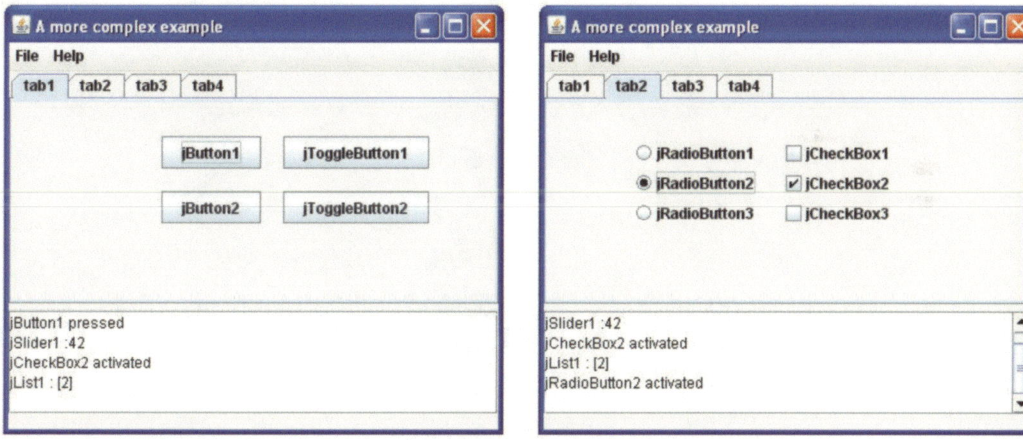

Fig. 14. Interface of Prg-ExeSw2 (written in Swing)

Each tablet provides a set of components that the user can choose to build up his interface. Although not a huge example, it is a rich one that focuses on different components and different actions.

Submitting the source program to the Java/Swing slicer described in this section, it produces a widget dependency graph like the one shown in Figure 15.

7. Conclusion

The need for maintaining, reusing, and re-engineering existing software systems has increased enormously over the past few years. Reusing and modifying legacy systems are complex and expensive tasks, because *program comprehension,* although required, is a difficult and time-consuming process. Thus, the need for methods and tools that facilitate program comprehension is urgent and strong. A variety of reverse engineering tools provide means to support this task. Reverse engineering aims at analyzing the software and representing it in an abstract form so that it is easier to understand what it does and how it works.

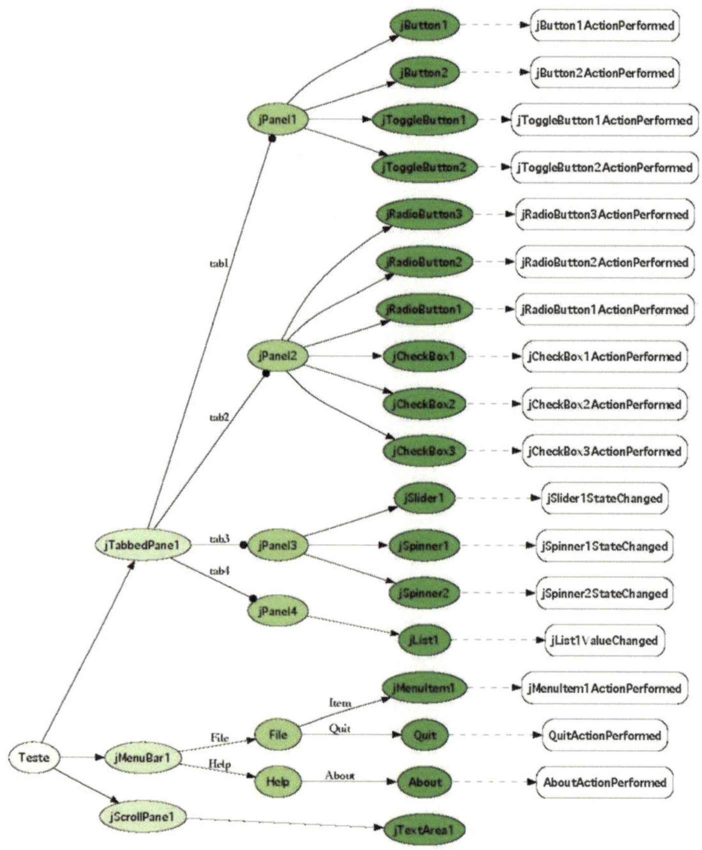

Fig. 15. Widget Dependence Graph for Prg-ExeSw2

In this context, we have shown along the chapter how slicing — a code analysis technique — can be used to derive the User Interface Abstract Model for an interactive application, aiming at reverse engineering and program comprehension.

From the Abstract Syntax Tree representation we are able to derive the *widget dependency graph* for a given program. That model can, then, be used to understand the behavior of the user interface or for verification purposes.

This approach has proved to be flexible and broader enough to be applied in real cases of software engineering. Also, it is applicable to different programming environments. To start, we have worked out two case studies: one in the functional side, using Haskell/wxHaskell, and another one in the object-oriented side, using Java/Swing. Now we plan to evolve, working in the .NET context with C#/Visual Basic and WinForms. At the moment only a subset of wxHaskell and Swing components are being considered by the prototypes we developed. Our first objective was to explore this approach and to assess its feasibility and usefulness. In the future, we will extend our implementation to handle more complex user interfaces.

8. References

Jean-Francois Bergeretti and Bernard A. Carre. Information-flow and data-flow analysis of while-programs. *ACM Trans. Program. Lang. Syst.*, 7(1):37—61, 1985.

J. Chen and S. Subramaniam. A gui environment to manipulate fsms for testing gui-based applications in java. In *HICSS '01: Proceedings of the 34th Annual Hawaii International Conference on System Sciences (HICSS-34)-Volume 9*, page 9061, Washington, DC, USA, 2001. IEEE Computer Society.

Eclipse. Abstract syntax tree. http://www.eclipse.org/articles/article. php?file=Article-JavaCodeManipulation_AST/index.html, April 2009.

GrammaTech. Dependence graphs and program slicing. 2009.

Yuri Gurevich. Logic and the challenge of computer science. http://research. microsoft.com/~gurevich/Books/book1.pdf, 1988.

Paul Hudak, Simon Peyton Jones, Philip Wadler, Brian Boutel, Jon Fairbairn, Joseph Fasel, Maria M. Guzman, Kevin Hammond, John Hughes, Thomas Johnsson, Dick Kieburtz, Rishiyur Nikhil, Will Partain, and John Peterson. Report on the programming language haskell: anon-strict, purely functional language version 1.2. *SIGPLANNot.*, 27(5):1-164, 1992.

Susan Horwitz and Thomas Reps. The use of program dependence graphs in software engineering. In *ICSE '92: Proceedings of the 14th international conference on Software engineering*, pages 392-411, New York, NY, USA, 1992. ACM.

Jeffrey Korn, Yih-Farn Chen, and Eleftherios Koutsofios. Chava: Reverse engineering and tracking of java applets. In *WCRE '99: Proceedings of the Sixth Working Conference on Reverse Engineering*, page 314, Washington, DC, USA, 1999. IEEE Computer Society.

Daan Leijen. wxHaskell - a portable and concise GUI library for Haskell. In *ACM SIGPLAN Haskell Workshop (HW'04)*. ACM Press, Setembro 2004.

R. Lammel and J. Visser. Typed Combinators for Generic Traversal. In *Proc. Practical Aspects of Declarative Programming PADL 2002*, volume 2257 of *LNCS*, pages 137-154. Springer-Verlag, Janeiro 2002.

R. Lammel and J. Visser. A Strafunski Application Letter. In V. Dahl and P. Wadler, editors, *Proc. of Practical Aspects of Declarative Programming (PADL'03)*, volume 2562 of *LNCS*, pages 357-375. Springer-Verlag, Janeiro 2003.

Ralf Lammel, Eelco Visser, and Joost Visser. The Essence of Strategic Programming. 18 p.; Draft; Available at http://www.cwi.nl/~ralf, Outubro15 2002.

R. Lammel, E. Visser, and J. Visser. Strategic programming meets adaptive programming, 2003.

Atif Memon, Ishan Banerjee, and Adithya Nagarajan. Gui ripping: Reverse engineering of graphical user interfaces for testing. In *WCRE 03: Proceedings of the 10th Working*

Conference on Reverse Engineering, page 260, Washington, DC, USA, 2003. IEEE Computer Society.

H. A. Muller and K. Klashinsky. Rigi-a system for programming-in-the-large. In *ICSE '88: Proceedings ofthe 10th international conference on Software engineering,* pages 80-86, Los Alamitos, CA, USA, 1988. IEEE Computer Society Press.

Atif M. Memon, Martha E. Pollack, and Mary Lou Soffa. Automated test oracles for guis. In *SIGSOFT '00/FSE-8: Proceedings of the 8th ACM SIGSOFT international symposium on Foundations of software engineering,* pages 30-39, New York, NY, USA, 2000. ACM.

Brad A. Myers. Why are human-computer interfaces difficult to design and implement? Technical report, Pittsburgh, PA, USA, 1993.

Tarja Systa, Kai Koskimies, and Hausi Muller. Shimba - an environment for reverse engineering java software systems. *Softw. Pract. Exper.,* 31(4):371—394, 2001.

R. F. Stark, J. Schmid, and E. Borger. *Java and the Java Virtual Machine: Definition, Verification and Validation.* Springer-Verlag, 2001.

F. Tip. A survey of program slicing techniques. *Journal of programming languages,* 3:121—189,1995.

Roger Took. Putting design into practice: formal specification and the user interface. Pages 63—96, 1990.

Eelco Visser, Zine el Abidine Benaissa, and Andrew Tolmach. Building program optimizers with rewriting strategies. *SIGPLANNot.,* 34(1):13—26, 1999.

Kathy Walrath, Mary Campione, Alison Huml, and Sharon Zakhour. *The JFC Swing Tutorial: A Guide to Constructing GUIs, Second Edition.* Addison Wesley Longman Publishing Co., Inc., Redwood City, CA, USA, 2004.

Mark Weiser. Program slicing. In *ICSE '81: Proceedings of the 5th international conference on Software engineering,* pages 439—449, Piscataway, NJ, USA, 1981. IEEE Press.

Baowen Xu, Ju Qian, Xiaofang Zhang, Zhongqiang Wu, and Lin Chen. A brief survey of program slicing. *SIGSOFTSoftw. Eng. Notes,* 30(2):1—36, 2005.

John Zukowski. *The Definitive Guide to Java Swing, Third Edition (Definitive Guide).* Apress, Berkely, CA, USA, 2005.

15

IMAGE QUALITY ENHANCEMENT BY APPLYING GENETIC ALGORITHM IN MEDIAN FILTERING

Sandra Sovilj-Nikic
University of Novi Sad
Serbia

1. Introduction

Images are often corrupted by impulse noise due to errors generated in noisy sensors or communication channels. Two types of impulse noise can be defined: 1) fixed-valued and 2) random-valued. Fixed-valued impulses occur when noisy pixel values are out of receiver's range and they can have one of two values (MIN or MAX). This type of noise is called "salt & pepper" noise and it appears as black and/or white impulses on the image. Another type of noise is generated after incorrect decoding of binary represented image. In this case noisy pixels can have arbitrary value.

In many applications it is very important to remove noise in the images before some subsequent processing such as edge detection, object recognition and image segmentation.

At the beginning of development of techniques in digital image processing, linear techniques are used extensively because of their mathematical simplicity and the existence of appropriate characteristics (e.g. principle of superposition) making them easy to design and implement. In the case where noise can be modulated as additive Gaussian noise linear techniques offer satisfactory performance for noise removal. However, in many cases the noise is impulsive and in this case linear techniques do not usually perform well. Another example where linear techniques fail is the case of nonlinear image degradations. Such degradations occur during image formation and during image transmission through nonlinear channels. The human visual perception mechanism has been shown to have nonlinear characteristics. Human vision is very sensitive to high-frequency information such as edges and fine details on the image (e.g. lines and corners). Therefore, high-frequency content of image is very important for visual perception. However, most of linear filters have low-pass characteristics. They tend to blur edges and to destroy lines and other fine details of image.

All above mentioned reasons led to leave linear techniques and to the use of nonlinear filtering techniques. One of nonlinear filters family includes filters based on order statistics (Pitas & Venetsanopoulos, 1992). The family of order statistics based filters is very rich, where the median filter is the best known. Median filter and its modification have shown good efficiency in suppressing impulse noise and capability of preserving image edges

(Pitas & Venetsanopoulos, 1991). Nevertheless, the median filters possess some disadvantages. The main disadvantage of median filter is location-invariant property, i.e. they are implemented uniformly across the entire image. They tend to alter both noise pixels and undisturbed good pixels. Therefore, they remove fine details in the image. Partition-based filtering is one of the concepts for eliminating disadvantages of median filtering.

In this chapter partition based median (PBM) filtering using genetic algorithm in the training process is proposed. With proposed PBM filter, at each location, observed vector is classified into one of M exclusive partitions, and an optimal particular filtering operation is then activated. The observation vector space is formed on differences between current pixel value and the outputs of the center weighted median (CWM) filters with variable center weights. The estimate at each location is formed as a linear combination of current pixel value and the outputs of CWM filters. Optimal weighting vector of each partition is derived using genetic algorithm in training the filter on the reference image. Optimal weights are derived to minimize the total square error of estimation at each location.

Performance of the proposed PBM filter has been evaluated by simulations on variety of test images. The proposed PBM filter in which genetic algorithm is used for optimization of the weighting vector for each partition had demonstrated better results in noise suppressing then competitive filters based on median filtering in terms of the SNR as well as the perceived image quality. The proposed filter outperforms other median based filters in removing different types of noise: impulse noise (fixed-valued and random-valued), Gaussian noise and mixed Gaussian and impulse noise.

In this chapter following introduction the definition of PBM filter and partition into regions are described. In section 3 application of genetic algorithm for solving the optimization problem is discussed. Finally in section 4 obtained results and comparison with competitive filters are given and discussed.

2. Definition of PBM filter

Schematic diagram of PBM filter is shown on Figure 1 (Chen & Wu, 2001).

Let $C = \{(c1, c2) \mid 1 \le c1 \le P,\ 1 \le c2 \le Q\}$ denote pixel coordinates of a digital image, where P and Q are its height and width, respectively. At each location $\mathbf{c}(c1, c2) \in C$ a filter window of size $W = 2n+1$ simetrically surrounding the current pixel, and

$$\mathbf{x(c)} = \{x_i(c) : i = 1,2,\ldots,2n+1\} \tag{1}$$

denotes set of observed pixels via filter window, where $x(c) = x_{n+1}$ is original or center pixel.

Another step in filtering is to apply CWM filters with variable center weights on input vector $\mathbf{x(c)}$ (Ko & Lee, 1991; Pitas & Venetsanopoulos, 1991). The output of CWM filter is described as:

$$y_k(c) = median(\mathbf{x}_{2k+1}(c)) = median(\mathbf{x}_{\omega}(c)) \tag{2}$$

where ω denotes center weight and $\omega = 2k+1$, k is nonnegative integer.

$$\mathbf{x}_{\omega}(c) = \{x_1(c), x_2(c), x_3(c),.., x_n(c), \omega \lozenge x_{n+1}(c), x_{n+2}(c),.., x_{2n+1}(c)\} \quad (3)$$

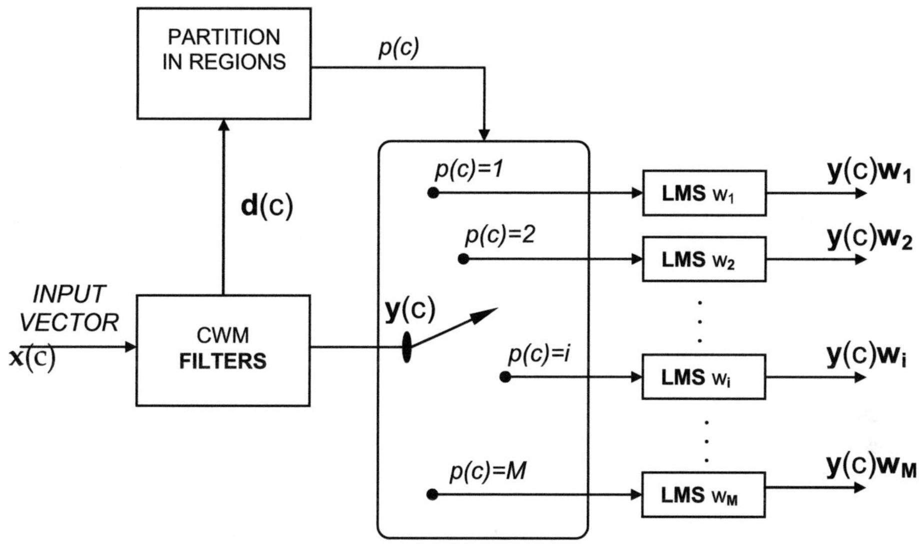

Fig. 1. Schematic diagram of PBM filter

Operator $\lozenge$ denotes repetition operation. Two limit cases exist in the CWM filtering. Output of CWM filter y_0 ($k=0, \omega=1$) corresponds to the output of standard median filter, and for $k \geq n$ CWM filter is an identity filter $y_k = x(c)$. Taking two limit cases into consideration, CWM filter with higher center wieght is superior in preserving fine details in the image than filter with smaller center weight. But, CWM filter with smaller center weight is better in noise suppressing. Therefore, we should find a compromise solution between preserving of fine details and noise suppressing. That was the reason for applying the CWM filter with variable center weights. In the proposed filtering scheme k lies in $[0, n-1]$.
At each location, for the current pixel, the following differences are defined:

$$d_k(c) = |y_k(c) - x(c)| \quad (4)$$

where $k = 0, 1, \ldots, n-1$ and $\mathrm{d_k}(c) \leq \mathrm{d_{k\text{-}1}}(c)$.
On the basis of these differences, it can be found out whether the current pixel is corrupted one. For instance, we can observe the difference $d_{n-1}(c)$. If it is too large, that implies the current pixel value is the biggest or the smallest in the set of observed pixels **x(c)** (1) and it is probably the corrupted pixel. On the other side, if the difference $d_0(c)$ is small, it can be concluded that the current pixel is uncorrupted one and it should be preserved unaltered.

The information about noise presence on the location $\mathbf{c}$ can be obtained on the basis of differences from $d_0(c)$ to $d_{n-1}(c)$.
At each location $\mathbf{c}$, the estimation of pixel value is derived as a linear combination of outputs of CWM filter with variable center weights and a current pixel value, which is equivalent to the output of the CWM filter with $k = n$ as follows:

$$\hat{x}(c) = \mathbf{y(c)} \cdot \mathbf{w}_{p(c)}^{\mathbf{T}} \tag{5}$$

where $p(c)$ corresponds to the partition index for $\mathbf{x(c)}$ which will be defined later and $\mathbf{y(c)}$ is the input vector for filtering at observed location:

$$\mathbf{y(c)} = [y_0(c), y_1(c), \dots, y_{n-1}(c), y_n(c)] = [y_0(c), y_1(c), \dots, y_{n-1}(c), x(c)] \tag{6}$$

Vector $\mathbf{w}_{p(c)} = \mathbf{w}_i = [w_{i,o}, w_{i,1}, \dots, w_{i,n}]$ represents weighting vector of the particular filter for the ith partition $(i = 1, 2, \dots, M)$. Optimal weighting vector for each partition is derived using genetic algorithm.
To control the dynamic range of outputs, weighting vector should satisfy a location-invariance constraint:

$$\mathbf{e}_{n+1} \cdot \mathbf{w}_i^{\mathbf{T}} = \mathbf{w}_i \cdot \mathbf{e}_{n+1}^{\mathbf{T}} = 1 \qquad (i = 1, 2, \dots, M) \tag{7}$$

where $\mathbf{e}_N = [1,1, \dots, 1]$ is $1 \times N$ vector.
If $x(c) = median(\mathbf{x(c)})$, then $y_k(c) = x(c)$ for any $k \geq 0$ and current pixel $x(c)$ remains unaltered. In this case, let $p(c) = i$, we have:

$$\hat{x}(c) = \mathbf{y(c)} \cdot \mathbf{w}_i^{\mathbf{T}} = \mathbf{e}_{n+1} \cdot x(c) \cdot \mathbf{w}_i^{\mathbf{T}} = x(c) \tag{8}$$

2.1 Region partitioning

At each location $\mathbf{c}$, difference vector is obtained by applying (4) as follows:

$$\mathbf{d(c)} = [d_0(c), d_1(c), \dots, d_{n-1}(c)] \in \mathbf{R}^n. \tag{9}$$

The difference vector space is divided into M exclusive regions, $\{\Omega_i : i = 1, 2, \dots, M\}$. The partition index for each input vector $\mathbf{x(c)}$ is given such that $p(c) = i$ for $\mathbf{d(c)} \in \Omega_i$. Partition in regions can be fulfilled by different methods, e.g. the scalar quantization, the vector quantization etc. Due to its simplicity and computational efficiency, scalar quantization has been chosen to apply for partitioning n-dimensional difference vector

space into regions. Quantization levels are determined experimentally and remain fixed through the simulations.
Let $\{q_{k,v} : v = 0, 1, \dots, L\}$ be a set of monotonically ascending points, i.e.:

$$q_{k,v} < q_{k,v+1} \quad , \quad 0 \le v \le L-1 \tag{10}$$

for the kth dimension of difference vector space, where $k = 0, 1, \dots, n-1$.
At each location, for each input vector $\mathbf{x(c)}$ and appropriate difference vector $\mathbf{d(c)}$ is defined vector of the quantization level indices as $\mathbf{z}_i = \lfloor z_{i,0}, z_{i,1}, \dots, z_{i,n-1} \rfloor$ for $i = 1, 2, \dots, M$.
In the other words scalar quantization is described as:

$$\mathbf{Q}(\mathbf{d(c)}) = \mathbf{z}_i \tag{11}$$

where $z_{i,k} = v$ if $q_{k,v} \le d_k(c) \le q_{k,v+1}$ for $k = 0, 1, \dots, n-1$.

	v						
k	0	1	2	3	4	5	6
0	0	5	20	35	50	70	256
1	0	5	15	25	35	55	256
2	0	5	10	15	25	35	256
3	0	2	5	10	15	20	256

Table 1. Quantization levels for $\{q_{k,v} : 0 \le k \le n-1,\ 0 \le v \le L\}$ obtained via a 3×3 $(n = 4,\ L = 6)$ filter window

In that way partitioning of n-dimensional space in $M = L^n$ regions is fulfilled, and unique vector $\mathbf{z}_i$ defines a distinct region for $i = 1, 2, \dots, M$. Experimentally determined quantization levels for 3×3 filter window are given in Table 1 (Chen & Wu, 2001). In this study 4-dimensional space has been partitioned in $M = L^n = 6^4 = 1296$ different regions.
Using the scalar quantization an estimation of partition index is fullfilled without multiplication which leads to the decrease of computational complexity in the training and the filtering process.

2.2 LMS weights optimization

Optimal weights are determined to minimize the mean square error, or equivalently the total square error:

$$\varepsilon = \sum_{c \in C} \left[s(c) - \hat{x}(c) \right]^2 \tag{12}$$

where $s(c)$ and $\hat{x}(c)$ denote the original pixel value and its estimate, respectively.
Taking partitioning of n-dimensional space in M exclusive regions into consideration we can write:

$$\varepsilon = \sum_{i=1}^{M} \left\{ \sum_{c:p(c)} \left[s(c) - \hat{x}(c) \right]^2 \right\} \tag{13}$$

where the inner sum, i.e. ε_i is error attributed to the pixels classified into the ith partiotion. Thus, entire error ε can be minimized by achieving the independent minimization of ε_i for $i = 1, 2, \ldots, M$

Following (5) we have:

$$\varepsilon_i = \sum_{c:p(c)=i} \left[s(c) - \hat{x}(c) \right]^2 = \sum_{c:p(c)=i} \left[s(c) - \mathbf{y(c)} \cdot \mathbf{w}_i^{\mathbf{T}} \right]^2 \tag{14}$$

Optimization problem is to find optimal weighting vector $\mathbf{w}_i$ of ith partition for $i = 1, 2, \ldots, M$ and ε_i of each partition should be minimal.

In this study genetic algorithm is used to derive optimal weighting vector $\mathbf{w}_i$ for each partition.

2.3 Recursive implementation

In this study PBM filter is implemented recursively because of obtained results through the simulations on variety of images. Superior results have been produced by the recursive PBM filter in removing noise than nonrecursive design.

The estimate of current pixel value in recursive filtering depends on past filter outputs, with input

$$\mathbf{x'(c)} = \left\{ \hat{x}_1(c), \hat{x}_2(c), \ldots, \hat{x}_n(c), x_{n+1}(c), x_{n+2}(c), \ldots, x_{2n+1}(c) \right\} \tag{15}$$

In the recursive PBM filtering the partition index for current pixel depends on previous filter outputs.

Recursive design of PBM filtering is shown on Figure 2 (Chen & Wu, 2001).

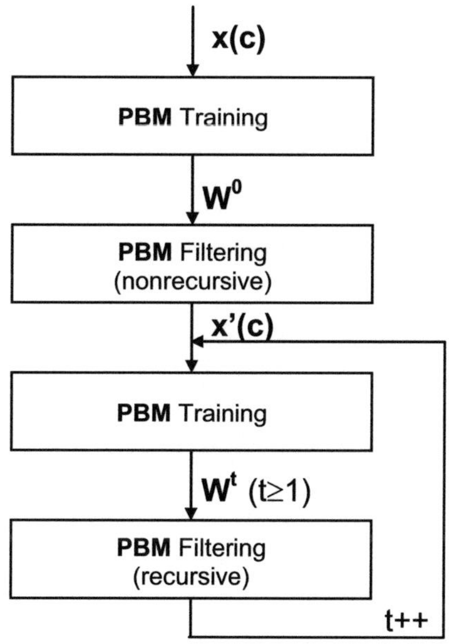

Fig. 2. Schematic diagram of recursive PBM filter

3. Optimization using genetic algorithm

Evolution algorithms are methods for solving optimization problems which are based on the principles of Darwin's evolution theory, i.e. natural selection and survival of the fittest (Koza, 1992; Michalewicz, 1996). The best known algorithms in this class include genetic algorithm, genetic programming, evolutionary programming, evolution strategies, classifier systems, and neural networks. All above mentioned algorithms are based on the same concept-simulating the evolution of organisms of some population through selection, recombination and mutation process (Michalewicz, 1996; Brezocnik, 2000).

Having in mind the nature of optimization problem and available data at the beginning of optimization process, it was decided that genetic algorithm will be used for solving the optimization problem. This choice has been shown as good one because the optimization process is not time-consuming, i.e. genetic algorithm converges very quickly.

3.1 Training process

Matrix of weighting vectors for each partition is obtained by training the filter over reference image. Optimal weights for each partition are obtained using genetic algorithm in the training process (Sovilj-Nikic S. & Sovilj-Nikic I., 2007). Structure of genetic algorithm is shown on Figure 3 (Sovilj-Nikic et al., 2008). Total square error of the current pixel value estimate between all combinations (previously memorized) of vector $\mathbf{y(c)}$ and the original pixel value should be minimal for each partition. In this study the number of memorized combinations was chosen to be 1000.

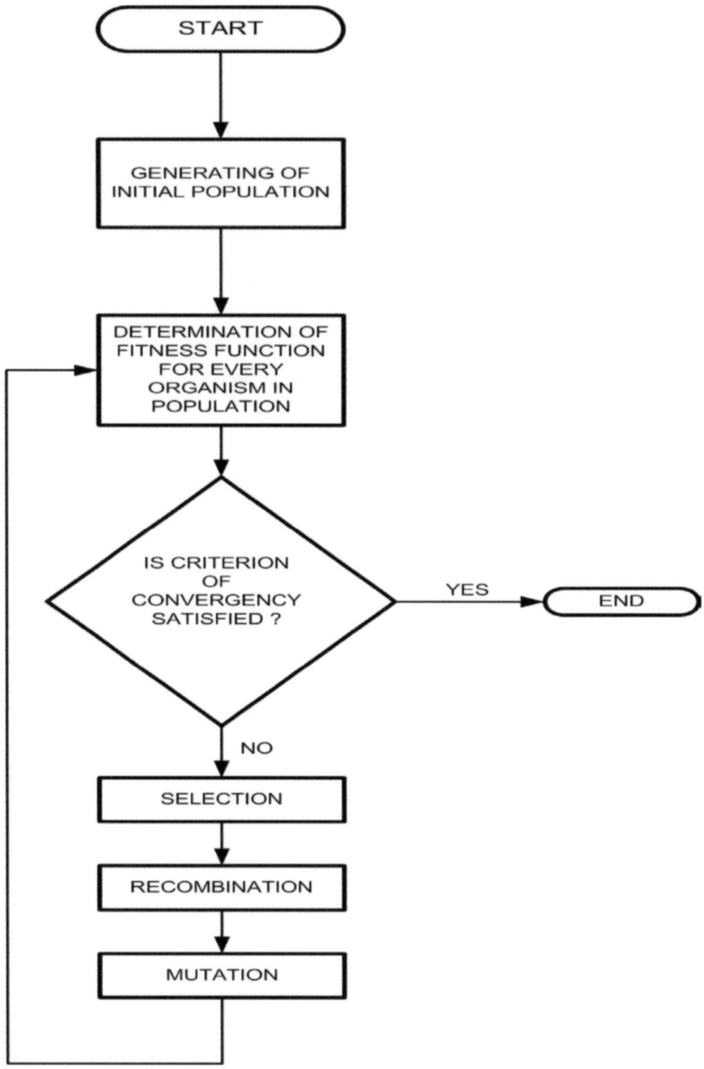

Fig. 3. Structure of genetic algorithm

3.1.1 Optimization function by applying genetic algorithm

Genetic algorithm has been applied for each partition and final result of that procedure is a matrix which consists of weighting vectors for each partition. First step in application of genetic algorithm is to choose population size, i.e. number of individuals in the population (Figure 4). Typical values of population size are from 20 to 500 individuals. Simulations on different values of population size have been shown that population of 120 individuals represents compromise solution for the optimization problem in this study regarding a quality of obtained solution and computational complexity of the algorithm. Individuals of population are generated randomly using Matlab's random numbers generator. Each individual represents potential problem solution, i.e. optimal weighting vector **w** which is one 1×5 vector. Columns of vector **w** are chromosomes (genes) of individuals. Range of values for individual chromosomes is $[-1,1]$ and weighting vectors satisfy location-invariance constraint:

$$\mathbf{e}_{n+1} \cdot \mathbf{w}^{\mathbf{T}} = \mathbf{w} \cdot \mathbf{e}_{n+1}^{\mathbf{T}} = 1 \tag{16}$$

where $\mathbf{e}_N = [1, 1, \dots, 1]$ is an $1 \times N$ vector.
After creating an initial population should evaluate fitness function for each individual in the population, In this case fitness function is a total square error ε, i.e. deviation between estimate of current pixel value and original (uncorrupted) pixel value:

$$\varepsilon = \left(s - \mathbf{y} \cdot \mathbf{w}^{\mathbf{T}}\right)^2 \tag{17}$$

where is:

s uncorrupted pixel value
$\mathbf{y}$ vector of CWM filter outputs
$\mathbf{w}$ weighting vector (individual of population)

After generating initial population comes iterative procedure of genetic operators (selection, crossover and mutation) application to the individuals. This procedure is repeated until the satisfaction of convergence criteria. If convergence criteria is not satisfied the fittest individual in the current population is found. That individual has been kept in the memory. Then, a new population is formed by selecting the more fit individuals. In this study tournament selection is applied to select potential parents. Using Matlab's random numbers generator two parents are chosen randomly and they create their two offsprings in the crossover operation. Crossover enables to exchange information between different potential solutions. In this study decade encoding and real arithmetic crossover is applyed (Michalewicz, 1996).
Crossovered offspring genes are formed as:

$$\begin{aligned} c1(i) &= \frac{k1 \cdot r1(i) + k2 \cdot r2(i)}{2} \\ c2(i) &= \frac{k2 \cdot r1(i) + k1 \cdot r2(i)}{2} \end{aligned} \tag{18}$$

where are:

$c1(i)$ and $c2(i)$ offspring genes at ith position
$r1(i)$ and $r2(i)$ parent genes at ith position
for $i = 1, 2, \dots, 5$

Coefficients *k1* and *k2* are selected randomly from range $[0.9,\ 1.0]$, taking the limitation for range of values of individual genes into consideration. Individual genes, i.e. elements of vector $\mathbf{w}$ have to be in range $[-1,\ 1]$. Offsprings become members of population instead two individuals which have the largest value of fitness function. Then using Matlab's random generator one individual is selected and also one its gene which will be alter.

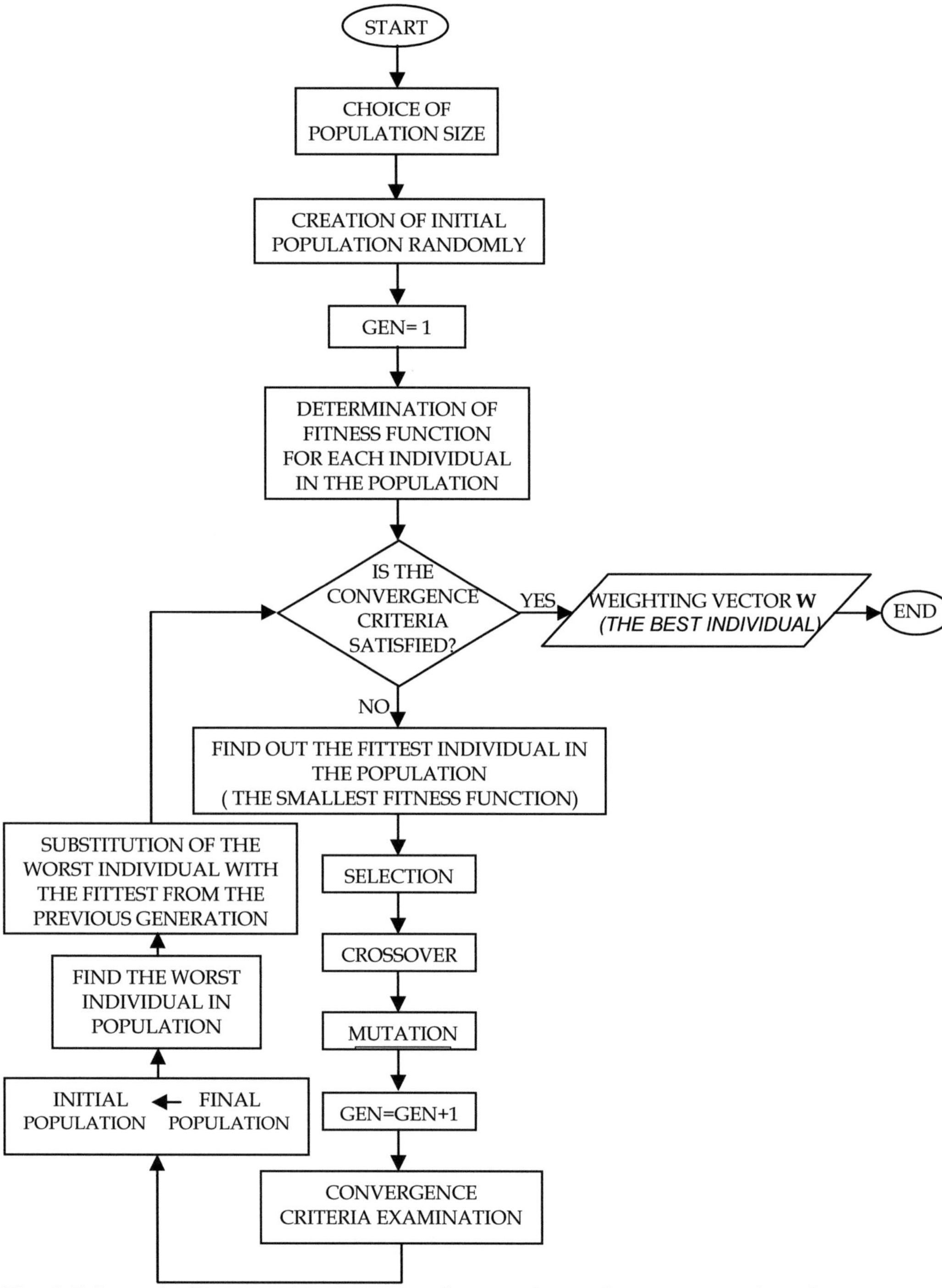

Fig. 4. Schematic diagram of optimization function by applying genetic algorithm

Mutation introduces new genetic material into population. Mutated gene of individual is formed as:

$$c1(i) = k \cdot r1(i) \tag{19}$$

where is:

$c1(i)$ mutated gene of individual at ith position

$r1(i)$ gene of individual at ith position before mutation

$i \in [1, 5]$

Coefficient k is selected randomly from range $[0.9,\ 1.0]$ with the same reason as crossover operation.
After mutation convergence criteria is examined. New population, after application of genetic operators, becomes initial population for the next generation. The worst individual in the current generation is replaced with a best one in the previous generation. Then, convergence criteria is tested and iterative procedure of applying genetic operators is repeated until the satisfaction of convergence criteria. Simulation have been shown that genetic algorithm converges after 50 generations. Satisfying of convergence criteria represents the end of genetic algorithm. And a result is the the fittest individual (with an optimal fitness function), i.e. optimal weighting vector **w** which in a linear combination with vector **y** gives the minimal error of current pixel value estimate.

4. Simulation results and comparison with competitive filters

Performance of PBM filter has been evaluated by simulations on variety of 256×256 test images. Within this study 5 different images (*Bridge, Lena, Camera, Apples, Parrot*) was analyzed. In simulations 3×3 filter window is used, and then $W = 2n + 1 = 9$, i.e. n=4. Therefore, $k = 0, 1, 2, 3$ and the difference vector space is 4-dimensional. Quantization levels are determined experimentally and they are shown in Table 1. Each dimension has $L = 6$ intervals in the range of $[0, 255]$ and the total number of regions is $M = L^n = 6^4 = 1296$. Simulations have been fulfilled on variety of images which have been corrupted with different type of noise:

1. IMPULSE NOISE
2. GAUSSIAN NOISE
3. MIXED GAUSSIAN AND IMPULSE NOISE

For a corruption by impulses with a noise ratio p, only p of total pixels are replaced with impulses and the others keep noise-free. Here, both fixed-valued and random-valued impulses are used. For gray-scale images, noise intensity in the first case corresponds to 0 or 255 with equal probability (i.e. $p/2$), while in the second case, it is uniformly distributed within $[0, 255]$. Another type of noise assumed is the zero-mean additive Gaussian noise with standard deviation σ. The mixed noise is also used by adding Gaussian noise and the fixed-valued impulse noise together.

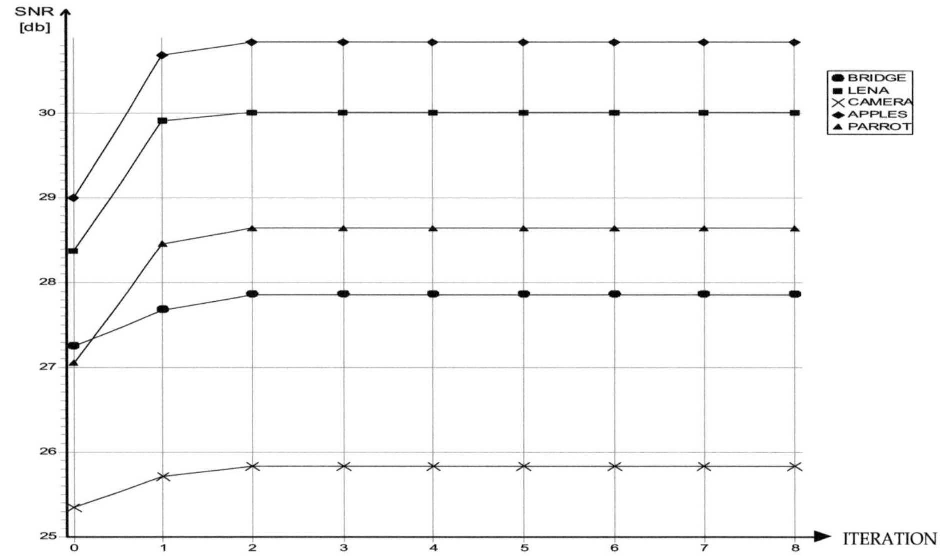

Fig. 5. Results of recursive PBM filtering for different images corrupted by fixed-valued impulses with p=20%

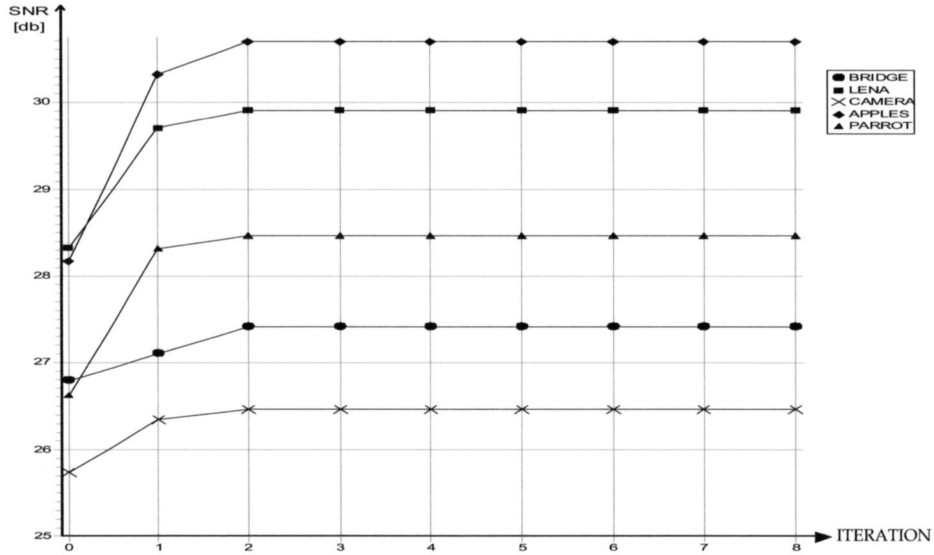

Fig. 6. Results of recursive PBM filtering for different images corrupted by random-valued impulses with p=20%

In this study PBM filter is implemented recursively, because of better results in SNR (signal-noise ratio) obtained by the recursive filtering over nonrecursive design. Results of recursive filtering are shown on Figure 5 and Figure 6 for various images corrupted by fixed-valued and random-valued impulses with p=20%.

Noticable gain has been achieved by recursive filtering and its value is image dependent. It is interesting to note that recursive filtering converges after two iterations of training. This can also see on Figure 5 and Figure 6.

4.1 Comparison with competitive filters

The performance of PBM filter is examined through comparison with competitive filters based on median filtering, including median filter (MED), CWM filter ($\omega = 3$) in recursive

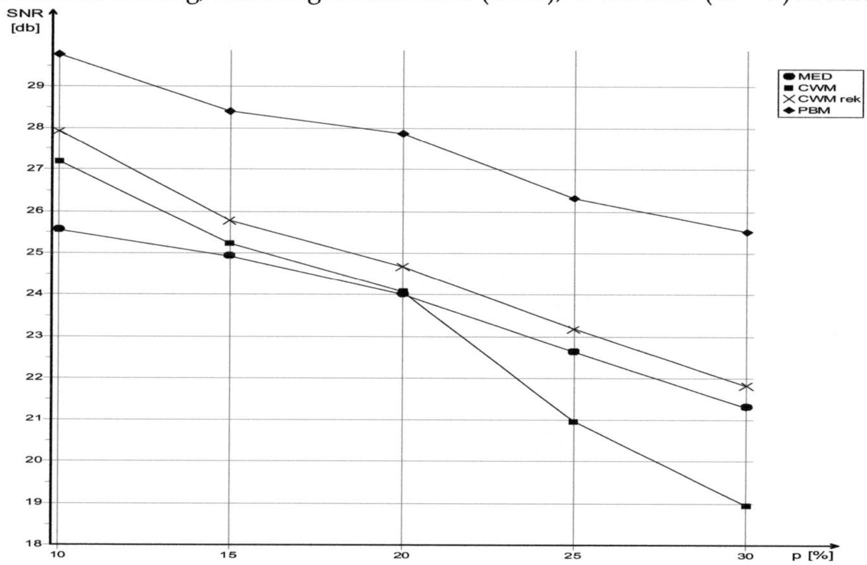

Fig. 7. Performance of different filters in filtering the Bridge image corrupted by fixed-valued impulses

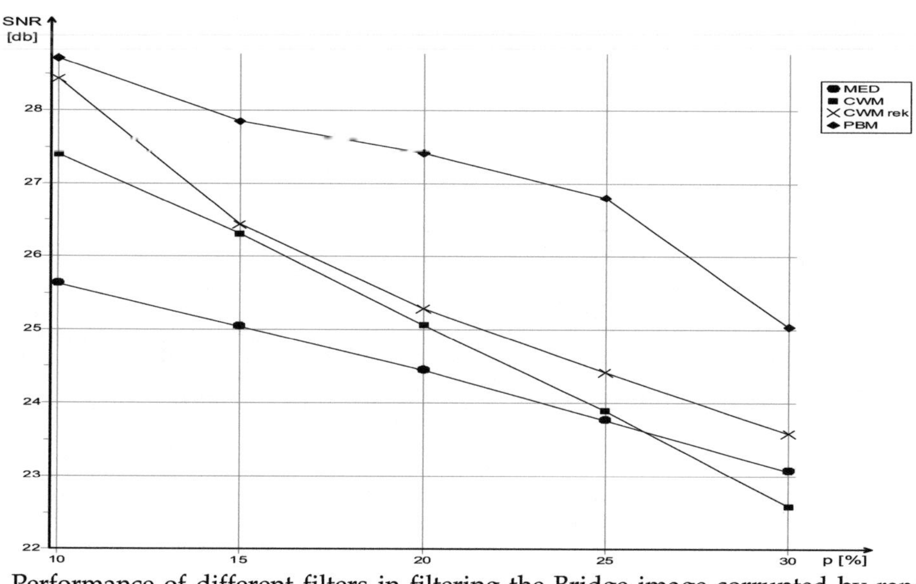

Fig. 8. Performance of different filters in filtering the Bridge image corrupted by random-valued impulses

and nonrecursive design, fuzzy median filter, florencio&schafer, SDROM (state dependent rank order median) filter in recursive and nonrecursive design and nonrecursive PBM filter. The comparative SNR results of filtering the *Bridge* image are given on Figure 7 and Figure 8 where *p* ranges from 10% to 30%. The PBM filter is trained assuming the corruption by 20% impulses, while the same type of noise is used in training and filtering.

FILTER	IMAGE				
	BRIDGE	LENA	CAMERA	APPLES	PARROT
MEDIAN	24.00	26.97	24.20	27.37	25.87
CWM	24.08	25.96	24.39	24.68	23.78
CWM RECURSIVE	24.53	27.36	25.30	27.81	26.03
FLORENCIO&SCHAFER	24.29	24.67	23.85	24.24	23.97
SDROM	25.43	27.55	24.54	27.77	26.20
SDROM RECURSIVE	26.71	29.51	25.48	30.41	28.35
FUZZY MEDIAN	27.42	28.70	25.67	28.25	28.41
PBM NONRECURSIVE	27.25	28.38.	25.35	29.00	27.05
PBM RECURSIVE	27.86	30.01	25.84	30.84	28.64

Table 2. Comparative results in SNR [dB] of filtering different images corrupted by fixed-valued impulse noise with p=20%

FILTER	IMAGE				
	BRIDGE	LENA	CAMERA	APPLES	PARROT
MEDIAN	24.44	27.68	25.25	28.33	25.86
CWM	25.05	28.43	25.76	26.70	25.19
CWM RECURSIVE	25.26	28.37	26.06	28.62	26.59
FLORENCIO&SCHAFER	23.31	24.03	23.02	22.81	22.42
SDROM	25.81	28.60	25.56	28.64	26.77
SDROM RECURSIVE	26.13	29.56	25.27	30.45	27.95
FUZZY MEDIAN	26.03	27.53	24.67	27.79	27.05
PBM NONRECURSIVE	26.79	28.33	25.74	28.17	26.62
PBM RECURSIVE	27.41	29.91	26.46	30.70	28.47

Table 3. Comparative results in SNR [dB] of filtering different images corrupted by random-valued impulse noise with p=20%

The PBM filter yields significant improvement over the other filters. Proposed filter has demonstrated exellent robustness in respect to impulse ratios, regardless of that used in the training.

Tables 2,3,4 and 5 present the comparative SNR results of removing different types of noise on various images. The proposed PBM filter yields better results in suppressing impulse noise (fixed-valued and random-valued), Gaussian noise as well as mixed Gaussian and impulse noise.

FILTER	IMAGE				
	BRIDGE	LENA	CAMERA	APPLES	PARROT
MEDIAN	24.37	26.95	25.15	27.75	26.07
CWM	25.14	26.73	25.75	27.10	26.21
CWM RECURSIVE	25.11	27.20	26.00	27.78	26.53
FLORENCIO&SCHAFER	23.34	24.17	23.95	24.39	23.84
SDROM	22.90	23.76	22.84	24.07	23.44
SDROM RECURSIVE	22.95	23.90	22.76	24.14	23.51
FUZZY MEDIAN	22.75	22.80	22.06	22.81	22.67
PBM NONRECURSIVE	26.13	27.53	26.63	27.87	27.02
PBM RECURSIVE	25.96	27.71	25.57	28.11	27.11

Table 4. Comparative results in SNR [dB] of filtering different images corrupted by Gaussian noise with $\sigma = 20$

FILTER	IMAGE				
	BRIDGE	LENA	CAMERA	APPLES	PARROT
MEDIAN	22.29	23.91	22.57	24.10	23.66
CWM	21.21	22.05	21.32	21.81	21.91
CWM RECURSIVE	22.61	24.08	23.09	24.07	23.84
FLORENCIO&SCHAFER	20.12	20.64	20.13	20.62	20.84
SDROM	21.06	22.07	21.09	22.15	21.95
SDROM RECURSIVE	22.06	23.15	21.95	23.36	22.89
FUZZY MEDIAN	21.92	22.27	21.48	22.21	22.22
PBM NONRECURSIVE	23.73	24.30	23.11	24.50	24.25
PBM RECURSIVE	24.09	25.87	23.88	26.48	25.71

Table 5. Comparative results in SNR [dB] of filtering different images corrupted by mixed Gaussian ($\sigma = 20$) and impulse noise (p=20%)

The performance of PBM filter proposed in this study in reducing different types of noise can also notice on Figure 9, Figure 10, Figure 11 and Figure 12. PBM filter yields better image quality with respect to noise suppression and detail preservation than the other methods, by producing a visually more pleasing image.

Original image

Noisy image

Image filtered by median filter

Image filtered by CWM filter

Image filtered by recursive CWM filter

Image filtered by recursive SDROM filter

Image filtered by SDROM filter

Image filtered by recursive PMB filter

Fig. 9. Comparison of the restoration performance of different filtering type for the Bridge image corrupted by 20% fixed-valued impulses

Original image

Noisy image

Image filtered by median filter

Image filtered by CWM filter

Image filtered by recursive CWM filter

Image filtered by recursive SDROM filter

Image filtered by SDROM filter

Image filtered by recursive PMB filter

Fig. 10. Comparison of the restoration performance of different filtering type for the Parrot image corrupted by 20% random-valued impulses

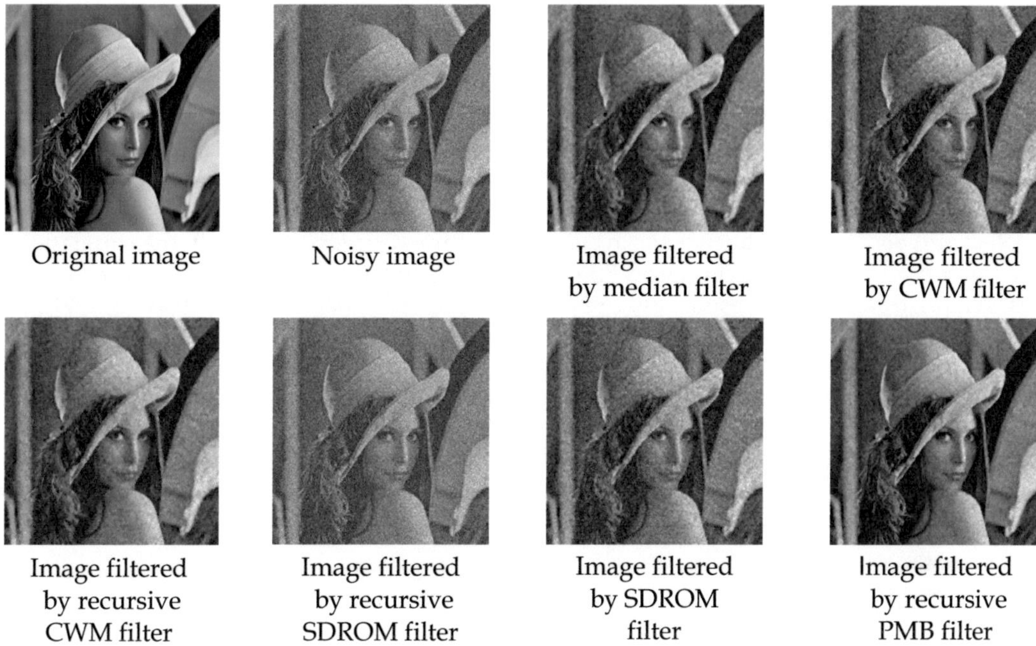

Fig. 11. Comparison of the restoration performance of different filtering type for the Lena image corrupted by Gaussian noise with $\sigma = 30$

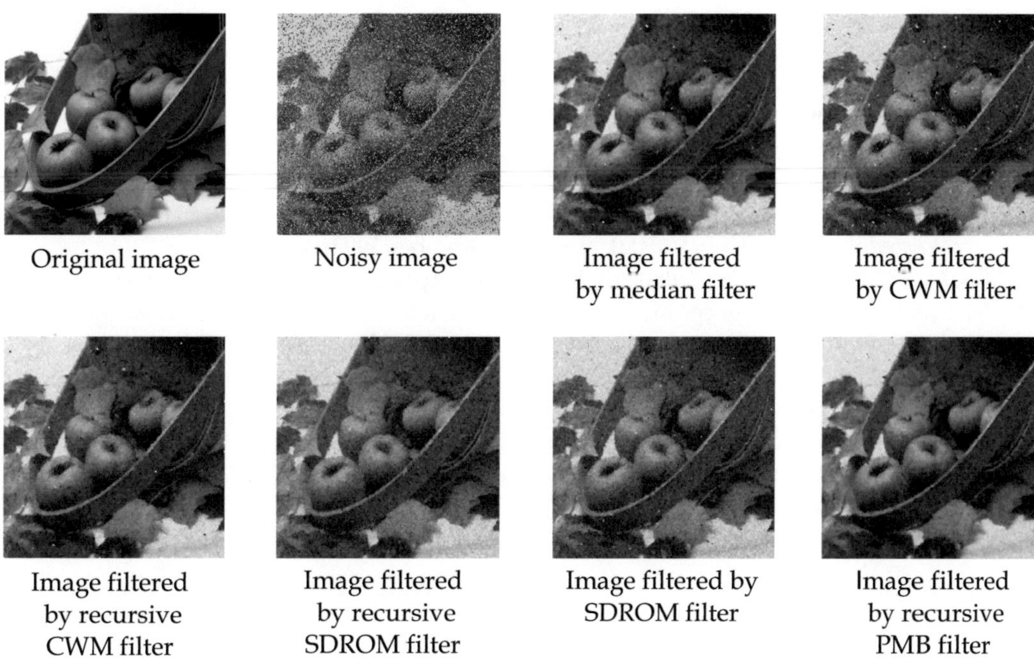

Fig. 12. Comparison of the restoration performance of different filtering type for the Apple image corrupted by mixed Gaussian noise ($\sigma = 20$) and impulse noise (p=20%)

5. Conclusion

In this chapter an adaptive filtering using genetic algorithm in the training process is proposed. In the proposed filtering scheme, at each location, observed vector is classified into one of *M* exclusive partitions, and an optimal particular filtering operation is then activated. Optimal weighting vector of each partition is derived using genetic algorithm in training the filter over a reference image. Recursive implementation of the proposed filter is applied and shown to produce better results than its nonrecursive design. In the simulations over variety of images, the proposed PBM filter using genetic algorithm in training process has demonstrated better results in suppressing different types of noise than competitive filters in terms of the SNR [dB] as well as the perceived image quality.

In the future, research will be directed to the forming of reference image which will provide more information for the genetic algorithm in the training process and improve the filtering process.

6. References

Brezocnik, M. (2000). Uporaba genetskega programiranja v inteligentnih proizvodnih sistemih, Fakulteta za strojnistvo, ISBN 86-435-0306-1, Maribor

Chen, T. & Wu, R. H. (2001). Application of Parition-Based Median Type Filter for Suppressing Noise in Images, *IEEE Trans. on Image Processing,* Vol. 10, (June 2001), pp. 829-836

Ko, S. J. & Lee, Y. H. (1991). Center Weighted Median Filters and Their Application to Image Enhancement, *IEEE Trans. on Circuits System,* Vol. 38, (September 1991). pp. 984-993

Koza, J. R. (1992). *Genetic Programming,* The MIT Press, Massachusetts

Michalewicz, Z. (1996). *Genetic Algorithms + Data Structures = Evolution Programs,* Springer-Verlag, ISBN 3-540-60676-9, Berlin

Pitas, I. & Venetsanopoulos, A. (1991). *Nonlinear Digital Filters-Principles and Applications,* Kluwer International Series, ISBN 0-7923-9049-0, Massachusetts

Pitas, I. & Venetsanopoulos, A. (1992), Order Statistics in Digital Image Processing, *Proceedings of the IEEE,* Vol. 80, No. 12, (December 1992), pp. 1893-1921

Sovilj-Nikic, I.; Sovilj, B. & Brezocnik,M. (2008). Application of Genetic Algorithm in Analysis of Influence of Gear Hob Geometric Parameters on the Tool Life, *Proceedings of ICMEN,* pp. 145-154, ISBN 978-960-243-649-3, Kallithea, October 2008, Aristoteles University of Thessaloniki, Thessaloniki

Sovilj-Nikic, S. & Sovilj-Nikic, I. (2007). Application of Genetic Algorithm in Median Filtering, *Proceedings of IMCSIT,* pp. 127-139, ISSN 1896-7094, Wisla, October 2007, Polish Information Processing Society in cooperation with IEEE Computer Society (Poland Chapter) and Systems Research Institute of the Polish Academy of Science, Katowice

Direction of Arrival Estimation using the PRIME Algorithm

H.K. Hwang and Zekeriya Aliyazicioglu
California State Polytechnic University, Pomona
CA, USA

1. Introduction

Instead of using a single sensor, an array processing system (Allen & Ghavami, 2005 and Trees, 2002) with innovative signal processing can enhance the resolution of signal parameters. An array sensor system has multiple sensors distributed in space. This array configuration provides spatial samplings of the received waveform. A sensor array has better performance than the single sensor in signal reception and parameter estimation. It also has the ability to identify multiple targets.

Array processing systems are used in a wide range of applications such as radar, sonar, seismology, mobile communications, and medical diagnostics (Forsythe, 1997, Leeet et al., 2005, Xu et al., 2001, Hwang & Grados, 2008, Aliyazicioglu & Hwang, 2008). For example, in defense applications, it is important to identify the direction of a possible threat. One example of a commercial application is to identify the direction of an emergency cell phone call in order to dispatch a rescue team to the proper location. Accurate estimation of a signal direction of arrival (DOA) has received a tremendous interest in communication and radar systems of commercial and military applications in the past decades.

This chapter describes the estimation of signal parameters such as signal frequency or DOA using an array processing systems and advanced signal processing algorithms. This chapter concentrates on the discussion of the *P*olynomial *R*oot *I*ntersection for *M*ulti-Dimensional *E*stimation (PRIME) algorithm (Hatke & Keith, 1994). Processing the received data by PRIME algorithm requires array processor. The PRIME algorithm can be considered the extension of the *Mu*ltiple *Si*gnals *C*lassification (MUSIC) (Schmidt, 1986) and Root MUSIC algorithms (Ren & William, 1997), which are based on the Eigen-analysis method.

To estimate the frequency of the sinusoid or the DOA of a narrowband signal using the conventional method suffers resolution limitation. For example, frequency resolution Δf using N point Fast Fourier Transform (FFT) is $\Delta f = 1/NT$, where T is the sampling period. Improved frequency resolution using FFT would require a large number of data samples. In many real time applications, using a large sample data is not always feasible. If there are multiple sinusoids with a frequency spacing less than Δf, FFT won't be able to resolve them.

The angle resolution of a conventional antenna is limited by the antenna mainlobe beamwidth. The mainlobe beamwidth is proportional to the signal wavelength and inversely proportional to the physical size of the antenna. Improving angle resolution by using large aperture antenna or operating at higher frequency is not always a viable solution. Certain systems such as aircraft antennas or missile seekers have physical size limitations; they cannot accommodate large aperture antennas. Higher frequency usually has a larger amount of atmospheric absorption; it may limit the detection range.

Rather than improve the DOA of frequency resolution by hardware improvement, an array processor together with an advanced signal processing algorithm provides an innovative solution that improves the resolution of parameter estimation. This chapter provides a brief review of the PRIME algorithm and its application in estimating a signal DOA.

Since the PRIME algorithm is closely related to MUSIC and root MUSIC, section 2 provides a brief review of the MUSIC algorithm. Computer simulations are used to demonstrate the enhanced resolution of MUSIC in temporal and spatial processing applications. The effects of estimation accuracy as a function of signal to noise ratio (SNR), and correlation matrix estimation based on different temporal averaging, are also discussed. Section 3 discusses the root MUSIC algorithm. Basic equations for frequency and angle estimations are derived. Some simulation examples demonstrate how to estimate signal parameters without having to use a scan vector. Finally, the extension of the root MUSIC to PRIME equivalent to estimate multiple parameters is discussed in section 4. Estimation of a signal DOA (elevation and azimuth angles) is used as a demonstration example. Estimation of two independent parameters requires two independent equations. These are derived from a subset and full array approaches and their simulation examples are discussed in section 4.

2. The MUSIC Algorithm

*Mu*ltiple *Si*gnals Classification (MUSIC) is one of the most commonly applied eigen-analysis methods. It works quite well both in frequency estimation or signal direction of arrival (DOA) estimation.

Consider the received data sequence u(n) consisting of L independent sinusoids in the white noise environment. The received data u(n) is expressed in Equation 2.1

$$u(n) = \sum_{k=1}^{L} A_k e^{j(2\pi f_k n+\theta_k)} + w(n),\ n = 1, 2, \ldots, N \tag{2.1}$$

where A_k, f_k, θ_k are the amplitude, frequency and phase of k independent sinusoids and w(n) is the white noise sequence.

Define the received data vector **u** as $\mathbf{u} = [u(1), u(2), \ldots, u(N)]^T$, then the data vector correlation matrix **R** is $\mathbf{R} = E[\mathbf{u}\mathbf{u}^H]$, where the superscript H represents the matrix complex conjugate transpose (Hermitian). Using the relationship of Equation (2.1) and independent noise assumption, matrix **R** can be expressed as Equation (2.2).

$$\mathbf{R} = \mathbf{SPS}^H + \sigma_w^2 \mathbf{I} \tag{2.2}$$

where $\mathbf{P} = \text{diag}[A_1^2, A_2^2, \ldots, A_L^2]$, $\mathbf{S} = \begin{bmatrix} e^{j2\pi f_1} & e^{j2\pi f_2} & \cdots & e^{j2\pi f_L} \\ e^{j2\pi 2f_1} & e^{j2\pi 2f_2} & \cdots & e^{j2\pi 2f_L} \\ \vdots & \vdots & \ddots & \vdots \\ e^{j2\pi Nf_1} & e^{j2\pi Nf_2} & \cdots & e^{j2\pi Nf_L} \end{bmatrix}$ and σ_w^2 is the noise variance and **I** is the identity matrix.

Let $\lambda_1, \lambda_2, \ldots, \lambda_N$, are the eigenvalues of the correlation matrix **R** and $\lambda_1 \geq \lambda_2 \geq \ldots \geq \lambda_N$, their associate eigenvectors are $\mathbf{q}_1, \mathbf{q}_2, \ldots, \mathbf{q}_N$ respectively.

If there are L independent signals, then eigenvectors $\mathbf{q}_1, \mathbf{q}_2, \ldots, \mathbf{q}_L$ span over the signal and noise subspace and eigenvectors $\mathbf{q}_{L+1}, \mathbf{q}_{L+2}, \ldots, \mathbf{q}_N$ span over the noise only subspace. Signal and noise subspace and noise only subspace are mutually orthogonal.

For frequency estimation, the MUSIC spectrum is computed according to Equation (2.3).

$$S_{MUSIC}(f) = \frac{1}{\mathbf{s}^H(f)\mathbf{V}_N\mathbf{V}_N^H\mathbf{s}(f)} \tag{2.3}$$

where $\mathbf{V}_N = [\mathbf{q}_{L+1}, \mathbf{q}_{L+2}, \ldots, \mathbf{q}_N]$, and $\mathbf{s}(f) = [1, e^{j2\pi f}, \ldots, e^{j2\pi(N-1)f}]^T$ is a scan vector that scans over all possible frequencies. If the scan frequency happens to be equal to one of the signal frequencies, then the scan vector is orthogonal to column space of $\mathbf{V}_N$. Thus the dominate peaks of $S_{MUSIC}(f)$ correspond to the L number of signals and frequencies.

The following example demonstrates the enhanced frequency resolution of the MUSIC algorithm.

Suppose there are 32 received data samples u(n), u(1), n = 0, 1, . . ., 31, where data sample u(n) consists of two equal amplitude sinusoids with normalized frequencies 0.115 and 0.135, and white noise. The signal to noise ratio = 10 dB.

$$u(n) = e^{j2\pi f_1 n} + e^{j(2\pi f_2 n + \theta)} + w(n) \tag{2.4}$$

where $f_1 = .115$, $f_2 = .135$, θ is random phase and w(n) is the white noise sequence.

The theoretical correlation matrix **R** is:

$$\mathbf{R}=\begin{bmatrix} 2+\sigma_w^2 & e^{-j2\pi 2_1}+e^{-j2\pi 2_2} & \cdots & e^{-j2\pi 2_1(M-1)}+e^{-j2\pi 2_2(M-1)} \\ e^{j2\pi 2_1}+e^{j2\pi 2_2} & 2+\sigma_w^2 & \cdots & e^{-j2\pi 2_1(M-2)}+e^{-j2\pi 2_2(M-2)} \\ \vdots & \vdots & \ddots & \vdots \\ e^{j2\pi 2_1(M-1)}+e^{j2\pi 2_2(M-1)} & e^{j2\pi 2_1(M-2)}+e^{j2\pi 2_2(M-2)} & \cdots & 2+\sigma_w^2 \end{bmatrix} \quad (2.5)$$

The estimated correlation matrix $\mathbf{\Phi}$ is computed from the following Equation.

$$\mathbf{\Phi} = \mathbf{A}^H\mathbf{A} \quad (2.6)$$

where $\mathbf{A}$ is the data matrix and matrix $\mathbf{A}^H$ is expressed as the following equation.

$$\mathbf{A}^H = \begin{bmatrix} u(M) & u(M+1) & \cdots & u(N) \\ u(M-1) & u(M) & \cdots & u(N-1) \\ \vdots & \vdots & \ddots & \vdots \\ u(1) & u(2) & \cdots & u(N-M+1) \end{bmatrix} \quad (2.7)$$

where M is the rank of matrix $\mathbf{A}$.

Figure 2.1 shows the spectrum plots of two sinusoids in white noise background. The signal to noise ratio (SNR) in this simulation is 10 dB. The blue curve is the spectrum by 256 point FFT method. Since there are only 32 data samples available, we padded an additional 224 zeros. This curve shows that the FFT method cannot resolve two closely frequency spaced signals. The green and red curves are the spectrum estimated by the MUSIC algorithm. The correlation matrix of the green curve is based on the theoretical equation defined by Equation (2.5); the correlation matrix of the red curve is a derivation based on the simulated data defined by Equation (2.6). Both curves show two clear peaks. The peaks of the green curve are at normalized frequencies of 0.1152 and 0.1348, respectively. They are very close to the true frequencies. The peaks of the red curve are at normalized frequencies of 0.1133 and 0.1387 respectively. They are a little bit off the true signal frequencies compared with the theoretical result. Also, their peaks are about 10 dB below the corresponding green curve. This Figure clearly shows that the MUSIC spectrum is very effective in resolving closely frequency spaced signals. A 5×5 matrix correlation matrix was used in this simulation study.

Figure 2.1 shows the performance degradation of the MUSIC algorithm based on finite received data samples. Increasing the sample number improves the estimation of correlation matrix and consequently an improved signal frequency estimation can be achieved. Figure 2.2 compares the performance of frequency estimation by the MUSIC algorithm with 32, 64 and 128 data samples. The red, green and blue curves in Figure 2.2 are MUSIC spectrum plots based on 32, 64 and 128 data samples. The peak frequencies are listed in Table 2.1. Table 2.1 and Figure 2.2 show that as the number of data sample increases, the estimated frequencies get closer to the true signal frequencies and the peaks of the MUSIC spectrum also increase.

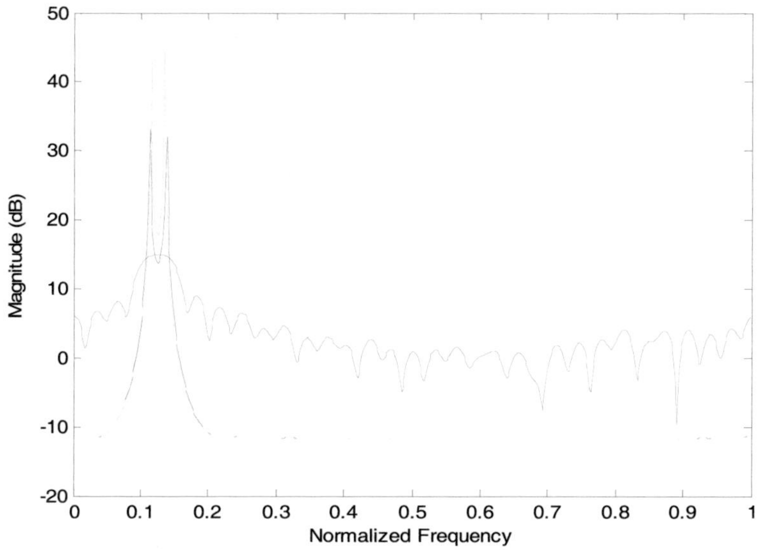

Fig. 2.1 Frequency Estimation by FFT and MUSIC Methods

	f_1	f_2
N = 32	0.1113	0.1387
N = 64	0.1152	0.1367
N=128	0.1152	0.1348

Table 2.1 Peak Frequencies of the MUSIC Spectrum

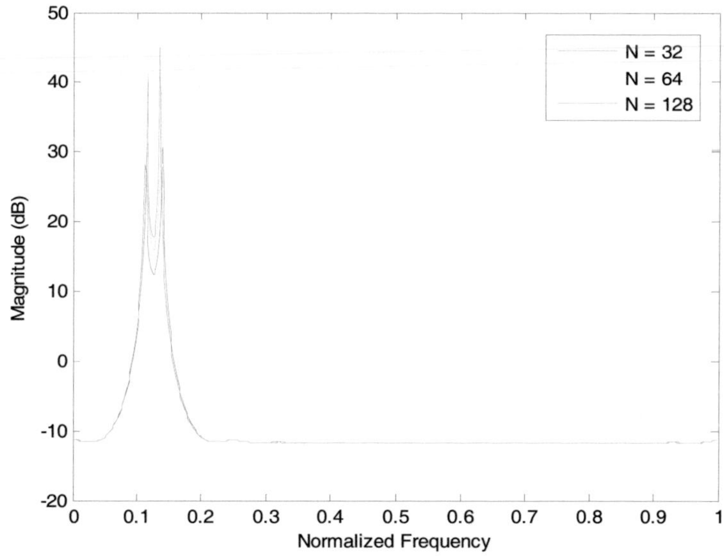

Fig. 2.2 Frequency Estimation by the MUSIC Method with 32, 64 and 128 Data Samples

Frequency estimation using the MUSIC algorithm can be considered as processing the received waveform in time domain (temporal) processing. This algorithm can also apply to spatial processing such as applications of sensor array systems.

Suppose there is a narrowband signal that impinges upon the uniformly spaced linear array antenna (ULA) with incident angle θ. The inter-element spacing of ULA d is $d = \lambda/2$, where λ is the signal wavelength. The ULA configuration is shown in Figure 2.3.

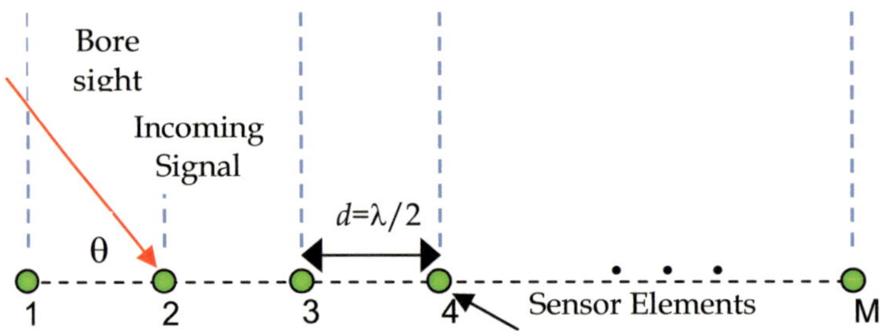

Fig. 2.3 Uniformly Spaced Linear Array Antenna

The narrowband waveform can be modeled as:

$$s(t) = m(t)\, e^{j2\pi f_c t} \tag{2.8}$$

where f_c is the center frequency.

If the signal impinges on the ULA with incident angle θ, the additional propagation path of the adjacent sensor is dcosθ. This additional path causes a propagation delay $\tau = d\cos\theta/c$ where c is the speed of light. If we choose the signal received by the first sensor $s_1(t)$ as the reference, the signal picked up by the kth sensor $s_k(t)$ is

$$s_k(t) = m[t - (k\text{-}1)\tau]\, e^{j2\pi f_c (t-(k-1)\tau)} \tag{2.9}$$

From the narrowband signal assumption, $m(t - (k\text{-}1)\,\tau) \approx m(t)$, and defining the electrical angle β as $\beta = -2\pi d\cos\theta/\lambda$, signal $s_k(t)$ can be expressed as

$$s_k(t) = s_1(t) e^{j(k-1)\beta} \tag{2.10}$$

If there are L independent signals impinging on the ULA with incident angle $\theta_1, \ldots, \theta_L$, in the presence of independent white noise with variance σ_w^2, then the theoretical spatial correlation matrix **R** of the ULA is

$$\mathbf{R} = \mathbf{SPS}^H + \sigma_w^2 \mathbf{I} \tag{2.11}$$

where matrices **P** and **S** are defined by:

$$\mathbf{P} = \text{diag}[P_1, \ldots, P_L] \tag{2.12}$$

$$\mathbf{S} = \begin{bmatrix} 1 & 1 & \cdots & 1 \\ e^{j\beta_1} & e^{j\beta_2} & \cdots & e^{j\beta_L} \\ \vdots & \vdots & \ddots & \vdots \\ e^{j(N-1)\beta_1} & e^{j(N-1)\beta_2} & \cdots & e^{j(N-1)\beta_L} \end{bmatrix} \tag{2.13}$$

and σ_w^2 is the noise variance, P_k, $k = 1, 2, \ldots, L$. are the power of kth signal.

The estimated spatial covariance matrix $\mathbf{\Phi}$ using temporal average method with M snapshots is given as:

$$\mathbf{\Phi} = \mathbf{A}^H\mathbf{A} \tag{2.14}$$

where $\mathbf{A}$ is the data matrix, matrix $\mathbf{A}^H$ is given by the following equation.

$$\mathbf{A}^H = [\mathbf{u}_1, \mathbf{u}_2, \ldots, \mathbf{u}_N] \tag{2.15}$$

and $\mathbf{u}_k = [u_1(k), u_2(k), \ldots, u_M(k)]^T$ is the received data vector of sensor array or the snapshot at sample time k, N is the number of snapshot.

The estimated correlation matrix $\mathbf{\Phi}$ asymptotically approaches the theoretical matrix $\mathbf{R}$ as the number of snapshots increases. Therefore in order to have an accurate estimation of the correlation matrix the observation time must be sufficiently long. However, some real time radar signal processing applications cannot afford a long observation time. Correlation matrix estimation techniques like the spatial smoothing method (Haykin, 2002) are better suited for use in time sensitive systems.

Equations (2.2), (2.11) show that both temporal and spatial processing have an identical mathematical form. The following example shows the application of spectral processing to estimate the signal DOA using the MUSIC algorithm. The scan vector $\mathbf{s}$ used in this application is $\mathbf{s}(\theta) = [1, e^{j\beta}, \ldots, e^{j(M-1)\beta}]^T$, where parameter β is related to the DOA angle by $\beta = -2\pi d\cos\theta/\lambda$.

Suppose there are two narrowband signals impinging upon the 16 element ULA from angles of 40° and 50°. The estimated signal DOA can be found from the peak of the MUSIC spectrum. The SNR in this simulation is 10 dB and the estimated correlation matrix is based on simulated data averaged over 32 snapshots. Figure 2.4 shows the simulation result of the estimated DOA using a ULA consisting of 6, 8 and 10 elements.

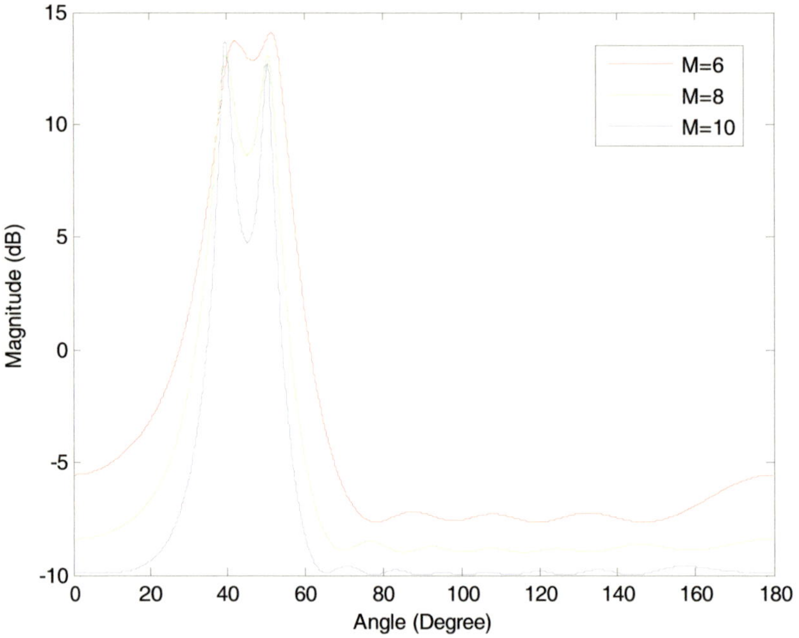

Fig. 2.4 DOA Estimation using ULA with 6, 8, 10 Elements

From Figure 2.4, with 6 element ULA (red curve), the MUSIC spectrum barely shows two peaks. As the number of elements increases to 8 (green curve) and 10 (blue curve), the MUSIC spectrum clearly shows two distinct peaks. The peak values of the green curve are at 39.6° and 50.1°, the peak values of the blue curve are at 39.8° and 50.3° respectively. The estimated DOA angles are fairly close to the true DOA angles.

Equation (2.14) shows the estimated correlation matrix based on temporal averaging over N snapshots. Increasing the number of snapshots N improves the estimation of the covariance matrix. Improving the estimation of the correlation matrix provides a more accurate DOA estimation. Figure 2.5 shows the DOA estimation using an 8 element ULA with an estimated covariance matrix based on temporal averaging over 16 (red curve), 32 (green curve) and 64 (blue curve) snapshots.

The peak values of the MUSIC spectrum in Figure 2.5 are listed in Table 2.2.

	θ_1	θ_2
N = 16	38.8°	50.8°
N = 32	39.6°	50.5°
N = 64	40.1°	49.9°

Table 2.2 Peak Values of the MUSIC Spectrum

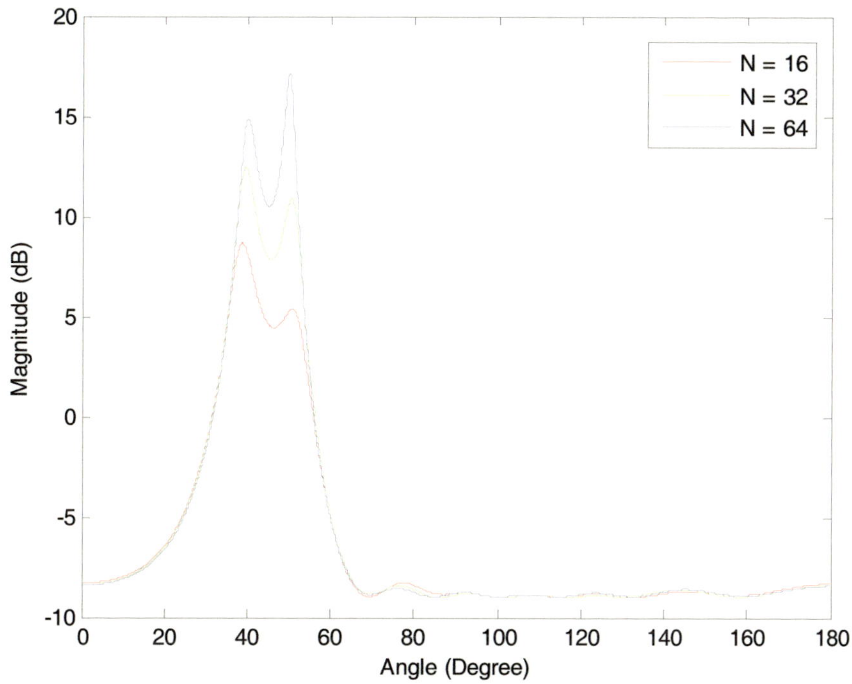

Fig. 2.5 DOA Estimation using an 8 Element ULA with Temporal Averaging over 16, 32, 64 Snapshots

Figure 2.5 and Table 2.2 show that the accuracy of the DOA estimation can be improved by increasing the number of snapshots in the correlation matrix estimation. Increasing the number of snapshots from 16 to 32 to 64 not only provides clearer peaks, but their peak values also increase.

3. Root Music Algorithm

To estimate frequency or signal DOA angles with the MUSIC algorithm requires using a scan vector to scan over all possible frequencies or over all possible direction angles. To obtain fine resolution, we need many frequency or angle sample points. Consequently, it requires high processing resources. Root MUSIC algorithm is a modification to MUSIC without using a scan vector. The estimated frequencies or DOA angles can be obtained by finding the L roots closest to unit circle of the following Equation.

$$J(z) = \mathbf{z}^H \mathbf{V}_N \mathbf{V}_N^H \mathbf{z} = 0 \tag{3.1}$$

where the steering vector **z** is

$$\mathbf{z} = [1, z^{-1}, z^{-2}, \ldots, z^{-(N-1)},]^T \tag{3.2}$$

and $z = e^{j2\pi f}$ for frequency estimation and $z = e^{j\beta}$ for angle estimation.

The frequency and angle are determined by the following Equations.

$$f_k = \frac{1}{2\pi}\arg(z_k) \quad , \quad k = 1, 2, \ldots, L \tag{3.3}$$

$$\theta_k = \cos^{-1}\left[\frac{\lambda}{2\pi d}\arg(z_k)\right], \quad k = 1, 2, \ldots, L \tag{3.4}$$

The roots of J(z) contain the directional information of the incoming signals. Ideally, the roots of J(z) corresponding to the signals' frequency or DOA would be on the unit circle, however due to the presence of noise the roots may not necessarily be exactly on the unit circle. In this case, the L roots closest to the unit circle represent the L incoming signals frequencies or DOA. These selected roots, by themselves, do not directly represent the frequency or incoming angle. For each root, the frequency or incoming angle can be found by computing Equations (3.3) and (3.4).

Consider a 16 elements ULA with an inter-element spacing that equals one half wavelength. If this were a conventional fixed antenna, its mainlobe beamwidth would be around 7°. This antenna array will not be able to resolve multiple signals if their angle separation is less than 7 degrees. Using the root MUSIC algorithm, this ambiguity can be easily resolved.

Let $x_i(1), x_i(2), \ldots, x_i(N)$ represent the received data samples from i^{th} element, where i = 1, 2, . . , M. The incoming data matrix **A** can be given

$$\mathbf{A}^H = \begin{bmatrix} x_1(1) & x_1(2) & .. & x_1(N) \\ x_2(1) & x_2(2) & .. & x_2(N) \\ \vdots & \vdots & :: & \vdots \\ x_M(1) & x_M(2) & .. & x_M(N) \end{bmatrix} \tag{3.5}$$

The estimated correlation matrix **Φ** is computer by

$$\mathbf{\Phi} = \mathbf{A}^H\mathbf{A} \tag{3.6}$$

From the estimated correlation matrix **Φ**, the eigenvalues can be computed. The columns of matrix $\mathbf{V}_N$ are the eigenvectors associated with the M-L smallest eigenvalues of matrix **Φ**. Once this matrix is available, the signals DOA can be derived from L roots of the polynomial J(z) closest to the unit circle.

If there are two signals impinging upon a 16 element ULA from angles of 40° and 46°, the roots computed from Equation (3.1) are shown in Figure 3.1. In this simulation, the number of snapshots N is 32 and the signal to noise ratio is 20 dB.

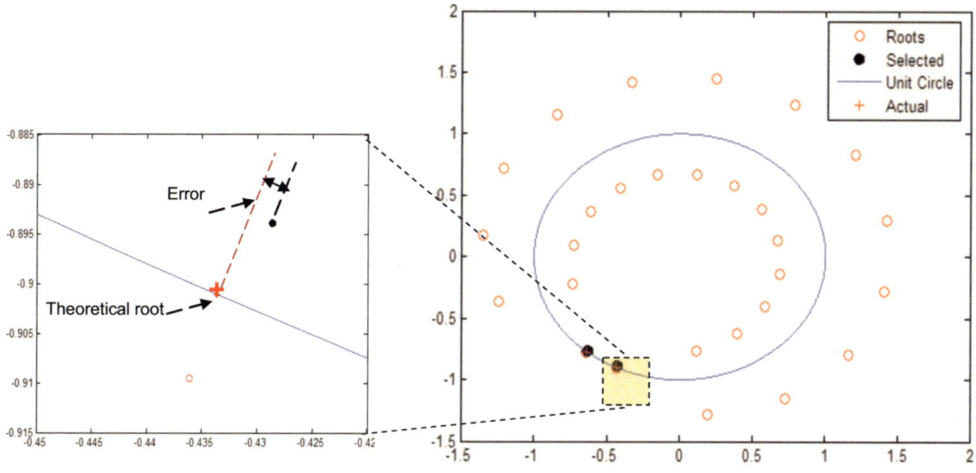

Fig. 3.1 Roots Polynomial J(z)

Figure 3.1 shows that when the angle separation between two signals is smaller than the mainlobe beamwidth, two distinct pairs of roots closest to the unit circle can easily be identified. It is shown in the zoom area that one of the roots is very close to the theoretical root of the signal DOA. Further reduce the angle separation to 3°, and 1.5°, and the results are very similar to Figure 3.1. Thus, the spatial resolution is improved by root MUSIC algorithm.

Equation (3.4) converts the roots of polynomial J(z) to the signal DOA. Assume there are two signals impinging on a 16 element ULA with 20 dB SNR and taking 32 snapshots, histograms of the estimated signal DOA with different angle separations are shown in Figure 3.2.

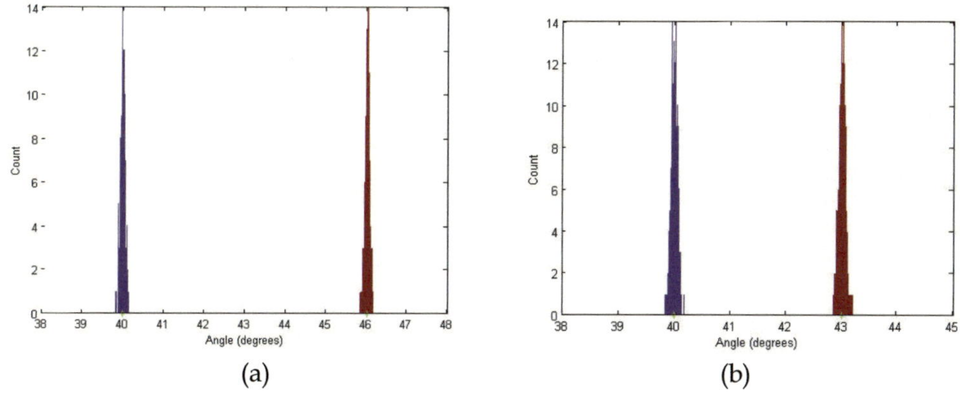

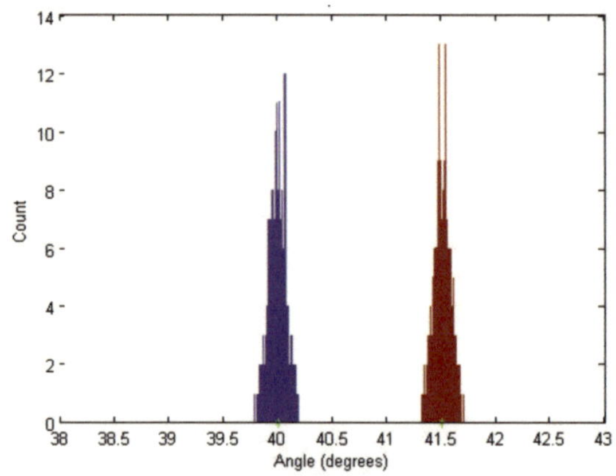

(c)

Fig. 3.2 Histograms of the Estimated Signal DOA for Angle Separation equal 6°, 3°, and 1.5°

The estimated means and variances based on 1000 trials are summarized in Table 3.1.

Angle Separation	6°		3°		1.5°	
True Angles	40°	46°	40°	43°	40°	41.5°
Estimated Mean	39.9972°	46.0041°	39.9998°	42.9995°	39.9999°	41.4987°
Variance	0.0009	0.0012	0.0023	0.0025	0.0047	0.0042

Table 3.1 Estimated Mean and Variance of DOAs for SNR = 20 dB

Figure 3.2 and Table 3.1 show that the estimation variance increases as the angle separation becomes smaller.

Increasing the estimated correlation matrix from 32 snapshots to 96 snapshots reduces the estimated variance. Figure 3.3 compares the histogram of the estimated signals' DOA for 20 dB SNR, and the signals' DOA are 40° and 41.5° for 32 and 96 snapshots. The estimated mean values and variances based on 1000 trials are listed in Table 3.2.

Number of Snapshots	32		96	
True Angles	40°	41.5°	40°	41.5°
Estimated Mean	39.9999°	41.4987°	39.9992°	41.5008°
Variance	0.0047	0.0042	0.0015	0.0016

Table 3.2 The Estimated Mean and Variance of DOAs for SNR = 20 dB

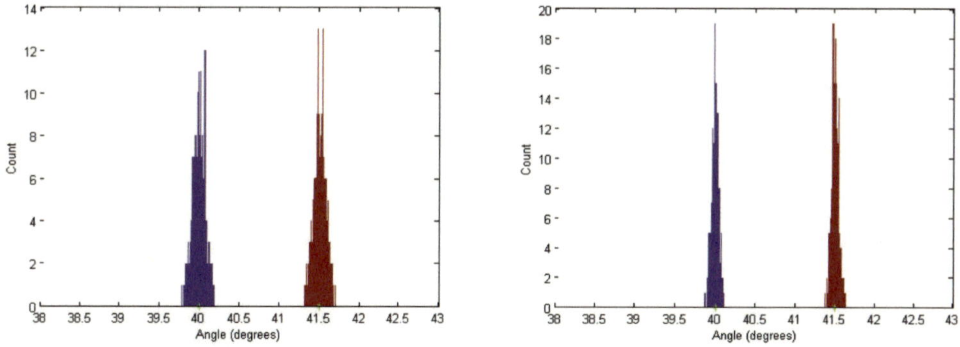

(a) (b)

Fig. 3.3 Histogram of the Estimated Signals' DOA with SNR = 20 dB and Signals' DOA are 40° and 41.5° (a) 32 Snapshots, (b) 96 Snapshots.

The above simulation results assume that the system operates in a high SNR environment. The SNR is 20 dB. If the SNR is only 5 dB, the simulation result yields a larger estimation variance. Figure 3.4 shows the histogram of the estimated signals' DOA for 5 dB SNR, and the signals' DOA are 40° and 46°. This result is based on 1000 independent simulations where the number of snapshots in each simulation is 32 and 96, respectively.

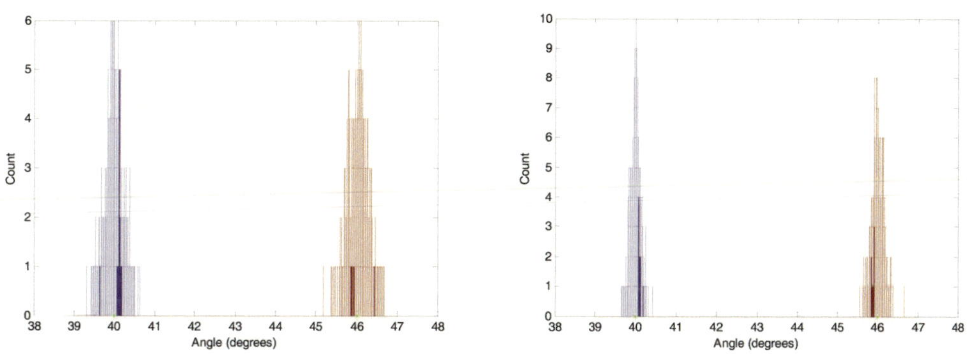

(a) (b)

Fig. 3.4 Histogram of the Estimated Signals' DOA with SNR = 5 dB, (a) 32 Snapshots (b) 96 Snapshots, Signals' DOA are 40° and 46°

The estimated mean values and variances based on 1000 trials for 5 dB SNR and the two different numbers of snapshots are listed in Table 3.3.

Number of Snapshots	32		96	
True Angles	40°	46°	40°	46°
Estimated Mean	39.9708°	46.0279°	39.9893°	46.0094°
Variance	0.0358	0.0430	0.0112	0.0140

Table 3.3 The Estimated Mean and Variance of DOAs for SNR = 5 dB

This simulation result shows that increases in the number of snapshots provide a better correlation matrix estimation; consequently, the estimation variance decreases.

4. PRIME Algorithm

Root MUSIC can only estimate one DOA angle. A signal impinging on the array anywhere on the cone with its axis aligned with the array elements yields the identical result. This angle ambiguity is shown in Figure 4.1. This angle ambiguity can be resolved by using a two dimensional array. The PRIME algorithm is a method that allows polynomial rooting techniques to be applied to multidimensional estimation.

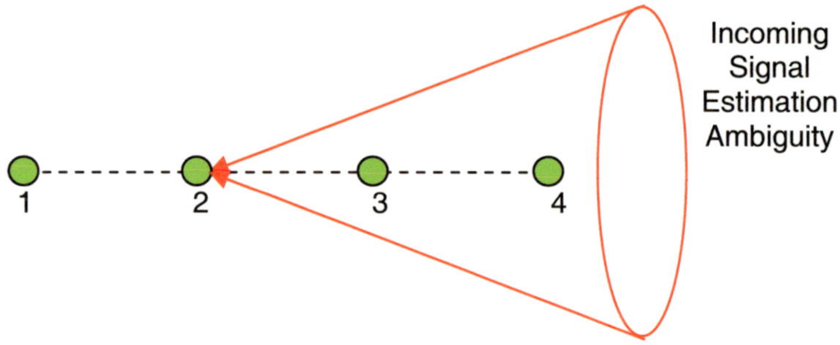

Fig. 4.1 Angle Ambiguity of ULA

Consider a general array of M sensors as shown in Figure 4.2. The coordinate of the ith sensor is $\mathbf{r}_i = [x_i, y_i, z_i]^T$, $i = 1, 2, \ldots, M$.

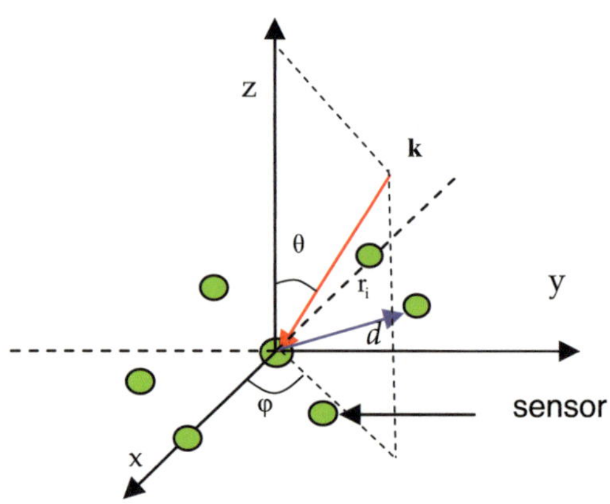

Fig. 4.2 An Array of M Sensors

Suppose a plane target signal waveform comes from the direction of $\mathbf{k} = [\sin\theta\cos\varphi, \sin\theta\sin\varphi, \cos\theta]^T$, where θ is the elevation angle and φ is the azimuth angle. The difference of the propagation path of this wave between the origin and the ith sensor Δd_i is

$$\Delta d_i = \mathbf{r}_i^T \mathbf{k} = \sin\theta\,(x_i\cos\varphi + y_i\sin\varphi) + z_i\cos\theta \tag{4.1}$$

The corresponding propagation time delay τ_i is

$$\tau_i = \Delta d_i / c \tag{4.2}$$

where c is the speed of light.

To avoid the effect of grating lobes, the distance between the two neighbor sensors has to be no more than one half of the wavelength. If the reference sensor is located at the origin, and a waveform received by the reference sensor due to signal coming from direction of **k** is x(t), then the received waveform at i^{th} sensor is $x_i(t) = x(t-\tau_i)$.

As shown in Figure 4.2, the array elements are placed on x-y plane, the elevation angle θ and azimuth angle φ uniquely define the signal DOA. For a narrowband signal, if the jth signal DOA is (θ_j, φ_j), the relative phase shift of kth element due to the jth signal is defined by the following Equation:

$$\beta_{k,j} = -\frac{2\pi}{\lambda}\sin\theta_j(x_k\cos\varphi_j + y_k\sin\varphi_j) \tag{4.3}$$

In Equation (4.3), each signal has two unknown parameters, elevation angle θ_j and azimuth angle φ_j, that need to be determined. Thus, to obtain the DOA angles, two independent polynomials must be constructed and solved. There are several different techniques to derive two independent polynomials.

The first approach constructs the two independent Equations from two distinct subsets. Two distinct null spaces matrices $\mathbf{V}_{1N}$ and $\mathbf{V}_{2N}$ can be derived from two different subsets. The two independent Equations are:

$$J_1(z, w) = \mathbf{a}^H(z,w)\mathbf{V}_{1N}\mathbf{V}_{1N}^H\mathbf{a}(z,w) \tag{4.4}$$

$$J_2(z, w) = \mathbf{b}^H(z,w)\mathbf{V}_{2N}\mathbf{V}_{2N}^H\mathbf{b}(z,w) \tag{4.5}$$

where variables $z = e^{j\frac{2\pi}{\lambda}x\sin\theta\cos\varphi}$, $w = e^{j\frac{2\pi}{\lambda}y\sin\theta\sin\varphi}$. Vectors **a** and **b** depend on the subset configurations. To guarantee the two Equations are independent, the two subsets cannot relate to each other by a linear shifting relation. There are many different ways to choose the distinct subsets. The accuracy of DOA estimation depends on the configuration of the subarrays.

The second approach constructs two independent equations by using the full array. The columns of matrices $\mathbf{V}_{1N}$ and $\mathbf{V}_{2N}$ are chosen from eigenvectors associates with M-L smallest eigenvalues of the correlation matrix. To guarantee two equations are independent, column vectors of matrices $\mathbf{V}_{1N}$ and $\mathbf{V}_{2N}$ cannot identical. Since the full array is used, the two polynomials are:

$$J_1(z, w) = \mathbf{a}^H(z,w)\mathbf{V}_{1N}\mathbf{V}_{1N}^H\mathbf{a}(z,w) \quad (4.6)$$

$$J_2(z, w) = \mathbf{a}^H(z,w)\mathbf{V}_{2N}\mathbf{V}_{2N}^H\mathbf{a}(z,w) \quad (4.7)$$

where vector **a** is the array manifold vector.

If the signal DOA is (θ, φ) and the estimated DOA is $(\hat{\theta}, \hat{\varphi})$, the estimated angle error α_e is given by the following equation.

$$\alpha_e = \cos^{-1}(\sin\theta\sin\hat{\theta}\cos\varphi\cos\hat{\varphi} + \sin\theta\sin\hat{\theta}\sin\varphi\sin\hat{\varphi} + \text{cosvcos}\,\hat{\theta}) \quad (4.8)$$

The estimated correlation matrix based on Equation (2.14) is different from theoretical equation (2.11). In theoretical equation, the signal and noise are assumed independent. However, the estimation based on finite number of data samples does not satisfy independent condition.

According to Equation (2.11) elements of correlation matrix contain no cross coupling terms between signal and noise. However, estimation the elements of correlation matrix based on finite received data samples contain cross couple terms. This cross couple terms degrade the estimation performance.

Suppose there is only one signal, the input waveform to the ith array element at sample time n $u_i(n)$ is

$$u_i(n) = Ae^{j(2\pi f_c n + \beta_i)} + w_i(n) \quad (4.9)$$

where $w_i(n)$ is the white noise with variance σ_w^2 and β_i is the relative signal phase of the ith element.

The element r_{ij} of the correlation matrix is

$$r_{ij} = \sum_{n=1}^{N} u_i(n)u_j^*(n) = \sum_{n=1}^{N}\left[Ae^{j(2\pi f_c n+\beta_i)} + w_i(n)\right]\left[Ae^{-j(2\pi f_c n+\beta_j)} + w_j^*(n)\right]$$

$$= NA^2 e^{j(\beta_i - \beta_j)} + \sum_{n=1}^{N} Ae^{j(2\pi f_c n+\beta_i)} w_j^*(n) + \sum_{n=1}^{N} Ae^{-j(2\pi f_c n+\beta_j)} w_i(n) + N\sigma_w^2\delta_{ij} \quad (4.10)$$

The term $NA^2e^{j(\beta_i-\beta_j)}$ is the component of r_{ij} due to the signal, $N\sigma_w^2\delta_{ij}$ is the component of r_{ij} due to the noise. $\sum_{n-1}^{N} Ae^{j(2\pi f_c n+\beta_i)} w_j^*(n) + \sum_{n-1}^{N} Ae^{-j(2\pi f_c n+\beta_j)} w_i(n)$ is the cross coupling term between the signal and noise is which has zero mean and variance is $2NA^2\sigma_w^2$.

If there are two signals impinging on the array, the input waveform to the ith array element $u_i(n)$ at sample time n is

$$u_i(n) = A_1e^{j(2\pi f_1 n+\beta_{i1})} + A_2e^{j(2\pi f_2 n+\theta+\beta_{i2})} + w_i(n) \tag{4.11}$$

where β_{i1} and β_{i2} are the corresponding electrical angles due to signal 1 and signal 2, f_1, f_2 are the frequencies of two signals, random phase θ represent the relative delay of two signals.

The element r_{ij} of the correlation matrix is

$$
\begin{aligned}
r_{ij} &= \sum_{n=1}^{N} u_i(n)u_j^*(n) \\
&= \sum_{n=1}^{N} \left[A_1e^{j(2\pi f_1 n+\beta_{i1})} + A_2e^{j(2\pi f_2 n+\theta+\beta_{i2})} + w_i(n)\right]\left[A_1e^{-j(2\pi f_1 n+\beta_{j1})} + A_2e^{-j(2\pi f_2 n+\theta+\beta_{j2})} + w_j^*(n)\right] \\
&= NA_1^2e^{j(\beta_{i1}-\beta_{j1})} + NA_2^2e^{j(\beta_{i2}-\beta_{j2})} + N\sigma_w^2\delta_{ij} + A_1A_2e^{j(\beta_{i1}-\beta_{j2}-\theta)}\sum_{n=1}^{N} e^{j2\pi\Delta fn} + A_1A_2e^{j(\beta_{i2}-\beta_{j1}+\theta)}\sum_{n=1}^{N} e^{-j2\pi\Delta fn} \\
&+ \sum_{n=1}^{N} A_1e^{j(2\pi f_1 n+\beta_{i1})} w_j^*(n) + \sum_{n=1}^{N} A_2e^{j(2\pi f_1 n+\beta_{i2}+\theta)} w_j^*(n) + \sum_{n=1}^{N} A_1e^{-j(2\pi f_2 n+\beta_{j1})} w_i(n) \\
&+ \sum_{n=1}^{N} A_2e^{-j(2\pi f_2 n+\theta+\beta_{j2})} w_i(n)
\end{aligned}
\tag{4.12}
$$

Terms $NA_1^2e^{j(\beta_{i1}-\beta_{j1})}$, $NA_2^2e^{j(\beta_{i2}-\beta_{j2})}$, $N\sigma_w^2\delta_{ij}$ are the contribution of r_{ij} due to two signals and noise. $A_1A_2e^{j(\beta_{i1}-\beta_{j2}-\theta)}\sum_{n=1}^{N} e^{j2\pi\Delta fn}$, $A_1A_2e^{j(\beta_{i2}-\beta_{j1}+\theta)}\sum_{n=1}^{N} e^{-j2\pi\Delta fn}$ are the cross coupling term of two signals. If the frequency offset between two signals $\Delta f = f_1 - f_2$ is $\Delta f = k/N$ and k is an integer, those terms will be zero. The last four terms $\sum_{n=1}^{N} A_1e^{j(2\pi f_1 n+\beta_{i1})} w_j^*(n)$, $\sum_{n=1}^{N} A_2e^{j(2\pi f_1 n+\beta_{i2}+\theta)} w_j^*(n)$, $\sum_{n=1}^{N} A_1e^{-j(2\pi f_2 n+\beta_{j1})} w_i(n)$ and $\sum_{n=1}^{N} A_2e^{-j(2\pi f_2 n+\theta+\beta_{j2})} w_i(n)$ are the coupling between two signals and noise, their mean values are zero. If there are more than two signals, then there will be even more coupling terms which will further degrade the performance.

The two dimensional array antenna in this simulation study is assumed to have seven elements arranged in a honeycomb configuration as shown in Figure 4.3. The inter-element spacing equals to half wavelength.

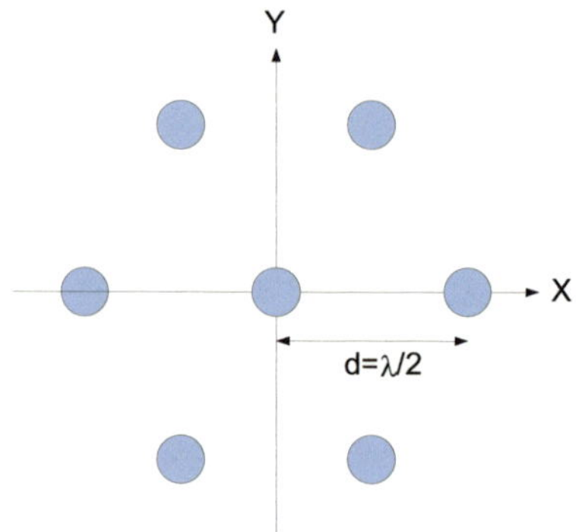

Fig. 4.3 Seven Element Array Antenna

4.1 Computer Simulations (Subset Approach)

Label the element number of the seven element antenna as in Figure 4.4. Since the inter-element spacing d = λ/2, where λ is the signal wavelength, then the variable z and w are:

$$z = e^{j\frac{\pi}{2}\sin\theta\cos\varphi} \tag{4.13}$$

$$w = e^{j\frac{\sqrt{3}\pi}{2}\sin\theta\sin\varphi} \tag{4.14}$$

The array manifold vector **a** of this array is given by

$$\mathbf{a} = [1\ \ z^2\ \ zw\ \ z^{-1}w\ \ z^{-2}\ \ z^{-1}w^{-1}\ \ zw^{-1}]^T \tag{4.15}$$

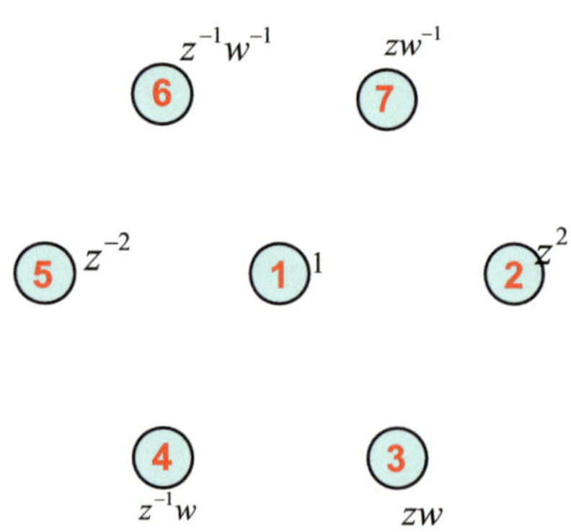

Fig. 4.4 Array Phase as a Function of z and w

Assume there is only one narrowband signal impinging on this array from angle $\theta = 50°$ and $\varphi = 35°$. The dimension of signal plus noise subspace is only one. The two different three element subsets are chosen from this array as shown in Figure 4.5. The first subset contains element (1, 4, 7), and the second subset contains element (1, 6, 7). The dimension of the noise only subspace in $\mathbf{V}_{1N}$ and $\mathbf{V}_{2N}$ is two. Two independent Equations can be constructed to define the signal DOA.

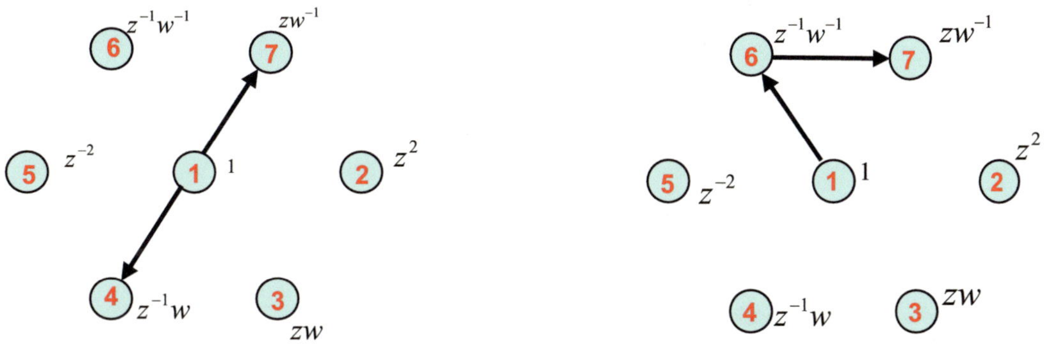

Fig. 4.5 Three Elements Subset Array Phase as a Function of z and w

The corresponding vector **a** and **b** would be

$$\mathbf{a} = [1 \;\; z^{-1}w \;\; zw^{-1}]^T \tag{4.16}$$

$$\mathbf{b} = [1 \;\; z^{-1}w^{-1} \;\; zw^{-1}]^T \tag{4.17}$$

The z, w roots from the Equations $J_1(z, w)$ and $J_2(z, w)$ are shown in Figure 4.6. This result is derived based on the SNR = 20 dB, and matrices $\mathbf{V}_{1N}$, $\mathbf{V}_{2N}$ are constructed from temporal averaging over 100 snapshots of the observed data.

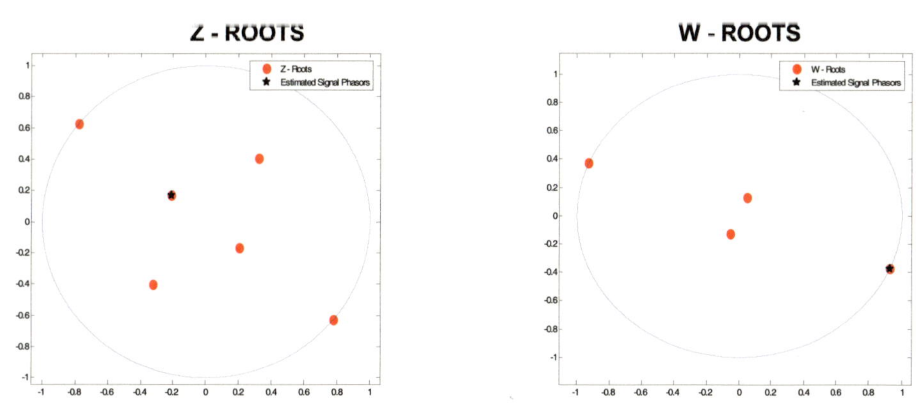

Fig. 4.6 Roots of $J_1(z, w)$ and $J_2(z, w)$ for SNR = 20 dB

Reduce the SNR to 5 dB, the roots of polynomials $J_1(z, w)$ and $J_2(z, w)$ are slightly different from roots shown in Figure 4.6. Their roots are shown in Figure 4.7.

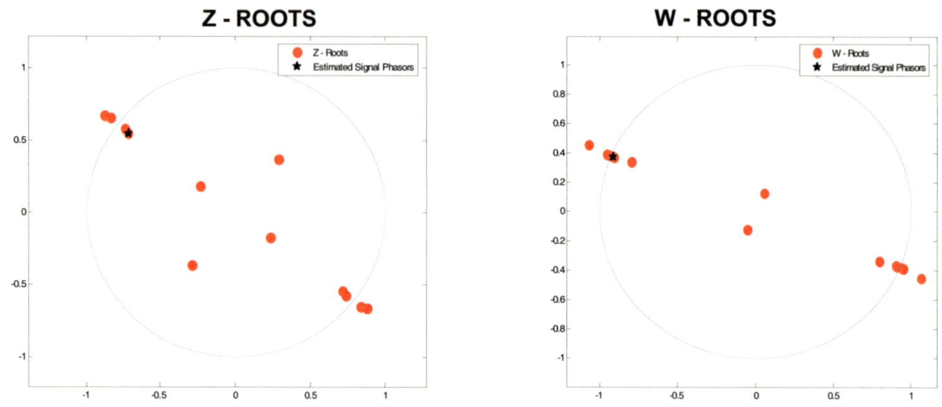

Fig. 4.7 Roots of $J_1(z, w)$ and $J_2(z, w)$ for SNR = 5 dB

The pair of roots closest to the unity are chosen to define the signal DOA. Once this pair of roots is identified, the elevation angle and azimuth angle can be computed by the following Equations.

$$\theta = \sin^{-1}\left(\frac{2}{\sqrt{3}\pi}\frac{1}{\sin\varphi}\arg(w)\right) \tag{4.18}$$

$$\varphi = \cos^{-1}\left(\frac{2}{\pi}\frac{1}{\sin\theta}\arg(z)\right) \tag{4.19}$$

where

$$\arg(u) = \tan^{-1}\left(\frac{\mathrm{Im}(u)}{\mathrm{Re}(u)}\right). \tag{4.20}$$

Simulation results based on 1000 independent trials using 3 element subsets at two different SNRs are shown in Figure 4.8. The variance and average error both increase with increased noise power as expected. The averaged estimation error for SNR = 20 dB and SNR = 5 dB are 0.206° and 1.187° respectively. The estimation variances are 0.019 and 0.602.

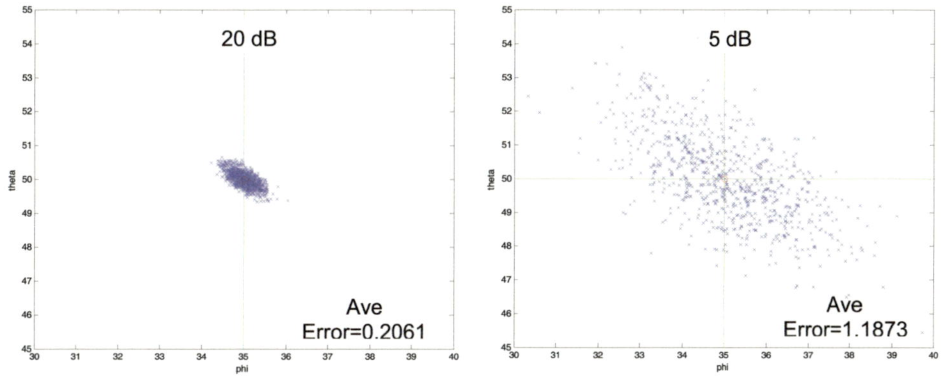

(a) (b)

Fig. 4.8 Estimated Signal DOA Based on 1000 Independent Simulations (a) SNR = 20 dB, (b) SNR = 5 dB

Increasing the subset from 3 elements to 4 elements improves the estimation accuracy. Suppose the elements of the two subsets are (1, 2, 6, 7) and (1, 4, 5, 7) as shown in Figure 4.9, then the corresponding vectors **a** and **b** are:

$$\mathbf{a} = [1 \;\; z^{2} \;\; z^{-1}w^{-1} \;\; zw^{-1}]^{T} \tag{4.21}$$

$$\mathbf{b} = [1 \;\; z^{-1}w \;\; z^{-2} \;\; zw^{-1}]^{T} \tag{4.22}$$

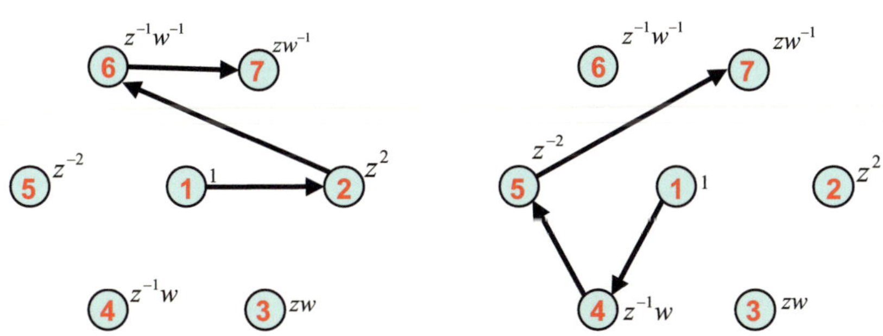

Fig. 4.9 Four Elements Subset Array Phase as a Function of z and w

The estimated signal DOA based on 1000 independent trials using 4 element subsets at 2 different SNR is shown in Figure 4.10. The variance and average error both increase with increased noise power as expected. The averaged estimation errors for SNR = 20 dB and SNR = 5 dB are 0.138° and 0.774° respectively. The estimation variances are 0.008 and 0.221.

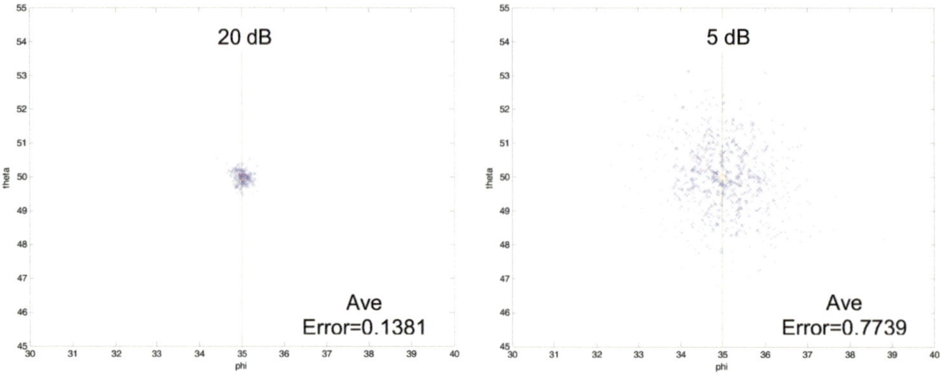

(a) (b)

Fig. 4.10 Estimated Signal DOA Based on 1000 Independent Simulations (a) SNR = 20 dB, (b) SNR = 5 dB

Figures 4.8 and 4.10 show that increasing the subset size improves the estimation accuracy. Choosing a larger subset increases the order of polynomials $J_1(z, w)$ and $J_2(z, w)$. Thus finding the roots of those polynomials requires more computation resources.

There are many different ways to pick the subsets from this seven element array. The 3 element subsets in the previous simulation are (1, 4, 7) and (1, 6, 7) respectively. If we choose different subsets consist of elements (1, 3, 6) and (1, 4, 7), the estimation variance is considerably smaller. Assume the SNR is 20 dB, scatter diagrams using subsets (1, 4, 7), (1, 6, 7) and (1, 3, 6), (1, 4, 7) based on 1000 independent simulations are shown in Figure 4.11. This new subsets reduces the estimation variance from 0.019 to 0.004, better than 6.7 dB improvement. This performance improvement is due to the fact that subset (1, 3, 6) spans over a larger region of the original array than subset (1. 6. 7).

(a) (b)

Fig. 4.11 Scatter Diagram for SNR = 20 dB using Subsets (a) (1, 4, 7) and (1, 6, 7), (b) (1, 3, 6) and (1, 4, 7)

Similar performance improvement is also observed in 4 element subsets. Figure 4.12 shows the scatter diagrams using different subsets (1, 2, 6, 7), (1, 4, 5, 7) and (1, 2, 3, 6), (1, 4, 5, 7) based on 1000 independent simulations. The SNR is assumed to be 20 dB.

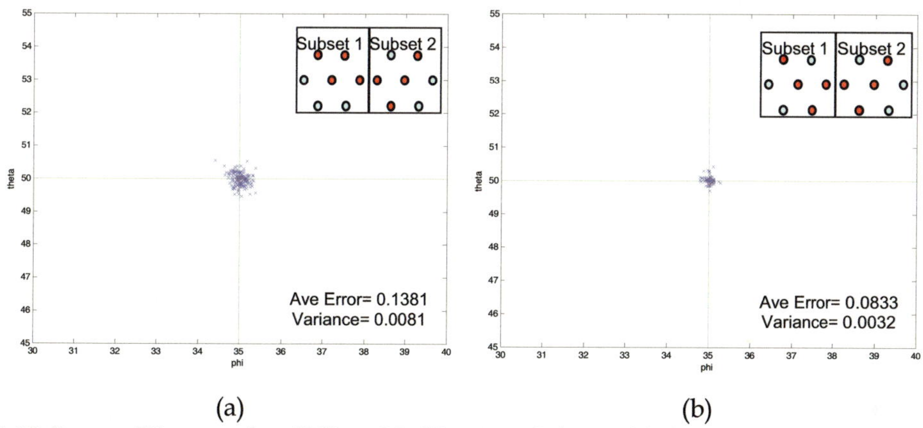

Fig. 4.12 Scatter Diagram for SNR = 20 dB using Subsets (a) (1, 2, 6, 7) and (1, 4, 5, 7) , (b) (1, 2, 3, 6) and (1, 4, 5, 7)

By using new pair of subsets, the estimation variance is reduced from 0.008 to 0.003; the improvement factor is better than 4 dB.

Correlation matrix estimation can be improved by increase the number of temporal averaging. Increase the number of temporal averaging enhances the estimation of the correlation matrix, consequently, the DOA estimation also improved. If the elements of the two subsets are (1, 2, 6, 7) and (1, 4, 5, 7), the SNR = 5 dB, the estimated DOA based on 100 and 1000 snapshots are shown in Figure 4.13.

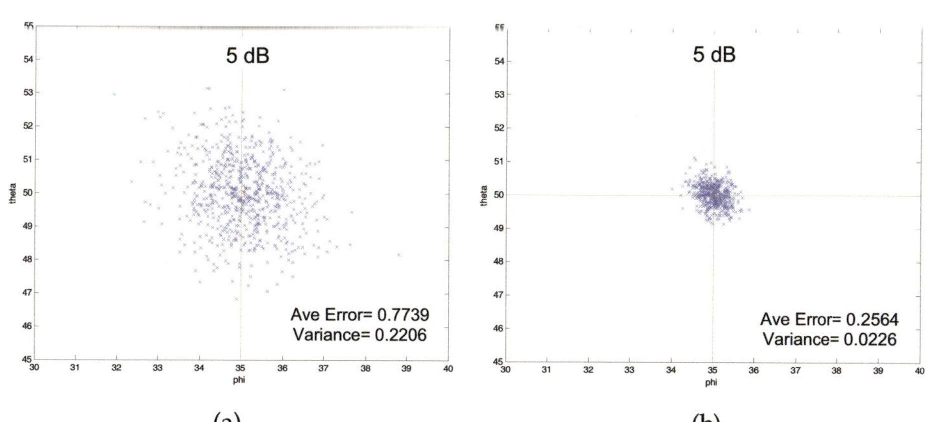

Fig. 4.13 Scatter Diagram for SNR = 5 dB (a) 100 Snapshots, (b) 1000 Snapshots

Figure 4.13 shows increasing the number of snapshots by a factor of 10, the estimation variance reduces from 0.2206 to 0.0226. A factor of 10 dB improvement is achieved.

The aperture of a seven element antenna is very small. If this is a conventional fixed antenna, then the mainlobe beamwidth is about 57°. This antenna will not be able to resolve multiple targets if their angle separation is less than 57°. This limitation can be easily resolved by using array antenna and PRIME processing algorithm.

Suppose there are two signals impinging on this array with DOA (θ = 60°, φ = 15°) and (θ = 50°, φ = 35°), the angle separation between those two target is 15.4°. If the SNR is 20 dB, the estimated DOA based on 1000 independent trials by using 4 element subsets with element (1, 2, 6, 7) and (1, 4, 5, 7) is shown in Figure 4.14.

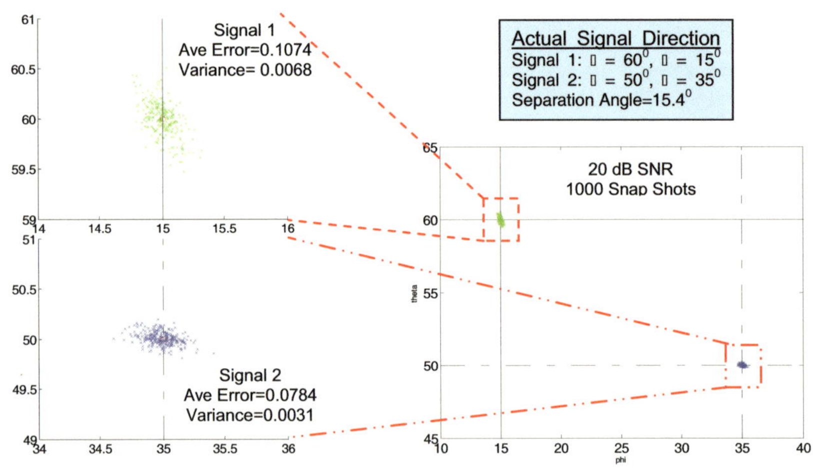

Fig. 4.14 Estimated DOA using 4 Element Subsets, Signals' Angle Spacing Approximately equal One Quarter of Mainlobe Beamwidth

Suppose the DOA of two signals are (θ = 50°, φ = 25°) and (θ = 50°, φ = 35°), the angle separation between those two targets is 8.4°. Under the same SNR and using identical subsets, the estimated signal DOA is shown in Figure 4.15.

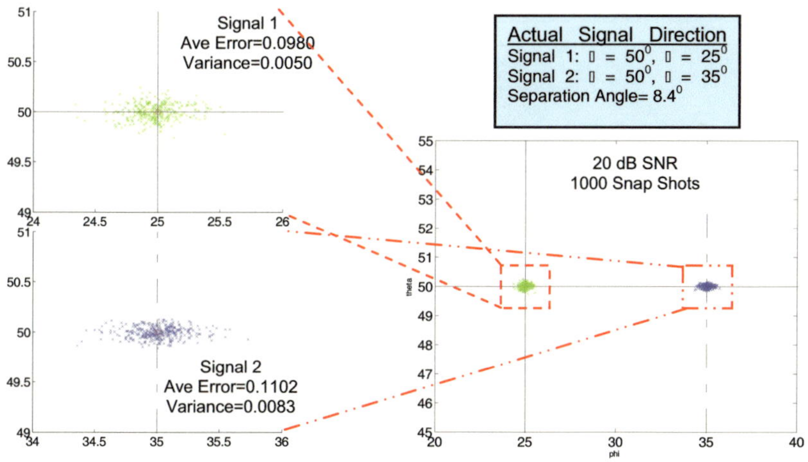

Fig. 4.15 Estimated DOA using 4 Element Subsets, Signals' Angle Spacing Approximately equal One Seventh of the Mainlobe Beamwidth

Figures 4.14 and 4.15 show that with the PRIME processing algorithm, the array antenna can resolve multiple targets even their angle separation is considerably less than the conventional antenna mainlobe beamwidth.

4.2 Computer Simulations (Full Array Approach

For full array approach, all array elements are used in the DOA estimation. The vector **a** in this approach is defined by Equation (4.15).

Assume there is only one narrowband signal impinging on the array antenna from angle θ = 30° and φ = 50°. The SNR is 5 dB. Since there is only one signal, eigenvectors $\mathbf{q}_2$, $\mathbf{q}_3$, $\mathbf{q}_4$, $\mathbf{q}_5$, $\mathbf{q}_6$, $\mathbf{q}_7$ span the noise only subspace. There are many degree of freedom choosing matrices $\mathbf{V}_{N1}$ and $\mathbf{V}_{N2}$. By choosing matrices $\mathbf{V}_{N1} = [\mathbf{q}_5, \mathbf{q}_7]$ and $\mathbf{V}_{N2} = [\mathbf{q}_6, \mathbf{q}_7]$ the scatter diagram of the estimated DOA is given in Figure 4.16. The average estimated elevation and azimuth errors for are $\alpha_\theta = 0.01°$ and $\alpha_\varphi = 0.05°$. The standard deviation of the estimated angle error is σ = 1.44°.

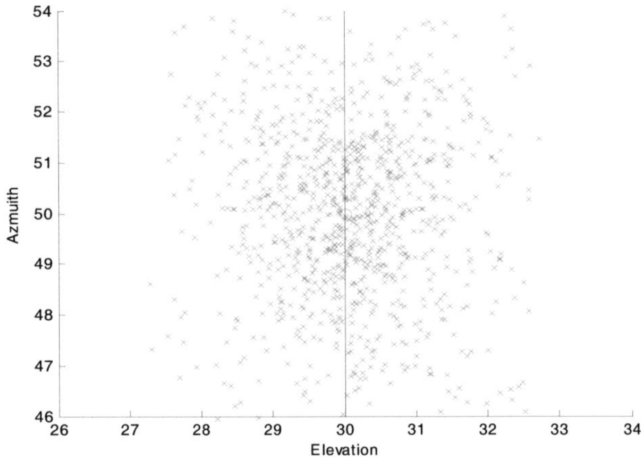

Fig. 4.16 Estimated Signal DOA Based on 1000 Independent Simulations for $\mathbf{V_{N1}} = [q_5, q_7]$, $\mathbf{V_{N2}} = [q_6, q_7]$

Choosing a different pair of matrices $\mathbf{V}_{N1}=[\mathbf{q}_2, \mathbf{q}_3]$ and $\mathbf{V}_{N2} =[\mathbf{q}_4, \mathbf{q}_5]$, the estimated DOA scatter diagram is shown in Figure 4.17. There are no common column vectors in matrices $\mathbf{V}_{N1}$ and $\mathbf{V}_{N2}$. The standard deviation of estimated angle error slightly decreases to 1.29°.

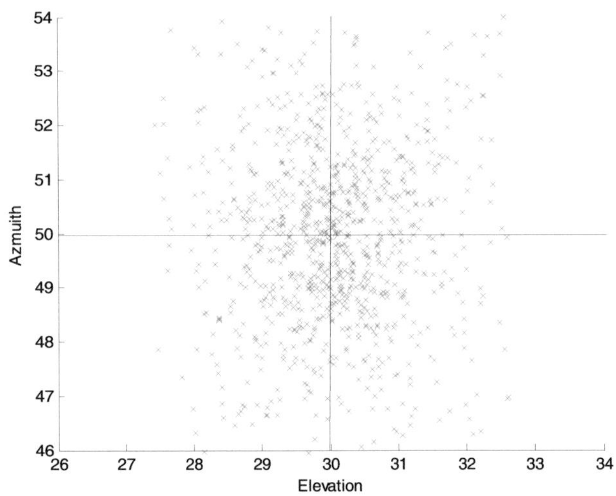

Fig. 4.17 Estimated Signal DOA Based on 1000 Independent Simulations for $V_{N1} = [q_2, q_3]$ and $V_{N2} = [q_4, q_5]$

Results from Figures 4.16 and 4.17 show the improvement of choosing matrices $\mathbf{V}_{N1}$, $\mathbf{V}_{N2}$ with no common column vectors is marginal.

Increasing the SNR from 5dB to 20dB improves the estimation accuracy for the full array approach. The estimated signal DOA based on 1000 independent simulation using $\mathbf{V}_{N1} = [\mathbf{q}_2, \mathbf{q}_3]$ and $\mathbf{V}_{N2} = [\mathbf{q}_4, \mathbf{q}_5]$ at 2 different SNR is shown in Figure 4.18. The variance and average error both increase with increased noise power as expected. The averaged elevation and azimuth estimation errors for SNR = 5 dB and SNR = 20 dB are $\alpha_{\theta 1}$ = 0.05°, $\alpha_{\varphi 1}$ = 0.02° and $\alpha_{\theta 2}$ = 0.00°, $\alpha_{\varphi 2}$ = 0.01°. The standard deviation of the estimated angle error decreases from 1.39° to 0.24° when the SNR improved from 5 dB to 20 dB.

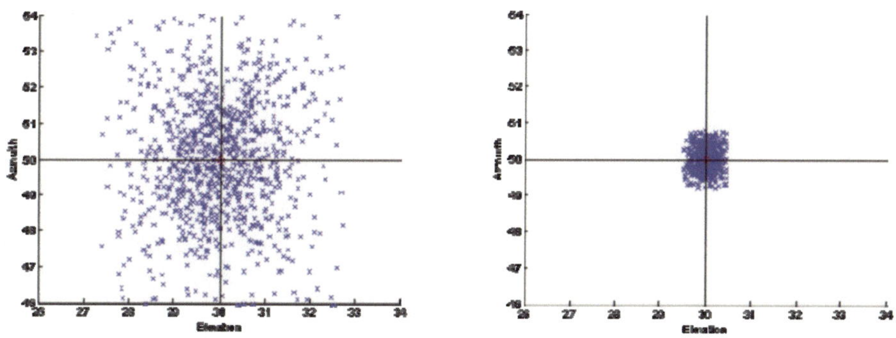

(a) (b)

Fig. 4.18 Estimated Signal DOA Based on 100 Snapshots (a) SNR = 5 dB, (b) SNR = 20 dB

The estimation of the correlation matrix can be improved by increasing the number of temporal averaging. Using $\mathbf{V}_{N1} = [\mathbf{q}_2, \mathbf{q}_3]$ and $\mathbf{V}_{N2} = [\mathbf{q}_4, \mathbf{q}_5]$ at 2 different SNR of 5 dB and 20dB, the estimated angles based on 1000 snapshots are shown in Figure 4.19. The averaged elevation and azimuth estimation errors for SNR = 5 dB and SNR = 20 dB are $\alpha_{\theta 1}$ = 0.01°, $\alpha_{\varphi 1}$ = 0.02° and $\alpha_{\theta 2}$ = 0.00°, $\alpha_{\varphi 2}$ = 0.01°. The standard deviation of the estimated angle error decreases from 0.41° to 0.08°.

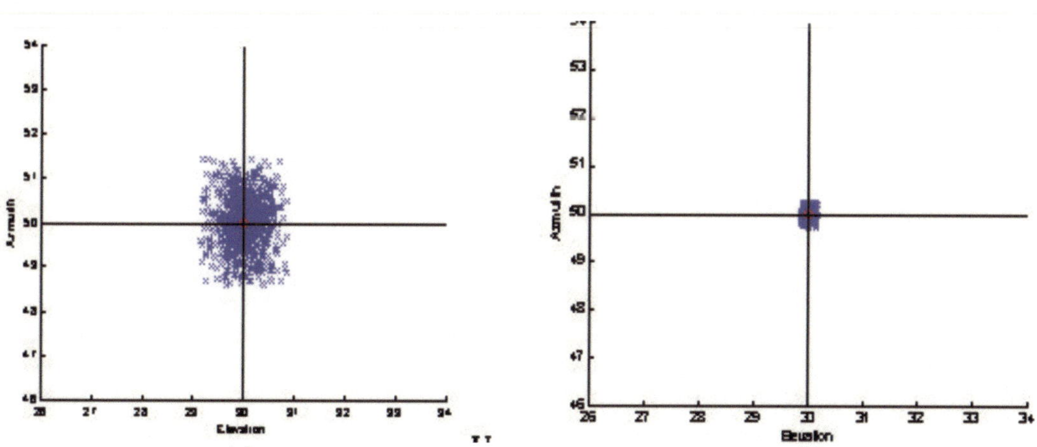

(a) (b)

Fig. 4.19 Estimated Signal DOA Based on 1000 snapshots (a) SNR = 5 dB, (b) SNR = 20 dB

Results of Figures 4.18 and 4.19 are summarized in Table 4.1.

	SNR = 5 dB	SNR = 20 dB
100 Snapshots	1.39°	0.24°
1000 Snapshots	0.41°	0.08°

Table 4.1 Standard Deviation of Estimation Error

Table 4.1 shows that the improved estimation can be achieved by either improve the estimation of correlation matrix by temporal averaging over larger number of samples or operating in a relatively noise free environment.

Suppose there are two signals impinging the array from DOA (30°, 30°) and (30°, 50°). The SNR is 20 dB, the frequency offset between two signals is $\Delta f = 1/200$, and the estimated correlation matrix is based on temporal averaging over 200 snapshots. The estimated DOA scatter diagram based on 200 independent simulations is shown in Figure 4.20. Since there are only two signals, eigenvectors $\mathbf{q}_3$, $\mathbf{q}_4$, $\mathbf{q}_5$, $\mathbf{q}_6$, $\mathbf{q}_7$ span over the noise only subspace. In this simulation, matrices $\mathbf{V}_{N1} = [\mathbf{q}_3, \mathbf{q}_4]$ and $\mathbf{V}_{N2} = [\mathbf{q}_5, \mathbf{q}_6]$. The average estimated elevation angle error for signals are $\alpha_{\theta 1} = 0.253°$, $\alpha_{\varphi 1} = 0.044°$ and $\alpha_{\theta 2} = 0.232°$, $\alpha_{\varphi 2} = 0.026°$. The standard deviation of the estimated angle errors are 0.591° and 0.497° respectively.

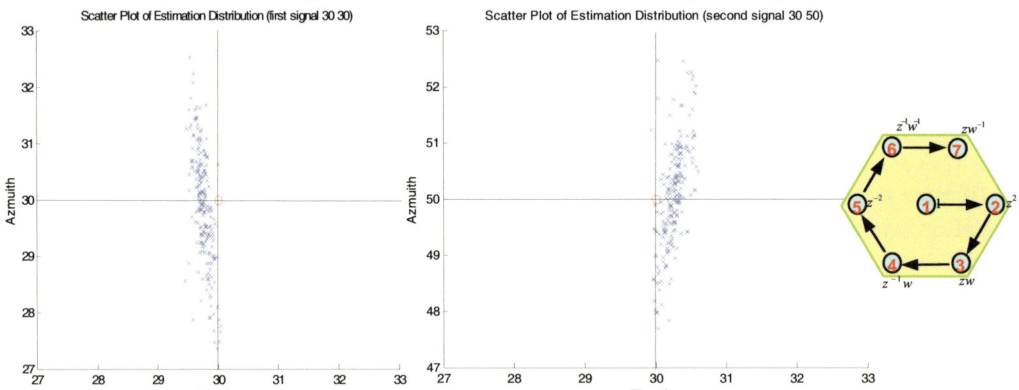

Fig. 4.20 Estimated DOA using Full Array for two Signals ($\Delta f = 1/200$)

The effect of correlation matrix estimation under different snapshots is shown in Figure 4.21. The blue and green bars are the standard deviation of angle estimation errors of two signals. Figure 4.21 shows that correlation matrix based on averaging over 100 snapshots has worst performance. Increase the temporal averaging to 180, 200 and 220 snapshots reduce the standard deviation of estimation error almost by a factor of two. The estimation error with 200 snapshots is better than 180 and 220 snapshots. This is due to the fact that Equation (4.12) indicates that if the product of snapshots and normalized frequency offset is an integer number, the coupling term due to different signals exactly cancel out, thus 200 snapshots provides better estimation than 180 or 220 snapshots. With 200 snapshots, the product of number of snapshots and normalized frequency offset equal 1, it provides the best estimation.

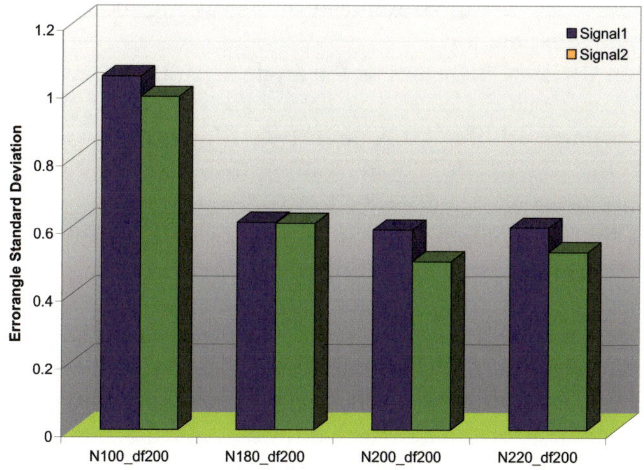

Fig. 4.21 Estimated DOA using 4 Element Subsets for two signals (Δf=1/100) under Different Snapshots.

5. Conclusions

This chapter investigates the possibility of combining the array antenna and advanced signal processing techniques to enhance the estimation of the direction of signal sources.

A conventional method to detect the direction of signal source is to use a fixed antenna to scan over certain searching region. Whenever there is a high received power from a particular direction, then we assume that is the signal DOA. This primitive estimation technique has many limitations. First its resolution is limited by the antenna mainlobe beamwidth. For small aperture antennas such as a missile seeker antenna, the resolution is very poor. Also if there are multiple signal sources, a conventional fixed antenna has difficulty in detecting them simultaneously.

Using the advanced signal processing techniques, the DOA estimation can be improved. One of the important algorithms based on eigen-analysis is the MUSIC algorithm. To guarantee MUSIC algorithm provides fine resolution, it needs a scan vector to scan large number of spatial sample points. Consequently, it requires large amount of processing power. Root MUSIC and PRIME algorithms are further refinements of MUSIC. Root MUSIC defines the signal parameter by finding the roots of its characteristic polynomial. For multi-dimensional estimation such as define the signals' DOA (elevation and azimuth angles), PRIME algorithm defines the simultaneous polynomials from either subset approach or full array approach. DOA information can be obtained from the roots of simultaneous equations. Thus Root MUSIC and PRIME improve the processing efficiency by eliminating the requirement of scan vector. Important conclusions of root MUSIC and PRIME algorithms are summarized as follows:

1. Both root MUSIC and PRIME algorithms provide much better resolution then the conventional fixed antenna.

2. The estimation variance can be reduced by increasing the number of snapshots in correlation matrix estimation.
3. The estimation variance increases as the angle separation between signals becomes smaller.
4. Estimation variance of the ULA and two dimensional array depend on the direction of the signal. A signal coming from the boresight has minimum estimation variance.
5. To guarantee that the polynomials constructed from array subsets are independent, the two subsets cannot relate to each other by a linear shifting relation.
6. The performance of the PRIME algorithm improves if the subsets elements span over the largest possible dimension, or the number of snapshots is increased.
7. The array antenna can resolve multiple targets even their angle separation is considerably less than the conventional antenna mainlobe beamwidth.
8. If there is frequency offset between multiple signals, the optimum number of temporal averaging N is to choose its value such that the multiplication of N and normalized frequency offset Δf to be an integer.

6. References

Aliyazicioglu Z. & Hwang H. K. (2008). Performance Analysis for DOA Estimation using the PRIME Algorithm, *10th International Conference on Signal and Image Processing*.

Allen, B & Ghavami M. (2005). *Adaptive Array Systems* Wiley, ISBN:978-0-470-86189-9

Forsythe, K. (1997). Utilizing Waveform Features for Adaptive Beamforming and Direction Finding with Narrowband Signals, *Lincoln Laboratory Journal* Vol: 10.2

Hatke, G. & Keith F. (1994). *A Class of Polynomial Rooting Algorithms for Joint Azimuth/Elevation Estimation Using Multidimensional Arrays, 28th Asilomar Conference on Signals, Systems and Computers*, p 694–699.

Haykin Simon (2002). *Adaptive Filter Theory,* Prentice Hall, ISBN 0130901261.

Hwang H. K. & Grados R. (2008) Multibeam Antenna and Antenna Beam Shaping using the Minimax Algorithm, *AIAA International Communications and Satellite Systems Conference.*

Lee, A.; Chen L.; Song A.; Wei J. & Hwang H. K. (2005). Simulation Study of Wideband Interference Rejection using Adaptive Array Antenna, *IEEE Aerospace Conference.*

Ren Q. S. & Willis A. J. (1997). Fast Root MUSIC Algorithm, *Electronic Letters.*

Schmidt, R. O. (1986). Multiple Emitter Location and Signal Parameter Estimation, *IEEE Trans. Antennas Propagation.*

Van Trees, H. L (2002). *Optimum Array Processing* Wiley, ISBN: 0471093904

Xu Y.; Feng W.; Hao J. & Hwang H. K. (2001). Adaptive Radar Clutter Suppression, *IEEE Ocean Conference.*

Some sufficient conditions for graphs to be (g, f, n)-critical graphs

Sizhong Zhou[a*], Hongxia Liu[b,c†] and Ziming Duan[d**]

*[a] *School of Mathematics and Physics, Jiangsu University of Science and Technology, Mengxi Road 2, Zhenjiang, Jiangsu 212003, People's Republic of China.*
Email: zsz_cumt@163.com

†[b] *School of Mathematics, Shandong University, Jinan, Shandong 250100, People's Republic of China.*

[c] *School of Mathematics and Informational Science, Yantai University, Yantai, Shandong 264005, People's Republic of China.*
Email: mqy7174@sina.com

**[d] *School of Science, China University of Mining and Technology, Xuzhou, Jiangsu 221008, People's Republic of China.*
Email: duanziming@163.com

Abstract. Let G be a graph of order p, and let a and b and n be nonnegative integers with $1< a < b$, and let g and f be two integer-valued functions defined on $V(G)$ such that $a \le g(x) \le f(x) \le b$ for all $x \in V(G)$. A (g, f)-factor of graph G is defined as a spanning sub graph F of G such that $g(x) \le d_F(x) \le f(x)$ for each $x \in V(G)$. Then a graph G is called a (g, f, n)-critical graph if after deleting any n vertices of G the remaining graph of G has a (g, f)-factor. In this paper, we prove that every graph G is a (g, f, n)-critical graph if its minimum degree is greater than $p + a + b \quad 2\sqrt{(a \mid 1)p \quad bn \mid 1}$. Furthermore, it is showed that the result in this paper is best possible in some sense.

Keywords: graph, minimum degree, $(g,$ f)-factor, (g, f, n)-critical graph.
PACS: 02.10.Ox

1. INTRODUCTION

In this paper, we consider a finite graph G with vertex set $V(G)$ and edge set $E(G)$, which has neither loops nor multiple edges. For any vertex x of G, we denote by $d_G(x)$ the degree of x in G. We denote by $\delta(G)$ the minimum vertex degree of G. For any $S \subseteq V(G)$, the subgraph of G induced by S is denoted by $G[S]$ and $G-S=G[V(G)\setminus S]$.

Let g and f be two nonnegative integer-valued functions defined on $V(G)$ such that $g(x) \le f(x)$ for each $x \in V(G)$. A (g,f)-factor of graph G is defined as a spanning subgraph F of G such that $g(x) \le d_F(x) \le f(x)$ for each $x \in V(G)$ (Where of course d_F-denotes the degree in F). If $g(x)=f(x)$ for each $x \in V(G)$, then a (g,f)-factor is called an f-factor. If $g(x)=a$ and $f(x)=b$ for all $x \in V(G)$, then a (g,f)-factor is called an $[a,b]$-factor. If $g(x)=f(x)=k$ for all $x \in V(G)$, then a (g,f)-factor is called a k-factor. A graph G is called a (g,f,n)-critical graph if after deleting any n vertices of G the remaining graph of G has a (g,f)-factor. If G is a (g,f,n)-critical graph, then we also say that G is (g,f,n)-critical. If $g(x)=f(x)$ for each $x \in V(G)$, then a (g,f,n)-critical graph is an (f,n)-critical graph. If $g(x)=a$ and $f(x)=b$ for all $x \in V(G)$, then a (g,f,n)-critical graph is an (a,b,n)-critical graph. If $a=b=k$, then an (a,b,n)-critical graph is simply called a (k,n)-critical graph. In particular, a $(1,n)$-critical graph is simply called an n-critical graph. The other notations and definitions not given in this paper can be found in [1].

Q. Yu [2] gave the characterization of n-critical graphs. O. Favaron [3] studied the properties of n-critical graphs. G. Liu and Q. Yu [4] studied the characterization of (k,n)-critical graphs. The characterization of (a,b,n)-critical graphs with $a<b$ was given by G. Liu and J. Wang[5]. S. Zhou [6,7,8,13] gave some sufficient conditions for graphs to be (a,b,n)-critical graphs. J. Li [9] showed two sufficient conditions for graphs to be (a,b,n)-critical graphs. S. Zhou [10] obtained a sufficient condition for graphs to be (g,f,n)-critical graphs. The characterization of (g,f,n)-critical graphs was given by J. Li and H. Matsuda [11]. In this paper, we obtain two new sufficient conditions for graphs to be (g,f,n)-critical graphs. The main results will be given in the following section. The following results on k-factors and (a,b,k)-critical graphs and (g,f,n)-critical graphs are known.

In [12], Y. Egawa and H. Enomoto proved the following result for the existence of k-factors.

Theorem 1.[12] Let $k \geq 2$ be an integer, and let G be a graph of order n, kn is even. If

$$\delta(G) > n + 2k - 2\sqrt{kn+1},$$

then G has a k-factor.

In [8], S. Zhou and M. Zong gave a sufficient condition for graphs to be (a,b,k)-critical graphs.

Theorem 2.[8] Let a,b and k be nonnegative integers such that $1 \leq a < b$ and G be a graph with order $n \geq \frac{(a-1)(a+1)(a+b)(a+b-1)}{a(b-1)} - \frac{(a+b)(ab+b-1)}{ab(b-1)} + k$. If $\delta(G) \geq a+k$, and

$$\max\{d_G(x), d_G(y)\} \geq \frac{an+bk}{a+b}$$

for any vertices x and y of $V(G)$ with $d(x,y)=2$. Then G is an (a,b,k)-critical graph.

In [10], S. Zhou showed a sufficient condition for graphs to be (g,f,n)-critical graphs.

Theorem 3.[10] Let G be a graph, and let g and f be two nonnegative integer-valued functions defined on $V(G)$ such that $g(x)<f(x)$ for each $x \in V(G)$. If $g(x) \le d_G(x)$ and $f(x)(d_G(y)-n) \ge d_G(x)g(y)$ for each $x,y \in V(G)$, then G is a $(g,f,$ n)-critical graph. Here n is a nonnegative integer.

2. THE PROOF OF MAIN THEOREMS

In this paper, we obtain a new sufficient condition for graphs to be (g,f,n)-critical graphs. Our result is the extension of Theorem 1.

Theorem 4. Let G be a graph of order p, and let a,b and n be nonnegative integers such that $1 \le a < b$, and let g and f be two integer-valued functions defined on $V(G)$ such that $a \le g(x) < f(x) \le b$ for each $x \in V(G)$. If

$$\delta(G) > p + a + b - 2\sqrt{(a+1)p - bn + 1}, \tag{1}$$

then G is a (g,f,n)-critical graph.

In Theorem 4, if $n=0$, then we obtain the following corollary.

Corollary 1. Let G be a graph of order p, and let a and b be integers such that $1 \le a < b$, and let g and f be two integer-valued functions defined on $V(G)$ such that $a \le g(x) < f(x) \le b$ for each $x \in V(G)$. If

$$\delta(G) > p + a + b - 2\sqrt{(a+1)p + 1},$$

then G has a (g,f)-factor.

According to Corollary 1 and the definition of $(g,f,$ n)-critical graph, we obtain easily the following result.

Theorem 5. Let G be a graph of order p, and let a,b and n be nonnegative integers such that $1 \le a < b$, and let g and f be two integer-valued functions defined on $V(G)$ such that $a \le g(x) < f(x) \le b$ for each $x \in V(G)$. If

$$\delta(G) > p + a + b - 2\sqrt{(a+1)p + 1} + n,$$

then G is a (g,f,n)-critical graph.

Let S and T be disjoint subsets of $V(G)$. We write $e_G(S,T) = |\{xy \in E(G) : x \in S, y \in T\}|$, $f(S) = \Sigma_{x \in S} f(x)$, $d_{G-S}(T) = \Sigma_{x \in T} d_{G-S}(x)$, and $g(T) = \Sigma_{x \in T} g(x)$. Our proof of Theorem 4 relies heavily on the following theorem.

Theorem 6.[11] Let G be a graph, $n \ge 0$ an integer, and let g and f be two integer-valued functions defined on $V(G)$ such that $g(x) < f(x)$ for each $x \in V(G)$. Then G is a (g,f,n)-

critical graph if and only if

$$\delta_G(S,T) = f(S)+d_{G-S}(T)-g(T) \\ \geq \max\{f(N) : N \subseteq S, |N| = n\}$$

for all disjoint subsets S and T of $V(G)$ with $|S| \geq n$.

Proof of Theorem 4. Suppose a graph G satisfies the condition of the theorem, but it is not a (g,f,n)-critical graph. Then, by Theorem 6, there exist disjoint subsets S and T of $V(G)$ with $|S| \geq n$ such that

$$\delta_G(S,T) = f(S) + d_{G-S}(T) - g(T) \leq \max\{f(N) : N \subseteq S, |N| = n\} - 1. \tag{2}$$

We choose subsets S and T such that $|T|$ is minimum and S and T satisfy (2).

Claim 1. $d_{G-S}(x) \leq g(x) - 1 \leq b-2$ for each $x \in T$.
Proof. Suppose that there exists a vertex $x \in T$ such that $d_{G-S}(x) \geq g(x)$. Then the subsets S and $T - \{x\}$ satisfy (2), which contradicts the choice of T.
Completing the proof of Claim 1.

If $T = \emptyset$, then by (2), $f(S) - 1 \geq \max\{f(N) : N \subseteq S, |N| = n\} - 1 \geq \delta_G(S,T) = f(S)$, a contradiction. Hence, $T \neq \emptyset$. Let

$$h = \min\{d_{G-S}(x) : x \in T\}.$$

According to Claim 1, we have

$$0 \leq h \leq b-2,$$

and

$$\delta(G) \leq h + |S|. \tag{3}$$

According to (2) and $|S| + |T| \leq p$, we get that

$$\begin{aligned} bn - 1 &\geq \max\{f(N) : N \subseteq S, |N| = n\} - 1 \\ &\geq \delta_G(S,T) = f(S) + d_{G-S}(T) - g(T) \\ &\geq (a+1)|S| + d_{G-S}(T) - (b-1)|T| \\ &\geq (a+1)|S| + h|T| - (b-1)|T| \\ &= (a+1)|S| - (b-h-1)|T| \\ &\geq (a+1)|S| - (b-h-1)(p-|S|) \\ &= (a+b-h)|S| - (b-h-1)p. \end{aligned}$$

Thus, we obtain

$$|S| \leq \frac{(b-h-1)p + bn - 1}{a+b-h}. \tag{4}$$

In view of (3) and (4), we have

$$\delta(G) \le h + |S| \le h + \frac{(b-h-1)p + bn - 1}{a+b-h}. \tag{5}$$

Let $f(h) = h + \frac{(b-h-1)p+bn-1}{a+b-h}$. In the range of $h \le a+b$, the function $f(h)$ attains its maximum value at $h = a+b-\sqrt{(a+1)p-bn+1}$. Since $0 \le h \le b-2$, then we have

$$\begin{aligned} f(h) &\le f(a+b-\sqrt{(a+1)p-bn+1}) \\ &= p+a+b-2\sqrt{(a+1)p-bn+1}, \end{aligned}$$

that is,

$$\delta(G) \le p+a+b-2\sqrt{(a+1)p-bn+1},$$

this contradicts (1).

From the argument above, we deduce the contradiction. Hence, G is a (g,f,n)-critical graph.
Completing the proof of Theorem 4.

The binding number $bind(G)$ of G is the minimum value of $\frac{|N_G(X)|}{|X|}$ taken over all non-empty subsets X of $V(G)$ such that $N_G(X) \ne V(G)$. The binding number condition on (a,b,k)-critical graphs was given by Sizhong Zhou and Jiashang Jiang [7].

Theorem 7.[7] Let G be a graph of order n, and let a,b and k be nonnegative integers such that $1 \le a < b$. If the binding number $bind(G) > \frac{(a+b-1)(n-1)}{bn-(a+b)-bk+2}$ and $n \ge \frac{(a+b-1)(a+b-2)}{b} + \frac{bk}{b-1}$, then G is an (a,b,k)-critical graph.
In Theorem 7, if $k=0$, then we get the following corollary.
Corollary 2. Let G be a graph of order n, and let a and b be two integers such that $1 \le a < b$. If the binding number $bind(G) > \frac{(a+b-1)(n-1)}{bn-(a+b)+2}$ and $n \ge \frac{(a+b-1)(a+b-2)}{b}$, then G has an $[a,b]$-factor.

Let a,b and k be nonnegative integers such that $1 \le a < b$. The proof of Theorem 7 relies heavily on the following theorem.

Theorem 8.[5] Let G be a graph of order $n \geq a + k + 1$. Then G is (a,b,k)-critical if and only if for any $S \subseteq V(G)$ and $|S| \geq k$

$$\sum_{j=0}^{a-1}(a-j)p_j(G-S) \leq b|S| - bk \text{, or}$$

$$\delta_G(S,T) = b|S| + d_{G-S}(T) - a|T| \geq bk,$$

where $T=\{x : x \in V(G) \setminus S,\ d_{G-S}(x) \leq a-1\}$.

Proof of Theorem 7. Suppose a graph G satisfies the condition of the theorem, but it is not an (a,b,k)-critical graph. Then, by Theorem 8, there exists a subset S of $V(G)$ with $|S| \geq k$ such that

$$\delta_G(S,T) = b|S| + d_{G-S}(T) - a|T| \leq bk - 1, \tag{6}$$

where $T=\{x : x \in V(G) \setminus S,\ d_{G-S}(x) \leq a-1\}$. We choose subsets S and T such that $|T|$ is minimum and S and T satisfy (6).

If $T = \emptyset$, then by (6), $bk-1 \geq \delta_G(S,T) = b|S| \geq bk$, a contradiction. Hence, $T \neq \emptyset$.

Let

$$h = \min\{d_{G-S}(x) : x \in T\}.$$

According to the definition of T, we have

$$0 \leq h \leq a - 1.$$

We shall consider various cases according to the value of h and derive contradictions.

Case 1. $h = 0$.

At first, we prove the following claim.

Claim 2. $\dfrac{bn-(a+b)-bk+2}{n-1} > 1.$

Proof. Since $n \geq \dfrac{(a+b-1)(a+b-2)}{b} + \dfrac{bk}{b-1}$, then we have

$$\begin{aligned} bn-(a+b)-bk+2-(n-1) &= (b-1)n-(a+b)-bk+3 \\ &\ge (b-1)\left(\frac{(a+b-1)(a+b-2)}{b}+\frac{bk}{b-1}\right)-(a+b)-bk+3 \\ &= \frac{(b-1)(a+b-1)(a+b-2)}{b}-(a+b)+3 \\ &\ge (a+b-2)-(a+b)+3>0 \end{aligned}$$

Thus, we have

$$\frac{bn-(a+b)-bk+2}{n-1}>1.$$

Completing the proof of Claim 2.

Let $m=|\{x : x\in T,\ d_{G-S}(x)=0\}|$, and let $Y=V(G)\setminus S$. Then $N_G(Y)\neq V(G)$ since h=0. In view of the definition of the binding number *bind*(G), we get that

$$|N_G(Y)|\ge bind(G)\,|Y|.$$

Thus, we obtain

$$n-m\ge|N_G(Y)|\ge bind(G)\,|Y|=bind(G)(n-|S|),$$

that is,

$$|S|\ge n-\frac{n-m}{bind(G)}. \tag{7}$$

Using $|S|+|T|\le n$ and (6) and (7) and Claim 2, we have

$$\begin{aligned} bk-1 &\ge \delta_G(S,T)=b|S|+d_{G-S}(T)-a|T| \\ &\ge b|S|-(a-1)|T|-m \\ &\ge b|S|-(a-1)(n-|S|)-m \\ &=(a+b-1)|S|-(a-1)n-m \\ &\ge (a+b-1)\left(n-\frac{n-m}{bind(G)}\right)-(a-1)n-m \\ &= bn-(a+b-1)\frac{n-m}{bind(G)}-m \\ &> bn-(a+b-1)\frac{(n-m)(bn-(a+b)-bk+2)}{(a+b-1)(n-1)}-m \\ &= bn-\frac{(n-m)(bn-(a+b)-bk+2)}{n-1}-m \end{aligned}$$

$$\geq bn - \frac{(n-1)(bn-(a+b)-bk+2)}{n-1} - 1$$
$$= bk + (a+b) - 3$$
$$\geq bk,$$

which is a contradiction.

Case 2. $1 \leq h \leq a-1$.

Let x_1 be a vertex in T such that $d_{G-S}(x_1)=h$, and let $Y = (V(G) \setminus S) \setminus N_{G-S}(x_1)$. Then $x_1 \in Y \setminus N_G(Y)$, so $Y \neq \emptyset$ and $N_G(Y) \neq V(G)$. In view of the definition of the binding number $bind(G)$, we obtain

$$\frac{|N_G(Y)|}{|Y|} \geq bind(G).$$

Thus, we get that

$$n-1 \geq |N_G(Y)| \geq bind(G)\,|Y| = bind(G)(n-h-|S|),$$

that is,

$$|S| \geq n-h-\frac{n-1}{bind(G)}. \tag{8}$$

By $|S|+|T| \leq n$ and (6) and (8), we obtain

$$bk-1 \geq \delta_G(S,T) = b|S| + d_{G-S}(T) - a|T|$$
$$\geq b|S| - (a-h)|T|$$
$$\geq b|S| - (a-h)(n-|S|)$$
$$= (a+b-h)|S| - (a-h)n$$
$$\geq (a+b-h)(n-h-\frac{n-1}{bind(G)}) - (a-h)n$$
$$> (a+b-h)(n-h-\frac{bn-(a+b)-bk+2}{a+b-1}) - (a-h)n,$$

that is,

$$bk-1 > (a+b-h)(n-h-\frac{bn-(a+b)-bk+2}{a+b-1}) - (a-h)n. \tag{9}$$

Let $f(h) = (a+b-h)(n-h-\frac{bn-(a+b)-bk+2}{a+b-1}) - (a-h)n$. In fact, the function $f(h)$ attains its minimum value at $h=1$ since $1 \leq h \leq a-1$ is an integer. Then, we have

$$f(h) \geq f(1).$$

Combining this with (9), we obtain

$$\begin{aligned} bk-1 > f(1) &= (a+b-1)(n-1-\frac{bn-(a+b)-bk+2}{a+b-1})-(a-1)n \\ &= (a+b-1)(n-1)-(bn-(a+b)-bk+2)-(a-1)n \\ &= bk-1, \end{aligned}$$

that is a contradiction.

From the argument above, we deduce the contradictions, so the hypothesis cannot hold. Hence, G is (a, b, k)-critical.
Completing the proof of Theorem 7.

Remark 1. Let us show that the condition $\delta(G) > p+a+b-2\sqrt{(a+1)p-bn+1}$ in Theorem 4 cannot be replaced by $\delta(G) \geq p+a+b-2\sqrt{(a+1)p-bn+1}$. Let $a=2$, $b=3$, and $n \geq 0$ an integer. Let $H = K_{n+1} \vee (K_a \cup K_a)$. Then $p=2a+n+1$ and $\delta(H)=a+n$. Thus, we obtain easily $p+a+b-2\sqrt{(a+1)p-bn+1} = a+n$, that is, $\delta(H) = p+a+b-2\sqrt{(a+1)p-bn+1}$. Let $S=V(K_{n+1}) \subseteq V(H)$, $T=V(Ka \cup K_a) \subseteq V(H)$. Since $a \leq g(x) < f(x) \leq b$ and $b=a+1$, then we have $g(x)=a$ and $f(x)=b=a+1$. Thus, we get

$$\begin{aligned} \delta_H(S,T) &= f(S)+d_{H-S}(T)-g(T) \\ &= b|S|+(a-1)|T|-a|T| \\ &= b|S|-|T| \\ &= b(n+1)-2a \\ &= bn+b-2a \\ &= bn-1 \qquad (\textit{Since } a=2 \textit{ and } b=3) \\ &< bn = \max\{f(N) : N \subseteq S, |N|=n\}. \end{aligned}$$

By Theorem 6, H is not a (g, f, n)-critical graph. In the above sense, the result of Theorem 4 is best possible.

Remark 2. We may adopt the similar way to argue the condition $\delta(G) > p+a+b-2\sqrt{(a+1)p+1}+n$ in Theorem 5, and the condition $\delta(G) > p+a+b-2\sqrt{(a+1)p+1}+n$ in Theorem 5 is the best possible in some sense.

Remark 3. Let us show that the condition $bind(G) > \frac{(a+b-1)(n-1)}{bn-(a+b)-bk+2}$ in Theorem 7 cannot be replaced by $bind(G) \geq \frac{(a+b-1)(n-1)}{bn-(a+b)-bk+2}$. Let $b > a \geq 2, k \geq 0$ be three integers such that $a+b+k$

is odd, and let $n=\frac{(a+b-1)(a+b-2)+(a+b-2)+(a+2b-1)k}{b}$ is an integer, and let $l=\frac{a+b+k-1}{2}$ and $m=n-2l=n-(a+b+k-1)=\frac{(a+b-1)(a-2)+(a+b-2)+(a+b-1)k}{b}$. Clearly, m is an integer. Let $H=K_m \vee lK_2$. Let $X=V(lK_2)$, for any $x \in X$, then $|N_H(X \setminus x)| = n-1$. By the definition of $bind(H)$, $bind(H) =\frac{|N_H(X\setminus x|}{|X\setminus x|}=\frac{n-1}{2l-1}=\frac{n-1}{a+b+k-2}=\frac{(a+b-1)(n-1}{bn-(a+b)-bk+2}$. Let $S=V(Km) \subseteq V(H)$, $T=V(lK_2) \subseteq V(H)$, then $|S| = m \geq k$, $|T| = 2l$.
Thus, we get

$$\begin{aligned}\delta_H(S,T) &= b|S|-a|T|+d_{H-S}(T)\\ &= b|S|-a|T|+|T|= b|S|-(a-1)|T|\\ &= b\frac{(a+b-1)(a-2)+(a+b-2)+(a+b-1)k}{b}-(a-1)(a+b+k-1)\\ &= bk-1<bk.\end{aligned}$$

By Theorem 8, H is not an (a,b,k)-critical graph. In the above sense, the result in Theorem 7 is best possible.

3. ACKNOWLEDGMENTS

The authors would like to thank the referees for their helpful comments and suggestions. This research was supported by Jiangsu Provincial Educational Department (07KJD110048).

4. REFERENCES

J. A. Bondy, U. S. R. Murty, *Graph Theory with Applications,* The Macmillan Press, London, 1976.

Qinglin Yu, "Characterizations of various matching extensions in graphs," *Australasian Journal of Combinatorics* 7, 55-64 (1993).

O. Favaron, "On k-factor-critical graphs," *Discussiones Mathematicae Graph Theory* **16**, 41-51 (1996).

Guizhen Liu, Qinglin Yu, "k-factors and extendability with prescribed components," *Congr. Numer.* **139**, 77-88 (1999).

Guizhen Liu, Jianfang Wang, "(a, b, k) -critical graphs," *Advances in Mathematics(China)* **27**, 536-540 (1998).

SizhongZhou, "Sufficient conditions for (a, b, k)-critical graphs," *Journal of Jilin University (Science Edition)(China)* **43**, 607-609 (2005).

Sizhong Zhou, Jiashang Jiang, "Notes on the binding numbers for (a, b, k)-critical graphs," *Bulletin of the Australian Mathematical Society* **76**, 307-314 (2007).

Sizhong Zhou, Minggang Zong, "Some new sufficient conditions for graphs to be (a, b, k)-critical graphs," *Ars Combinatoria,* to appear.

Jianxiang Li, "Sufficient conditions for graphs to be (a, b, n)-critical graphs," *Mathematica Applicata (China)* **17**, 450-455 (2004).

Sizhong Zhou, "Some sufficient conditions for graphs to have (g, f)-factors," *Bulletin of the Australian Mathematical Society* **75**, 447-452 (2007).

Jianxiang Li, H. Matsuda, "On $(g, f,$ n)-critical graphs," *Ars Combinatoria* **78**, 71-82 (2006).

Y. Egawa, H. Enomoto, "Sufficient conditions for the existence of k-factors," *Recent Studies in Graph Theory,* Vishwa International Publication, India, 96-105 (1989).

Sizhong Zhou, "Binding number conditions for (a, b, k) -critical graphs," *Bulletin of the Korean Mathematical Society* **45**, 53-57 (2008).

Metacomputing with Federated Method Invocation

Michael Sobolewski
Texas Tech University
Lubbock, TX

1. Introduction

The term "grid computing" originated in the early 1990s as a metaphor for accessing computer power as easy as an electric power grid. Today there are many definitions of grid computing (Foster et al., 2001) with a varying focus on architectures, resource management and access, virtualization, provisioning, and sharing between heterogeneous compute domains. Thus, diverse compute resources across different administrative domains form a *compute grid* for the shared and coordinated use of resources in dynamic, distributed, and virtual computing organizations. These organizations are dynamic subsets of departmental grids, enterprise grids, and global grids, which allow programs to use shared resources—collaborative compute federations.

A *computer* as a programmable device that performs symbol processing, especially one that can process, store and retrieve large amounts of data very quickly, requires a computing platform (runtime) to operate. *Computing platforms* that allow software to run require a *processor, operating system*, and *programming environment* with related runtime libraries or user agents. Therefore, the grid requires a *platform* that describes a kind of framework to allow software to run utilizing virtual organizations. Different platforms of grids can be distinguished along with corresponding types of virtual federations. However, in order to make any grid-based computing possible, computational modules have to be defined in terms of *platform data, operations*, and *relevant control strategies*.

For a grid program, the control strategy is a plan for achieving the desired results by applying the platform operations to the data in the required sequence and by leveraging the dynamically federating resources. We can distinguish three generic grid platforms, which are described below.

Programmers use abstractions all the time. The source code written in a software language is an abstraction of machine language. From machine language to object-oriented programming, layers of abstractions have accumulated like geological strata. Every generation of programmers uses its era's programming languages and tools to build programs of next generation. Each programming language reflects a relevant abstraction, and usually the type and quality of the abstraction implies the complexity of problems we are able to solve.

Procedural languages provide an abstraction of an underlying machine language. An executable file represents a computing component whose content is interpreted as a program by the underlying native processor. A request can be submitted to a *grid resource broker* to execute a machine code in a particular way, e.g., by parallelizing and collocating it dynamically to the right processors in the grid. That can be done, for example, with the Nimrod-G grid resource broker scheduler ("Nimrod", n.d.) or the Condor-G high-throughput scheduler (Thain, 2003). Both rely on Globus/GRAM (Grid Resource Allocation and Management) protocol (Sotomayor & Childers, 2005). In this type of grid, called a *compute grid*, executable files are moved around the grid to form virtual federations of required processors. This approach is reminiscent of batch processing in the era when operating systems were not yet developed. A series of programs ("jobs") is executed on a computer without human interaction or the possibility to view any results before the execution is complete.

We consider a true grid program as the abstraction of hierarchically organized collection of component programs that makes decisions about when and how to run them. This abstraction is a *metaprogram*—a program that manipulates other programs as its data. Nowadays the same computing abstraction is usually applied to the program executing on a single computer as to the metaprogram executing in the grid of computers, even though the executing environments (platforms) are structurally completely different. Most grid programs are still written using software languages (generating native processor code) such as FORTRAN, C, C++, Java, and interpreted languages such as Perl and Python the way it usually works on a single host. The current trend is still to have these programs and scripts define grid computational modules as *services*. Thus, most grid computing modules are developed using the same abstractions and, in principle, run the same way on the grid as on a single processor. There is presently no grid programming methodologies to deploy a metaprogram that will dynamically federate all needed services in the grid according to a control strategy aligned with the consistent *service algorithmic logic*. Applying the same programming abstractions to the grid as to a single computer does not foster transitioning from the current phase of early grid adopters to public recognition and then to mass adoption phases.

The reality at present is that grid resources are still very difficult for most users to access, and that detailed programming must be carried out by the user through command line and script execution to carefully tailor jobs on each end to the resources on which they will run, or for the data structure that they will access. This produces frustration for the user, delays in the adoption of grid techniques, and a multiplicity of specialized "grid-aware" tools that are not, in fact, aware of each other that defeat the basic purpose of the compute grid. Thinking more explicitly about grid programming languages than software languages may be our best tool for dealing with real world complexity. By understanding the principles that run across languages, appreciating which language traits are best suited for which type of application (service), and knowing how to craft the relevant infrastructure we can bring these languages to synergistic life and deal efficiently with the evolving complexity of distributed computing.

Instead of moving executable files around the compute grid, we can autonomically provision the corresponding computational components as uniform services on the grid. All grid services can be interpreted as instructions (metainstructions) of the *metacompute grid*. Now we can submit a metaprogram in terms of metainstructions to the *grid platform* that manages a dynamic federation of service providers and related resources, and enables the metaprogram to interact with the service providers according to the metaprogram control strategy. We consider a *service* as interface type, for example identified as a Java interface. A provider can implement multiple interfaces, thus can provide multiple services. While grid computing is about utilizing virtual organization, metacomputing is about utilizing virtual processor with its instruction set in terms of services.

The term "metacomputing" was coined around 1987 by NCSA Director, Larry Smarr ("Metacomputing", n.d.). "The metacomputer is, simply put, a collection of computers held together by state-of-the-art technology and *balanced* so that, to the individual user, it looks and acts like a single computer. The constituent parts of the resulting *metacomputer* could be housed locally, or distributed between buildings, even continents ("Metacomputer", n.d.).

We can distinguish three types of grids depending on the nature of computational platforms: *compute grids* (*cGrids*), *metacompute grids* (*mcGrids*), and the hybrid of the previous two—*intergrids* (*iGrids*). Note that a cGrid is a virtual federation of processors (roughly CPUs) that execute submitted executable codes with the help of a grid resource broker. However, a mcGrid is a federation of service providers managed by the mcGrid operating system. Thus, the latter approach requires a metaprogramming methodology while in the former case the conventional procedural programming languages are used. The hybrid of both cGrid and mcGrid abstractions allows for an iGrid to execute both programs and metaprograms as depicted in Fig. 1, where platform layers P1, P2, and P3 correspond to resources, resource management, and programming environment correspondingly.

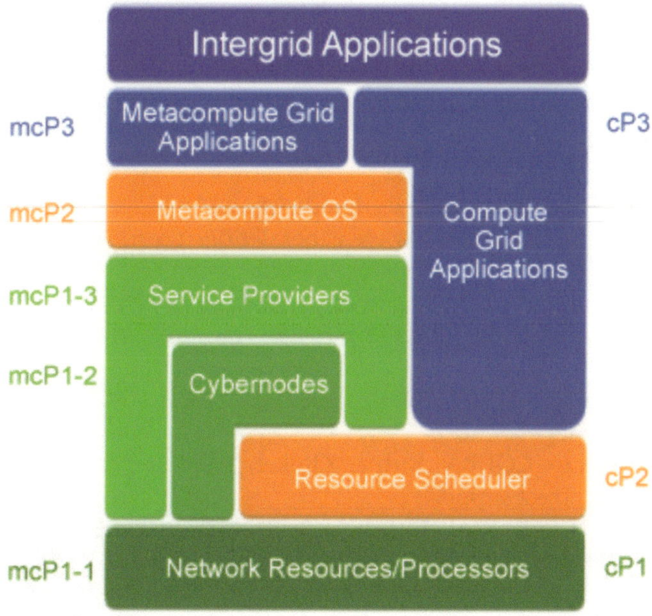

Fig. 1. Three types of grids: metacompute grid, compute grid, and intergrid. A cybernode provides a lightweight dynamic virtual processor, turning heterogeneous compute resources into homogeneous services available to the metacomputing OS ("Project Rio", n.d.)

One of the first mcGrids was developed under the sponsorship of the National Institute for Standards and Technology (NIST)—the Federated Intelligent Product Environment (FIPER)

(Röhl et al., 2000; Sobolewski, 2002). The goal of FIPER is to form a federation of distributed services that provide engineering data, applications, and tools on a network. A highly flexible software architecture had been developed (1999-2003), in which engineering tools like computer-aided design (CAD), computer-aided engineering (CAE), product data management (PDM), optimization, cost modeling, etc., act as federating service providers and service requestors.

The Service-ORiented Computing EnviRonment (SORCER) builds on the top of FIPER to introduce a metacomputing operating system with all system services necessary, including a federated file system and autonomic resource management, to support service-oriented metaprogramming. It provides an integrated solution for complex metacomputing applications. The SORCER metacomputing environment adds an entirely new layer of abstraction to the practice of grid computing—exertion-oriented (EO) programming with complementary federated method invocation. The EO programming makes a positive difference in service-oriented programming primarily through a new metaprogramming abstraction as experienced in many service-oriented computing projects including systems deployed at GE Global Research Center, GE Aviation, Air Force Research Lab, and SORCER Lab.

This chapter is organized as follows. Section 2 gives overview of RPC generations; Section 3 provides a brief description of two service-oriented architectures used in grid computing with a related discussion of distribution transparency; Section 4 describes the SORCER metacomputing philosophy and its federated method invocation; Section 5 describes the SORCER compute grid; Section 6 describes federated file system; Section 7 presents autonomic resource management; Section 8 explains the notion of intergrid and future development, and Section 9 provides concluding remarks.

2. Generations of Remote Procedure Call

Socket-based communication forces us to design distributed applications using a read/write (input/output) interface, which is not how we generally design non-distributed applications based on procedure call (request/response) communication. In 1983, Birrell and Nelson devised remote procedure call (RPC) (Birrell & Nelson, 1983), a mechanism to allow programs to call procedures on other hosts. So far, six RPC generations can be distinguished:

1. First generation RPCs—Sun RPC (ONC RPC) and DCE RPC, which are language, architecture, and OS independent;
2. Second generation RPCs—CORBA (Ruh & Klinker, 1999) and Microsoft DCOM-ORPC, which add distributed object support;
3. Third generation RPC—Java RMI (Pitt & McNiff, 2001) is conceptually similar to the second generation but supports the semantics of object invocation in different address spaces that are built for Java only. Java RMI fits cleanly into the language with no need for standardized data representation, external interface definition language, and with behavioral transfer that allows remote objects to perform operations that are determined at runtime;
4. Fourth generation RPC—next generation of Java RMI, Jini Extensible Remote Invocation ("Package net.jini.jeri", n.d) with dynamic proxies, smart proxies, network security, and

with dependency injection by defining exporters, end points, and security properties in deployment configuration files;

5. Fifth generation RPCs—Web/OGSA Services RPC (McGovern et al., 2003; Sotomayor & Childers, 2005) and the XML movement including Microsoft WCF/.NET;
6. Sixth generation RPC—Federated Method Invocation (FMI) (Sobolewski, 2007), allows for concurrent invocations on multiple federating compute resources (virtual metaprocessor) in the evolving SORCER environment (Sobolewski, 2008b).

All the RPC generations listed above are based on a form of service-oriented architecture (SOA) discussed in Section 3. However, CORBA, RMI, and Web/OGSA service providers are in fact object-oriented wrappers of network interfaces that hide object distribution and ignore the real nature of network through classical object abstractions that encapsulate network connectivity by using existing network technologies. The fact that object-oriented languages are used to create these object wrappers does not mean that developed distributed objects have a great deal to do with object-oriented distributed programming. For example, CORBA defines many services, and implementing them using distributed objects does not make them well structured with core object-oriented features: encapsulation, instantiation, and polymorphism. Similarly in Java RMI, marking objects with the Remote interface does not help to cope with network-centric messaging, for example when calling on a dead stub. Network centricity here means that sending a message to a remote object, in fact is sending it onto the network in the first place, and then dispatching it to a live remote object provided by the network in runtime and uniformly. Network-centric messaging should encapsulate object discovery, fault detection, recovery, partial failure, and others.

Each platform and its programming language used reflect a relevant abstraction, and usually the type and quality of the abstraction implies the complexity of problems we are able to solve. For example, a procedural language provides an abstraction of an underlying machine language. Building on the object-oriented distributed paradigm is the service object-oriented infrastructure exemplified by the Jini service architecture ("Jini architecture specification", n.d.; Edwards, 2000) in which the network objects come together on-the-fly to play their predefined roles. In the Service-ORiented Computing EnviRonmet (SORCER) developed at Texas Tech University ("SORCER Research Group", n.d.)), a service provider is a remote object that accepts network requests to participate in a collaboration—a process by which service providers work together to seek solutions that reach beyond what any one of them could accomplish on their own. While conventional objects encapsulate explicitly *data* and *operations*, the network requests called *exertions* encapsulate explicitly *data*, *operations*, and *control strategy*. An exertion can federate concurrently and transparently on multiple hosts according to its *control strategy* by hiding all low-level Jini networking details as well.

The SORCER metacomputing environment adds an entirely new layer of abstraction to the practice of grid computing—*exertion-oriented (EO) programming*. The EO programming makes a positive difference in service-oriented programming primarily through a new metacomputing platform as experienced in many grid-computing projects including applications deployed at GE Global Research Center, GE Aviation, Air Force Research Lab, and SORCER Lab. The new abstraction is about managing object-oriented distributed system complexity laid upon the complexity of the network of computers—metacomputer.

An exertion submitted onto the network dynamically binds to all relevant and currently available service providers in the object-oriented distributed system. The providers that dynamically participate in this invocation are collectively called an *exertion federation*. This

federation is also called a *virtual metaprocessor* since federating services are located on multiple processors held together by the EO infrastructure so that, to the requestor submitting the exertion, it looks and acts like a single processor.
The SORCER environment provides the means to create interactive EO programs (Sobolewski & Kolonay, 2006) and execute them using the SORCER runtime infrastructure presented in Section 4. Exertions can be created using interactive user agents downloaded on-the-fly from service providers. Using these interfaces, the user can create, execute, and monitor the execution of exertions within the EO platform. The exertions can be persisted for later reuse, allowing the user to quickly create new applications or EO programs on-the-fly in terms of existing, usually persisted for reuse exertions.
SORCER is based on the evolution of concepts and lessons learned in the FIPER project ("FIPER", n.d.), a $21.5 million program founded by NIST (National Institute of Standards and Technology). Academic research on FMI and EO programming has been established at the SORCER Laboratory, TTU, ("SORECE Research Group", n.d) where twenty-eight SORCER related research studies have been investigated so far ("SORCER Research Topics", n.d.).

3. SOA and Distribution Transparency

Various definitions of a Service-Oriented Architecture (SOA) leave a lot of room for interpretation. In general terms, SOA is a software architecture using loosely coupled software services that integrates them into a distributed computing system by means of service-oriented programming. Service providers in the SOA environment are made available as independent service components that can be accessed without a priori knowledge of their underlying platform or implementation. While the client-server architecture separates a client from a server, SOA introduces a third component, a service registry, as illustrated in Fig. 2 (the left chart). In SOA, the client is referred to as a service requestor and the server as a service provider. The provider is responsible for deploying a service on the network, publishing its service to one or more registries, and allowing requestors to bind and execute the service. Providers advertise their availability on the network; registries intercept these announcements and collect published services. The requestor looks up a service by sending queries to registries and making selections from the available services. Requestors and providers can use discovery and join protocols to locate registries and then publish or acquire services on the network.

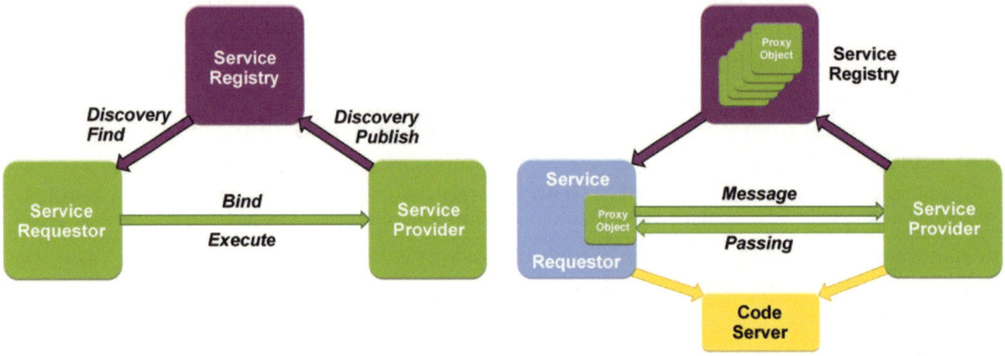

Fig. 2. SOA versus SOOA

We can distinguish the *service object-oriented architecture* (SOOA), where providers are network (*call/response*) objects accepting remote invocations, from the *service protocol oriented architecture* (SPOA), where a communication (*read/write*) protocol is fixed and known beforehand by the provider and requestor. Based on that protocol and a service description obtained from the service registry, the requestor can bind to the service provider by creating a proxy used for remote communication over the fixed protocol. In SPOA a service is usually identified by a name. If a service provider registers its service description by name, the requestors have to know the name of the service beforehand.

In SOOA, a proxy—an object implementing the same service interfaces as its service provider—is registered with the registries and it is always ready for use by requestors. Thus, in SOOA, the service provider publishes the proxy as the active surrogate object with a codebase annotation, e.g., URLs to the code defining proxy behavior (RMI and Jini ERI). In SPOA, by contrast, a passive service description is registered (e.g., an XML document in WSDL for Web/OGSA services, or an interface description in IDL for CORBA); the requestor then has to generate the proxy (a stub forwarding calls to a provider) based on a service description and the fixed communication protocol (e.g., SOAP in Web/OGSA services, IIOP in CORBA). This is referred to as a bind operation. The proxy binding operation is not required in SOOA since the requestor holds the active surrogate object obtained via the registry. The surrogate object is already bound to the provider that registered it with its appropriate network configuration and its code annotations.

Web services and OGSA services cannot change the communication protocol between requestors and providers while the SOOA approach is protocol neutral ("Waldo", n.d.). In SOOA, how the object proxy communicates with a provider is established by the contract between the provider and its published proxy and defined by the provider implementation. The proxy's requestor does not need to know who implements the interface or how it is implemented. So-called smart proxies (Jini ERI) can grant access to local and remote resources; they can also communicate with multiple providers on the network regardless of who originally registered the proxy. Thus, separate providers on the network can implement different parts of the smart proxy interface. Communication protocols may also vary, and a single smart proxy can also talk over multiple protocols including efficient application-specific protocols.

SPOA and SOOA differ in their method of discovering the service registry (see Fig. 2). SORCER uses dynamic discovery protocols to locate available registries (lookup services) as defined in the Jini architecture ("Jini architecture specification", n.d.). Neither the requestor who is looking up a proxy by its interfaces nor the provider registering a proxy needs to know specific locations. In SPOA, however, the requestor and provider usually do need to know the explicit location of the service registry—e.g., the IP address of an ONC/RPC portmapper, a URL for RMI registry, a URL for UDDI registry, an IP address of a COS Name Server—to open a static connection and find or register a service. In deployment of Web and OGSA services, a UDDI registry is sometimes even omitted when WSDL descriptions are shared via files; in SOOA, lookup services are mandatory due to the dynamic nature of objects identified by service types (e.g., Java interfaces). Interactions in SPOA are more like client-server connections (e.g., HTTP, SOAP, IIOP), often in deployment not requiring to use service registries at all.

Let us emphasize the major distinction between SOOA and SPOA: in SOOA, a proxy is created and always owned by the service provider, but in SPOA, the requestor creates and owns a proxy which has to meet the requirements of the protocol that the provider and requestor agreed upon a priori. Thus, in SPOA the protocol is always a generic one, reduced to a common denominator—one size fits all—that leads to inefficient network communication in many cases. In SOOA, each provider can decide on the most efficient protocol(s) needed for a particular distributed application.

Service providers in SOOA can be considered as independent network objects finding each other via service registries and communicating through message passing. A collection of these objects sending and receiving messages—the only way these objects communicate with one another—looks very much like a service object-oriented distributed system.

However, do you remember the eight fallacies ("Fallacies", n.d.) of network computing? We cannot just take an object-oriented program developed without distribution in mind and make it a distributed system ignoring the unpredictable network behavior. Most RPC systems, except Jini, hide the network behavior and try to transform local communication into remote communication by creating distribution transparency based on a local assumption of what the network might be. However every single distributed object cannot do that in a uniform way as the network is a heterogeneous distributed system and cannot be represented completely within a single entity.

The network is dynamic, cannot be constant, and introduces latency for remote invocations. Network latency also depends on potential failure handling and recovery mechanisms, so we cannot assume that a local invocation is similar to remote invocation. Thus, complete distribution transparency—by making calls on distributed objects as though they were local—is impossible to achieve in practice. The distribution is simply not just an object-oriented implementation of a single distributed object; it is a metasystemic issue in object-oriented distributed programming. In that context, Web/OGSA services define distributed objects, but do not have anything common with object-oriented distributed systems that, for example, the Jini programming model and service architecture emphasize.

Object-oriented programming can be seen as an attempt to abstract both *data* representing a managed state of computational module and related *operations* in an entity called *object*. Thus, object-oriented program be seen as a collection of cooperating *objects* communicating via *message* passing, as opposed to a traditional view in which a program may be seen as a list of instructions to the computer. Instead of *objects* and *messages*, in EO programming *service providers* and *exertions* constitute a program. An *exertion* is a kind of meta-request sent onto the network. Thus, the exertion is considered as the *specification of a collaboration* that encapsulates *data* for the collaboration, related *operations*, and *control strategy*. The operations specify implicitly the required service providers on the network. The active exertion creates at runtime a federation of providers to execute service collaboration according to the exertion's control strategy. Thus, the active exertion is the *metaprogram* and its *metashell* (by analogy to the Unix shell, but here distributed) that submits the request onto the network to run the collaboration in which all providers pass to one other the component exertions only. This type of metashell was created for the SORCER metacompute operating system (see Fig. 3)—the exemplification of SOOA with autonomic management of system resources and domain-specific service providers to run EO programs.

No matter how complex and polished the individual operations are, it is often the quality of the *glue* that determines the power of the distributed computing system. SORCER defines the object-oriented distribution and glue for EO programming (Sobolewski, 2008a). It uses indirect federated remote method invocation (Sobolewski, 2007) with no location of service provider explicitly specified in exertions. A specialized infrastructure of distributed services supports discovery/join protocols for the metashell, federated file system, autonomic resource management, and the rendezvous providers responsible for coordination of executing federations. The infrastructure defines SORCER's *object-oriented distributed* modularity, extensibility, and reuse of providers and exertions—key features of object-oriented distributed programming that are usually missing in SPOA programming environments. Object proxying with discovery/join protocols provides for provider protocol, location, and implementation neutrality missing in SPOA programming environments as well.

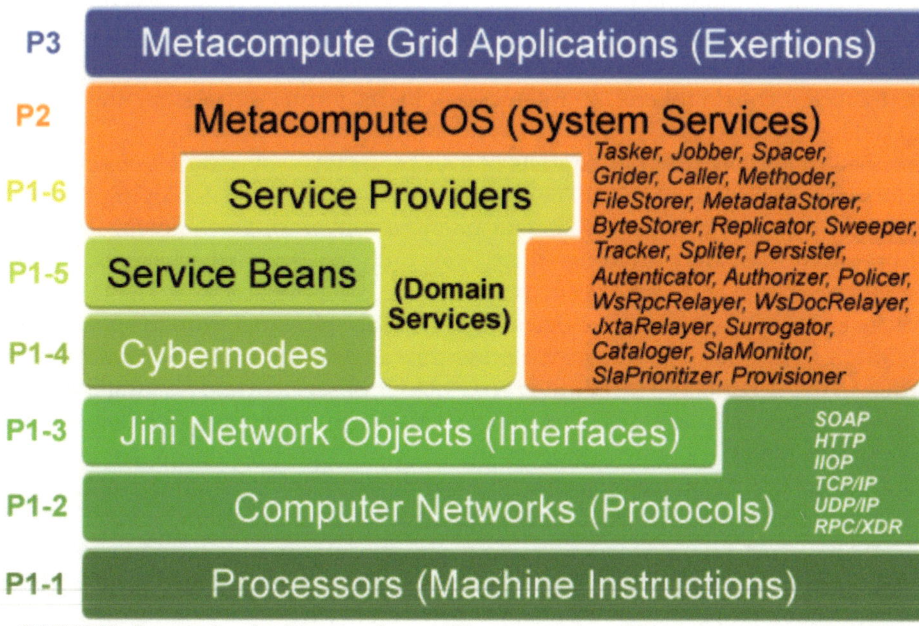

Fig. 3. SORCER layered platform, where P1 resources, P2 resource management, P3 programming environment

4. Metacompute Grid

SORCER is a federated service-to-service (S2S) metacomputing environment that treats service providers as network peers with well-defined semantics of a federated service object-oriented architecture (FSOOA). It is based on Jini semantics of services ("Jini Architecture", n.d.) in the network and the Jini programming model (Edwards, 2000) with explicit leases, distributed events, transactions, and discovery/join protocols. While Jini focuses on service management in a networked environment, SORCER is focused on EO programming and the execution environment for exertions (see Fig. 3).

An *exertion* is a metaprogram that specifies how a *collaboration* is realized by a collection (federation) of service providers and associations playing specific roles used in a specific way (Sobolewski, 2008c). An *exertion collaboration* specifies a view of cooperating providers and their services—a projection of service federation. It describes the required links between providers that play the roles of collaboration, as well as the attributes required that specify the participating providers. Several exertions may describe different projections of the same collection of providers—*federation*. Please note that conventional objects encapsulate explicitly *data* and *operations*, but *exertions* encapsulate explicitly *data, operations*, and *control strategy*. The exertion participants in the federation collaborate transparently according to its *control strategy* managed by the SORCER metacompute OS based on the Triple Command Pattern presented at the end in this Section.

The exertion collaboration defines an *exertion interaction*. The *exertion interaction* specifies how invocations of operations are sent between service providers in a collaboration to perform a specific behavior. The interaction is defined in the context of exertion's control strategy. From the computing platform point of view, exertions are entities considered at the programming level, interactions at the operating system level, and federations at the processor level. Thus exertions are programs that define collaborations. The operating system manages collaborations as interactions in its virtual processor—the dynamically formed federations (see Fig. 3).

As described in Section 3, SOOA consists of four major types of network objects: providers, requestors, registries, and proxies. The provider is responsible for deploying the service on the network, publishing its proxy to one or more registries, and allowing requestors to access its proxy. Providers advertise their availability on the network; registries intercept these announcements and cache proxy objects to the provider services. The requestor looks up proxies by sending queries to registries and making selections from the available service types. Queries generally contain search criteria related to the type and quality of service. Registries facilitate searching by storing proxy objects of services and making them available to requestors. Providers use discovery/join protocols to publish services on the network; requestors use discovery/join protocols to obtain service proxies on the network. The SORCER metacompute OS uses Jini discovery/join protocols to implement its FSOOA.

In FSOOA, a service provider is an object that accepts exertions from service requestors to form a collaboration. An exertion encapsulates service data, operations, and control strategy. A *task exertion* is an elementary service request, a kind of elementary remote instruction (elementary statement) executed by a single service provider or a small-scale federation. A composite exertion called a *job exertion* is defined hierarchically in terms of tasks and other jobs, including control flow exertions. A job exertion is a kind of network procedure executed by a large-scale federation. Thus, the executing exertion is a service-oriented program that is dynamically bound to all required and currently available and on-demand provisioned, if needed, service providers on the network. This collection of providers identified at runtime is called an *exertion federation*. While this sounds similar to the object-oriented paradigm, it really is not. In the object-oriented paradigm, the object space is a program itself; here the exertion federation is the *execution environment* for the exertion, and the exertion is the *specification* of service collaboration. This changes the programming paradigm completely. In the former case a single computer hosts the object space, whereas in the latter case the parent and its component exertions along with bound service providers are hosted by the network of computers.

The overlay network of all service providers is called the *service grid* and an exertion federation is called a *virtual metaprocessor* (see Fig. 4). The *metainstruction set* of the metaprocessor consists of all operations offered by all providers in the grid. Thus, a service-oriented program is composed of metainstructions with its own service-oriented control strategy and service context representing the metaprogram data. Service signatures specify metainstructions—collaboration participants in SORCER. Each signature primarily is defined by a service type (interface name), operation in that interface, and a set of optional attributes. Four types of signatures are distinguished: `PROCESS`, `PREPROCESS`, `POSTPROCESS`, and `APPEND`. A `PROCESS` signature—of which there is only one allowed per exertion—defines the dynamic late binding to a provider that implements the signature's interface. The service context (Zhao & Sobolewski, 2001; Sobolewski, 2008a) describes the data that tasks and jobs work on. An `APPEND` signature defines the context received from the provider specified by this signature. The received context is then appended in runtime to the service context later processed by `PREPROCESS`, `PROCESS`, and `POSTPROCESS` operations of the exertion. Appending a service context allows a requestor to use actual network data in runtime not available to the requestor when the exertion is submitted. A metacompute OS allows for an exertion to create and manage dynamic federation and transparently coordinate the execution of all component exertions within the federation. Please note that these metacomputing concepts are defined differently in traditional grid computing where a job is just an executing process for a submitted executable code with no federation being formed for the executable.

An exertion can be activated by calling exertion's `exert` operation:

```
Exertion.exert(Transaction):Exertion,
```

where a parameter of the `Transaction` type is required when a transactional semantics is needed for all participating nested exertions within the parent one. Thus, EO programming

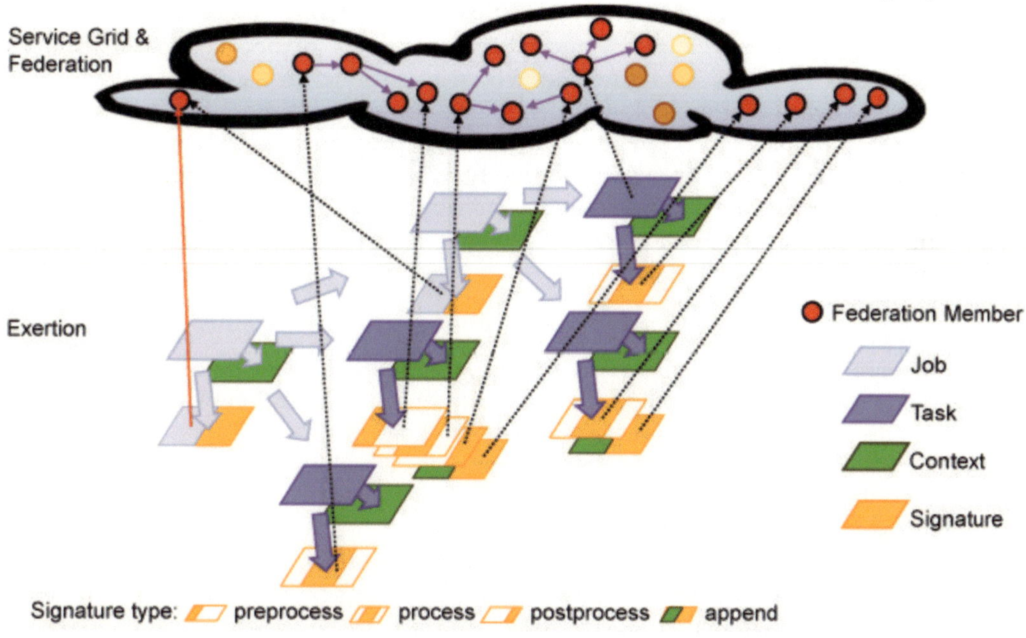

Fig. 4. An exertion federation. The solid line (the first from the left) indicates the originating invocation: `Exertion.exert(Transaction)`. The top-level exertion with component exertions is depicted below the service grid (a cloud). Late bindings to all participants defined by signatures are indicated by dashed lines. The participants form the exertion federation (metaprocessor).

allows us to submit an exertion onto the network and to perform executions of exertion's signatures on various service providers indirectly (see Fig. 4), but where does the service-to-service communication come into play? How do these services communicate with one another if they are all different? Top-level communication between services, or the sending of service requests, is done through the use of the generic `Servicer` interface and the operation `service` that all SORCER services are required to provide:

```
Servicer.service(Exertion, Transaction):Exertion.
```

This top-level service operation takes an exertion as an argument and gives back an exertion as the return value.

So why are exertions used rather than directly calling on a provider's method and passing service contexts? There are two basic answers to this. First, passing exertions helps to aid with the network-centric messaging. A service requestor can send an exertion implicitly out onto the network—`Exertion.exert()` —and any service provider can pick it up. The provider can then look at the interface and operation requested within the exertion, and if it doesn't implement the desired interface or provide the desired method, it can continue forwarding it to another service provider who can service it. Second, passing exertions helps with fault detection and recovery. Each exertion has its own completion state associated with it to specify if it has yet to run, has already completed, or has failed. Since full exertions are both passed and returned, the user can view the failed exertion to see what method was being called as well as what was used in the service context input nodes that may have caused the problem. Since exertions provide all the information needed to execute a task including its control strategy, a user would be able to pause a job between tasks, analyze it and make needed updates. To figure out where to resume an exertion, the executing provider would simply have to look at the exertion's completion states and resume the first one that wasn't completed yet. In other words, EO programming allows the user, *not programmer* to update the metaprogram on-the-fly, what practically translates into creating new collaborative applications during the exertion runtime.

Despite the fact that every Servicer can accept any exertion, Servicers have well defined roles in the S2S platform (see Fig. 3):

a) Taskers - process service tasks
b) Jobbers - process service jobs
c) Spacers - process tasks and jobs via exertion space for space-based computing (Freeman, 1999). See also secure space computing with exertions in (Kerr & Sobolewski, 2008).
d) Contexters - provide service contexts for `APPEND` Signatures
e) FileStorers - provide access to federated file system providers (Sobolewski, 2005; Berger, & Sobolewski, 2007) (see Section 6 for details)
f) Catalogers - Servicer registries
g) SlaMonitors - provide management of SLAs for QoS exertions (see Section 7);
h) Provisioners - provide on-demand provisioning of services by SERVME (see Section 7);
i) Persisters - persist service contexts, tasks, and jobs to be reused for interactive EO programming
j) Relayers - gateway providers; transform exertions to native representation, for example integration with Web services (McGovern et al., 2003) and JXTA ("JXTA", n.d.)
k) Autenticators, Authorizers, Policers, KeyStorers - provide support for service security
l) Auditors, Reporters, Loggers - support for accountability, reporting, and logging
m) Griders, Callers, Methoders - support compute grid (see Section 4)

n) Generic ServiceTasker, ServiceJobber, and ServiceSpacer implementations are used to configure domain-specific providers via dependency injection—configuration files for smart proxying and embedding business objects, called service beans, into service providers;

o) Notifiers - use third party services for collecting provider notifications for time consuming programs and disconnected requestors (Lapinski & Sobolewski, 2003).

An exertion can be created interactively (Sobolewski, 2006) or programmatically (using SORCER APIs), and its execution can be monitored and debugged (Soorianarayanan & Sobolewski, 2006) in the overlay service network via service user interfaces ("The Service UI Project", n.d.) attached to providers and installed on-the-fly by generic service browsers ("Inca X", n.d). Service providers do not have mutual associations prior to the execution of an exertion; they come together dynamically (federate) for all nested tasks and jobs in the exertion. Domain specific providers within the federation, or *task peers*, execute service tasks. Rendezvous peers coordinate exertion jobs: *Jobber* or *Spacer* are two of the SORCER platform control-flow services. However, a job can be sent to any peer. A peer that is not a rendezvous peer is responsible for forwarding the job to an available rendezvous peer and returning results to its direct requestor. Thus implicitly, any peer can handle any exertion type. Once the exertion execution is complete, the federation dissolves and the providers disperse to seek other exertions to join.

An Exertion is activated by calling its `exert` operation. The SORCER API defines the following three related operations:

1. `Exertion.exert(Transaction):Exertion` - join the federation; the activated exertion binds to the available provider specified by the exertion's `PROCESS` signature;
2. `Servicer.service(Exertion, Transaction):Exertion` - request a service in the federation initiated by any bounding provider; and
3. `Exerter.exert(Exertion, Transaction):Exertion` - execute the argument exertion by the provider accepting the service request in 2) above. Any component exertions of the exerted one are processed as in 1) above.

This above Triple Command pattern (Sobolewski, 2007) defines various implementations of these interfaces: `Exertion` (metaprogram), `Servicer` (generic peer provider), and `Exerter` (service provider exerting a particular type of `Exertion`). This approach allows for the P2P environment (Sobolewski, 2008a) via the `Servicer` interface, extensive modularization of Exertions and Exerters, and extensibility from the triple design pattern so requestors can submit onto the network any EO programs they want with or without transactional semantics. The Triple Command pattern is used as follows:

1. An exertion can be activated by calling `Exertion.exert()`. The `exert` operation implemented in `ServiceExertion` uses `ServiceAccessor` to locate in runtime the provider matching the exertion's `PROCESS` signature.
2. If the matching provider is found, then on its access proxy the `Servicer.service()` method is invoked.
3. When the requestor is authenticated and authorized by the provider to invoke the method defined by the exertion's `PROCESS` signature, then the provider calls its own `exert` operation: `Exerter.exert()`.
4. `Exerter.exert()` operation is implemented by `ServiceTasker`, `ServiceJobber`, and `ServiceSpacer`. The `ServiceTasker` peer calls by reflection the application method specified in the `PROCESS` signature of the task exertion. All application domain methods

of provider interface have the same signature: a single `Context` type parameter and a `Context` type return value. Thus an application interface implemented by the application provider looks like an RMI (Pitt, 2001) interface with the above simplification on the common signature for all interface operations.

The exertion activated by a service requestor can be submitted directly or indirectly to the matching service provider. In the direct approach, when signature's access type is `PUSH`, the exertion's `ServicerAccessor` finds the matching service provider against the service type and attributes of the `PROCESS` signature and submits the exertion to the matching provider. The execution order of signatures is defined by signature priorities, if the exertion's flow type is `SEQUENTIAL`; otherwise they are dispatched in parallel. EO programming has a branch exertion (`IfExertion`) and loop exertions (`WhileExertion`, `ForExertion`) as well as two mechanisms for nonlinear control flow (`BreakExertion`, `ContinueExertion`) (Sobolewski, 2008a).

A Job instance specifies a "block" of component tasks and other jobs. It is the distributed analog of a procedure in conventional programming languages. However, in EO programming it is a composite of exertions that makeup the network interaction. A Job can reflect a workflow with branching and looping by applying control flow exertions (Sobolewski, 2008a).

To illustrate a very flexible distributed control strategy of EO programs, let's consider the case presented in Fig. 5. This control strategy defines a virtual mapping of the control flow defined by the exertion e_1 onto the interactions of dynamically created federation. A rectangular frame outlines providers in that federation.

The following control flow exertions are defined in SORCER:

1. | (e_1, ..., e_n) – sequential exertion;
2. || (e_1, ..., e_n) – parallel exertion;
3. ⊣ (e_1, e_2, e_3) – the `if` exertion: if e_1`.isTrue() then` do e_2 `else do` e_3; and
4. *(e_1, e_2) or *(e), if e_1 = e_2 and e_1 = e – the `while` exertion: `do` e_2 `while` e_1`.isTrue()`.

Using the above notation the federation in Fig. 5 can be described by as follows: exertion e_1 = | | (e_2, *(e_3)), where e_2 = | (e_4, e_5) and e_5 = *(⊣ (e_6, e_7, e_8)), and e_6 evaluates to true.

Alternatively, when signature's access type is `PULL`, a `ServiceAccessor` can use a `Spacer` provider and simply drops (writes) the exertion into the shared exertion space to be pulled by a matching provider. In Fig. 6 four use cases are presented to illustrate push vs. pull exertion processing with either `PUSH` or `PULL` access types. We assume here that an exertion is a job with two component exertions executed in parallel (sequence numbers with a and b), i.e., the job's signature flow type is `PARALLEL`. The job can be submitted directly to either Jobber (use cases: 1—access is `PUSH`, and 2—access is `PULL`) or Spacer (use cases: 3 —access is `PUSH`, and 4—access is `PULL`) depending on the interface defined in its `PROCES` signature. Thus, in cases 1 and 2 the signature's interface is Jobber and in cases 3 and 4 the signature's interface is Spacer as shown in Fig. 6. The exertion's ServicerAccessor delivers the right service proxy dynamically, either for a Jobber or Spacer. If the access type of the parent exertion is `PUSH`, then all the component exertions are directly passed to servicers matching their `PROCESS` signatures (case 1 and 3), otherwise they are written into the exertion space by a Spacer (case 2 and 4). In the both cases 2 and 4, the component exertions are pulled from the exertion space by servicers matching their signatures as soon as they are available. Thus,

Spacers provide efficient load balancing for processing the exertion space. The fastest available servicer gets an exertion from the space before other overloaded or slower servicers can do so. When an exertion consists of component jobs with different access and flow types, then we have a *hybrid* case when the collaboration potentially executes concurrently with multiple *pull* and *push* subcollaborations at the same time.

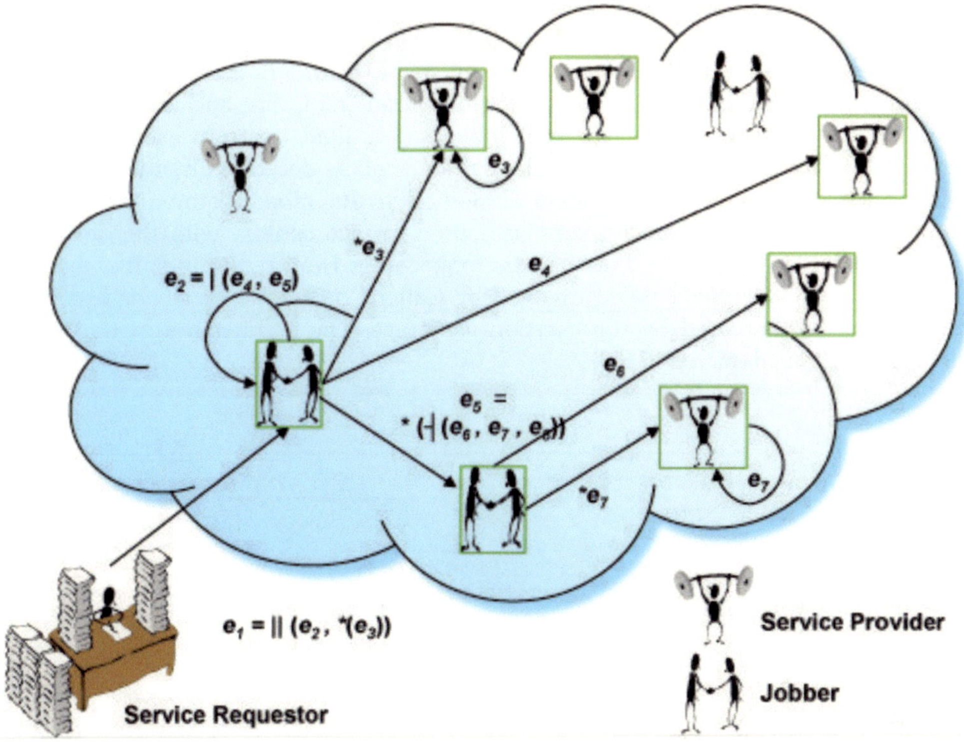

Fig. 5. SORCER metacompute OS finds the right service provider to whom a component exertion has to be bound as defined by its `PROCES` signature at runtime.

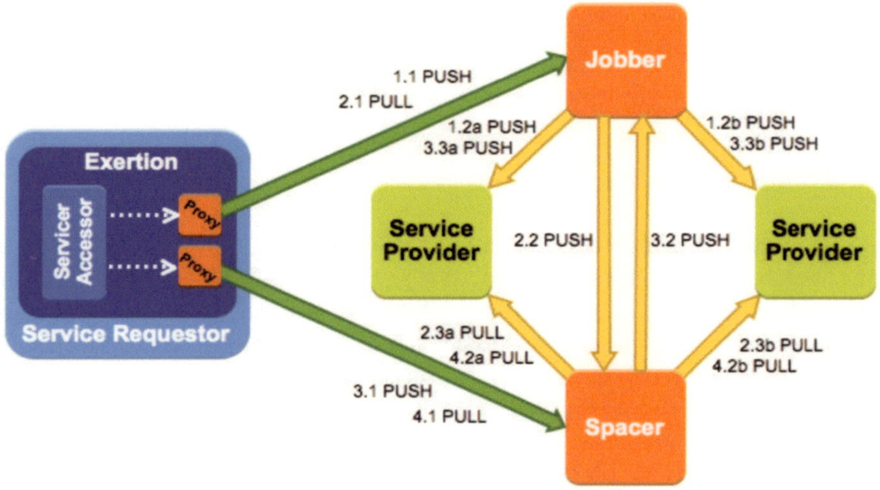

Fig. 6. Push vs. pull exertion processing

5. Compute Grid

To use legacy applications, SORCER supports a traditional approach to grid computing similar to those found in Condor (Thain, 2003) and Globus (Sotomayor, 2005). Here, instead of exertions being executed by services providing business logic for collaborating exertions, the business logic comes from the service requestor's executable codes that seek compute resources on the network.

The cGrid services in the SORCER environment include Griders accepting exertions and collaborating with Jobbers and Spacers as cGrid schedulers. Caller and Methoder services are used for task execution received from Jobbers or pulled up from exertion space via Spacers. Callers execute provided codes via a system call as described by the standardized Caller's service context of the submitted task. Methoders download required Java code (task method) from requestors to process any submitted service context with the downloaded code accordingly. In either case, the business logic comes from requestors; it is executable code specified in the service context invoked by Callers, or mobile Java code executed by Methoders that is annotated by the exertion signature. The architecture of the SORCER cGrid, called SGrid is depicted in Fig. 7.

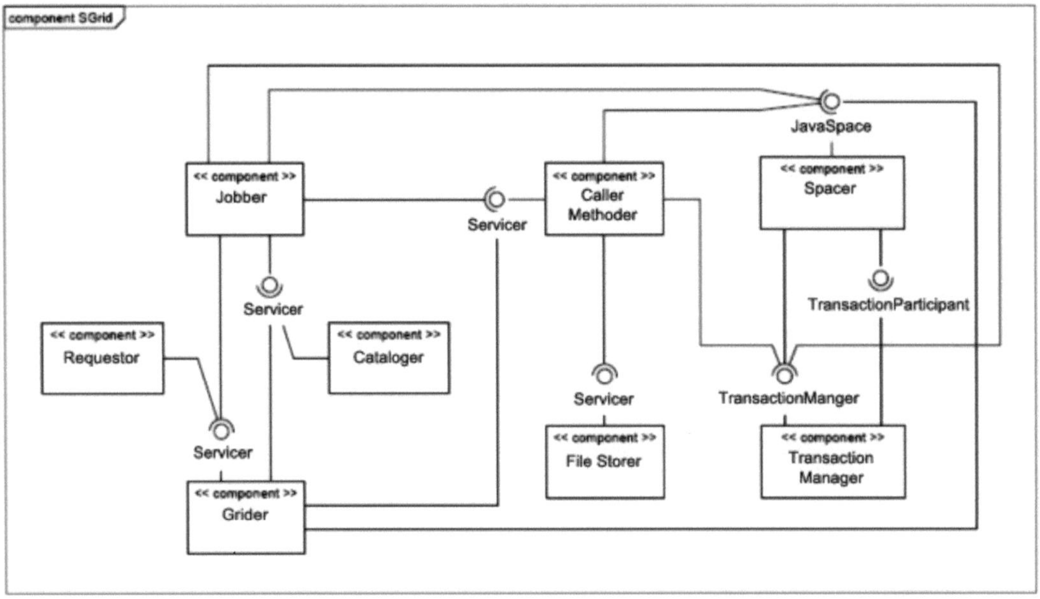

Fig. 7. SGrid component diagram

The SORCER cGrid with Methoders was used to deploy an algorithm called Basic Local Alignment Search Tool (BLAST) (Alschul, 1990) to compare newly discovered, unknown DNA and protein sequences against a large database with more than three gigabytes of known sequences. BLAST (C++ code) searches the database for sequences that are identical or similar to the unknown sequence. This process enables scientists to make inferences about the function of the unknown sequence based on what is understood about the similar sequences found in the database. Many projects at the USDA–ARS Research Unit, for example, involve as many as 10,000 unknown sequences, each of which must be analyzed via the BLAST algorithm. A project involving 10,000 unknown sequences requires about

three weeks to complete on a single desktop computer. The S-BLAST implemented in SORCER (Khurana et al., 2005), a federated form of the BLAST algorithm, reduces the amount of time required to perform searches for large sets of unknown sequences. S-BLAST is comprised of BlastProvider (with the attached BLAST Service UI), Jobbers, Spacers, and Methoders. Methoders in S-BLAST download Java code (a service task method) that initializes a required database before making a system call on the BLAST code. Armed with the S-BLAST's cGrid and seventeen commodity computers, projects that previously took three weeks to complete can now be finished in less than one day.
The SORCER cGrid with Griders, Jobbers, Spacers, and Callers has been successfully deployed with the Proth program (C code to search for large prime factors of Fermat numbers) and easy-to-use zero-install service UI attached to a Grider using the SILENUS federated file system.

6. Federated File System

The SILENUS federated file system (Berger & Sobolewski, 2005; Berger & Sobolewski, 2007a) was developed to provide data access and persistence storage for metaprograms. It complements the centralized file store developed for FIPER (Sobolewski et al., 2003) with the true P2P services. The SILENUS system itself is a collection of service providers that use the SORCER exertion-oriented framework for communication.

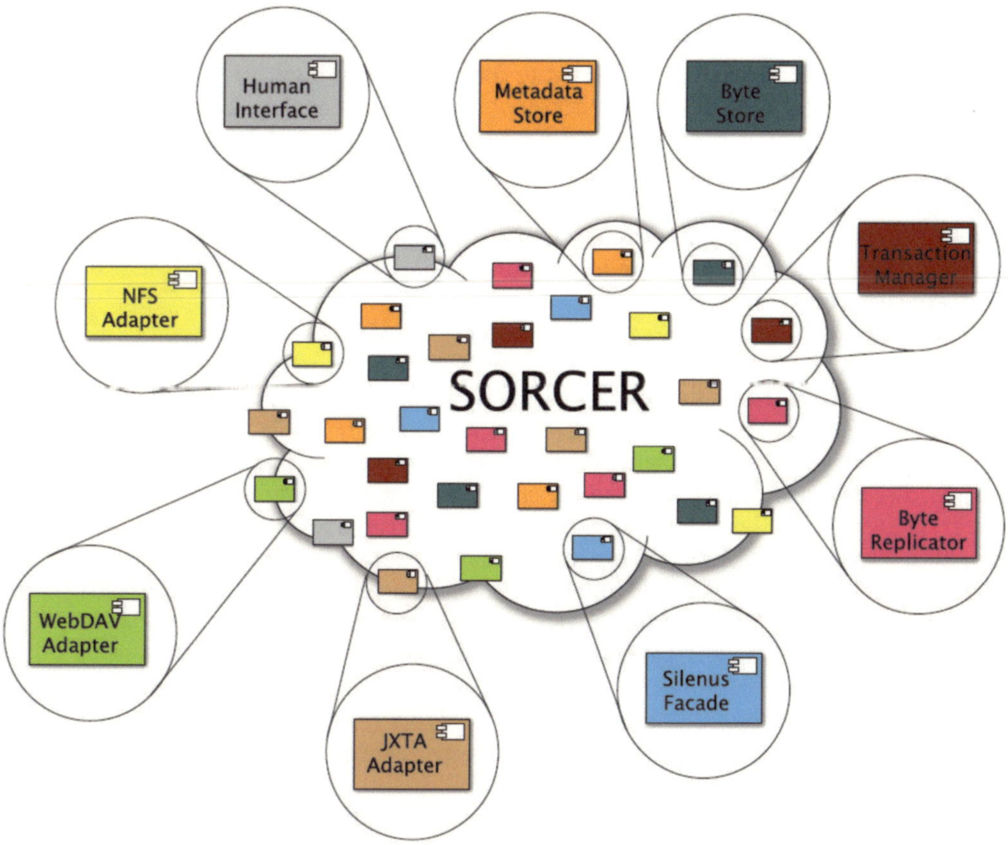

Fig. 8. SILENUS file system components for the SORCER platform

In classical client-server file systems, a heavy load may occur on a single file server. If multiple service requestors try to access large files at the same time, the server can be overloaded. In P2P architecture, every provider is a client and a server at the same time. The load can be balanced between all peers if files are spread across all of them. The SORCER architecture splits up the functionality of the metaprocessor into smaller service peers (Servicers), and this approach was applied to the distributed file system as well.

The SILENUS federated file system is comprised of several network services that run within the SORCER environment as illustrated in Fig. 8.

These services include a byte store service for holding file data, a metadata service for holding metadata information about the files, several optional optimizer services, and façade (Grand, 1999) services to assist in accessing federating services. SILENUS is designed so that many instances of these services can run on a network, and the required services will federate together to perform the necessary functions of a file system. In fact the SILENUS system is completely decentralized, eliminating all potential single points of failures. SILENUS services can be broadly categorized into gateway components, data services, and management services. Each byte store provides fast access to the underlying native file system on the provider's host while each metadata provider allows creating, listing, and traversing directories persisted in the provider's embedded relational database. All metadata databases are synchronized in runtime for all file modifications and updates.

The SILENUS façade service provides a gateway service to the SILENUS federations for requestors that want to use the file system. Since the metadata and actual file contents are stored by different services, there is a need to coordinate communication between these two services. The façade service itself is a combination of a control component, called the coordinator, and a smart proxy component that contains needed inner proxies provided dynamically by the coordinator. These inner proxies facilitate direct P2P communications for file upload and download between the requestor and SILENUS federating services such as metadata and byte stores, if needed with the participation of the Jini transaction manager when transactional semantics is required for updates to both metadata and byte store service concurrently.

Core SILENUS services have been successfully deployed as SORCER services along with WebDAV and NFS adapters. The SILENUS file system scales very well with a virtual disk space adjusted as needed by the corresponding number of required byte store providers and the appropriate number of metadata stores required to satisfy the needs of current users and service requestors. The system handles several types of network and computer outages by utilizing disconnected operation and data synchronization mechanisms. It provides a number of user agents including a zero-install file browser attached to the SILENUS façade. Also a simpler version of SILENUS file browser is available for smart MIDP phones.

In most file systems it is impossible or impracticable to ask the user which conflicting option to choose. The SILENUS file system provides support for disconnected operation. A new dual-time vector clock based synchronization mechanism (Berger & Sobolewski, 2007b) detects and orders events properly. It detects also possible conflicts and resolves them in a consistent manner without user interactions. To solve a conflict, the SILENUS system uses virtual duplication. Virtual duplication addresses the issue of local consistency and requires no direct user interaction. The approach based on dual-time vector clock synchronization provides complete and consistent support for dynamically federating services and changing overlay networks.

The FICUS framework (Turner & Sobolewski, 2007) is an extension to SILENUS. FICUS supports storing very large files (Turner & Sobolewski, 2007) by providing two services: a splitter service and a tracker service. When a file is uploaded to the file system, the splitter service determines how that file should be stored. If a file is sufficiently large, the file will be split into multiple parts, or chunks, and stored across many byte store services. Once the upload is complete, a tracker service keeps a record of where each chunk was stored. When a user requests to download the full file later on, the tracker service can be queried to determine the location of each chunk and the file can be reassembled in parallel to the original form.

To achieve availability and reliability of files, SILENUS provides data redundancy in the form of file replication. It uses an active replication scheme which means that all replicas are treated as if they are the original. The drawback of this scheme is that it requires a lot of coordination in that if an update occurs on one replica then all of the replicas need to be updated. The coordination is currently implemented in SILENUS; however there is no management of these replicas after creation. A separate framework called LOCO (Hard & Sobolewski, 2009) has been developed to dynamically manage replicas and to provide quality of service for data store providers. It monitors user's access habits so that it can make logical decisions on where to replicate the files to. It will also dynamically manage the number of times each file is replicated depending on file size, available storage space at each byte store provider, and the byte store host type (e.g., server, desktop, laptop). The LOCO framework is an extension to SILENUS and is comprised of four services: a Locator service, Sweeper service, Replicator service, and a Resource Usage Store service.

LOCO will replicate a file for several reasons, if a byte store becomes unavailable then all of the files that were located there will be replicated and if a file is uploaded into the system LOCO will decide on an appropriate number of times to replicate the file. LOCO may also delete certain replicas, for example, if a byte store becomes unavailable and all of the files stored there are replicated, then when that byte store becomes available again LOCO may choose to delete some of the replicas.

LOCO also makes several qualities of service guarantees to data store providers. First, a file will not be replicated to a storage location that already contains the file or replica of the file. Second, a minimum number of replicas, which may be specified by the user or the locator service, will be maintained as long as there are enough storage locations present in the network to satisfy the number.

7. Autonomic Resource Management

Federated computing environments offer requestors the ability to dynamically invoke services offered by collaborating providers in the entire service grid. Without an efficient resource management, however, the assignment of providers to customer's requests cannot be optimized and cannot offer high reliability without relevant SLA guarantees. A SLA-based SERViceable Metacomputing Environment (SERVME) (Rubach & Sobolewski, 2009) capable of matching providers based on QoS requirements and performing autonomic provisioning and deprovisioning of services according to dynamic requestor needs has beed developed for the SORCER metaoperating system. In SERVME an exertion signature includes an SLA Context that encapsulates all QoS/SLA related data. SERVME builds on the SORCER environment by extending its interfaces and adding new QoS/SLA service

providers. It is a generic resource management framework in terms of common QoS/SLA data structures and extensible communication interfaces hiding all implementation details.
Along with the QoS/SLA object model SERVME defines basic components and communication interfaces as depicted in the UML component diagram illustrated in Fig. 9. We distinguish two forms of autonomic provisioning: monitored and on-demand. In monitored provisioning the provisioner (Rio Provisioner (Rio Project, n.d.)) deploys a requested collection of providers, then monitors them for presence and in the case of any failure in the collection, the provisioner makes sure that the required number of providers is always on the network as defined by a provisioner's deployment descriptor. On-demand provisioning refers to a type of provisioning (On-demand Provisioner) where the actual provider is presented to the requestor, once a subscription to the requested service is successfully processed. In both cases, if services become unavailable, or fail to meet processing requirements, the recovery of those service providers to available compute resources is enabled by Rio provisioning mechanisms.
The basic components are defined as follows:

- QosProviderAccessor is a component used by the service requestor (customer) that is responsible for processing the exertion request containing QosContext in its signature. If the exertion type is Task then QosCatalog is used, otherwise a relevant rendezvous peer: Jobber, Spacer is used.
- QosCatalog is an independent service that acts as an extended Lookup Service (QoS LUS). The QosCatalog uses the functional requirements as well as related non-functional QoS requirements to find a service provider from currently available in the network. If a matching provider does not exist, the QosCatalog may provision the needed one.
- SlaDispatcher is a component built into each service provider. It performs two roles. On one hand, it is responsible for retrieving the actual QoS parameter values from the operating system in which it is running, and on the other hand, it exposes the interface used by QosCatalog to negotiate, sign and manage the SLA with its provider.
- SlaPrioritizer is a component that allows controlling the prioritization of the execution of exertions according to the organizational requirements of SlaContext.
- QosMonitor UI provides an embedded GUI that allows the monitoring of provider's QoS parameters at runtime.
- SlaMonitor is an independent service that acts as a registry for negotiated SLA contracts and exposes the user interface (UI) for administrators to allow them to monitor, update or cancel active SLAs.
- On-demandProvisioner is a SERVME provider that enables on-demand provisioning of services in cooperation with the Rio Provisioner ("Rio", n.d.) The QosCatalog uses it when no matching service provider can be found that meets requestor QoS requirements. We distinguish two forms of autonomic provisioning: monitored and on-demand. In monitored provisioning the Rio Provisioner deploys a requested collection of providers, then monitors them for presence and in the case of any failure in the collection, the Provisioner makes sure that the required number of providers is always on the network as defined by a provisioner's deployment descriptor. On-demand provisioning refers to a type of provisioning (On-demand Provisioner) when the actual provider is presented to the requestor, once a subscription to the requested service is successfully processed. In both cases, if services become unavailable, or fail to meet

processing requirements, the recovery of those service providers to available compute resources is enabled by Rio Project provisioning mechanisms.

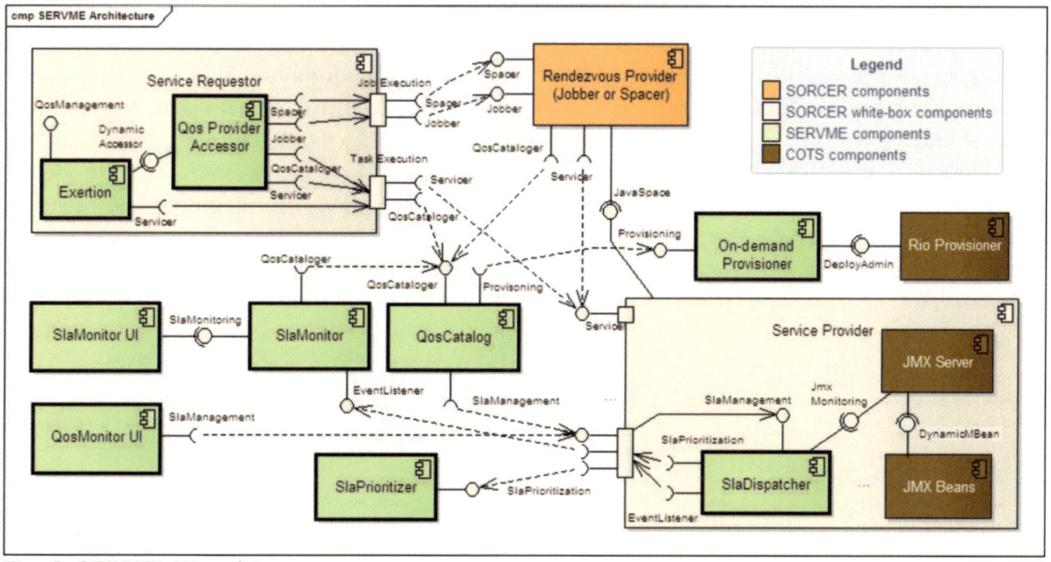

Fig. 9. SERVEME architecture

The SERVME framework is integrated directly into the federated metacomputing environment. As described in Section 4, the service requestor submits the exertion with QoS requirements (QosContext) into the network by invoking `Exertion.exert()` operation. If the exertion is of Task type, then QosProviderAccessor via QosCalatog finds in runtime a matching service provider with a corresponding SLA.

If the SLA can be directly provided then the contracting provider approached by the QosCalatog returns it in the form of SlaContext, otherwise a negotiation can take place for the agreeable SlaContext between the requestor and provider. The provider's SlaDispatcher drives this negotiation in cooperation with SlaPrioritizer and the exertion's requestor.

If the task contains multiple signatures then the provider is responsible for contracting SLAs for all other signatures of the task before the SLA for its `PROCESS` signature is guaranteed.

However, if the submitted exertion is of Job type, then QosProviderAccessor via QosCalatog finds in runtime a matching rendezvous provider with a guaranteed SLA. Before the guaranteed SLA is returned, the rendezvous provider recursively acquires SLAs for all component exertions as described above depending on the type (Task or Job) of component exertion.

8. SORCER iGrid and Future Development

In Section 4 and 5 two complementary platforms: metacompute grid and compute grid are described respectively. As indicated in Fig. 1 the hybrid of both types of grids is feasible to create *intergrid* (iGrid) applications that take advantage of both platforms synergistically. Legacy applications can be reused directly in cGrids and new complex, for example concurrent engineering applications (Sobolewski & Ghodous, 2005) can be defined in mcGrids, for example using EO programming.

Relayers are SORCER gateway providers that transform exertions to native representations and vice versa. The following exertion gateways have been developed: JxtaRelayer for JXTA ("JXTA", n.d.), and WsRpcRelayer and WsDocRelayer for for RPC and document style Web services, respectively (SORCER Research Topics, n.d.). Relayers exhibit native and mcGrid behavior by implementing dual protocols. For example a JxtaRelayer (1) in Fig. 10 is at the same time a Servicer (1-) in the mcGrid and a JXTA peer (1--) implementing JXTA interfaces. Thus it shows up also in SORCER mcGrid and in the JXTA cGrid as well. Native cGrid providers can play the SORCER role (as SORCER wrappers), thus are available in the iGrid along with mcGrid providers. For example, a JAXTA peer 4-- implements the Servicer interface, so shoes up in the JXTA iGrid as provider 4. Also, native cGrid providers via corresponding relayers can access iGrid services (bottom-up in Fig. 10). Thus, the iGrid is a projection of Servicers onto mcGrids and cGrds.

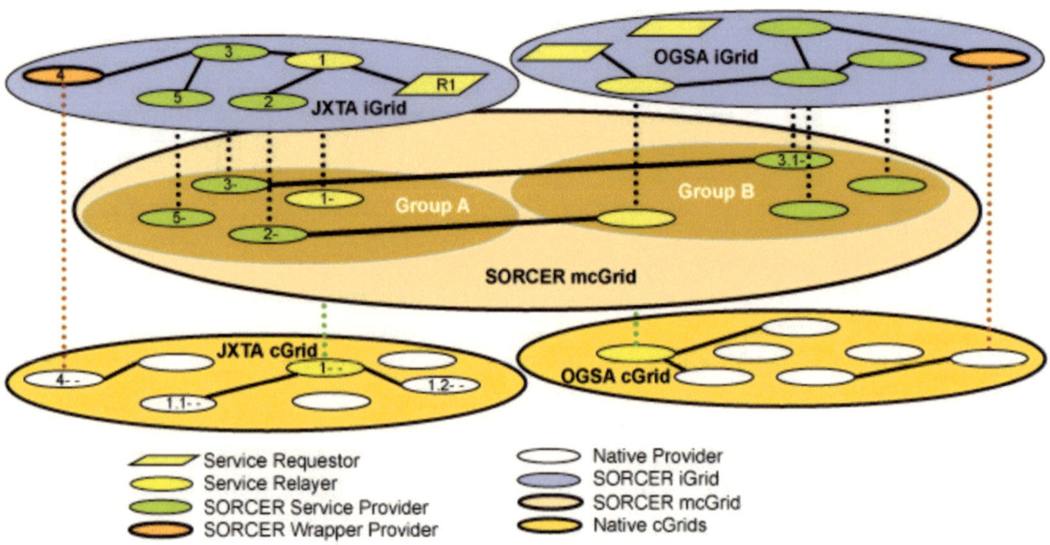

Fig. 10. Integrating and wrapping cGrids with SORCER mcGrids. Two requestors, one in JXTA iGrid, one in OGSA iGrid submits exertion to a corresponding relayer. Two federations are formed that include providers from the two horizontal layers below the iGrid layer (as indicated by continuoues and dashed links).

The iGrid-integrating model is illustrated in Fig. 10, where horizontal native technology grids (bottom) are seamlessly integrated with horizontal SORCER mcGrids via the SORCER operating system services. Through the use of open standards-based communication—Jini, Web Services, Globus/OGSA, and Java interoperability—iGrid leverages mcGrid's FSOOA with its inherent provider proxy protocol, location, and implementation neutrality along with the flexibility of EO programming with its complementary metacompute federated OS. To clarify iGrid interactions, let's consider the requestor R1 submitting the exertion to provider 1. The JxtaRelayer 1 is a version of Jobber that is able to route exertions directly to JXTA peers. At the level of iGrid a federation consisting of five providers is formed (1,2, 3, 4, and 5). The relayer interacts with two JXTA peers 1.1-- and 1.2-- for two-component exertion from R1. Providers 2, 3, and 5 are projected into the SORCER mcGrid, and the provider 3- collaborates with the provider 3.1-. The native JXA peer 4-- is used via the Servicer wrapper 4. Thus, the federation of five iGrid services (1, 2, 3, 4, and 5) projects a federation of ten federating services (1-, 1--, 1.1--, 1.2--, 2-, 3-, 3.1-, 4, 4--, and 5-) in the SORCER mcGrid and JXTA cGrid. In fact, service 1-, 2-, 3-, and 5- are the same Servicers as services 1, 2, 3, and 5 correspondingly.

9. Conclusions

A distributed system is not just a collection of static distributed objects—it is the network of dynamic objects that come and go. From the object-oriented point of view, the network of dynamic objects is the *problem domain* of object-oriented distributed system that requires relevant abstractions in the *solution space*—metacomputing with FMI. The exertion-based programming introduces the new abstraction of the solution space with *service providers* and *exertions* instead of object-oriented conventional *objects* and *messages*. Exertions not only encapsulate operations, data, and control strategy, they encapsulate related collaborations of dynamic service providers as well. From the metacomputing platform point of view, exertions are entities considered at the programming level, collaborative interactions at the operating system level, and federations at the processor level. Thus, exertions are programs that define dynamic collaborations. The SORCER operating system manages collaborations as interactions in its virtual processor—the dynamically formed federations that use FMI.

Service providers can be easily deployed in SORCER by injecting implementation of domain-specific interfaces into the FMI framework. The providers register proxies, including smart proxies, via dependency injection using twelve methods investigated already. Executing a top-level exertion, by sending it onto the network, means forming a federation of currently available and on-demand provisioned, if needed, domain-specific providers at runtime. The federation processes service contexts of all nested exertions collaboratively as specified by control strategies of the top-level and component exertions. The fact that control strategy is exposed directly to the user in a modular way allows him/her to create new applications on-the-fly. For the updated control strategy only, the new federation becomes the new implementation of the updated exertion—a truly creative metaprogramming. When the federation is formed then each exertion operation has its corresponding method (code) on the network available. Services, as specified by exertion signatures, are invoked only indirectly by passing exertions on to providers via service object proxies that in fact are access proxies allowing for service providers to enforce security policies on access to required services. If the access to use the operation is granted, then the operation defined by an exertion's `PROCESS` signature is invoked by reflection.

The FMI framework allows the P2P computing via the Servicer interface, extensive modularization of Exertions and Exerters, and extensibility from the Triple Command design pattern. The presented EO programming methodology with SORCER metacompute OS with its federated file system (SILENUS/FICUS/LOCO) and resource management (SERVME) has been successfully deployed and tested in multiple concurrent engineering and large-scale distributed applications (Röhl et al., 2000; Burton et al., 2002; Kolonay et al., 2002; Kao et al., 2003; Goel & Sobolewski, 2005; Goel et al., 2007; Kolonay et al., 2007; Goel et al., 2008).

To work effectively in large, distributed environments, concurrent engineering teams need a service-oriented programming methodology along with common design process, discipline-independent representations of designs, and general criteria for decision making.

Distributed multidisciplinary analysis and optimization are essential for decision making in engineering design that provide a foundation for service-oriented concurrent engineering (Sobolewski & Ghodous, 2005). It is believed that incremental improvements will not suffice, and so we plan to continue the development of *Service-Oriented Optimization Toolkit with EO Programming for Distributed High Fidelity Engineering Design Optimization* as the validation test case for SORCER iGrid. This approach brings together many ideas and results from twenty eight research studies completed at the SORCER Lab and AFRL, to investigate how *Variable-Filter-Evaluation Design Pattern* for distributed functional composition, comprehensive security, and *Dynamic Proxying with Dependency Injection* can be used to address several fundamental challenges posed by the emerging metacomputing based on FMI for *Distributed High Fidelity Engineering Design Optimization* in real world complex and high performance computing applications.

10. Acknowledgments

This work was partially supported by Air Force Research Lab, Air Vehicles Directorate, Multidisciplinary Technology Center, the contract number F33615-03-D-3307, Algorithms for Federated High Fidelity Engineering Design Optimization. I would like to express my gratitude to all those who helped me in my SORCER research. I would like to thank all my colleagues at GE Global Research Center, AFRL/RBSD, and my students at the SORCER Lab, TTU. They shared their views, ideas, and experience with me, and I am very thankful to them for that. Especially I would like to express my gratitude to Dr. Ray Kolonay, my technical advisor at AFRL/RBSD for his support, encouragement, and advice.

11. References

Berger, M. & Sobolewski, M. (2005). SILENUS – A Federated Service-oriented Approach to Distributed File Systems, In: *Next Generation Concurrent Engineering*, Sobolewski, M., and Ghodous, P. (Ed.), pp. 89-96, ISPE Inc./Omnipress, ISBN 0-9768246-0-4

Berger, M. & Sobolewski, M. (2007a). Lessons Learned from the SILENUS Federated File System, In: *Complex Systems Concurrent Engineering*, Loureiro, G. and L.Curran, R. (Ed.), pp. 431-440, Springer Verlag, ISBN: 978-1-84628-975-0

Berger M. & Sobolewski, M. (2007b). A Dual-time Vector Clock Based Synchronization Mechanism for Key-value Data in the SILENUS File System, *IEEE Third International Workshop on Scheduling and Resource Management for Parallel and Distributed Systems* (SRMPDS '07), Hsinchu, Taiwan

Birrell, A. D. & Nelson, B. J. (1983). Implementing Remote Procedure Calls, XEROX CSL-83-7

Burton, S. A.; Tappeta, R.; Kolonay, R. M. & Padmanabhan, D (2002). Turbine Blade Reliability-based Optimization Using Variable-Complexity Method, 43rd AIAA/ASME/ASCE/AHS/ASC Structures, Structural Dynamics, and Materials Conference, Denver, Colorado. AIAA 2002-1710

Edwards W.K. (2000) *Core Jini*, 2nd ed., Prentice Hall

Fallacies of Distributed Computing. Accessed on: April 24, 2009. Available at: http://en.wikipedia.org/wiki/Fallacies_of_Distributed_Computing

FIPER: Federated Intelligent Product EnviRonmet. Available at: http://sorcer.cs.ttu.edu/fiper/fiper.html. Accessed on: April 24, 2009.

Foster I.; Kesselman C. & Tuecke S. (2001). The Anatomy of the Grid: Enabling Scalable Virtual Organizations, *International J. Supercomputer Applications*, 15(3)

Freeman, E.; Hupfer, S. & Arnold, K. *JavaSpaces™ Principles, Patterns, and Practice*, Addison-Wesley, ISBN: 0-201-30955-6

Goel, S.; Talya S. & Sobolewski, M. (2005). Preliminary Design Using Distributed Service-based Computing, *Proceeding of the 12th Conference on Concurrent Engineering: Research and Applications*, In: *Next Generation Concurrent Engineering*, Sobolewski, M., and Ghodous, P. (Ed.), pp. 113-120, ISPE Inc./Omnipress, ISBN 0-9768246-0-4

Goel S., Shashishekara, Talya S.S., Sobolewski M. (2007). Service-based P2P overlay network for collaborative problem solving, *Decision Support Systems*, Volume 43, Issue 2, March 2007, pp. 547-568

Goel, S.; Talya, S.S. & Sobolewski, M. (2008). Mapping Engineering Design Processes onto a Service-Grid: Turbine Design Optimization, *International Journal of Concurrent Engineering: Research & Applications*, Concurrent Engineering, Vol.16, pp 139-147

Hard, C. & Sobolewski, M (2009). File Location Management in Federated Computing Environments, *International Journal of Recent Trends in Engineering (Computer Science)*, Vol. 1, No. 1, June 2009, pp. 512-517.

Grand M. (1999). Patterns in Java, Volume 1, Wiley, ISBN: 0-471-25841-5

Inca X™ Service Browser for Jini Technology. Available at: http://www.incax.com/index.htm?http://www.incax.com/service-browser.htm. Accessed on: April 24, 2009.

JXTA. Available at: https://jxta.dev.java.net/. Accessed on: April 24 2009.

Jini architecture specification, Version 2.1. Available at: http://www.sun.com/software/jini /specs/jini1.2html/jini-title.html. Accessed on: January 15, 2008(2001)

Kao, K. J.; Seeley, C.E.; Yin, S.; Kolonay, R.M.; Rus, T. & Paradis, M.J. (2003). Business-to-Business Virtual Collaboartion of Aircraft Engine Combustor Design, Proceedings of *DETC'03* ASME 2003 Design Engineering Technical Conferences and Computers and Information in Engineering Conference, Chicago, Illinois

Kerr, D. & Sobolewski, M. (2008). Secure Space Computing with Exertions, *3rd Annual Symposium on Information Assurance* (ASIA'08), Albany, NY.

Khurana, V.; Berger, M. & Sobolewski, M. (2005). A Federated Grid Environment with Replication Services. *Next Generation Concurrent Engineering*. ISPE/Omnipress, ISBN 0-9768246-0-4, pp. 97-103.

Kolonay, R.M.; Sobolewski; M., Tappeta, R.; Paradis. M. & Burton, S. (2002). Network-Centric MAO Environment. The Society for Modeling and Simulation International, Westrn Multiconference, San Antonio, TX

Kolonay, R. M.; Thompson, E.D.; Camberos, J.A. & Eastep, F. (2007). Active Control of Transpiration Boundary Conditions for Drag Minimization with an Euler CFD Solver, AIAA-2007-1891, 48th AIAA/ASME/ASCE/AHS/ASC Structures, Structural Dynamics, and Materials Conference, Honolulu, Hawaii

Lapinski, M. & Sobolewski, M. (2003). Managing Notifications in a Federated S2S Environment, *International Journal of Concurrent Engineering: Research & Applications*, Vol. 11, pp. 17-25

Metacomputing: Past to Present, Retrieved April 24, 2009, from: http://archive.ncsa.uiuc.edu/Cyberia/MetaComp/MetaHistory.html

Metacomputer: One from Many, April 24, 2009, from: http://archive.ncsa.uiuc.edu/Cyberia/MetaComp/MetaHome.html

McGovern J.; Tyagi S.; Stevens M.E. & Mathew S. (2003). Morgan Kaufmann

Nimrod: Tools for Distributed Parametric Modelling. Retrieved April 24, 2009, from: http://www.csse.monash.edu.au/~davida/nimrod/nimrodg.htm.

Package net.jini.jeri. Available at: http://java.sun.com/products/jini/2.1/doc/api/net/jini/jeri/package-summary.html. Accessed on: April 24, 2009

Pitt E. & McNiff K. (2001). *java.rmi: The Remote Method Invocation Guide*, Addison-Wesley Professional

Project Rio, A Dynamic Service Architecture for Distributed Applications. Available at: https://rio.dev.java.net/. Accessed on: April 24, 2009

Röhl, P.J.; Kolonay, R.M.; Irani, R.K.; Sobolewski, M. & Kao, K. (2000). A Federated Intelligent Product Environment, AIAA-2000-4902, 8th AIAA/USAF/NASA/ISSMO Symposium on Multidisciplinary Analysis and Optimization, Long Beach, CA

Rubach, P. & Sobolewski, M. (2009). Autonomic SLA Management in Federated Computing Environments, *Proceedings of the 2009 International Conference on Parallel Processing Workshops (ICPPW 2009)*, Vienna, Austria. IEEE Computer Society, ISBN 978-0-7695-3803-7, pp. 314-321.

Ruh W.A.; Herron T. & Klinker P. (1999). IIOP Complete: Understanding CORBA and Middleware Interoperability, Addison-Wesley

Sampath, R.; Kolonay, R. M. & Kuhne, C. M. (2002). 2D/3D CFD Design Optimization Using the Federated Intelligent Product Environment (FIPER) Technology. AIAA-2002-5479, 9th AIAA/ISSMO Symposium on Multidisciplinary Analysis and Optimization, Atlanta, GA

Sobolewski M. (2002). Federated P2P services in CE Environments, Advances in Concurrent Engineering, A.A. Balkema Publishers, 2002, pp. 13-22

Sobolewski, M., Soorianarayanan, S., Malladi-Venkata, R-K. (2003). Service-Oriented File Sharing, Proceedings of the IASTED Intl., Conference on Communications, Internet, and Information technology, pp. 633-639, ACTA Press

Sobolewski, M. & Ghodous, P. (Ed.). (2005). *Next Generation Concurrent Engineering: Smart and Concurrent Integration of Product Data, Services, and Control Strategies,* ISPE, Inc., ISBN 0-9768246-0-4

Sobolewski M., Kolonay R. (2006). Federated Grid Computing with Interactive Service-oriented Programming, International Journal of Concurrent Engineering: Research & Applications, Vol. 14, No 1, pp. 55-66

Sobolewski M. (2007). Federated Method Invocation with Exertions, Proceedings of the IMCSIT Conference, PTI Press, ISSN 1896-7094, pp. 765-778

Sobolewski, M. (2008a). Exertion Oriented Programming, IADIS, vol. 3 no. 1, pp. 86-109, ISBN: ISSN: 1646-3692

Sobolewski, M (2008b). SORCER: Computing and Metacomputing Intergrid, 10th International Conference on Enterprise Information Systems, Barcelona, Spain (2008).

Sobolewski, M. 2008c). Federated Collaborations with Exertions, 17h IEEE International Workshop on Enabling Technologies: Infrastructures for Collaborative Enterprises, Rome, Italy

Soorianarayanan, S. & Sobolewski, M. (2004). Monitoring Federated Services in CE, *Concurrent Engineering: The Worldwide Engineering Grid*, Tsinghua Press and Springer Verlag, pp. 89-95

SORCER Research Group. Available at: http://sorcer.cs.ttu.edu/ or http://sorcersoft.org. Accessed on: April 24, 2009.

SORCER Research Topics. Available at: http://sorcer.cs.ttu.edu/theses/ or http://sorcersoft.org/theses/. Accessed on: April 24, 2009

Sotomayor B. & Childers L. (2005). *Globus® Toolkit 4: Programming Java Services*, Morgan Kaufmann

Thain D.; Tannenbaum T.; Livny M. (2003). Condor and the Grid. In: Grid Computing: Making The Global Infrastructure a Reality, Fran Berman, Anthony J.G. Hey, and Geoffrey Fox, (Ed.),. John Wiley

Turner, A. & Sobolewski, M. (2007). FICUS—A Federated Service-Oriented File Transfer Framework, *Complex Systems Concurrent Engineering*, Loureiro, G. and L.Curran, R. (Ed.). Springer Verlag, ISBN: 978-1-84628-975-0, pp. 421-430

The Service UI Project. Available at: http://www.artima.com/jini/serviceui/index.html. Accessed on: April 24, 2009

Waldo J. The End of Protocols, Available at: http://java.sun.com/developer/technicalArticles/jini/protocols.html. Accessed on: April 24 15, 2009.

Zhao, S.; and Sobolewski, M. (2001). Context Model Sharing in the FIPER Environment, Proc. of the 8th *Int. Conference on Concurrent Engineering: Research and Applications*, Anaheim, CA

NEW STOCHASTIC DEPENDENCES PARADIGM AND ITS APPLICATION IN PROBABILISTIC MODELING

Jerzy K. Filus
Department of Mathematics and Computer Science
Oakton Community College, Des Plaines, Il 60016, USA
email: jfilus@oakton.edu

Lidia Z. Filus
Department of Mathematics
Northeastern Illinois University, Chicago, IL 60625, USA
email: L-Filus@neiu.edu

Abstract. We present a quite **simple pattern** that, by a properly defined conditioning, allows to describe a wide range of new stochastic dependences (virtually, it is the **type of the multivariate normal kind of the dependencies extended to** numerous **other** multivariate cases**).**

We then construct a variety of stochastic models in form of multivariate probability distributions. The key element of the theory is the obtained a quite easy method for constructing various classes of conditional pdfs $\mathbf{g_k (y \mid x_1, \dots ,x_k)}$ of random variable's, here denoted by Y, given realizations of some other (explanatory) random variables $X_1, \dots ,$ X_k. The latter variables are either independent or posses some known joint probability distribution. The striking easiness in their construction and a significant universality for a variety of anticipated applications, suggest a possibility of employing them in a variety of areas that sometimes seem to be remote from each other.

Some of the main applications of the considered constructions pattern are practical problems associated with the **statistical regression.** Here, the paradigm, relies on **replacing** (or 'extending'**),** whenever possible a regression model, typically used in the form of the conditional expectation $\mathbf{E[\,Y \mid x_1, \dots ,x_k\,]}$ by the corresponding (one, but not necessarily unique) conditional pdf $\mathbf{g_k (y \mid x_1, \dots ,x_k)}$**.** In this case, the original regression model is simply the expectation of the latter conditional pdf.

Nevertheless, in this work we rather concentrate on modeling of multi component **systems reliability** as well as similar **biomedical** problems. One of the main reasons for this preference is the fact that the reliability examples bring better clarity for demonstration of the common '*stochastic model – real world*' relation.

As for the reliability application, we model (by means of the introduced general stochastic dependence) a parallel two component system with respect to its stochastically dependent components life times.

1. On A General Continuous Stochastic Dependences Pattern; Introductory Part

1.1 The pattern for stochastic dependences is a basic ingredient of **stochastic models** that we construct and explore. The motivation for the constructions is both a recognition and anticipation of a strong potential for applications of the obtained models in a variety of everyday' phenomena that are "by nature" random. The **pattern,** determines a general method that is fundamental for all the constructions that are or can be performed in the presented framework**.** Roughly speaking, this method relies on what follows. Given **(any)** two random quantities $\mathbf{X_1}$, $\mathbf{X_2}$ representing, say, two objects u_1, u_2 respectively **(**whose **"physical"** meaning is to a large extend "arbitrary"**)** such that the magnitude of a given realization (or outcome) $\mathbf{x_1}$ of the random variable X_1, "stochastically **influences"** magnitude of a possible realization $\mathbf{x_2}$ of the random variable X_2. The way the value $\mathbf{x_1}$ of the quantity $\mathbf{X_1}$ "acts" on a possible outcome $X_2 = x_2$ of the other quantity, is described 'indirectly' in terms of **changes in the X_2's probability distribution,** rather than in terms of direct changes in X_2 itself.

Our Objective is to present an analytic description of a "measure" that reflects a particular situation in modeled reality. Among several possibilities we basically concentrate on two. The first possibility is to investigate the distribution's changes through changes in its original hazard rate, see [9]. This approach strongly applies to determining dependent life-times distributions in reliability (see [2] and also [4, 9, 10, 12]) or in some **biomedical** problems [3]. Note, however, that the mechanism of changes in the hazard (failure) rate, presented here, is essentially **different than** the one that was described for the first time in 1961 by **Freund** in [9]**.**
The second possibility we consider requires a somewhat more general procedure. In this case we tend to find a description of changes in the probability distribution or the corresponding density through corresponding (hypothetical) **changes of the density's parameters,** see [5 – 8]. Thus, in this case, the pattern relies on (statistical) 'measuring' change of the (original) pdf 's **parameter** value(s) θ_2. The changed value of that parameter is assumed to be functionally **dependent on** a magnitude of the first random realization of quantity ($X_1 = \mathbf{x_1}$)**.**

1.2 In other words, we develop a powerful while still simple, **method** for determining **stochastic dependences** of various kinds of random variables as well as of random vectors. Application of this method to various practical problems of the 'real life' produces a remarkably wide range of flexible **stochastic models.**
Roughly speaking, a huge variety of models and their more specific versions is based on a simple observation that the **stochastic dependence** of a random quantity, say **Y (**whose cdf, in an absence of considered in this work stresses is denoted by $F(y; \theta)$ **)** on a set of other **(explanatory)** random variables $\{ X_1, \ldots ,X_k \}$ can nicely be described in a proper mathematical model.

For a more compact definition of the stochastic dependence suppose that an elementary random **event** $(X_1, \ldots, X_k) = (x_1, \ldots, x_k)$ has happened.
Mathematically, we define the dependence as a result of rather new, but quite "obvious", kind of the **transformations:**

$$(x_1, \ldots, x_k) \rightarrow F(y; \theta), \tag{1}$$

that we propose to call **"weak"**, or "stochastic" in a contrast to the ordinary "strong" or **"algebraic" transformation** $(X_1, \ldots, X_k) \rightarrow Y$**.**
Among several ways the weak transformation can be determined, we have chosen possibly the simplest by claiming that the **impact** of the random quantities (say, **"stresses"**) $X_1, \ldots, X_k$ **on the cdf** of the quantity of interest **Y,** exhibits itself as an impact on the scalar or vector parameter θ of the cdf. **$F(y; \theta)$.**
Thus the defined above weak transformation can be shorten to the relation:

$$\theta \rightarrow \theta(x_1, \ldots, x_k), \tag{2}$$

where the symbol 'θ' alone, represents the cdf's **parameter** original numerical value i.e., the value in an absence of the stresses $X_1, \ldots, X_k$.
The new (random) value $\theta(X_1, \ldots, X_k) \neq \theta$, of the parameter of the Y's cdf may, in most general case, be considered as just **any continuous function** (!) of its k arguments. However, for the sake of tractability of further **statistical verification** of the so constructed models, it may become necessary to limit the class of the continuous functions to some **parametric classes**. Thus, the statistical parametric procedures will be concerned now with a given functions' class (such as the exponential, say $\theta(x) = \{A\exp[\, bx \,]\}$ or power, polynomials etc **...**) parameters, instead of the original numerical values of the previous parameter θ itself. In general, the number of such a function's parameters (for example, the **parameters A, b** in the above exponential model for the transformed value of θ, where it also may assumed, that $\theta = A$) should not be much more than double number of the original parameters θ.
Notice, that the so obtained new cdf **$F(y; \theta(x_1, \ldots, x_k))$**, virtually is the defined **conditional distribution of Y** given an elementary event $(X_1, \ldots, X_k) = (x_1, \ldots, x_k)$ and, actually the so defined stochastic **dependence** of **Y** from the $(X_1, \ldots, X_k)$ embraces **the core idea** of an emerging new theory (compare this concept with the very similar structure of the classical **multivariate normal pdf).**
Obviously, the ordinary product of the conditional pdf, say :

$$f(y \mid x_1, \ldots, x_k) = f(y; \theta(x_1, \ldots, x_k)) \tag{3}$$

and the joint pdf **$g(x_1, \ldots, x_k)$** of the "explanatory" variables $X_1, \ldots, X_k$ provides the (k+1) – variate joint pdf **$h(y, x_1, \ldots, x_k)$**. In that way, most of the multivariate distributions can be constructed within the theory presented here. Notice also the important fact that there is no need for any assumptions concerning classes of probability distributions of all underlying random variables such as $Y, X_1, \ldots, X_k$. As a matter of fact, any of the variables, may belong to **any class of probability distributions (!).** Moreover, the procedures delineated here are expected to extend the classical **regression** methods. Namely, one can extend the regression

models, typically met in form of the **conditional expectations** **E [Y | x_1, ... ,x_k]** to the ones defined as the conditional probability **distributions** **F(y | x_1, ... ,x_k),** whose densities (if exist) are given by **(3).** Notice an obvious fact, that their expectations are the same as in classical models for the regression.
Considering the various stochastic models, obtained by the **common paradigm**, given by the scheme expressed in (1), (2) and (3) one finds that the **generality** of the described modeling **method** may lead to a number of possible applications. The applications can likely spread out over many "physically" different areas of the real world. We hope that the considered here method will turn out to be fruitful in solving variety of practical problems.
Nevertheless, regardless of that remoteness of application areas the **mathematical** (probabilistic) methods and the models' **structure is very similar,** sometimes just 'identical' in some of "totally different" fields.
In our opinion, the most "natural" and relatively easy approach to explain the general idea is the following two components system **reliability' modeling** case.

We have decided that in the next section this (first) topic in reliability will be a little more elaborated than some other, mathematically similar, that will follow after.

2. The Reliability of Two Component Parallel System

Now, we start to investigate each of the system components' **failure mechanism** as being subjected to the following **two,** associated each to other, **patterns** of the components interactions. The first scheme we call:
"Micro-shocks → Micro-damages" phenomena.

This relationship is considered in a junction with the second that may be understood as a method of a "translation" some 'physical' phenomena to a proper mathematical model as (the second)**: "Micro-damages → Micro-hazard rate** (probability) **changes"** scheme. We apply a **continuous** approximation approach to this phenomena. In that setting we also describe cumulation **(**in the chosen model) of the stochastic micro-effects **(**or equivalently: the 'probability micro-changes'**)** by means of the calculus Riemann integral formalism.

Generally speaking, we encounter the following two situations.
The (random) **life-times** of two physical units **u_1, u_2** are estimated in **two distinct conditions** by use of the common statistical methods.
At first, both the units u_1, u_2 are tested, in separation of each other in, say "laboratory" **'off-system'** conditions. It is assumed that, as a result one obtains good enough estimations of the (**"baseline"**) probability distributions **$F_1(x_1)$, F_2 (x_2) of** the life-times **T_1, T_2 .**
Because of the physical separation at this stage of the research **(**that eventually may be considered as first stage of "mental experiment"**)** the resulting life-times T_1, T_2, of the units are stochastically **independent.**
At the **second stage** of the procedure the units are considered as components installed (in parallel) into the system. Now, as we assume**, "side-effects"** of various physical phenomena, associated with operating of any of the components, contribute to the failure mechanism of the other. Therefore, unlike in the previous off-system conditions, **additional** physical **stresses** are put on each of the two system components u_1, u_2.

As a result of the component's "harmful" activities, some **changes** in the other component's physical structure, such as **micro-damages,** occur. These micro-damages accelerate (or, in some cases delay) the processes leading to the component failures.
The objective is to find as "good" as possible stochastic **model** for such a system's reliability.
(For a similar construction's pattern, see [9]).
For this sake, one should admit that the physical phenomena associated with processes of the components interaction may turn out to be too complicated to be followed and analyzed adequately in traditional deterministic ways. This is the reason we rely on stochastic description by constructing a **joint probability distribution** of the "in-system" component life-times $\mathbf{X_1, X_2}$.

The **key idea** to start with the construction is: Express the **stochastic dependences** in terms of some extra (due to the new 'in-system' conditions) **increments** in the 'original' (off-system) component **failure rates,** say $\boldsymbol{\lambda_1(x_1)}$, $\boldsymbol{\lambda_2(x_2)}$.
Recall, these failure (hazard) rates are associated with the 'original' life-time cdfs $F_1(x_1)$, $F_2(x_2)$ **of** $\mathbf{T_1, T_2}$ (so the changes in one equivalently parallel changes in other).
On the physical part of the problem, the mutual impact of any component on the other can be explained in the following manner. During the components' in-system performance either of the two creates such a situation that the other component is "constantly bombarded" by a **string of** harmful (or beneficial) **"micro-shocks".** Each such a "micro-shock" causes a corresponding **"micro-damage"** in the affected unit's physical constitution. Interpreting that **physical processes** 'language' **into** the 'language' of the **corresponding probabilistic** facts, one can say that the micro-damages of the components are equivalent to corresponding small **(micro) changes in** the original **failure (hazard) rates (**probability distribution**)** of their life-times.
On the other hand, each such a micro-damage is very small so that there is no practical possibility as to detect immediately any significant effect. However, after a time period long enough, the **micro-damages cumulate** their effects so that after that time the difference in the corresponding probability distributions may become quite significant.
To express the "smallness" of the micro-effects and then their significant accumulation, in the language related to the constructed **analytical model** we utilize (as it is frequently applied in modeling such phenomena like many those considered in physics) the familiar calculus notions of an **'infinitesimal quantity'** and that of the Riemann integral. Here, the integral will be applied as a "formal tool" to "sum up"(in the approximating analytical model) 'all' of the "infinitely many infinitesimal damages" in terms of the related micro-changes in the given value of the component's baseline failure rate (or in a distribution's parameter(s) **).** As a result of that integration over some finite time interval (of the component functioning) of length t one obtains a finite, practically recognizable, probabilistic quantity, say $\boldsymbol{\varphi}$ **(t;).**
Generally speaking, we apply a **continuous description** as a "smoothing" approximation to that kind of physical reality.
The goal is to **construct** a proper **bi-variate probability distribution of** the system component life-times $\mathbf{X_1, X_2}$, which is a common type of the stochastic models in the system reliability investigations.
For the classical examples, see [9, 12]; also see [4 - 8].

3. The Reliability Problem's Analytical Solution

In accordance with the general concept described in section 1 let us consider the previous two component' lifetimes X_1, X_2, as a "tandem" such that each of the two random variables is "explanatory variable" for the other.
In this section we will find the joint probability distribution of the random vector (X_1, X_2) in terms of its **joint survival function** $\mathbf{S(x_1, x_2) = Pr(X_1 > x_1 , X_2 > x_2)}$.
Recall, that the joint survival function $s^*(x_1, x_2)$ of the independent off-system component life-times T_1, T_2 is given by the following 'product form':

$$s^*(x_1, x_2) = \exp[- \int_0^{x_1} \lambda_1(t_1)\, d t_1 - \int_0^{x_2} \lambda_2(t_2)\, d t_2], \tag{4}$$

where $\lambda_1(t_1)$, $\lambda_2(t_2)$ are the components' off-system (baseline) failure rates.
When the components u_1, u_2 work in the system then, in accordance with the adopted (in the analytical model) assumption, in "every" infinitesimal small time interval $[\tau_k , \tau_k + d\tau_k)$ an occurrence of an infinitesimal **micro-damage** of the component, say u_k, $k = 1, 2$; (that is caused by '**side effects**' accompanying an activity of the component u_m, where $m = 1, 2;$ $m \neq k$) results in an **infinitesimal increment** $\alpha_{k\,m}(\tau_k)\, d\tau_k$ **of** the u_k's failure rate.
For every 'past' time instant τ_k, that increment is given by a predetermined quantity $\alpha_{k\,m}(\tau_k)$ that, in a stochastic way reflects "an amount" of the physical influence of a component u_m on the component u_k. That quantity is chosen (and then must be **statistically estimated and verified** for fit to data available) to be a continuous function of all the past epochs τ_k the micro-damages occurred.
All the **stochastic** effects $\alpha_{k\,m}(\tau_k)d\tau_k$ (of the physical micro-damage's) "sum up" over the time. Each of their "partial accumulation" (created from the time zero, up to the "current" epoch, say t_k) is expressed as the following Riemann integral:

$$\varphi_k(t_k) = (\int_0^{t_k} \alpha_{k\,m}(\tau_k)\, d\tau_k, \ (k \neq m). \tag{5}$$

This integral is a non decreasing continuous function of the current time t_k as is taken over all time intervals $[0, t_k]$, with $0 \le t_k \le x_k < \infty$, for $k = 1, 2$.
Both the variables x_k ($k = 1, 2$) as present in the foregoing condition are the arguments of the survival function (4).
At every "current" time instant t_k, the '**in-system' failure rate** $r_k(t_k)$ of the component u_k ($k = 1, 2$) is defined to be a simple arithmetic sum of the 'off-system' baseline failure rate $\lambda_k(t_k)$ and the "additional failure rate" given by the integral

$$\varphi_k(t_k) = \int_0^{t_k} \alpha_{k\,m}(\tau_k)\, d\tau_k, \ (k \neq m).$$

This integral will be thought off as a measure of a "magnitude" of the u_k's micro-damage's accumulation up to the current time epoch t_k.

Thus, at every time epoch t_k one obtains the following formula for the 'in-system' **failure rate** $r_k(t_k)$ of the component u_k:

$$r_k(t_k) = \lambda_k(t_k) + \int_0^{t_k} \alpha_{km}(\tau_k)\, d\tau_k, \tag{6}$$

as $k, m = 1, 2,$ and $k \neq m$.

We consider the failure rate formula (6) to be valid for each time argument t_k satisfying $0 \leq t_k \leq x$, where x = minimum (x_1, x_2) is considered to be the time of the first failure in the system. From the above one obtains the following survival function:

$$S_1(x) = \Pr(\min(X_1, X_2) > x), \quad \text{with } x = \min(x_1, x_2)),$$

for the first order statistics **X** of the set of random variables: $\{X_1, X_2\}$. That is:

$$S_1(x) = \exp\left[-\int_0^x r_1(t_1)\, dt_1 - \int_0^x r_2(t_2)\, dt_2\right], \tag{7}$$

where $r_1(t_1)$ and $r_2(t_2)$ are given by (1) for $k = 1, 2$.

These two functions represent **the 'in system' failure rates** of the components u_1 and u_2 respectively (at the time instances t_1, t_2), both prior to the time, say x, after which the first failure in the system occurs. In other words, (7) represents the **reliability function $S_1(x)$ of the system as a whole if its reliability structure is series.**

Continuing with the concept of **parallel** reliability structure, we consider the system's residual life -time's failure rate, say $r_k(t)$ i.e., the failure rate of either surviving component c_k at any time t satisfying $x \leq t \leq y$. Recall that **x, y** are the time epochs of the first and the second failure in the system respectively. For that period of time we have chosen the following failure pattern.

Namely, we define the failure rate $r_k(t)$ in the time interval **[x, y]** as the following arithmetic sum:

$$r_k(t) = \lambda_k(t) + \int_0^x \alpha_{km}(\tau)\, d\tau \tag{8}$$

In this context, **the integral** $\int_0^x \alpha_{km}(\tau)\, d\tau$ **is constant** over time past x which 'now' is fixed **(** $k, m = 1, 2,$ and $k \neq m$ **).**

The reason for its constancy is based on a simple observation that in the time interval $[x, y]$ only (one) component c_k is working in the system, and thus the process of the micro - damages accumulation is terminated as the time x passed. This integral (present as a part in (9), (9*) that follow) is an additional part of the overall failure rate $r_k(t)$ of component c_k, and may be understood as a **measure of "memory"** of the micro-incentives the c_k received before the other component c_m, stopped its activity at time x. For more on that see Remark 1.

The Final Formula for the joint survival function $\mathbf{S(x_1, x_2) = Pr(X_1 > x_1 , X_2 > x_2)}$ of the in-system component life-times $\mathbf{X_1, X_2}$ is given as follows:

$$\Pr(X_1 > x_1, X_2 > x_2 \mid X_1 \le X_2) = \exp\Big[- \int_0^{x_1} \{\lambda_1(t_1) + \int_0^{t_1} \alpha_{1,2}(\tau_1)\, d\tau_1\}\, dt_1 - \int_0^{x_1} \{\lambda_2(t_2) + \int_0^{t_2} \alpha_{2,1}(\tau_2)\, d\tau_2\}\, dt_2\Big] \exp\Big[- \int_{x_1}^{x_2} \{\lambda_2(t_2)\, dt_2\} - (x_2 - x_1) \int_0^{x_1} \alpha_{2,1}(\tau_1)\, d\tau_1 \Big]; \qquad (9)$$

$$\Pr(X_1 > x_1, X_2 > x_2 \mid X_1 > X_2) = \exp\Big[- \int_0^{x_2} \{\lambda_2(t_2) + \int_0^{t_2} \alpha_{2,1}(\tau_2)\, d\tau_2\}\, dt_2 \quad \int_0^{x_2} \{\lambda_1(t_1) + \int_0^{t_1} \alpha_{1,2}(\tau_1)\, d\tau_1\}\, dt_1\Big] \exp\Big[- \int_{x_2}^{x_1} \{\lambda_1(t_1)\, dt_1\} - (x_1 - x_2) \int_0^{x_2} \alpha_{1,2}(\tau_1)\, d\tau_1 \Big]. \qquad (9^*)$$

If in both the formulas (9), (9*) one sets $x_2 = 0$, then one obtains the **marginal** probability distribution **of** $\mathbf{X_1}$ to be the same as the original probability distribution $\mathbf{F_1(x_1)}$ of the off-system life-time T_1, **related to** the given in advance original failure rate $\boldsymbol{\lambda_1(t_1)}$**.** The similar result one obtains when imposing in (9), (9*) the condition $x_1 = 0$.
The latter condition yields the marginal distribution of the $\mathbf{X_2}$ to be equal $\mathbf{F_2(x_2)}$.
As the conclusion one derives the following surprising property , shared by all the models that obey the pattern expressed by (9), (9*).

Property 1. For any joint probability distribution $\mathbf{S(x_1, x_2)}$ that satisfies the pattern, defined by (9), (9*), the given in advance original probability distributions $F_1(x_1)$, $F_2(x_2)$ of the off-system life-times T_1, T_2 **are preserved !** as **the marginal distributions** of the joint probability distribution of the in-system life-times X_1, X_2 (of the considered units u_1, u_2).

From the Property 1, the following conclusion can be derived.

Corollary. Suppose we are given a pair of probability distributions $G_1(x_1)$, $G_2(x_2)$ that belong to any class of probability distribution functions, whose all members posses continuous failure (hazard) rates, say $\lambda_1(t_1)$, $\lambda_2(t_2)$.
If one puts any arbitrary single pair of such distributions into the scheme defined by (9), (9*) then, as a result one can generate a wide class of the bivariate survival functions $S(x_1, x_2)$, whose marginals remain to be the $G_1(x_1)$, $G_2(x_2)$. The class of the so obtained bivariate

probability distributions "given the (fixed) marginals $G_1(x_1)$, $G_2(x_2)$" is determined by the family of all the continuous functions $\alpha_{i,j}(\tau_i)$, (i, j = 1, 2, with $i \neq j$) that produce all the integrals in (9), (9*) finite.

So, in this particular sense one can consider **the "bivariate Weibull, gamma (in particular, exponential), the extreme value"** and other joint probability distributions.

Realize, however that the marginal distributions $\mathbf{G_1(x_1)}$, $\mathbf{G_2(x_2)}$, in Corollary 1 also may represent two **distinct distribution classes.** The last possibility may be utilized in modeling reliability of two stochastically dependent units (such as system components) each one subjected to a different failure mechanism. Apparently such cases often are realistic.

Example 1 As a particular class of bivariate survival functions $S(x_1, x_2)$, satisfying the pattern given by (9), (9*), we now choose a class of bivariate exponential distributions given by two arbitrary constant failure rates λ_1, λ_2 for the marginals.
We also restrict the dependence structure. In this case it is assumed to be determined only by two arbitrary **constant** functions $\alpha_{1,2}(\ )$, $\alpha_{2,1}(\ )$. Recall, they represent the rates of increment in the failure (hazard) rate of the unit u_1 caused by u_2 and that failure rate increment of u_2, caused by u_1, respectively.
The resulting class of the **joint exponential survival functions** can be expressed by the more specific following formulas:

$$\mathbf{Pr(X_1 > x_1, X_2 > x_2 \mid X_1 \leq X_2) = \exp\left[-\int_0^{x_1}\{\lambda_1 + \int_0^{t_1} \alpha_{1,2}\, d\tau_1\}\, dt_1 - \int_0^{x_1}\{\lambda_2 + \int_0^{t_2} \alpha_{2,1}\, d\tau_2\}\, dt_2\right] \exp\left[-\int_{x_1}^{x_2}\{\lambda_2\, dt_2\} - (\alpha_{2,1} x_1)(x_2 - x_1)\right];} \tag{10}$$

$$\mathbf{Pr(X_1 > x_1, X_2 > x_2 \mid X_1 > X_2) = \exp\left[-\int_0^{x_2}\{\lambda_2 + \int_0^{t_2} \alpha_{2,1}\, d\tau_2\}\, dt_2 - \int_0^{x_2}\{\lambda_1 + \int_0^{t_1} \alpha_{1,2}\, d\tau_1\}\, dt_1\right] \exp\left[-\int_{x_2}^{x_1}\{\lambda_1\, dt_1\} - (\alpha_{1,2}\, x_2)(x_1 - x_2)\right].} \tag{10*}$$

(Recall, that any power transformation applied to the random variables X_1, X_2 yields the corresponding bivariate **Weibull model.)** Upon simplifying assumption that

$\alpha_{1,2}(\ ) = \alpha_{2,1}(\ ) = \alpha =$ **constant,** both the formulas (10), (10*) reduce to the following single one:

$$\mathbf{Pr(X_1 > x_1, X_2 > x_2) = \exp[-\lambda_1 x_1 - \lambda_2 x_2 - \alpha x_1 x_2].} \tag{11}$$

Thus, as a special case one obtains the first bivariate exponential **Gumbel** probability distribution **as (perhaps a first time)** the system **reliability model** (see [11]).

Remark 1. Return, for a while to the integral $\int_0^x \alpha_{k\,m}(\tau)\,d\tau$, discussed in this section in association with the formula (8). In the models presented in this paper this additional (constant over the time interval [x , y], where **x, y** denote the times of the first and the second failure in the system, respectively) value of the e_k's failure rate can be interpreted as a measure of **"an amount of memory"** of the two components past interaction. The memory is assumed to be kept by any survived component $\mathbf{u}_k$ after the failure of the other component $\mathbf{u}_m$ (k, m = 1, 2).
Actually, the assumption of preserving the whole memory for all the residual time is rather strong and for many 'physical' (real) entities not realistic.
As usually, the reason it was adopted in this work was the common need to preserve a reasonable level of the simplicity.

Once it was done, **next step** in a process of the models construction would be adopting the models to more realistic situations when the **memory varies.**
Consider the following two phenomena. In the first, one assumes that due to some kind of "elasticity" of the units, **no memory** at all is kept by any component after the first failure.
To adopt our previous models to this case we set the extra failure rates given by the integrals

$\int_0^{x_1} \alpha_{2,1}(\tau_1)\,d\tau_1$, $\int_0^{x_2} \alpha_{1,2}(\tau_2)\,d\tau_2$, present in (9), (9*), respectively **to zero.**

In the second case, typical, for example in **biomedical phenomena,** the **memory** does not vanish but instead **decays** with the time (as result of 'rest' or **'recovery').** To describe that case we can multiply the considered here integrals by continuous functions (called the **"forgetting factors")** decreasing with the time, from one to zero, and then integrate the so obtained products over the remaining time. Thus, in expressions (9), (9*) we replace the integrals:

$$(x_2 - x_1)\int_0^{x_1} \alpha_{2,1}(\tau_1)\,d\tau_1, \text{ and } (x_1 - x_2)\}\int_0^{x_2} \alpha_{1,2}(\tau_2)\,d\tau_2,$$

by the following expressions:

$$\gamma^{-1}\exp\{-\gamma(x_2 - x_1)\}\int_0^{x_1} \alpha_{2,1}(\tau_1)\,d\tau_1, \text{ and } \gamma^{-1}\exp\{-\gamma(x_1 - x_2)\}\int_0^{x_2} \alpha_{1,2}(\tau_2)\,d\tau_2,$$

where γ is (to be estimated) a positive constant that may be called the **"coefficient of decay".**
In such a way one obtains other variants of the stochastic models defined earlier in this work.

Remark 2 Observe that the dependence of the units u_1, u_2 failure mechanisms and its stochastic description in section 2 somehow resembles the multiple shock models pretty frequently met in literature. See for example "a successive damage model" in [3] . As for the difference, in all such models the shocks were considered to form a discrete kind of sets (mostly finite). Also unlike with the failure mechanisms we consider, every single shock from that (discrete) set is a significant, in the sense it always could cause the unit's failure with a positive probability. Nevertheless, these differences may only be regarded as a usual conceptual difference between discrete and continuous approach to basically similar phenomena. The continuous model is only thought off as an approximating limiting transition if a number of weak "shocks" becomes very large and is "densely" redistributed over the time. Therefore, the ("smoothed") model of the failure mechanism as described in section 2, we propose to call "Continuous 'micro shock - micro damage' model", whenever in reliability framework. In more general settings we propose to call it Continuous "micro action" → "micro effect" model that might, for example, be applied for a joint description of such random quantities like 'level of employment versus rate of inflation ' in a macro economy investigations or in other similar circles of practical problems.

4. Other Applications of the Dependence Paradigm

The pattern of the stochastic dependence, applied to reliability in previous sections, can naturally be extended to the (mathematically similar) modeling of a variety **bio-medical** phenomena and related, in many cases random, quantities, (for that see [3]). A simple but vivid illustration of that kind of the modeling problems provides the following example of actuary investigations.

Example 2. One of the pretty recently considered **actuary problems** (see [11]) is to improve **stochastic predictions** on residual life-times for potential clients of a given age, who possibly widowed in a recent time.
Two situations are considered and compared. Either a candidate for a given insurance plan was living all the past life as a single or spent a significant of part of life in a marriage. It is assumed that "at present" she or he is widowed.
The problem is based on **statistical** data **evidence,** which indicates that the two life-styles significantly result in statistically **different** (in the sense of expected value or of an underlying probability distribution) residual life-times for the two groups of the persons. The persons besides are supposed to be "identical" with respect to any other essential criteria that may influence the life-times. The statistical findings suggest that some physical, psychological or mental **interactions** between the spouses in marriage produce some additional stresses, which positively or negatively affect the client's residual life-time or, more precisely, its probability distribution. Also they suggest that, even if the person widows, a "memory" of past experiences remains in a person's psychophysical structure, affecting her/his residual life-time.

Phenomena, like the one above, seem to be typical in many other similar situations that can be present in a variety aspects of the real world, especially those of human' life conditions and accompanying events.
The problem of estimating the (random) length of a human's residual life time is vital for life **insurance** companies, and requires a use of advanced statistical methods. It is well known that the average residual life time or well being of a person at a specific age (besides of his / her "genetics") depends on a variety of factors, the essential ones being "**stresses**" (and corresponding times of their duration) such as smoking tobacco, excessive drinking alcohol, the length of time being exposed to especially harsh conditions such as prison, war or other.

In the vast majority of cases where statistical methods are employed, it is customary that the conclusions derived from, say, randomized experiments or other tests, are reduced (in the case of smoking versus nonsmoking, for example) to dichotomous statements on the existence of the influence of a given stress on the residual life time, or lack of such influence (given a significance level). In these cases, there is often **lack of information on any quantified** relationship between the **life time**'s stochastic characteristics (such as, for example, expectations, quantiles, hazard rates or other) and an 'amount' of stress a person endured. In the case of tobacco smoking this amount can be measured as, for example, a product (or some other function) of the time period of duration and the intensity (amount of nicotine per day) of the given stress.

5. The 'Micro-Incentives → Micro-Effects' Scheme and the Related Stochastic Dependences' Pattern. General Formulation.

A comparison of the, given above, reliability and bio-medical examples exhibits a common idea, in stochastic modeling procedures. The range of possible applications turns out to be remarkably wide, entering far beyond the context of the reliability investigations.
The essence of the considered, in this work general pattern , first of all relies on reviling a **relation** (if exists) **of,** say, **"parallelism"** between some ('continuous') **"physical** interactions" of two or more observed entities, on one side, **and** the corresponding infinitesimal changes in the **mathematical** (probabilistic) model's parameters on the other side.
This, rather a new pattern of the (physical versus stochastic) dependence can be considered as an extension of the **reliability scheme's** (described in Example 1) that, as a whole, could be illustrated, by the following 'diagram':

"('micro-shocks' – 'micro-damages') versus ('micro-probability -changes')", (12)

where the 'physical' parallels the 'stochastic'. In (12), the meaning the word "versus" is the same as the meaning of the "parallels". The choice between the two words was dictated by the (partly 'esthetic') structure of the above diagram.
Realize that the above pattern for reliability problems can be extended to a significantly more general domain of the phenomena. Consequently, the diagram (12) can be replaced by the following, more general, diagram:

"('micro-incentives' – 'micro-physical changes') versus

('micro-probability -changes')". (13)

The pattern described by (12) is special case of that given by (13).
To explain the **similarities** between the reliability settings and other (if appropriate) types of 'real world' phenomena we refer to Example 2, as well as to a huge number of particular situation ranging from **econometric** problems (like, possibly, stock market predictions) to the bio-medicals.

Look, for example, at the relationship between a human's smoking tobacco (or other stress), during a given time period and a probability distribution of his/ her **life time: Y.**
Physically, this problem may be "imagined" as "constant attacks" on the human's body by a sequence of very small "pieces" of the harmful substance that result in a corresponding sequence of small micro-changes (damages) in some parts of the human's body. An effect of any single piece of the substance's (in this case, say the nicotine) activity is usually too small to be observed or even admitted. However, these effects cumulate and after some, sufficiently long period of time, the total sum of them makes a significant **contribution** (a "change") to the biochemical processes that are "responsible" for an illness (such as hard attack) or death by accelerating them.
As a corresponding stochastic effect the probability distribution of the life time **Y** may be **changed** making the **probabilities** (or equivalently the **hazard rates)** of shorter life times **higher** than the corresponding probabilities (the baseline hazard rate) for, the statistically the same but differing by that "**smoking** factor", persons.
Probably, in most of the cases, the 'physics' of the described above phenomena may be too fugitive or complicated to be reasonably describable in terms of deterministic scientific (including a 'biomedical description') language.
The introduced in this paper **probabilistic approach** is thought off as a **shortcut,** that eventually may lead to a useful stochastic model.
For the stochastic model we have chosen a **continuous** one, despite **discrete nature of** the physical **reality.** As this is a common procedure, applied, first of all, in science and engineering, a continuous approximating description, of being considered 'real-life' phenomena, stand for analytically nice and sufficiently precise models (both, deterministic and stochastic) if some (smoothing) conditions are satisfied.
In our case, the two such conditions are assumed to be satisfied: **1.** Every string of micro-incentives as well as that of the resulting 'micro-physical changes', only contains very small pieces of, say "micro-actions". **2.** The time-distance between any such two consecutive actions is also very small, so that a number of such actions in some reasonably long time interval is "large".

That smallness and a large number of the micro-changes that occur during any sufficiently long time interval allows for averaging and smoothing the phenomena.
According to this possibility we treat, within the mathematical stochastic model (only) all the micro-changes as '**infinitesimals',** which are "continuously redistributed" along the time.
That reasoning and the analytical efficiency of the mathematical calculus facilities, made us to chose the **continuous** model(s) as the approximation(s) of the 'real life' phenomena, that unfortunately are, by the nature, discrete.

In the following section we give an example of the one more and very important application of the introduced in this work, kind of the stochastic dependences.

6. On the 'Extended Regression' Paradigm

Consider, once more, the conditional density $\mathbf{g_j}$ $(\mathbf{x_j} \mid \mathbf{x_1}, \dots, \mathbf{x_{j-1}})$ that represents the main object (as the general model) of the presented theory. Now, we admit the meaning of the random variables **Y** and the $X_1, \dots, X_k$, to be 'arbitrary', with $\mathbf{X_1}, \dots, \mathbf{X_k}$ considered as 'any' **explanatory** (random) variables for the **Y,** that is considered to be the actual variable (or random vector) of interest. The random variables $\mathbf{X_1, \ldots, X_k}$ may either be independent or, if not, their joint probability distribution is, in general, assumed to be known.

We may restrict our investigation to each **single unit** (as characterized by the quantity **'Y'),** separately, just for 'practical' needs, while resigning from developing a more general theory, that would involve classes or "populations" of those units. In such a 'practical' framework instead of the model that contains the probability distribution of the explanatory random variables $\mathbf{X_1, \ldots, X_k}$ one must rely on their deterministic realizations $x_1, \ldots, x_k$, as they can be known, in each single case, 'post factum', by direct observations followed by proper measurements. The way out from this limitation could be, whenever possible, an (approximating) assumption on stochastic independence of the r. variables $\mathbf{X_1, \ldots, X_k}$.

The crucial fact, behind the above description, is that the so defined and relatively easily achievable (!) **stochastic dependences** of a considered random variable **Y** on the random variables $\mathbf{X_1, \ldots, X_k}$, may directly lead to a modification and **enrichment of the classical regression methodology.**

Recall, that **the dependence** of the **Y** on the random variables $X_1, \ldots, X_k$ is not a direct 'functional' one. **Instead of** usually considered direct (explicit) influence of the realizations $\mathbf{x_1, \ldots, x_k}$ **on value of Y,** here the given realizations **"only" influence** (explicitly) the **probability distribution** of the **Y.**
The new (conditional) probability distribution of **Y** (after it "enters to interaction with some physical impacts" characterized by the random quantities $X_1, \ldots, X_k$) is obtained by a **direct transformation of** the original (baseline) distribution' **parameters** into their new values, that are continuously dependent on the realizations $\mathbf{x_1, \ldots, x_k}$ of the "impacts".

This is obvious that the pattern for the class of all the obtained conditional pdfs $g(y \mid x_1, \ldots, x_k)$ may provide significantly more information on the random quantity **Y** than just when one considers its conditional **expectation only.** Nevertheless the latter **is** included in the **"extended regression model": $g(y \mid x_1, \ldots, x_k)$,** simply as its expectation. Also realize that in the considered paradigm the normality assumption for the $g(y \mid x_1, \ldots, x_k)$ is quite not necessary as it becomes natural that $g(y \mid \ldots)$ can be **arbitrary probability density** in the variable **y.**
The progress, we believe has been made in comparison to the present state of the art, first of all relies on allowing any cdf's parameter **(**in particular, an expectation and variance in the case of normal distribution **)** to be **arbitrary continuous function** of the_**explanatory** (random) **variables.** We find that there is no necessity to restrict these functions to linear or to simple polynomials only. The use (as the models) of most of the common (parameter)-functions (such as the power, exponential, logarithmic, some trigonometric or their combinations), in general **does not involve** estimation **of much more unknown parameters** than it is used with the simple polynomial or even linear function' application.

The kind of the "regression techniques", here suggested, may too be compared with a more familiar (to reliability oriented readers), procedure associated with the well known **accelerated test models** for the life-time of some technical devices. In that case the

explanatory variables $X_1, \ldots, X_k$, that here we consider in a more general setting, can be interpreted as various kinds of, say, random **loads** or stresses that may eventually be multiplied by (also random) times these loads are to be endured by the tested units.
This subject is, for example, very well elaborated in [13].

Other illustration is associated with the common **actuary** problem as to estimate residual life-time of a given age client who smoked tobacco during a time period **T** with an intensity of **X** milligrams of nicotine per day. Supposing the client' **residual life-time Y** is approximate by a normal pdf **N(μ, σ)** in an absence of smoking. If, however, the smoking took place, then we may hypothetically assume that the average life-time μ "somehow" depends on the **(random**, in case of the whole population of the clients **or** a known **deterministic** in each individual case) **load Z** that is strictly proportional to the product of **TX** associated with smoking **tobacco.**
This stochastic relationship between the life-time and the 'smoking amount', may be explicitly given by the following conditional (normal in y) **pdf of the residual life-time Y:**

$$g(y \mid x, t) = [\sigma(xt)\sqrt{(2\pi)}]^{-1} \exp[-(y - \mu(xt))^2 / 2[\sigma(x t)]^2], \qquad (14)$$

where **μ(xt) and σ(xt)** are arbitrary (reasonable) continuous functions of the **product xt.** Having known joint pdf f(x, t) of the T and X (across the smokers population) we may find the unconditioned pfd of the time Y just by integrating out the variables t, x from the product **g(y | x, t)** f(x, t) that represents the trivariate joint pdf h(x, t, y) of the random vector (**Y**, T, X).
As hypothetical parameter functions, implicitly present in the model (14), we may, for example, consider the functions $\mu(xt) = \mu + a(xt) + A(xt)^r$, **(with possibly a = 0, while A, r being positive real numbers), and σ (x t) = constant** (in this particular case). For many more examples on that see [5,6,8].

7. References

[1] B. C. Arnold, E. Castillo and J. M. Sarabia, *Conditionally Specified Distributions*, Lecture Notes in Statistics - 73, New York: Springer- Verlag, 1992.
[2] R. E. Barlow and F. Proschan, *Statistical Theory of Reliability and Life Testing*, Holt, Rinehart and Winston, New York, 1975.
[3] D. Collett, *Modeling Survival Data in Medical Research*, Chapman & Hall / CRC Text in Statistical Science Series, A CRC Press Company, 2003.
[4] J. K. Filus, "On a Type of Dependencies between Weibull Life times of System Components," *Reliability Engineering and System Safety*, Vol.31, No.3, 267-280, 1991.
[5] J. K. Filus, L. Z. Filus, *A Class of Generalized Multivariate Normal Densities*. Pakistan Journal of Statistics, 1, Vol 16, 11- 32, 2000.
[6] J. K. Filus, L. Z. Filus, *On Some New Classes of Multivariate Probability Distributions*. Pakistan Journal of Statistics, 1, Vol 22, 21 – 42, 2006
[7] J. K. Filus, L. Z. Filus, *On Methods for Construction New Multivariate Probability Distributions in System Reliability Framework*. 12th International Conference on Reliability and Quality in Design, ISSAT 2006, Chicago, USA, Conference Proceedings, pp 245 -252.

[8] J. K. Filus, L. Z. Filus, *On New Multivariate* Probability Distributions and Stochastic Processes with System *Reliability and Maintenance Applications.* Methodology and Computing in Applied Probability Journal, 9, 426-446, 2007.

[9] J. E. Freund, "A Bivariate Extension of the Exponential Distribution," *J. Amer. Statist. Assoc.,* Vol 56, 971- 77, 1961.

[10] P. Hougaard, "Fitting a Multivariate Failure Time Distribution", IEEE Transactions on Reliability, Vol 38, No. 4, 444-448, 1989.

[11] S. Kotz, N. Balakrishnan and N. L. Johnson, *Continuous Multivariate Distributions,* Volume 1. Second Edition. J. Wiley & Sons, Inc, New York, Chichester, Weinheim, Brisbane, Singapore, Toronto, 2000.

[12] A. W. Marshall and I. Olkin, "A Generalized Bivariate Exponential Distribution," *Journal of Applied Probability* 4, 291-303, 1967.

[13] W. Q. Meeker and L. A. Escobar, *Statistical Methods for Reliability Data,* J. Wiley & Sons, Inc, New York, 1998.

Introduction to AdaIndex—An Adaptive Similarity Search Algorithm in General Metric Spaces

Tao Ban and Youki Kadobayashi
National Institute of Information and Communication Technology
Japan

1. Introduction

Because of the ever-increasing amount of digital information created, captured, and replicated, we are faced today with a rapidly expanding amount of published information. It would be hard to survive this information explosion without the search engines that are readily accessible on the web, PC, and various database servers. In these systems, *similarity search* techniques (Samet, 2005; Zezula et al., 2006) always play an essential rule to efficiently retrieve user-relevant information from a large amount of data with limited computational resources. Meanwhile, similarity search has also been a prominent data preprocessing operation in fields such as data mining, signal processing, multimedia information retrieval, computational biology, pattern recognition, etc.

One popular approach for similarity search is mapping data objects into feature vectors and then conducting search in the feature space. Such a method is computationally efficient because the geometrical properties of the feature space and the vector representation of the data help to speed up the search. However, it also introduces the undesirable element of indirection into the process, especially for sophisticated applications where finding the vector representation of the data is itself an open question. A more direct approach is to define a distance function between objects and then build indexing structures based on the distance. Researches have shown that if the distance function satisfies some basic conditions, namely, non-negativity, identity, symmetry, and triangle inequality, efficient algorithms can be formulated for fast similarity search (Chávez et al., 2001; Gisli & Samet, 2003; Samet, 2005; Zezula et al., 2006). Such a distance function, usually called a metric, together with the data domain, is commonly known as a metric space. Since defining a metric between objects can be accomplished more intuitively than mapping objects to feature vectors, the metric space model has found numerous applications in processing complex data such as multimedia objects, texts, protein sequences, images, etc.

Similarity hashing methods known as Distance Index (D-index) (Dohnal et al., 2003) and its descendants incorporate multiple principles for advanced search efficiency. Assuming that the database objects are stored in the secondary storage, D-index aims to build an indexing structure with advanced search performance by incorporating the following principles in the algorithm. First, it organizes objects into a hierarchical structure composed of multiple levels, where an individual level is further hashed into separable buckets by some split function. At query time, the levels are sequentially accessed. Because objects in difference buckets are search-separable up to some predefined margin ρ —minimum distance between objects from two separable sets—at most one bucket per level needs to be accessed for queries with search range $r \leq \rho$. Thus D-index supports a bounded search cost in the level with regards to both distance computation and disk access. Second, with the pivot filtering technique from (Micó et al., 1994; Vidal, 1994), further reduction in distance computations is achieved in the accessed bucket. According to the experiments in (Dohnal et al., 2003), D-index showed preferable results in terms of reduction of distance calculations compared with other popular metric index methods. Moreover, by storing compact clusters of objects in the separable buckets into disk pages, it also offered an excellent IO management performance.

D-index has built a good framework for metric search especially for queries with comparatively small radii. However, the pivot selection strategy suggested in (Dohnal et al., 2003) does not support balanced data partitioning in the structure and thus leads to increase in the number of distance computation and IO accesses at query time. Another problem of D-index is the tuning of parameter ρ : On the one hand, a large ρ value will leads to too many objects assigned into the inseparable regions, resulting in uncontrollable separable-set volume and number of levels. On the other hand, a small ρ value is always related with degenerated search separable property for the separable buckets. Moreover, for a complicated dataset, a ρ value uniformly performs well for all levels may even not exist.

In this paper, we present an adaptive indexing structure termed AdaIndex (Ban et al., 2009), which overcomes the above problems of D-index in the following way. When partitioning the objects into separable sets, D-index fixes the margin and leaves the formulation of the separable sets to a pivot selection procedure. On the contrary, in AdaIndex, we fix the size of the separable sets and try to maximize the margin between separable sets. The alternated strategy will lead to the following benefits. First, the number of pivots no longer influences the formulation of the separate sets so that we gain degrees of freedom to tune the number of pivots in the index structure. Thus, we can either select more pivots to improve the search performance or reduce the number to implement the index structure on a system with limited storage. Second, the maximization of the margin will result in better search performance of the pivoting rules, substantially reducing the side computations at query time. Finally, with the objects evenly partitioned into search separable sets, more efficient IO management can be supported by the algorithm.

2. Related Works on Metric Search

Before specifying the previously known search algorithms designed for metric spaces, we will first review the properties of a metric space and commonly used metric query types.

2.1 Similarity Search in Metric Spaces

Let D be the domain of objects, $d:D\times D\rightarrow R$ a distance function on D. The tuple $M=(D,d)$ is called a *metric space,* if $\forall x,y,z\in D$, the following conditions hold (Brin, 1995):

$$d(x,y) \geq 0, \quad \text{non-negativity;}$$
$$d(x,y) = 0 \Leftrightarrow x = y, \quad \text{Identity;}$$
$$d(x,y) = d(y,x), \quad \text{Symmetry;}$$
$$d(x,y) + d(y,z) \geq d(x,z), \quad \text{triangle equality.}$$

A metric query is generally defined by a query object q and a proximity condition. There are two types of queries that are widely used: the *range query* and the *nearest neighbour query.* The range query can be specified as: Given a metric space $M=(D,d)$, a finite set $X\subset D$, a query $q\in D$, and a range $r\in R$, the answer set for a query q with range r is the set

$$R(q,r,X)=\{x_i | d(q,x_i)\leq r, x_i\in X\}. \tag{1}$$

Note that *point query* is a special case of range query, with $r=0$. For the nearest-neighbour query, the closet object to q is retrieved as the answer set. The concept can be easily generalized to search for the k nearest neighbours of q, thus the answer set for a k NN query is

$$K(q,k,X) = K := \{K \subseteq X, |K| = k, \forall x_i \in K, y_j \in X \setminus K, d(q,x_i) \leq d(q,y_j)\}. \tag{2}$$

For simplicity, we confine our discussion to the range query, which is the most widely explored search type. All of the discussions can be easily extended to k NN queries by maintaining a list of k candidates seen so far and using the largest distance among the candidates as the search range r in a range query. Discussions on other kinds of queries, e.g., reverse NN query, similarity join, and a combination of the enumerated search types, can be found in (Samet, 2005; Zezula et al., 2006).

2.2 Metric Search Structures

Popular indexing structures designed for similarity search in a metric space can be largely grouped into three categories: metric tree structures, distance-matrix based approaches, and hybrid methods.

The metric tree approaches include some well known methods such as the Vantage Point tree (VPT) (Yianilos, 1994), Burhard-Keller tree (BKT) (Burkhard & Keller, 1973), Generalized Hyperplane tree (GHT) (Uhlmann, 1991), Geometric Near-neighbour Access tree (GNAT) (Brin, 1995) and Metric tree (M-tree) (Ciaccia et al., 1997). When the search index is built, objects in the database are grouped into geographically adjacent clusters presented as nodes, organized into a tree-like hierarchical structure. At query time, the tree is traversed in a certain order; and to prevent direct comparison of the query object with the indexed objects, some so called pivoting rules are applied to the nodes or individual objects.

The distance-matrix based approaches refer to the methods such as AESA (Vidal, 1986; Vidal, 1994), LAESA (Micó et al., 1994), Reduced Overhead AESA (Vilar, 1995), etc., where pre-computed distances are used to characterize the indexed objects. At a preprocessing step, distances between the indexed objects and a group of selected anchoring objects, termed pivots, are computed and stored. At query time, these distances are employed to estimate unknown distances, i.e., the distances from the query object to the indexed objects, and objects which do not qualify the search criterion are skipped without direct comparison.

Distance-matrix based indexing methods provide promising performance boost in terms of distance-computation reduction. Their disadvantage lies in the enormous and sometimes infeasible space requirements. The hybrid methods try to combine both the partitioning principle, i.e., data clustering in the metric tree approaches, and the pre-computed distances technique into a single index structure. The so called D-index algorithm (Dohnal et al., 2003; Dohnal, 2004) which is an improvement on the Similarity Hashing method (SH) (Gennaro et al., 2001), is built upon a completely different principle from the metric tree approaches. D-index builds a multi-tier hashing structure, where each tier is consisted of search separable sets, organized in buckets. The structure supports easy insertion and bounded search costs for range queries up to a pre-defined search radius: at most one bucket need to be accessed at each level. Meanwhile, buckets can be arranged in to sequential disk pages so that IO cost can be saved when all objects in the bucket are all pruned during the search.

Note that there are some metric tree structures which also take advantage of the pre-computed distance, e.g., the Multi Vantage Point Tree (MVPT) (Bozkaya & Ozsoyoglu, 1997), the GNAT, and M-tree, etc. In fact, for any metric search algorithm, an extra pre-computed distance matrix can always help to substantially reduce the number of distance computations. In (Fredriksson, 2007), the author suggests applying the AESA technique to most of the existing metric search structures to efficiently reduce the number of distance computations during the search. This idea is best illustrated by the TLAESA (Gomez-Ballester et al., 2006) algorithm.

3. Metric Search by D-index

The AdaIndex algorithm introduced is partly inspired by the D-index algorithm. In this section, we will give a brief review on D-index. More detailed description of the algorithm can be found in (Dohnal et al., 2003; Dohnal, 2004).

3.1 Hashing the Dataset

In D-index, the ρ -split functions are defined to hash objects into search-separable clusters. An example is the bps (ball-partitioning split) function. With a predefined margin ρ , a bps uniquely determines the belongingness of an object $x \in X$:

$$bps^{1,\rho}(x_i) = \begin{cases} 0 & \text{if} \quad d(x_i, p) \le d_m - \rho, \\ 1 & \text{if} \quad d(x_i, p) > d_m + \rho, \\ - & \quad \text{otherwise}, \end{cases} \tag{3}$$

where p is a pivot and d_m the median of the distances from p to all $x_i \in X$. The superscript 1 denotes the order of the split function, i.e., the number of pivots involved. The subset characterized by the symbol '$-$' is called the *exclusion set*, noted as E. The subsets denoted by $S^{1,\rho}_{[0]}(X)$ and $S^{1,\rho}_{[1]}(X)$ are called *separable sets* according to the *separable property:*

$$d(x_i,x_j)>2\rho, \text{forall } x_i \in S^{1,\rho}_{[0]}(X), x_j \in S^{1,\rho}_{[1]}(X). \tag{4}$$

To partition the dataset into more separable sets, higher order ρ-split functions are composed by combining multiple first order ρ-split functions. Given m *bps* split functions, the joint m-order split function is denoted as $bps^{m,\rho}$, and the return value can be seen as a string $b=[b_1,b_2,\cdots,b_m]$, where $b_i \in \{0,1,-\}$. The following hashing operator $<\cdot>$ returns an integer value in the range $[0,\cdots,2^m]$ for any string.

$$<b>=\begin{cases} 2^m, & \text{if } \exists j \ \ b_j=-, \\ [b_1,b_2,\cdots,b_m]_2=\sum_{j=1}^{m} 2^{m-j} b_j & \text{otherwise.} \end{cases} \tag{5}$$

Thus through the ρ-split function and the hashing function, a mapping is defined from $x_i \in X$ to an integer $c \in [0,2^m]$. The objects are grouped into 2^m separable subsets where the separable property still holds, and an *exclusion set*, E_H, which holds the remaining objects.

The *bps* function is defined by multiple pivots and the associated median distances. D-index applies incremental selection to select pivots. At the beginning, a set $P=\{p_1\}$ with a maximized $\mu_i (i=1)$ is chosen from the objects, where μ_i is the expectation of the inter-object distances in the feature space defined by the pivots, formally,

$$\mu_i = \underset{x\in X, y\in X}{E} \max_{s=1}^{i-1} | d(x,p_l) - d(y,p_l) | . \tag{6}$$

At step i, with the previously selected pivot set fixed, p_i is chosen from the dataset with the maximum μ_i. This process is repeated until a desired number of pivots are determined.

3.2 Storage Architecture

The storage architecture of D-index consists of a two dimensional array of *buckets* storing data objects. On the first level, an m_1-order *bps* function is applied to the dataset and a list of separable sets are obtained. Each separable set is organized as a bucket which represents a metric region and manages all the objects falling into the region. In the next level, another *bps* function is applied to the exclusion set of the former level to form new separable sets. The algorithm repeats this procedure for a given number of times, H, or until the exclusion set cannot be further scattered. Finally, the exclusion set on the final level forms the exclusion bucket of the multi-level storage structure. To deal with overflow problems and file growth, a bucket is implemented as an elastic structure consisting of a necessary number of fixed-size *blocks*.

3.3 Search Operations

Given a D-index structure, the search algorithm guides the search procedure. For brevity, we only discuss the range search algorithm with $r \le \rho$. Refer to (Dohnal et al., 2003) for fully specified general range search and nearest neighbour search algorithms. For a range query $R(q,r,X)$ with $r \le \rho$, with ρ set to zero, if $bps_h^{m_h,0}(q)$ yields a value smaller than 2^{m_h}, only one separable bucket will be accessed at each level. Otherwise, the query sphere drops into the exclusion set and there will be some chance to skip all the separable sets in the level. Consequently, at most one separable bucket is accessed at each level. In the simple range search algorithm, we assume all levels are accessed as well as the global exclusion bucket. This algorithm requires $H+1$ bucket accesses, which is the upper bound to the more sophisticated algorithm specified in (Dohnal et al., 2003).

In D-index, special techniques are applied to speed up the search within a bucket. Generally, a bucket structure consists of a header plus a dynamic list of fixed-size blocks accommodating the objects. In the header, information on the pivots as well as the distances from all the objects in the bucket to these pivots is stored. Thus, the following pivoting rule (Vidal, 1994) can be applied to avoid unnecessary distance computations in the bucket. Let p_i be a pivot and x be an object in the bucket. Then for query $R(q,r,X)$, we have

$$|d(x,p)-d(q,p)|>r \Rightarrow d(q,x)>r. \qquad (7)$$

This pivoting rule follows directly from the triangle inequality. Note that when the objects in the bucket are all pruned by the pivoting rule, bucket access can be avoided.

4. Metric Search by AdaIndex

The proposed AdaIndex is designed for similarity search in generic metric spaces. Despite of a similar hierarchical storage structure for the indexed objects, AdaIndex differentiates itself from D-index by the design philosophy. In the following, we mainly follow the terminology from D-index to save the introduction of another group of terms with similar meanings.

4.1 Partitioning the Dataset

In AdaIndex, we use the split functions to hash objects into search-separable clusters. A *Kbps* (K-nearest-neighbour ball-partitioning split) function is defined by a tuple (p_m, K), where p_m is a pivot and K the size of the neighbouring set to the pivot. Let the distance from p_m to its K th nearest neighbour be d_K. Then a *bps* uniquely determines the belongingness of any object x_i in the indexed dataset X:

$$Kbps^1(x_i)=\begin{cases} 1 & \text{if} \quad d(x_i,p_m) \le d_K, \\ 0 & \text{if} \quad d(x_i,p_m) > d_K. \end{cases} \qquad (8)$$

The superscript 1 denotes the order of the split function. To partition the dataset into more subsets, we compose higher order split functions by combining multiple first order *Kbps* functions. Given M $Kbps$ functions, the joint M -order split function is denoted as $Kbps^M$, and the return value can be seen as a string $b=[b_1,b_2,\cdots,b_m,\cdots,b_M]$, $b_m\in\{0,1\}$. The following $<\cdot>$ operator returns an integer value in $[0,M]$ for any string b:

$$<b>=\begin{cases} m, & \text{if } \exists m \quad b_m=1, \\ 0, & \text{otherwise.} \end{cases} \tag{9}$$

We call the neighbouring subset associated with a pivot the separable set and the objects which do not belong to any of the separable sets are assigned to an exclusion set. If the pivots are selected to be far from each other, then we can achieve a better separable ability for the separable sets. Fig. 1a shows an example where a collection of objects are divided into three separable sets, S_1 , S_2 , S_3 , and an exclusion set E .

To make sure no object will be assigned to multiple subsets, we endow an order among the pivots—the neighbour of the previously selected pivots are removed before a subsequent pivot takes effect.

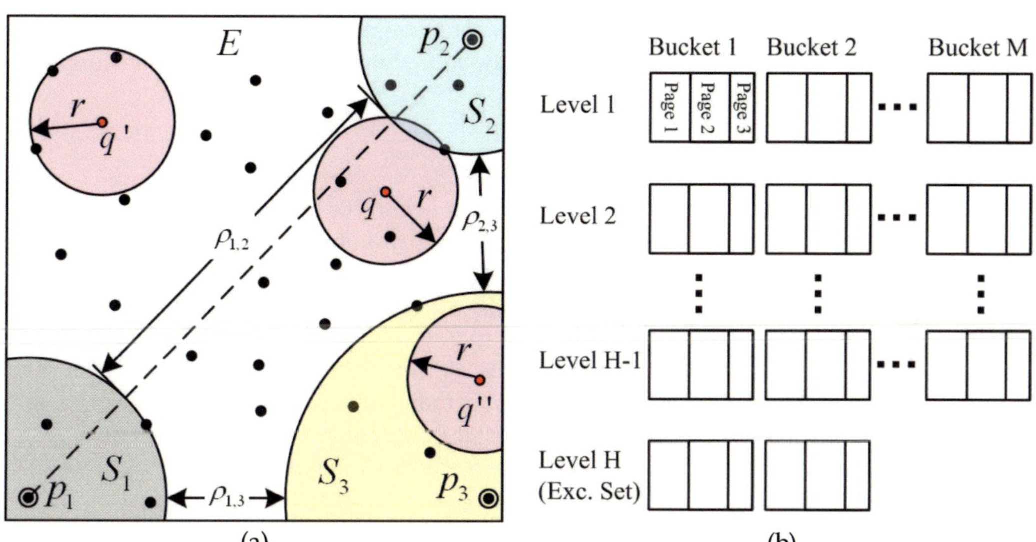

Fig. 1. AdaIndex data structure. (a) Single level partition on a 2D dataset, $K=3$, $M=3$. (b) The multilevel storage structure of AdaIndex.

4.2 Search Separable ability

In Fig. 1a, we call the minimal distance between two separable sets an adaptive margin, noted as $\rho_{i,j}$. The feature that two separable sets satisfies

$$d(x_1,x_2) > \rho_{i,j}, \quad \forall x_1\in S_i, x_2\in S_j. \tag{10}$$

is the so called search *separable property* in D-index. This property indicates that if the search radius $r\le\rho_{i,j}$, then for an arbitrary query object q , only one of S_i and S_j needs to be accessed. For example, for query q in Fig. 1a, the query sphere intersects S_2, and because of the search separable property, objects in S_1 and S_3 can be safely pruned. Of course, there is some chance that the query sphere falls exclusively into the exclusion set and thus no separable set needs to be accessed in the level, e.g., query q' in Fig. 1a. Obviously, the margins among separable sets give a good measure on the search difficulty in the level and need to be maximized for better search performance.

4.3 Multi-level Structure

Naturally, the margins of the separable sets diminish as more pivots are added. A simple but effective approach to obtaining large margins between separable sets is to formulate a hierarchical structure. Following D-index, the data structure associated with the separable sets defined by an M -order *Kbps* function is called a level. Note that because the objects in the exclusion set do not satisfy the search separable property so that group pruning is not supported. Moreover, as the objects in the exclusion set can not be organized into geometrically compact groups, the random access of the objects will degenerate the IO performance of the algorithm. Hence when the exclusion set of a level is still too large, we create an additional level structure with new split functions applied to form more separable sets. This process is repeated until the exclusion set is empty. Though the last level usually contains a flexible number of separable sets, in the following, we will not make difference of it from other preceding levels.

4.4 Pivot Selection

Another approach to increasing the margin of the separable sets is to incorporate some specific strategy in the pivot selection procedure. As well known is the literature, selection of pivots greatly affects the search performance for any search algorithm. We adopt the so-called farthest point clustering (Gonzalez, 1985) to select the set of M pivots, P. The pivots can be found following the algorithm specified in Alg. 1. It starts from the initialization of the pivot set with a pivot randomly selected from X (line 2); and then selects the next pivot as the object which is farthest away from the current pivot set (line 13). This process is repeated until a predefined number of pivots are chosen. When a pivot is selected, a separable set is created and the pivot together with its K nearest neighbours (line 8) is associated with the set.

Alg. 1 Pivot selection and separable set creation.

Inputs: X, M, K;
$P \leftarrow \phi$; $S_m \leftarrow \phi, m = 1, \cdots, M$;
Randomly select $p_1 \in X$;
for $m = 1$ **to** M **do**
    $P \leftarrow P \cup p_m$; $X \leftarrow X \setminus p_m$; $S_m \leftarrow S_m \cup p_m$;
    $d_K \leftarrow d(p_m, x_K)$, where x_K is the Kth neighbor of p_m in X;
    for $x_i \in X$ **do**
        if $d(x_i, p_m) \le d_K$ **then**
            $S_m \leftarrow S_m \cup x_i$; $X \leftarrow X \setminus x_i$; // assign KNNs to the set
        else
            $d_i \leftarrow \min_{p_m \in P} d(x_i, p_m)$; // update distance to the pivot set
        end if
    end for
    $p_m \leftarrow x_j$, where $d(x_j, P) = \max_{x_i \in X} d(x_i, P)$; // select next pivot
end for
return P, S_m;

Alg. 1. Algorithm for pivot selection and separable set creation.

4.5 Storage Architecture

Like in D-index, AdaIndex consists of a two dimensional array of buckets which deal with IO and search operations of objects in the separable sets, as shown in Fig. 1b. In the vertical picture, the bucket lists for all H levels are ordered sequentially. In the horizontal picture at a given level, a list of separable sets is obtained from the M-order *Kbps* function on the exclusion set of the previous level. Each of these separable sets is organized as a bucket. Based on the nature of the data, when necessary, a bucket is implemented as an elastic structure consisting of a necessary number of fixed-size blocks (disk pages), which is the basic disk access unit of the database system.

4.6 Search Operation

Given an AdaIndex structure, the range search algorithm guides the algorithm to traverse the structure for qualified objects. As shown in Alg. 2 the search algorithm sequentially traverses the H levels in the AdaIndex structure. When visiting a level, the algorithm first computes the distances from the query object to the pivots in the level and then applies the following pivoting rules to all separable sets (Fukunaga & Narendra, 1975). Let the maximal and minimal distances between a pivot p and the objects in separable set S be δ_{max} and δ_{min}, and suppose they are pre-stored in the index structure. Then, we have

Rule 1 (Fig. 2a): S contains no answer to the query, if $d(q,p)-r>\delta_{max}$;

Rule 2 (Fig. 2b): S contains no answer to the query, if $d(q,p)+r<\delta_{min}$.

If the above two rules fail at a separable set, the set is retrieved from the disk for further examination. To avoid unnecessary distance computations in the set, we make use of another two pivoting rules (Kamgar-Parsi & Kanal, 1985). Suppose the distances between an object x in the separable set and a pivot p are pre-stored in the index structure, we have

Rule 3 (Fig. 2c): x is not an answer to the query, if $d(x,p)+r<d(q,p)$;

Rule 4 (Fig. 2d): x is not an answer to the query, if $d(x,p)-r>d(q,p)$.

If Rules 3 and 4 fail at an object x , then distance $d(x,q)$ is directly computed. And when the distance function is invoked, the answer set is updated if x satisfies the query. Note that rules 3 and 4 are equivalent to the pivoting rule in equation (7).

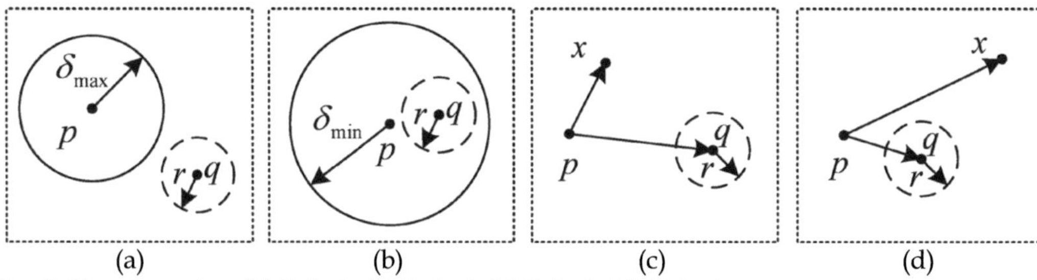

Fig. 2. Pivoting rules. (a) Rule 1. (b) Rule 2. (c) Rule 3. (d) Rule 4.

Rules 1 and 2 are able to prune multiple objects at a time and thus we call them *group-prune rules*. Rules 3 and 4 are called *object-prune rules* since they prune one object at a time. Obviously, the object-prune rules are the special cases of group-prune rules when there is only one object contained in the separable set. If an object can be pruned by the group-prune rules, then it can be pruned by the object-prune rules as well, given the necessarily pre-stored distances. Thus application of the object-prune rules is the key to the reduction of invoked distance computations at query time. On the other hand, the group-prune rules can substantially avoid unnecessary side computations, i.e., application of the object-prune rules. Moreover, storing δ_{max} and δ_{min} is usually much cheaper than holding an array of distances in the main memory. Hence the group-prune rules also contribute to the search performance, especially for applications with computationally less intensive distance functions and tighter storage limit.

Alg. 2 Range search algorithm for AdaIndex.

Inputs: X, q, r;
$A \leftarrow \emptyset$; // answer set
for $h = 1$ **to** H **do** // sequentially traverse all levels
  $C \leftarrow \{S_m, m = 1, \cdots, M\}$; // yet not pruned separable sets
  for $m = 1$ **to** M **do**
    $d_m = metric(q, p_m)$; // distance computation
    if $d_m \le r$ **then** $A \leftarrow A \cup p_m$; **end if** // update answer set
    for $l = 1$ **to** M **do** // prune separable sets by p_m
      if $d_m - r > \delta_{max}[l, m]$ **or** $d_m + r < \delta_{min}[l, m]$ **then** // Rules 1&2
        $C \leftarrow C \setminus S_l$; // separable set pruned
      end if
    end for
  end for
  for all $S_m \in C$ **do** // explore the remaining separable sets
    Load $x_l(l = 1, \cdots, K)$ from disk; // IO access
    for $m = 1$ **to** M **do** // prune individual objects by p_m
      for $l = 1$ **to** K **do**
        if $d[l, m] + r < d_m$ **or** $d[l, m] - r > d_m$ **then** // Rules 3&4
        else
          $d'_l = metric(x_l, q)$; // distance computation
          if $d'_l \le r$ **then** $A \leftarrow A \cup p_m$; **end if** // update answer set
        end if
      end for
    end for
  end for
end for
return A;

Alg. 2. Range search algorithm.

5. Experiments

In this section, we will evaluate the efficacy of the AdaIndex algorithm. The performance of the index structures is measured by three criteria, i.e., distance calculations, disk accesses, and side computations. In each of the reported experiments, the indexed set, the validation set, and the query set are independently drawn from the same uniform distribution in N-dimensional unit hyper-cubes. The coordinates of the data points are never directly used and only the inter-object distances are taken as inputs to the algorithm. We set the indexed dataset size to 10,000, the validation set size to 100, and the query set size to 1,000. If not otherwise specified, the search range is set to retrieve about 5% of the data from the database and the results are averaged over 100 queries for the validation and 1,000 queries for testing.

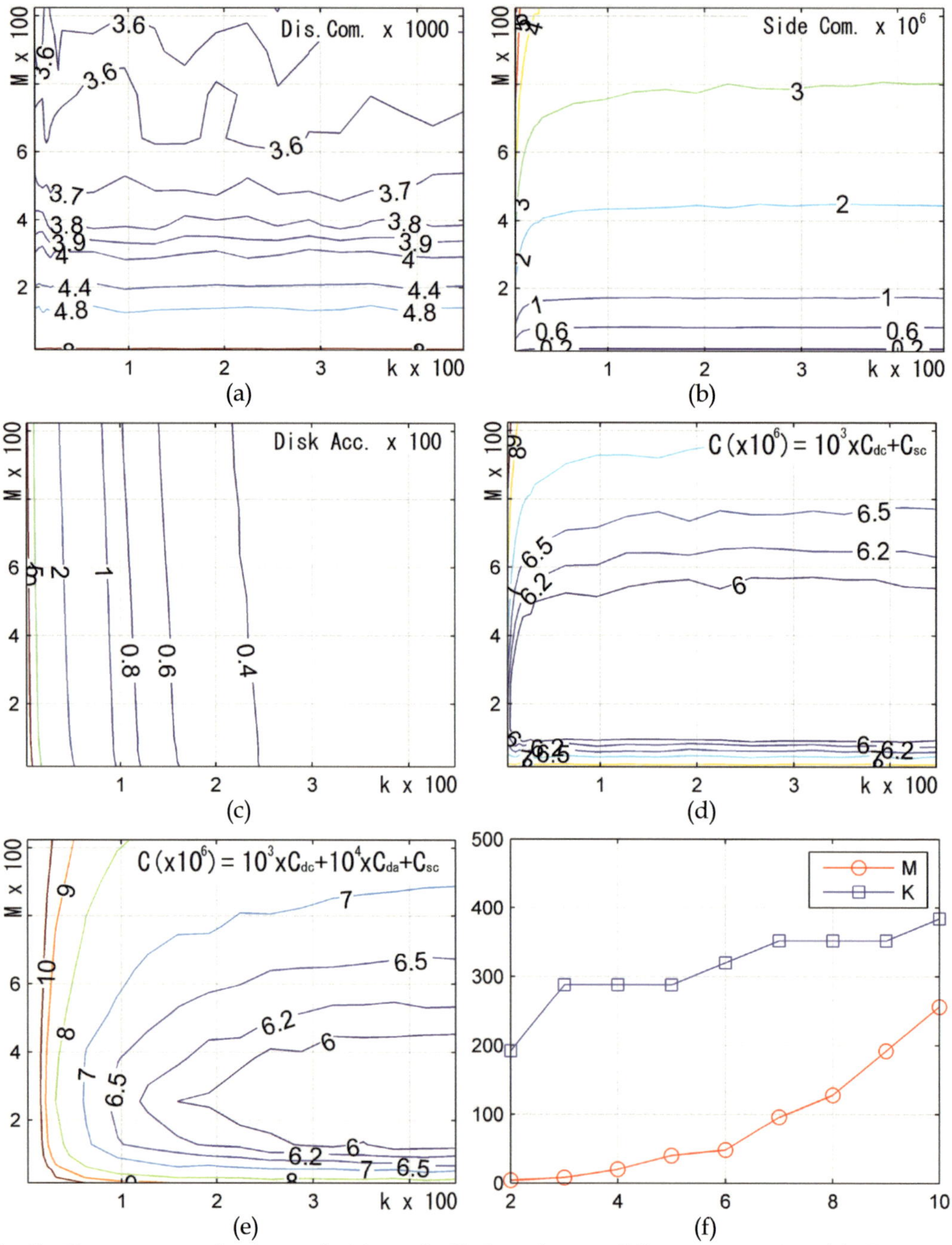

Fig. 3. Parameter selection of M and K based on different criteria. (a) Distance computation. (b) Disk access. (c) Side computation. (d) Disk computation plus side computation. (e) Integrated overall cost. (f) Selected parameters for 2–10 dimensional simulation datasets.

5.1 Parameter Selection

There are three parameters in AdaIndex, i.e., the number of pivots in the level, M , the size of a separable set, K , and the number of levels in the structure, H . Because H is uniquely determined by M and K , hereafter we only discuss how to tune M and K . To find appropriate values of M and K with better search efficiency, we conduct a grid search process: Given a list of values for M and a list for K , for each possible pair of parameters, we build an AdaIndex structure and test its performance on a validation set. The parameters with the best search performance are employed to build an index structure for evaluation on the test set.

In the following, we illustrate the above parameter tuning process of a 10-D dataset. The distance computations, disk accesses, and side computations against M and K averaged over the validation set are shown as contours in Fig. 3. In Fig. 3a, we can see that M is the deterministic factor for the number of distance computations at query time. The reason is obvious: M determines the storage cost of the index structure, and intuitively, more stored information in the data structure will lead to more prevented distance computations. Fig. 3b shows the number of disk access for difference parameter settings. Here, we assume an ideal situation that a separable set can always be stored in a disk page. And thus it is obvious that the larger the value of K , the less disk accesses during the search. However, in a practical application where the object size is not ignorable to the size of a disk page, the contours may vary a lot. Consider the other extreme case that an object always takes one or more disk pages. Obviously, this time the number of disk accesses will correlate exactly to the number of distance computations. From the above two extreme cases, we can see that for an application, whatever the ratio of the object size to the disk-page size, the actual contours of disk accesses will feature some combined properties in Fig. 3a and Fig. 3b. In fact, the larger the ratio of the object size to disk-page size, the flatter the slope of the contours. Fig. 3c presents the contour of side computations during the search. Similar as in Fig. 3a, the number of pivots is the deterministic factor for side computations. However, at this time, the effect of adding more pivots are minus—the more pivots employed the more side computations invoked during the search.

Above we have shown some basic principals for parameter tuning for a given evaluation criterion. It is worth noting that in a real application, computational cost of the search usually involves more than one factor from the above. However, the selection of parameters based on multiple criteria seems somewhat contradictive. Thus it will be interesting to explore some strategy on parameter tuning on multiple criteria. We adopt the weighting technique to solve this problem. For a given application, it is easy to estimate a pair of weight coefficients α and β such that the overall computation cost of a query can be computed as

$$C=\alpha C_{\mathrm{dc}}+\beta C_{\mathrm{da}}+C_{\mathrm{sc}}. \quad (11)$$

Here, C_{sc} is the number of side computations which are taken as reference, C_{dc} the number of distance computations, and C_{da} the number of disk accesses. Base on the above definition, we can again employ the grid search method to select a group of parameters which gives optimal computational cost for the application. Fig. 3d shows the contours of the overall computational cost for α=1,000 and β=0 , i.e., the IO costs are neglected. We can see that for a quite wide range of parameters, i.e., $M \in [80,500]$ and $K \in [40,450]$, the search performance is near optimal. Fig. 3e shows the result when the IO costs are considered by setting $\beta = 10{,}000$. The acceptable range of parameter shrinks to be around $M \in [110,370]$ and $K \in [250,450]$.

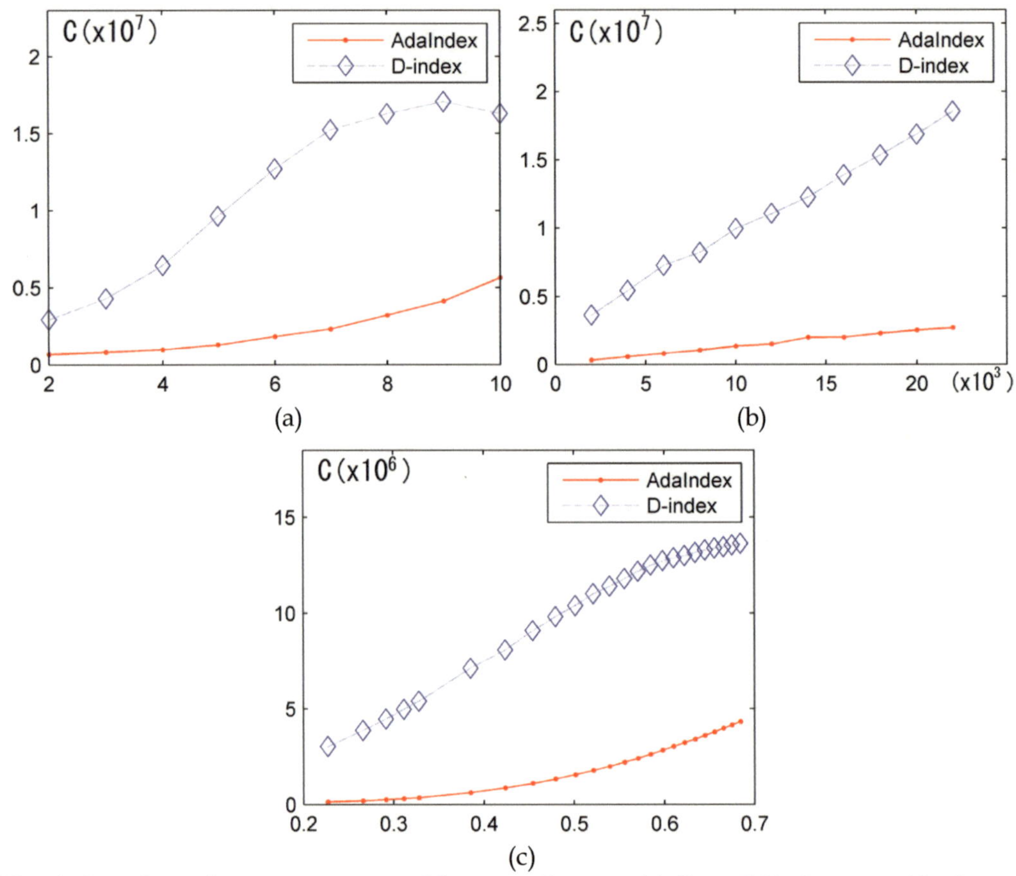

Fig. 4. Search performance measured by overall costs. (a) On a 5-D dataset with dynamic search range. (b) On a 5-D datasets with varying sample size. (c) On multi-dimensional datasets.

5.2 Performance Evaluation

In this section, we evaluate the search performance of AdaIndex on uniformly distributed data in N-dimensional Euclidean spaces. Fig. 3f shows the selected parameters for $N = 2,\cdots,10$. We set $\alpha = 1{,}000$ and $\beta = 10{,}000$ for all datasets. And for reference, we also report the results of D-index.

In the first experiment, we show how the search range r influences the search performance of AdaIndex. The evaluation is done on a 5-D dataset. The search range is gradually increased with the answer set growing from about 0.2% to 20% of the indexed set. As shown in Fig. 4a, the overall cost of AdaIndex increases almost linearly with the search range, especially when the search range is small. For all the search ranges, AdaIndex results in much less overall cost than D-index since it avoids more distance computations during the search.

Then we test the performance of AdaIndex for datasets with varying sample size. AdaIndex and D-index are built on 5-D datasets up to size 20,000. In the evaluation, we fix the search range for retrieving about 5% of the data. The curves of the overall cost against the dataset size are shown in Fig. 4b. It is obvious that the number of distance calculations for AdaIndex increases linearly as indexed data in the structure increases. Compared with D-index, the search performance of AdaIndex is more preferable.

The aim of the last experiment is to show the performance of AdaIndex on datasets with different dimensions. The algorithms are tested against datasets with dimensions up to 10. It is easy to learn from Fig. 4c that the search difficulty increases gradually as the dimension grows because of the so called curse of dimensionality. In spite of the increased difficulty, AdaIndex again shows a much better performance than D-index.

Above all, AdaIndex has shown stable performance in a variety of simulated experiments. For all the tested datasets, it always has a preferable performance than D-index.

6. Conclusion

In this chapter, we have presented the AdaIndex, an adaptive index algorithm for efficient similarity search in general metric spaces. AdaIndex has incorporated the following principles to speed up the search. First, it borrows the idea from D-index to create a hierarchical data structure so that the search can be efficiently conducted in parallel mode. Second, on an individual level, the objects are partitioned into compact clusters and are managed by the bucket structure for effective IO management. Then, with the maximized search separable property among the buckets and the advanced pivoting rules, AdaIndex supports significant reduction in distance computations. Another very important property of the AdaIndex algorithm is its adaptivity for varying applications. Given a group of cost coefficients for different types of computational cost, we can easily apply the introduced grid search method for an index structure with optimal overall performance.

7. References

Ban, T.; Guo, S.; Xu, Q.; & Kadobayashi, Y. (2009). AdaIndex: an adaptive index structure for fastsimilarity search in metric spaces, *Lecture Notes in Computer Science,* Vol. 5864, pp. 729–737.

Bozkaya, T. & Ozsoyoglu, Z. M. (1997). Distance-based indexing for high-dimensional metric spaces, *Proceedings of the ACM International Conference on Management of Data (SIGMOD 1997),* pp. 357–368, ACM Press.

Brin, S. (1995). Near neighbor search in largemetric spaces, *Proceedings of the 21st International Conference on Very Large Data Bases,* pp. 574–584.

Burkhard, W. A. & Keller, R. M. (1973). Some approaches to best-match file searching, *Communications of the ACM,* Vol. 16, No. 4, pp. 230–236.

Chávez, E.; Navarro, G.; & Marroquin, J. L. (2001). Searching in Metric Spaces, *ACM Computing Surveys*, Vol. 33, No. 3, pp. 273–321.

Ciaccia, P.; Patella, M.; & Zezula, P. (1997). M-tree: an efficient access method for similarity search in metric spaces, *Preceedings of the 23rd International Conference on Very Large Data Bases*, pp. 426–435.

Dohnal, V.; Gennaro, C.; Savino, P.; & Zezula, P. (2003). D-Index: distance searching index for metric data sets, *Multimedia Tools and Applications*, Vol. 21, No. 1, pp. 9–33.

Dohnal, V. (2004). *Indexing Structures for Searching in Metric Spaces*, PhD thesis, Faculty of Informatics, Masaryk University in Brno, Czech Republic.

Fredriksson, K. (2007). Engineering efficient metric indexes, *Pattern Recognition Letters*, Vol. 28, No. 1, pp. 75–84.

Fukunaga, L. & Narendra, P. M. (1975). A branch and bound algorithm for computing k-nearest neighbors, *IEEE Transactions on Computers*, Vol. 24, No. 7, pp. 750–753.

Gennaro, C.; Savino, P.; & Zezula, P. (2001). Similarity search in metric databases through hashing, *Proceedings of the 3rd ACM Multimedia 2001 Workshop on Multimedia Information Retrieval (MIR 2001)*, pp. 1–5.

Gisli, H. R. & Samet, H. (2003). Index-driven similarity search in metric spaces, *ACM Transactions on Database Systems*, Vol. 28, pp. 517–580.

Gomez-Ballester E.; Micó L.; & Oncina J. (2006). Some approaches to improve tree-based nearest neighbor search algorithms, *Pattern Recognition Letters*, Vol. 39, pp. 171–179.

Gonzalez, T. F. (1985). Clustering to minimize the maximum intercluster distance, *Theoretical Computer Science*, Vol. 38, pp. 293–306.

Kamgar-Parsi, B. & Kanal, L. N. (1985). An improved branch and bound algorithm for computing k-nearest neighbors, *Pattern Recognition Letters*, Vol. 3, No. 1, pp. 7–12.

Micó, M. L.; Oncina, J.; & Vidal, E. (1994). A new version of the nearest-neighbor approximating and eliminating search algorithm (AESA) with linear preprocessing time and memory requirements, *Pattern Recognition Letters*, Vol. 15, No. 1, pp. 9–17.

Samet, H. (2005). *Foundations of Multidimensional and Metric Data Structures*, Morgan Kaufmann Publishers Inc., San Francisco, CA, USA.

Uhlmann, J. K. (1991). Satisfying general proximity/similarity queries with metric trees, *Information Processing Letters*, Vol. 40, No. 4, pp. 175–179.

Vidal, E. (1986). An algorithm for finding nearest neighbors in (approximately) constant average time, *Pattern Recognition Letters*, Vol. 4, pp. 145–157.

Vidal, E. (1994). New formulation and improvements of the nearest-neighbor approximating and eliminating search algorithm (AESA), *Pattern Recognition Letters*, Vol. 15, No. 1, pp. 1–7.

Vilar, J. M. (1995). Reducing the overhead of the AESA metric space nearest neighbor searching algorithm, *Information Processing Letters*, Vol. 56, No. 5, pp. 265–271.

Yianilos, P. N. (1993). Data structures and algorithms for nearest neighbor search in general metric spaces, *ACM-SIAM Symposium on Discrete Algorithms 1993*, pp. 311–321.

Zezula, P.; Amato, G.; Dohnal, V.; & Batko, M. (2006). *Similarity Search – The Metric Space Approach*, Springer.

21

Scenario Analysis of the Mobile Voice Services Market

HANNU VERKASALO*, KIM LINDQVIST, HEIKKI HÄMMÄINEN
** hannu.verkasalo@tkk.fi*
+358 40 5959663
Helsinki University of Technology
Department of Communications and Networking
P.O. Box 3000, FI-02015 TKK, Finland

Abstract

Internet services shake the dynamics of the mobile industry. This paper studies the future of mobile voice with a scenario analysis method. A group of industry experts is interviewed to obtain a set of variables reflecting the uncertainties of the mobile voice market. These variables are used in describing the future evolution of mobile voice. With iterative interviews the two most important variables (mobile market structure and access mode in multi-radio networks) are defined, and four industry scenarios introduced. The mobile industry is found to be on a verge of horisontalization. The structural form of the market determines how mobile voice services are deployed in the future. The mobile industry is gradually moving towards the Internet. In this evolution, alternative wireless technologies are seen as the main source of disruption, with either one-operator or multi-operator terminal support. Also the regulation of mobile networks and services is found to play a significant role. Together the dominant market form (horizontal or vertical orientation) and techno-economic context (single-operator or multi-operator model) determine whether incumbent operators will retain strong position in the future.

Keywords: mobile voice, mobile Internet, mobile services, operator business

1. Motivation

Voice is still the most successful mobile service, and most of the operator revenue comes from circuit-switched mobile voice. However, for long the evolution of mobile networks has evolved towards packet-switched technologies, and today's new mobile devices enable seamless wireless Internet connectivity. According to Nokia's estimations, the number of mobile subscriptions is likely to surpass three billion in 2008 [1]. The number of Internet connections is much lower, about 1 billion in 2005 [2] [36]. The all-IP movement is taking place [3], pushing the Internet towards the mobile world. Consequently various kinds of Internet services from web browsing to email have emerged in the mobile domain [4], the mobile VoIP (*mobile voice-over-IP*), however, being still a newcomer service.

The motivation to study mobile VoIP can be divided into three key trends that will inevitably take place in the mobile service domain: 1. There will be a non-decreasing demand for mobile voice services; 2. Fixed-to-mobile substitution will evolve further; 3. Packet-switched mobile connectivity will emerge. The biggest uncertainties regarding mobile VoIP include the business models to commercialize the IP-based mobile voice service and the players who will provision these services.

The current telecom world is characterized by a strong vertical orientation in which operators commonly run both the network and services [5]. Service innovation suffers because of the closed "walled garden" business models. The world of Internet is much different. This is because of two reasons. First, the end-to-end connectivity induces application-level development independent of the connectivity and networking layers. Second, the Internet services have evolved quickly mainly because of network-edge based innovation (i.e. the openness towards developers). The potential disruption resulting from the clash of the Internet and mobile telecom world is inevitable [6] [7]. Not only do individual companies face a new business environment in which to operate, but also the whole ecosystem experiences shocks, that might lead into new ways of doing business and serving end-users [8].

The mobile VoIP business presents an interesting playground as both incumbent telecom operators and challenger Internet players are providing IP-based voice [9]. Technically the uncertainty factors are low, and much more interest should be targeted at the potential business impact. Therefore the research question of the paper is: *"What are the possible future scenarios of the mobile VoIP business?"*

2. Background

2.1 Industry structure and value networks

Porter [10] models industry structures through his famous *value chain* framework. In the value chain framework Porter emphasizes the different stages that are needed in producing the final product from raw materials, as well as the division of company functions into core and support functions. In addition to core functions such as operations and sales, support functions such as R&D are typically needed in the process. Porter defines vertical integration as the extent of value chain coverage taking place inside one firm. In other words, companies that take care of a major part of the value chain are vertically integrated, whereas companies that focus on one part of the value chain only, contracting and outsourcing extensively with external companies, are not vertically integrated. In this paper operators are considered vertically integrated as they do play a role on many layers of the mobile service value chain, whereas Internet companies typically focus on services thus having less vertical integration. According to Kraft [11] the concept of vertical integration and its link to competitive dynamics is one of the major determinants of industry evolution.

Porter [10] makes a contribution by discussing vertical integration, industry structures and strategic role of firm boundaries. Harrigan [12] suggests that companies can apply various strategies, and the industry structure is an outcome of the strategic choices the individual companies apply in making up the ecosystem. Verkasalo [8] uses this theoretical background in comparing mobile business ecosystems in different countries against each other. He uses the term *dominant market ecosystem* in referring to the currently dominating form of the industry business ecosystem.

The complex production and business network management processes should be understood [13], and *value networks* are a more comprehensive metaphor than value chains. Mitchell and Singh [13] suggest that many approaches to vertical integration exist, and rather than choosing from two extreme choices companies should consider a whole portfolio of strategic paths. The concept of value chain cannot be easily used when analyzing industries [14], and therefore a more suitable term is *value network*. A number of studies exist applying or discussing value networks [15] [16] [17], one common thing being that they all consider value-creation dynamics as a more complex process than what the value chain framework suggests. In this paper, as the focus is on the role of mobile VoIP in transforming the mobile voice industry, the value network ideology with associated company clusters and hot-spots [18] is a natural approach. A business ecosystem is considered as a structured community of companies creating value [19. The term ecosystem highlights that all of the companies involved in the value-creation process are important in keeping the ecosystem alive. Ecosystems and other metaphors are needed when taking a holistic look at mobile industry evolution without focusing solely on one firm only [20].

2.2 Cellular and Internet business ecosystems

Operators deploy vertically oriented business models in the mobile industry. Cellular operators have invested in access and core networks, and they typically manage their networks quite independently. In some markets so called virtual network operators (MVNOs) have, however, emerged. MVNOs rent capacity from cellular network operators, and run their own subscriber management systems. So called service operators run their own brands and services only, their partners taking care of the technical infrastructure and network access. [21] [5] However, a typical cellular business ecosystem is vertically integrated. In many countries technical fragmentation exists (e.g. USA) thus making it difficult to achieve horizontal economies of scale in the mobile industry, whereas in some countries operators can lock the customer into their services by controlling, for example, the design of mobile terminals (e.g. Japan, see [7] and [22]).

The Internet world leverages modular technical infrastructures. PCs have spread all over the world, and operating systems in general support various add-on applications and open Internet networking. It is even difficult to define what the Internet is really all about. Email services, web browsing, streaming multimedia, instant messaging – they are all Internet services. Because of horizontally oriented technical and business architectures the innovative context is more open than in the mobile industry. People increasingly communicate with each other over the Internet (instead of only accessing content), and overlay networks (e.g. P2P and VoIP) are some of the most hyped new trends [23]. Innovative business approaches can be seen on the network edge (e.g. Skype leverages add-on goods sales, and Google generates advertisement-based revenue).

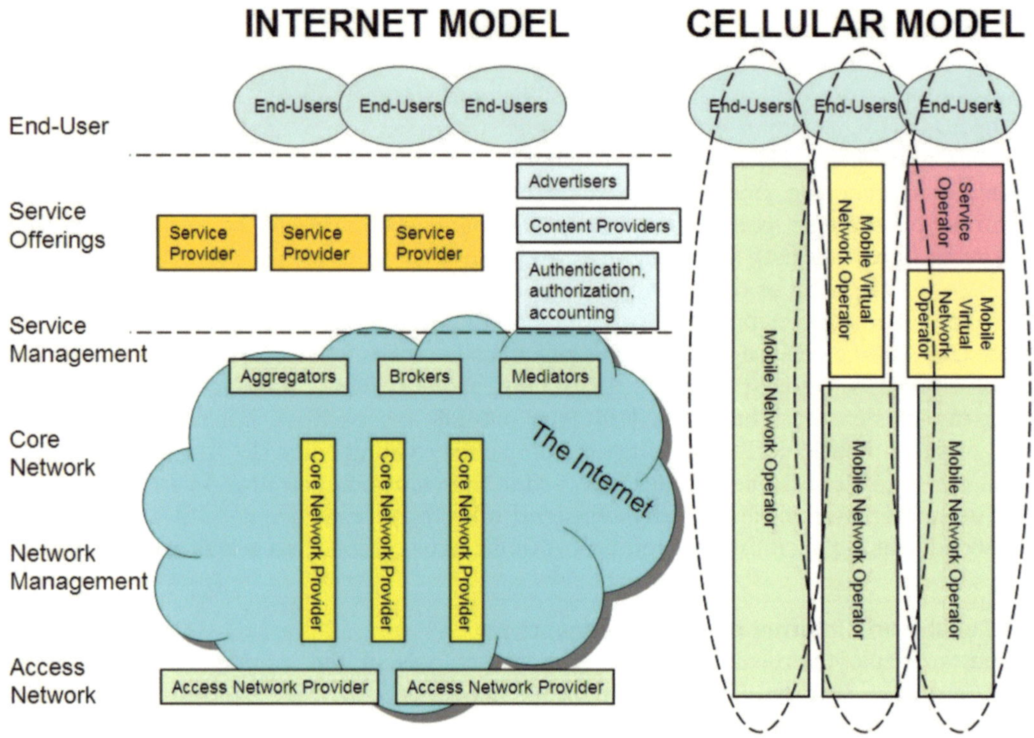

Fig. 1. - Internet vs. cellular model of service delivery

The figure above compares the different ecosystems. Though the illustration above is a simplification, the differences in the horizontal/vertical forms of the Internet and mobile industries are quite evident in practice. The difference in the market structure of these two industries is already pinpointed in [24] and [25].

2.3 Disruptive potential of mobile VoIP

Christensen [26] introduces the idea of disruptive innovation. In a disruptive evolution initially a low cost challenger technology overtakes the dominant market technology, though the initial technical performance is inferior to the dominant design. From the business perspective disruptive services are considered as *"...new services that create significant changes in a business model"* [27]. Disruptive services shake dominant business models by introducing new innovations, at the same time making older services obsolete (consider e.g. Amazon's online book store). Hardagon [28] discusses breakthroughs, suggesting that radical innovations emerge typically when different worlds or paradigms are combined together. From this perspective the mobile Internet is an interesting concept. The mobile industry and the Internet business have emerged much separately from each other. Both industries generate significant producer and consumer surplus, in other words economic value-added. Radical potential exists if these two worlds are combined together. Ville Saarikoski [6] claims that indeed the mobile Internet could represent one of the radical forces transforming the incumbent business models of the mobile industry.

Internet services represent potential sources of disruption in the domain of mobile services. As the dominant mobile business models in Europe are largely operator-centric, the emergence of the Internet business logic might weaken the power of operators and thus have an effect on the whole ecosystem. Data services provide the biggest venue for disruption, as the packet data interface to the Internet makes it possible for many of the known Internet services to be deployed in mobile handsets. Verkasalo [8] calls these as spill-over effects of the fixed Internet. This also works the other way round. Incumbent mobile services can be replaced with Internet-based services. In this sense the mobile VoIP is an important topic, as the technical standards and solutions are ready (SIP; Skype; IMS, GAN), and voice is the most important (see the figure below) and widely used [4], still cellular-based, service used in mobile devices.

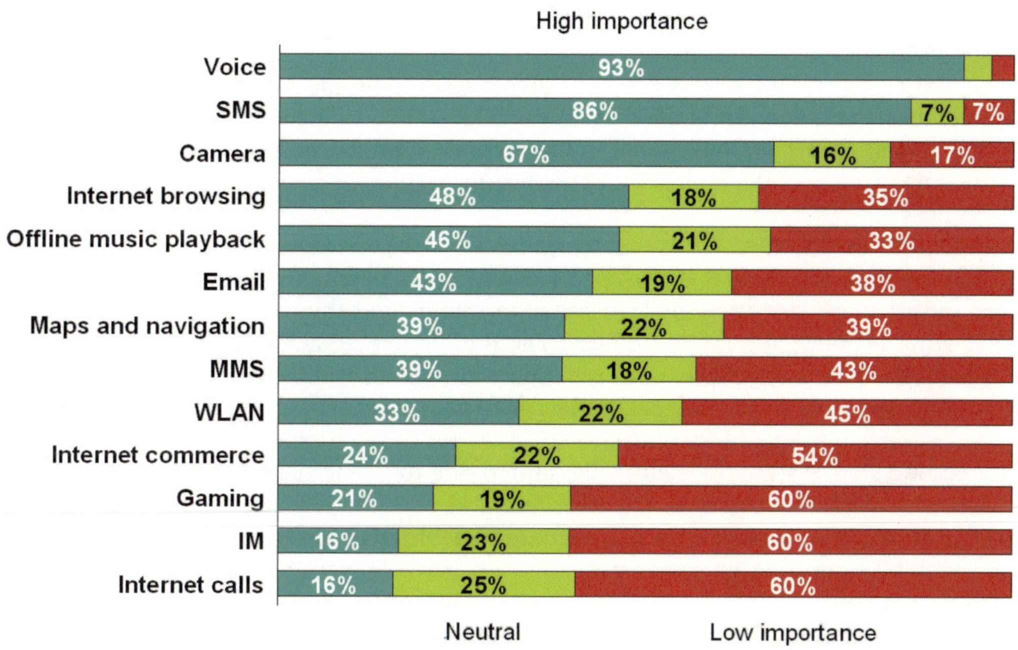

Fig. 2. - Importance of mobile services (adopted from the Finnish smartphone study 2007; [34] [35])

Along the lines of Christensen [26], challenger mobile VoIP services could in optimal conditions overtake the dominant circuit-switched voice service. The circuit-switched mobile voice already faces competition from Skype type of Internet solutions that complement the basic voice service with additional features such as chat, presence, voice mailbox and file transfer - all for free. A zero-cost alternative might catch interest in special circumstances at first, such as in international voice roaming [29].

As Figure 1 presents, the Internet model is horizontally layered. This means that the access and core networks are managed separately, and services are provided on top of the network. Little vertical integration exists. Overlay networks further utilize the horizontal structure of the Internet [23]. As the Internet is based on the layered OSI model [30], it is no surprise that also Internet business is much horizontally oriented with little vertical linkage between the actors of different layers. If this Internet model evades to the mobile domain, the most extreme outcomes would involve the break-up of the vertically oriented ecosystems. Alternative mobile access networks might emerge (e.g. WiFi, WiMAX), the business logic of incumbent cellular operators might change (orientation towards bit-pipe strategies), and services may be deployed on the edge of the network in the fashion of the Internet. Fixed-to-mobile Internet spill-over effects [8] and network externalities [31] are likely to drive the emergence of the mobile Internet. Most new data services have new value propositions. However, the mobile VoIP represents a perfect substitute to circuit-switched voice.

3. Scenario Analysis of Mobile Voice Market

3.1 Scenario analysis method

Scenario analysis is used in this paper to demonstrate how the long-term development of the mobile voice market can be modeled. The value-added of the scenario analysis is not in the final scenarios per se, but instead in the process of understanding on the one hand the fundamental drivers of the industry and on the other hand the new emerging forces shaping the business.

For scenario analysis, see [32] and [14]. In scenario analysis fundamental and certain drivers of the industry are first identified. In order to understand the uncertain, one has to first realize what is going to happen for sure. The underlying certain drivers include the non-decreasing need for voice services, migration from fixed to mobile services, and movement from circuit-switched services to packet data services.

In the second step of scenario analysis the underlying dynamic variables are identified. This can be done with, for example, expert interviews and Porter's five forces analysis. The objective is to come up with a list of uncertain variables that have an impact on the future. These variables are then grouped, dependencies between variables are controlled for by excluding dependent variables, and the most important uncertainties are constructed into key scenario variables that represent as the dimensions of the final model. The scenario analysis is iterative, and expert interviews are used to validate the developed framework. The interviews for this paper are held in Finland in June 2007, except for a preliminary interview with Ficora in February 2007. A list of interviewees is presented below.

Name	Title	Company
Klaus Nieminen	Senior Adviser	Ficora
Jaakko Kuosmanen	Managing Director	ICT Turku
Juha Korsimaa	Senior Direc. Operat.	Fujitsu
Tapani Nevanpää	Development Direct.	TeliaSonera
Mika Julkunen	Project Manager	TeliaSonera
Jarkko Utriainen	Head of Buss.Intellig.	DNA Finland
Niklas Koløter	CEO	Ipon Communications

Table 1. – List of interviewees

3.2 Uncertain elements of structure

The table below introduces the constructed uncertain elements of structure. They include all the uncertain elements of structure that affect the business around mobile VoIP.

Table 2. - Uncertain elements of structure of mobile VoIP

Threat of new entrants

- Do VoIP service providers pose a threat for the Finnish MNOs?
- Do international operators pose a threat for the Finnish MNOs?
- How will the regulation deal with proprietary voice services?
- Is the regulation of interconnecting PSTN and cellular changing?
- What is the significance of network effect of Internet communities?
- Will flat rate pricing introduce challengers on the service business?
- Does the mobile data access support all type of traffic?

Bargaining power of buyers

- How wide is the consumer/corporate demand for mobile VoIP?
- How price sensitivity affects the rate of switching a service?
- How do users adopt alternative roaming methods?
- Do the users deploy alternative mobile access technologies?

Intensity of rivalry

- How do the mobile operators' react with the Internet phenomenon?
- How are the license terms set for alternative wireless networks?
- Are the mobile operators going to deploy the alternative wireless technologies?
- Is the regulator going to continue handset bundling?
- Does the MNO's value reside on the network infrastructure or on the customer population?

Threat of substitutes

- What is the level of software modularity in mobile phones?
- Will service bundling become popular with handset bundling?
- Do alternative radio interfaces become popular on mobile phones?
- How do the Internet services affect the vertical mobile market?
- Do instant messengers pose a threat to voice services?
- Do switching costs have any significance on customer behavior?
- Is mobile VoIP able to replace or partially substitute CS voice?
- Are Internet businesses able to capitalize on the mobile market?

Bargaining power of suppliers

- Does the supplier group hold any potential entrants?

- Are suppliers able to bypass the mobile operators in the value chain?
- Will the big suppliers support mobile VoIP on mobile handsets?

3.3 Identifying the causal factors behind the scenario variables

Before using the uncertainties in constructing the scenarios, the possible interdependencies between the variables need to be cut down. This is done by dividing the uncertainties into two categories. 1. *Independent uncertainties*: Those elements the uncertainty of which is independent of other elements of structure. The sources of uncertainty may be inside or outside the industry. 2. *Dependent uncertainties:* Those elements of structure that will be largely or completely determined by the independent uncertainties." Only independent variables can be used in scenario construction as they are not dependent on other variables. Dependent variables are set after the assumptions about independent variables are resolved. Each dependent variable then becomes part of the scenarios. [14]

The most important scenario variables are derived from the list of uncertain elements of structure by combining the relevant dimensions into a set of independent variables. Most of the uncertain elements of structure have synergies with each other and thus they need to be merged into consistent higher level variables. The six most important scenario variables that are formulated with this method (the first two are identified as the most important ones in the interviews) include:

1. *What is going to be the dominating market structure?*
2. *What is the access mode in multi-radio networks?*
3. *What is going to be the pricing structure of mobile communications?*
4. *Is the market dominated by local or global service operators?*
5. *What is the level of consumer demand for alternative communication methods?*
6. *How is regulation of mobile telephony going to deal with the alternative mobile voice services?*

The most important scenario variables are chosen to be the dimensions upon which the final scenarios are constructed. The chosen scenario variables of the future mobile VoIP business are here presented with the causal factors driving them. As Table 3 depicts, there are several causalities that underlie both scenario variables.

Scenario Variable	Causal factors
Market structure of mobile industry	▪ Do the international service providers or operators enter the Finnish market? ▪ Will the regulation support mobile voice service with the alternative wireless technologies? ▪ What is the level of software modularity in mobile phones? ▪ What is the level of significance of Internet communities and rich voice services? ▪ Does the MNO's value reside in the network infrastructure or in the customer population?

Access mode in multi-radio wireless networks?	▪ How are the license terms set for access networks? ▪ Do the network providers choose to compete or cooperate? ▪ Do alternative wireless technologies ever become a success? ▪ Are the operators going to deploy alternative wireless technologies?

Table 3. - Causal factors determining the uncertainties of the mobile voice business

3.4 Dimensioning the scenario variables

Before introducing the final scenarios some dimensioning of the variables need to be conducted. Two most important scenario variables are dimensioned in two distinct dimensions. Firstly, the uncertainty in the dominating future market structure is dimensioned between *vertical market structure* and *horizontal market structure*. Secondly, uncertainty in the development of enabler technologies is dimensioned between *single-operator* access mode and *multi-operator* access mode.

Market structure of the mobile industry is divided into two dimensions, even though the complexity of the variable enables a wider assessment, too. However, the current dimensioning is found essential in answering the question whether the dominating market structure is going to be horizontal or vertical. The mobile operators can either produce the VoIP services in-house and act also as content providers, or act only as network providers and give up in the services business. According to Vesa [5], vertical or horizontal market structure, together with the level of architecture modularity are the main dimensions that define the mobile market structure. In this paper the definition of market structure is, however, based on the distinction between vertical and horizontal orientation only.

In *vertical market structure* the first observation (and assumption also for the future) is that the convergence of the mobile industry (with the Internet) is currently rather weak, providing the incumbent operators' an asset to deploy mobile networks under their sole control. In Finland the status quo is mainly a closed group of mobile operators (DNA Finland, Elisa, TeliaSonera) who control the market and thus characterize the vertical form of mobile market structure. However, as more access networks emerge, the challenger players can provide comparable voice services in the mobile domain and thus challenge the mobile operators in mobile voice business. On the other hand, mobile operators are expected to provide mobile VoIP with GAN and IMS technologies to maintain their market dominance and avoid the threat of opening the walled gardens.

In h*orizontal market structure the c*onvergence of mobile industries and mobile service providers is found significant, the synergy of alternative wireless communication channels and VoIP applications putting pressure on the dominance of mobile operators. New value networks, as presented in [33], are expected to leverage the potential for new innovations. In this sense, this paper observes not only the emergence of mobile VoIP, but also other internet services on mobile handsets.

Horizontal market structure of mobile communications would be actually a continuation to the current wired broadband market in which the households are provided with connections of unlimited use with unrestricted content. The wired broadband market illustrates the structure of horizontal markets and justifies the expectations that the horizontal structure becomes dominating also in the mobile industry.

The perspective of **access mode in multi-radio networks** studies whether mobile phones enable multi-radio connectivity options. The uncertainty in this scenario variable derives from the fact whether the set of different radio technologies will be supported independently of each other or are they bundled together. Furthermore, the access mode variable holds also the uncertainty over whether the network selection is performed by the user or by the network itself. The uncertainty in this scenario variable is divided into two dimensions; *single-operator* access mode and *multi-operator* access mode.

The *single-operator access mode* describes the relationship of a network operator and multiple network access technologies. In the single-operator mode the mobile handset is able to access the network only through one predefined set of access technologies, the operator-controlled set of alternatives. Similarly, any network that is not managed by the network operator will not be accessible with the mobile phone. In single-operator mode the network interface of mobile handset is expected to be closed for any other network service than the one that is provided by the network operator. This has already been seen because of mobile operators that use SIM-lock on their bundled mobile handsets. Users may have some contribution to the selection as long as the selected network belongs to the predefined set of access networks. In single-operator mode the wireless networks are expected to operate cooperatively. Network based handovers are expected to be the key thing to make this work. Low-cost access technologies are favored and more expensive networks utilized only when needed. The system can, for example, favor WiFi over 3G and to utilize the latter only when the user misses WiFi coverage.

In the *multi-operator mode* the access networks and their providers are seen in a competitive context. Furthermore, in the multi-operator mode the network access selection is notably more open than in the single-operator mode. The horizontal market structure is favored in the multi-operator mode as voice services that support multi-operator mode are more likely horizontally layered than vertically integrated.

3.5 Constructing the scenarios

In order to construct the final scenarios, the two most important scenario variables are combined into internally consistent scenarios. The dimensioning, depicted below, describes the scenarios. The dimensions are combined into the final scenarios, presented as consistent combinations of the independent scenario variables. As presented in the figure below, four final scenarios are formulated

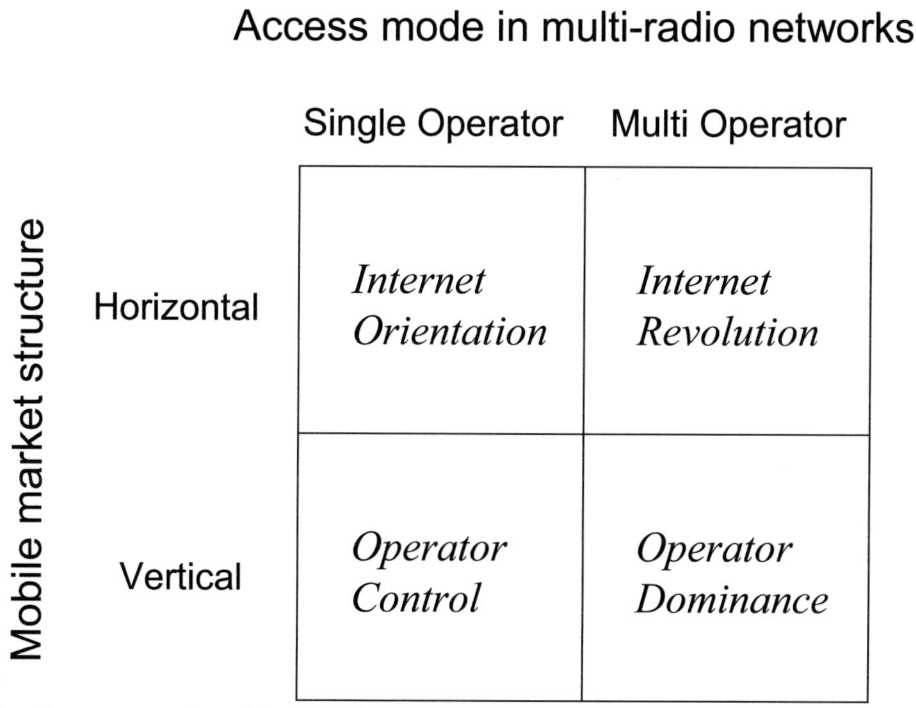

Fig. 3. - Future scenarios of the mobile voice market

3.6 Scenarios of the future mobile voice market

The initial setting on the current mobile industry forms a scenario that has not been defined with the formal scenario construction process. This scenario is, however, only a prolongation of the current situation in terms of the immaturity of the mobile VoIP business and thus also a continuation to the current vertical market structure. In the current situation the slowness of regulative decisions gives the mobile operators an asset to continue their current business models and prepare for future actions. At the same time VoIP service providers that still need to operate under the PSTN regulation are suffering from the slowdown of fixed telephony. This leads to a vanishing customer population and high interconnection costs from PSTN to cellular. In the current situation the high entry barriers keep the VoIP market unattractive for challenger VoIP service providers. The following sections present the special characteristics of the alternative scenarios. The scenarios are not projected to be mutually exclusive but rather to partially coexist.

This first scenario - ***operator control*** - continues partly from the current situation. In this scenario the market structure of the mobile industry is the same as now, meaning that the mobile operators have maintained their vertically integrated value networks by offering both the voice service and the network connections. Customers also call similarly as today, the only difference being that the terminal is able to deploy several different (operator-controlled) access technologies, with the condition that they are provided by the same operator. Terminals still require a SIM card or equivalent to operate (no multi-operator support).

In Figure 4 (appendix) the operator A provides both the voice service and the network access. Several wireless technologies are supported, and also, as the distinction between VoIP and cellular is vague, it is presumable that a single subscription might be able to deploy both the CS voice and VoIP service in parallel. In this scenario the mobile operators are the strongest candidates in providing mobile VoIP, as they are currently the only players controlling wide area wireless networks (3G). However, the technical development with alternative wireless carriers poses this scenario a threat - challenger access providers being able to operate as a combined network access and VoIP operator, thus creating a competing service from the perspective of incumbent mobile operators. Similarly, the challenger wireless network operators are a threat when combined with an externally provided voice service. However, this setting leads the focus towards the scenario *Internet orientation*.

Emergence of alternative radio technologies poses this scenario a risk to either allow the market to reach a more horizontal structure. As the mobile industry obtains currently a vertically integrated structure, radical structural changes are not expected to happen rapidly. Thus the mobile operators will have good possibilities to organize their technologies and business models to better meet the future demand.

The second scenario - ***Internet orientation*** - assumes that the mobile industry converges with the Internet world. In this scenario the convergence of the industries is pushing the mobile industry to form a horizontal structure although the divergence and interoperability of wireless network technologies has not yet matured sufficiently to provide a ubiquitous wireless Internet. In this scenario the mobile operators are expected to head towards flat-rate pricing and perhaps ultimately also towards bit-pipe operator business models. Similarly, as with the previous scenario, the characteristic of this scenario is to be slightly fragmented between the old telecom world and new Internet world. However, the role of service providers is emphasized even more than in the previous scenario as the amount of services and applications is not limited to only one service operator. This scenario supports also the distinction between network operators and service providers the way they are presented in the Communications Market Act in Finland.

Figure 5 (appendix) illustrates the market dynamics of this scenario. Operator B is a virtual operator providing VoIP service to its customers, whereas operator C has an exclusive right to provide the network access for the customers of operator B. More accurately, the operator C manages all the connections to the mobile handset, either due to legacy business models in mobile communications or due to monopolistic control over the various network technologies.

Compared to the current situation, the biggest difference in this scenario is the separation of the services industry and network business. In addition, a strongly tied relationship is expected to materialize between the end-user, and the network access provider instead of the voice service provider. Other than voice based mobile Internet services are expected to find this scenario rather attractive as the huge penetration of open mobile terminals with Internet connectivity opens a completely new market for them. If the horizontal market structure dominates the mobile industry, it would also imply that the future evolution leads towards the scenario *Internet revolution* - if the multi-operator access mode is being facilitated.

In the third scenario - ***operator dominance*** - the most relevant matter is the significant market power of mobile operators that is difficult to overtake by challenger actors. Mobile operators are considered vertically integrated in this scenario and a term *master mobile operator* is introduced to describe an operator that provides both the voice service and the network access. The main characteristic of this scenario, however, is the control over wireless technologies. Alternative networks that are not managed by the mobile operator are inaccessible with the mobile handset, if the end-user is willing to continue using the same voice subscription. In order to change the network provider, also the VoIP service should be changed. In other words the vertical silos take place, but on the other hand mobile terminals support multiple operators, and SIM cards (or equivalent) are not needed.

Figure 6 (appendix) illustrates the dynamics between the different operators in this scenario. Operator A is seen as a master operator in this scenario. Operator C is an alternative network access provider with whom the Operator A has made a contract so that Operator A's customers are able to deploy Operator C's network in places where Operator A has no network coverage. In an international level the cooperative contracting between network operators is better known as *roaming agreements*. On a national level the same concept is referred with a term *national roaming*. Regulation of communication markets on its current form supports this scenario. Pricing of interconnection and inability to route traffic to cellular networks are problems for new mobile VoIP service providers and proprietary solutions. If the competitiveness of these alternative services is hindered by the regulation it will lead to a situation where the mobile industry will not converge and the horizontal model will not dominate.

In the fourth scenario - ***Internet revolution*** - the market structure is strongly horizontal and the distinction between services and network accesses is clear. There are many ways to deploy mobile VoIP services; the end-user can either self manage both the VoIP service and the wireless network access selection, or the services can be combined by an external service aggregator. Furthermore, in the latter case the service aggregation can also be driven by the voice service provider or by the network operator. For example the network operator may recommend certain VoIP services alongside with the mobile network subscription. Or the other way round, the service provider may recommend certain network operators. The main characteristic of this scenario is, however, that the end-user may use several wireless network operators.

Figure 7 (appendix) illustrates this scenario. The end-user uses operator B's voice service but accesses the service through network operators A and C. Thus the market has horizontal structure and the user utilizes several network operators to access the voice service. Interoperability of the networks will probably set the highest demand for this scenario. Utilization of multiple access networks together with the support for seamless operability and mobile use will not be an easy task. Some sort of interoperability has been seen also in the previous scenarios as all the scenarios serve the idea of multiple radio interfaces. However, all the other scenarios more or less concentrate on providing the service within the same operator or within a collaboration of a set of operators. The scenario of Internet revolution assumes the access mode to be completely open and the services to be surrounded by a competitive context.

This final scenario itself is a bit vaguely defined, but it is also the most distinct to the current industry structure. Main issues rising in this scenario include the question of wireless connections taking over the wired connections. Other issues would be content-independent communications which will ultimately lead to a distinction of access providers and service providers and further to an issue of funding the services. Currently the VoIP telephony is riding on a crest of the wave by allowing free calls inside the VoIP domain. However, in the future this does not look promising and other revenue models need to be discovered.

4. Conclusion

Legacy cellular business ecosystems are much different from Internet ecosystems. Whereas strong operators have traditionally controlled mobile business ecosystems through vertical silos, Internet business models are horizontally oriented. Internet services are moving to the mobile domain due to the migration towards packet switched mobile networks. One of the most important mobile services is voice, which is likely to retain its fundamental position among communication services in the future, too. This paper sets out to model the future of mobile voice through scenario analysis.

The constituted future scenarios on the development of mobile voice communications describe the current market situation and mirror the future prospects of the evolving mobile voice market. All the scenarios are based on the findings of the analysis of business dynamics. The final outcome of the analysis is that the future market structure depends on two independent variables; *mobile market structure* and *access mode in multi-radio networks.* These variables are dimensioned into two to present prospective aspects of the market. Four final scenarios are formulated based on these dimensions.

First of the scenarios, *operator control*, continues closely from the current situation, the only difference being the expected emergence of mobile VoIP through multiple radio networks (all operated by the controlling operator). In this scenario the voice is not a separate service from the network connection. Instead, a scenario called *Internet orientation* is introduced to continue from the current situation with separation of service providers and network access providers. In these two scenarios the biggest difference is whether the mobile operator controls voice calls or whether the deployment of VoIP is open to rivalry. The common thing is that the network operator has a lock-in to the end-user (no multiple operators supported).

The two latter scenarios are partly continuations of the previous scenarios. Scenario *operator dominance* is probably most attractive for the mobile operators as it depicts the future to be fully controlled by the mobile operators, also in terms of controlling the VoIP usage. In this scenario, however, the terminals support multiple operators, leading the industry to a battle ground of few dominating operators operating vertical silos. *Internet revolution* is the opposite of operator dominance, stating the operators to be only bit-pipes and the actual service providers to be chosen by end-users. In the Internet revolution the use of open access networks is emphasized, which is not believed to be possible in the scenario operator dominance.

5. References

Nokia. (2005). Nokia defines strategy and targets for continued profitable growth. Press release, 1.12.2005. http://www.nokia.com/A4136002?newsid=1023902. Referred 20.2.2007.

Computer Industry Almanac Inc. (2005). Worldwide Internet Users Top 1 Billion in 2005. http://www.c-i-a.com/pr0106.htm. Referred 20.2.2007.

Alahuhta, P. & Jurvansuu, M. & Pentikäinen, H. (2004). Roadmap for network technologies and services. Tekes, Helsinki, Finland, *Technology Review 162/2004*. ISBN 952-457-176-5.

Verkasalo, H. (2007). Insights on the Evolution of the Finnish Mobile Service Market. Submitted for publication at Conference on Telecommunication Techno-Economics CTTE) 2007, 14-15 June 2007, Helsinki, Finland.

Vesa, J. (2005). *Mobile Services in the Networked Economy*. IRM Press, Hershey, PA, USA.

Saarikoski, V. (2006). *The Odyssey of the Mobile Inter*net. Doctoral Dissertation. University of Oulu, Finland.

Funk, J. (2004). *Mobile Disruption - the technologies and applications driving the mobile internet,* Wiley January 2004.

Verkasalo, H. (2007). *A Cross-Country Comparison of Mobile Service and Handset Usage.* Licentiate's paper, Helsinki University of Technology, Networking Laboratory, Finland.

Osterwalder, A. & Ondrus, J. & Pigneur, Y. (2005). Skype's disruptive potential in the telecom market: a systematic comparison of business models. HEC Lausanne Working paper, May 2005.

Porter, M. (1980). *Competitive Strategy,* Free Press, New York, 1980.

Kraft, J. (2003). Vertical structure of the industry and competition: An analysis of the evolution of the info-communications industry. *Telecommunications Policy, 27, 625-649.*

Harrigan, KR. (1984). Formulating vertical integration strategies. *Academy of Management Review, 9 (4), 638-652.*

Mitchell, W. & Singh, K. (1996). Precarious Collaboration: Business Survival after Partnerships shut Down of Form New Partnerships, *Strategic Management Journal,* 1996, 17.

Porter, M. (1985). *Competitive Advantage,* Free Press, New York, 1985.

Normann, R. & Ramirez, R. (1993). From value chain to value constellation: Designing interactive strategy. *Harvard Business Review, July-August 1993, 65-77.*

Timmers, P. (1999). *Electronic commerce - Strategies and models for business-to-business trading.* London: John Wiley.

Berger, S. & Sturgeon, T. & Kurz, C. & Voskamp, U. & Wittke, V. (1999). *Globalization, value networks and national models.* Memorandum prepared for the IPC Globalization Meteting, October 8 (1999), MIT.

Pursiainen, H. & Leppävuori, I. (2002). *Analysis of the Finnish mobile cluster - Any potential in mobile services.* Helsinki: Ministry of Transport and Communications, Finland.

Moore, JF. (1993). Predators and pray: A new ecology of competition. *Harvard Business Review, May-June, 75-86.*

Afuah, A. (2001). Dynamic boundaries of the firm: Are firms better off being vertically integrated in the face of a technological change? *Academy of Management Journal, 44 (6), 1211-1220.*

Kiiski, A. (2007). *Impact of Virtual Operators on Mobile Market.* Licentiate's Paper. Networking Laboratory. Helsinki University of Technology.

Funk, J. (2006). Mobile phone industry: A microcosm of deregulation, globalization, and technological change in the Japanese economy. In R. Taplin (Ed.), *Japanese Telecommunications Market and Policy in Transition*. London: Routledge.

Clark DD. & Lehr W. & Bauer SJ. & Faratin P. & Sami R. & Wroclawski J. (2006). Overlay Networks and Future of the Internet. *Journal of Communications and Strategies*, 3(63), pp 1-21, 2006.

Noam, EM. (1987). The Public Telecommunications Network: A Concept in Transition. *Journal of Communication, Winter, pp.30-48.*

Noam, EM. (1994). Beyond liberalization: From the network of networks to the system of systems. *Telecommunication Policy, vol.18(4), pp.286-294.*

Christensen, CM. (1997). *The Innovator's Dilemma*. Harvard Business School Press.

Barsi, T. (2002). Disruptive technology vs. disruptive applications. Telephony Online. http://telephonyonline.com/news/telecom_disruptive_technology_vs/index.html . Referred 6.6.2006.

Hargadon, A. (2003). *How Breakthroughs Happen - The Surprising Truth About How Companies Innovate,* Boston Massachusetts, Harvard Business School Press, 2003.

Kumar, RKR. (2006). International Mobile Roaming Alternatives: An Impact Analysis. Presented at World Telecommunications Congress 2006 - Emerging Telecom Opportunities. WTC, Budapest, Hungary, 1-3 May, 2006.

Zimmermann, H. (1980). OSI Reference Model — The ISO Model of Architecture for Open Systems Interconnection. *IEEE Transactions on Communications, vol. 28, no. 4, April 1980, pp. 425 - 432.*

Katz, ML. & Shapiro, C. (1985). Network Externalities, Competition, and Compatibility. American Economic Review. *American Economic Association, vol. 75(3), pages 424-40, June.*

Karlson, B. & Bri, A. & Link, J. & Lönnqvist, P. & Norling, C. (2003). *Wireless Foresight: Scenarios of the Mobile World in 2015*. John Wiley and Sons, 2003.

Shapiro, C. & Varian, HR. (1998). *Information Rules: A Strategic Guide to the Network Economy.* Boston, MA: Harvard Business School Press.

Verkasalo, H. & Hämmäinen, H. (2007). A Handset-Based Platform for Measuring Mobile Service Usage. *INFO: The Journal of Policy, Regulation and Strategy. Vol 9 No 1, 2007.*

Verkasalo H. (2005). *Handset-Based Monitoring of Mobile Customer Behavior.* Master's Paper Series. Networking Laboratory. Department of Electrical and Telecommunications Engineering. Helsinki University of Technology.

ITU. (2007). Key Global Indicators for the World of Telecommunication Service Sector. Referred 1.9.2007.

Appendices

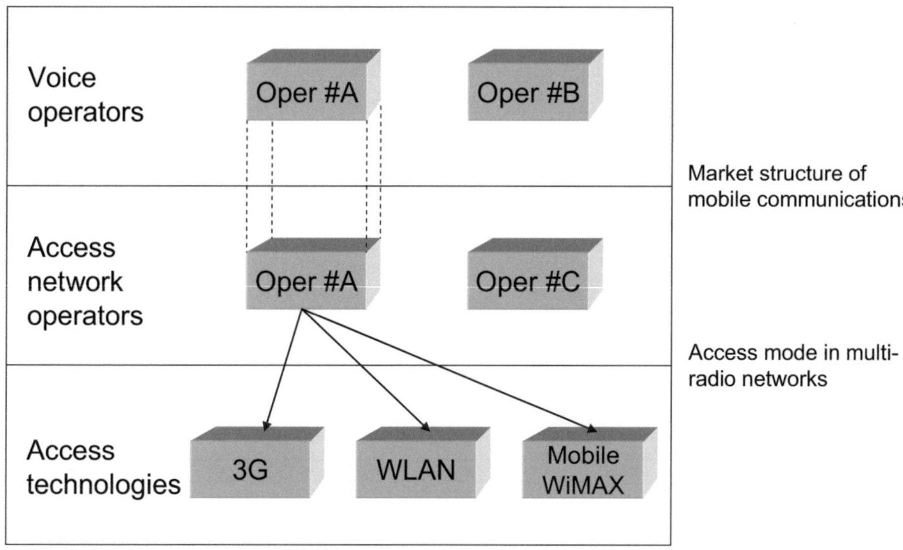

Fig. 4. - Illustration of scenario "Operator control"

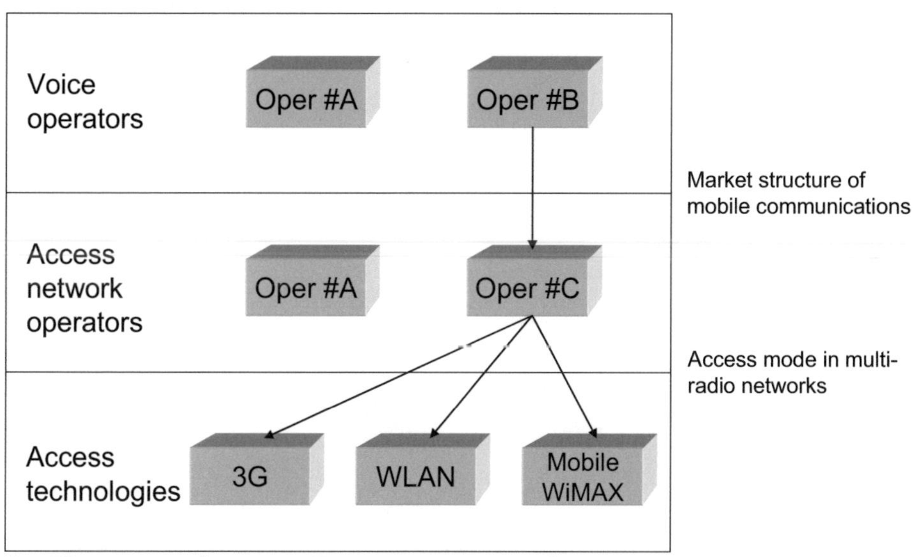

Fig. 5. - Illustration of scenario "Internet orientation"

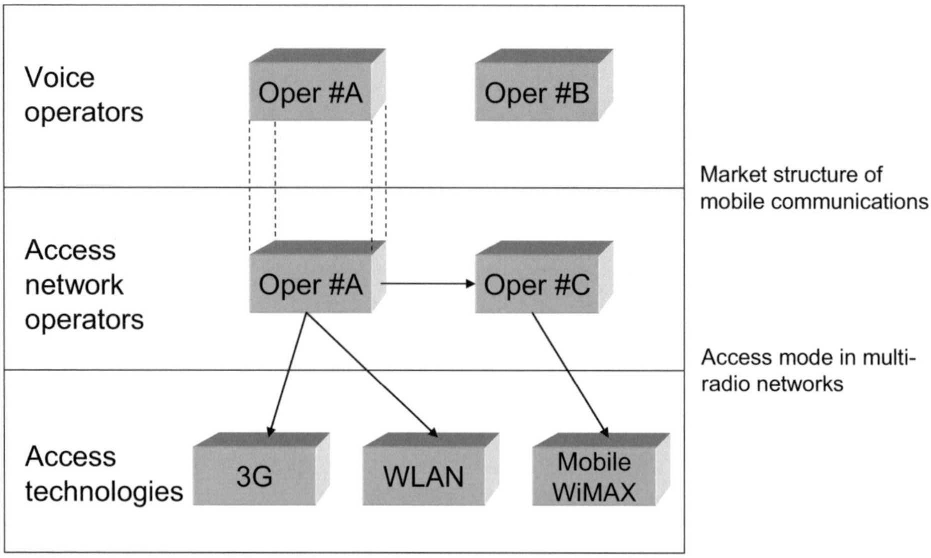

Fig. 6. - Illustration of scenario "Operator dominance"

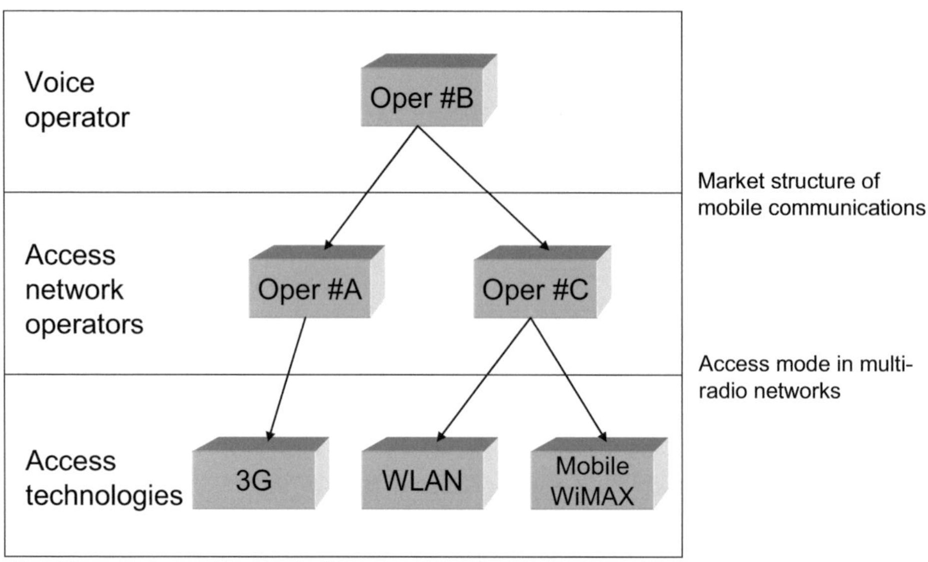

Fig. 7. - Illustration of scenario "Internet revolution"

Next Generation of Electronic Patient Record: Moving from Information to Knowledge-based

Lau, Adela
School of Nursing, The Hong Kong Polytechnic University
Hong Kong, China

Abstract

WHO has defined three standards for classification and terminology used in Healthcare Information Systems: ICD (International Classification of Disease), ICF (International Classification of Functioning, Disability and Health) and ICHI (International Classification of Health Intervention). They are used for clinical and diagnosis coding, classification of the health components of functioning and disability, and classifying procedure codes in medicine respectively. These classifications provide the terminology to describe clinical data and diagnosis. To represent the semantic meaning of e-patient records, WHO launched a project of implementation of ICD-10 plus, ICD-11 draft and ICD-11 Ontology in March of 2007. The new ICD standard guides the classification and representation of knowledge of clinical data. So, what is the next generation of e-patient record? How does the e-patient record move from being information-based to being knowledge-based? What kinds of research questions need to be tackled in the new evolution of e-patient records?

1. Introduction

WHO defined three standards for classification and terminology used in Healthcare Information Systems. ICD is an international classification of disease for clinical and diagnosis coding (World Health Organization[a], 2008). The classification ICF (International Classification of Functioning, Disability and Health) complements ICD, which contains information on diagnosis and health condition, but not on functional status (World Health Organization[b], 2008). ICHI (International Classification of Health Intervention) is for classifying procedure codes in medicine (World Health Organization[c], 2008). The vision of ICD (World Health Organization, 2007) is to assist in public health policy, resource allocation and monitoring outcomes by recording mortality, morbidity and other population health parameters. In addition, ICD aims to support clinical decisions and health system management and to be integrated into routine practice in different settings, including primary care, more specialized clinical care and research.

In order to transfer the e-patient record from an information to a knowledge-based system, the new vision of ICD aims to guide the classification and representation of knowledge of clinical data. It expands the level of detail of classification entities by linking them to standard description of signs, symptoms and other descriptors of illness (World Health Organization, 2007). Thus, the new version of ICD (10 plus, 11) is appropriate for using electronic health records for knowledge capture and sharing. To represent knowledge adequately, the classification will be built using ontological tools with various domains such as constellations of signs and symptoms, severity and course, as well as genetic and other information. This ontological approach enables standardized information processing and communication by computers in e-health applications, and facilitates knowledge capture and sharing across different healthcare information systems. Therefore, the aims of this paper are to discuss what the next generation of e-patient record might look like, how the e-patient record moves from being information-based to being knowledge-based, and what research questions are to be tackled in the new evolution of the e-patient record.

2. How ICD Standards Facilitate Knowledge Capture and Sharing

As stated in the white paper on ICD (World Health Organization, 2007), ICD-10 Plus is a web application that allows users to enter structured proposals for ICD revision for standardization of the exchange and communication of e-patient records. ICD11 draft aims to define the ICD ontology. The selected expert can use a wiki-like structured joint-authoring tool to define the health/medical terminology (e.g. the name of each entity, relevant inclusion and exclusion terms and a textual description), taxonomy rules (e.g. in what chapter or section in the classification tree, and whether it is a disease, disorder, injury, syndrome, sign, symptom, other), and clinical and/or research rules for diagnosis and place them into the WHO web portal. Expert drafting groups will use terminology/ontology tools such as SNOMED (The International Health Terminology Standards Development Organisation, 2008) and/or any other terminology (NANDA International, 2007; National Cancer Institute, 2008) to identify core constructs and concepts of ICD11. A taxonomic review, clarification and comment on the proposed ontology will be carried out by WHO experts, scientific peer review and the public afterward. Thus, ICD11 facilitates creating knowledge linkages and algorithms for symptom-diagnosis or diagnosis-treatment decision support. Since ICD11 standardizes the health/clinical/medical terminology and medical records so that the patient data can be represented and exchanged in semantic manner, it supports and facilitates knowledge capture, creation and sharing in health/nursing/ medical diagnosis and treatment.

3. Next Generation of E-patient Record

The next generation of e-patient record can be divided into four layers (see figure 1 below). The data and transaction layer has the traditional healthcare transaction information systems, such as e-patient record and medical insurance claim systems for storing and archiving the patient's personal profile, insurance profile, clinical data and transaction data. Thus, this layer is designed for data input and is used by the clinical professional such as the nurse, physician and accounting manager for their daily activities.

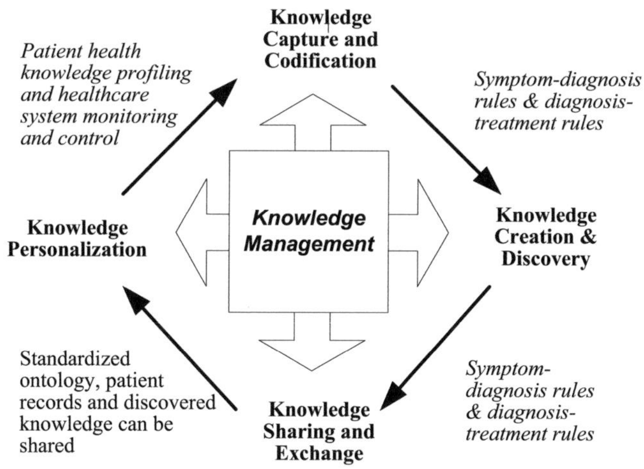

Fig. 1. The information architecture of the next generation of e-patient record

On top of the data and transaction layer, the ontology layer provides the health/clinical/medical ontological tools such as ICD11 for ontology management and ontology-based patient record management. Ontology management provides the services of co-authoring, mapping and exchanging the ontologies from different sources. The defined ontology is stored in ontology databases. Ontology-based patient record management parses and processes the ontology from the ontology databases for implementing the ontology-based patient records. In addition, this layer provides a patient record mapping service to map different record standards and formats of healthcare information systems for patient record exchange.

The information layer on top of the ontological layer provides the service of health/clinical/medical information retrieval and reporting. Healthcare management and policy makers can retrieve the information and report on population health, healthcare outcomes, and administration plans. This enables the healthcare management and policy maker to better plan infection control and disaster prevention, healthcare initiatives, and healthcare resources allocation and scheduling.

On top of the information layer, the knowledge layer provides the services of medical intelligence, personalized patient record management and health monitoring and alerts. By using the symptom-diagnosis and diagnosis-treatment rules defined in the ontology, medical knowledge and a knowledge base can be created for decision support. In addition, since all e-patient records are stored in semantic manner using computing power and artificial intelligence, similar cases and medical rules can be discovered. This facilitates the development of a case-based, rule-based or expert-based clinical/medical intelligence system. Further, the symptoms, diseases and treatment from different cases can be related and evaluated to generate a clinical/medical outcome assessment. Most importantly, the patient's health profile can be personalized and evaluated by relating the patient's medical records with the signs and symptoms, symptoms with diagnosis, diagnosis with disease, and disease with treatment knowledge. As a result, the patient's health can be monitored and alerted. In addition, the captured rules can be used to generate a health/medical knowledge map or knowledge base. By using the health/medical knowledge map and patient records, population health status and distribution can be captured so that infection and disease control can be exercised. Lastly, by reviewing the healthcare system and the health of the population, health professional knowledge capital and assets can be measured and planned.

4. Transforming E-patient Record from Information-based into Knowledge-based

In the past few years, researchers have studied how to develop and integrate the medical ontologies (Charlet et al., 2006; Jon et al., 2007; Lee et al., 2006; Meton et al., 2006) and apply them to medical knowledge management (Dieng-Kuntz et al., 2006; Haung & Chen, 2007; Shah et al., 2007). Thus, the next generation of e-patient records will transfer from being information-based to being knowledge-based (see figure 2 below). All the health/clinical/ medical ontologies are standardized and mapped. The health/clinical/medical knowledge such as symptom-diagnosis rules, diagnosis-treatment rules, etc., is captured and codified. By using the patient records data and ontological representation and rules, new health/clinical/medical knowledge can be created and discovered. The ontology, patient records and new health/clinical/medical knowledge are shared and exchanged over the virtual integrated platform so that patient health knowledge profiling and healthcare system monitoring and control can be exercised.

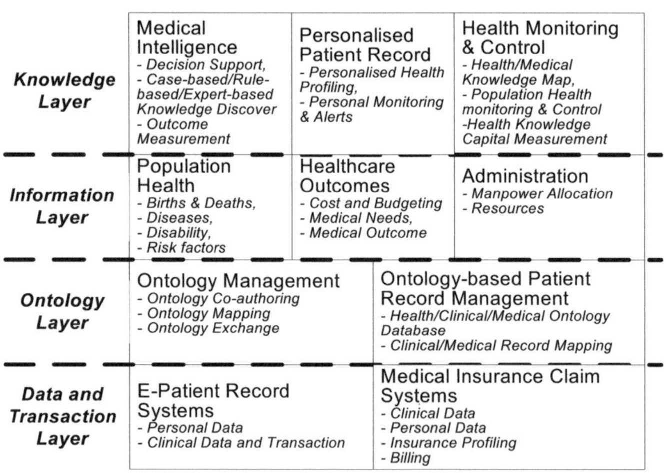

Fig. 2. Transformation from information-based to knowledge-based records in the next generation of e-patient record

In summary, the next generation of e-patient record has the new features of semantic patient record management, health/clinical/medical knowledge representation, integrated ontology-based e-patient record, virtual medical knowledge collaboration, sharing and exchange, medical, clinical and healthcare reporting, monitoring and forecasting, intelligent

medical knowledge repository, personalized health knowledge management, and healthcare system knowledge management and capital measurement.
Research Questions to be Tackled in Next Generation of E-patient Record

Therefore, the research questions to be tackled in the next generation of e-patient records include (but are not limited to):

- How to apply wiki-features and technologies to develop a co-authoring platform for ontology creation and sharing?
- How semantic web representation language and technologies represent the semantic meaning of the e-patient record?
- How to construct a knowledge map of medical symptoms, diagnosis and treatment as a knowledge base?
- What knowledge can be discovered from the symptom-diagnosis rules and diagnosis-treatment rules of medical ontologies and e-patient records?
- Research on the algorithms of ontology-based text mining to discover knowledge, such as symptom-diagnosis, diagnosis-treatment, etc., from e-patient records.
- How to map different clinical/medical ontologies such as ICD10, SNOMED, NCI ontology, Gene Ontology, MGED Ontology, MedDRA, VANDFRT, LOINC, and GALEN across different healthcare information systems?
- What web services and semantic web technologies are to be used for virtual patient record exchange and sharing?
- How to apply web/knowledge management technologies for personalizing patient records and profiles?
- How to apply data and text mining techniques for health monitoring and alerts?

5. Conclusions

The next generation of e-patient record standardizes the health/clinical/medical terminology. All the patient data can be represented in a semantic manner so that it facilitates knowledge capture, creation and sharing in health/nursing/medical diagnosis and treatment. The research questions to be tackled for the next generation of e-patient records cover the research topics of ontology knowledge representation and co-authoring, the ontology engineering process, social network analysis, knowledge repositories, text mining, knowledge discovery and knowledge intellectual capital measurement.

6. References

Charlet, J.; Bachimont, B. & Jaulent, Marie-Christine. (2006). Building medical ontologies by terminology extraction from texts: An experiment for the intensive care units. *Computers in Biology and Medicine*, Vol. 36, No. 7-8, (Jul-Aug 2006) pp.857-870.

Dieng-Kuntz, R.; Minier, D.; Ruzicka, M.; Corby, F.; Corby, O. & Alamarguy, L. (2006). Building and using a medical ontology for knowledge management and cooperative work in a health care network. *Computers in Biology and Medicine*, Vol. 36, No. 7-8, (Jul-Aug 2006), pp.871-892.

Huang, M.J. & Chen, M.Y. (2007). Integrated design of the intelligent web-based Chinese Medical Diagnostic System (CMDS) - Systematic development for digestive health. *Expert Systems with Applications*, Vol. 32, No. 2, Pp.658-673.

Jon, P.; Wang, Y.F. & Budd, P. (2007). An automated system for conversion of clinical notes into SNOMED clinical terminology. *ACM International Conference Proceeding Series*; Vol. 249, (Jan 2007) , pp.219–226.

Lee, Y.Y.; Supekar, K. & Geller, J. (2006). Ontology integration: Experience with medical terminologies. *Computers in Biology and Medicine*, Vol. 36, No. 7-8, (Jul-Aug 2006) pp.893-919.

Melton, G.B.; Parsons, S.; Morrison, F.P.; Rothschild, A.S.; Markatou, M. & Hripcsak, G. (2006). Inter-patient distance metrics using SNOMED CT defining relationships. *Journal of Biomedical Informatics*, Vol. 39, No. 6, (Dec 2006), pp.697-705.

NANDA International. "Nursing Diagnoses: Definitions & Classification", 2007. NANDI-I. Avaliable at http://www.nanda.org [Access 3rd Mar 2008].

National Cancer Institute. "Cancer Topics", 2007. Avaliable at http://www.cancer.gov/cancertopics [Access 3rd Mar 2008].

Shah, N.H.; Rubin, D.L.; Espinosa, I.; Montgomery, K. & Musen, M.A. (2007). Annotation and query of tissue microarray data using the NCI Thesaurus, *BMC Bioinformatics*, (Aug 2007), pp.296 – 303. [Access 3rd Mar 2008].

The International Health Terminology Standards Development Organisation. "Systematized Nomenclature of Medicine", last updated in 2008. Avaliable at http://www.snomed.org/ [Access 1st Apr 2008].

World Health Organization. "Production of ICD-11: The overall revision process. WHO White Paper", Mar 2007. Avaliable at http://www.who.int/classifications/icd/ICDRevision/en/index.html [Access 2rd Apr 2008].

World Health Organization[a]. "International classification of disease", last updated in 2008. Avaliable at http://www.who.int/classifications/icd/en/ [Access 4th Apr 2008].

World Health Organization[b]. "International Classification of Functioning, Disability and Health", last updated in 2008. Avaliable at http://www.who.int/classifications/icf/en/ [Access 4th Apr 2008].

World Health Organization[c]. "International Classification of Health Interventions", last updated in 2008. Avaliable at http://www.who.int/classifications/ichi/en/ Access 4th Apr 2008].